Customer service analysis	Database design Database querying and reporting	Chapter 8
Sales lead and customer analysis	Database design Database querying and reporting	Chapter 11
Blog creation and design	Blog creation tool	Chapter 12

Internet Skills

Using online software tools for job hunting and career development	Chapter 1
Using online interactive mapping software to plan efficient transportation routes	Chapter 2
Researching product information Evaluating Web sites for auto sales	Chapter 3
Researching travel costs using online travel sites	Chapter 4
Searching online databases for products and services	Chapter 5
Using Web search engines for business research	Chapter 6
Researching and evaluating business outsourcing services	Chapter 7
Researching and evaluating supply chain management services	Chapter 8
Evaluating e-commerce hosting services	Chapter 9
Using shopping bots to compare product price, features, and availability	Chapter 10
Analyzing Web site design	Chapter 11
Using Internet newsgroups for marketing	Chapter 12

Analytical, Writing, and Presentation Skills *

Business Problem	Chapter
Management analysis of a business	Chapter 1
Value chain and competitive forces analysis Business strategy formulation	Chapter 3
Employee productivity analysis	Chapter 6
Disaster recovery planning	Chapter 7
Locating and evaluating suppliers	Chapter 8
Developing an e-commerce strategy	Chapter 9
Formulating a corporate privacy policy	Chapter 12

Essentials of Management Information Systems

Tenth Edition

Kenneth C. Laudon
New York University

Jane P. Laudon
Azimuth Information Systems

PEARSON

Boston   Columbus   Indianapolis   New York   San Francisco   Upper Saddle River
Amsterdam   Cape Town   Dubai   London   Madrid   Milan   Munich   Paris   Montreal   Toronto
Delhi   Mexico City   Sao Paulo   Sydney   Hong Kong   Seoul   Singapore   Taipei   Tokyo

Editorial Director: Sally Yagan
Executive Editor: Bob Horan
Editorial Project Manager: Kelly Loftus
Editorial Assistant: Ashlee Bradbury
Director of Marketing: Maggie Moylan
Senior Marketing Manager: Anne Fahlgren
Senior Managing Editor: Judy Leale
Senior Production Project Manager: Karalyn Holland
Senior Operations Supervisor: Arnold Vila
Operations Specialist: Maura Zaldivar
Associate Director of Design: Blair Brown

Art Director: Steve Frim
Cover Illustrator and Designer: Bobby Starnes Electrographics
Media Project Manager: Allison Longley
Media Project Manager, Production: Lisa Rinaldi
Full Service Project Management: Azimuth Interactive, Inc.
Composition: Azimuth Interactive, Inc.
Printer/Binder: Courier/Kendallville
Cover Printer: Lehigh-Phoenix Color/Hagarstown
Text Font: 10.5/12.5 Times LT Std, 9.5pt

Library of Congress Cataloging-in-Publication Information is Available

10 9 8 7 6 5 4 3 2 1

ISBN 10: 0-13-266855-6
ISBN 13: 978-0-13-266855-2

About the Authors

Kenneth C. Laudon is a Professor of Information Systems at New York University's Stern School of Business. He holds a B.A. in Economics from Stanford and a Ph.D. from Columbia University. He has authored twelve books dealing with electronic commerce, information systems, organizations, and society. Professor Laudon has also written over forty articles concerned with the social, organizational, and management impacts of information systems, privacy, ethics, and multimedia technology.

Professor Laudon's current research is on the planning and management of large-scale information systems and multimedia information technology. He has received grants from the National Science Foundation to study the evolution of national information systems at the Social Security Administration, the IRS, and the FBI. Ken's research focuses on enterprise system implementation, computer-related organizational and occupational changes in large organizations, changes in management ideology, changes in public policy, and understanding productivity change in the knowledge sector.

Ken Laudon has testified as an expert before the United States Congress. He has been a researcher and consultant to the Office of Technology Assessment (United States Congress), Department of Homeland Security, and to the Office of the President, several executive branch agencies, and Congressional Committees. Professor Laudon also acts as an in-house educator for several consulting firms and as a consultant on systems planning and strategy to several Fortune 500 firms.

At NYU's Stern School of Business, Ken Laudon teaches courses on Managing the Digital Firm, Information Technology and Corporate Strategy, Professional Responsibility (Ethics), and Electronic Commerce and Digital Markets. Ken Laudon's hobby is sailing.

Jane Price Laudon is a management consultant in the information systems area and the author of seven books. Her special interests include systems analysis, data management, MIS auditing, software evaluation, and teaching business professionals how to design and use information systems.

Jane received her Ph.D. from Columbia University, her M.A. from Harvard University, and her B.A. from Barnard College. She has taught at Columbia University and the New York University Stern School of Business. She maintains a lifelong interest in Oriental languages and civilizations.

The Laudons have two daughters, Erica and Elisabeth, to whom this book is dedicated.

Brief Contents

Complete Contents

Preface

We wrote this book for business school students who want an in-depth look at how today's business firms use information technologies and systems to achieve corporate objectives. Information systems are one of the major tools available to business managers for achieving operational excellence, developing new products and services, improving decision making, and achieving competitive advantage. Students will find here the most up-to-date and comprehensive overview of information systems used by business firms today.

When interviewing potential employees, business firms often look for new hires who know how to use information systems and technologies to achieve bottom-line business results. Regardless of whether you are an accounting, finance, management, operations management, marketing, or information systems major, the knowledge and information you find in this book will be valuable throughout your business career.

What's New in This Edition

CURRENCY

The 10th edition features all new opening, closing and "Interactive Session" cases. The text, figures, tables, and cases have been updated through November 2011 with the latest sources from industry and MIS research.

NEW FEATURES

- New Video Cases Package: 24 video case studies (2 per chapter) and 12 instructional videos are available online.
- Additional discussion questions are provided for each chapter.
- Management checklists are found throughout the book; they are designed to help future managers make better decisions.
- Over 40 Learning Tracks are available online for additional coverage.

NEW TOPICS

- Expanded coverage of business intelligence and business analytics
- Expanded coverage of cloud computing and cloud software tools
- Private and public clouds
- Social graph
- Social e-commerce
- Social marketing
- Social search
- Social CRM
- Apps ecosystem
- Windows 8
- Android, iOS, and Chrome operating systems
- Multitouch interface

- Tablet computers
- Microblogging
- IPv6
- Expanded coverage of collaboration systems and tools
- Identity management
- Augmented reality
- Mobile application development
- Cloud and mobile security
- HTML5

What's New in MIS?

Plenty. In fact, there's a whole new world of doing business using new technologies for managing and organizing. What makes the MIS field the most exciting area of study in schools of business is the continuous change in technology, management, and business processes. (Chapter 1 describes these changes in more detail.)

A continuing stream of information technology innovations is transforming the traditional business world. Examples include the emergence of cloud computing, the growth of a mobile digital business platform based on smartphones, tablet computers, and not least, the use of social networks by managers to achieve business objectives. Most of these changes have occurred in the last few years. These innovations are enabling entrepreneurs and innovative traditional firms to create new products and services, develop new business models, and transform the day-to-day conduct of business. In the process, some old businesses, even industries, are being destroyed while new businesses are springing up.

For instance, the emergence of online media and entertainment stores—driven by millions of consumers who prefer iPods and smartphones—has forever changed the older business model of distributing music on physical devices, such as records and CDs. Online video rentals are similarly transforming the old model of distributing films through theaters and then through DVD rentals. New high-speed broadband connections to the home have supported these two business changes.

E-commerce is back, generating over $310 billion in revenues in 2010, and estimated to grow to over $435 billion in 2015 at about 10% annually. Amazon's revenues grew 40 percent in 2010, despite the recession, while offline retail grew by 4 percent. E-commerce is changing how firms design, produce and deliver their products and services. E-commerce has reinvented itself again, disrupting the traditional marketing and advertising industry and putting major media and content firms in jeopardy. Facebook and other social networking sites such as YouTube, Twitter, and Tumblr, exemplify the new face of e-commerce in the 21st Century. They sell services. Social e-commerce, and social network marketing, where consumers rely on friends for product news and purchases, are increasingly a normal part of business at major Fortune 500 firms. When we think of e-commerce we tend to think of selling physical products. While this iconic vision of e-commerce is still very powerful and the fastest growing form of retail in the U.S., growing up alongside is a whole new value stream based on selling services, not goods. It's a services model of e-commerce. Information systems and technologies are the foundation of this new services-based e-commerce.

Likewise, the management of business firms has changed: With new mobile smartphones, high-speed wireless Wi-Fi networks, and wireless tablet computers, remote salespeople on the road are only seconds away from their managers' questions and oversight. Managers on the move are in direct, continuous contact with their employees and customers. The growth of enterprise-wide information systems with extraordinarily rich data means that managers no longer operate in a fog of confusion, but instead have online, nearly instant, access to the really important information they need for accurate and timely decisions. In addition to their public uses on the Web, wikis, blogs, and Twitter microblogs are becoming important corporate tools for communication, collaboration, and information sharing.

The Tenth Edition: The Comprehensive Solution for the MIS Curriculum

Since its inception, this text has helped to define the MIS course around the globe. This edition continues to be authoritative, but is also more customizable, flexible, and geared to meeting the needs of different colleges, universities, and individual instructors.

This book is now part of a complete learning package that includes the core text and an extensive offering of supplemental materials on the Web.

The core text consists of 12 chapters with hands-on projects covering the most essential topics in MIS. An important part of the core text is the Video Case Study and Instructional Video Package: 24 video case studies (2 per chapter) plus 12 instructional videos that illustrate business uses of information systems, explain new technologies, and explore concepts. Videos are keyed to the topics of each chapter.

In addition, for students and instructors who want to go deeper into selected topics, there are over 40 online Learning Tracks that cover a variety of MIS topics in greater depth.

MyMISLab provides more in-depth coverage of chapter topics, career resources, additional case studies, supplementary chapter material, and data files for hands-on projects.

THE CORE TEXT

The core text provides an overview of fundamental MIS concepts using an integrated framework for describing and analyzing information systems. This framework shows information systems composed of people, organization, and technology elements and is reinforced in student projects and case studies.

Chapter Organization
Each chapter contains the following elements:
- A chapter-opening case describing a real-world organization to establish the theme and importance of the chapter
- A diagram analyzing the opening case in terms of the people, organization, and technology model used throughout the text

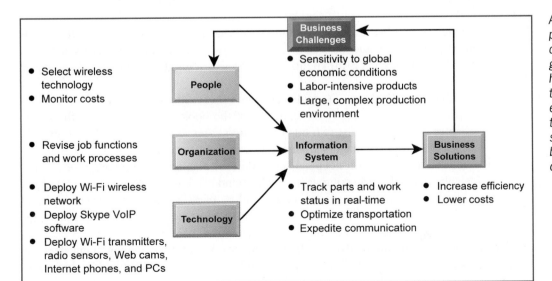

A diagram accompanying each chapter-opening case graphically illustrates how people, organization, and technology elements work together to create an information system solution to the business challenges discussed in the case.

- A series of Learning Objectives

- Two Interactive Sessions with Case Study Questions and MIS in Action projects

- A Learning Tracks section identifying supplementary material in MyMISLab

- A Review Summary keyed to the Student Learning Objectives

- A list of Key Terms that students can use to review concepts

- Review questions for students to test their comprehension of chapter material

- Discussion questions raised by the broader themes of the chapter

- A series of Hands-on MIS Projects consisting of two Management Decision Problems, a hands-on application software project, and a project to develop Internet skills

- A pointer to downloadable video cases

- A Collaboration and Teamwork project to develop teamwork and presentation skills, with options for using open source collaboration tools

- A chapter-ending case study for students to apply chapter concepts

KEY FEATURES

We have enhanced the text to make it more interactive, leading-edge, and appealing to both students and instructors. The features and learning tools are described in the following sections:

Business-Driven with Real-World Business Cases and Examples

The text helps students see the direct connection between information systems and business performance. It describes the main business objectives driving the use of information systems and technologies in corporations all over the world: operational excellence; new products and services; customer and supplier intimacy; improved decision making; competitive advantage; and survival. In-text examples and case studies show students how specific companies use information systems to achieve these objectives.

We use only current 2011 examples from business and public organizations throughout the text to illustrate the important concepts in each chapter. All the case studies describe companies or organizations that are familiar to students, such as Google, Facebook, Disney World, Walmart, Procter & Gamble, and JetBlue.

Interactivity

There's no better way to learn about MIS than by doing MIS! We provide different kinds of hands-on projects where students can work with real-world business scenarios and data, and learn first hand what MIS is all about. These projects heighten student involvement in this exciting subject.

- **Online Video Case Package.** Students can watch short videos online, either in-class or at home or work, and then apply the concepts of the book to the analysis of the video. Every chapter contains at least two business video cases (24 videos in all) that explain how business firms and managers are using information systems, describe new management practices, and explore concepts discussed in the chapter. Each video case consists of a video about a real-world company, a background text case, and case study questions. These video cases enhance students' understanding of MIS topics and the relevance of MIS to the business world. In addition, there are 12 Instructional Videos that describe developments and concepts in MIS keyed to respective chapters.

- **Management Decision Problems.** Each chapter contains two management decision problems that teach students how to apply chapter concepts to real-world business scenarios requiring analysis and decision making.

- **Collaboration and Teamwork Projects**. Each chapter features a collaborative project that encourages students working in teams to use Google Sites, Google Docs, and other open-source collaboration tools. The first team project in Chapter 1 asks students to build a collaborative Google Site.
- **Hands-on MIS Projects.** Every chapter concludes with a Hands-on MIS Projects section containing three types of projects: two Management Decision Problems, a hands-on application software exercise using Microsoft Excel, Access, or Web page and blog creation tools, and a project that develops Internet business skills. A Dirt Bikes USA running case in MyMISLab provides additional hands-on projects for each chapter.

Two real-world business scenarios per chapter provide opportunities for students to apply chapter concepts and practice management decision making.

2. Applebee's is the largest casual dining chain in the world, with over 1,800 locations throughout the United States and 20 other countries. The menu features beef, chicken, and pork items, as well as burgers, pasta, and seafood. Applebee's CEO wants to make the restaurant more profitable by developing menus that are tastier and contain more items that customers want and are willing to pay for despite rising costs for gasoline and agricultural products. How might business intelligence help management implement this strategy? What pieces of data would Applebee's need to collect? What kinds of reports would be useful to help management make decisions on how to improve menus and profitability?

Students practice using software in real-world settings.

The database includes fields for store identification number, sales region number, item number, item description, unit price, units sold, and the weekly sales period when the sales were made.

ID	Store No	Sales Region	Item No	Item Description	Unit Price	Units Sold	Week Ending
1	1	South	2005	17" monitor	$229.00	28	8/28/2009
2	1	South	2005	17" monitor	$229.00	30	9/25/2009
3	1	South	2005	17" monitor	$229.00	9	10/30/2009
4	1	South	3006	101 Keyboard	$19.95	30	8/28/2009
5	1	South	3006	101 Keyboard	$19.95	35	9/25/2009
6	1	South	3006	101 Keyboard	$19.95	39	10/30/2009
7	1	South	6050	PC Mouse	$8.95	28	8/28/2009
8	1	South	6050	PC Mouse	$8.95	3	9/25/2009
9	1	South	6050	PC Mouse	$8.95	38	10/30/2009
10	1	South	8500	Desktop CPU	$849.95	25	8/28/2009

Record: 1 of 10   No Filter   Search

Develop some reports and queries to make this information more useful for running the business. Sales and production managers want answers to the following questions:
- Which products should be restocked?
- Which stores and sales regions would benefit from a promotional campaign and

Each chapter features a project to develop Internet skills for accessing information, conducting research, and performing online calculations and analysis.

IMPROVING DECISION MAKING: USING WEB TOOLS TO CONFIGURE AND PRICE AN AUTOMOBILE

Software skills: Internet-based software
Business skills: Researching product information and pricing

In this exercise, you will use software at car-selling Web sites to find product information about a car of your choice and use that information to make an important purchase decision. You will also evaluate two of these sites as selling tools.

You are interested in purchasing a new Ford Escape (or some other car of your choice). Go to the Web site of CarsDirect (www.carsdirect.com) and begin your investigation. Locate the Ford Escape. Research the various Escape models, choose one you prefer in terms of price, features, and safety ratings. Locate and read at least two reviews. Surf the Web site of the manufacturer, in this case Ford (www.ford.com). Compare the information available on Ford's Web site with that of CarsDirect for the Ford Escape. Try to locate the lowest price for the car you want in a local dealer's inventory. Suggest improvements for CarsDirect.com and Ford.com.

- **Interactive Sessions.** Two short cases in each chapter have been redesigned as Interactive Sessions to be used in the classroom (or on Internet discussion boards) to stimulate student interest and active learning. Each case concludes with two types of activities: case study questions and MIS in Action. The case study questions provide topics for class discussion, Internet discussion, or written assignments. MIS in Action features hands-on Web activities for exploring issues discussed in the case more deeply.

ASSESSMENT AND AACSB ASSESSMENT GUIDELINES

The Association to Advance Collegiate Schools of Business (AACSB) is a not-for-profit corporation of educational institutions, corporations and other organizations that seeks to improve business education primarily by accrediting university business programs. As a part of its accreditation activities, the AACSB has developed an Assurance of Learning Program designed to ensure that schools do in fact teach students what they promise. Schools are required to state a clear mission, develop a coherent business program, identify student learning objectives, and then prove that students do in fact achieve the objectives.

We have attempted in this book to support AACSB efforts to encourage assessment-based education. The front end papers of this edition identify student learning objectives and anticipated outcomes for our Hands-on MIS projects. On the Laudon Web site is a more inclusive and detailed assessment matrix that identifies the learning objectives of each chapter and points to all the available assessment tools for ensuring students in fact do achieve

Each chapter contains two Interactive Sessions on People, Organizations, or Technology using real-world companies to illustrate chapter concepts and issues.

INTERACTIVE SESSION: ORGANIZATIONS — Burton Snowboards Speeds Ahead with Nimble Business Processes

When we hear "snowboarding," we tend to think of snow-covered slopes, acrobatic jumps, and high-flying entertainment. We don't usually think of improving business process efficiency. But snowboarding is business for Burton Snowboards, an industry pioneer and market leader. Founded in 1977 by Jake Burton Carpenter and headquartered in Burlington, Vermont, Burton designs, manufactures, and markets equipment, clothing, and related accessories for snowboarders. Today, Burton is a global enterprise that serves customers in 27 countries and has offices in Japan, Austria, and throughout the United States.

At its peak, Burton controlled over 40 percent of the U.S. snowboarding market, and it remains the market leader amidst a growing number of competitors. Now, as Burton continues to expand into a global company, it has a new set of problems: improving its systems for inventory, supply chain, purchasing, and customer service.

structure, and the company gained proficiency with SAP enterprise software in the process. Burton aims for standard, traditional versions of software whenever possible, realizing that with more bells and whistles comes increased maintenance costs and steeper learning curves to understanding the software.

SAP analysts helped Burton identify the top five transactions that were the most critical to its business operations and that needed optimization from a systems standpoint. Burton had to identify unnecessarily complicated processes, backlogs, and design gaps in the flow of its business processes. For example, the available-to-promise process was taking hours to complete. (Available to promise, in response to customer order enquiries, reports on available quantities of a requested product and delivery due dates.) Burton wanted to speed up this process so that its dealers and retail customers would have more precise information about the availability of products not currently in

MIS in Action projects encourage students to learn more about the companies and issues discussed in the case studies.

CASE STUDY QUESTIONS

1. Analyze Burton using the value chain and competitive forces models.

2. Why are the business processes described in this case such an important source of competitive advantage for Burton?

3. Explain exactly how these process improvements enhance Burton's operational performance and decision making.

MIS IN ACTION

Visit Burton Snowboards' Web site, then answer the following questions:

1. What is the purpose of this Web site? How does it support the company's goals?

2. What functions at this Web site are related to the business processes discussed in this case? How did improving those processes impact the Web site?

the learning objectives. Because each school is different and may have different missions and learning objectives, no single document can satisfy all situations. The authors will provide custom advice on how to use this text in their colleges with different missions and assessment needs. Please e-mail the authors or contact your local Pearson Prentice Hall representative for contact information.

For more information on the AACSB Assurance of Learning Program, and how this text supports assessment-based learning, please visit the Web site for this book.

Customization and Flexibility: New Learning Track Modules:

Our Learning Tracks feature gives instructors the flexibility to provide in-depth coverage of the topics they choose. There are over 40 Learning Tracks available to instructors and students. A Learning Tracks section at the end of each chapter directs students to short essays or additional chapters in MyMISLab.

This supplementary content takes students deeper into MIS topics, concepts and debates; reviews basic technology concepts in hardware, software, database design, telecommunications, and other areas; and provide additional hands-on software instruction. The 10th Edition includes new Learning Tracks on Creating a Pivot Table with Microsoft Excel PowerPivot, Service Platforms, and additional coverage of computer hardware and software technology.

Author-Certified Test Bank and Supplements

- **Author-Certified Test Bank.** The authors have worked closely with skilled test item writers to ensure that higher level cognitive skills are tested. Test bank multiple choice questions include questions on content, but also include many questions that require analysis, synthesis, and evaluation skills.
- **Annotated Slides.** The authors have prepared a comprehensive collection of PowerPoint slides to be used in your lectures. Many of these slides are the same as used by Ken Laudon in his MIS classes and executive education presentations. Each of the slides is annotated with teaching suggestions for asking students questions, developing in-class lists that illustrate key concepts, and recommending other firms as examples in addition to those provided in the text. The annotations are like an Instructor's Manual built into the slides and make it easier to teach the course effectively.

Student Learning-Focused

Student Learning Objectives are organized around a set of study questions to focus student attention. Each chapter concludes with a Review Summary and Review Questions organized around these study questions.

MyMISLab

MyMISLab is a Web-based assessment and tutorial tool that provides practice and testing while personalizing course content and providing student and class assessment and reporting. Your course is not the same as the course taught down the hall. Now, all the resources both you and your students need for course success are in one place – flexible and easily organized and adapted for your individual course experience. Visit www.mymislab.com to see how you can Teach. Learn. Experience. MIS.

Career Resources

The Instructor's Resource section of the Laudon Web site also provides extensive Career Resources, including job-hunting guides and instructions on how to build a Digital Portfolio demonstrating the business knowledge, application software proficiency, and Internet skills acquired from using the text. The portfolio can be included in a resume or job application or used as a learning assessment tool for instructors.

Instructional Support Materials

Instructor's Resource Center

Most of the support materials described in the following sections are conveniently available for adopters on the online Instructor Resource Center (IRC). The IRC includes the Image Library (a very helpful lecture tool), Instructor's Manual, Lecture Notes, Test Item File and TestGen, and PowerPoint slides.

Image Library

The Image Library is an impressive resource to help instructors create vibrant lecture presentations. Almost every figure and photo in the text is provided and organized by chapter for convenience. These images and lecture notes can be imported easily into Microsoft PowerPoint to create new presentations or to add to existing ones.

Instructor's Manual

The Instructor's Manual features not only answers to review, discussion, case study, and group project questions but also an in-depth lecture outline, teaching objectives, key terms, teaching suggestions, and Internet resources.

Test Item File

The Test Item File is a comprehensive collection of true–false, multiple-choice, and essay questions. The questions are rated by difficulty level and the answers are referenced by section. The test item file also contains questions tagged to the AACSB learning standards. An electronic version of the Test Item File is available in TestGen and TestGen conversions are available for BlackBoard or WebCT course management systems. All TestGen files are available for download at the Instructor Resource Center.

PowerPoint Slides

PowerPoint slides are available. The slides illuminate and build on key concepts in the text.

Video Cases and Instructional Videos

Instructors can download step-by-step instructions for accessing the video cases from the Instructor Resources page at www.pearsonhighered.com/laudon. See page xix for a list of video cases and instructional videos.

Learning Track Modules

Over forty Learning Tracks provide additional coverage topics for students and instructors. See page xx for a list of the Learning Tracks available for this edition.

VIDEO CASES

Chapter	Video
Chapter 1: Business Information Systems in Your Career	Case 1: UPS Global Operations with the DIAD IV Case 2: IBM, Cisco, Google: Global Warming by Computer
Chapter 2: Global E-Business: and Collaboration	Case 1: How FedEx Works: Enterprise Systems Case 2: Oracle's Austin Data Center Instructional Video 1: FedEx Improves Customer Experience with Integrated Mapping & Location Data
Chapter 3: Achieving Competitive Advantage with Information Systems	Case 1: National Basketball Association: Competing on Global Delivery With Akamai OS Streaming Case 2: Customer Relationship Management for San Francisco's City Government
Chapter 4: IT Infrastructure: Hardware and Software	Case 1: Hudson's Bay Company and IBM: Virtual Blade Platform Case 2: Salesforce.com: SFA on the iPhone and iPod Touch Instructional Video 1: Google and IBM Produce Cloud Computing Instructional Video 2: IBM Blue Cloud Is Ready-to-Use Computing Instructional Video 3: What the Hell Is Cloud Computing? Instructional Video 4: What Is AJAX and How Does it Work? Instructional Video 5: Yahoo's FireEagle Geolocation Service
Chapter 5: Foundations of Business Intelligence: Databases and Information Management	Case 1: Maruti Suzuki Business Intelligence and Enterprise Databases Case 2: Data Warehousing at REI: Understanding the Customer
Chapter 6: Telecommunications, the Internet, and Wireless Technology	Case 1: Cisco Telepresence: Meeting Without Traveling Case 2: Unified Communications Systems With Virtual Collaboration: IBM and Forterra Instructional Video 1: AT&T Launches Managed Cisco Telepresence Solution Instructional Video 2: CNN Telepresence Instructional Video 3: Microsoft: Unified Communications and POS Malaysia Management
Chapter 7: Securing Information Systems	Case 1: IBM Zone Trusted Information Channel (ZTIC) Case 2: Open ID and Web Security Instructional Video 1: The Quest for Identity 2.0 Instructional Video 2: Identity 2.0
Chapter 8: Achieving Operational Excellence and Customer Intimacy: Enterprise Applications	Case 1: Sinosteel Strengthens Business Management with ERP Applications Case 2: Ingram Micro and H&R Block Get Close to Their Customers
Chapter 9: E-Commerce: Digital Markets, Digital Goods	Case 1: M-Commerce: The Past, Present, and Future Case 2: Ford AutoXchange B2B Marketplace
Chapter 10: Improving Decision Making and Managing Knowledge	Case 1: L'Oréal: Knowledge Management Using Microsoft SharePoint Case 2: IdeaScale Crowdsourcing: Where Ideas Come to Life Case 3: Antivia: Community-based Collaborative Business Intelligence Case 4: IBM and Cognos: Business Intelligence and Analytics for Improved Decision Making
Chapter 11: Building Information Systems and Managing Projects	Case 1: IBM: Business Process Management in a Service-Oriented Architecture Case 2: Startup Appcelerator For Rapid Rich App Development Instructional Video 1: Salesforce and Google: Developing Sales Support Systems with Online Apps
Chapter 12: Ethical and Social Issues in Information Systems	Case 1: Net Neutrality: Neutral Networks Work Case 2: Data Mining for Terrorists and Innocents

LEARNING TRACKS

Chapter	Learning Tracks
Chapter 1: Business Information Systems in Your Career	How Much Does IT Matter? The Changing Business Environment of IT Business Information Value Chain Emerging Mobile Digital Platform
Chapter 2: Global E-Business: and Collaboration	Systems From a Functional Perspective Collaboration, Team Work and Information Systems Challenges of Using Business Information Systems Organizing the Information Systems Function
Chapter 3: Achieving Competitive Advantage with Information Systems	Challenges of Information Systems for Competitive Advantage Primer on Business Process Design and Documentation Primer on Business Process Management
Chapter 4: IT Infrastructure: Hardware and Software	How Computer Hardware and Software Works Service Level Agreements Cloud Computing The Open Source Software Initiative Evolution of IT Infrastructure Technology Drivers of IT Infrastructure IT Infrastructure: Management Opportunities, Challenges, and Solutions
Chapter 5: Foundations of Business Intelligence: Databases and Information Management	Database Design, Normalization, and Entity-Relationship Diagramming Introduction to SQL Hierarchical and Network Data Models
Chapter 6: Telecommunications, the Internet, and Wireless Technology	Computing and Communications Services Provided by Commercial Communications Vendors Broadband Network Services and Technologies Cellular System Generations Wireless Applications for CRM, Supply Chain Management, and Healthcare Introduction to Web 2.0
Chapter 7: Securing Information Systems	The Booming Job Market in IT Security The Sarbanes-Oxley Act Computer Forensics General and Application Controls for Information Systems Software Vulnerability and Reliability Management Challenges of Security and Control
Chapter 8: Achieving Operational Excellence and Customer Intimacy: Enterprise Applications	SAP Business Process Map Business Processes in Supply Chain Management and Supply Chain Metrics Best Practice Business Processes in CRM Software Service Platforms
Chapter 9: E-Commerce: Digital Markets, Digital Goods	E-Commerce Challenges: The Story of Online Groceries Build an E-Commerce Business Plan Hot New Careers in E-Commerce E-Commerce Payment Systems
Chapter 10: Improving Decision Making and Managing Knowledge	Building and Using Pivot Tables The Expert System Inference Engine Business Intelligence Challenges of Knowledge Management Systems
Chapter 11: Building Information Systems and Managing Projects	Capital Budgeting Methods for Information Systems Investments Enterprise Analysis (Business Systems Planning) and Critical Success Factors Unified Modeling Language (UML) IT Investments and Productivity
Chapter 12: Ethical and Social Issues in Information Systems	Developing a Corporate Code of Ethics for IT

Acknowledgments

The production of any book involves valued contributions from a number of persons. We would like to thank all of our editors for encouragement, insight, and strong support for many years. We thank Bob Horan for guiding the development of this edition and Karalyn Holland for her role in managing the project.

Special thanks go to Barbara Ellestad and our supplement authors for their work. We are indebted to William Anderson for his assistance in the writing and production of the text and to Megan Miller for her help during production. We thank Diana R. Craig for her assistance with database and software topics.

Special thanks to colleagues at the Stern School of Business at New York University; to Professor Bernard Merkle of California Lutheran University for his close read of our text and many suggestions; to Professor Lawrence Andrew of Western Illinois University; to Professor Detlef Schoder of the University of Cologne; to Professor Walter Brenner of the University of St. Gallen; to Professor Lutz Kolbe of the University of Gottingen; to Professor Donald Marchand of the International Institute for Management Development; and to Professor Daniel Botha of Stellenbosch University who provided additional suggestions for improvement. Thank you to Professor Ken Kraemer, University of California at Irvine, and Professor John King, University of Michigan, for more than a decade's long discussion of information systems and organizations. And a special remembrance and dedication to Professor Rob Kling, University of Indiana, for being my friend and colleague over so many years.

We also want to especially thank all our reviewers whose suggestions helped improve our texts. Reviewers for this edition include the following

Andrew Cromey - University South Carolina Beaufort
Don Danner – San Francisco State University
Steven Hunt – Morehead State University
Robert Michatek - University South Carolina Beaufort
Richard Potter - University of Illinois, Chicago
Gerrald Reed - Washburn Institute of Technology
Daniel Schmidt - Washburn Institute of Technology
Ludwig Slusky - California State University, Los Angeles
David Teneyuca – University of Texas, San Antonio
Fred Westfall – Troy University
Michael Yates – Robert Morris University

Information Systems in the Digital Age

PART I

Part I introduces the major themes and the problem-solving approaches that are used throughout this book. While surveying the role of information systems in today's businesses, this part raises several major questions: What is an information system? Why are information systems so essential in businesses today? How can information systems help businesses become more competitive? What do I need to know about information systems to succeed in my business career?

Business Information Systems in Your Career

CHAPTER 1

STUDENT LEARNING OBJECTIVES

After completing this chapter, you will be able to answer the following questions:

1. How are information systems transforming business, and what is their relationship to globalization?

2. Why are information systems so essential for running and managing a business today?

3. What exactly is an information system? How does it work? What are its people, organizational, and technology components?

4. How will a four-step method for business problem solving help you solve information system-related problems?

5. How will information systems affect business careers, and what information systems skills and knowledge are essential?

CHAPTER OUTLINE

SHORTENING LINES AT DISNEY WORLD: TECHNOLOGY TO THE RESCUE

No one likes standing in line at Orlando's Walt Disney World, least of all parents with several young children in tow. In recent years, the average Magic Kingdom visitor only had time for nine rides because of lengthy waits and crowded restaurants and walkways. Disney's management is unhappy with these long lines as well, and is using information technology to change that experience.

Disney handles over 30 million visitors each year, many of them during peak family vacation times, such as Christmas, Thanksgiving, and summer vacations. Disney has been treating crowd control as a science for a long time, and now it wants to quicken the pace even more. Customers accustomed to video games and smartphones expect entertainment to be immediately available.

Disney World's management would genuinely like to make its guests happier. In order to increase revenue at Disney's theme parks, it must try to wring more expenditures from existing customers. So it's definitely in Disney's interest to invest in giving guests faster and better access to fun if that encourages them to return more often. And if

© manley099, 2011, iStockPhoto LP.

Disney can also increase guests' average number of restaurant or shop visits, this will boost per capita spending as well.

Beneath the Cinderella Castle lies a Disney Operational Command Center, which uses video cameras, digital park maps, computer programs, and other tools to spot gridlock before it forms and immediately launch countermeasures. The center's information systems determine ride capacity in part by analyzing airline bookings, hotel reservations, and historic attendance data. Satellites supply up-to-the-minute weather analysis. Employees monitor flat-screen televisions displaying various Disney attractions outlined in red, yellow, and green. They are constantly on the lookout for ways to speed up lines or make more efficient use of Disney facilities.

As Bob Schlinger, a writer on Disney for the Frommers.com travel site notes, "you only have so many options once the bathtub is full." So, for example, if the outline for the Pirates of the Caribbean ride changes from green to yellow, the center might alert managers to launch more boats. Alternatively, managers might choose to dispatch Captain Jack Sparrow or Goofy to entertain people as they wait in line. Video game stations help visitors pass the time at wait areas for rides such as Space Mountain.

If Fantasyland is overcrowded but nearby Tomorrowland has more room, the command center might route a miniparade called "Move it! Shake it! Celebrate it!" into the less-crowded area to attract guests in that direction. Other command center technicians monitor restaurants to see if additional registers need to be opened or if more greeters are required to hand menus to people waiting to order. By using information technology to improve the flow of crowds, the Operational Command Center has managed to raise the average number of daily rides for Disney World visitors to 10.

Disney has started to harness mobile technology. Disney's own mobile application called Mobile Magic provides additional tools for guiding visitors more efficiently, including displaying wait times for rides and the ability to locate Disney characters, such as Sleeping Beauty, along with directions to where they are entertaining visitors.

Sources: Chad Storlie, "Walt Disney-Learning from the Military," Military.com, January 4, 2011; Jeremy Olson, "Surviving Disney World," *Minneapolis Star-Tribune*, April 4, 2011; and Brooks Barnes, "Disney Tackles Major Theme Park Problem: Lines," *The New York Times*, December 27, 2010.

The challenges facing Disney World and other theme parks show why information systems are so essential today. There is a limit to the number of people Disney World can handle at one time. In order to keep increasing revenue, Disney needs to find more efficient and productive ways to utilize its existing facilities. In Disney's case, this means encouraging customers to spend more time on the premises and also to make repeat visits.

The chapter-opening diagram calls attention to important points raised by this case and this chapter. To increase revenue, Disney management chose to use information technology to improve the customer experience. Disney uses video cameras, television displays, and specialized computer software to calculate visitor capacity, identify gridlock, and launch activities that will help re-flow crowds. In addition to reducing wait times, Disney uses information technology to provide new interactive services, such as video games to guests waiting in line, and mobile applications to help visitors navigate the theme park more efficiently.

It is also important to note that using information technology for crowd control has changed the way Disney World runs its business. Disney World's systems for managing people in lines changed procedures for ticketing, crowd management, and ordering food from restaurants. These changes had to be carefully planned to make sure they enhanced service, efficiency, and profitability.

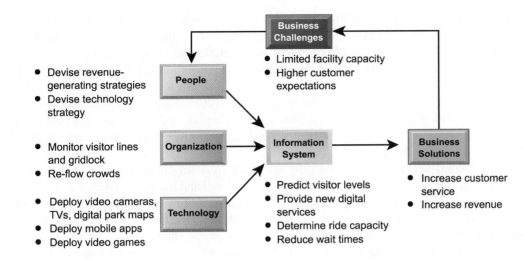

1.1 The Role of Information Systems in Business Today

It's not business as usual in America any more, or the rest of the global economy. In 2011, American businesses will invest nearly $1 trillion in information systems hardware, software, and telecommunications equipment—more than half of all capital investment in the United States. In addition, they will spend another $450 billion on business and management consulting and services, much of which involves redesigning firms' business operations to take advantage of these new technologies. More than half of all business investment in the United States each year involves information systems and technologies, and these expenditures grew at around 7 percent in 2011, far faster than the economy as a whole (BEA, 2011; Gartner 2011).

HOW INFORMATION SYSTEMS ARE TRANSFORMING BUSINESS

You can see the results of this massive spending around you every day by observing how people conduct business. Cell phones, smartphones, tablet computers, e-mail, and online conferencing over the Internet have all become essential tools of business. In 2011, more than 131 million businesses had dot-com Internet sites registered. Approximately 232 million Americans are online, 19 million purchase something every day on the Internet, 40 million research a product, and 116 million use a search engine. What this means is that if you and your business aren't connected to the Internet and wireless networks, chances are you are not being as effective as you could be (Pew Internet and American Life, 2011).

Despite the economic downturn, in 2011 FedEx moved over 900 million packages in the United States, mostly overnight, and United Parcel Service (UPS) moved more than 3.6 billion packages, as businesses sought to sense and respond to rapidly changing customer demand, reduce inventories to the lowest possible levels, and achieve higher levels of operational efficiency. The growth of e-commerce has had a significant impact on UPS's shipping volume. Supply chains have become more fast paced, with companies of all sizes depending on the delivery of just-in-time inventory to help them compete. Companies today manage their inventories in near real time in order to reduce their overhead costs and get to market faster. If you are not a part of this new supply chain management economy, chances are your business is not as efficient as it could be.

As newspaper readership continues to decline, 106 million people read at least some of their news online, 70 million read actual newspapers online, and 88 million use a social networking site like Facebook, Tumblr, or Google+. Over 100 million bank online, and around 74 million now read blogs, creating an explosion of new writers, readers, and new forms of customer feedback that did not exist before. Adding to this mix of new social media, about 33 million people use Twitter, the online and cellular text messaging service, including 75 percent of Fortune 500 firms communicating with their customers. This means your customers are empowered and able to talk to each other about your business products and services. Do you have a solid online customer relationship program in place? Do you know what your customers are saying about your firm? Is your marketing department listening?

E-commerce and Internet advertising are growing in 2011 at around 14 percent despite an economic recession at a time when traditional advertising and commerce are flat. Google's online ad revenues surpassed $28 billion in 2010. Is your advertising department reaching this new Web-based customer?

New federal security and accounting laws require many businesses to keep e-mail messages for five years. Coupled with existing occupational and health laws requiring firms to store employee chemical exposure data for up to 60 years, these laws are spurring the growth of digital information now estimated to be 1.8 zettabytes (1.8 trillion gigabytes), equivalent to more than 50,000 Libraries of Congress. Does your compliance department meet the minimal requirements for storing financial, health, and occupational information? If they don't, your entire business may be at risk.

Briefly, it's a new world of doing business, one that will greatly affect your future business career. Along with the changes in business come changes in jobs and careers. No matter whether you are a finance, accounting, management, marketing, operations management, or information systems major, how you work, where you work, and how well you are compensated will all be affected by business information systems. The purpose of this book is to help you understand and benefit from these new business realities and opportunities.

WHAT'S NEW IN MANAGEMENT INFORMATION SYSTEMS?

Lots! What makes management information systems the most exciting topic in business is the continual change in technology, management use of the technology, and the impact on business success. New businesses and industries appear, old ones decline, and successful firms are those that learn how to use the new technologies. Table 1.1 summarizes the major new themes in business uses of information systems. These themes will appear throughout the book in all the chapters, so it might be a good idea to take some time now and discuss these with your professor and other students.

In the technology area are three interrelated changes: (1) the mobile digital platform composed of smartphones and tablet devices, (2) the growth of online software as a service, and (3) the growth in "cloud computing," where more and more business software runs over the Internet.

IPhones, Android phones, BlackBerrys, and high definition tablet computers are not just gadgets or entertainment outlets. They represent new emerging computing and media platforms based on an array of new hardware and software technologies. More and more business computing is moving from PCs and desktop machines to these mobile devices. Managers are increasingly using these devices to coordinate work, communicate with employees, and provide information for decision making. In 2012, more than half of Internet users will access the Web through mobile devices. Apple and Google no longer refer to their smartphones as "computers" but as "media and communications devices" (that just happen to have dual core processors and 32 gigabytes of storage.) To a large extent these devices change the character of corporate computing.

Managers routinely use so-called "Web 2.0" technologies like social networking, collaboration tools, and wikis in order to make better, faster decisions. As management behavior changes, how work gets organized, coordinated, and measured also changes. By connecting employees working on teams and projects, the social network is where works gets done, where plans are executed, and where managers manage. Collaboration spaces are where employees meet one another, even when they are separated by continents and time zones.

The strength of cloud computing, and the growth of the mobile digital platform, mean that organizations can rely more on telework, remote work, and distributed decision making. This same platform means firms can outsource more work, and rely on markets (rather

TABLE 1.1

What's New in MIS

Change	Business Impact
TECHNOLOGY	
Cloud computing platform emerges as a major business area of innovation	A flexible collection of computers on the Internet begins to perform tasks traditionally performed on corporate computers, reducing infrastructure costs.
Growth in software as a service (SaaS)	Major business applications are now delivered online as an Internet service rather than as boxed software or custom systems.
A mobile digital platform emerges to compete with the PC as a business system and as a software platform	Apple opens its iPhone software to developers, and then opens its App Store on iTunes where business users can download hundreds of thousands of applications to support collaboration, location-based services, and communication with colleagues. Small, portable, lightweight, low-cost, tablet computers become a major part of IT budgets.
PEOPLE	
Managers adopt online collaboration and social networking software to improve coordination, collaboration, and knowledge sharing	Google Apps, Google Sites, Microsoft Windows SharePoint Services, and IBM Lotus Connections are used by over 100 million business professionals worldwide to support blogs, project management, online meetings, personal profiles, social bookmarks, and online communities.
Business intelligence applications accelerate	More powerful data analytics and interactive dashboards provide real-time performance information to managers to enhance management control and decision making.
Virtual meetings proliferate	Managers adopt telepresence video conferencing and Web conferencing technologies to reduce travel time, and cost, while improving collaboration and decision making.
ORGANIZATIONS	
Web 2.0 applications are widely adopted by firms	Web-based services enable employees to interact as online communities using social networks, blogs, wikis, texting, and instant messaging services. Facebook and Google+ create new opportunities for businesses to collaborate with customers and vendors.
Telework gains momentum in the workplace	The Internet, Wi-Fi, cellular networks, and smart mobile devices make it possible for growing numbers of people to work away from the traditional office. Fifty-five percent of U.S. businesses have some form of remote work program.
Co-creation of business value	Sources of business value shift from products to solutions and experiences, and from internal sources to networks of suppliers and collaboration with customers. Supply chains and product development become more global and collaborative; customer interactions help firms define new products and services.

than employees) to build value. It also means that firms can collaborate with suppliers and customers to create new products, or make existing products more efficiently.

You can see some of these trends at work in the Interactive Session on Organizations. Millions of managers and employees rely heavily on the mobile digital platform to coordinate suppliers and shipments, satisfy customers, and organize work activities. A business day without these mobile devices or Internet access would be unthinkable. As you read this case, note how the emerging mobile platform greatly enhances the accuracy, speed, and richness of decision making.

INTERACTIVE SESSION: ORGANIZATIONS Running the Business from the Palm of Your Hand

Can you run your company from the palm of your hand? Perhaps not entirely, but there are many functions today that can be performed using an iPhone, iPad, BlackBerry, or other mobile handheld device.

The BlackBerry has been the favorite mobile handheld for business because it was optimized for e-mail and messaging, with strong security and tools for accessing internal corporate systems. Now that's changing. Companies large and small are starting to deploy Apple's iPhone and iPad as well as Android mobile devices to conduct more of their work. They are enhancing their security systems so that mobile users can remotely access proprietary corporate resources with confidence.

For some, these handhelds have become indispensible. TCHO Chocolate is a start-up that uses custom-developed machinery to create unique chocolate flavors. Owner Timothy Childs developed an iPhone app that enables him to remotely log into each chocolate-making machine, control time and temperature, turn the machines on and off, and receive alerts about when to make temperature changes. The iPhone app also enables him to remotely view several video cameras that show how the TCHO Flavor Lab is doing. TCHO employees also use the iPhone to exchange photos, e-mail, and text messages.

Using handhelds to run the business is not limited to small companies. General Electric (GE) is one of the world's largest companies, producing aircraft engines, locomotives and other transportation equipment, kitchen and laundry appliances, lighting, electric distribution and control equipment, generators and turbines, and medical imaging equipment. GE is also a leading provider of financial services, aviation, clean energy, media, and health care technology. This giant multinational was an early adopter of mobile technology. GE employees use their iPads to access e-mail, contacts, documents, and electronic presentations. GE's Mobile Center of Excellence has developed dozens of iPhone and iPad applications, including industry-specific diagnostic and monitoring tools and business intelligence tools that help decision makers find patterns and trends in large volumes of data. The company's Transformer Monitoring app helps manage gas turbine inventory and electronic transformers throughout the world, with the ability to zoom in from a global map to a specific transformer and read all of the key performance indicators. A PDS Movement Planner app lets service personnel monitor railway tracks and obtain diagnostic information on locomotives.

With operations in 60 countries, Dow Corning offers more than 7,000 products and services for consumer and industrial applications, from adhesives to lubricants, delivered as fluids, solids, gels, and powders. A Roambi Visualizer app lets Dow Corning executives use their iPhones to quickly view and analyze real-time data from their core corporate system, including sales figures, trends, and projections. It presents managers with simple, intuitive dashboards of complex data. According to Executive Vice President and Chief Financial Officer Don Sheets, "In 15 seconds I can get a sense of whether there's a financial performance issue I need to get involved with."

Dow Corning's Analytics App for the iPhone monitors Web site traffic and online sales for the company's XIAMETER brand of standard silicone products. Analytics App interfaces with Google Analytics. When Dow Corning rolls out XIAMETER Web sites across the globe, executives will be able to monitor what content is and isn't being used whether they are home, traveling, or at the office.

Sunbelt Rentals, based in Fort Mill, South Carolina, is one of the largest equipment rental companies in the United States, with a $2 billion inventory of rental equipment. More than 1,200 company employees, including sales staff, field personnel, and executives, are equipped with iPhones to interact with contacts and stay abreast of calendar events. In addition to using iPhones for e-mail, scheduling, and contact management, Sunbelt deployed a custom application called Mobile SalesPro, which ties multiple systems and databases into a single package for the sales team. This application connects the corporate point-of-sale system, inventory control and management system, and enterprise system, which integrates data from many different business functions. Users are able to share sales quotes based on the most up-to-date information on rental rates and equipment availability. With this application, Sunbelt's sales team can respond immediately to customer requests while they are at a job site.

SAP has developed a Business One mobile application for the iPhone, which enables users to stay connected to business and customer data in real time when they are away from the office. (Business One is a single software system integrating all core business functions across the company, including financials, sales, customer relationship management, inventory, and operations.)

The mobile application enables sales managers to receive alerts on specific events, such as deviations from approved discounts, while sales reps can retrieve and update customer records as well as manage their appointments in real time. Managers are able to check inventory availability and access detailed information about products in stock. Management at Coolshop.dk, an independent distributor of interactive entertainment products in the Nordic countries, uses the Business One mobile application to rapidly access customer information and changes in margins, prices and inventory when traveling away from the office.

Sources: Doug Henschen, "Mobilizing Enterprise Apps: The Next Big Leap," *Information Week*, February 12, 2011; Hande Bolukbasi, "Putting the Business in the Palm of Your Hand-Literally," *SAPInsider*, January 1, 2011; and Apple iPhone in Business Profiles, www.apple.com, accessed April 28, 2011.

CASE STUDY QUESTIONS

1. What kinds of applications are described here? What business functions do they support? How do they improve operational efficiency and decision making?

2. Identify the problems that businesses in this case study solved by using mobile digital devices.

3. What kinds of businesses are most likely to benefit from equipping their employees with mobile digital devices such as iPhones, iPads, and BlackBerrys?

4. One company deploying iPhones has said, "The iPhone is not a game changer, it's an industry changer. It changes the way that you can interact with your customers and with your suppliers." Discuss the implications of this statement.

MIS IN ACTION

Explore the Web site for either the Apple iPhone, the BlackBerry, or an Android smartphone, such as the Droid Incredible or Samsung Fascinate, then answer the following questions:

1. List and describe the capabilities of each of these devices and give examples of how they could be used by businesses.

2. List and describe three downloadable business apps for each device and describe their business benefits.

GLOBALIZATION CHALLENGES AND OPPORTUNITIES: A FLATTENED WORLD

Prior to 1492 and the voyages of Columbus and others to the Americas, there was no truly global economic system of trade that connected all the continents on earth. After the fifteenth century, a global trading system began to emerge. The world trade that ensued after these voyages

iPhone and iPad Business Applications

1. *Salesforce Mobile*
2. *FedEx Mobile for iPhone*
3. *Cisco WebEx Meeting Center*
4. *iSchedule*
5. *iWork*
6. *Documents to Go*
7. *PDF Reader Pro*
8. *BizXpenseTracker*

© sd619, 2011, iStockPhoto, LP.

Whether it's attending an online meeting, checking orders, working with files and documents, or obtaining business intelligence, Apple's iPhone and iPad offer unlimited possibilities for business users. Both devices have a stunning multitouch display, full Internet browsing, digital camera, and capabilities for messaging, voice transmission, and document management. These features make each an all-purpose platform for mobile computing and business.

has brought the peoples and cultures of the world much closer together. The "industrial revolution" was really a worldwide phenomenon energized by expansion of trade among nations. Until the Internet was invented and refined, the global economy was ineffcient because it was difficult and costly to communicate from one corner of the earth to another.

By 2005, journalist Thomas Friedman wrote an influential book declaring the world was now "flat," by which he meant that the Internet and global communications had greatly expanded the opportunities for people to communicate with one another, and reduced the economic and cultural advantages of developed countries. U.S. and European countries were in a fight for their economic lives, competing for jobs, markets, resources, and even ideas with highly educated, motivated populations in low-wage areas in the less developed world (Friedman, 2007). This "globalization" presents you and your business with both challenges and opportunities.

A growing percentage of the economy of the United States and other advanced industrial countries in Europe and Asia depends on imports and exports. In 2011, more than 33 percent of the U.S. economy resulted from foreign trade, both imports and exports. In Europe and Asia, the number exceeds 50 percent. Half of the Fortune 500 U.S. firms derive at least half their revenues from foreign operations. For instance, more than 50 percent of Intel's revenues in 2010 came from overseas sales of its microprocessors, and the same is true for Internet titans like Google, Amazon, Apple, Microsoft, and Facebook. Toys for chips: 80 percent of the toys sold in the United States are manufactured in China, while about 90 percent of the PCs manufactured in China use American-made Intel or Advanced Micro Design (AMD) chips. Apple's iPhone is assembled in China, but 90 percent of the value comes from the United States and Europe in the form of parts and designs.

It's not just goods that move across borders. So too do jobs, some of them high-level jobs that pay well and require a college degree. In the past decade, the United States lost several million manufacturing jobs to offshore, low-wage producers. But manufacturing is now a very small part of U.S. employment (less than 12 percent). In a normal year, about 300,000 service jobs move offshore to lower-wage countries, many of them in less-skilled information system occupations, but also include "tradable service" jobs in architecture, financial services, customer call centers, consulting, engineering, and even radiology.

On the plus side, the U.S. economy creates over 3.5 million new jobs in a normal year. Employment in information systems and the other service occupations listed previously have expanded in sheer numbers, wages, productivity, and quality of work. Outsourcing has actually accelerated the development of new systems in the United States and worldwide. In the midst of an economic recession, jobs in information systems are among the most in demand.

The challenge for you as a business student is to develop high-level skills through education and on-the-job experience that cannot be outsourced. The challenge for your business is to avoid markets for goods and services that can be produced offshore much less expensively. The opportunities are equally immense. You can learn how to profit from the lower costs available in world markets and the chance to serve a marketplace with billions of customers. You have the opportunity to develop higher-level and more profitable products and services. You will find throughout this book examples of companies and individuals who either failed or succeeded in using information systems to adapt to this new global environment.

What does globalization have to do with management information systems? That's simple: everything. The emergence of the Internet into a full-blown international communications system has drastically reduced the costs of operating and transacting on a global scale. Communication between a factory floor in Shanghai and a distribution center in Sioux Falls, South Dakota, is now instant and virtually free. Customers now can shop in a worldwide marketplace, obtaining price and quality information reliably 24 hours a day. Firms producing goods and services on a global scale achieve extraordinary cost reductions by finding low-cost suppliers and managing production facilities in other countries. Internet service firms, such as Google and eBay, are able to replicate their business models and services in multiple countries without having to redesign their expensive fixed-cost information systems infrastructure.

BUSINESS DRIVERS OF INFORMATION SYSTEMS

What makes information systems so essential today? Why are businesses investing so much in information systems and technologies? They do so to achieve six important business objectives: operational excellence; new products, services, and business models; customer and supplier intimacy; improved decision making; competitive advantage; and survival.

Operational Excellence

Businesses continuously seek to improve the efficiency of their operations in order to achieve higher profitability. Information systems and technologies are some of the most important tools available to managers for achieving higher levels of efficiency and productivity in business operations, especially when coupled with changes in business practices and management behavior.

Walmart, the largest retailer on Earth, exemplifies the power of information systems coupled with brilliant business practices and supportive management to achieve world-class operational efficiency. In 2010, Walmart achieved more than $405 billion in sales—nearly one-tenth of retail sales in the United States—in large part because of its Retail Link system, which digitally links its suppliers to every one of Walmart's 8,400 stores worldwide. As soon as a customer purchases an item, the supplier monitoring the item knows to ship a replacement to the shelf. Walmart is the most efficient retail store in the industry, achieving sales of more than $450 per square foot, compared to its closest competitor, Target, at $425 a square foot, with other large retail firms producing less than $12 a square foot.

Amazon, the largest online retailer on earth, generating $34 billion in sales in 2010, invested $1.7 billion in information systems so that when one of its estimated 121 million customers searches for a product, Amazon can respond in milliseconds with the correct product displayed (and recommendations for other products).

New Products, Services, and Business Models

Information systems and technologies are a major enabling tool for firms to create new products and services, as well as entirely new business models. A **business model** describes how a company produces, delivers, and sells a product or service to create wealth. Today's music industry is vastly different from the industry in 2000. Apple Inc. transformed an old business model of music distribution based on vinyl records, tapes, and CDs into an online, legal distribution model based on its own operating system and iTunes store. Apple has prospered from a continuing stream of innovations, including the original iPod, iPod nano, iTunes music service, iPhone, and iPad.

© 2011, Transpara.

Transpara's Mobile Dashboard delivers comprehensive and accurate information for decision making. The graphical overview of key performance indicators helps managers quickly spot areas that need attention.

Customer and Supplier Intimacy

When a business really knows its customers and serves them well, the way they want to be served, the customers generally respond by returning and purchasing more. This raises revenues and profits. Likewise with suppliers: the more a business engages its suppliers, the better the suppliers can provide vital inputs. This lowers costs. How to really know your customers, or suppliers, is a central problem for businesses with millions of offline and online customers.

The Mandarin Oriental in Manhattan and other high-end hotels exemplify the use of information systems and technologies to achieve customer intimacy. These hotels use computers to keep track of guests' preferences, such as their preferred room temperature, check-in time, frequently dialed telephone numbers, and television programs, and store these data in a giant data repository. Individual rooms in the hotels are networked to a central network server computer so that they can be remotely monitored or controlled. When a customer arrives at one of these hotels, the system automatically changes the room conditions, such as dimming the lights, setting the room temperature, or selecting appropriate music, based on the customer's digital profile. The hotels also analyze their customer data to identify their best customers and to develop individualized marketing campaigns based on customers' preferences.

JCPenney exemplifies the benefits of information systems-enabled supplier intimacy. Every time a dress shirt is bought at a JCPenney store in the United States, the record of the sale appears immediately on computers in Hong Kong at TAL Apparel Ltd., a giant contract manufacturer that produces one in eight dress shirts sold in the United States. TAL runs the numbers through a computer model it developed and decides how many replacement shirts to make, and in what styles, colors, and sizes. TAL then sends the shirts to each JCPenney store, completely bypassing the retailer's warehouses. In other words, JCPenney's surplus shirt inventory is near zero, as is the cost of storing it.

Improved Decision Making

Many business managers operate in an information fog bank, never really having the right information at the right time to make an informed decision. Instead, managers rely on forecasts, best guesses, and luck. The result is over- or underproduction of goods and services, misallocation of resources, and poor response times. These poor outcomes raise costs and lose customers. In the past 10 years, information systems and technologies have made it possible for managers to use real-time data from the marketplace when making decisions.

For instance, Verizon Corporation, one of the largest regional Bell operating companies in the United States, uses a Web-based digital dashboard to provide managers with precise real-time information on customer complaints, network performance for each locality served, and line outages or storm-damaged lines. Using this information, managers can immediately allocate repair resources to affected areas, inform consumers of repair efforts, and restore service fast.

Competitive Advantage

When firms achieve one or more of these business objectives—operational excellence; new products, services, and business models; customer/supplier intimacy; and improved decision making—chances are they have already achieved a competitive advantage. Doing things better than your competitors, charging less for superior products, and responding to customers and suppliers in real time all add up to higher sales and higher profits that your competitors cannot match. Apple Inc., Walmart, and UPS are industry leaders because they know how to use information systems for this purpose.

Survival

Business firms also invest in information systems and technologies because they are necessities of doing business. Sometimes these necessities are driven by industry-level changes. For instance, after Citibank introduced the first automated teller machines (ATMs) in the New York region to attract customers through higher service levels, its competitors rushed to provide ATMs to their customers to keep up with Citibank. Today, virtually all banks in the United States have regional ATMs and link to national and international ATM networks, such as CIRRUS. Providing ATM services to retail banking customers is simply a requirement of being in and surviving in the retail banking business.

Many federal and state statutes and regulations create a legal duty for companies and their employees to retain records, including digital records. For instance, the Toxic Substances Control Act (1976), which regulates the exposure of U.S. workers to more than 75,000 toxic chemicals, requires firms to retain records on employee exposure for 30 years. The Sarbanes-Oxley Act (2002), which was intended to improve the accountability of public firms and their auditors, requires public companies to retain audit working papers and records, including all e-mails, for five years. Firms turn to information systems and technologies to provide the capability to respond to these information retention and reporting requirements. The Dodd–Frank Act (2010) requires financial service firms to greatly expand their public reporting on derivatives and other financial instruments.

1.2 Perspectives on Information Systems and Information Technology

So far we've used *information systems and technologies* informally without defining the terms. **Information technology (IT)** consists of all the hardware and software that a firm needs to use in order to achieve its business objectives. This includes not only computer machines, disk drives, and mobile handheld devices but also software, such as the Windows or Linux operating systems, the Microsoft Office desktop productivity suite, and the many thousands of computer programs that can be found in a typical large firm. "Information systems" are more complex and can be best understood by looking at them from both a technology and a business perspective.

WHAT IS AN INFORMATION SYSTEM?

An **information system (IS)** can be defined technically as a set of interrelated components that collect (or retrieve), process, store, and distribute information to support decision making, coordinating, and control in an organization. In addition, information systems may also help managers and workers analyze problems, visualize complex subjects, and create new products.

Information systems contain information about significant people, places, and things within the organization or in the environment surrounding it. By **information** we mean data that have been shaped into a form that is meaningful and useful to human beings. **Data**, in contrast, are streams of raw facts representing events occurring in organizations or the physical environment before they have been organized and arranged into a form that people can understand and use.

A brief example contrasting information and data may prove useful. Supermarket checkout counters scan millions of pieces of data, such as bar codes, that describe the product. Such pieces of data can be totaled and analyzed to provide meaningful information, such as the total number of bottles of dish detergent sold at a particular store, which brands of dish detergent were selling the most rapidly at that store or sales territory, or the total amount spent on that brand of dish detergent at that store or sales region (see Figure 1.1).

Three activities in an information system produce the information that organizations need to make decisions, control operations, analyze problems, and create new products or services. These activities are input, processing, and output (see Figure 1.2). **Input** captures or collects raw data from within the organization or from its external environment. **Processing** converts this raw input into a meaningful form. **Output** transfers the processed information to the people who will use it or to the activities for which it will be used. Information systems also require **feedback**, which is output that is returned to appropriate members of the organization to help them evaluate or correct the input stage.

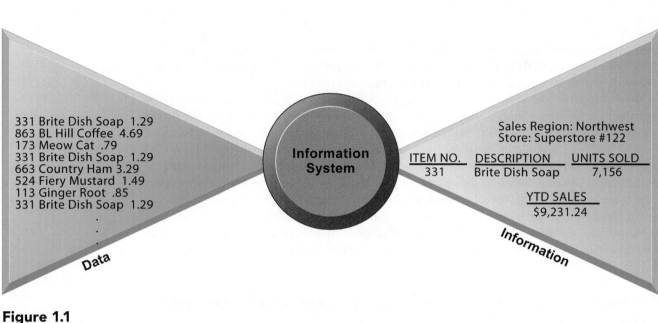

331 Brite Dish Soap 1.29
863 BL Hill Coffee 4.69
173 Meow Cat .79
331 Brite Dish Soap 1.29
663 Country Ham 3.29
524 Fiery Mustard 1.49
113 Ginger Root .85
331 Brite Dish Soap 1.29

Data

Information System

Information

Sales Region: Northwest
Store: Superstore #122

ITEM NO.	DESCRIPTION	UNITS SOLD
331	Brite Dish Soap	7,156

YTD SALES
$9,231.24

Figure 1.1
Data and Information
*Raw data from a supermarket checkout counter can be processed and organized to produce
meaningful information, such as the total unit sales of dish detergent or the total sales revenue from
dish detergent for a specific store or sales territory.*

In Disney World's systems for controlling crowds, the raw input consists of data from
airline bookings and hotel reservations, satellite weather data, historic attendance data
for the date being analyzed, and images of crowds from video cameras stationed at key
locations throughout the park. Computers store these data and process them to calculate
projected total attendance for a specific date as well as attendance figures and wait times for

Figure 1.2
**Functions of an
Information System**
*An information system
contains information
about an organization
and its surrounding
environment. Three
basic activities—input,
processing, and
output—produce the
information organiza-
tions need. Feedback
is output returned to
appropriate people or
activities in the orga-
nization to evaluate
and refine the input.
Environmental actors,
such as customers,
suppliers, competitors,
stockholders, and regu-
latory agencies, interact
with the organization and
its information systems.*

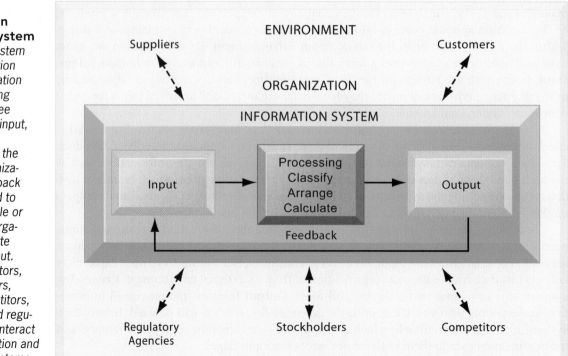

each ride and restaurant at various times during the day. The systems indicate which rides or attractions are too overcrowded, which have spare capacity, and which can add capacity. The system provides meaningful information such as the number of guests attending on a particular day or time period, the average wait time per ride, the average number of restaurant and shop visits, the average number of rides guests squeezed into a single day's visit, and the average amount spent per customer during a specific time period. Such information helps Disney management gauge the theme park's overall efficiency and profitability.

Although computer-based information systems use computer technology to process raw data into meaningful information, there is a sharp distinction between a computer and a computer program and an information system. Electronic computers and related software programs are the technical foundation, the tools and materials, of modern information systems. Computers provide the equipment for storing and processing information. Computer programs, or software, are sets of operating instructions that direct and control computer processing. Knowing how computers and computer programs work is important in designing solutions to organizational problems, but computers are only part of an information system.

A house is an appropriate analogy. Houses are built with hammers, nails, and wood, but these alone do not make a house. The architecture, design, setting, landscaping, and all of the decisions that lead to the creation of these features are part of the house and are crucial for solving the problem of putting a roof over one's head. Computers and programs are the hammer, nails, and lumber of computer-based information systems, but alone they cannot produce the information a particular organization needs. To understand information systems, you must understand the problems they are designed to solve, their architectural and design elements, and the organizational processes that lead to these solutions.

IT ISN'T SIMPLY TECHNOLOGY: THE ROLE OF PEOPLE AND ORGANIZATIONS

To fully understand information systems, you will need to be aware of the broader organization, people, and information technology dimensions of systems (see Figure 1.3) and their power to provide solutions to challenges and problems in the business environment. We refer to this broader understanding of information systems, which encompasses an understanding of the people and organizational dimensions of systems as well as the technical dimensions of systems, as **information systems literacy**. Information systems literacy includes a behavioral as well as a technical approach to studying information systems. **Computer literacy**, in contrast, focuses primarily on knowledge of information technology.

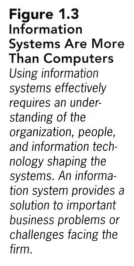

Figure 1.3
Information Systems Are More Than Computers
Using information systems effectively requires an understanding of the organization, people, and information technology shaping the systems. An information system provides a solution to important business problems or challenges facing the firm.

The field of **management information systems (MIS)** tries to achieve this broader information systems literacy. MIS deals with behavioral issues as well as technical issues surrounding the development, use, and impact of information systems used by managers and employees in the firm.

DIMENSIONS OF INFORMATION SYSTEMS

Let's examine each of the dimensions of information systems—organizations, people, and information technology.

Organizations

Information systems are an integral part of organizations. And although we tend to think about information technology changing organizations and business firms, it is, in fact, a two-way street: The history and culture of business firms also affects how the technology is used and how it should be used. In order to understand how a specific business firm uses information systems, you need to know something about the structure, history, and culture of the company.

Organizations have a structure that is composed of different levels and specialties. Their structures reveal a clear-cut division of labor. A business firm is organized as a hierarchy, or a pyramid structure, of rising authority and responsibility. The upper levels of the hierarchy consist of managerial, professional, and technical employees, whereas the lower levels consist of operational personnel. Experts are employed and trained for different business functions, such as sales and marketing, manufacturing and production, finance and accounting, and human resources. Information systems are built by the firm in order to serve these different specialties and different levels of the firm. Chapter 2 provides more detail on these business functions and organizational levels and the ways in which they are supported by information systems.

An organization accomplishes and coordinates work through this structured hierarchy and through its **business processes**, which are logically related tasks and behaviors for accomplishing work. Developing a new product, fulfilling an order, and hiring a new employee are examples of business processes.

Most organizations' business processes include formal rules that have been developed over a long time for accomplishing tasks. These rules guide employees in a variety of procedures, from writing an invoice to responding to customer complaints. Some of these business processes have been written down, but others are informal work practices, such as a requirement to return telephone calls from coworkers or customers, that are not formally documented. Information systems automate many business processes. For instance, how a customer receives credit or how a customer is billed is often determined by an information system that incorporates a set of formal business processes.

Each organization has a unique **culture**, or fundamental set of assumptions, values, and ways of doing things, that has been accepted by most of its members. Parts of an organization's culture can always be found embedded in its information systems. For instance, the United Parcel Service's concern with placing service to the customer first is an aspect of its organizational culture that can be found in the company's package tracking systems.

Different levels and specialties in an organization create different interests and points of view. These views often conflict. Conflict is the basis for organizational politics. Information systems come out of this cauldron of differing perspectives, conflicts, compromises, and agreements that are a natural part of all organizations.

People

A business is only as good as the people who work there and run it. Likewise with information systems—they are useless without skilled people to build and maintain them, and without people who can understand how to use the information in a system to achieve business objectives.

For instance, a call center that provides help to customers using an advanced customer relationship management system (described in later chapters) is useless if employees are not adequately trained to deal with customers, find solutions to their problems, and leave the customer feeling that the company cares for them. Likewise, employee attitudes about their jobs, employers, or technology can have a powerful effect on their abilities to use information systems productively.

Business firms require many different kinds of skills and people, including managers as well as rank-and-file employees. The job of managers is to make sense out of the many situations faced by organizations, make decisions, and formulate action plans to solve organizational problems. Managers perceive business challenges in the environment, they set the organizational strategy for responding to those challenges, and they allocate the human and financial resources to coordinate the work and achieve success. Throughout, they must exercise responsible leadership.

But managers must do more than manage what already exists. They must also create new products and services and even re-create the organization from time to time. A substantial part of management responsibility is creative work driven by new knowledge and information. Information technology can play a powerful role in helping managers develop novel solutions to a broad range of problems.

As you will learn throughout this text, technology is relatively inexpensive today, but people are very expensive. Because people are the only ones capable of business problem solving and converting information technology into useful business solutions, we spend considerable effort in this text looking at the people dimension of information systems.

Technology

Information technology is one of many tools managers use to cope with change and complexity. **Computer hardware** is the physical equipment used for input, processing, and output activities in an information system. It consists of the following: computers of various sizes and shapes; various input, output, and storage devices; and telecommunications devices that link computers together.

Computer software consists of the detailed, preprogrammed instructions that control and coordinate the computer hardware components in an information system. Chapter 4 describes the contemporary software and hardware platforms used by firms today in greater detail.

Data management technology consists of the software governing the organization of data on physical storage media. More detail on data organization and access methods can be found in Chapter 5.

Networking and telecommunications technology, consisting of both physical devices and software, links the various pieces of hardware and transfers data from one physical location to another. Computers and communications equipment can be connected in networks for sharing voice, data, images, sound, and video. A **network** links two or more computers to share data or resources, such as a printer.

The world's largest and most widely used network is the **Internet**. The Internet is a global "network of networks" that uses universal standards (described in Chapter 6) to connect millions of different networks in nearly 200 countries around the world.

The Internet has created a new "universal" technology platform on which to build new products, services, strategies, and business models. This same technology platform has internal uses, providing the connectivity to link different systems and networks within the firm. Internal corporate networks based on Internet technology are called **intranets**. Private intranets extended to authorized users outside the organization are called **extranets**, and firms use such networks to coordinate their activities with other firms for making purchases, collaborating on design, and performing other interorganizational work. For most business firms today, using Internet technology is a business necessity and a competitive advantage.

The **World Wide Web** is a service provided by the Internet that uses universally accepted standards for storing, retrieving, formatting, and displaying information in a page format on the Internet. Web pages contain text, graphics, animations, sound, and video and are linked to other Web pages. By clicking on highlighted words or buttons on a Web page, you can link to related pages to find additional information and links to other locations on the Web. The Web can serve as the foundation for new kinds of information systems such as UPS's Web-based package tracking system.

All of these technologies, along with the people required to run and manage them, represent resources that can be shared throughout the organization and constitute the firm's **information technology (IT) infrastructure**. The IT infrastructure provides the foundation, or *platform*, on which the firm can build its specific information systems. Each organization must carefully design and manage its information technology infrastructure so that it has the set of technology services it needs for the work it wants to accomplish with information systems. Chapters 4 through 7 of this text examine each major technology component of information technology infrastructure and show how they all work together to create the technology platform for the organization.

The Interactive Session on Technology describes some of the typical technologies used in computer-based information systems today. UPS invests heavily in information systems technology to make its business more efficient and customer oriented. It uses an array of information technologies including bar code scanning systems, wireless networks, large mainframe computers, handheld computers, the Internet, and many different pieces of software for tracking packages, calculating fees, maintaining customer accounts, and managing logistics. As you read this case, try to identify the problem this company was facing, what alternative solutions were available to management, and how well the chosen solution worked.

Let's identify the organization, people, and technology elements in the UPS package tracking system we have just described. The organization element anchors the package tracking system in UPS's sales and production functions (the main product of UPS is a service—package delivery). It specifies the required procedures for identifying packages with both sender and recipient information, taking inventory, tracking the packages en route, and providing package status reports for UPS customers and customer service representatives.

The system must also provide information to satisfy the needs of managers and workers. UPS drivers need to be trained in both package pickup and delivery procedures and in how to use the package tracking system so that they can work efficiently and effectively. UPS customers may need some training to use UPS in-house package tracking software or the UPS Web site.

UPS's management is responsible for monitoring service levels and costs and for promoting the company's strategy of combining low cost and superior service. Management decided to use automation to increase the ease of sending a package using UPS and of checking its delivery status, thereby reducing delivery costs and increasing sales revenues.

The technology supporting this system consists of handheld computers, bar code scanners, wired and wireless communications networks, desktop computers, UPS's central computer, storage technology for the package delivery data, UPS in-house package tracking software, and software to access the World Wide Web. The result is an information system solution to the business challenge of providing a high level of service with low prices in the face of mounting competition.

1.3 Understanding Information Systems: A Business Problem-Solving Approach

Our approach to understanding information systems is to consider information systems and technologies as solutions to a variety of business challenges and problems. We refer to this as a "problem-solving approach." Businesses face many challenges and problems, and information systems are one major way of solving these problems. All of the

INTERACTIVE SESSION: TECHNOLOGY   UPS Competes Globally with Information Technology

United Parcel Service (UPS) started out in 1907 in a closet-sized basement office. Jim Casey and Claude Ryan—two teenagers from Seattle with two bicycles and one phone—promised the "best service and lowest rates." UPS has used this formula successfully for more than a century to become the world's largest ground and air package-delivery company. It's a global enterprise with over 400,000 employees, 93,000 vehicles, and the world's ninth largest airline.

Today UPS delivers 15.6 million packages and documents each day in the United States and more than 220 other countries and territories. The firm has been able to maintain leadership in small-package delivery services despite stiff competition from FedEx and Airborne Express by investing heavily in advanced information technology. UPS spends more than $1 billion each year to maintain a high level of customer service while keeping costs low and streamlining its overall operations.

It all starts with the scannable bar-coded label attached to a package, which contains detailed information about the sender, the destination, and when the package should arrive. Customers can download and print their own labels using special software provided by UPS or by accessing the UPS Web site. Before the package is even picked up, information from the "smart" label is transmitted to one of UPS's computer centers in Mahwah, New Jersey, or Alpharetta, Georgia, and sent to the distribution center nearest its final destination.

Dispatchers at this center download the label data and use special software to create the most efficient delivery route for each driver that considers traffic, weather conditions, and the location of each stop. UPS estimates its delivery trucks save 28 million miles and burn 3 million fewer gallons of fuel each year as a result of using this technology. To further increase cost savings and safety, drivers are trained to use "340 Methods" developed by industrial engineers to optimize the performance of every task from lifting and loading boxes to selecting a package from a shelf in the truck.

The first thing a UPS driver picks up each day is a handheld computer called a Delivery Information Acquisition Device (DIAD), which can access a wireless cell phone network. As soon as the driver logs on, his or her day's route is downloaded onto the handheld. The DIAD also automatically captures customers' signatures along with pickup and delivery information. Package tracking information is then transmitted to UPS's computer network for storage and processing. From there, the information can be accessed worldwide to provide proof of delivery to customers or to

respond to customer queries. It usually takes less than 60 seconds from the time a driver presses "complete" on a DIAD for the new information to be available on the Web.

Through its automated package tracking system, UPS can monitor and even re-route packages throughout the delivery process. At various points along the route from sender to receiver, bar code devices scan shipping information on the package label and feed data about the progress of the package into the central computer. Customer service representatives are able to check the status of any package from desktop computers linked to the central computers and respond immediately to inquiries from customers. UPS customers can also access this information from the company's Web site using their own computers or mobile phones. UPS now has mobile apps and a mobile Web site for iPhone, BlackBerry, and Android smartphone users.

Anyone with a package to ship can access the UPS Web site to track packages, check delivery routes, calculate shipping rates, determine time in transit, print labels, and schedule a pickup. The data collected at the UPS Web site are transmitted to the UPS central computer and then back to the customer after processing. UPS also provides tools that enable customers, such as Cisco Systems, to embed UPS functions, such as tracking and cost calculations, into their own Web sites so they can track shipments without visiting the UPS site.

A Web-based Post Sales Order Management System (OMS) manages global service orders and inventory for critical parts fulfillment. The system enables high-tech electronics, aerospace, medical equipment, and other companies anywhere in the world that ship critical parts to quickly assess their critical parts inventory, determine the most optimal routing strategy to meet customer needs, place orders online, and track parts from the warehouse to the end user. An automated e-mail or fax feature keeps customers informed of each shipping milestone and can provide notification of any changes to flight schedules for commercial airlines carrying their parts.

UPS is now leveraging its decades of expertise managing its own global delivery network to manage logistics and supply chain activities for other companies. It created a UPS Supply Chain Solutions division that provides a complete bundle of standardized services to subscribing companies at a fraction of what it would cost to build their own systems and infrastructure. These services include supply chain design and management, freight forwarding, customs brokerage, mail services, multimodal transportation, and financial services, in addition to logistics services.

Intralox, LLC, of Harahan, Louisiana, is a producer of conveyor belt technologies with close to 60,000 manufacturing customers worldwide. To improve service to key customers in Mexico, Intralox worked with UPS to overhaul its shipping model. UPS implemented a UPS Trade Direct Cross Border solution that consolidates multiple Intralox orders at a UPS Supply Chain Solutions facility in Laredo, Texas, then moves bulk shipments to the border, reducing Intralox's transportation costs. UPS Supply Chain Solutions then

clears the bulk shipment through Mexican customs as a single entry, saving Intralox more money by eliminating multiple brokerage fees. The bulk shipment is received at a third-party logistics partner's facility in Nuevo Laredo, Mexico, where it is broken down into individual orders and delivered to individual customers at domestic rates.

Sources: Bob DuBois, "UPS Mobile Goes Global," UPS Compass, January 27, 2011; "Intralox and UPS: Streamlining Efficiencies South of the Border,"www. ups.com, accessed April 30, 3011; Jennifer Levitz, "UPS Thinks Out of the Box on Driver Training," *Wall Street Journal,* April 6, 2010; Agam Shah, "UPS Invests $1 Billion in Technology to Cut Costs," *Bloomberg BusinessWeek,* March 25, 2010.

CASE STUDY QUESTIONS

1. What are the inputs, processing, and outputs of UPS's package tracking system?

2. What technologies are used by UPS? How are these technologies related to UPS's business strategy?

3. What strategic business objectives do UPS's information systems address?

4. What would happen if UPS's information systems were not available?

MIS IN ACTION

Explore the UPS Web site (www.ups.com) and answer the following questions:

1. What kind of information and services does the Web site provide for individuals, small businesses, and large businesses? List these services.

2. Go to the Business Solutions portion of the UPS Web site. Browse the UPS Business Solutions by category (such as shipment delivery, returns, or international trade) and write a description of all the services UPS provides for one of these categories. Explain how a business would benefit from these services.

Using a handheld computer called a Delivery Information Acquisition Device (DIAD), UPS drivers automatically capture customers' signatures along with pickup, delivery, and time card information. UPS information systems use these data to track packages while they are being transported.

© Bill Aron, 2011, PhotoEdit Inc.

cases in this book illustrate how a company used information systems to solve a specific problem.

The problem-solving approach has direct relevance to your future career. Your future employers will hire you because you are able to solve business problems and achieve business objectives. Your knowledge of how information systems contribute to problem solving will be very helpful to both you and your employers.

THE PROBLEM-SOLVING APPROACH

At first glance, problem solving in daily life seems to be perfectly straightforward: A machine breaks down, parts and oil spill all over the floor, and, obviously, somebody has to do something about it. So, of course, you find a tool around the shop and start repairing the machine. After a cleanup and proper inspection of other parts, you start the machine, and production resumes.

No doubt some problems in business are this straightforward. But few problems are this simple in the real world of business. In real-world business firms, a number of major factors are simultaneously involved in problems. These major factors can usefully be grouped into three categories: *organization, technology,* and *people.* In other words, a whole set of problems is usually involved.

A MODEL OF THE PROBLEM-SOLVING PROCESS

There is a simple model of problem solving that you can use to help you understand and solve business problems using information systems. You can think of business problem-solving as a four-step process (see Figure 1.4). Most problem solvers work through this model on their way to finding a solution. Let's take a brief look at each step.

Problem Identification
The first step in the problem-solving process is to understand what kind of problem exists. Contrary to popular beliefs, problems are not like basketballs on a court simply waiting to be picked up by some "objective" problem solver. Before problems can be solved, there must be agreement in a business that a problem exists, about what the problem is, about what its causes are, and about what can be done about the problem given the limited resources of the

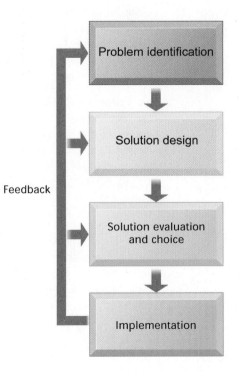

**Figure 1.4
Problem Solving Is
a Continuous Four-
Step Process**
*During implementa-
tion and thereafter, the
outcome must be contin-
ually measured and
the information about
how well the solution is
working is fed back to
the problem solvers. In
this way, the identifica-
tion of the problem can
change over time, solu-
tions can be changed,
and new choices made,
all based on experience.*

organization. Problems have to be properly defined by people in an organization before they can be solved.

For instance, what at first glance what might seem like a problem with employees not adequately responding to customers in a timely and accurate manner might in reality be a result of a older, out-of-date information system for keeping track of customers. Or it might be a combination of both poor employee incentives for treating customers well and an outdated system. Once you understand this critical fact, you can start to solve problems creatively. Finding answers to these questions will require fact gathering, interviews with people involved in the problem, and analysis of documents.

In this text, we emphasize three different and typical dimensions of business problems: organizations, technology, and people (see Table 1.2). Typical organizational problems include poor business processes (usually inherited from the past), unsupportive culture, political in-fighting, and changes in the organization's surrounding environment. Typical technology problems include insufficient or aging hardware, outdated software, inadequate database capacity, insufficient telecommunications capacity, and the incompatibility of old systems with new technology. Typical people problems include employee training, difficulties of evaluating performance, legal and regulatory compliance, ergonomics, poor or indecisive management, and employee support and participation. When you begin to analyze a business problem, you will find these dimensions are helpful guides to understanding the kind of problem with which you are working.

Solution Design

The second step is to design solutions to the problem(s) you have identified. As it turns out, there are usually a great many "solutions" to any given problem, and the choice of solution often reflects the differing perspectives of people in an organization. You should try to consider as many different solutions as possible so that you can understand the range of possible solutions. Some solutions emphasize technology; others focus on change in the organization and people aspects of the problem. As you will find throughout the text,

TABLE 1.2

Dimensions of
Business Problems

Dimension	Description
Organizational dimensions	Outdated business processes
	Unsupportive culture and attitudes
	Political conflict
	Turbulent business environment, change
	Complexity of task
	Inadequate resources
Technology dimensions	Insufficient or aging hardware
	Outdated software
	Inadequate database capacity
	Insufficient telecommunications capacity
	Incompatibility of old systems with new technology
	Rapid technological change and failure to adopt new technology
People dimensions	Lack of employee training
	Difficulties of evaluating performance
	Legal and regulatory compliance
	Work environment
	Lack of employee support and participation
	Indecisive management
	Poor management
	Wrong incentives

most successful solutions result from an integrated approach in which new technologies are accompanied by changes in organization and people.

Solution Evaluation and Choice

Choosing the "best" solution for your business firm is the next step in the process. Some of the factors to consider when trying to find the "best" single solution are the cost of the solution, the feasibility of the solution for your business given existing resources and skills, and the length of time required to build and implement the solution. Also very important at this point are the attitudes and support of your employees and managers. A solution that does not have the support of all the major interests in the business can quickly turn into a disaster.

Implementation

The best solution is one that can be implemented. Implementation of an information system solution involves building the solution and introducing it into the organization. This includes purchasing or building the software and hardware—the technology part of the equation. The software must be tested in a realistic business setting; then employees need to be trained, and documentation about how to use the new system needs to be written.

You will definitely need to think about change management. **Change management** refers to the many techniques used to bring about successful change in a business. Nearly all information systems require changes in the firm's business processes and, therefore, changes in what hundreds or even thousands of employees do every day. You will have to design new, more efficient business processes, and then figure out how to encourage employees to adapt to these new ways of doing business. This may require meeting sessions to introduce the change to groups of employees, new training modules to bring employees quickly up to speed on the new information systems and processes, and, finally, some kind of rewards or incentives to encourage people to enthusiastically support the changes.

Implementation also includes the measurement of outcomes. After a solution has been implemented, it must be evaluated to determine how well it is working and whether any additional changes are required to meet the original objectives. This information is fed back to the problem solvers. In this way, the identification of the problem can change over time, solutions can be changed, and new choices made, all based on experience.

Problem Solving: A Process, Not an Event

It is often assumed that once a problem is "solved," it goes away and can be forgotten about. And it is easy to fall into the trap of thinking about problem solving as an event that is "over" at some point, like a relay race or a baseball game. Often in the real world this does not happen. Sometimes the chosen solution does not work, and new solutions are required.

For instance, the U.S. National Aeronautics and Space Administration (NASA) spent more than $1 billion to fix a problem with shedding foam on the space shuttle. Experience proved the initial solution did not work. More often, the chosen solution partially works but needs a lot of continuous changes to truly "fit" the situation. Initial solutions are often rough approximations at first of what ultimately "works." Sometimes, the nature of the problem changes in a way that makes the initial solution ineffective. For instance, hackers create new variations on computer viruses that require continually evolving antivirus programs to hold in check. For all these reasons, problem solving is a continuous process rather than a single event.

THE ROLE OF CRITICAL THINKING IN PROBLEM SOLVING

It is amazingly easy to accept someone else's definition of a problem or to adopt the opinions of some authoritative group that has "objectively" analyzed the problem and offers quick solutions. You should try to resist this tendency to accept existing definitions of any problem. Through the natural flow of decision making, it is essential that you try to maintain some distance from any specific solution until you are sure you have properly identified the problem, developed understanding, and analyzed alternatives. Otherwise, you may leap off in the wrong direction, solve the wrong problem, and waste resources. You will have to engage in some critical-thinking exercises.

Critical thinking can be briefly defined as the sustained suspension of judgment with an awareness of multiple perspectives and alternatives. It involves at least four elements:

- Maintaining doubt and suspending judgment
- Being aware of different perspectives
- Testing alternatives and letting experience guide
- Being aware of organizational and personal limitations

Simply following a rote pattern of decision making, or a model, does not guarantee a correct solution. The best protection against incorrect results is to engage in critical thinking throughout the problem-solving process.

First, maintain doubt and suspend judgment. Perhaps the most frequent error in problem solving is to arrive prematurely at a judgment about the nature of the problem. By doubting all solutions at first and refusing to rush to a judgment, you create the necessary mental conditions to take a fresh, creative look at problems, and you keep open the chance to make a creative contribution.

Second, recognize that all interesting business problems have many dimensions and that the same problem can be viewed from different perspectives. In this text, we have emphasized the usefulness of three perspectives on business problems: technology, organizations, and people. Within each of these very broad perspectives are many subperspectives, or views. The *technology perspective*, for instance, includes a consideration of all the components in the firm's IT infrastructure and the way they work together. The *organization perspective* includes a consideration of a firm's business processes, structure, culture, and politics. The *people perspective* includes consideration of the firm's management, as well as employees as individuals and their interrelationships in workgroups.

You will have to decide for yourself which major perspectives are useful for viewing a given problem. The ultimate criterion here is usefulness: Does adopting a certain perspective tell you something more about the problem that is useful for solving the problem? If not, reject that perspective as being not meaningful in this situation and look for other perspectives.

The third element of critical thinking involves testing alternatives, or modeling solutions to problems, letting experience be the guide. Not all contingencies can be known in advance, and much can be learned through experience. Therefore, experiment, gather data, and reassess the problem periodically.

THE CONNECTION BETWEEN BUSINESS OBJECTIVES, PROBLEMS, AND SOLUTIONS

Now let's make the connection between business information systems and the problem-solving approach. At the beginning of this chapter we talked about the six reasons business firms invest in information systems and technologies. We identified six business objectives of information systems: operational excellence; new products, services, and business models; customer/supplier intimacy; improved decision making; strategic advantage; and survival. When firms cannot achieve these objectives, they become "challenges" or "problems" that receive attention. Managers and employees who are aware of these challenges often turn to information systems as one of the solutions, or the entire solution.

Review the diagram at the beginning of this chapter. The diagram shows how Disney World's systems solved the business problem presented by the need to increase revenue with a limited amount of guest capacity and higher customer expectations. These systems provide a solution that takes advantage of multiple technologies, including satellite data feeds, high-definition television displays, digital mapping, and mobile applications. They improved business performance by reducing wait times for rides and restaurants and for providing pleasurable experiences that encouraged guests to visit multiple times and spend more during each visit. The diagram illustrates how people, technology, and organizational elements work together to create the system.

Each chapter of this text begins with a diagram similar to this one to help you analyze the chapter-opening case. You can use this diagram as a starting point for analyzing any information system or information system problem you encounter.

1.4 Information Systems and Your Career

Looking out to 2018, the U.S. economy will create 12.6 million new jobs and 24 million existing jobs will open up as their occupants retire. More than 95 percent of the new jobs will be created in the service sector. The vast majority of these new jobs and replacement jobs will require a college degree to perform (Statistical Abstract, 2010; U.S. Bureau of Labor Statistics, 2011).

What this means is that U.S. business firms are looking for candidates who have a broad range of problem-solving skills—the ability to read, write, and present ideas—as well as the technical skills required for specific tasks. Regardless of your business school major, or your future occupation, information systems and technologies will play a major and expanding role in your day-to-day work and your career. Your career opportunities, and your compensation, will in part depend on your ability to help business firms use information systems to achieve their objectives.

HOW INFORMATION SYSTEMS WILL AFFECT BUSINESS CAREERS

In the following sections, we describe how specific occupations will be affected by information systems and what skills you should be building in order to benefit from this emerging labor market based on the research of the Bureau of Labor Statistics (Bureau of Labor Statistics, 2011; U.S. Census, 2011).

Accounting

There are about 1.6 million accountants in the U.S. labor force today, and the field is expected to expand by 22 percent by the year 2018, adding nearly 300,000 new jobs, and a similar number of jobs to replace retirees. This above-average growth in accounting is in part driven by new accounting laws for public companies, greater scrutiny of public and private firms by government tax auditors, and a growing demand for management and operational advice.

Accountants rely heavily on information systems to summarize transactions, create financial records, organize data, and perform financial analysis. As a result of new public laws, accountants require an intimate knowledge of data bases, reporting systems, and networks in order to trace financial transactions. Because so many transactions are occurring over the Internet, accountants need to understand online transaction and reporting systems, and how systems are used to achieve management accounting functions in an online, wireless, and mobile business environment.

Finance

If you include financial analysts, stock analysts, insurance underwriters, and related financial service occupations, there are currently about 2.2 million managers in finance. Financial managers develop financial reports, direct investment activities, and implement cash management strategies. These financial occupations are expected to grow by about 20 percent a year to 2018, and add 185,000 new jobs, with replacements adding another 100,000 openings.

Financial managers play important roles in planning, organizing, and implementing information system strategies for their firms. Financial managers work directly with a firm's board of directors and senior management to ensure investments in information systems help achieve corporate goals and achieve high returns. The relationship between information systems and the practice of modern financial management and services is so strong that many advise finance majors to also co-major in information systems (and vice versa).

Marketing

No field has undergone more technology-driven change in the past five years than marketing and advertising. The explosion in e-commerce activity described earlier means that eyeballs are moving rapidly to the Internet. As a result, Internet advertising is the fastest growing form of advertising, reaching $29 billion in 2011. Product branding and customer communication are moving online at a fast pace.

There are about 1.8 million, public relations, sales, and advertising managers in the U.S. labor force. This field is growing faster than average at about 12 percent, and is expected to add more than 234,000 jobs by 2018 and replace an additional 100,000 employees who are retiring. There is a much larger group of 2.6 million nonmanagerial employees in marketing-related occupations (art, design, entertainment, sports, and media) and more than 15.9 million employees in sales. These occupations together are expected to create an additional 3.3 million jobs by 2018. Marketing and advertising managers deal with large databases of customer behavior both online and offline in the process of creating brands and selling products and services. They develop reports on product performance, retrieve feedback from customers, and manage product development. These managers need an understanding of how enterprise-wide systems for product management, sales force management, and customer relationship management are used to develop products that consumers want, to manage the customer relationship, and to manage an increasingly mobile sales force.

Operations Management in Services and Manufacturing

The growing size and complexity of modern industrial production and the emergence of huge global service companies have created a growing demand for employees who can coordinate and optimize the resources required to produce goods and services. Operations management as a discipline is directly relevant to three occupational categories: industrial production managers, administrative service managers, and operations analysts.

Production managers, administrative service managers, and operations analysts will be employing information systems and technologies every day to accomplish their jobs, with extensive use of database and analytical software.

Management

Management is the largest single group in the U.S. business labor force with more than 15 million members, not including an additional 627,000 management consultants. Overall, the management corps in the United States is expected to expand faster than other occupational groups, adding about 3.2 million new jobs by 2018, with about 2 million openings in this period to replace retirements. There are more than 20 different types of managers tracked by the Bureau of Labor Statistics, all the way from chief executive officer, to human resource managers, production managers, project managers, lodging managers, medical managers, and community service managers.

The job of management has been transformed by information systems. Arguably, it would be impossible to manage business firms today, even very small firms, without the extensive use of information systems. Nearly all U.S. managers use information systems and technologies every day to accomplish their jobs, from desktop productivity tools to applications coordinating the entire enterprise. Managers today manage through a variety of information technologies without which it would be impossible to control and lead the firm.

The job of management requires extensive use of information systems to support decision making and to monitor the performance of the firm.

© nyul, 2011, iStockPhoto LP.

Information Systems

The information systems field is arguably one of the most fast-changing and dynamic of all the business professions because information technologies are among the most important tools for achieving business firms' key objectives. The explosive growth of business information systems has generated a growing demand for information systems employees and managers who work with other business professionals to design and develop new hardware and software systems to serve the needs of business. Of the top 20 fastest growing occupations through 2018, five are information systems occupations.

There are about 300,000 information system managers in the United States, with an estimated growth rate of 17 percent through 2018, expanding the number of new jobs by more than 50,000 new positions, with an additional 36,000 new hires required for replacements. As businesses and government agencies increasingly rely on the Internet for communication and computing resources, system and network security management positions are growing very rapidly. One of the fastest growing U.S. occupational groups is network systems and data communications analysts, with a projected growth rate of 50 percent.

Outsourcing and Offshoring The Internet has created new opportunities for outsourcing many information systems jobs, along with many other service sector and manufacturing jobs. There are two kinds of outsourcing: outsourcing to domestic U.S. firms and offshore outsourcing to low-wage countries, such as India and eastern European countries. Even this distinction blurs as domestic service providers, such as IBM, develop global outsourcing centers in India.

The most common and successful offshore outsourcing projects involve production programming and system maintenance programming work, along with call center work related to customer relationship management systems. However, inflation in Indian wages for technology work, coupled with the additional management costs incurred in outsourcing projects, is leading to a counter movement of jobs back to the United States. Moreover, although technical IS jobs can be outsourced easily, all those management and organizational tasks required in systems development—including business process design, customer interface, and supply chain management—often remain in the United States. The net result is that offshore outsourcing will increase demand in the United States for managerial IS positions.

Given all these factors in the IT labor market, on what kinds of skills should information system majors focus? Following is a list of general skills we believe will optimize employment opportunities:

- An in-depth knowledge of how new and emerging hardware and software can be used by business firms to make them more efficient and effective, enhance customer and supplier intimacy, improve decision making, achieve competitive advantage, and ensure firm survival. This includes an in-depth understanding of databases, database design, implementation, and management.
- An ability to take a leadership role in the design and implementation of new information systems, work with other business professionals to ensure systems meet business objectives, and work with software packages providing new system solutions.

INFORMATION SYSTEMS AND YOUR CAREER: WRAP-UP

Looking back at the information system skills required for specific majors, there are some common themes that affect all business majors. Following is a list of these common requirements for information system skills and knowledge:

- All business students, regardless of major, should understand how information systems and technologies can help firms achieve business objectives such as achieving operational efficiency, developing new products and services, and maintaining customer intimacy.
- Perhaps the most dominant theme that pervades this review of necessary job skills is the central role of databases in a modern firm. Each of the careers we have just described relies heavily in practice on databases.
- With the pervasive growth in databases comes inevitably an exponential growth in digital information and a resulting challenge to managers trying to understand all this information. Regardless of major, business students need to develop skills in analysis of information and helping firms understand and make sense out of their environments. Business analytics and intelligence are important skill sets to analyze the mountains of big data being produced by the online environment of business firms.
- All business majors need to be able to work with specialists and system designers who build and implement information systems. This is necessary to ensure that the systems that are built actually service business purposes and provide the information and understanding required by managers and employees.
- Each of the business majors will be impacted by changes in the ethical, social, and legal environment of business. Business school students need to understand how information systems can be used to meet business requirements for reporting to government regulators and the public and how information systems impact the ethical issues in their fields.

HOW THIS BOOK PREPARES YOU FOR THE FUTURE

This book is explicitly designed to prepare you for your future business career. It provides you with the necessary knowledge and foundational concepts for understanding the role of information systems in business organizations. You will be able to use this knowledge to identify opportunities for increasing the effectiveness of your business. You will learn how to use information systems to improve operations, create new products and services, improve decision making, increase customer intimacy, and promote competitive advantage.

Equally important, this book develops your ability to use information systems to solve problems that you will encounter on the job. You will learn how to analyze and define a business problem and how to design an appropriate information system solution. You will deepen your critical-thinking and problem-solving skills. The following features of the text and the accompanying learning package reinforce this problem-solving and career orientation.

A Framework for Describing and Analyzing Information Systems

The text provides you with a framework for analyzing and solving problems by examining the people, organizational, and technology components of information systems. This framework is used repeatedly throughout the text to help you understand information systems in business and analyze information systems problems.

A Four-Step Model for Problem Solving

The text provides you with a four-step method for solving business problems, which we introduced in this chapter. You will learn how to identify a business problem, design alternative solutions, choose the correct solution, and implement the solution. You will be asked to use this problem-solving method to solve the case studies in each chapter. Chapter 11 will show you how to use this approach to design and build new information systems.

Hands-On MIS Projects for Stimulating Critical Thinking and Problem Solving

Each chapter concludes with a series of hands-on MIS projects to sharpen your critical-thinking and problem-solving skills. These projects include two Management Decision Problems, hands-on application software problems, and projects for building Internet skills. For each of these projects, we identify both the business skills and the software skills required for the solution.

Career Resources

To make sure you know how the text is directly useful in your future business career, we've added a full set of Career Resources to help you with career development and job hunting.

Digital Portfolio MyMISLab includes a template for preparing a structured digital portfolio to demonstrate the business knowledge, application software skills, Internet skills, and analytical skills you have acquired in this course. You can include this portfolio in your resume or job applications. Your professors can also use the portfolio to assess the skills you have learned.

Career Resources A Career Resources section in MyMISLab shows you how to integrate what you have learned in this course in your resume, cover letter, and job interview to improve your chances for success in the job market.

LEARNING TRACKS

The following Learning Tracks provide content relevant to topics covered in this chapter:

1. How Much Does IT Matter?
2. Changing Business Environment for Information Technology
3. Business Information Value Chain
4. The Emerging Mobile Digital Platform

Review Summary

1 **How are information systems transforming business, and what is their relationship to globalization?** E-mail, online conferencing, and cell phones have become essential tools for conducting business. Information systems are the foundation of fast-paced supply chains. The Internet allows businesses to buy, sell, advertise, and solicit customer feedback online. The Internet has stimulated globalization by dramatically reducing the costs of producing, buying, and selling goods on a global scale.

2 **Why are information systems so essential for running and managing a business today?** Information systems are a foundation for conducting business today. In many industries, survival and even existence is difficult without extensive use of information technology. Businesses use information systems to achieve six major objectives: operational excellence; new products, services, and business models; customer/supplier intimacy; improved decision making; competitive advantage; and day-to-day survival.

3 **What exactly is an information system? How does it work? What are its people, organization, and technology components?** From a technical perspective, an information system collects, stores, and disseminates information from an organization's environment and internal operations to support organizational functions and decision making, communication, coordination, control, analysis, and visualization. Information systems transform raw data into useful information through three basic activities: input, processing, and output. From a business perspective, an information system provides a solution to a problem or challenge facing a firm and represents a combination of people, organization, and technology elements.

The people dimension of information systems involves issues such as training, job attitudes, and management behavior. The technology dimension consists of computer hardware, software, data management technology, and networking/telecommunications technology, including the Internet. The organization dimension of information systems involves issues such as the organization's hierarchy, functional specialties, business processes, culture, and political interest groups.

4 **How will a four-step method for business problem solving help you solve information system-related problems?** Problem identification involves understanding what kind of problem is being presented, and identifying people, organizational, and technology factors. Solution design involves designing several alternative solutions to the problem that has been identified. Evaluation and choice entails selecting the best solution, taking into account its cost and the available resources and skills in the business. Implementation of an information system solution entails purchasing or building hardware and software, testing the software, providing employees with training and documentation, managing change as the system is introduced into the organization, and measuring the outcome. Problem solving requires critical thinking in which one suspends judgment to consider multiple perspectives and alternatives.

5 **How will information systems affect business careers, and what information system skills and knowledge are essential?** Business careers in accounting, finance, marketing, operations management, management and human resources, and information systems all will need an understanding of how information systems help firms achieve major business objectives; an appreciation of the central role of databases; skills in information analysis and business intelligence; sensitivity to the ethical, social, and legal issues raised by systems; and the ability to work with technology specialists and other business professionals in designing and building systems.

Key Terms

Business model, 11
Business processes, 16
Change management, 23
Computer hardware, 17
Computer literacy, 15
Computer software, 17
Critical thinking, 24
Culture, 16
Data, 13
Data management
  technology, 17

Extranets, 17
Feedback, 13
Information, 13
Information system (IS), 13
Information systems
  literacy, 15
Information technology
  (IT), 13
Information technology (IT)
  infrastructure, 18
Input, 13

Internet, 17
Intranets, 17
Management information
  systems (MIS), 16
Network, 17
Networking and telecommu-
  nications technology, 17
Output, 13
Processing, 13
World Wide Web, 18

Review Questions

1. How are information systems transforming business, and what is their relationship to globalization?
- Describe how information systems have changed the way businesses operate and their products and services.
- Describe the challenges and opportunities of globalization in a "flattened" world.

2. Why are information systems so essential for running and managing a business today?
- List and describe the six reasons why information systems are so important for business today.

3. What exactly is an information system? How does it work? What are its people, organization, and technology components?
- List and describe the organizational, people, and technology dimensions of information systems.
- Define an information system and describe the activities it performs.
- Distinguish between data and information and between information systems literacy and computer literacy.
- Explain how the Internet and the World Wide Web are related to the other technology components of information systems.

4. How will a four-step method for business problem solving help you solve information system-related problems?
- List and describe each of the four steps for solving business problems.
- Give some examples of people, organizational, and technology problems found in businesses.
- Describe the relationship of critical thinking to problem solving.
- Describe the role of information systems in business problem solving.

5. How will information systems affect business careers, and what information system skills and knowledge are essential?
- Describe the role of information systems in careers in accounting, finance, marketing, management, and operations management, and explain how careers in information systems have been affected by new technologies and outsourcing.
- List and describe the information system skills and knowledge that are essential for all business careers.

Discussion Questions

1. What are the implications of globalization when you have to look for a job? What can you do to prepare yourself for competing in a globalized business environment? How would knowledge of information systems help you compete?

2. If you were setting up the Web site for Disney World visitors, what people, organi-

zational, and technology issues might you encounter?

3. Identify some of the people, organizational, and technology issues that UPS had to address when creating its successful information systems.

Hands-On MIS Projects

The projects in this section give you hands-on experience in analyzing financial reporting and inventory management problems, using data management software to improve management decision making about increasing sales, and using Internet software for researching job requirements.

MANAGEMENT DECISION PROBLEMS

1. Snyders of Hanover, which sells about 80 million bags of pretzels, snack chips, and organic snack items each year, had its financial department use spreadsheets and manual processes for much of its data gathering and reporting. Hanover's financial analyst would spend the entire final week of every month collecting spreadsheets from the heads of more than 50 departments worldwide. She would then consolidate and re-enter all the data into another spreadsheet, which would serve as the company's monthly profit-and-loss statement. If a department needed to update its data after submitting the spreadsheet to the main office, the analyst had to return the original spreadsheet, then wait for the department to re-submit its data before finally submitting the updated data in the consolidated document. Assess the impact of this situation on business performance and management decision making.

2. Dollar General Corporation operates deep-discount stores offering housewares, cleaning supplies, clothing, health and beauty aids, and packaged food, with most items selling for $1. Its business model calls for keeping costs as low as possible. The company has no automated method for keeping track of inventory at each store. Managers know approximately how many cases of a particular product the store is supposed to receive when a delivery truck arrives, but the stores lack technology for scanning the cases or verifying the item count inside the cases. Merchandise losses from theft or other mishaps have been rising and now represent over 3 percent of total sales. What decisions have to be made before investing in an information system solution?

IMPROVING DECISION MAKING: USING DATABASES TO ANALYZE SALES TRENDS

Software skills: Database querying and reporting
Business skills: Sales trend analysis

In this project, you will start out with raw transactional sales data and use Microsoft Access database software to develop queries and reports that help managers make better decisions about product pricing, sales promotions, and inventory replenishment. In MyMISLab, you can find a Store and Regional Sales Database developed in Microsoft Access. The database contains raw data on weekly store sales of computer equipment in various sales regions. The database includes fields for store identification number, sales region, item number, item description, unit price, units sold, and the weekly sales period when the sales were made.

Use Access to develop some reports and queries to make this information more useful for running the business. Sales and production managers want answers to the following questions:

- Which products should be restocked?
- Which stores and sales regions would benefit from a promotional campaign and additional marketing?
- When (what time of year) should products be offered at full price, and when should discounts be used?

You can easily modify the database table to find and report your answers. Print your reports and results of queries.

IMPROVING DECISION MAKING: USING THE INTERNET TO LOCATE JOBS REQUIRING INFORMATION SYSTEMS KNOWLEDGE

Software skills: Internet-based software
Business skills: Job searching

Visit a job-posting Web site such as Monster.com. Spend some time at the site examining jobs for accounting, finance, sales, marketing, and human resources. Find two or three descriptions of jobs that require some information systems knowledge. What information systems knowledge do these jobs require? What do you need to do to prepare for these jobs? Write a one- to two-page report summarizing your findings.

Video Cases

Video Cases and Instructional Videos illustrating some of the concepts in this chapter are available. Contact your instructor to access these videos.

Collaborating and Teamwork

Creating a Web Site for Team Collaboration

Form a team with three or four classmates. Then use the tools at Google Sites to create a Web site for your team. You will need to create a Google account for the site and specify the collaborators (your team members) who are allowed to access the site and make contributions. Specify your professor as the viewer of the site so that person can evaluate your work. Assign a name to the site. Select a theme for the site, and change the colors and fonts. Add features for project announcements and a repository for team documents, source materials, illustrations, electronic presentations, and Web pages of interest. You can add other features if you wish. Use Google to create a calendar for your team. After you complete this exercise, you can use this Web site and calendar for your other team projects.

BUSINESS PROBLEM-SOLVING CASE

Are Electronic Medical Records a Cure for Health Care?

During a typical trip to the doctor, you'll often see shelves full of folders and papers devoted to the storage of medical records. The majority of medical records are currently paper-based, making these records very difficult to access and share. It has been said that the U.S. health care industry is the world's most inefficient information enterprise.

Inefficiencies in medical record keeping are one reason why health care costs in the United States are the highest in the world. And since administrative costs and medical recordkeeping account for about 12 percent of U.S health care spending, improving medical recordkeeping systems has been targeted as a major path to cost savings and even higher health care quality. Enter electronic medical record (EMR) systems.

An electronic medical record system contains all of a person's vital medical data, including personal information, a full medical history, test results, diagnoses, treatments, prescription medications, and the effect of those treatments. A physician would be able to immediately and directly access needed information from the EMR without having to pore through paper files. If the record holder went to the hospital, the records and results of any tests performed at that point would be immediately available online. Having a complete set of patient information at their fingertips would help physicians prevent prescription drug interactions and avoid redundant tests. By analyzing data extracted from electronic patient records, Southeast Texas Medical Associates in Beaumont, Texas, improved patient care, reduced complications, and slashed its hospital readmission rate by 22 percent in 2010.

Many experts believe that electronic records will reduce medical errors and improve care, create less paperwork, and provide quicker service, all of which will lead to dramatic savings in the future, as much as $80 billion per year. The U.S. government's short-term goal is for all health care providers in the United States to have EMR systems in place that meet a set of basic functional criteria by the year 2015. Its long-term goal is to have a fully-functional nationwide electronic medical recordkeeping network. The consulting firm Accenture estimates that approximately 50 percent of U.S. hospitals are at risk of incurring penalties by 2015 for failing to meet federal requirements.

The challenges of setting up individual EMR systems, let alone a nationwide system, are daunting. Many smaller medical practices are finding it difficult to afford the costs and time commitment to upgrade their recordkeeping systems. In 2011, 71 percent of physicians and 90 percent of hospitals in the United States were still using paper medical records. Less than 2 percent of U.S. hospitals had electronic medical record systems that were fully functional.

It's also unlikely that the many different types of EMR systems being developed and implemented right now will be compatible with one another in 2015 and beyond, jeopardizing the goal of a national system where all health care providers can share information. No nationwide software standards for organizing and exchanging medical information have been put in place. And there are many other smaller obstacles that health providers, health IT developers, and insurance companies will need to overcome for electronic health records to catch on nationally, including patients' privacy concerns, data quality issues, and resistance from health care workers.

Economic stimulus money provided by the American Recovery and Reinvestment Act was available to health care providers in two ways. First, $2 billion was provided up front to hospitals and physicians to help set up electronic records. Another $17 billion is available to reward providers that successfully implement electronic records by 2015.

In addition to stimulus payments, the federal government plans to assess penalties on practices that fail to comply with the new electronic recordkeeping standards. Providers that cannot meet the standards by 2015 will have their Medicare and Medicaid reimbursements slowly reduced by 1 percent per year until 2018, with further, more stringent penalties coming beyond that time if a sufficiently low number of providers are using electronic health records.

Electronic medical recordkeeping systems typically cost around $30,000 to $50,000 per doctor. This would burden many providers, especially medical practices with fewer than four doctors and hospitals with fewer than 50 beds. Smaller providers are also less likely to have begun digitizing their records compared to their larger counterparts.

Implementing an EMR system also requires physicians and other health care workers to change the way they work. Answering patient phone calls, examining patients, and writing prescriptions will need to incorporate procedures for accessing and updating electronic medical records; paper-based records will have to be converted into electronic form, most likely with codes assigned for various treatment options and data structured to fit the record's format. Training can take up to 20 hours of a doctor's time, and doctors are extremely time-pressed. Health care professionals will resist these systems if they add steps to their work flow and compound the frustration of performing required tasks. The Obama administration is working on standards to improve EMR usability.

Many smaller practices and hospitals have balked at the transition to EMR systems for these reasons, but the evidence of systems in action suggests that the move may be well worth the effort if the systems are well-designed. The most prominent example of electronic medical records in use today is the U.S. Veterans Affairs (VA) system of doctors and hospitals. The VA system switched to digital records years ago, and far exceeds the private sector and Medicare in quality of preventive services and chronic care. The 1,400 VA facilities use VistA, record-sharing software developed by the government that allows doctors and nurses to share patient history. A typical VistA record lists all of the patient's health problems; weight and blood pressure since beginning treatment at the VA system; images of the patient's x-rays, lab results, and other test results; lists of medications; and reminders about upcoming appointments.

But VistA is more than a database; it also has many features that improve quality of care. For example, nurses scan tags for patients and medications to ensure that the correct dosages of medicines are going to the correct patients. This feature reduces medication errors, which is one of the most common and costly types of medical errors, and speeds up treatment as well. The system also generates automatic warnings based on specified criteria. It can notify providers if a patient's blood pressure goes over a certain level or if a patient is overdue for a regularly scheduled procedure like a flu shot or a cancer screening. Devices that measure patients' vital signs can automatically transmit their results to the VistA system, which automatically updates doctors at the first sign of trouble.

The 40,000 patients in the VA's in-home monitoring program reduced their hospital admissions by 25 percent and the length of their hospital stays by 20 percent. More patients receive necessary periodic treatments under VistA (from 27 percent to 83 percent for flu vaccines and from 34 percent to 84 percent for colon cancer screenings).

Patients also report that the process of being treated at the VA is effortless compared to paper-based providers. That's because instant processing of claims and payments are among the benefits of EMR systems. Insurance companies traditionally pay claims around two weeks after receiving them, despite quickly processing them soon after they are received; governmental regulations only require insurers to pay claims within 15 days of their receipt. Additionally, today's paper-based health care providers must assign the appropriate diagnostic codes and procedure codes to claims. Because there are thousands of these codes, the process is even slower, and most providers employ someone solely to perform this task. Electronic systems hold the promise of immediate processing, or "real-time claims adjudication" just like when you pay using a credit card, because claim data would be sent immediately and diagnostic and procedure code information are automatically entered.

VistA is far from the only option for doctors and hospitals starting the process of updating their records. Many health technology companies are eagerly awaiting the coming spike in demand for their EMR products and have developed a variety of different health record structures. Humana, Aetna, and other health insurance companies are helping to defray the cost of setting up EMR systems for some doctors and hospitals. Humana has teamed up with health IT company athenahealth to subsidize EMR systems for approximately 100 primary care practices within Humana's network. Humana pays most of the bill and offers further rewards for practices meeting governmental performance standards. Aetna and IBM have launched a cloud-based system that will pool patient records and can be licensed to doctors both inside and outside of Aetna.

There are two problems with the plethora of options available to health care providers. First, there are likely to be many issues with the sharing of medical data between different systems. While the majority of EMR systems are likely to satisfy the specified criteria of reporting data electronically to governmental agencies, they may not be able to report the same data to one another, a key requirement for a nationwide system. Many fledgling systems are designed using VistA as a guide, but many are not. Even if medical data are easily shared, it's another problem altogether for doctors to actually locate the information they need quickly and easily. Many EMR systems have no capacity to drill down for more specific data, forcing doctors to wade through large repositories of information they don't need to find the one piece of data that they do need. EMR vendors are developing search engine technology intended for use in medical records. Only after EMR systems become more widespread will the extent of the problems with data sharing and accessibility become clearer.

The second problem is that there is a potential conflict of interest for the insurance companies involved in the creation of health record systems. While most insurers are adamant that only doctors and patients will be able to access data in these systems, many prospective patients are skeptical. In 2009, a poll conducted for National Public Radio found that 59 percent of respondents said they doubted the confidentiality of online medical records; even if the systems are secure, the perception of poor privacy could affect the success of the system and quality of care provided. A poorly designed EMR network would amplify these concerns.

Sources: Steve Lohr, "Seeing Promise and Peril in Digital Records," *New York Times*, July 17, 2011; Russ Britt, "Digital Health Push Woos Tech Firms, Pains Doctors, MarketWatch, June 2, 2011; Marianne Kolbasuk McGee, "Better Clinical Analytics Means Better Clinical Care," *Information Week*, May 21, 2011; Eric Engleman, "More Physicians Adopting Electronic Health Records, U.S. Reports," *Bloomberg News*, April 26, 2011; Jeff Goldman, "Implementing Electronic Health Records: Six Best Practices," *CIO Insight*, March 7, 2011; Robin Lloyd, "Electronic Health Records Face Human Hurdles More than Technological Ones," *Scientific American*, April 16, 2011; Katherine Gammon, "Connecting Electronic Medical Records," *Technology Review*, August 9, 2010; David Talbot, "The Doctor Will Record Your Data Now," Technology Review, July 23, 2010; Tony Fisher and Joyce Montanari, "The Current State of Data in Health Care," InformationManagement. com, June 15, 2010; and Jacob Goldstein, "Can Technology Cure Health Care?", *The Wall Street Journal*, April 13, 2010.

Case Study Questions

1. Identify and describe the problem in this case.
2. What people, organization, and technology factors are responsible for the difficulties in building electronic medical record systems? Explain your answer.
3. What is the business, political, and social impact of not digitizing medical records (for individual physicans, hospitals, insurers, patients, and the U.S. government)?
4. What are the business and social benefits of digitizing medical recordkeeping?
5. Are electronic medical record systems a good solution to the problem of rising health care costs in the United States? Explain your answer.

Global E-business and Collaboration

CHAPTER 2

STUDENT LEARNING OBJECTIVES

After completing this chapter, you will be able to answer the following questions:

1. What major features of a business are important for understanding the role of information systems?

2. How do systems serve different management groups in a business?

3. How do systems that link the enterprise improve organizational performance?

4. Why are systems for collaboration and teamwork so important and what technologies do they use?

5. What is the role of the information systems function in a business?

CHAPTER OUTLINE

AMERICA'S CUP 2010: USA WINS WITH INFORMATION TECHNOLOGY

The BMW Oracle Racing organization won the 33rd America's Cup yacht race in Valencia, Spain on February 18, 2010. The BMW Oracle boat USA, backed by software billionaire Larry Ellison, beat Alinghi, the Swiss boat backed by Ernesto Bertarelli, a Swiss billionaire. It's always a spectacle when two billionaires go head-to-head for the prize. Lots and lots of money, world-class talent, and in this case, the best technologies and information systems in the world. In the end, the 114-foot USA won handily the first two races of a best-of-three series, reaching speeds over 35 miles an hour, three times faster than the wind. As far as experts can figure, USA is the fastest sailboat in history.

What kind of technology can you get for a $300 million sailboat? Start with the physical structure: a three hulled trimaran, 114 feet long, fashioned from carbon fiber shaped into a form descended from Polynesian outrigger boats over a thousand years old. The hull is so light it only extends six inches into the water. Forget about a traditional mast (that's the pole that holds up the sails) and sails too. Think about a 233-foot airplane wing also made from carbon fiber that sticks up from the boat deck 20 stories high. Instead of cloth sails, think about an aeronautical fabric stretched over a

© PCN Photography, 2011, Alamy.

carbon fiber frame that is hydraulically controlled to assume any shape you want. The result is a wing, not a sail, whose shape can be changed from near flat to quite curved, just like an aircraft wing.

Controlling this wickedly sleek sailboat requires a lightning-fast collection of massive amounts of data, powerful data management, rapid real-time data analysis, quick decision making, and immediate measurement of the results. In short, all the information technologies needed by a modern business firm. When you can perform all these tasks thousands of times in an hour, you can incrementally improve your performance and have an overwhelming advantage over less IT-savvy opponents on race day.

For USA, this meant using 250 sensors on the wing, hull, and rudder to gather real-time data on pressure, angles, loads, and strains to monitor the effectiveness of each adjustment. The sensors track 4,000 variables, 10 times a second, producing 90 million data points an hour. Managing all these data is Oracle Database 11g data management software. The data are wirelessly transferred to a tender ship running Oracle 11g for near real-time analysis using a family of formulas (called velocity prediction formulas) geared to understanding what makes the boat go fast. Oracle's Application Express presentation graphics summarize the millions of data points and present the boat managers with charts that make sense of the information. The data are also sent to Oracle's Austin data center for more in-depth analysis. Using powerful data analysis tools, USA managers were able to find relationships they had never thought about before. Over several years of practice, from day one to the day before the race, the crew of USA could chart a steady improvement in performance.

Each crew member wore a small mobile handheld computer on his wrist to display data on the key performance variables customized for that person's responsibilities, such as the load balance on a specific rope or the current aerodynamic performance of the wing sail. Rather than stare at the sails or the sea, the crew had to be trained to sail like pilots looking at instruments. The helmsman turned into a pilot looking at data displayed on his sunglasses with an occasional glance at the deck crew, sea state, and competitors.

Professional and amateur sailors across the world wondered if the technology had transformed sailing into something else. Winner Larry Ellison sets the rules for the next race, and many sailors hoped Ellison would go back to traditional single hull sail boats run by people and not computers. But this will not happen. Instead, in 2011, Ellison embraced the new multihull design for the next America's Cup, to be held in San Francisco in September 2013. All 2013 competitors will be racing essentially identical 72-foot multihull boats. To train the next generation of "sailors," Ellison has built a fleet of 45-foot, scaled-down America's cup boats with the idea of "meeting the expectations of the Facebook generation, not the Flintstone generation." Ellison will be enhancing the IT component of the race with a focus on data collection, analysis, presentation, and performance-based decision making. He's even invited the public aboard via wireless high definition television cameras placed on all the boats in an effort to turn America's cup racing into a popular sporting event.

Sources: Adam Fisher, "Winging It," Americascup.com, August 23, 2011; Jeff Erickson, "Sailing Home with the Prize," *Oracle Magazine*, May/June 2010; Jeff Erickson, "America's Cup: Oracle Data Mining Supports Crew and BMW ORACLE Racing," Sail-world.com, September 24, 2010; www.americascup.com, accessed September 5, 2011; and www.bmworacleracing.com, accessed September 5, 2011.

The experience of BMW Oracle's USA in the 2010 America's Cup competition illustrates how much organizations today, even those in traditional sports such as sailing, rely on information systems to improve their performance and remain competitive. It also shows the difference information systems make a difference in an organization's ability to innovate, execute, and in the case of business firms, grow profits.

The chapter-opening diagram calls attention to important points raised by this case and this chapter. The America's Cup contenders were confronted with both a challenge and opportunity. Both were locked in the world's most competitive sailing race. They staffed their crews with the best sailors in the world, but sailing ability was not enough. There were

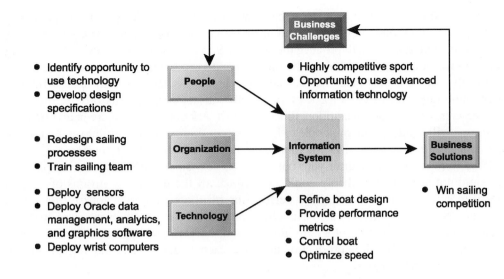

opportunities for improving sailing performance by changing and refining the design of the competing vessels using information systems intensively for this purpose.

Because Oracle was one of the world's leading information technology providers, the company was a natural for using the most advanced information technology to continually improve USA's design and performance. But information technology alone would not have produced a winning boat. The Oracle team had to revise many of the processes and procedures used in sailing to take advantage of the technology, including training experienced sailors to work more like pilots with high-tech instruments and sensors. Oracle won the America's Cup because it had learned how to apply new technology to improve the processes of designing and sailing a competitive sailboat.

2.1 Components of a Business

A **business** is a formal organization whose aim is to produce products or provide services for a profit—that is, to sell products at a price greater than the costs of production. Customers are willing to pay this price because they believe they receive a value greater than or equal to the sale price. Business firms purchase inputs and resources from the larger environment (suppliers who are often other firms). Employees of the business firm transform these inputs by adding value to them in the production process.

There are, of course, nonprofit firms and government agencies that are complex formal organizations that produce services and products but do not operate in order to produce a profit. Nevertheless, even these organizations consume resources from their environments, add value to these inputs, and deliver their outputs to constituents and customers. In general, the information systems found in government and nonprofit organizations are remarkably similar to those found in private industry.

ORGANIZING A BUSINESS: BASIC BUSINESS FUNCTIONS

Imagine you want to set up your own business. Simply deciding to go into business is the most important decision, but next is the question of what product or service to produce (and hopefully sell). The decision of what to produce is called a *strategic choice* because it determines your likely customers, the kinds of employees you will need, the production methods and facilities needed, the marketing themes, and many other choices.

Once you decide what to produce, what kind of organization do you need? First, you need to develop a production division—an arrangement of people, machines, and business processes (procedures) that will produce the product. Second, you need a sales and marketing group who will attract customers, sell the product, and keep track of after-sales issues, such as warranties and maintenance. Third, once you generate sales, you will need a finance and accounting group to keep track of financial transactions, such as orders, invoices, disbursements, and payroll. In addition, this group will seek out sources of credit and finance. Finally, you will need a group of people to focus on recruiting, hiring, training, and retaining employees. Figure 2.1 summarizes the four basic functions found in every business.

If you were an entrepreneur or your business was very small with only a few employees, you would not need, and probably could not afford, all these separate groups of people. Instead, in small firms, you would be performing all these functions yourself or with a few others. No wonder small firms have a high mortality rate! In any event, even in small firms, the four basic functions of a firm are required. Larger firms often will have separate departments for each function: production and manufacturing, sales and marketing, finance and accounting, and human resources.

Figure 2.1 is also useful for thinking about the basic entities that make up a business. The five basic entities in a business with which it must deal are: suppliers, customers, employees, invoices/payments, and, of course, products and services. There are many other entities that a business must manage and monitor, but these are the basic ones at the foundation of any business.

BUSINESS PROCESSES

Once you identify the basic business functions and entities for your business, your next job is to describe exactly how you want your employees to perform these functions. What specific tasks do you want your sales personnel to perform, in what order, and on what schedule? What steps do you want production employees to follow as they transform raw resources into finished products? How will customer orders be fulfilled? How will vendor bills be paid?

The actual steps and tasks that describe how work is organized in a business are called **business processes**. A business process is a logically related set of activities that define how specific business tasks are performed. Business processes also refer to the unique ways in which work, information, and knowledge are coordinated in a specific organization.

Figure 2.1
The Four Major Functions of a Business
Every business, regardless of its size, must perform four functions to succeed. It must produce the product or service; market and sell the product or service; keep track of accounting and financial transactions; and perform basic human resources tasks, such as hiring and retaining employees.

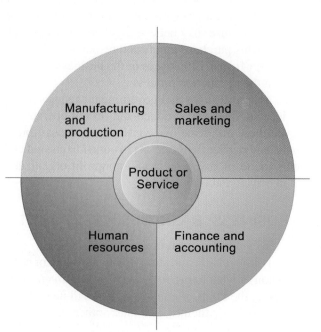

TABLE 2.1

Examples of Functional
Business Processes

Functional Area	Business Process
Manufacturing and production	Assembling the product
	Checking for quality
	Producing bills of materials
Sales and marketing	Identifying customers
	Making customers aware of the product
	Selling the product
Finance and accounting	Paying creditors
	Creating financial statements
	Managing cash accounts
Human resources	Hiring employees
	Evaluating employees' job performance
	Enrolling employees in benefits plans

Every business can be seen as a collection of business processes. Some of these processes are part of larger encompassing processes. Many business processes are tied to a specific functional area. For example, the sales and marketing function would be responsible for identifying customers, and the human resources function would be responsible for hiring employees. Table 2.1 describes some typical business processes for each of the functional areas of business.

Other business processes cross many different functional areas and require coordination across departments. Consider the seemingly simple business process of fulfilling a customer order (see Figure 2.2). Initially, the sales department receives a sales order. The order goes to accounting to ensure the customer can pay for the order either by a credit verification or request for immediate payment prior to shipping. Once the customer credit is established, the production department has to pull the product from inventory or produce the product.

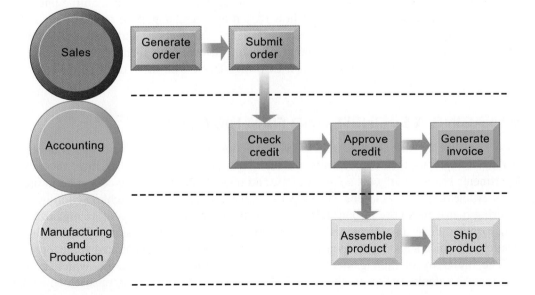

**Figure 2.2
The Order
Fulfillment Process**
*Fulfilling a customer
order involves a complex
set of steps that requires
the close coordination
of the sales, accounting,
and manufacturing
functions.*

Next, the product needs to be shipped (and this may require working with a logistics firm, such as UPS or FedEx). A bill or invoice is then generated by the accounting department, and a notice will be sent to the customer indicating that the product has shipped. Sales has to be notified of the shipment and prepare to support the customer by answering calls or fulfilling warranty claims.

What at first appears to be a simple process, fulfilling an order, turns out to be a very complicated series of business processes that require the close coordination of major functional groups in a firm. Moreover, to efficiently perform all these steps in the order fulfillment process requires a great deal of information and the rapid flow of information within the firm, with business partners such as delivery firms, and with the customer. The particular order fulfillment process we have just described is not only *cross-functional*, it is also *interorganizational* because it includes interactions with delivery firms and customers who are outside the boundaries of the organization. Ordering raw materials or components from suppliers would be another interorganizational business process.

To a large extent, the efficiency of a business firm depends on how well its internal and interorganizational business processes are designed and coordinated. A company's business processes can be a source of competitive strength if they enable the company to innovate or to execute better than its rivals. Business processes can also be liabilities if they are based on outdated ways of working that impede organizational responsiveness and efficiency. The chapter-opening case describing the processes used to sail the 2010 winning America's Cup boat clearly illustrates these points, as do many other cases in this text.

How Information Technology Enhances Business Processes

Exactly how do information systems enhance business processes? Information systems automate many steps in business processes that were formerly performed manually, such as checking a client's credit, or generating an invoice and shipping order. But today, information technology can do much more. New technology can actually change the flow of information, making it possible for many more people to access and share information, replacing sequential steps with tasks that can be performed simultaneously, and eliminating delays in decision making. It can even transform the way the business works and drive new business models. Ordering a book online from Amazon.com and downloading a music track from iTunes are entirely new business processes based on new business models that are inconceivable without information technology.

That's why it's so important to pay close attention to business processes, both in your information systems course and in your future career. By analyzing business processes, you can achieve a very clear understanding of how a business actually works. Moreover, by conducting a business process analysis, you will also begin to understand how to change the business to make it more efficient or effective. Throughout this book we examine business processes with a view to understanding how they might be changed, or replaced, by using information technology to achieve greater efficiency, innovation, and customer service. Chapter 3 discusses the business impact of using information technology to redesign business processes, and MyMISLab has a Learning Track with more detailed coverage of this topic.

MANAGING A BUSINESS AND FIRM HIERARCHIES

What is missing from Figures 2.1 and 2.2 is any notion of how to coordinate and control the four major functions, their departments, and their business processes. Each of these functional departments has its own goals and processes, and they obviously need to cooperate in order for the whole business to succeed. Business firms, like all organizations, achieve coordination by hiring managers whose responsibility is to ensure all the various parts of an organization work together. Firms coordinate the work of employees in various divisions by developing a hierarchy in which authority (responsibility and accountability) is concentrated at the top.

The hierarchy of management is composed of **senior management**, which makes long-range strategic decisions about products and services as well as ensures financial performance of the firm; **middle management**, which carries out the programs and plans of senior management; and **operational management**, which is responsible for monitoring the daily activities of the business. **Knowledge workers**, such as engineers, scientists, or architects, design products or services and create new knowledge for the firm, whereas **data workers**, such as secretaries or clerks, assist with administrative work at all levels of the firm. **Production or service workers** actually produce the product and deliver the service (Figure 2.3).

Each of these groups has different needs for information given their different responsibilities. Senior managers need summary information that can quickly inform them about the overall performance of the firm, such as gross sales revenues, sales by product group and region, and overall profitability. Middle managers need more specific information on the results of specific functional areas and departments of the firm, such as sales contacts by the sales force, production statistics for specific factories or product lines, employment levels and costs, and sales revenues for each month or even each day. Operational managers need transaction-level information, such as the number of parts in inventory each day or the number of hours logged on Tuesday by each employee. Knowledge workers may need access to external scientific databases or internal databases with organizational knowledge. Finally, production workers need access to information from production machines, and service workers need access to customer records in order to take orders and answer questions from customers.

THE BUSINESS ENVIRONMENT

So far we have talked about business as if it operated in a vacuum, but nothing could be further from the truth. In fact, business firms depend heavily on their environments to supply capital, labor, customers, new technology, services and products, stable markets and legal systems, and general educational resources. Even a pizza parlor cannot survive long without a supportive environment that delivers the cheese, tomato sauce, and flour!

Figure 2.4 summarizes the key actors in the environment of every business. To stay in business, a firm must monitor changes in its environment and share information with the key entities in that environment. For instance, a firm must respond to political shifts, respond to changes in the overall economy (such as changes in labor rates and price inflation), keep track of new technologies, and respond to changes in the global business environment (such as foreign exchange rates). In its immediate environment, firms need to track and share information with suppliers, customers, stockholders, regulators, and logistic partners (such as shipping firms).

Figure 2.3
Levels in a Firm
Business organizations are hierarchies consisting of three principal levels: senior management, middle management, and operational management. Information systems serve each of these levels. Scientists and knowledge workers often work with middle management.

Figure 2.4
The Business Environment
To be successful, an organization must constantly monitor and respond to—or even anticipate—developments in its environment. A firm's environment includes specific groups with which the business must deal directly, such as customers, suppliers, and competitors as well as the broader general environment, including socioeconomic trends, political conditions, technological innovations, and global events.

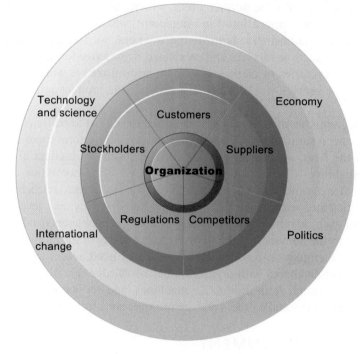

Business environments are constantly changing: New developments in technology, politics, customer preferences, and regulations happen all the time. In general, when businesses fail, it is often because they failed to respond adequately to changes in their environments.

Changes in technology, such as the Internet, are forcing entire industries and leading firms to change their business models or suffer failure. Apple's iTunes and other online music download services are making the music industry's traditional business model based on distributing music on CDs obsolete. Another example is the photography business. Digital photography has forced Eastman Kodak to downsize and move into digital cameras and Internet photography services because most of the consumer marketplace no longer wants to use traditional cameras with film.

THE ROLE OF INFORMATION SYSTEMS IN A BUSINESS

Until now we have not mentioned information systems. But from the brief review of business functions, entities, and environments, you can see the critical role that information plays in the life of a business. Up until the mid 1950s, firms managed all this information and information flow with paper records. During the past 50 years, more and more business information and the flow of information among key business actors in the environment has been computerized.

Businesses invest in information systems as a way to cope with and manage their internal production functions and to cope with the demands of key actors in their environments. Specifically, as we noted in Chapter 1, firms invest in information systems for the following business objectives:

- To achieve operational excellence (productivity, efficiency, agility)
- To develop new products and services
- To attain customer intimacy and service (continuous marketing, sales, and service; customization and personalization)
- To improve decision making (accuracy and speed)
- To achieve competitive advantage
- To ensure survival

2.2 Types of Business Information Systems

Now it is time to look more closely at how businesses use information systems to achieve these goals. Because there are different interests, specialties, and levels in an organization, there are different kinds of systems. No single system can provide all the information an organization needs.

A typical business organization will have systems supporting processes for each of the major business functions—sales and marketing, manufacturing and production, finance and accounting, and human resources. You can find examples of systems for each of these business functions in the Learning Tracks for this chapter. Functional systems that operated independently of each other are becoming a thing of the past because they cannot easily share information to support cross-functional business processes. They are being replaced with large-scale cross-functional systems that integrate the activities of related business processes and organizational units. We describe these integrated cross-functional applications later in this section.

A typical firm will also have different systems supporting the decision-making needs of each of the main management groups described earlier. Operational management, middle management, and senior management each use a specific type of system to support the decisions they must make to run the company. Let's look at these systems and the types of decisions they support.

SYSTEMS FOR MANAGEMENT DECISION MAKING AND BUSINESS INTELLIGENCE

A business firm has systems to support decision making and work activities at different levels of the organization. They include transaction processing systems and systems for business intelligence.

Transaction Processing Systems

Operational managers need systems that keep track of the elementary activities and transactions of the organization, such as sales, receipts, cash deposits, payroll, credit decisions, and the flow of materials in a factory. **Transaction processing systems (TPS)** provide this kind of information. A transaction processing system is a computerized system that performs and records the daily routine transactions necessary to conduct business, such as sales order entry, hotel reservations, payroll, employee record keeping, and shipping.

The principal purpose of systems at this level is to answer routine questions and to track the flow of transactions through the organization. How many parts are in inventory? What happened to Mr. Williams's payment? To answer these kinds of questions, information generally must be easily available, current, and accurate.

At the operational level, tasks, resources, and goals are predefined and highly structured. The decision to grant credit to a customer, for instance, is made by a lower-level supervisor according to predefined criteria. All that must be determined is whether the customer meets the criteria.

Figure 2.5 illustrates a TPS for payroll processing. A payroll system keeps track of money paid to employees. An employee time sheet with the employee's name, social security number, and number of hours worked per week represents a single transaction for this system. Once this transaction is input into the system, it updates the system's file (or database—see Chapter 5) that permanently maintains employee information for the organization. The data in the system are combined in different ways to create reports of interest to management and government agencies and to send paychecks to employees.

Managers need TPS to monitor the status of internal operations and the firm's relations with the external environment. TPS are also major producers of information for the other systems and business functions. For example, the payroll system illustrated in Figure 2.5,

Figure 2.5
A Payroll TPS
A TPS for payroll processing captures employee payment transaction data (such as a timecard). System outputs include online and hard copy reports for management and employee paychecks.

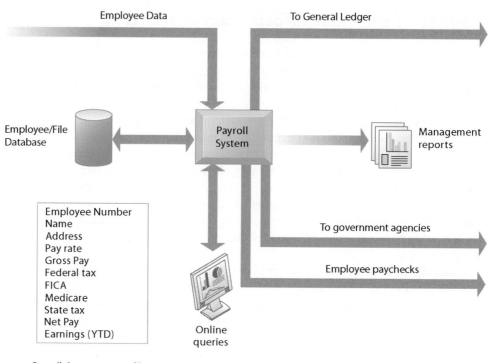

Payroll data on master file

along with other accounting TPS, supplies data to the company's general ledger system, which is responsible for maintaining records of the firm's income and expenses and for producing reports such as income statements and balance sheets. It also supplies employee payment history data for insurance, pension, and other benefits calculations to the firm's human resources function, and employee payment data to government agencies such as the U.S. Internal Revenue Service and Social Security Administration.

Transaction processing systems are often so central to a business that TPS failure for a few hours can lead to a firm's demise and perhaps that of other firms linked to it. Imagine what would happen to UPS if its package tracking system were not working! What would the airlines do without their computerized reservation systems?

The Interactive Session on Technology describes the impact on airline travel when automated baggage handling systems are not working properly. As you read this case, try to identify the transactions being processed and how the data generated from these systems impact business performance.

Systems for Business Intelligence

Firms also have business intelligence systems that focus on delivering information to support management decision making. **Business intelligence** is a contemporary term for data and software tools for organizing, analyzing, and providing access to data to help managers and other enterprise users make more informed decisions. Business intelligence addresses the decision-making needs of all levels of management. This section provides a brief introduction to business intelligence. You'll learn more about this topic in Chapters 5 and 10.

Business intelligence systems for middle management help with monitoring, controlling, decision-making, and administrative activities. In Chapter 1, we defined management information systems as the study of information systems in business and management. The term **management information systems (MIS)** also designates a specific category of information systems serving middle management. MIS provide middle managers with reports on the organization's current performance. This information is used to monitor and control the business and predict future performance.

INTERACTIVE SESSION: TECHNOLOGY Can Airlines Solve Their Baggage Handling

It's been a rough decade for the airline industry. Terrorism scares, rising fuel prices, and overall economic malaise have combined to damage airline companies' bottom lines. In 2007, nearly every major airline began charging baggage fees to generate revenue. Travelers were already unhappy about the poor baggage handling service they received, but paying for often spotty and unreliable baggage handling service was one of the biggest sources of customer dissatisfaction throughout the industry.

To promote customer goodwill as well as reduce costs, airlines developed state-of-the-art baggage handling systems designed to drastically cut down on the number of bags delayed or lost. Statistics suggest these systems are working. Overall, the airline industry rate for lost luggage has improved by 38 percent over similar figures from two years ago, when nearly 2.5 million bags were lost or delayed.

Some of the improvement in the numbers of bags lost or mishandled is because passengers are bringing fewer bags to avoid baggage charges. But updated baggage handling systems have been the major reason for the improvement. Baggage handling systems must perform several key roles: they must move bags from the check-in area to the departure gate, move bags from gate to gate, and move bags from the arrival gate to the baggage claim. The systems must be both accurate and fast, and baggage should move from its current location to its destination faster than travelers can get there.

Baggage handling systems are among the most complex systems in the systems universe because they involve a wide variety of sensors, actuators, mechanical devices, and computers. These systems use over 3 million lines of software program code. Some of the advanced technology used in baggage-handling systems includes destination-coded vehicles (DCVs), automatic bar code scanners, use of radio frequency identification (RFID) tags, and high-tech conveyors equipped with sorting machines.

At check-in, fliers' bags are tagged. The tags contain your flight information and a bar code that all of the computers in the baggage handling system can read. When computers in the system scan the bar code, they process the information it contains and determine where to send your bag. After being scanned once, the system always knows where your bag is at any point.

Bags are deposited into DCVs to transport them to gates quickly. DCVs are unmanned carts that can load and unload bags without stopping movement. These carts move on tracks like miniature rollercoasters

along a "highway" that spans the airport. Computers throughout the system keep track of the location of each bag, its destination, and the time it is needed at that destination. The system can optimize the routes taken by the carts to get the bags needed most urgently to their destinations fastest

Because DCVs move at high speed and do not come to a full stop to receive baggage, the conveyors must be extremely precise, depositing bags where they are needed at just the right time for maximum efficiency. Once bags reach the gate, they enter a sorting station where airline employees use computer terminals to send bags to the correct plane. Increasingly, system vendors are turning to RFID tags attached to each piece of baggage rather than bar code tags. RFID tags are wireless devices that transmit their location and contents, and make it far easier to track packages than bar codes which are silent and passive. They are unfortunately much more expensive than simple bar code tags.

Baggage handling systems can be extremely expensive, but if implemented successfully, pay for themselves. Lost and mishandled baggage is a major expense for airlines, and reducing the incidence of lost and mishandled baggage creates significant yearly savings. According to the International Air Transport Association, a mishandled bag costs an airline, on average, $100, and the global, airline-industry price tag for mishandled baggage is $2.5 billion per year.

In 2007 US Airways lost nine bags for every thousand travelers. After implementing a new baggage handling system at its terminals, that figure dropped to three lost bags for every thousand travelers. US Airways spent $16 million on scanning technology and other associated costs of their baggage handling system, but the company says the system now saves $25 million per year and has boosted customer satisfaction.

In 2007, Delta Airlines emerged from bankruptcy to overhaul many of its outdated systems, including its baggage handling system. Between 2008 and 2010, Delta installed optical scanners to read baggage tag bar codes, widened and extended its system of baggage conveyor belts, and installed a central control room to monitor conveyor belts and baggage carousels in Atlanta and most of its other airport terminals. The airline recorded a top-notch baggage handling record of just 2.93 mishandled bags per 1,000 passengers. Bags now take less than 10 minutes to travel from terminal to terminal — a process that took as long as 30 minutes with the older system. In 2011, Delta added a service that allows passengers to track their checked bags from scanning at check-in, to the flight they're loaded on, and then arrival at baggage claim.

New baggage systems are not flawless. In July 2010, a software glitch shut down the baggage handling system at an American Airlines terminal at JFK airport. A piece of software failed in the bar code scanning device, forcing airline employees to sort luggage by hand, delaying some flights and causing a luggage pileup at the ticket counter. The largest baggage system modernization program failure occurred at the Denver International in the period 1993–2005. After spending $250 million, the airport authority finally

abandoned the effort and returned to older manual methods, which have slowly been upgraded by 2011. The system itself was not a trivial undertaking with 4,000 vehicles, 5.5 miles of conveyors, and 22 miles of track. The Denver failure provided important lessons for system modernization programs that followed, and overall, better baggage handling technology is greatly improving service for flyers.

Sources: Timothy W. Martin, "Delta Lets Fliers Check Bags," *Wall Street Journal*, April 23, 2011; Scott McCartney. "Better Odds of Getting Your Bags." *Wall Street Journal*, December 2, 2010; David B. Caruso, "Baggage System Breakdown Delays Flights at JFK," Associated Press, July 30, 2010.

CASE STUDY QUESTIONS

1. What types of transactions are handled by baggage handling systems?

2. What are the people, organization, and technology components of baggage handling systems?

3. What is problem these baggage handling systems are trying to solve? Discuss the business impact of this problem. Are today's baggage handling systems a solution to this problem? Explain.

4. What kinds of management reports can be generated from the data from these systems?

MIS IN ACTION

1. Do a search on "airline baggage handling technology" and identify suppliers of baggage handling systems to the airlines industry. Choose one supplier and describe how its systems work. How are they different from the systems described above?

2. Go to ibm.com/luggage and watch the video case study of the IBM baggage handling system installed at Schiphol Airport in Amsterdam. The video claims that Schiphol's system is the most advanced in the world. Review this case and discuss whether or not this claim is justified.

3. One of the largest baggage system modernization program failures in history occurred at the Denver International Airport in the period 1995–2005. Do a search on "Denver baggage system failure" and write a brief report on why this project failed.

MIS summarize and report on the company's basic operations using data supplied by transaction processing systems. The basic transaction data from TPS are compressed and usually presented in reports that are produced on a regular schedule. Today, many of these reports are delivered online. Figure 2.6 shows how a typical MIS transforms transaction-level data from inventory, production, and accounting into MIS files that are used to provide managers with reports. Figure 2.7 shows a sample report from this system.

MIS typically provide answers to routine questions that have been specified in advance and have a predefined procedure for answering them. For instance, MIS reports might list the total pounds of lettuce used this quarter by a fast-food chain or, as illustrated in Figure 2.7, compare total annual sales figures for specific products to planned targets. These systems generally are not flexible and have little analytical capability. Most MIS use simple routines, such as summaries and comparisons, as opposed to sophisticated mathematical models or statistical techniques.

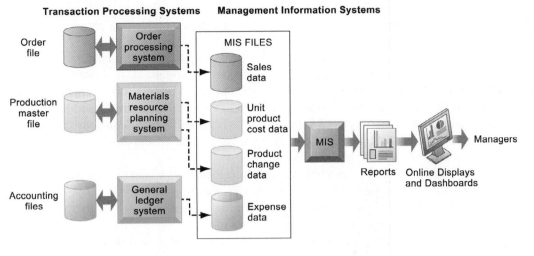

Figure 2.6
How Management Information Systems Obtain Their Data from the Organization's TPS
In the system illustrated by this diagram, three TPS supply summarized transaction data to the MIS reporting system at the end of the time period. Managers gain access to the organizational data through the MIS, which provides them with the appropriate reports.

Other types of business intelligence systems support more non-routine decision making. **Decision-support systems (DSS)** focus on problems that are unique and rapidly changing, for which the procedure for arriving at a solution may not be fully predefined in advance. They try to answer questions such as these: What would be the impact on production schedules if we were to double sales in the month of December? What would happen to our return on investment if a factory schedule were delayed for six months?

Although DSS use internal information from TPS and MIS, they often bring in information from external sources, such as current stock prices or product prices of competitors. These systems are employed by "super-user" managers and business analysts who want to use sophisticated analytics and models to analyze data.

An interesting, small, but powerful, DSS is the voyage-estimating system of a subsidiary of a large American metals company that exists primarily to carry bulk cargoes of coal, oil, ores, and finished products for its parent company. The firm owns some vessels, charters others, and bids for shipping contracts in the open market to carry general cargo. A voyage-estimating system calculates financial and technical voyage details. Financial calculations include ship/time costs (fuel, labor, capital), freight rates for various types of

Consolidated Consumer Products Corporation Sales by Product and Sales Region: 2012

PRODUCT CODE	PRODUCT DESCRIPTION	SALES REGION	ACTUAL SALES	PLANNED	ACTUAL versus PLANNED
4469	Carpet Cleaner	Northeast	4,066,700	4,800,000	0.85
		South	3,778,112	3,750,000	1.01
		Midwest	4,867,001	4,600,000	1.06
		West	4,003,440	4,400,000	0.91
	TOTAL		16,715,253	17,550,000	0.95
5674	Room Freshener	Northeast	3,676,700	3,900,000	0.94
		South	5,608,112	4,700,000	1.19
		Midwest	4,711,001	4,200,000	1.12
		West	4,563,440	4,900,000	0.93
	TOTAL		18,559,253	17,700,000	1.05

Figure 2.7
Sample MIS Report
This report, showing summarized annual sales data, was produced by the MIS in Figure 2.6.

cargo, and port expenses. Technical details include a myriad of factors, such as ship cargo capacity, speed, port distances, fuel and water consumption, and loading patterns (location of cargo for different ports).

The system can answer questions such as the following: Given a customer delivery schedule and an offered freight rate, which vessel should be assigned at what rate to maximize profits? What is the optimal speed at which a particular vessel can optimize its profit and still meet its delivery schedule? What is the optimal loading pattern for a ship bound for the U.S. West Coast from Malaysia? Figure 2.8 illustrates the DSS built for this company. The system operates on a powerful desktop personal computer, providing a system of menus that makes it easy for users to enter data or obtain information.

The voyage-estimating DSS we have just described draws heavily on models. Other business intelligence systems are more data-driven, focusing instead on extracting useful information from massive quantities of data. For example, Intrawest—the largest ski operator in North America—collects and stores large amounts of customer data from its Web site, call center, lodging reservations, ski schools, and ski equipment rental stores. It uses custom software to analyze these data to determine the value, revenue potential, and loyalty of each customer so managers can make better decisions on how to target their marketing programs. The system segments customers into seven categories based on needs, attitudes, and behaviors, ranging from "passionate experts" to "value-minded family vacationers." The company then e-mails video clips that would appeal to each segment to encourage more visits to its resorts.

Business intelligence systems also address the decision-making needs of senior management. Senior managers need systems that focus on strategic issues and long-term trends, both in the firm and in the external environment. They are concerned with questions such as: What will employment levels be in five years? What are the long-term industry cost trends? What products should we be making in five years?

Executive support systems (ESS) help senior management make these decisions. They address non-routine decisions requiring judgment, evaluation, and insight because there is no agreed-on procedure for arriving at a solution. ESS present graphs and data from many sources through an interface that is easy for senior managers to use. Often the information is delivered to senior executives through a **portal**, which uses a Web interface to present integrated personalized business content. You will learn more about other applications of portals in Chapter 10.

ESS are designed to incorporate data about external events, such as new tax laws or competitors, but they also draw summarized information from internal MIS and DSS. They

Figure 2.8
Voyage-Estimating Decision-Support System
This DSS operates on a powerful PC. It is used daily by managers who must develop bids on shipping contracts.

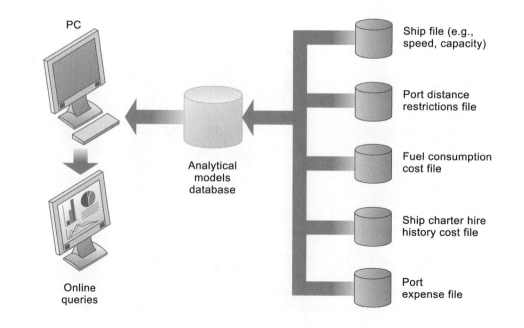

PC

Analytical models database

Online queries

Ship file (e.g., speed, capacity)

Port distance restrictions file

Fuel consumption cost file

Ship charter hire history cost file

Port expense file

filter, compress, and track critical data, displaying the data of greatest importance to senior managers. Increasingly, such systems include business intelligence analytics for analyzing trends, forecasting, and "drilling down" to data at greater levels of detail.

For example, the CEO of Leiner Health Products, the largest manufacturer of private-label vitamins and supplements in the United States, has an ESS that provides on his desktop a minute-to-minute view of the firm's financial performance as measured by working capital, accounts receivable, accounts payable, cash flow, and inventory. The information is presented in the form of a **digital dashboard**, which displays on a single screen graphs and charts of key performance indicators for managing a company. Digital dashboards are becoming an increasingly popular tool for management decision makers.

Contemporary business intelligence and analytics technology has enabled a whole new style of management called, variously, "information driven management," or "management by facts." Here, information is captured at the factory floor (or sales floor) level, immediately entered into enterprise systems, and then sent to corporate headquarters executive dashboards for analysis within a matter of hours or seconds. It's real-time management. The Interactive Session on Organizations illustrates information-driven management at work.

SYSTEMS FOR LINKING THE ENTERPRISE

Reviewing all the different types of systems we have just described, you might wonder how a business can manage all the information in these different systems. You might also wonder how costly it is to maintain so many different systems. Additionally, you might wonder how all these different systems can share information and how managers and employees are able to coordinate their work. In fact, these are all important questions for businesses today.

Enterprise Applications

Getting all the different kinds of systems in a company to work together has proven a major challenge. Typically, corporations are put together both through normal "organic" growth and through acquisition of smaller firms. Over a period of time, corporations end up with a

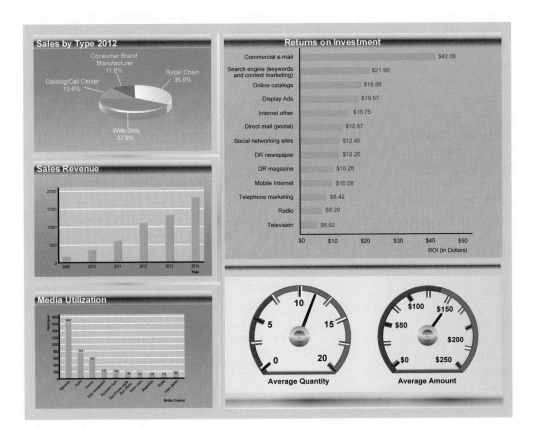

A digital dashboard delivers comprehensive and accurate information for decision making often using a single screen. The graphical overview of key performance indicators helps managers quickly spot areas that need attention.

INTERACTIVE SESSION: ORGANIZATIONS   Piloting Valero with Real-Time Management

If you haven't heard of Valero don't worry. It's largely unknown to the public, although investors recognize it as one of the largest oil refiners in the United States. Valero Energy is a top-10 Fortune company headquartered in San Antonio, Texas, with 2010 annual revenues of $89.2 billion. Valero owns 14 refineries in the United States, Canada, and Aruba that produce gasoline, distillates, jet fuel, asphalt, petrochemicals, lubricants, and other refined products. The company also owns 10 ethanol plants located in the Midwest with a combined ethanol production capacity of about 1.1 billion gallons per year.

In 2008, Valero's chief operating officer (COO) called for the development of the "Refining Dashboard" that would display real-time data related to plant and equipment reliability, inventory management, safety, and energy consumption. Using a series of monitors on the walls of the headquarters operations center room, with a huge central monitor screen showing a live display of the company's Refining Dashboard, the COO and other plant managers can review the performance of the firm's major refineries in the United States and Canada.

The COO and his team review the performance of each refinery in terms of how each plant is performing compared to the production plan of the firm. For any deviation from planned daily or monthly targets, up or down, the plant manager is expected to provide the group an explanation, and a description of corrective actions. The headquarters group can drill down from executive level to refinery level and individual system-operator level displays of performance.

Valero's Refining Dashboard is available on the Web to plant managers in remote locations. The data are refreshed every five minutes. The dashboard taps directly into the firm's SAP Manufacturing Integration and Intelligence application, in which where each plant's history of production and current production data is stored. Valero's management estimates that the dashboards have saved $140 million per year for the plants where they are in use, with anticipated total savings of $230 million per year when they are rolled out to all Valero refineries.

Valero's Refining Dashboard has been so successful that the firm is developing separate dashboards that show detailed statistics on power consumption for each unit of the firm, and each plant. Using the shared data, managers will be able to share with one another best practices, and make changes in equipment to reduce energy consumption while maintaining production targets. The Dashboard system has the unintended advantage of helping managers learn more about how their company actually operates, and how to improve it.

How helpful are Valero's executive dashboards? How much of a difference do they make? Valero's stock price plummeted from $70 in January 2008, to about $17 in November 2008, rising to about $26 by May 2011. As it turns out, changes in refining efficiency are only one factor affecting profitability. Valero's profitability is heavily driven by the spread between the price of refined products and the price of crude oil, referred to as the "refined product margin." The global economic slowdown beginning in 2008 and extending through 2010 weakened demand for refined petroleum products, which put pressure on refined product margins throughout 2009 and 2010. This reduced demand, combined with increased inventory levels, caused a significant decline in diesel and jet fuel profit margins.

The price of crude and aggregate petroleum demand are largely beyond the control of Valero management. Although Valero's dashboard focuses on one of the things management can control within a narrow range (namely refining costs), the dashboard does not display a number of strategic factors beyond its control, which nevertheless powerfully impact company performance. Bottom line: a powerful dashboard system does not turn an unprofitable operation into a profitable one.

Another limitation of information-driven management using dashboards such as Valero's is that it is most appropriate for industries such as oil refining where the process is relatively unchanging, well known and understood, and very central to the revenues of a firm. Dashboard systems say nothing about innovation in product, marketing, sales, or any other area of the firm where innovation is important. Apple Corporation did not invent the Apple iPhone using a performance dashboard although it might have such a dashboard to monitor iPhone manufacturing and sales. Managers have to be sensitive to, and reflect upon, all the factors that shape the success of their business even if they are not reflected in the firm's dashboards.

Sources: Valero Energy Corporation, Form 10-K Annual Report for the fiscal year ended December 31, 2010, filed with the Securities and Exchange Commission, February 25, 2011; www.valero.com, accessed May 17, 2011; and Doug Henschen, "Execs Want Focus on Goals, Not Just Metrics," *Information Week*, November 13, 2009.

CASE STUDY QUESTIONS

1. What people, organization, and technology issues had to be addressed when developing Valero's dashboard?

2. What measures of performance do dashboards display? Give examples of several management decisions that would benefit from the information provided by Valero's dashboards.

3. What kinds of information systems are required for Valero to maintain and operate its refining dashboard?

4. How effective are Valero's dashboards in helping management pilot the company? Explain your answer.

5. Should Valero develop a dashboard to measure the many factors in its environment which it does not control? Why or why not?

MIS IN ACTION

Visit Valero.com and click on its Summary Annual Report. Based on this report, what other corporate dashboards might be appropriate for senior management?

collection of systems, most of them older, and face the challenge of getting them all to "talk" with one another and work together as one corporate system. There are several solutions to this problem.

One solution is to implement **enterprise applications**, which are systems that span functional areas, focus on executing business processes across the business firm, and include all levels of management. Enterprise applications help businesses become more flexible and productive by coordinating their business processes more closely and integrating groups of processes so they focus on efficient management of resources and customer service.

There are four major enterprise applications: enterprise systems, supply chain management systems, customer relationship management systems, and knowledge management systems. Each of these enterprise applications integrates a related set of functions and business processes to enhance the performance of the organization as a whole. Figure 2.9 shows that the architecture for these enterprise applications encompasses processes spanning the entire organization and, in some cases, extending beyond the organization to customers, suppliers, and other key business partners.

Enterprise Systems Firms use **enterprise systems**, also known as *enterprise resource planning (ERP)* systems, to integrate business processes in manufacturing and production, finance and accounting, sales and marketing, and human resources into a single software system. Information that was previously fragmented in many different systems is stored in a single comprehensive data repository where it can be used by many different parts of the business.

For example, when a customer places an order, the order data flow automatically to other parts of the company that are affected by them. The order transaction triggers the warehouse to pick the ordered products and schedule shipment. The warehouse informs the factory to replenish whatever has been depleted. The accounting department is notified to send the customer an invoice. Customer service representatives track the progress of the order through every step to inform customers about the status of their orders. Managers are able to use firm-wide information to make more precise and timely decisions about daily operations and longer-term planning.

Figure 2.9
Enterprise
Application
Architecture
*Enterprise applications
automate processes
that span multiple busi-
ness functions and
organizational levels and
may extend outside the
organization.*

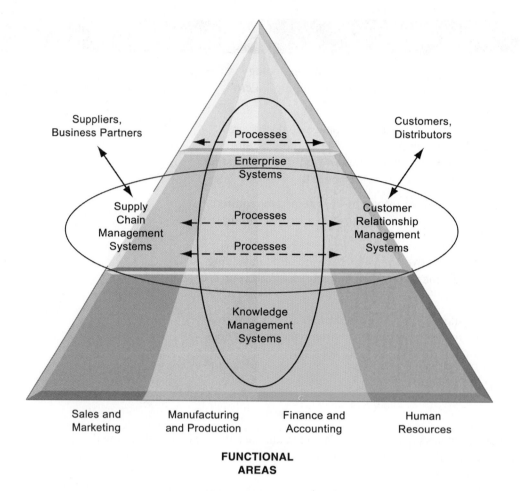

**FUNCTIONAL
AREAS**

Supply Chain Management Systems Firms use **supply chain management (SCM)
systems** to help manage relationships with their suppliers. These systems help suppliers,
purchasing firms, distributors, and logistics companies share information about orders,
production, inventory levels, and delivery of products and services so that they can source,
produce, and deliver goods and services efficiently. The ultimate objective is to get the right
amount of their products from their source to their point of consumption in the least amount
of time and at the lowest cost. These systems increase firm profitability by lowering the
costs of moving and making products and by enabling managers to make better decisions
about how to organize and schedule sourcing, production, and distribution.

Supply chain management systems are one type of **interorganizational system** because
they automate the flow of information across organizational boundaries. You will find
examples of other types of interorganizational information systems throughout this text
because such systems make it possible for firms to link electronically to customers and to
outsource their work to other companies.

Customer Relationship Management Systems Firms use **customer relationship
management (CRM) systems** to help manage their relationships with their customers.
CRM systems provide information to coordinate all of the business processes that deal
with customers in sales, marketing, and service to optimize revenue, customer satisfaction,
and customer retention. This information helps firms identify, attract, and retain the most
profitable customers; provide better service to existing customers; and increase sales.

Knowledge Management Systems Some firms perform better than others because they
have better knowledge about how to create, produce, and deliver products and services.
This firm knowledge is unique, difficult to imitate, and can be leveraged into long-term

strategic benefits. **Knowledge management systems (KMS)** enable organizations to better manage processes for capturing and applying knowledge and expertise. These systems collect all relevant knowledge and experience in the firm, and make it available wherever and whenever it is needed to improve business processes and management decisions. They also link the firm to external sources of knowledge.

We examine enterprise systems and systems for supply chain management and customer relationship management in greater detail in Chapter 8. We discuss collaboration systems that support knowledge management in this chapter and cover other types of knowledge management applications in Chapter 10.

Intranets and Extranets

Enterprise applications create deep-seated changes in the way the firm conducts its business, offering many opportunities to integrate important business data into a single system. They are often costly and difficult to implement. Intranets and extranets deserve mention here as alternative tools for increasing integration and expediting the flow of information within the firm, and with customers and suppliers.

Intranets are simply internal company Web sites that are accessible only by employees. The term "intranet" refers to an internal network, in contrast to the Internet, which is a public network linking organizations and other external networks. Intranets use the same technologies and techniques as the larger Internet, and they often are simply a private access area in a larger company Web site. Extranets are company Web sites that are accessible to authorized vendors and suppliers, and often used to coordinate the movement of supplies to the firm's production apparatus.

For example, Six Flags, which operates 19 theme parks throughout North America, maintains an intranet for its 2,500 full-time employees that provides company-related news and information on each park's day-to-day operations, including weather forecasts, performance schedules, and details about groups and celebrities visiting the parks. We describe the technology for intranets and extranets in more detail in Chapter 6.

E-BUSINESS, E-COMMERCE, AND E-GOVERNMENT

The systems and technologies we have just described are transforming firms' relationships with customers, employees, suppliers, and logistic partners into digital relationships using networks and the Internet. So much business is now enabled by or based upon digital networks that we use the terms *electronic business* and *electronic commerce* frequently throughout this text.

Electronic business, or **e-business**, refers to the use of digital technology and the Internet to execute the major business processes in the enterprise. E-business includes activities for the internal management of the firm and for coordination with suppliers and other business partners. It also includes **electronic commerce**, or **e-commerce**. E-commerce is the part of e-business that deals with the buying and selling of goods and services over the Internet. It also encompasses activities supporting those market transactions, such as advertising, marketing, customer support, security, delivery, and payment.

The technologies associated with e-business have also brought about similar changes in the public sector. Governments on all levels are using Internet technology to deliver information and services to citizens, employees, and businesses with which they work. **E-government** refers to the application of the Internet and networking technologies to digitally enable government and public sector agencies' relationships with citizens, businesses, and other arms of government. In addition to improving delivery of government services, e-government can make government operations more efficient and also empower citizens by giving them easier access to information and the ability to network electronically with other citizens. For example, citizens in some states can renew their driver's licenses or apply for unemployment benefits online, and the Internet has become a powerful tool for instantly mobilizing interest groups for political action and fund-raising.

2.3 Systems for Collaboration and Teamwork

With all these systems and information, you might wonder how is it possible to make sense of them? How do people working in firms pull it all together, work towards common goals, and coordinate plans and actions? Information systems can't make decisions, hire or fire people, sign contracts, agree on deals, or adjust the price of goods to the marketplace. In addition to the types of systems we have just described, businesses need special systems to support collaboration and teamwork.

WHAT IS COLLABORATION?

Collaboration is working with others to achieve shared and explicit goals. Collaboration focuses on task or mission accomplishment and usually takes place in a business, or other organization, and between businesses. You collaborate with a colleague in Tokyo having expertise on a topic about which you know nothing. You collaborate with many colleagues in publishing a company blog. If you're in a law firm, you collaborate with accountants in an accounting firm in servicing the needs of a client with tax problems. Collaboration can be short-lived, lasting a few minutes, or longer term, depending on the nature of the task and the relationship among participants. Collaboration can be one-to-one or many-to-many.

Employees may collaborate in informal groups that are not a formal part of the business firm's organizational structure or they may be organized into formal teams. **Teams** are part of the organization's business structure for getting things done. Teams have a specific mission that someone in the business assigned to them. They have a job to complete. The members of the team need to collaborate on the accomplishment of specific tasks and collectively achieve the team mission. The team mission might be to "win the game," or "increase online sales by 10 percent," or "prevent insulating foam from falling off a space shuttle." Teams are often short-lived, depending on the problems they tackle and the length of time needed to find a solution and accomplish the mission.

Collaboration and teamwork are more important today than ever for a variety of reasons.

- *Changing nature of work.* The nature of work has changed from factory manufacturing and pre-computer office work where each stage in the production process occurred independently of one another, and was coordinated by supervisors. Work was organized into silos. Within a silo, work passed from one machine tool station to another, from one desktop to another, until the finished product was completed. Today, our jobs require much closer coordination and interaction among the parties involved in producing the service or product. A recent report from the consulting firm McKinsey and Company argued that 41 percent of the U.S. labor force is now composed of jobs where interaction (talking, e-mailing, presenting, and persuading) is the primary value-adding activity. Moreover, "interaction" jobs are the fastest growing: 70 percent of all new jobs created since 1998 are "interaction" jobs. Even in factories, workers today often work in production groups, or pods.

- *Growth of professional work.* "Interaction" jobs tend to be professional jobs in the service sector that require close coordination, and collaboration. Professional jobs require substantial education, and the sharing of information and opinions to get work done. Each actor on the job brings specialized expertise to the problem, and all the actors need to take one another into account in order to accomplish the job.

- *Changing organization of the firm.* For most of the industrial age, managers organized work in a hierarchical fashion. Orders came down the hierarchy, and responses moved back up the hierarchy. Today, work is organized into groups and teams, who are expected to develop their own methods for accomplishing the task. Senior managers observe and measure results, but are much less likely to issue detailed orders or operating procedures. In part this is because expertise has been pushed down in the organization, as have decision-making powers.

- *Changing scope of the firm.* The work of the firm has changed from single location to multiple locations—offices or factories throughout a region, a nation, or even around the globe. For instance, Henry Ford developed the first mass-production automobile plant at a single Dearborn, Michigan factory. In 2011 Ford employed over 164,000 employees at 90 plants and facilities worldwide. With this kind of global presence, the need for close coordination of design, production, marketing, distribution, and service obviously takes on new importance and scale. Large global companies need to have teams working on a global basis.

- *Emphasis on innovation.* We tend to think of innovations in business and science as coming from great individuals, but more commonly these individuals are working with a team of brilliant colleagues, and all have been preceded by a long line of earlier innovators and innovations. Think of Bill Gates and Steve Jobs (founders of Microsoft and Apple), both of whom are highly regarded innovators, and both of whom built strong collaborative teams to nurture and support innovation in their firms. Their initial innovations derived from close collaboration with colleagues and partners. Innovation, in other words, is a group and social process, and most innovations derive from collaboration among individuals in a lab, a business, or government agencies. Strong collaborative practices and technologies are believed to increase the rate and quality of innovation.

- *Changing culture of work and business.* Most research on collaboration supports the notion that diverse teams produce better and faster outputs than individuals working on their own. Popular notions of the crowd ("crowdsourcing," and the "wisdom of crowds") also provide cultural support for collaboration and teamwork.

BUSINESS BENEFITS OF COLLABORATION AND TEAMWORK

Many articles and books that have been written about collaboration, some of them by business executives and consultants, and a great many by academic researchers in a variety of businesses. Nearly all of this research is anecdotal. Nevertheless, among both business and academic communities there is a general belief that the more a business firm is "collaborative," the more successful it will be, and that collaboration within and among firms is more essential than in the past. A recent global survey of business and information systems managers found that investments in collaboration technology produced organizational improvements that returned over four times the amount of the investment, with the greatest benefits for sales, marketing, and research and development functions (Frost and White, 2009). Another study of the value of collaboration also found that the overall economic benefit of collaboration was significant: for every word seen by an employee in e-mails from others, $70 of additional revenue was generated (Aral, Brynjolfsson, and Van Alstyne, 2007).

Table 2.2 summarizes some of the benefits of collaboration identified by previous writers and scholars. Figure 2.10 graphically illustrates how collaboration is believed to impact business performance.

BUILDING A COLLABORATIVE CULTURE

Collaboration won't take place spontaneously in a business firm, especially if there is no supportive culture. Business firms, especially large firms, had in the past a reputation for being "command and control" organizations where the top leaders formulated the really

TABLE 2.2

Business Benefits of Collaboration

Benefit	Rationale
Productivity	People working together can complete a complex task faster than the same number of people working in isolation from one another. There will be fewer errors.
Quality	People working collaboratively can communicate errors, and corrective actions faster than if they work in isolation. There will be a reduction in buffers and time delay among production units.
Innovation	People working collaboratively in groups can come up with more innovative ideas for products, services, and administration than the same number working in isolation from one another. There are advantages in group diversity and "the wisdom of crowds."
Customer service	People working together in teams can solve customer complaints and issues faster and more effectively than if they were working in isolation from one another.
Financial performance (profitability, and sales growth)	As a result of all of the above, collaborative firms have sales, superior sales, sales growth, and financial performance.

important matters, and then ordered lower-level employees to execute senior management plans. The job of middle management supposedly was to pass messages back and forth, up and down the hierarchy.

To some extent this is a caricature of how firms used to behave in the 1950s to1990s, but caricatures often have some truth. Command and control firms required lower-level employees to carry out orders without asking too many questions, with no responsibility to improve processes, and with no rewards for teamwork or team performance. If your work group needed help from another work group, that was something for the bosses

Figure 2.10
Requirements for Collaboration
Successful collaboration requires an appropriate organizational structure and culture, along with appropriate collaboration technology.

to figure out. You never communicated horizontally, always vertically, so management could control the process. As long as employees showed up for work, and performed the job satisfactorily, that's all that was required. Together, the expectations of management and employees formed a culture, a set of assumptions about common goals and how people should behave. It is surprising how many business firms still operate this way.

A collaborative business culture is very different. Senior managers are responsible for achieving results, but rely on teams of employees to achieve and implement the results. Policies, products, designs, processes, and systems are much more dependent on teams at all levels of the organization to devise, to create, and to build. Teams are rewarded for their performance, and individuals are rewarded for their performance in a team. You might be a brilliant star on a failed team and receive only half the rewards. The function of middle managers is to build the teams, coordinate their work, and monitor their performance. In a collaborative culture, senior management establishes collaboration and teamwork as vital to the organization, and it actually implements collaboration for the senior ranks of the business as well.

TOOLS AND TECHNOLOGIES FOR COLLABORATION AND TEAMWORK

A collaborative, team-oriented culture won't produce benefits if there are no information systems in place to enable collaboration. Currently there are hundreds of tools designed to deal with the fact that, in order to succeed in our jobs, we are all much more dependent on one another, our fellow employees, customers, suppliers and managers. Table 2.3 lists the most important types of collaboration software tools. Some high-end tools like IBM's Lotus Notes are expensive, but powerful enough for global firms. Others are available online for free (or with premium versions for a modest fee) and are suitable for small businesses. Let's look more closely at some of these tools.

E-mail and Instant Messaging (IM)

E-mail and instant messaging have been embraced by corporations as a major communication and collaboration tool supporting interaction jobs. Their software operates on computers, mobile phones, and other wireless handheld devices, and includes features for sharing files as well as transmitting messages. Many instant messaging systems allow users to engage in real-time conversations with multiple participants simultaneously. Gartner technology consultants have reported that instant messaging is becoming the "de facto tool" for voice, video, and text chat for 95 percent of employees in big companies.

Social Networking

We've all visited social networking sites such as Facebook and Twitter, which feature tools to help people share their interests and interact. Internal social networking tools are quickly becoming a corporate tool for sharing ideas and collaborating among interaction-based jobs in the firm. The internal social networks are set up so that companies are able to determine who sees particular files and who belongs to specific groups on the network. IBM's Lotus

E-mail and instant messaging	White boarding
Collaborative writing	Web presenting
Collaborative reviewing/editing	Work scheduling
Event scheduling	Document sharing (including wikis)
File sharing	Mind mapping
Screen sharing	Large-audience Webinars
Audio conferencing	Co-browsing
Video conferencing	

TABLE 2.3

Fifteen Categories of Collaborative Software Tools

Notes collaboration software now has a Community Tools component with social networking features. Salesforce.com added a social networking tool called Chatter, which enables users to follow coworkers, receive broadcasted updates about projects, and post messages on other colleagues' profiles. Yammer is an enterprise social network service used for private communication within organizations or between organizational members and pre-designated groups.

Wikis

Wikis are a type of Web site that makes it easy for users to contribute and edit text content and graphics without any knowledge of Web page development or programming techniques. The most well-known wiki is Wikipedia, the largest collaboratively edited reference project in the world. It relies on volunteers, makes no money, and accepts no advertising.

Wikis are ideal tools for storing and sharing company knowledge and insights. Intel Corporation employees built their own internal wiki, and it has been edited over 100,000 times and viewed more than 27 million times by Intel employees. The most common search is for the meaning of Intel acronyms such as EASE for "employee access support environment." Other popular resources include a page about software engineering processes at the company. Wikis are a major repository for unstructured corporate knowledge because they are so much less costly than formal knowledge management systems, and they can be much more dynamic and current.

Virtual Worlds

Virtual worlds, such as Second Life, are online 3-D environments populated by "residents" who have built graphical representations of themselves known as avatars. Organizations such as Northrup Grumman, Cigna Corporation, Intel, and IBM, have used this virtual world to stage online meetings, trade shows, training sessions, and other corporate events. Real-world people represented by avatars meet, interact, and exchange ideas at these virtual locations using voice or text chat.

Private virtual world platforms such as OpenSim now offer virtual world capabilities to companies who need more security than can be provided by a public platform such as Second Life. Siemens Corporate Research used OpenSim to create a secure private environment where employees represented as avatars work with virtual models of products. They are able to discuss the appearance, functionality, and environmental impact of products without incurring travel costs (Korolov, 2011).

Internet-Based Collaboration Environments

There are now suites of software products providing multi-function platforms for workgroup collaboration among teams of employees who work together from many different locations. Numerous collaboration tools are available, but the most widely used are Internet-based audio conferencing and video conferencing systems, online software services such as Google Apps/Google Sites, and corporate collaboration systems such as Lotus Notes and Microsoft SharePoint.

Virtual Meeting Systems In an effort to reduce travel expenses, many companies, both large and small, are adopting videoconferencing and Web conferencing technologies. Companies such as Heinz, General Electric, Pepsico, and Wachovia are using virtual meeting systems for product briefings, training courses, strategy sessions, and even inspirational chats.

A videoconference allows individuals at two or more locations to communicate simultaneously through two-way video and audio transmissions. High-end videoconferencing systems feature **telepresence** technology, an integrated audio and visual environment which allows a person to give the appearance of being present at a location other than his or her true physical location. Free or low-cost Internet-based systems such as Skype group videoconferencing and ooVoo are of lower quality, but still useful for smaller companies. Apple's FaceTime and Google video chat tools are useful tools for one-to-one videoconferencing.

Companies of all sizes are finding Web-based online meeting tools such as Cisco WebEx, Microsoft Office Live Meeting, and Adobe Connect especially helpful for training and sales presentations. These products enable participants to share documents and presentations in conjunction with audioconferencing and live video via Webcam.

Google Apps/Google Sites One of the most widely used "free" online services for collaboration is Google Apps/Google Sites. Google Sites allows users to quickly create online group-editable Web sites. Google Sites is one part of the larger Google Apps suite of tools. Google Sites users can design and populate Web sites in minutes and can, without any advanced technical skills, post a variety of files including calendars, text, spreadsheets, and videos for private, group, or public viewing and editing.

Google Apps work with Google Sites and include the typical desktop productivity office software tools (word processing, spreadsheets, presentation, contact management, messaging, and mail). A Premier edition charging businesses $50 per year for each user offers 25 gigabytes of mail storage, a 99.9 percent uptime guarantee for e-mail, tools to integrate with the firm's existing infrastructure, and 24/7 phone support. Table 2.4 describes some of the capabilities of Google Apps/GoogleSites.

Microsoft SharePoint Microsoft SharePoint is the most widely adopted collaboration system for small and medium-sized firms that use Microsoft server and networking products. Some larger firms have adopted it as well. SharePoint is a browser-based collaboration and document management platform, combined with a powerful search engine that is installed on corporate servers.

SharePoint has a Web-based interface and close integration with everyday tools such as Microsoft Office desktop software products. Microsoft's strategy is to take advantage of its "ownership" of the desktop through its Microsoft Office and Windows products. For Microsoft, the path towards enterprise-wide collaboration starts with the Office desktop and Microsoft network servers. SharePoint software makes it possible for employees to share their Office documents and collaborate on projects using Office documents as the foundation.

SharePoint products and technologies provide a platform for Web-based collaboration at the enterprise level. SharePoint can be used to host Web sites that organize and store information in one central location to enable teams to coordinate work activities, collaborate on and publish documents, maintain task lists, implement workflows, and share information via wikis and blogs. Because SharePoint stores and organizes information in one place, users can find relevant information quickly and efficiently while working together closely on tasks, projects, and documents.

Here is a list of SharePoint's major capabilities:

- Provides a single workspace for teams to coordinate schedules, organize documents, and participate in discussions, within the organization or over an extranet.
- Facilitates creation and management of documents with the ability to control versions, view past revisions, and enforce document-specific security and maintain document libraries.

Google Apps/Google Sites Capability	Description
Google Calendar	Private and shared calendars; multiple calendars.
Google Gmail	Google's free online e-mail service, with mobile access capabilities.
Google Talk	Instant messaging, text, voice, and video chat.
Google Docs	Online word processing, electronic presentation software, spreadsheets; online editing, sharing, publishing.
Google Sites	Team collaboration sites for sharing of documents, schedules, calendars, searching documents; creation of group wikis.

TABLE 2.4

Google Apps/Google Sites Collaboration Features

- Provides announcements, alerts, and discussion boards to inform users when actions are required or changes are made to existing documentation or information.
- Supports personalized content and both personal and public views of documents and applications
- Provides templates for blogs and wikis to help teams share information and brainstorm.
- Provides tools to manage document libraries, lists, calendars, tasks, and discussion boards offline, and to synchronize changes when reconnected to the network.
- Provides enterprise search tools for locating people, expertise, and content.

Sony Electronics, a leading provider of consumer and professional electronics products with more 170,000 employees around the world, uses Microsoft Office SharePoint Server 2010 to improve information access, enhance collaboration, and make better use of experts inside the company. Sony uses SharePoint's wiki tools to capture and organize employees' insights and comments into a company-wide body of knowledge, and its people search feature to identify employees with expertise about specific projects and research areas. The company also used SharePoint to create a central file-sharing repository. This helps employees collaboratively write, edit, and exchange documents and eliminates the need to e-mail documents back and forth. All of these improvements have cut development time on key projects from three to six months to three to six weeks. (Microsoft, 2010).

Lotus Notes For very large firms (Fortune 1000 and Russell 2000 firms) the most widely used collaboration tool is IBM's Lotus Notes. Lotus Notes was an early example of groupware, a collaborative software system with capabilities for sharing calendars, collective writing and editing, shared database access, and electronic meetings, with each participant able to see and display information from others and other activities. Notes is now Web-enabled with enhancements for social networking (Lotus Connections) and a scripting and application development environment so that users can build custom applications to suit their unique needs.

Notes software installed on the user's client computer allows the machine to be used as a platform for e-mail, instant messaging (working with Lotus Sametime), Web browsing, and calendar/resource reservation work, as well as for interacting with collaborative applications. Notes also provides blogs, wikis, RSS aggregators, CRM, and help desk systems.

Thousands of employees at hundreds of large firms such as the Toshiba, Air France, and Global Hyatt Corporation use IBM Lotus Notes as their primary collaboration and teamwork tools. Firmwide installations of Lotus Notes at a large Fortune 1000 firm may cost millions of dollars a year and require extensive support from the corporate information systems department. Very large firms adopt IBM Lotus Notes because this system promises higher levels of security and reliability, and the ability to retain control over sensitive corporate information.

For example, the Magnum AS Group, which specializes in wholesale and retail sales of pharmaceuticals and medical supplies throughout the Baltic States, uses Lotus Notes to manage more than 500,000 documents and meet strict regulatory requirements. The software provides a central document repository with full version control for all company documentation, which includes written documents, spreadsheets, images, PDF files, and emails. Users are able to find the latest version of a document with a single search. Documents can only be edited by authorized users, enhancing security and simplifying compliance with the stringent regulations and audit requirements of the international pharmaceuticals industry (IBM, 2010).

Large firms in general do not feel secure using popular online software services for "strategic" applications because of the implicit security concerns, and the dependency on external vendor's computing resources. Most experts agree, however, that these concerns will diminish as experience with online tools grows, and the sophistication of online software service suppliers increases to protect security and reduce vulnerability. Table 2.5 describes additional popular online collaboration tools.

TABLE 2.5

Other Popular Online Collaboration Tools

Tool	Description
Socialtext	An enterprise server-based collaboration environment that provides social networking, Twitter-like micro-blogging, and wiki workspaces; includes integrated weblogs, distributed spreadsheets, and a personal home page for every user.
Zoho Notebook Project	Allows collection of and collaborating on text, line drawings, images, Web pages, video, RSS feeds; includes project management (task management, work flow, reports, time tracking, forums, and file sharing)
Basecamp	Enables sharing of to-do lists, files, message boards, project milestone tracking
Onehub	Provides customizable work spaces for online collaboration; enables project and file sharing.
WorkZone	Enables collaboration with file sharing; includes project management, customization, and security

Checklist for Managers: Evaluating and Selecting Collaboration Software Tools

With so many collaboration tools and services available, how do you choose the right collaboration technology for your firm? To answer this question, you need a framework for understanding just what problems these tools are designed to solve. One framework that has been helpful for us to talk about collaboration tools is the time/space collaboration matrix developed by a number of collaborative work scholars (Figure 2.11).

The time/space matrix focuses on two dimensions of the collaboration problem: time and space. For instance, you need to collaborate with people in different time zones and you

Socialtext's enterprise social networking products including microblogging, blogs, wikis, profiles, and social spreadsheets enable employees to share vital information and work together in real time. Built on a flexible Web-oriented architecture, Socialtext integrates with virtually any traditional system of record, such as CRM and ERP, enabling companies to discuss, collaborate, and take action on key business processes.

Figure 2.11
The Time/Space
Collaboration Tool
Matrix
Collaboration technologies can be classified in terms of whether they support interactions at the same or different time or place, and whether these interactions are remote or co-located.

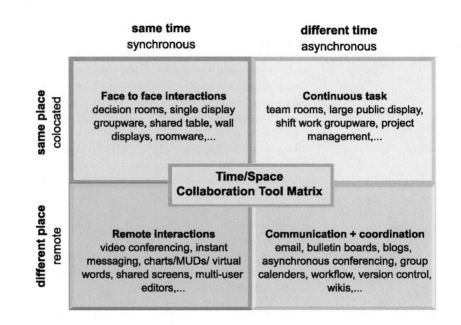

cannot all meet at the same time. Midnight in New York is noon in Bombay, so this makes it difficult to have a video conference. Time is clearly an obstacle to collaboration on a global scale.

Place (location) also inhibits collaboration in large global or even national and regional firms. Assembling people for a physical meeting is made difficult by the physical dispersion of distributed firms (firms with more than one location), the cost of travel, and the time limitations of managers.

The collaboration technologies described previously are ways of overcoming the limitations of time and space. Using this time/space framework will help you to choose the most appropriate collaboration and teamwork tools for your firm. Note that some tools are applicable in more than one time/place scenario. For example, Internet collaboration suites such as Lotus Notes have capabilities for both synchronous (instant messaging, electronic meeting tools) and asynchronous (e-mail, wikis, document editing) interactions.

Here's a "to-do" list to get started. If you follow these six steps, you should be led to investing in the correct collaboration software for your firm at a price you can afford, and within your risk tolerance.

1. What are the collaboration challenges facing the firm in terms of time and space? Locate your firm in the time/space matrix. Your firm can occupy more than one cell in the matrix. Different collaboration tools will be needed for each situation.

2. Within each cell of the matrix where your firm faces challenges, exactly what kinds of solutions are available? Make a list of vendor products.

3. Analyze each of the products in terms of their cost and benefits to your firm. Be sure to include the costs of training in your cost estimates, and the costs of involving the information systems department, if needed.

4. Identify the risks to security and vulnerability involved with each of the products. Is your firm willing to put proprietary information into the hands of external service providers over the Internet? Is your firm willing to risk its important operations to systems controlled by other firms? What are the financial risks facing your vendors? Will they be here in three to five years? What would be the cost of making a switch to another vendor in the event the vendor firm fails?

5. Seek the help of potential users to identify implementation and training issues. Some of these tools are easier to use than others.

6. Make your selection of candidate tools, and invite the vendors to make presentations.

2.4 The Information Systems Function in Business

We've seen that businesses need information systems to operate today and that they use many different kinds of systems. But who is responsible for running these systems? Who is responsible for making sure the hardware, software, and other technologies used by these systems are running properly and are up to date? End users manage their systems from a business standpoint, but managing the technology requires a special information systems function.

In all but the smallest of firms, the **information systems department** is the formal organizational unit responsible for information technology services. The information systems department is responsible for maintaining the hardware, software, data storage, and networks that comprise the firm's IT infrastructure. We describe IT infrastructure in detail in Chapter 4.

THE INFORMATION SYSTEMS DEPARTMENT

The information systems department consists of specialists, such as programmers, systems analysts, project leaders, and information systems managers. **Programmers** are highly trained technical specialists who write the software instructions for computers. **Systems analysts** constitute the principal liaisons between the information systems groups and the rest of the organization. It is the systems analyst's job to translate business problems and requirements into information requirements and systems. **Information systems managers** are leaders of teams of programmers and analysts, project managers, physical facility managers, telecommunications managers, or database specialists. They are also managers of computer operations and data entry staff. Also, external specialists, such as hardware vendors and manufacturers, software firms, and consultants, frequently participate in the day-to-day operations and long-term planning of information systems.

In many companies, the information systems department is headed by a **chief information officer (CIO)**. The CIO is a senior manager who oversees the use of information technology in the firm. Today's CIOs are expected to have a strong business background as well as information systems expertise, and to play a leadership role in integrating technology into the firm's business strategy. Large firms today also have positions for a chief security officer, chief knowledge officer, and chief privacy officer, all of whom work closely with the CIO.

The **chief security officer (CSO)** is in charge of information systems security for the firm and is responsible for enforcing the firm's information security policy (see Chapter 7). (Where information systems security is separated from physical security, this position is sometimes called the chief information security officer [CISO]). The CSO is responsible for educating and training users and information systems specialists about security, keeping management aware of security threats and breakdowns, and maintaining the tools and policies chosen to implement security.

Information systems security and the need to safeguard personal data have become so important that corporations collecting vast quantities of personal data have established positions for a **chief privacy officer (CPO)**. The CPO is responsible for ensuring that the company complies with existing data privacy laws.

The **chief knowledge officer (CKO)** is responsible for the firm's knowledge management program. The CKO helps design programs and systems to find new sources of knowledge or to make better use of existing knowledge in organizational and management processes. **End users** are representatives of departments outside of the information systems group for whom applications are developed. These users are playing an increasingly large role in the design and development of information systems.

In the early years of computing, the information systems group was composed mostly of programmers who performed highly specialized but limited technical functions. Today, a growing proportion of staff members are systems analysts and network specialists, with the information systems department acting as a powerful change agent in the organization. The information systems department suggests new business strategies and new information-based products and services, and coordinates both the development of the technology and the planned changes in the organization.

INFORMATION SYSTEMS SERVICES

Services provided by the information systems department include the following:

- Computing platforms provide computing services that connect employees, customers, and suppliers into a coherent digital environment, including large mainframes, desktop and laptop computers, and mobile handheld devices.
- Telecommunications services provide data, voice, and video connectivity to employees, customers, and suppliers.
- Data management services store and manage corporate data, and provide capabilities for analyzing the data.
- Application software services provide development and support services for the firm's business systems, including enterprise-wide capabilities, such as enterprise resource planning, customer relationship management, supply chain management, and knowledge management systems, that are shared by all business units.
- Physical facilities management services develop and manage the physical installations required for computing, telecommunications, and data management services.
- IT management services plan and develop the infrastructure, coordinate with the business units for IT services, manage accounting for the IT expenditure, and provide project management services.
- IT standards services provide the firm and its business units with policies that determine not only which information technology will be used, but when, and how.
- IT educational services provide training in system use to employees and offer managers training in how to plan for and manage IT investments.
- IT research and development services provide the firm with research on potential future information systems projects and investments that could help the firm differentiate itself in the marketplace.

In the past, firms generally built their own software and managed their own computing facilities. As our discussion of collaboration systems has shown, many firms are turning to external vendors to provide these services (see also Chapters 4 and 11) and are using their information systems departments to manage these service providers.

LEARNING TRACKS

The following Learning Tracks provide content relevant to topics covered in this chapter:

1. Systems from a Functional Perspective
2. IT Enables Collaboration and Teamwork
3. Challenges of Using Business Information Systems
4. Organizing the Information Systems Function

Review Summary

1 **What major features of a business are important for understanding the role of information systems?** A business is a formal complex organization producing products or services for a profit. Businesses have specialized functions, such as finance and accounting, human resources, manufacturing and production, and sales and marketing. Business organizations are arranged hierarchically into levels of management. A business process is a logically related set of activities that define how specific business tasks are performed. Business firms must monitor and respond to their surrounding environments.

2 **How do systems serve different management groups in a business?** Systems serving operational management are transaction processing systems (TPS), such as payroll or order processing, that track the flow of the daily routine transactions necessary to conduct business. Business intelligence serve multiple levels of management, and help employees make more informed decisions. Management information systems (MIS) and decision-support systems (DSS) support middle management. Most MIS reports condense information from TPS and are not highly analytical. DSS support management decisions that are unique and rapidly changing using advanced analytical models and data analysis capabilities. Executive support systems (ESS) support senior management by providing data that are often in the form of graphs and charts delivered via portals and dashboards using many sources of internal and external information.

3 **How do systems that link the enterprise improve organizational performance?** Enterprise applications are designed to coordinate multiple functions and business processes. Enterprise systems integrate the key internal business processes of a firm into a single software system to improve coordination and decision making. Supply chain management systems help the firm manage its relationship with suppliers to optimize the planning, sourcing, manufacturing, and delivery of products and services. Customer relationship management (CRM) systems coordinate the business processes surrounding the firm's customers. Knowledge management systems enable firms to optimize the creation, sharing, and distribution of knowledge. Intranets and extranets are private corporate networks based on Internet technology. Extranets make portions of private corporate intranets available to outsiders.

4 **Why are systems for collaboration and teamwork so important and what technologies do they use?** Collaboration is working with others to achieve shared and explicit goals. Collaboration and teamwork have become increasingly important in business because of globalization, the decentralization of decision making, and growth in jobs where interaction is the primary value-adding activity. Collaboration is believed to enhance innovation, productivity, quality, and customer service. Effective collaboration today requires a supportive organizational culture as well as information systems and tools for collaborative work. Collaboration tools include e-mail and instant messaging, wikis, videoconferencing systems, virtual worlds, social networking systems, cell phones, and Internet collaboration platforms such as Google Sites/Apps, Microsoft SharePoint, and Lotus Notes.

5 **What is the role of the information systems function in a business?** The information systems department is the formal organizational unit responsible for information technology services. It is responsible for maintaining the hardware, software, data storage, and networks that comprise the firm's IT infrastructure. The department consists of specialists, such as programmers, systems analysts, project leaders, and information systems managers, and is often headed by a CIO.

Key Terms

Business, 39

Business intelligence, 46

Business processes, 40

Chief information officer
  (CIO), 65

Chief knowledge officer
  (CKO), 65

Chief privacy officer
  (CPO), 65

Chief security officer
  (CSO), 65

Collaboration, 56

Customer relationship
  management (CRM)
  systems, 54

Data workers, 43

Decision-support systems
  (DSS), 49

Digital dashboard, 51

Electronic business
  (e-business), 55

Review Questions

1. What major features of a business are important for understanding the role of information systems?
- Define a business and describe the major business functions.
- Define business processes and describe the role they play in organizations.
- Identify and describe the different levels in a business firm and their information needs.
- Explain why environments are important for understanding a business.

2. How do systems serve different management groups in a business?
- Define business intelligence systems.
- Describe the characteristics of transaction processing systems (TPS) and role they play in a business.
- Describe the characteristics of management information systems (MIS), decision support systems (DSS), and executive support systems (ESS) and explain how each type of system helps managers make decisions.

3. How do systems that link the enterprise improve organizational performance?
- Explain how enterprise applications improve organizational performance.
- Define enterprise systems, supply chain management systems, customer relationship management systems, and knowledge management systems and describe their business benefits.
- Explain how intranets and extranets help firms improve business performance.

4. Why are systems for collaboration and teamwork so important and what technologies do they use?
- Define collaboration and teamwork and explain why they have become so important in business today.
- List and describe the business benefits of collaboration.
- Describe a supportive organizational culture for collaboration.
- List and describe the various types of collaboration and communication systems.

5. What is the role of the information systems function in a business?
- Describe how the information systems function supports a business.
- Compare the roles played by programmers, systems analysts, information systems managers, the chief information officer (CIO), chief security officer (CSO), and chief knowledge officer (CKO).

Discussion Questions

1. How could information systems be used to support the order fulfillment process illustrated in Figure 2.2? What are the most important pieces of information these systems should capture? Explain your answer.

2. Identify the steps that are performed in the process of selecting and checking out a book from your college library and the information that flows among these activities. Diagram the process. Are there any ways this process could be adjusted to improve the performance of your library or your school? Diagram the improved process.

3. How might the BMW Oracle team have used collaboration systems to improve the design and performance of the America's Cup boat USA? Which system features would be the most important for these tasks?

Hands-on MIS Projects

The projects in this section give you hands-on experience analyzing opportunities to improve business processes with new information system applications, using a spreadsheet to improve decision making about suppliers, and using Internet software to plan efficient transportation routes.

MANAGEMENT DECISION PROBLEMS

1. Don's Lumber Company on the Hudson River features a large selection of materials for flooring, decks, moldings, windows, siding, and roofing. The prices of lumber and other building materials are constantly changing. When a customer inquires about the price on pre-finished wood flooring, sales representatives consult a manual price sheet and then call the supplier for the most recent price. The supplier in turn uses a manual price sheet, which has been updated each day. Often, the supplier must call back Don's sales reps because the company does not have the newest pricing information immediately on hand. Assess the business impact of this situation, describe how this process could be improved with information technology, and identify the decisions that would have to be made to implement a solution.
2. Henry's Hardware is a small family business in Sacramento, California. The owners must use every square foot of store space as profitably as possible. They have never kept detailed inventory or sales records. As soon as a shipment of goods arrives, the items are immediately placed on store shelves. Invoices from suppliers are only kept for tax purposes. When an item is sold, the item number and price are rung up at the cash register. The owners use their own judgment in identifying items that need to be reordered. What is the business impact of this situation? How could information systems help Henry and Kathleen run their business? What data should these systems capture? What decisions could the systems improve?

IMPROVING DECISION MAKING: USE A SPREADSHEET TO SELECT SUPPLIERS

Software skills: Spreadsheet date functions, data filtering, DAVERAGE function
Business skills: Analyzing supplier performance and pricing

In this exercise, you will learn how to use spreadsheet software to improve management decisions about selecting suppliers. You will filter transactional data on suppliers based on several different criteria to select the best suppliers for your company.

You run a company that manufactures aircraft components. You have many competitors who are trying to offer lower prices and better service to customers, and you are trying to determine whether you can benefit from better supply chain management. In MyMISLab, you will find a spreadsheet file that contains a list of all of the items that your firm has ordered from its suppliers during the past three months. The fields in the spreadsheet file include vendor name, vendor identification number, purchaser's order number, item identification number and item description (for each item ordered from the vendor), cost per item, number of units of the item ordered (quantity), total cost of each order, vendor's accounts payable terms, order date, and actual arrival date for each order.

Prepare a recommendation of how you can use the data in this spreadsheet database to improve your decisions about selecting suppliers. Some criteria to consider for identifying preferred suppliers include the supplier's track record for on-time deliveries, suppliers offering the best accounts payable terms, and suppliers offering lower pricing when the same item can be provided by multiple suppliers. Use your spreadsheet software to prepare reports to support your recommendations.

ACHIEVING OPERATIONAL EXCELLENCE: USING INTERNET SOFTWARE TO PLAN EFFICIENT TRANSPORTATION ROUTES

In this exercise, you will use MapQuest software to map out transportation routes for a business and select the most efficient route.

You have just started working as a dispatcher for Cross-Country Transport, a new trucking and delivery service based in Cleveland, Ohio. Your first assignment is to plan a delivery of office equipment and furniture from Elkhart, Indiana (at the corner of E. Indiana Ave. and Prairie Street) to Hagerstown, Maryland (corner of Eastern Blvd. N. and Potomac Ave.). To guide your trucker, you need to know the most efficient route between the two cities. Use MapQuest to find the route that is the shortest distance between the two cities. Use MapQuest again to find the route that takes the least time. Compare the results. Which route should Cross-Country use?

Video Cases

Video Cases and Instructional Videos illustrating some of the concepts in this chapter are available. Contact your instructor to access these videos.

Collaboration and Teamwork

Describing Management Decisions and Systems

With a team of three or four other students, find a description of a manager in a corporation in *BusinessWeek, Fortune*, the *Wall Street Journal*, or another business publication, or do your research on the Web. Gather information about what the manager's company does and the role he or she plays in the company. Identify the organizational level and business function where this manager works. Make a list of the kinds of decisions this manager has to make and the kinds of information the manager would need for those decisions. Suggest how information systems could supply this information. If possible, use Google Sites to post links to Web pages, team communication announcements, and work assignments. Use Google Docs to develop a presentation of your findings for the class.

BUSINESS PROBLEM-SOLVING CASE

Collaboration and Innovation at Procter & Gamble

Look in your medicine cabinet. No matter where you live in the world odds are that you'll find many Procter & Gamble (P&G) products that you use every day. P&G is the largest manufacturer of consumer products in the world and one of the top 10 largest companies in the world by market capitalization. The company is known for its successful brands, as well as its ability to develop new brands and maintain its brands' popularity with unique business innovations. Popular P&G brands include Pampers, Tide, Bounty, Folgers, Pringles, Charmin, Swiffer, Crest, and many more. The company has approximately 127,000 employees in more than 80 countries, and its leading competitor is Britain-based Unilever. Founded in 1837 and headquartered in Cincinnati, Ohio, P&G has been a mainstay in the American business landscape for well over 150 years. In 2010, it earned nearly $79 billion in revenue.

P&G's business operations are divided into three main units: Beauty Care, Household Care, and Health and Well-Being, each of which are further subdivided into more specific units. In each of these divisions, P&G has three main focuses as a business. It needs to maintain the popularity of its existing brands, via advertising and marketing; it must extend its brands by developing new products under those brands; and it must innovate and create new brands entirely from scratch. Because so much of P&G's business is built around brand creation and management, it's critical that the company facilitate collaboration between researchers, marketers, and managers. And because P&G is such a big company, and makes such a wide array of products, achieving these goals is a daunting task.

P&G spends 3.4 percent of revenue on innovation, which is more than twice the industry average of 1.6 percent. Their research and development teams consist of 8,000 scientists spread across 30 sites globally. Though the company has an 80 percent "hit" rate on ideas that lead to products, making truly innovative and groundbreaking new products is very difficult in an extremely competitive field like consumer products. What's more, the creativity of bigger companies like P&G has been on the decline, with the top consumer goods companies accounting for only 5 percent of patents filed on home care products in the early 2000s.

Finding better ways to innovate and develop new ideas is critical in a marketplace like consumer goods, and for any company as large as P&G, finding methods of collaboration that are effective across the enterprise can be difficult. That's why P&G has been active in implementing IT that fosters effective collaboration and innovation. The social networking and collaborative tools popularized by Web 2.0 have been especially attractive to P&G management, starting at the top with former CEO A.G. Lafley. Lafley was succeeded by Robert McDonald in 2010, but has been a major force in revitalizing the company.

When Lafley became P&G's CEO in 2000, he immediately asserted that by the end of the decade, the company would generate half of its new product ideas using sources from outside the company, both as a way to develop groundbreaking innovations more quickly and to reduce research and development costs. At the time, Lafley's proclamation was considered to be visionary, but in the past 10 years, P&G has made good on his promise.

The first order of business for P&G was to develop alternatives to business practices that were not sufficiently collaborative. The biggest culprit, says Joe Schueller, Innovation Manager for P&G's Global Business Services division, was perhaps an unlikely one: e-mail. Though it's ostensibly a tool for communication, e-mail is not a sufficiently collaborative way to share information; senders control the flow of information, but may fail to send mail to colleagues who most need to see it, and colleagues that don't need to see certain e-mails will receive mailings long after they've lost interest. Blogs and other collaborative tools, on the other hand, are open to anyone interested in their content, and attract comments from interested users.

However, getting P&G employees to actually use these newer products in place of e-mail has been a struggle for Schueller. Employees have resisted the changes, insisting that newer collaborative tools represent more work on top of e-mail, as opposed to a better alternative. People are accustomed to e-mail, and there's significant organizational inertia against switching to a new way of doing things. Some P&G processes for sharing knowledge were notoriously inefficient. For instance, some researchers used to write up their experiments using Microsoft Office applications, then print them out and glue them page by page into notebooks. P&G was determined to implement more efficient and collaborative methods of communication to supplant some of these outdated processes.

To that end, P&G launched a total overhaul of its collaboration systems, led by a suite of Microsoft products. The services provided include instant messaging, unified communications (which integrates services for voice transmission, data transmission, instant messaging, e-mail, and electronic conferencing), Microsoft Live Communications Server functionality, Web conferencing with Live Meeting, and content management with SharePoint. According to P&G, over 80,000 employees use instant messaging, and 20,000 use

Microsoft Outlook, which provides tools for e-mail, calendaring, task management, contact management, note taking, and Web browsing. Outlook works with Microsoft Office SharePoint Server to support multiple users with shared mailboxes and calendars, SharePoint lists and meeting schedules.

P&G also adopted Teamcenter product lifecycle collaboration software from Siemens, which supports sharing of 3D visual product data. Teamcenter is based on Microsoft Sharepoint, so that it works side by side with P&G employees' existing Microsoft software tools, enabling more people to participate in project lifecycle processes.

The presence of these tools suggests more collaborative approaches are taking hold. Researchers use the tools to share the data they've collected on various brands; marketers can more effectively access the data they need to create more highly targeted ad campaigns; and managers are more easily able to find the people and data they need to make critical business decisions.

Companies like P&G are finding that one vendor simply isn't enough to satisfy their diverse needs. That introduces a new challenges: managing information and applications across multiple platforms. For example, P&G found that Google search was inadequate because it doesn't always link information from within the company, and its reliance on keywords for its searches isn't ideal for all of the topics for which employees might search. P&G decided to implement a new search product from start-up Connectbeam which allows employees to share bookmarks, tag content with descriptive words that appear in future searches, and facilitates social networks of coworkers to help them find and share information more effectively.

The results of the initiative have been immediate. For example, when P&G executives traveled to meet with regional managers, there was no way to integrate all the reports and discussions into a single document. One executive glued the results of experiments into Word documents and passed them out at a conference. Another executive manually entered his data and speech into PowerPoint slides, and then e-mailed the file each report to his colleagues. One result was that the same report ended up in countless individual mailboxes. Now, P&G's IT department can create a Microsoft SharePoint page where that executive can post all of his presentations. Using SharePoint, the presentations are stored in a single location, but are still accessible to employees and colleagues in other parts of the company. Another collaborative tool, InnovationNet, contains over 5 million research-related documents in digital format accessible via a browser-based portal. That's a far cry from experiments glued in notebooks.

One concern P&G had when implementing these collaborative tools was that if enough employees didn't use them, the tools would be much less useful for those that did use them. Collaboration tools are like other networks—the more people connected to the network the greater the value to all participants. Collaborative tools grow in usefulness as more and more workers contribute their information and insights. They also allow employees quicker access to the experts within the company who have needed information and knowledge. But these benefits are contingent on the majority of company employees using the tools.

Another major innovation for P&G was its large-scale adoption of Cisco TelePresence conference rooms at many locations across the globe. For a company as large as P&G, telepresence is an excellent way to foster collaboration between employees across not just countries, but continents. In the past, telepresence technologies were prohibitively expensive and overly prone to malfunction. Today, the technology makes it possible to hold high-definition meetings over long distances. P&G boasts the world's largest rollout of Cisco telepresence technology. P&G estimates that 35 percent of its employees use telepresence regularly. In some locations, usage is as high as 70 percent.

Benefits of telepresence include significant travel savings, more efficient flow of ideas, and quicker decision making. Decisions that once took days now take minutes. Laurie Heltsley, P&G's director of global business services, noted that the company has saved $4 for every $1 invested in the 70 high-end telepresence systems it has installed over the past few years. These high-definition systems are used four times as often as the company's earlier versions of videoconferencing systems.

Sources: Dennis McCafferty, "How Apple, Nike, and Procter & Gamble Jump the S Curve," *CIO Insight*, April 5, 2011; "Procter & Gamble Creates a Collaborative Community," www.siemens.com, accessed May 9, 2011; Computerworld Honors Program 2008 www.pg.com, accessed May 9, 2011; "Procter & Gamble Revolutionizes Collaboration with Cisco TelePresence," www.cisco.com, accessed May 9, 2011; and "IT's Role in Collaboration at Procter & Gamble," *Information Week*, February 1, 2007.

Case Study Questions

1. What is Procter & Gamble's business strategy? What is the relationship of collaboration and innovation to that business strategy?

2. How is P&G using collaboration systems to execute its business model and business strategy? List and describe the collaboration systems and technologies it is using and the benefits of each.

3. What problems do collaboration systems solve for P&G?

4. Why were some collaborative technologies slow to catch on at P&G?

5. Compare P&G's old and new processes for writing up and distributing the results of a research experiment.

6. Why would telepresence be such a useful collaborative tool for a company like P&G?

7. Can you think of other ways P&G could use collaboration to foster innovation?

Achieving Competitive Advantage with Information Systems

CHAPTER 3

STUDENT LEARNING OBJECTIVES

After completing this chapter, you will be able to answer the following questions:

1. How does Porter's competitive forces model help companies develop competitive strategies using information systems?

2. How do the value chain and value web models help businesses identify opportunities for strategic information system applications?

3. How do information systems help businesses use synergies, core competencies, and network-based strategies to achieve competitive advantage?

4. How do competing on a global scale and promoting quality enhance competitive advantage?

5. What is the role of business process management (BPM) in enhancing competitiveness?

CHAPTER OUTLINE

VERIZON, AT&T, AND SKYPE: WHICH DIGITAL STRATEGY WILL PREVAIL?

Verizon and AT&T are the two largest telecommunications companies in the United States. In addition to voice communication, customers use their networks to surf the Internet; send e-mail, text, and video messages; share photos; watch videos and high-definition TV; and conduct videoconferences around the globe. All of these products and services are digital.

Competition in this industry is exceptionally intense and fast-changing. Both companies have tried to prevail by refining their wireless, landline, and high-speed Internet networks and expanding the range of products, applications, and services available to customers. Wireless services are the most profitable, and smartphone customers are the most desirable of all because they typically pay higher monthly rates for wireless data service plans. (Each iPhone owner pays an average of more than $90 per month to AT&T.)

For a number of years, Verizon tried to blunt competition by making heavy technology investments in both its landline and wireless networks. Its wireless network was considered the most far-reaching and reliable in the United States. AT&T took a different path, partnering with other companies to capitalize on their

© Jose Luis Gutierrez, 2011, iStockPhoto LP.

technology innovations. The company contracted with Apple Computer to be the exclusive network for its iPhone. The iPhone's streamlined design, touch screen, exclusive access to the Apple iTunes music service, and 500,000 downloadable applications made it an instant hit. Since its debut in 2007, the iPhone was AT&T's primary growth engine.

Now that's all changing. In February 2011, Verizon was allowed to sell a version of the Apple iPhone that worked on its wireless network. Verizon further hedged its bets by offering leading-edge smartphones based on Google's highly-popular Android operating system. AT&T countered in March 2011 by announcing its intention to buy T-Mobile USA, a deal that would make it the largest wireless carrier in the United States. The newly combined company, combining AT&T's 95.5 million wireless subscribers with T-Mobile's 33.7 million subscribers, would account for 42 percent of all US wireless subscribers. (Verizon has roughly 31 percent.)

And it looks like the competitive balance is about to shift again. In May 2011, Microsoft acquired Skype, a service that allows users to make voice and video calls over the Internet for free or for a very low cost. Skype's smartphone app allows mobile users to avoid paying higher fees to wireless carriers. Microsoft will be able to incorporate Skype into its other products, such as its Office productivity programs, Xbox video game system, and Windows Phone 7 mobile operating system, enabling its users to be seamlessly connected at work and at home.

Industry analysts predict that the majority of consumers will eventually move from landline telephones or from paying for mobile phone calls by the minute, to communicating over the Internet using services like Skype. People won't need to spend so much on mobile phones or land lines to make video calls. This will eat into the profits of Verizon and AT&T, which have been able to charge premium rates for their digital communication services.

Sources: Nick Wingfield, "Microsoft Dials Up Change" *Wall Street Journal*, May 11, 2011; Jenna Wortham, "With Android Phones, Verizon Is in Position to Gain Lost Ground," *New York Times*, January 6, 2011, and "As Verizon's IPhone Sales Begin, Gauging the Effects on AT&T," *New York Times*, February 9, 2011; Andrew Ross Sorkin, Michael J. De La Merced, and Jenna Wortham, "AT&T to Buy T-Mobile USA For $39 Million," *New York Times*, March 20, 2011; Nick Bilton, "Skype, Even for $8.5 Billion, Could Be a Deal," *New York Times*, May 10, 2011; and Roger Cheng, "For Telecom Firms, Smartphones Rule," *Wall Street Journal*, July 19, 2010.

The story of Verizon, AT&T, and Skype illustrates some of the ways that information systems help businesses compete—and also the challenges of sustaining a competitive advantage. The telecommunications industry in which these companies operate is extremely crowded and competitive, with telecommunications companies vying with cable companies, upstarts such as Skype, and each other to provide a wide array of digital services as well as voice transmission. To meet the challenges of surviving and prospering in this environment, Verizon and AT&T focused on different competitive strategies using information technology.

The chapter-opening diagram calls attention to important points raised by this case and this chapter. Both companies identified opportunities to use information technology to offer new products and services. AT&T offered enhanced wireless services for the iPhone, while Verizon initially focused on high-capacity, high-quality network services. AT&T's strategy initially emphasized keeping costs low while capitalizing on innovations from other technology vendors. Verizon's strategy involved high up-front costs to build a high-capacity network infrastructure, and it also focused on providing a high level of network reliability and customer service.

This case study clearly shows how difficult it is to sustain a competitive advantage. Exclusive rights to use the highly popular iPhone on its network brought AT&T millions of new customers and enhanced its competitive position. But this competitive advantage has diminished now that Verizon offers a version of the iPhone as well as popular Android smartphones. Acquiring T-Mobile would enable AT&T to shift its strategy to emphasize network heft and breadth of coverage. Competition from Skype, which will affect wireless service pricing, may also tilt the competitive balance among the various wireless carriers.

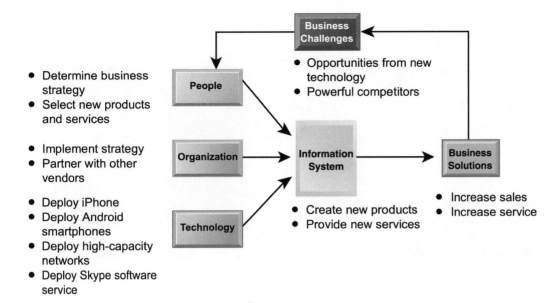

- Determine business strategy
- Select new products and services

- Implement strategy
- Partner with other vendors

- Deploy iPhone
- Deploy Android smartphones
- Deploy high-capacity networks
- Deploy Skype software service

3.1 Using Information Systems to Achieve Competitive Advantage

In almost every industry you examine, you will find that some firms do better than most others. There's almost always a standout firm. In the automotive industry, Toyota is considered a superior performer. In pure online retail, Amazon is the leader; in offline retail Walmart, the largest retailer on earth, is the leader. In online music, Apple's iTunes is considered the leader with more than 75 percent of the downloaded music market, and in the related industry of digital music players, the iPod is the leader. In Web search, Google is considered the leader.

Firms that "do better" than others are said to have a competitive advantage over others: They either have access to special resources that others do not, or they are able to use commonly available resources more efficiently—usually because of superior knowledge and information assets. In any event, they do better in terms of revenue growth, profitability, or productivity growth (efficiency), all of which ultimately in the long run translate into higher stock market valuations than their competitors.

But why do some firms do better than others and how do they achieve competitive advantage? How can you analyze a business and identify its strategic advantages? How can you develop a strategic advantage for your own business? And how do information systems contribute to strategic advantages? One answer to these questions is Michael Porter's competitive forces model.

PORTER'S COMPETITIVE FORCES MODEL

Arguably, the most widely used model for understanding competitive advantage is Michael Porter's **competitive forces model** (see Figure 3.1). This model provides a general view of the firm, its competitors, and the firm's environment. Recall in Chapter 2 we described the importance of a firm's environment and the dependence of firms on environments. Porter's model is all about the firm's general business environment. In this model, five competitive forces shape the fate of the firm.

Figure 3.1
Porter's Competitive Forces Model
In Porter's competitive forces model, the strategic position of the firm and its strategies are determined not only by competition with its traditional direct competitors but also by four forces in the industry's environment: new market entrants, substitute products, customers, and suppliers.

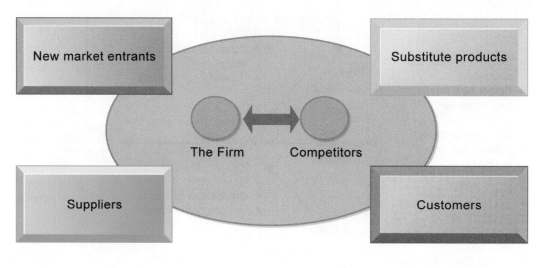

Traditional Competitors

All firms share market space with other competitors who are continuously devising new, more efficient ways to produce by introducing new products and services, and attempting to attract customers by developing their brands and imposing switching costs on their customers.

New Market Entrants

In a free economy with mobile labor and financial resources, new companies are always entering the marketplace. In some industries, there are very low barriers to entry, whereas in other industries, entry is very difficult. For instance, it is fairly easy to start a pizza business or just about any small retail business, but it is much more expensive and difficult to enter the computer chip business, which has very high capital costs and requires significant expertise and knowledge that is hard to obtain. New companies have several possible advantages: They are not locked into old plants and equipment, they often hire younger workers who are less expensive and perhaps more innovative, they are not encumbered by old worn-out brand names, and they are "more hungry" (more highly motivated) than traditional occupants of an industry. These advantages are also their weakness: They depend on outside financing for new plants and equipment, which can be expensive; they have a less-experienced workforce; and they have little brand recognition.

Substitute Products and Services

In just about every industry, there are substitutes that your customers might use if your prices become too high. New technologies create new substitutes all the time. Even oil has substitutes: Ethanol can substitute for gasoline in cars; vegetable oil for diesel fuel in trucks; and wind, solar, coal, and hydro power for industrial electricity generation. Likewise, Internet telephone service can substitute for traditional telephone service, and fiber-optic telephone lines to the home can substitute for cable TV lines. And, of course, an Internet music service that allows you to download music tracks to an iPod is a substitute for CD-based music stores. The more substitute products and services in your industry, the less you can control pricing and the lower your profit margins.

Customers

A profitable company depends in large measure on its ability to attract and retain customers (while denying them to competitors), and charge high prices. The power of customers grows if they can easily switch to a competitor's products and services, or if they can force a business and its competitors to compete on price alone in a transparent marketplace where there is little product differentiation, and all prices are known instantly (such as on the Internet). For instance, in the used college textbook market on the Internet, students (customers) can find multiple suppliers of just about any current college textbook. In this case, online customers have extraordinary power over used-book firms.

Suppliers

The market power of suppliers can have a significant impact on firm profits, especially when the firm cannot raise prices as fast as suppliers can. The more suppliers a firm has, the greater control it can exercise over those suppliers in terms of price, quality, and delivery schedules. For instance, manufacturers of laptop PCs almost always have multiple competing suppliers of key components, such as keyboards, hard drives, and display screens.

INFORMATION SYSTEM STRATEGIES FOR DEALING WITH COMPETITIVE FORCES

What is a firm to do when faced with all these competitive forces? And how can the firm use information systems to counteract some of these forces? How do you prevent substitutes and inhibit new market entrants? How do you become the most successful firm in an industry in terms of profit and share price (two measures of success)?

Basic Strategy 101: Align the IT with the Business Objectives

The basic principle of IT strategy for a business is to ensure the technology serves the business, and not the other way around. The research on IT and business performance has found that (a) the more successfully a firm can align its IT with its business goals, the more profitable it will be, and (b) only about one-quarter of firms achieve alignment of IT with business. About half of a business firm's profits can be explained by alignment of IT with business (Luftman, 2003; Henderson, et al., 1996).

Most businesses get it wrong: IT takes on a life of its own and does not serve management and shareholder interests very well. Instead of business people taking an active role in shaping IT to the enterprise, they ignore it, claim to not understand IT, and tolerate failure in the IT area as just a nuisance to work around. Such firms pay a hefty price in poor performance. Successful firms and managers understand what IT can do and how it works, take an active role in shaping its use, and measure its impact on revenues and profits.

So how do you as a manager achieve this alignment of IT with business? In the following sections, we discuss some basic ways to do this, but here's a summary:

- Identify your business strategy and goals.
- Break these strategic goals down into concrete activities and processes.
- Identify how you will measure progress towards the business goals (e.g. metrics).
- Ask yourself "How can information technology help me achieve progress towards our business goals and how it will improve our business processes and activities?"
- Measure actual performance. Let the numbers speak.

Let's see how this works out in practice. There are four generic strategies, each of which often is enabled by using information technology and systems: low-cost leadership, product differentiation, focus on market niche, and strengthening customer and supplier intimacy.

Low-Cost Leadership

Use information systems to achieve the lowest operational costs and the lowest prices. The classic example is Walmart. By keeping prices low and shelves well stocked using a legendary inventory replenishment system, Walmart became the leading retail business in the United States. Walmart's continuous replenishment system sends orders for new merchandise directly to suppliers as soon as consumers pay for their purchases at the cash register. Point-of-sale terminals record the bar code of each item passing the checkout counter and send a purchase transaction directly to a central computer at Walmart headquarters. The computer

Supermarkets and large retail stores such as Walmart use sales data captured at the checkout counter to determine which items have sold and need to be reordered. Walmart's continuous replenishment system transmits orders to restock directly to its suppliers. The system enables Walmart to keep costs low while fine-tuning its merchandise to meet customer demands.

© kali9, 2011, iStockPhoto LP.

collects the orders from all Walmart stores and transmits them to suppliers. Suppliers can also access Walmart's sales and inventory data using Web technology.

Because the system replenishes inventory with lightning speed, Walmart does not need to spend much money on maintaining large inventories of goods in its own warehouses. The system also enables Walmart to adjust purchases of store items to meet customer demands. Competitors, such as Sears, have been spending 24.9 percent of sales on overhead. By using systems to keep operating costs low, Walmart pays only 16.6 percent of sales revenue for overhead. (Operating costs average 20.7 percent of sales in the retail industry.)

Walmart's continuous replenishment system is also an example of an **efficient customer response system**. An efficient customer response system directly links consumer behavior to distribution and production and supply chains. Walmart's continuous replenishment system provides such an efficient customer response. Dell Computer Corporation's assemble-to-order system, described in the following discussion, is another example of an efficient customer response system.

Product Differentiation

Use information systems to enable new products and services, or greatly change the customer convenience in using your existing products and services. For instance, Google continuously introduces new and unique search services on its Web site, such as Google Maps. Apple created iPod, a unique portable digital music player, plus a unique online Web music service where songs can be purchased for $.69 to $1.29 each. Apple has continued to innovate with its multimedia iPhone, iPad tablet computer, and iPod video player.

Manufacturers and retailers are using information systems to create products and services that are customized and personalized to fit the precise specifications of individual customers. For example, Nike sells customized sneakers through its Nike iD program on its Web site. Customers are able to select the type of shoe, colors, material, outsoles, and even a logo of up to eight characters. Nike transmits the orders via computers to specially-equipped plants in China and Korea. The sneakers cost only $10 extra and take about three weeks to reach the customer. This ability to offer individually tailored

Amazon: One-click shopping	Amazon holds a patent on one-click shopping that it licenses to other online retailers	
Online music: Apple iPod and iTunes	An integrated handheld player backed up with an online library of over 10 million songs	
Golf club customization: Ping	Customers can select from more than 1 million different golf club options; a build-to-order system ships their customized clubs within 48 hours	
Online person-to-person payment: PayPal.com	Enables transfer of money between individual bank accounts and between bank accounts and credit card accounts	

TABLE 3.1

IS-Enabled New Products and Services Providing Competitive Advantage

products or services using the same production resources as mass production is called **mass customization**.

Table 3.1 lists a number of companies that have developed IS-based products and services that other firms have found difficult to copy.

Focus on Market Niche

Use information systems to enable a specific market focus, and serve this narrow target market better than competitors. Information systems support this strategy by producing and analyzing data for finely tuned sales and marketing techniques. Information systems enable companies to analyze customer buying patterns, tastes, and preferences closely so that they efficiently pitch advertising and marketing campaigns to smaller and smaller target markets.

The data come from a range of sources—credit card transactions, demographic data, purchase data from checkout counter scanners at supermarkets and retail stores, and data collected when people access and interact with Web sites. Sophisticated software tools find patterns in these large pools of data and infer rules from them that can be used to guide decision making. Analysis of such data drives one-to-one marketing where personal messages can be created based on individualized preferences. For example, Hilton Hotels' OnQ system analyzes detailed data collected on active guests in all of its properties to determine the preferences of each guest and each guest's profitability. Hilton uses this information to give its most profitable customers additional privileges, such as late checkouts. Contemporary customer relationship management (CRM) systems feature analytical capabilities for this type of intensive data analysis (see Chapters 2 and 8).

Strengthen Customer and Supplier Intimacy

Use information systems to tighten linkages with suppliers and develop intimacy with customers. Toyota, Ford, and other automobile manufacturers have information systems that give their suppliers direct access to their production schedules, enabling suppliers to decide how and when to ship supplies to the plants where cars are assembled. This allows suppliers more lead time in producing goods. On the customer side, Amazon.com keeps track of user preferences for book and CD purchases, and can recommend titles purchased by others to its customers. Strong linkages to customers and suppliers increase **switching costs** (the cost of switching from one product or service to competitor) and loyalty to your firm.

Table 3.2 summarizes the competitive strategies we have just described. Some companies focus on one of these strategies, but you will often see firms pursuing several of them simultaneously. Starbucks, discussed in the Interactive Session on Technology, is an example.

INTERACTIVE SESSION: TECHNOLOGY   Technology Helps Starbucks Find New Ways to Compete

Starbucks is the world's largest specialty coffee retailer, with more than 16,850 coffee shops in about 40 countries. For years, Starbucks has continued to grow throughout the United States and internationally, opening franchises at an impressive rate. From 2002 to 2007 alone, the company tripled the number of stores it operated worldwide. Starbucks offers a unique experience: high-end specialty coffees and beverages, friendly and knowledgeable servers, and customer-friendly coffee shops. This was a winning formula for many years and enabled Starbucks to charge premium prices.

During the economic downturn beginning in 2008 profits plunged. Customers complained that the company had lost its hip, local feel and had become more like a fast-food chain. Many coffee drinkers went in search of cheaper alternatives from McDonald's and Dunkin' Donuts for their coffee fixes. Starbucks stock lost over 50 percent by the end of 2008. Major changes were in order.

Starbucks used the opportunity to overhaul its business using several different strategies simultaneously. First, the company has revamped its in-store technology and sought to integrate its business processes with wireless technology and the mobile digital platform. Also, rather than copy the practices of competitors, Starbucks pursued a more aggressive product differentiation strategy, intended to emphasize the high quality of its beverages and efficient and helpful customer service. At the same time, however, Starbucks also focused on becoming 'lean', like many of its competitors, eliminating inefficiency wherever possible.

When Starbucks set out to improve its customer experience, it found that more than a third of its customers are active users of smartphones. The company set out to implement several features and improvements that would appeal to this segment of its customer base. First, Starbucks implemented a technology that allows customers to pay using a smartphone app. The app is integrated with the Starbucks Card system, which allows regular customers to pay with a pre-paid and rechargeable card at any Starbucks branch. When customers make a purchase using the app, a cashier scans a bar code displayed on the phone, and the resulting sale is charged to the customer's Starbucks Card account. Customers report that paying using this app, available for all major smartphone operating systems, is much faster than traditional forms of payment.

Many of Starbucks' most loyal customers regularly spend time using the free Wi-Fi wireless network offered in each store. A majority of these customers also use mobile devices to connect to the in-store Wi-Fi networks. Recognizing this, Starbucks launched what it calls the "Starbucks Digital Network", a portal designed specifically for mobile devices as opposed to traditional Web browsers. The site is optimized for all major smartphone operating systems (iOS, Android, and BlackBerry), and responds to the multi-touch capability of devices like the iPad.

The Starbucks Digital Network site was developed in partnership with Yahoo and functions as a content portal. Starbucks customers using the site will receive free *Wall Street Journal* access, select free iTunes downloads, and a wide variety of other content. The site will integrate with Foursquare, a location-based social networking site for mobile devices. This arrangement will allow users to check in and receive award points using Starbucks' site. Because Starbucks has the most Foursquare check-ins of any company to date, this feature has been popular with customers.

Rather than serve ads on the site, Starbucks has opted to offer the site free of advertising, hoping that striking deals with content providers will make it a profitable venture. Even if the Starbucks Digital Network is not highly profitable, analysts suggest that the site is an effective way for Starbucks to improve its relationship with its most valuable customers and a creative use of the mobile digital platform to enhance customer satisfaction.

In addition to revamping their business to better serve the needs of their mobile users, Starbucks has made a concerted effort to become more efficient, reduce waste, and use the time saved to provide better customer service. Starbucks set out to streamline the business processes used in each of its stores so that baristas do not need to bend down to scoop coffee, cutting down on idle time while waiting for coffee to drain, and finding ways to reduce the amount of time each employee spends making a drink. Starbucks created a 10-person "lean team" whose job is to travel the country visiting franchises and coaching them in lean techniques made famous by automaker Toyota's production system.

Store labor costs Starbucks about $2.5 billion, amounting to 24 percent of its annual revenue. If Starbucks is able to reduce the time each employee spends making a drink, the company can make more drinks with the same number of workers or with fewer workers. Alternatively, Starbucks could use this time savings to give baristas more time to interact with customers and hopefully improve the Starbucks experience.

Wireless technology enhanced Starbucks' business process simplification effort. Starbucks district managers use the in-store wireless networks to run store operations and to connect to the company's private corporate network and systems. Starbucks district managers were equipped with Wi-Fi enabled laptops for this purpose. Before the in-store wireless networks were implemented, a district manager who oversaw 10 stores had to visit each store, review its operations, develop a list of items on which to follow up, and then drive to a Starbucks regional office to file reports and send e-mail. Instead of running the business from cubicles in regional headquarters, Starbucks district managers can do most of their work sitting at a table in one of the stores they oversee. The time saved from going back and forth to regional offices can be used to observe how employees are serving customers and improve their training. Implementing Wi-Fi technology enabled Starbucks to increase the in-store presence of district managers by 25 percent without adding any extra managers.

Dating to 2008, the weakened economy forced Starbucks to close 900 stores, renegotiate some rents, cut prices on some of their big ticket items, and begin offering price-reduced specials, such as a breakfast sandwich and a drink for $3.95. Cost reductions from procedural changes made it possible for Starbucks to offer these lower prices.

Major fast-food chains already used these techniques. While some baristas have resisted the changes, and analysts were skeptical that the changes would take hold, Starbucks attributes much of its recent uptick in profits to its efforts to go lean. Starbucks CEO Howard Schultz said that "the majority of cost reductions we've achieved come from a new way of operating and serving our customers", and also added that the time and money saved was also allowing the company to improve its customer engagement. By 2011, Starbucks had returned to profitability and continuing growth, with plans to open 500 new stores, in large part because of the success of each these changes.

Sources: Trefis Team, "Starbucks Brews Up Smartphone Payment Platform," *Forbes*, February 7, 2011, http://blogs.forbes.com/greatspeculations/2011/02/17/starbucks-brews-up-smartphone-payment-platform/; Ryan Kim, "Starbucks' New Portal Designed with Mobile in Mind," *Business Week*, September 2, 2010; Starbucks Form 10-K for Fiscal Year ended October 3, 2010; Julie Jargon, "Latest Starbucks Buzzword: 'Lean' Japanese Techniques," *The Wall Street Journal*, August 4, 2009.

CASE STUDY QUESTIONS

1. Analyze Starbucks using the competitive forces and value chain models.
2. What is Starbucks' business strategy? Assess the role played by technology in this business strategy.
3. How much has technology helped Starbucks compete? Explain your answer.

MIS IN ACTION

Visit Starbucks' Web site, then answer the following questions:

1. What functions are provided by the Web site?
2. How does the Web site support Starbucks' business strategy?

TABLE 3.2

Four Basic Competitive Strategies

Strategy	Description	Example
Low-cost leadership	Use information systems to produce products and services at a lower price than competitors while enhancing quality and level of service	Walmart
Product differentiation	Use information systems to differentiate products, and enable new services and products	Google, eBay, Apple, Starbucks
Focus on market niche	Use information systems to enable a focused strategy on a single market niche; specialize	Hilton Hotels, Harrah's
Customer and supplier intimacy	Use information systems to develop strong ties and loyalty with customers and suppliers	Toyota Corporation, Amazon

Implementing any of these strategies is no simple matter. But it is possible, as evidenced by the many firms that obviously dominate their markets and that have used information systems to enable their strategies. As shown by the cases throughout this book, successfully using information systems to achieve a competitive advantage requires a precise coordination of technology, organizations, and people. Indeed, as many have noted with regard to Walmart, Apple, and Amazon, the ability to successfully implement information systems is not equally distributed, and some firms are much better at it than others.

THE INTERNET'S IMPACT ON COMPETITIVE ADVANTAGE

Because of the Internet, the traditional competitive forces are still at work, but competitive rivalry has become much more intense (Porter, 2001). Internet technology is based on universal standards that any company can use, making it easy for rivals to compete on price alone and for new competitors to enter the market. Because information is available to everyone, the Internet raises the bargaining power of customers, who can quickly find the lowest-cost provider on the Web. Profits have been dampened. Table 3.3 summarizes some of the potentially negative impacts of the Internet on business firms identified by Porter.

The Internet has nearly destroyed some industries and has severely threatened others. For instance, the printed encyclopedia industry and the travel agency industry have been nearly decimated by the availability of substitutes over the Internet. Likewise, the Internet has had a significant impact on the retail, music, book, retail brokerage, software, telecommunications, and travel industries. The chapter-ending case provides a detailed discussion of the Internet's impact on publishing.

However, the Internet has also created entirely new markets, formed the basis for thousands of new products, services, and business models, and provided new opportunities for building brands with very large and loyal customer bases. Amazon, eBay, iTunes, YouTube, Facebook, Travelocity, and Google are examples. In this sense, the Internet is "transforming" entire industries, forcing firms to change how they do business.

TABLE 3.3

Impact of the Internet on Competitive Forces and Industry Structure

Competitive Force	Impact of the Internet
Substitute products or services	Enables new substitutes to emerge with new approaches to meeting needs and performing functions
Customers' bargaining power	Shifts bargaining power to customers due to the availability of global price and product information
Suppliers' bargaining power	Tends to raise bargaining power over suppliers in procuring products and services; however, suppliers can benefit from reduced barriers to entry and from the elimination of distributors and other intermediaries standing between them and their users
Threat of new entrants	Reduces barriers to entry, such as the need for a sales force, access to channels, and physical assets; it provides a technology for driving business processes that makes other things easier to do
Positioning and rivalry among existing competitors	Widens the geographic market, increasing the number of competitors and reducing differences among competitors; makes it more difficult to sustain operational advantages; puts pressure to compete on price

THE BUSINESS VALUE CHAIN MODEL

Although the Porter model is very helpful for identifying competitive forces and suggesting generic strategies, it is not very specific about what exactly to do, and it does not provide a methodology to follow for achieving competitive advantages. If your goal is to achieve operational excellence, where do you start? Here's where the business value chain model is helpful.

The **value chain model** highlights specific activities in the business where competitive strategies can best be applied (Porter, 1985) and where information systems are most likely to have a strategic impact. This model identifies specific, critical leverage points where a firm can use information technology most effectively to enhance its competitive position. The value chain model views the firm as a series or chain of basic activities that add a margin of value to a firm's products or services. These activities can be categorized as either primary activities or support activities (see Figure 3.2).

Primary activities are most directly related to the production and distribution of the firm's products and services, which create value for the customer. Primary activities include inbound logistics, operations, outbound logistics, sales and marketing, and service. Inbound logistics includes receiving and storing materials for distribution to production. Operations transforms inputs into finished products. Outbound logistics entails storing and distributing finished products. Sales and marketing includes promoting and selling the firm's products. The service activity includes maintenance and repair of the firm's goods and services.

Support activities make the delivery of the primary activities possible and consist of organization infrastructure (administration and management), human resources (employee recruiting, hiring, and training), technology (improving products and the production process), and procurement (purchasing input).

You can ask at each stage of the value chain, "How can we use information systems to improve operational efficiency and improve customer and supplier intimacy?" This will force you to critically examine how you perform value-adding activities at each stage and how the business processes might be improved. For example, value chain analysis would

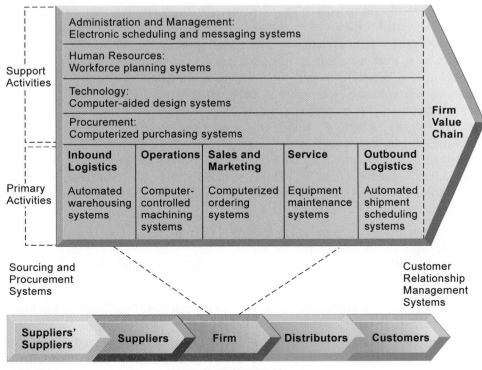

**Figure 3.2
The Value Chain Model**
This figure provides examples of systems for both primary and support activities of a firm and of its value partners that would add a margin of value to a firm's products or services.

indicate that Verizon, described in the chapter-opening case, should improve its processes for product development and quality control. You can also begin to ask how information systems can be used to improve the relationship with customers and with suppliers who lie outside the firm value chain but belong to the firm's extended value chain where they are absolutely critical to your success. Here, supply chain management systems that coordinate the flow of resources into your firm, and customer relationship management systems that coordinate your sales and support employees with customers, are two of the most common system applications that result from a business value chain analysis. We discuss these enterprise applications in detail later in Chapter 8.

Using the business value chain model will also cause you to consider benchmarking your business processes against your competitors or others in related industries, and identifying industry best practices. **Benchmarking** involves comparing the efficiency and effectiveness of your business processes against strict standards and then measuring performance against those standards. Industry **best practices** are usually identified by consulting companies, research organizations, government agencies, and industry associations as the most successful solutions or problem-solving methods for consistently and effectively achieving a business objective.

Once you have analyzed the various stages in the value chain at your business, you can come up with candidate applications of information systems. Then, once you have a list of candidate applications, you can decide which to develop first. By making improvements in your own business value chain that your competitors might miss, you can achieve competitive advantage by attaining operational excellence, lowering costs, improving profit margins, and forging a closer relationship with customers and suppliers. If your competitors are making similar improvements, then at least you will not be at a competitive disadvantage—the worst of all cases!

Extending the Value Chain: The Value Web

Figure 3.2 shows that a firm's value chain is linked to the value chains of its suppliers, distributors, and customers. After all, the performance of most firms depends not only on what goes on inside a firm but also on how well the firm coordinates with direct and indirect suppliers, delivery firms (logistics partners, such as FedEx or UPS), and, of course, customers.

How can information systems be used to achieve strategic advantage at the industry level? By working with other firms, industry participants can use information technology to develop industry-wide standards for exchanging information or business transactions electronically, which force all market participants to subscribe to similar standards. Such efforts increase efficiency, making product substitution less likely and perhaps raising entry costs—thus discouraging new entrants. Also, industry members can build industry-wide, IT-supported consortia, symposia, and communications networks to coordinate activities concerning government agencies, foreign competition, and competing industries.

Looking at the industry value chain encourages you to think about how to use information systems to link up more efficiently with your suppliers, strategic partners, and customers. Strategic advantage derives from your ability to relate your value chain to the value chains of other partners in the process. For instance, if you are Amazon.com, you would want to build systems that

- Make it easy for suppliers to display goods and open stores on the Amazon site
- Make it easy for customers to pay for goods
- Develop systems that coordinate the shipment of goods to customers
- Develop shipment tracking systems for customers

In fact, this is exactly what Amazon has done to make it one of the Web's most satisfying online retail shopping sites.

Internet technology has made it possible to create highly synchronized industry value chains called value webs. A **value web** is a collection of independent firms that use information technology to coordinate their value chains to produce a product or service for a market collectively. It is more customer driven and operates in a less linear fashion than the traditional value chain.

Figure 3.3 shows that this value web synchronizes the business processes of customers, suppliers, and trading partners among different companies in an industry or in related industries. These value webs are flexible and adaptive to changes in supply and demand. Relationships can be bundled or unbundled in response to changing market conditions. Firms will accelerate time to market and to customers by optimizing their value web relationships to make quick decisions on who can deliver the required products or services at the right price and location.

SYNERGIES, CORE COMPETENCIES, AND NETWORK-BASED STRATEGIES

A large corporation is typically a collection of businesses. Often, the firm is organized financially as a collection of strategic business units, and the returns to the firm are directly tied to the performance of all the units. For instance, General Electric—one of the largest industrial firms in the world—is a collection of aerospace, heavy manufacturing, electrical appliance, medical imaging, electronics, and financial services firms called business units. Information systems can improve the overall performance of these business units by promoting communication, synergies, and core competencies among the units.

Synergies

Synergies develop when the output of some units can be used as inputs to other units, or two organizations can pool markets and expertise, and these relationships lower costs and generate profits. Recent bank and financial firm mergers, such as the merger of Bank of America and Countrywide Financial and JPMorgan Chase and Washington Mutual occurred precisely for this purpose.

One use of information technology in these synergy situations is to tie together the operations of disparate business units so that they can act as a whole. For example, acquiring Countrywide Financial enabled Bank of America to expand its mortgage lending business and acquire a large pool of new customers that might be interested in its credit

Figure 3.3
The Value Web
The value web is a networked system that can synchronize the value chains of business partners within an industry to respond rapidly to changes in supply and demand.

cards, consumer banking, and other financial products. Information systems would help the merged companies consolidate operations, lower retailing costs, and increase cross-marketing of financial products.

Enhancing Core Competencies

Another use of information systems for competitive advantage is to think about ways that systems can enhance core competencies. The argument is that the performance of all business units can increase insofar as these business units develop, or create, a central core of competencies. A **core competency** is an activity for which a firm is a world-class leader. Core competencies may involve being the world's best miniature parts designer, the best package delivery service, or the best thin-film manufacturer. In general, a core competency relies on knowledge that is gained over many years of experience and a first-class research organization, or simply key people who follow the literature and stay abreast of new external knowledge.

Any information system that encourages the sharing of knowledge across business units enhances competency. Such systems might encourage or enhance existing competencies and help employees become aware of new external knowledge; such systems might also help a business leverage existing competencies to related markets.

For example, Procter & Gamble (P&G), a world leader in brand management and consumer product innovation, uses a series of systems to enhance its core competencies. P&G uses an intranet called InnovationNet to help people working on similar problems share ideas and expertise. The system connects those working in research and development (R&D), engineering, purchasing, marketing, legal affairs, and business information systems around the world, using a portal to provide browser-based access to documents, reports, charts, videos, and other data from various sources. InnovationNet added a directory of subject matter experts who can be tapped to give advice or collaborate on problem solving and product development, and created links to outside research scientists and 150 entrepreneurs who are searching for new, innovative products worldwide.

Network-Based Strategies

Internet and networking technology have spawned strategies that take advantage of firms' abilities to create networks or network with each other. Network-based strategies include the use of network economics and a virtual company model.

Business models based on a network may help firms strategically by taking advantage of **network economics**. In traditional economics—the economics of factories and agriculture—production experiences diminishing returns. The more any given resource is applied to production, the lower the marginal gain in output, until a point is reached where the additional inputs produce no additional outputs. This is the law of diminishing returns, and it is one foundation of modern economics.

In some situations, the law of diminishing returns does not work. For instance, in a network, the marginal costs of adding another participant are about zero, whereas the marginal gain is much larger. The larger the number of subscribers in a telephone system or the Internet, the greater the value to all participants because each user can interact with more people. It is no more expensive to operate a television station with 1,000 subscribers than with 10 million subscribers. The value of a community of people grows with size, whereas the cost of adding new members is inconsequential.

From this network economics perspective, information technology can be strategically useful. Internet sites can be used by firms to build *communities of users*—like-minded customers who want to share their experiences. This can build customer loyalty and enjoyment, and build unique ties to customers. EBay, the giant online auction site, and iVillage, an online community for women, are examples. Both businesses are based on networks of millions of users, and both companies have used the Web and Internet communication tools to build communities. The more people offering products on eBay, the more valuable the eBay site is to everyone because more products are listed, and more competition among suppliers lowers prices. Network economics also provide strategic benefits to commercial software vendors. The value of their software and complementary software products increases as more people use them, and there is a larger installed base to justify continued use of the product and vendor support.

Another network-based strategy uses the model of a virtual company to create a competitive business. A **virtual company**, also known as a *virtual organization*, uses networks to link people, assets, and ideas, enabling it to ally with other companies to create and distribute products and services without being limited by traditional organizational boundaries or physical locations. One company can use the capabilities of another company without being physically tied to that company. The virtual company model is useful when a company finds it cheaper to acquire products, services, or capabilities from an external vendor or when it needs to move quickly to exploit new market opportunities and lacks the time and resources to respond on its own.

Fashion companies, such as GUESS, Ann Taylor, Levi Strauss, and Reebok, enlist Hong Kong-based Li & Fung to manage production and shipment of their garments. Li & Fung handles product development, raw material sourcing, production planning, quality assurance, and shipping. Li & Fung does not own any fabric, factories, or machines, outsourcing all of its work to a network of more than 7,500 suppliers in 37 countries all over the world. Customers place orders to Li & Fung over its private extranet. Li & Fung then sends instructions to appropriate raw material suppliers and factories where the clothing is produced. The Li & Fung extranet tracks the entire production process for each order. Working as a virtual company keeps Li & Fung flexible and adaptable so that it can design and produce the products ordered by its clients in short order to keep pace with rapidly changing fashion trends.

DISRUPTIVE TECHNOLOGIES: RIDING THE WAVE

Sometimes a technology and resulting business innovation comes along to radically change the business landscape and environment. These innovations are loosely called "disruptive." (Christensen, 2003). In some cases, **disruptive technologies** are substitute products that perform as well or better than anything currently produced. The automobile substituted for the horse-drawn carriage; the Apple iPod for portable CD players; digital photography for process film photography. In these cases, entire industries are put out of business.

In other cases, disruptive technologies simply extend the market, usually with less functionality and much less cost, than existing products. Eventually they turn into low-cost competitors for whatever was sold before. Disk drives are an example: small hard disk drives used in PCs extended the market for computer disk drives by offering cheap digital storage for small files on small computers. Eventually, small PC hard disk drives became the largest segment of the disk drive marketplace.

Some firms are able to create these technologies and ride the wave to profits, whereas others learn quickly and adapt their business; still others are obliterated because their products, services, and business models become obsolete. There are also cases where no firms benefit, and all gains go to consumers (firms fail to capture any profits). Table 3.4 provides examples of some disruptive technologies.

Disruptive technologies are tricky. Firms that invent disruptive technologies as "first movers" do not always benefit if they lack the resources to exploit the technology or fail to see the opportunity. The MITS Altair 8800 is widely regarded as the first PC, but its inventors did not take advantage of their first mover status. Second movers, so-called "fast followers" such as IBM and Microsoft, reaped the rewards. Citibank's ATMs revolutionized retail banking, but they were copied by other banks. Now all banks use ATMs, with the benefits going mostly to the consumers.

TABLE 3.4

Disruptive
Technologies: Winners
and Losers

Technology	Description	Winners and Losers
Microprocessor chips (1971)	Thousands and eventually millions of transistors on a silicon chip	Microprocessor firms win (Intel, Texas Instruments) while transistor firms (GE) decline
Personal computers (1975)	Small, inexpensive, but fully functional desktop computers	PC manufacturers (HP, Apple, IBM), and chip manufacturers prosper (Intel), while mainframe (IBM) and minicomputer (DEC) firms lose
Digital photography 1975	Using charge-coupled device (CCD) image sensor chips to record images	CCD manufacturers and traditional camera companies win, manufacturers of film products lose
World Wide Web (1989)	A global database of digital files and "pages" instantly available	Owners of online content, news benefit while traditional publishers (newspapers, magazines, and broadcast television) lose
Internet music, video, TV services	Repositories of downloadable music, video, TV broadcasts on the Web	Owners of Internet platforms, telecommunications providers owning Internet backbone (AT&T, Verizon), local Internet service providers win, while content owners and physical retailers lose (Tower Records, Blockbuster)
PageRank algorithm	A method for ranking Web pages in terms of their popularity to supplement Web search by key terms	Google is the winner (they own the patent), while traditional key word search engines (Alta Vista) lose
Software as Web service	Using the Internet to provide remote access to online software	Online software services companies (Salesforce.com) win, while traditional "boxed" software companies (Microsoft, SAP, Oracle) lose

3.2 Competing on a Global Scale

Look closely at your jeans or sneakers. Even if they have a U.S. label, they were probably designed in California and stitched together in Hong Kong or Guatemala using materials from China or India. Call Microsoft Support, or Verizon Support, and chances are good you will be speaking to a customer service representative located in India.

Consider the path to market for an iPhone, which is illustrated in Figure 3.4. The iPhone was designed by Apple engineers in the United States, sourced with more than 100 high-tech components from around the world, and assembled in China. Among the iPhone's major suppliers, Samsung Electronics in South Korea has supplied the flash memory and applications processor. The iPhone 4's accelerator and gyroscope are made in Italy and France by STMicroelectronics, and its electronic compass is made by AKM Semiconductor in Japan. Germany's Infineon Technologies supplies chips that send and receive phone calls and data. Texas Instruments (TI) supplies the touch screen controller, while South Korea's LG Display makes the high-definition display screen. Foxconn, a Chinese division of Taiwan's Hon Hai Group, is in charge of manufacturing and assembly.

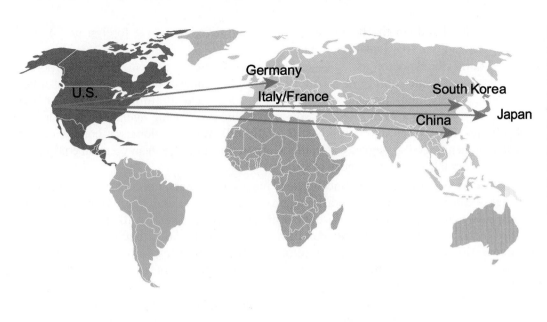

Figure 3.4
Apple iPhone's Global Supply Chain
Apple designs the iPhone in the United States, and relies on suppliers in the United States, Germany, Italy, France, and South Korea for other parts. Final assembly occurs in China.

Firms pursuing a global strategy benefit from economies of scale and resource cost reduction (usually wage cost reduction). Apple spread design, sourcing, and production for its iPhone over multiple countries overseas to reduce logistics, tariffs, and labor costs. Digital content firms that produce Hollywood movies are able to sell millions more copies of DVDs of popular films by using foreign markets.

THE INTERNET AND GLOBALIZATION

Up until the mid-1990s, competing on a global scale was dominated by huge multinational firms, such as General Electric, General Motors, Toyota, and IBM. These large firms could afford huge investments in factories, warehouses, and distribution centers in foreign countries and proprietary networks and systems that could operate on a global scale. The emergence of the Internet into a full-blown international communications system has drastically reduced the costs of operating on a global scale, deepening the possibilities for large companies but simultaneously creating many opportunities for small and medium-sized firms.

The global Internet, along with internal information systems, puts manufacturing firms in nearly instant contact with their suppliers. Internet telephony permits millions of service calls to U.S. companies to be answered in India and Jamaica, just as easily and cheaply as if the help desk were in New Jersey or California. Likewise, the Internet makes it possible to move very large computer files with hundreds of graphics, or complex industrial designs, across the globe in seconds.

Small and medium-sized firms have created an entirely new class of "micromultinational firms." For instance, CEO Brad Oberwager runs Sundia, a company that sells premium cut fruit to more than 6,000 grocery and convenience stores in the United States and Canada out of his San Francisco home. Oberwager has employees in other parts of the United States as well as in India and the Philippines, and they use Web-based information systems to manage and coordinate. A Sundia employee in the Philippines is able to take orders from a Boston grocery store for watermelon juice made from Mexican fruit. The juice is squeezed in Washington State and payment goes to Oberwager in California.

GLOBAL BUSINESS AND SYSTEM STRATEGIES

There are four main ways of organizing businesses internationally: domestic exporter, multinational, franchiser, and transnational, each with different patterns of organizational structure or governance. In each type of global business organization, business functions may be centralized (in the home country), decentralized (to local foreign units), and coordinated (all units participate as equals).

The **domestic exporter** strategy is characterized by heavy centralization of corporate activities in the home country of origin. Production, finance/accounting, sales/marketing, human resources, and strategic management are set up to optimize resources in the home country. International sales are sometimes dispersed using agency agreements or subsidiaries, but foreign marketing is still totally reliant on the domestic home base for marketing themes and strategies. Caterpillar Corporation and other heavy capital equipment manufacturers fall into this category of firm.

A **multinational** strategy concentrates financial management and control out of a central home base while decentralizing production, sales, and marketing operations to units in other countries. The products and services on sale in different countries are adapted to suit local market conditions. The organization becomes a far-flung confederation of production and marketing facilities operating in different countries. Many financial service firms, along with a host of manufacturers such as Ford Motor Co. and Intel Corporation, fit this pattern.

Franchisers have the product created, designed, financed, and initially produced in the home country but rely heavily on foreign personnel for further production, marketing, and human resources. Food franchisers, such as McDonald's and Starbucks, fit this pattern. McDonald's created a new form of fast-food chain in the United States and continues to rely largely on the United States for inspiration of new products, strategic management, and financing. Nevertheless, local production of some items, local marketing, and local recruitment of personnel are required.

Transnational firms have no single national headquarters but instead have many regional headquarters and perhaps a world headquarters. In a **transnational** strategy, nearly all the value-adding activities are managed from a global perspective without reference to national borders, optimizing sources of supply and demand wherever they appear and taking advantage of any local competitive advantages. There is a strong central management core of decision making but considerable dispersal of power and financial muscle throughout the global divisions. Few companies have actually attained transnational status, but Citigroup, Sony, and Nestlé are attempting this transition.

Nestlé S.A., the largest food and beverage company in the world, is one of the world's most globalized companies, with nearly 280,000 employees at 500 facilities in 200 countries. Nestlé launched a $2.4 billion initiative to adopt a single set of business processes and systems for procurement, distribution, and sales management using mySAP enterprise software. All of Nestlé's worldwide business units use the same processes and systems for making sales commitments, establishing factory production schedules, billing customers, compiling management reports, and reporting financial results. Nestlé has learned how to operate as a single unit on a global scale.

GLOBAL SYSTEM CONFIGURATION

Figure 3.5 depicts four types of systems configurations for global business organizations. *Centralized systems* are those in which systems development and operation occur totally at the domestic home base. *Duplicated systems* are those in which development occurs at the home base but operations are handed over to autonomous units in foreign locations. *Decentralized systems* are those in which each foreign unit designs its own unique solutions and systems. *Networked systems* are those in which systems development and operations occur in an integrated and coordinated fashion across all units.

As can be seen in Figure 3.5, domestic exporters tend to have highly centralized systems in which a single domestic systems development staff develops worldwide applications. Multinationals allow foreign units to devise their own systems solutions based on local needs with few, if any, applications in common with headquarters (the exceptions being financial reporting and some telecommunications applications). Franchisers typically develop a

SYSTEM CONFIGURATION	Strategy			
	Domestic Exporter	Multinational	Franchiser	Transnational
Centralized	X			
Duplicated			X	
Decentralized	x	X	x	
Networked		x		X

Figure 3.5
Global Business Organization and Systems Configurations
The large Xs show the dominant patterns, and the small Xs show the emerging patterns. For instance, domestic exporters rely predominantly on centralized systems, but there is continual pressure and some development of decentralized systems in local marketing regions.

single system, usually at the home base, and then replicate it around the world. Each unit, no matter where it is located, has identical applications. Firms such as Nestle organized along transnational lines use networked systems that span multiple countries using powerful telecommunications networks and a shared management culture that crosses cultural barriers.

3.3 Competing on Quality and Design

Quality has developed from a business buzzword into a very serious goal for many companies. Quality is a form of differentiation. Companies with reputations for high quality, such as Lexus or Nordstrom, are able to charge premium prices for their products and services. Information systems have a major contribution to make in this drive for quality. In the services industries in particular, quality strategies are generally enabled by superior information systems and services.

WHAT IS QUALITY?

Quality can be defined from both producer and customer perspectives. From the perspective of the producer, quality signifies conformance to specifications or the absence of variation from those specifications. The specifications for a telephone might include one that states the strength of the phone should be such that it will not be dented or otherwise damaged by a drop from a four-foot height onto a wooden floor. A simple test will allow this specification to be measured.

A customer definition of quality is much broader. First, customers are concerned with the quality of the physical product—its durability, safety, ease of use, and installation. Second, customers are concerned with the quality of service, by which they mean the accuracy and truthfulness of advertising, responsiveness to warranties, and ongoing product support. Finally, customer concepts of quality include psychological aspects: the company's knowledge of its products, the courtesy and sensitivity of sales and support staff, and the reputation of the product.

Today, as the quality movement in business progresses, the definition of quality is increasingly from the perspective of the customer. Customers are concerned with getting value for their dollar and product fitness, performance, durability, and support.

Many companies have embraced the concept of **total quality management (TQM)**. Total quality management makes quality the responsibility of all people and functions within an organization. TQM holds that the achievement of quality control is an end in itself. Everyone is expected to contribute to the overall improvement of quality—the engineer who avoids design errors, the production worker who spots defects, the sales representative who presents the product properly to potential customers, and even the secretary who avoids typing mistakes. TQM derives from quality management concepts developed by American quality experts, such as W. Edwards Deming and Joseph Juran, but the Japanese popularized it.

Another quality concept that is widely implemented today is six sigma, which Amazon. com used to reduce errors in order fulfillment. **Six sigma** is a specific measure of quality, representing 3.4 defects per million opportunities. Most companies cannot achieve this level of quality but use six sigma as a goal to implement a set of methodologies and techniques for improving quality and reducing costs. Studies have repeatedly shown that the earlier in the business cycle a problem is eliminated, the less it costs the company. Thus, quality improvements not only raise the level of product and service quality but they can also lower costs.

HOW INFORMATION SYSTEMS IMPROVE QUALITY

Let's examine some of the ways companies face the challenge of improving quality to see how information systems can be part of the process.

Reduce Cycle Time and Simplify the Production Process

Studies have shown that one of the best ways to reduce quality problems is to reduce **cycle time**, which refers to the total elapsed time from the beginning of a process to its end. Shorter cycle times mean that problems are caught earlier in the process, often before the production of a defective product is completed, saving some of the hidden production costs. Finally, finding ways to reduce cycle time often means finding ways to simplify production steps. The fewer steps in a process, the less time and opportunity for an error to occur. Information systems help eliminate steps in a process and critical time delays.

800-Flowers, a multimillion-dollar company selling flowers by telephone or over the Web, used to be a much smaller company that had difficulty retaining its customers. It had poor service, inconsistent quality, and a cumbersome manual order-taking process. Telephone representatives had to write each order, obtain credit card approval, determine which participating florist was closest to the delivery location, select a floral arrangement, and forward the order to the florist. Each step in the manual process increased the chance of human error, and the whole process took at least a half hour. Owners Jim and Chris McCann installed a new information system that downloads orders taken in telecenters or over the Web to a central computer and electronically transmits them to local florists. As a result, orders are more accurate and arrive at the florist within two minutes.

Benchmark

Companies achieve quality by using benchmarking to set standards for products, services, and other activities, and then measuring performance against those standards. Companies may use external industry standards, standards set by other companies, internally developed standards, or some combination of the three. L.L.Bean, the Freeport, Maine, outdoor clothing company, used benchmarking to achieve an order-shipping accuracy of 99.9 percent. Its old batch order fulfillment system could not handle the surging volume and variety of items to be shipped. After studying German and Scandinavian companies with leading-edge order fulfillment operations, L.L.Bean carefully redesigned its order fulfillment process and information systems so that orders could be processed as soon as they were received and shipped within 24 hours.

Use Customer Demands to Improve Products and Services

Improving customer service, and making customer service the number one priority, will improve the quality of the product itself. Delta Airlines decided to focus on its customers, installing a customer care system at its airport gates. For each flight, the airplane seating chart, reservations, check-in information, and boarding data are linked in a central database. Airline personnel can track which passengers are on board regardless of where they checked in and use this information to help passengers reach their destination quickly, even if delays cause them to miss connecting flights.

Computer-aided design (CAD) systems improve the quality and precision of product design by performing much of the design and testing work on the computer.

© Wojtek Kryczka, 2011, iStockPhoto LP.

Improve Design Quality and Precision

Computer-aided design (CAD) software has made a major contribution to quality improvements in many companies, from producers of automobiles to producers of razor blades. A **computer-aided design (CAD) system** automates the creation and revision of designs, using computers and sophisticated graphics software. The software enables users to create a digital model of a part, a product, or a structure, and make changes to the design on the computer without having to build physical prototypes.

Troy Lee Designs, which makes sports helmets, recently invested in CAD design software that could create the helmets in 3-D. The technology defined the shapes better than traditional methods, which involved sketching an idea on paper, hand-molding a clay model, and shipping the model to Asian factories to create a plastic prototype. Production is now about six months faster and about 35 percent cheaper, with Asian factories about to produce an exact replica after receiving the digital design via e-mail (Maltby, 2010).

Improve Production Precision and Tighten Production Tolerances

For many products, quality can be enhanced by making the production process more precise, thereby decreasing the amount of variation from one part to another. CAD software often produces design specifications for tooling and manufacturing processes, saving additional time and money while producing a manufacturing process with far fewer problems. The user of this software is able to design a more precise production system, a system with tighter tolerances, than could ever be done manually.

3.4 Competing on Business Processes

Technology alone is often not enough to make organizations more competitive, efficient, or quality-oriented. The organization itself needs to be changed to take advantage of the power of information technology. These changes may require minor adjustments in work activities, but, often, entire business processes will need to be redesigned. Business process management (BPM) addresses these needs.

WHAT IS BUSINESS PROCESS MANAGEMENT?

Business process management (BPM) is an approach to business which aims to continuously improve business processes. BPM uses a variety of tools and methodologies to understand existing processes, design new processes, and optimize those processes. BPM is never concluded because continuous improvement requires continual change. Companies practicing business process management need to go through the following steps:

1. **Identify processes for change:** One of the most important strategic decisions that a firm can make is not deciding how to use computers to improve business processes, but rather understanding what business processes need improvement. When systems are used to strengthen the wrong business model or business processes, the business can become more efficient at doing what it should not do. As a result, the firm becomes vulnerable to competitors who may have discovered the right business model. Considerable time and cost may also be spent improving business processes that have little impact on overall firm performance and revenue. Managers need to determine what business processes are the most important and how improving these processes will help business performance.

2. **Analyze existing processes:** Existing business processes should be modeled and documented, noting inputs, outputs, resources, and the sequence of activities. The process design team identifies redundant steps, paper-intensive tasks, bottlenecks, and other inefficiencies.

Figure 3.6 illustrates the "as-is" process for purchasing a book from a physical bookstore. Consider what happens when a customer visits a physical bookstore and searches its shelves for a book . If he or she finds the book, that person takes it to the checkout counter and pays for it via credit card, cash, or check. If the customer is unable to locate the book, he or she

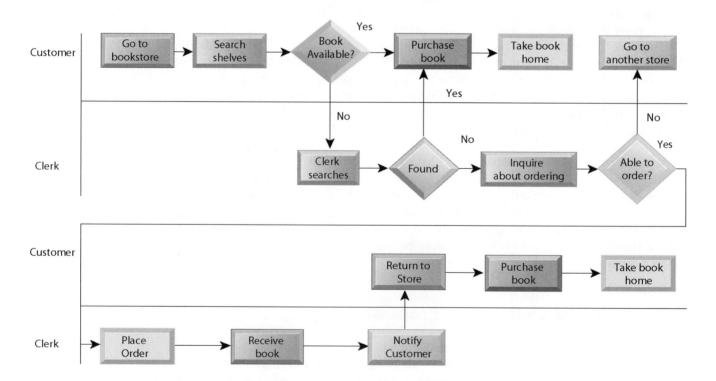

Figure 3.6
As-Is Business Process for Purchasing a Book from a Physical Bookstore
Purchasing a book from a physical bookstore requires many steps to be performed by both the seller and the customer.

must ask a bookstore clerk to search the shelves or check the bookstore's inventory records to see if it is in stock. If the clerk finds the book, the customer purchases it and leaves. If the book is not available locally, the clerk inquires about ordering it for the customer, either from the bookstore's warehouse or from the book's distributor or publisher. Once the ordered book arrives at the bookstore, a bookstore employee telephones the customer with this information. The customer would have to go to the bookstore again to pick up the book and pay for it. If the bookstore is unable to order the book for the customer, the customer would have to try another bookstore. You can see that this process has many steps and might require the customer to make multiple trips to the bookstore.

3. **Design the new process:** Once the existing process is mapped and measured in terms of time and cost, the process design team will try to improve the process by designing a new one. A new streamlined "to-be" process will be documented and modeled for comparison with the old process.

Figure 3.7 illustrates how the book purchasing process can be redesigned by taking advantage of the Internet. The customer accesses an online bookstore over the Internet from his or her computer. He or she searches the bookstore's online catalog for the book he or she wants. If the book is available, the customer orders the book online, supplying credit card and shipping address information, and the book is delivered to the customer's home. If the online bookstore does not carry the book, the customer selects another online bookstore and searches for the book again. This process has far fewer steps than that for purchasing the book in a physical bookstore, requires much less effort on the part of the customer, and requires less sales staff for customer service. The new process is therefore much more efficient and time-saving.

The new process design needs to be justified by showing how much it reduces time and cost or enhances customer service and value. Management first measures the time and cost of the existing process as a baseline. In our example, the time required for purchasing a book from a physical bookstore might range from 15 minutes (if the customer immediately finds what he or she wants) to 30 minutes if the book is in stock but has to be located by sales staff. If the book has to be ordered from another source, the process might take one or two weeks and another trip to the bookstore for the customer. If the customer lives far away from the bookstore, the time to travel to the bookstore would have to be factored in. The bookstore will have to pay the costs for maintaining a physical store and keeping the book in stock, for sales staff on site, and for shipment costs if the book has to be obtained from another location.

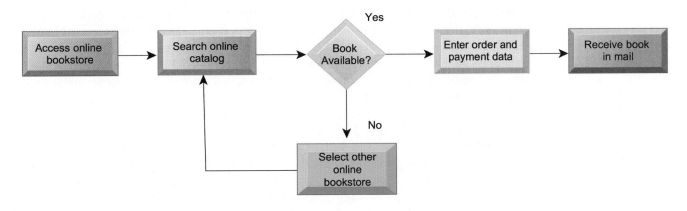

Figure 3.7
Redesigned Process for Purchasing a Book Online
Using Internet technology makes it possible to redesign the process for purchasing a book so that it only has a few steps and consumes much fewer resources.

The new process for purchasing a book online might only take several minutes, although the customer might have to wait several days or weeks to receive the book in the mail and will have to pay a small shipping charge. But the customer saves time and money by not having to travel to the bookstore or make additional visits to pick up the book. Book sellers' costs are lower because they do not have to pay for a physical store location or for local inventory.

4. **Implement the new process:** Once the new process has been thoroughly modeled and analyzed, it must be translated into a new set of procedures and work rules. New information systems or enhancements to existing systems may have to be implemented to support the redesigned process. The new process and supporting systems are rolled out into the business organization. As the business starts using this process, problems are uncovered and addressed. Employees working with the process may recommend improvements.

5. **Continuous measurement:** Once a process has been implemented and optimized, it needs to be continually measured. Why? Processes may deteriorate over time as employees fall back on old methods, or they may lose their effectiveness if the business experiences other changes.

Over 100 software firms provide tools for various aspects of BPM, including IBM, Oracle, and Tibco. These tools help businesses identify and document processes requiring improvement, create models of improved processes, capture and enforce business rules for performing processes, and integrate existing systems to support new or redesigned processes. BPM software tools also provide analytics for verifying that process performance has been improved and for measuring the impact of process changes on key business performance indicators.

The Interactive Session on Organizations provides an example of a company that benefited competitively from business process management. As with any company that rapidly expands from a small business to a global brand, Burton Snowboards found that some of its business processes had become outdated. Burton has made serious efforts to improve these processes and turn their weaknesses into strengths.

Business Process Reengineering

Many business process improvements are incremental and ongoing, but occasionally, more radical change is required. Our example of a physical bookstore redesigning the book purchasing process so that it can be carried out online is an example of this type of radical, far-reaching change. This radical rethinking and redesign of business processes is called **business process reengineering (BPR).**

When properly implemented, BPR can lead to dramatic gains in productivity and efficiency, even changing the way the business is run. In some instances, it drives a "paradigm shift" that transforms the nature of the business itself. This actually happened in book retailing when Amazon challenged traditional physical bookstores with its online retail model. By radically rethinking the way a book can be purchased and sold, Amazon and other online bookstores have achieved remarkable efficiencies, cost reductions, and a whole new way of doing business.

BPM poses challenges. Executives report that the largest single barrier to successful business process change is organizational culture. Employees do not like unfamiliar routines, and often try to resist change. This is especially true of business process reengineering projects because the organizational changes are so far-reaching. Managing change is neither simple nor intuitive, and companies committed to extensive process improvement need a good change management strategy (see Chapter 11).

INTERACTIVE SESSION: ORGANIZATIONS   Burton Snowboards Speeds Ahead with Nimble Business Processes

When we hear "snowboarding," we tend to think of snow-covered slopes, acrobatic jumps, and high-flying entertainment. We don't usually think of improving business process efficiency. But snowboarding is business for Burton Snowboards, an industry pioneer and market leader. Founded in 1977 by Jake Burton Carpenter and headquartered in Burlington, Vermont, Burton designs, manufactures, and markets equipment, clothing, and related accessories for snowboarders. Today, Burton is a global enterprise that serves customers in 27 countries and has offices in Japan, Austria, and throughout the United States.

At its peak, Burton controlled over 40 percent of the U.S. snowboarding market, and it remains the market leader amidst a growing number of competitors. Now, as Burton continues to expand into a global company, it has a new set of problems: improving its systems for inventory, supply chain, purchasing, and customer service.

Stocking and managing inventory is a difficult problem for Burton, whose inventory changes dramatically depending on product line updates and the time of the year. Burton takes feedback from its customers very seriously, and will move quickly to meet their needs. For instance, if a rider tests a jacket and recommends repositioning a zipper, Burton's production line must be able to make this modification quickly and easily. Being dynamic and adaptable is a competitive necessity.

Burton has implemented and currently maintains SAP enterprise software, an Oracle database, a SUSE Linux enterprise server, and commodity hardware. That's a long way from a lone woodworking shop in Vermont. Before making these upgrades, Burton's information systems were a hodgepodge of inconsistently implemented and underutilized software. The company had to manually allocate product to customers and orders. In 1997, Burton first deployed SAP to begin upgrading its IT landscape, and the company has continued to use SAP since that time. But Burton needed to do more with its systems.

Two of Burton's IT goals, established by CIO Kevin Ubert, are to "strengthen the foundation," and keep their systems "simple, standard, (and) supportable." The 'foundation' Ubert referred to is SAP Enterprise Resource Planning (ERP) software. Rather than buying new software to solve IT problems, Burton decided that it would explore basic functionalities of SAP enterprise resource planning (ERP) software that it had not used yet. Often, Burton could resolve problems this way without adding new layers of complexity to its IT infra-

structure, and the company gained proficiency with SAP enterprise software in the process. Burton aims for standard, traditional versions of software whenever possible, realizing that with more bells and whistles comes increased maintenance costs and steeper learning curves to understanding the software.

SAP analysts helped Burton identify the top five transactions that were the most critical to its business operations and that needed optimization from a systems standpoint. Burton had to identify unnecessarily complicated processes, backlogs, and design gaps in the flow of its business processes. For example, the available-to-promise process was taking hours to complete. (Available to promise, in response to customer order enquiries, reports on available quantities of a requested product and delivery due dates.) Burton wanted to speed up this process so that its dealers and retail customers would have more precise information about the availability of products not currently in stock. Completing this process now takes 20 minutes.

Other processes in need of improvement included the order-to-cash process (receiving and processing customer sales, including order entry, fulfillment, distribution, and payment); the handling of overdue purchase orders in the procure-to-pay process, which consists of all the steps from purchasing goods from a supplier to paying the supplier; and the electronic data interchange (EDI) inventory feed extract transaction. Burton has an assortment of warehouses which pass inventory data to one another automatically using EDI systems. Thousands of items are moving from warehouse to warehouse and thousands of transactions occur each day at each warehouse. Burton found that the process of reporting inventory was inefficient, and both suppliers and customers could not easily determine up-to-date information on which items were in stock at which warehouse. SAP and Burton worked together to improve communication between warehouses and supply chain efficiency.

A management dashboard developed with the help of SAP shows how smoothly a critical process is running at a certain point in time. Information from the dashboard helps Burton's key users discover inconsistencies, gaps, or other areas that they should be monitoring more closely.

All of these process improvements proved especially valuable during what Burton calls its "reorder" season. Burton's dealers place orders to stock their stores well before winter sets in. As consumers start buying the merchandise, the dealers reorder with Burton to replenish their stock or to buy new products. Now they are able to see more timely product availability data, and receive orders more rapidly.

Sources: Lauren Bonneau, "How Burton Snowboards Remains as Nimble as Its Riders," SAP InsiderPROFILES, April-June 2011 and "Burton Snowboards Inc. Company Profile," Reference for Business, accessed May 2011.

CASE STUDY QUESTIONS

1. Analyze Burton using the value chain and competitive forces models.

2. Why are the business processes described in this case such an important source of competitive advantage for Burton?

3. Explain exactly how these process improvements enhance Burton's operational performance and decision making.

MIS IN ACTION

Visit Burton Snowboards' Web site, then answer the following questions:

1. What is the purpose of this Web site? How does it support the company's goals?

2. What functions at this Web site are related to the business processes discussed in this case? How did improving those processes impact the Web site?

LEARNING TRACKS

The following Learning Tracks provide content relevant to topics covered in this chapter:

1. Challenges of Information Systems for Competitive Advantage
2. Primer on Business Process Management
3. Primer on Business Process Design

Review Summary

1 **How does Porter's competitive forces model help companies develop competitive strategies using information systems?** In Porter's competitive forces model, the strategic position of the firm, and its strategies, are determined by competition with its traditional direct competitors. They are also greatly affected by new market entrants, substitute products and services, suppliers, and customers. Information systems help companies compete by maintaining low costs, differentiating products or services, focusing on market niche, strengthening ties with customer and suppliers, and increasing barriers to market entry with high levels of operational excellence. Information systems are most successful when the technology is aligned with business objectives.

2 **How do the value chain and value web models help businesses identify opportunities for strategic information system applications?** The value chain model highlights specific activities in the business where competitive strategies and information systems will have the greatest impact. The model views the firm as a series of primary and support activities that add value to a firm's products or services. Primary activities are directly related to production and distribution, whereas support activities make the delivery of primary activities possible. A firm's value chain can be linked to the value chains of its suppliers, distributors, and customers. A value web consists of information systems that enhance competitiveness at the industry level by promoting the use of standards and industry-wide consortia, and by enabling businesses to work more efficiently with their value partners.

3 **How do information systems help businesses use synergies, core competences, and network-based strategies to achieve competitive advantage?** Because firms consist of multiple business units, information systems achieve additional efficiencies or enhanced services by tying together the operations of disparate business units. Information systems help businesses leverage their core competencies by promoting the sharing of knowledge across business units. Information systems facilitate business models based on large networks of users or subscribers that take advantage of network economics. A virtual company strategy uses networks to link to other firms so that a company can use the capabilities of other companies to build, market, and distribute products and services. Disruptive technologies provide strategic opportunities, although "first movers" do not necessarily obtain long-term benefit.

4 **How do competing on a global scale and promoting quality enhance competitive advantage?** Information systems and the Internet can help companies operate internationally by facilitating coordination of geographically dispersed units of the company and communication with faraway customers and suppliers. Information systems can enhance quality by simplifying a product or service, facilitating benchmarking, reducing product development cycle time, and improving quality and precision in design and production.

5 **What is the role of business process management (BPM) in enhancing competitiveness?** Organizations often have to change their business processes in order to execute their business strategies successfully. If these business processes use technology, they can be redesigned to make the technology more effective. BPM combines and streamlines the steps in a business process to eliminate repetitive and redundant work and to achieve dramatic improvements in quality, service, and speed. BPM is most effective when it is used to strengthen a good business model and when it strengthens processes that have a major impact on firm performance.

Key Terms

Benchmarking, 86	Cycle time, 94	Quality, 93
Business process management (BPM), 96	Disruptive technologies, 89	Six sigma, 94
Best practices, 86	Domestic exporter, 92	Support activities, 85
Business process reengineering (BPR), 98	Efficient customer response system, 80	Switching costs, 81
Competitive forces model, 77	Franchiser, 92	Total quality management (TQM), 93
Computer-aided design (CAD) system, 95	Mass customization, 81	Transnational, 92
Core competency, 88	Multinational, 92	Value chain model, 85
	Network economics, 88	Value web, 86
	Primary activities, 85	Virtual company, 89

Review Questions

1. How does Porter's competitive forces model help companies develop competitive strategies using information systems?
- Define Porter's competitive forces model and explain how it works.
- List and describe four competitive strategies enabled by information systems that firms can pursue.
- Describe how information systems can support each of these competitive strategies and give examples.
- Explain why aligning IT with business objectives is essential for strategic use of systems.

2. How do the value chain and value web models help businesses identify opportunities for strategic information system applications?
- Define and describe the value chain model.
- Explain how the value chain model can be used to identify opportunities for information systems.
- Define the value web and show how it is related to the value chain.
- Explain how the value web helps businesses identify opportunities for strategic information systems.
- Describe how the Internet has changed competitive forces and competitive advantage.

3. How do information systems help businesses use synergies, core competencies, and network-based strategies to achieve competitive advantage?
- Explain how information systems promote synergies and core competencies.
- Describe how promoting synergies and core competencies enhances competitive advantage.
- Explain how businesses benefit by using network economics.
- Define and describe a virtual company and the benefits of pursuing a virtual company strategy.
- Explain how disruptive technologies create strategic opportunities.

4. How do competing on a global scale and promoting quality enhance competitive advantage?
- Describe how globalization has increased opportunities for businesses.
- List and describe the four main ways of organizing a business internationally and the types of systems configuration for global business organizations.
- Define quality and compare the producer and consumer definitions of quality.
- Describe the various ways in which information systems can improve quality.

5. What is the role of business process management (BPM) in enhancing competitiveness?
- Define BPM and explain how it helps firms become more competitive.
- Distinguish between BPM and business process reengineering (BPR).
- List and describe the steps companies should take to make sure BPM is successful.

Discussion Questions

1. It has been said that there is no such thing as a sustainable competitive advantage. Do you agree? Why or why not?

2. What are some of the issues to consider in determining whether the Internet would provide your business with a competitive advantage?

3. It has been said that the advantage that leading-edge retailers such as Walmart have over competitors isn't technology-it's their management. Do you agree? Why or why not?

Hands-on MIS Projects

The projects in this section give you hands-on experience identifying information systems to support a business strategy and to solve a customer retention problem, using a database to improve decision making about business strategy, and using Web tools to configure and price an automobile.

MANAGEMENT DECISION PROBLEMS

1.   Macy's, Inc., through its subsidiaries, operates approximately 800 department stores in the United States. Its retail stores sell a range of merchandise, including apparel, home

furnishings, and housewares. Senior management has decided that Macy's needs to tailor merchandise more to local tastes, and that the colors, sizes, brands, and styles of clothing and other merchandise should be based on the sales patterns in each individual Macy's store. How could information systems help Macy's management implement this new strategy? What pieces of data should these systems collect to help management make merchandising decisions that support this strategy?

2.   Despite aggressive campaigns to attract customers with lower mobile phone prices, Sprint Nextel has been losing large numbers of monthly contract subscribers. Management wants to know why so many customers are leaving Sprint and what can be done to entice them back. Are customers deserting because of poor customer service, uneven network coverage, wireless service charges, or competition from carriers with Apple iPhone service? How can the company use information systems to help find the answer? What management decisions could be made using information from these systems?

IMPROVING DECISION MAKING: USING A DATABASE TO CLARIFY BUSINESS STRATEGY

Software skills: Database querying and reporting; database design
Business skills: Reservation systems; customer analysis

In In this exercise, you'll use database software to analyze the reservation transactions for a hotel and use that information to fine-tune the hotel's business strategy and marketing activities.

In MyMISLab, you'll find a database for hotel reservation transactions developed in Microsoft Access with information about The President's Inn hotel in Cape May, New Jersey. At the Inn, 10 rooms overlook side streets, 10 rooms have bay windows with limited views of the ocean, and the remaining 10 rooms in the front of the hotel face the ocean. Room rates are based on room choice, length of stay, and number of guests per room. Room rates are the same for one to four guests. Fifth and sixth guests must pay an additional $20 per person per day. Guests staying for seven days or more receive a 10 percent discount on their daily room rates.

The owners currently use a manual reservation and bookkeeping system, which is unable to provide management with immediate data about the hotel's daily operations and revenue. Use the database to develop reports on average length of stay per room type, average visitors per room type, base revenue per room (i.e., length of visit multiplied by the daily rate) during a specified period of time, and strongest customer base. After answering these questions, write a brief report about the Inn's current business situation and suggest future strategies.

IMPROVING DECISION MAKING: USING WEB TOOLS TO CONFIGURE AND PRICE AN AUTOMOBILE

Software skills: Internet-based software
Business skills: Researching product information and pricing

In this exercise, you will use software at car-selling Web sites to find product information about a car of your choice and use that information to make an important purchase decision. You will also evaluate two of these sites as selling tools.

You are interested in purchasing a new Ford Escape (or some other car of your choice). Go to the Web site of CarsDirect (www.carsdirect.com) and begin your investigation. Locate the Ford Escape. Research the various Escape models, choose one you prefer in terms of price, features, and safety ratings. Locate and read at least two reviews. Surf the Web site of the manufacturer, in this case Ford (www.ford.com). Compare the information available on Ford's Web site with that of CarsDirect for the Ford Escape. Try to locate the lowest price for the car you want in a local dealer's inventory. Suggest improvements for CarsDirect.com and Ford.com.

Video Cases

Video Cases and Instructional Videos illustrating some of the concepts in this chapter are available. Contact your instructor to access these videos.

Collaboration and Teamwork

Identifying Opportunities for Strategic Information Systems

With your team of three or four students, select a company described in the *Wall Street Journal*, *Fortune*, *Forbes*, or another business publication. Visit the company's Web site to find additional information about that company and to see how the firm is using the Web. On the basis of this information, analyze the business. Include a description of the organization's features, such as important business processes, culture, structure, and environment, as well as its business strategy. Suggest strategic information systems appropriate for that particular business, including those based on Internet technology, if appropriate. If possible, use Google Sites to post links to Web pages, team communication announcements, and work assignments; to brainstorm; and to work collaboratively on project documents. Try to use Google Docs to develop a presentation of your findings for the class.

BUSINESS PROBLEM-SOLVING CASE

Will Technology Save the Publishing Industry?

The publishing industry is grappling with disruptive technologies that may transform its business models and the way we buy and read books. What is the impact of the Internet and e-book technology on book and newspaper publishing? Who will win and who will lose out, and how will the struggle play out?

Newspapers are the most troubled segment of the publishing industry, due to the availability of alternatives to the printed newspaper and publishers' inability to protect valuable content from being distributed for free over the Internet. Over 60 percent of newspapers have reduced news staff in the past three years and about the same percentage report reducing the size of their newspapers. Readership has been declining for about a decade and advertising is down 15 percent a year. Alternative online sources of news such as Yahoo, Google, and blogs have become major sources of news for many Americans, especially younger readers.

At first glance, the online newspaper industry appears to be a classic case of a disruptive technology destroying a traditional business model based on physical products and physical distribution. But the newspapers have much valuable content worth preserving and they have acquired a huge online audience. Next to social networks, newspapers have the largest online audience of any media, and online newspaper readership is growing by 17 percent each year. Contrary to popular opinion, they are one of the most successful forms of online content to date. The problem is that online newspapers are not generating enough revenue online from paying readers or from advertising. They are trying to revamp their business models to address this problem. In the past, the papers did not charge for online content, and so the content became freely available across the Web. Aggregators such as Google and Yahoo News were able to repackage this content for their viewers free of charge.

What can newspaper publishers do to stem the flow of red ink? One option is to share revenue with Internet partners such as Google and Yahoo. Another is to charge fees for newspaper content delivered to new reading devices, including smartphones, e-readers, iPads, and tablets, which enable online newspapers to be read everywhere. A third option is to charge fees for "premium" news and opinion. But because advertising remains a major source of revenue, the newspapers must clearly figure out how to grow their online revenue fast enough to offset their losses from print advertising.

The Internet has been steadily taking advertising share from other traditional media, like print newspapers and magazines. While television still dominates ad spending, the Internet now ranks second and is expected to capture a 20 percent share of marketers' ad budgets in 2011, according to the eMarketer research firm. If this trend continues, and there is every indication that it will, more companies will be placing ads in online newspapers, and this source of revenue should grow.

What about book publishing? Many physical bookstores have disappeared, especially small mom-and-pop stores competing against large chains such as Barnes & Noble as well as against online booksellers. The chains themselves have lost sales to online retailers such as Amazon. Book publishing is holding steady (U.S. consumers purchased 3.2 billion books in 2010) but book readership is flat. Young people are reading less than in the past while the expanding elderly population is reading more.

When e-readers were first developed and e-books first started to become popular, many analysts speculated that they would threaten the continued livelihood of the publishing industry. That has not happened. Instead, e-books have become a new channel for book content distribution. E-book sales are skyrocketing, thanks to the popularity of Amazon's Kindle e-book reader and the iPad. What remains unanswered is whether e-books are cannibalizing sales of physical printed books or whether they are extending book readership to a larger audience.

Amazon's Kindle was the first e-reader to realize the promise of e-books. Analysts expect that Amazon will sell 17.5 million Kindles in 2011, generating $2 billion in revenue, as well as 310 million e-books, good for another $1.7 billion in revenue. Meanwhile, sales for Apple's iPad have been so brisk that Apple called demand for the device "staggering." The design of the iPad appeals to many readers of magazines, newspapers, and illustrated books, and publishers view the iPad as a better potential platform for textbooks than the Kindle.

Publishing companies have begun investing more resources in the Kindle and iPad as delivery platforms for their books and less money in traditional delivery platforms, like print news and bound books. Textbook publishers are working on iPad versions of their offerings; newspapers have apps out for the iPad and offer Kindle subscriptions to readers; and major publishers are contracting with software companies to convert existing files to e-reader compatible products.

The publishing industry views e-books as a big potential boost to sagging sales numbers. The difficult part is developing a fee structure that will make e-book delivery profitable for publishers as well as the device manufacturers. How can publishers overcome the lower profit margins involved in selling an e-book compared to a physical book?

Amazon, Apple, Google, and a host of other smaller companies are competing with one another to offer appealing e-book delivery platforms and pricing models. Apple announced in February 2011 that it would receive a 30 percent fee for each sale of digital content sold through its App Store. Apple also prohibited app developers from placing links to external Web sites within their apps, effectively preventing these developers from guiding their app users to product offerings that would not be subject to Apple's fees. Apple believes that because it is bringing so many new customers to the publishers on the iPad and iPhone, they have a legitimate claim to a portion of the resulting profits.

Apple also plans to prevent publishers and other content providers from receiving data about their iPad customers unless customers gives permission beforehand. Apple, meanwhile, will have access to much of this information. Publishing companies have strenuously objected, arguing that they need this information to successfully market and advertise their products. Apple says the rule protects the privacy of iPad owners.

For many publishers, removing their content from the iPad is not a realistic response to their problems with Apple's new rules. In fact, Apple's bargaining position is so dominant that some analysts believe there is an antitrust case to be made against them. The changes are slated to take effect later in 2011.

One company hoping to capitalize on this dissatisfaction is Google. Rather than relying on any particular e-reader or developing a device of its own, Google hopes to offer a more "open" model that allows readers to access books using any Web browser. (Kindle users can only buy books from an Amazon store and can only read those books on devices using Kindle software; the same goes for Apple and the App Store or iBooks.) Google's advantage is that it is not tied down to any individual device, and as the number of e-readers continues to grow, this advantage will become even more significant. This model will also give Google a much larger reach. Instead of just e-reader users, Google's target audience will be the 190 million monthly Internet users in the United States, and Google hopes to profit from the detailed information it will acquire about its e-book customers

Google's e-book venture, Google Editions, will allow users to buy books directly from Google or associated online retailers, including smaller, independent bookstores. When users buy a book this way, it's added to an online library tied to a Google account, as opposed to buying from the App Store or Kindle store, where the book is tied to the device on which it was purchased.

Google has also opened a payment system for these books and other digital content that will allow publishers to keep more revenues than under Apple's new system. This system, called Google One Pass, allows publishers to set their prices, grants publishers more control over customer data, and gives Google only a 10 percent cut of each sale. Readers using One Pass can log into their Google accounts, visit the Web sites of participating publishers, and pay for any content, any time.

So far, Germany's largest newspaper publisher and largest magazine publisher have adopted One Pass, and other publishers in France, Spain, and the United States have followed suit. Many major U.S. publishers already have their own infrastructure to sell, fulfill, and authenticate digital subscriptions, but these publishers still want to make their publications available on Android-powered devices. Google's offering is also far more appealing to smaller publishers and independent e-book sellers.

Other Google initiatives may work against book publishers' interests and profits. Google Books is Google's project to scan the world's 150 million books and make them available via Google's search engine. Publishers and lawmakers have raised copyright and intellectual property concerns, but a 2008 settlement allowed Google to continue scanning and did not disallow the possibility of serving ads in tandem with pages from books. A federal court overturned the 2008 ruling, but Google hopes to resolve the legal issues surrounding the project.

Companies are just starting to experiment with ways to place ads that readers will tolerate in books. Wowio, a lesser-known digital bookstore, has had success selling ad space in e-books downloaded from its site onto iPads and Kindles. The books are heavily discounted or free to readers. Wowio charges $1 to $3 for e-books with ads served in various says, and shares the revenue with publishers, who can then distribute ad revenue to their authors as they see fit. In the past, ads in books quickly became irrelevant after the book had been in circulation for a time, but with e-books, highly targeted advertisements can be inserted and replaced with ease.

Other e-book advertising possibilities include sponsorships that give readers free books; videos, graphics, and text that appear only when books are opened; and ads that appear along the border of digital pages. The popularity of e-books and e-readers has convinced advertisers to give e-book advertising a chance, but it remains to be seen whether readers will buy e-books containing ads without a significant price decrease compared to ad-free e-books.

Educators are also excited about the potential of tablets like the iPad to revolutionize learning at all levels. The iPad is portable, has a large, clear screen, a flat design that allows students to keep eye contact with their teachers, and is robust enough to handle a variety of multimedia. Schools in New York City, Chicago, California, and a host of other areas throughout the United States have launched iPad pilot programs to replace physical textbooks with electronic versions and to use this device for new interactive learning experiences. Textbook publishers are already making headway in their efforts to convert their books to iPad-compatible formats, and Houghton Mifflin Harcourt has developed the first iPad-specific algebra program, which has been used in pilot programs at several California schools.

It's possible that instead of destroying the publishing industry, technology just might save it.

Sources: Emily Steel, "Big Pop Seen for Online Ads," *Wall Street Journal*, June 8, 2011; Efrati, Amir Mary Lane, and Russell Adams, "Google Elbows Apple, Woos Publishers." *Wall Street Journal*, February 17, 2011; Yukari Iwatani Kane and Russell Adams, "Apple Retreats in Publisher Fight, *Wall Street Journal*, June 9, 2011 and "Apple Opens a Door, Keeps Keys." *Wall Street Journal*, February 16, 2011; Amir Efrati and Jeffrey A. Trachtenberg, "Judge Rejects Google Books Settlement," *Wall Street Journal*, March 23, 2011; Winnie Hu, "Math that Moves: Schools Embrace the iPad," *New York Times*, January 4, 2011; David Carnoy, "iFlow Reader Developer Rages at Apple," reviews.cnet.com, May 12, 2011; L. Gordon Crovitz. "From Gutenberg to Zoobert." *Wall Street Journal*, August 8, 2010; Jeffrey A. Trachtenberg, Jessica E. Vascellaro, and Amir Efrati. "Google Set to Launch E-Book Venture." *Wall Street Journal*, December 1, 2010; and Emily Steel, "Marketers Test Ads in E-Books," *Wall Street Journal* (December 13, 2010).

Case Study Questions

1. Evaluate the impact of the Internet on newspaper and book publishers using the value chain and competitive forces models.

2. How are newspapers and book publishers changing their business models to deal with the Internet and e-book technology?

3. How can newspaper and book publishers take better advantage of the Internet? What will it take for them to benefit from e-books? Explain your answer.

4. Will technology be able to save the newspaper and book publishing industries? Explain your answer.

Information Technology Infrastructure

PART
II

Part II provides the technical foundation for understanding information systems by examining hardware, software, databases, networking technologies, and tools and techniques for security and control. This part answers questions such as these: What technologies and tools do businesses today need to accomplish their work? What do I need to know about these technologies to make sure they enhance the performance of my firm? How are these technologies likely to change in the future?

IT Infrastructure: Hardware and Software

CHAPTER 4

STUDENT LEARNING OBJECTIVES

After completing this chapter, you will be able to answer the following questions:

1. What are the components of IT infrastructure?

2. What are the major computer hardware, data storage, input, and output technologies used in business?

3. What are the major types of computer software used in business?

4. What are the most important contemporary hardware and software trends?

5. What are the principal issues in managing hardware and software technology?

CHAPTER OUTLINE

BART SPEEDS UP WITH A NEW IT INFRASTRUCTURE

The Bay Area Rapid Transit (BART) is a heavy-rail public transit system that connects San Francisco to Oakland, California, and other neighboring cities to the east and south. BART has provided fast, reliable transportation for more than 35 years and now carries more than 346,000 passengers each day over 104 miles of track and 43 stations. It provides an alternative to driving on bridges and highways, decreasing travel time and the number of cars on the Bay Area's congested roads. It is the fifth busiest rapid transit system in the United States.

BART recently embarked on an ambitious modernization effort to overhaul stations, deploy new rail cars, and extend routes. This modernization effort also encompassed BART's information technology infrastructure. BART's information systems were no longer state-of-the art, and they were starting to affect its ability to provide good service. Aging homegrown financial and human resources systems could no longer provide information rapidly enough for making timely decisions and were too unreliable to support its 24/7 operations.

BART upgraded both its hardware and software. It replaced old legacy mainframe applications with Oracle's PeopleSoft Enterprise applications running on HP Integrity

© Jyeshern Cheng, 2011, iStockPhoto LP.

blade servers and the Oracle Enterprise Linux operating system. This configuration provides more flexibility and room to grow because BART is able to run the PeopleSoft software in conjunction with new applications it could not previously run.

BART wanted to create a high-availability IT infrastructure using grid computing where it could match computing and storage capacity more closely to actual demand. BART chose to run its applications on a cluster of servers using a grid architecture. Multiple operating environments share capacity and computing resources that can be provisioned, distributed, and redistributed as needed over the grid.

In most data centers, a distinct server is deployed for each application, and each server typically uses only a fraction of its capacity. BART uses virtualization to run multiple applications on the same server, increasing server capacity utilization to 50 percent or higher. This means fewer servers can be used to accomplish the same amount of work.

With blade servers, if BART needs more capacity, it can add another server to the main system. Energy usage is minimized because BART does not have to purchase computing capacity it doesn't need and the blade servers' stripped down modular design minimizes the use of physical space and energy.

By using less hardware and existing computing resources more efficiently, BART's grid environment savings saves power and cooling costs. Consolidating applications onto a shared grid of server capacity is expected to reduce energy usage by about 20 percent.

Sources: David Baum, "Speeding into the Modern Age," *Profit*, February 2010; www.bart.gov, accessed May 22, 2011; and Steve Clouther, "The San Francisco Bay Area Rapid Transit Uses IBM Technology to Improve Safety and Reliability," ARC Advisory Group, October 7, 2009.

BART has been widely praised as a successful modern rapid transit system, but its operations and ability to grow where needed were hampered by an outdated IT infrastructure. BART's management felt the best solution was to invest in new hardware and software technologies that were more cost-effective, efficient, and energy-saving.

The chapter-opening diagram calls attention to important points raised by this case and this chapter. Management realized that in order to keep providing the level of service expected by Bay Area residents, it had to modernize its operations, including the hardware and software used for running the organization. The IT infrastructure investments it made had to support BART's business goals and contribute to improving its performance. Other goals included reducing costs and also "green" goals of reducing power and materials consumption.

By replacing its legacy software and computers with blade servers on a grid and more modern business software, BART was able to reduce wasted computer resources not used for processing, use existing resources more efficiently, and cut costs and power consumption. New software tools make it much easier to develop new applications and services. BART's IT infrastructure is easier to manage and capable of scaling to accommodate growing processing loads and new business opportunities. This case shows that the right hardware and software investments not only improve business performance but can also contribute to important social goals, such as conservation of power and materials.

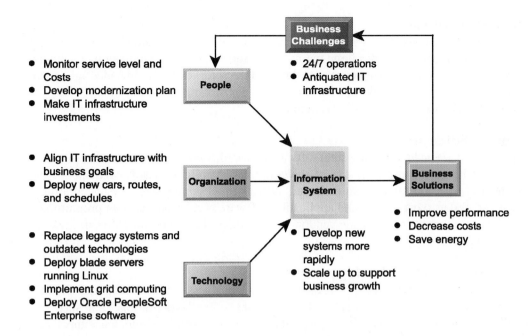

- Monitor service level and Costs
- Develop modernization plan
- Make IT infrastructure investments

- Align IT infrastructure with business goals
- Deploy new cars, routes, and schedules

- Replace legacy systems and outdated technologies
- Deploy blade servers running Linux
- Implement grid computing
- Deploy Oracle PeopleSoft Enterprise software

Business Challenges

People

- 24/7 operations
- Antiquated IT infrastructure

Organization

Information System

Technology

- Develop new systems more rapidly
- Scale up to support business growth

Business Solutions

- Improve performance
- Decrease costs
- Save energy

4.1 IT Infrastructure: Computer Hardware

If you want to know why businesses worldwide spend about $3.6 trillion every year on computing and information systems, just consider what it would take for you personally to set up a business or manage a business today. Businesses require a wide variety of computing equipment, software, and communications capabilities simply to operate and solve basic business problems. Obviously, you need computers, and, as it turns out, a wide variety of computers are available, including desktops, laptops, and handhelds.

Do your employees travel or do some work from home? You will want to equip them with laptop computers (over half the computers sold in the U.S. are laptops). If you are employed by a medium to large business, you will also need larger server computers, perhaps an entire data center or server farm with hundreds or even thousands of servers. A **data center** is a facility housing computer systems and associated components, such as telecommunications, storage, security systems, and backup power supplies.

You will also need plenty of software. Each computer will require an operating system and a wide range of application software capable of dealing with spreadsheets, documents, and data files. Unless you are a single-person business, you will most likely want to have a network to link all the people in your business together and perhaps your customers and suppliers. As a matter of fact, you will probably want several networks: a local area network connecting employees in your office, and remote access capabilities so employees can share e-mail and computer files while they are out of the office. You will also want all your employees to have access to landline phone systems, cell phone networks, and the Internet. Finally, to make all this equipment and software work harmoniously, you will also need the services of trained people to help you run and manage this technology.

All of the elements we have just described combine to make up the firm's *information technology (IT) infrastructure*, which we first defined in Chapter 1. A firm's IT infrastructure provides the foundation, or platform, for supporting all the information systems in the business.

INFRASTRUCTURE COMPONENTS

Today's IT infrastructure is composed of five major components: computer hardware, computer software, data management technology, networking and telecommunications technology, and technology services (see Figure 4.1). These components must be coordinated with each other.

Computer Hardware

Computer hardware consists of technology for computer processing, data storage, input, and output. This component includes large mainframes, servers, desktop and laptop computers, and mobile devices for accessing corporate data and the Internet. It also includes equipment for gathering and inputting data, physical media for storing the data, and devices for delivering the processed information as output.

Computer Software

Computer software includes both system software and application software. **System software** manages the resources and activities of the computer. **Application software** applies the computer to a specific task for an end user, such as processing an order or generating a mailing list. Today, most system and application software is no longer custom programmed but rather is purchased from outside vendors. We describe these types of software in detail in Section 4.2.

Data Management Technology

In addition to physical media for storing the firm's data, businesses need specialized software to organize the data and make them available to business users. **Data management software** organizes, manages, and processes business data concerned with inventory, customers, and vendors. Chapter 5 describes data management software in detail.

Networking and Telecommunications Technology

Networking and telecommunications technology provides data, voice, and video connectivity to employees, customers, and suppliers. It includes technology for running a company's internal networks, services from telecommunications/telephone services companies, and technology for running Web sites and linking to other computer systems through the Internet. Chapter 6 provides an in-depth description of these technologies.

Technology Services

Businesses need people to run and manage the infrastructure components we have just described and to train employees in how to use these technologies for their work. Chapter 2 described the role of the information systems department, which is the firm's internal business unit set up for this purpose. Today, many businesses supplement their in-house

Figure 4.1
IT Infrastructure Components
A firm's IT infrastructure is composed of hardware, software, data management technology, networking technology, and technology services.

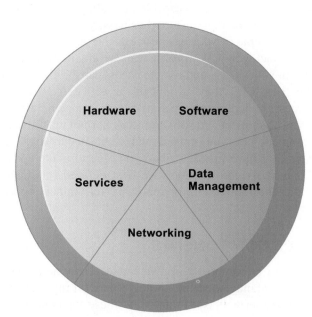

information systems staff with external technology consultants. Even large firms do not have the staff, the skills, the budget, or the necessary experience to implement and run the wide array of required technologies. When businesses need to make major system changes or implement an entirely new IT infrastructure, they typically turn to external consultants to help them with systems integration.

Systems integration means ensuring that the new infrastructure works with the firm's older, so-called legacy systems and that the new elements of the infrastructure work with one another. **Legacy systems** are generally older transaction processing systems created for older computers that continue to be used to avoid the high cost of replacing or redesigning them.

There are thousands of technology vendors supplying IT infrastructure components and services and an equally large number of ways of putting them together. This chapter is about the hardware and software components of infrastructure you will need to run a business. Chapter 5 describes the data management component, and Chapter 6 is devoted to the networking and telecommunications technology component. Chapter 7 deals with hardware and software for ensuring that information systems are reliable and secure, and Chapter 8 discusses software for enterprise applications.

TYPES OF COMPUTERS

Business firms face many different challenges and problems that can be solved by computers and information systems. In order to be efficient, firms need to match the right computer hardware to the nature of the business challenge, neither overspending nor underspending for the technology.

Computers come in an array of sizes with differing capabilities for processing information, from the smallest handheld devices to the largest mainframes and supercomputers. If you're working alone or with a few other people in a small business, you'll probably be using a desktop or laptop **personal computer (PC)**. You might carry around a mobile device with substantial computing capability, such as a BlackBerry, iPhone, or iPad. If you're doing advanced design or engineering work requiring powerful graphics or computational capabilities, you might use a **workstation**, which fits on a desktop but has more powerful mathematical and graphics-processing capabilities than a PC.

If your business has a number of computers networked together or maintains a Web site, it will need a **server**. Server computers are specifically optimized to support a computer network, enabling users to share files, software, peripheral devices (such as printers), or other network resources.

Servers have become important components of firms' IT infrastructures because they provide the hardware platform for electronic commerce. By adding special software, they can be customized to deliver Web pages, process purchase and sale transactions, or exchange data with systems inside the company. You will sometimes find many servers linked together to provide all the processing needs for large companies. If your company has to process millions of financial transactions or customer records, you will need multiple servers or a single large mainframe to solve these challenges.

Mainframe computers first appeared in the mid-1960s, and are still used by large banks, insurance companies, stock brokerages, airline reservation systems, and government agencies to keep track of hundreds of thousands, or even millions, of records and transactions. A **mainframe** is a large-capacity, high-performance computer that can process large amounts of data very rapidly. Airlines, for instance, use mainframes to process upwards of 3,000 reservation transactions per second.

IBM, the leading mainframe vendor, has repurposed its mainframe systems so they can be used as giant servers for large-scale enterprise networks and corporate Web sites. A single IBM mainframe can run enough instances of Linux or Windows server software to replace thousands of smaller Windows-based servers.

A **supercomputer** is a specially designed and more sophisticated computer that is used for tasks requiring extremely rapid and complex calculations with thousands of variables, millions of measurements, and thousands of equations. Supercomputers traditionally have been used in engineering analysis of structures, scientific exploration and simulations, and military work, such as classified weapons research and weather forecasting. A few private business firms use supercomputers. For instance, Volvo and most other automobile manufacturers use supercomputers to simulate vehicle crash tests.

If you are a long-term weather forecaster, such as the National Oceanic and Atmospheric Administration (NOAA), or the National Hurricane Center, and your challenge is to predict the movement of weather systems based on hundreds of thousands of measurements, and thousands of equations, you would want access to a supercomputer or a distributed network of computers called a grid.

Grid computing involves connecting geographically remote computers into a single network to create a "virtual supercomputer" by combining the computational power of all computers on the grid. Grid computing takes advantage of the fact that most computers in the United States use their central processing units on average only 25 percent of the time, leaving 75 percent of their capacity available for other tasks. By using the combined power of thousands of PCs and other computers networked together, the grid is able to solve complicated problems at supercomputer speeds at far lower cost.

The business case for using grid computing involves cost savings, speed of computation, and agility, as noted in the chapter-opening case. The chapter-opening case shows that by running its applications on clustered servers on a grid, BART eliminated unused computer resources, used existing resources more efficiently, and reduced costs and power consumption.

Computer Networks and Client/Server Computing

Unless you are in a small business with a stand-alone computer, you'll be using networked computers for most processing tasks. The use of multiple computers linked by a communications network for processing is called **distributed processing**. **Centralized processing**, in which all processing is accomplished by one large central computer, is much less common.

One widely used form of distributed processing is **client/server computing**. Client/server computing splits processing between "clients" and "servers." Both are on the network, but each machine is assigned functions it is best suited to perform. The **client** is the user point of entry for the required function and is normally a desktop or laptop computer. The user generally interacts directly only with the client portion of the application. The server provides the client with services. Servers store and process shared data and also perform functions such as managing printers, backup storage, and network activities such as security, remote access, and user authentication. Figure 4.2 illustrates the client/server computing concept. Computing on the Internet uses the client/server model (see Chapter 6).

Figure 4.2 illustrates the simplest client/server network, consisting of a client computer networked to a server computer, with processing split between the two types of machines. This is called a *two-tiered client/server architecture*. Whereas simple client/server networks can be found in small businesses, most corporations have more complex, multitiered (often called **N-tier**) **client/server architectures**, in which the work of the entire network is

Figure 4.2
Client/Server
Computing
In client/server computing, computer processing is split between client machines and server machines linked by a network. Users interface with the client machines.

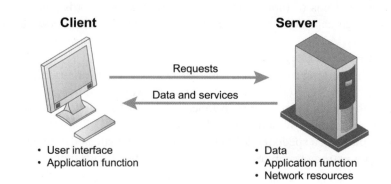

Client

Requests

Data and services

Server

• User interface
• Application function

• Data
• Application function
• Network resources

balanced over several different levels of servers, depending on the kind of service being requested (see Figure 4.3).

For instance, at the first level a **Web server** will serve a Web page to a client in response to a request for service. Web server software is responsible for locating and managing stored Web pages. If the client requests access to a corporate system (a product list or price information, for instance), the request is passed along to an **application server**. Application server software handles all application operations between a user and an organization's back-end business systems. The application server may reside on the same computer as the Web server or on its own dedicated computer. Chapters 5 and 6 provide more detail on other pieces of software that are used in multitiered client/server architectures for e-commerce and e-business.

STORAGE, INPUT, AND OUTPUT TECHNOLOGY

In addition to hardware for processing data, you will need technologies for data storage, and input and output. Storage and input and output devices are called *peripheral devices* because they are outside the main computer system unit.

Secondary Storage Technology

Electronic commerce and electronic business, and regulations such as Sarbanes-Oxley, have made storage a strategic technology. The amount of data that companies now need to store is doubling every 12 to 18 months. The principal storage technologies are magnetic disks, optical disc, magnetic tape, and storage networks.

Magnetic Disks The most widely used secondary storage medium today is the *magnetic disk*. PCs have *hard drives*, and large mainframe or midrange computer systems have multiple hard disk drives because they require immense disk storage capacity in the gigabyte and terabyte range. Earlier generation PCs used floppy disks for storage, but they have been largely supplanted by *USB flash drives,* also known as USB drives. A USB flash drive provides portable flash memory storage by plugging into a computer's USB port. It can provide up to 256 gigabytes of portable storage capacity and is small enough to fit into a pocket.

Servers and computers with large storage requirements use a disk technology called *RAID (Redundant Array of Inexpensive Disks)*. RAID devices package more than 100 disk drives, a controller chip, and specialized software into a single, large unit delivering data over multiple paths simultaneously.

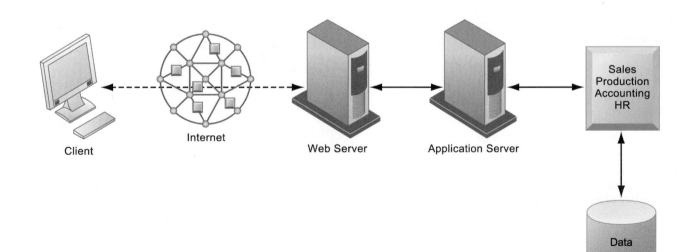

Figure 4.3
A Multitiered Client/Server Network (N-Tier)
In a multitiered client/server network, client requests for service are handled by different levels of servers.

Optical Discs These discs use laser technology to store large quantities of data, including sound and images, in a highly compact form. They are available for both PCs and large computers. **CD-ROM (compact disc read-only memory)** for PCs is a 4.75-inch compact disc that can store up to 660 megabytes. CD-ROM is read-only storage, but *CD-RW (CD-ReWritable)* discs are rewritable. **Digital video discs (DVDs)** are optical discs the same size as CD-ROMs but of even higher capacity, storing a minimum of 4.7 gigabytes of data. DVDs are now the favored technology for storing video and large quantities of text, graphics, and audio data, and rewritable *(DVD-RW)* discs are widely used in personal computer systems.

Magnetic Tape Some companies still use **magnetic tape,** an older storage technology that is used for secondary storage of large quantities of data that are needed rapidly but not instantly. It stores data sequentially and is relatively slow compared to the speed of other secondary storage media.

Storage Networking Large firms are turning to network-based storage technologies to deal with the complexity and cost of mushrooming storage requirements. **Storage area networks (SANs)** connect multiple storage devices on a separate high-speed network dedicated to storage. The SAN creates a large central pool of storage that can be rapidly accessed and shared by multiple servers (see Figure 4.4).

Input and Output Devices

Human beings interact with computer systems largely through input and output devices. **Input devices** gather data and convert them into electronic form for use by the computer, whereas **output devices** display data after they have been processed. Table 4.1 describes the principal input and output devices.

CONTEMPORARY HARDWARE TRENDS

The exploding power of computer hardware and networking technology has dramatically changed how businesses organize their computing power, putting more of this power on networks and mobile handheld devices. Let's look at seven hardware trends: the emerging

Figure 4.4
A Storage Area Network (SAN)
A typical SAN consists of a server, storage devices, and networking devices, and is used strictly for storage. The SAN stores data on many different types of storage devices, providing data to the enterprise. The SAN supports communication between any server and the storage unit as well as between different storage devices in the network.

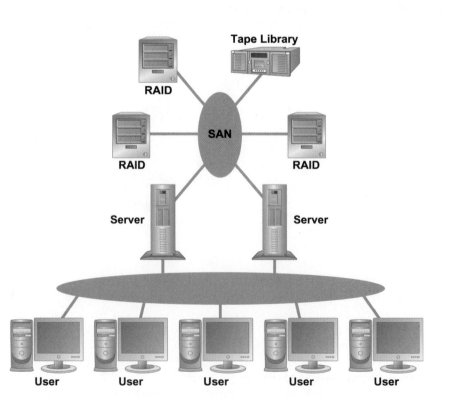

TABLE 4.1

Input and Output Devices

Input Device	Description
Keyboard	Principal method of data entry for text and numerical data.
Computer mouse	Handheld device with point-and-click capabilities for controlling a cursor's position on a computer display screen and selecting commands. Trackballs and touch pads often are used in place of the mouse as pointing devices on laptop PCs.
Touch screen	Device that allows users to interact with a computer by touching the surface of a sensitized display screen. Used in kiosks in airports, retail stores, and restaurants and in multitouch devices such as the iPhone, IPad, and multitouch PCs.
Optical character recognition	Device that can translate specially designed marks, characters, and codes into digital form. The most widely used optical code is the bar code. The codes can include time, date, and location data in addition to identification data.
Magnetic ink character recognition (MICR)	Technology used primarily in check processing for the banking industry. Characters on the bottom of a check identify the bank, checking account, and check number and are preprinted using special magnetic ink, for translation into digital form for the computer.
Pen-based input	Handwriting-recognition devices, such as pen-based tablets, notebooks, and notepads, that convert the motion made by an electronic stylus pressing on a touch-sensitive tablet screen into digital form.
Digital scanner	Device that translates images, such as pictures or documents, into digital form.
Audio input	Voice input devices that convert spoken words into digital form for processing by the computer. Microphones and tape cassette players can serve as input devices for music and other sounds.
Sensors	Devices that collect data directly from the environment for input into a computer system. For instance, today's farmers can use sensors to monitor the moisture of the soil in their fields to help them with irrigation.

Output Device	Description
Monitor	Display screen consisting of a flat-panel display or (in older systems) a cathode ray tube (CRT).
Printers	Devices that produce a printed hard copy of information output. They include impact printers (such as dot matrix printers) and nonimpact printers (such as laser, inkjet, and thermal transfer printers).
Audio output	Voice output devices that convert digital output data back into intelligible speech. Other audio output, such as music, can be delivered by speakers connected to the computer.

mobile digital platform, nanotechnology, virtualization, cloud computing, green computing, high-performance/power-saving processors, and autonomic computing.

The Emerging Mobile Digital Platform

Chapter 1 pointed out that new mobile digital computing platforms have emerged as alternatives to PCs and larger computers. Cell phones and smartphones such as the BlackBerry and iPhone have taken on many functions of handheld computers, including transmission of data, surfing the Web, transmitting e-mail and instant messages, displaying digital content, and exchanging data with internal corporate systems. The new mobile platform also includes small low-cost lightweight subnotebooks called netbooks optimized for wireless communication and Internet access, **tablet computers** such as the iPad, and digital e-book readers such as Amazon's Kindle with some Web access capabilities.

In a few years, smartphones and tablet computers will be the primary means of accessing the Internet, with business computing moving increasingly from PCs and desktop machines to these mobile devices. For example, senior executives at General Motors are using smartphone applications that drill down into vehicle sales information, financial performance, manufacturing metrics, and project management status.

Nanotechnology

Over the years, microprocessor manufacturers have been able to exponentially increase processing power while shrinking chip size by finding ways to pack more transistors into less space. They are now turning to nanotechnology to shrink the size of transistors down to the width of several atoms. **Nanotechnology** uses individual atoms and molecules to create computer chips and other devices that are thousands of times smaller than current technologies permit. IBM and other research labs have created transistors from nanotubes and other electrical devices and have developed a manufacturing process for producing nanotube processors economically (Figure 4.5).

Virtualization

Virtualization is the process of presenting a set of computing resources (such as computing power or data storage) so that they can all be accessed in ways that are not restricted by physical configuration or geographic location. Virtualization enables a single physical resource (such as a server or a storage device) to appear to the user as multiple logical resources. For example, a server or mainframe can be configured to run many instances of an operating system so that it acts like many different machines. Virtualization also enables multiple physical resources (such as storage devices or servers) to appear as a single logical resource, as would be the case with storage area networks or grid computing. Virtualization

Figure 4.5
Examples of Nanotubes
Nanotubes are tiny tubes about 10,000 times thinner than a human hair. They consist of rolled up sheets of carbon hexagons and have potential uses as minuscule wires or in ultrasmall electronic devices and are very powerful conductors of electrical current.

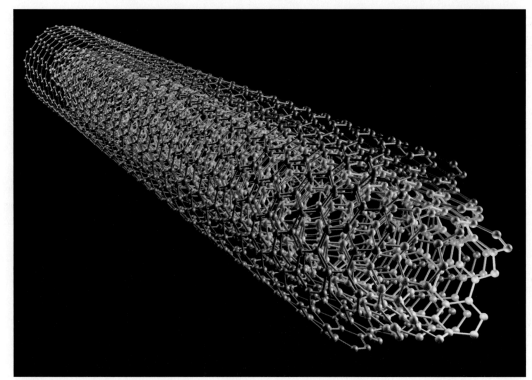

makes it possible for a company to handle its computer processing and storage using computing resources housed in remote locations. VMware is the leading virtualization software vendor for Windows and Linux servers. Microsoft offers its own Virtual Server product and has built virtualization capabilities into the newest version of Windows Server.

By providing the ability to host multiple systems on a single physical machine, virtualization helps organizations increase equipment utilization rates, conserving data center space and energy usage. Most servers run at just 15–20 percent of capacity, and virtualization can boost server utilization rates to 70 percent or higher. Higher utilization rates translate into fewer computers required to process the same amount of work, as illustrated by BART's experience with virtualization in the chapter-opening case. Virtualization also facilitates centralization and consolidation of hardware administration. It is now possible for companies and individuals to perform all of their computing work using a virtualized IT infrastructure, as is the case with cloud computing.

Cloud Computing

Cloud computing is a model of computing in which computer processing, storage, software, and other services are provided as a pool of virtualized resources over a network, primarily the Internet. These "clouds" of computing resources can be accessed on an as-needed basis from any connected device and location. Figure 4.6 illustrates the cloud computing concept.

The U.S. National Institute of Standards and Technology (NIST) defines cloud computing as having the following essential characteristics (Mell and Grance, 2009).

- **On-demand self-service:** Consumers can obtain computing capabilities such as server time or network storage as needed automatically on their own.
- **Ubiquitous network access:** Cloud resources can be accessed using standard network and Internet devices, including mobile platforms.
- **Location independent resource pooling:** Computing resources are pooled to serve multiple users, with different virtual resources dynamically assigned according to user demand. The user generally does not know where the computing resources are located.
- **Rapid elasticity:** Computing resources can be rapidly provisioned, increased, or decreased to meet changing user demand.
- **Measured service:** Charges for cloud resources are based on amount of resources actually used.

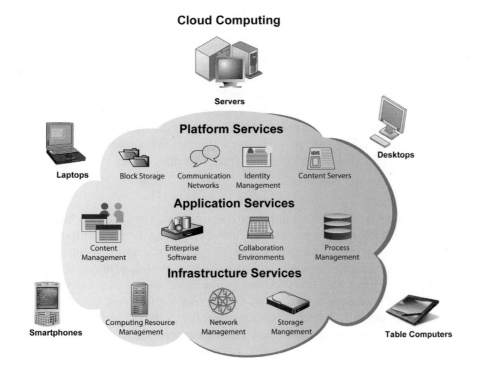

Figure 4.6
Cloud Computing Platform
In cloud computing, hardware and software capabilities are a pool of virtualized resources provided over a network, often the Internet. Businesses and employees have access to applications and IT infrastructure anywhere and at any time.

Cloud computing consists of three different types of services:

- **Cloud infrastructure as a service:** Customers use processing, storage, networking, and other computing resources from cloud service providers to run their information systems. For example, Amazon uses the spare capacity of its IT infrastructure to provide a broadly based cloud environment selling IT infrastructure services. These include its Simple Storage Service (S3) for storing customers' data and its Elastic Compute Cloud (EC2) service for running their applications. Users pay only for the amount of computing and storage capacity they actually use. (See the chapter-ending case study.)
- **Cloud platform as a service:** Customers use infrastructure and programming tools supported by the cloud service provider to develop their own applications. For example, IBM offers a Smart Business Application Development & Test service for software development and testing on the IBM Cloud. Another example is Salesforce.com's Force.com, which allows developers to build applications that are hosted on its servers as a service.
- **Cloud software as a service:** Customers use software hosted by the vendor on the vendor's cloud infrastructure and delivered over a network. Leading examples are Google Apps, which provides common business applications online and Salesforce.com, which also leases customer relationship management and related software services over the Internet. Both charge users an annual subscription fee, although Google Apps also has a pared-down free version. Users access these applications from a Web browser, and the data and software are maintained on the providers' remote servers.

A cloud can be private or public. A **public cloud** is owned and maintained by a cloud service provider, such as Amazon Web Services, and made available to the general public or industry group. A **private cloud** is operated solely for an organization. It may be managed by the organization or a third party and may exist on or off premise. Like public clouds, private clouds are able to allocate storage, computing power, or other resources seamlessly to provide computing resources on an as-needed basis. Companies that want flexible IT resources and a cloud service model while retaining control over their own IT infrastructure are gravitating toward these private clouds. (See the chapter-ending case study.)

Since organizations using public clouds do not own the infrastructure, they do not have to make large investments in their own hardware and software. Instead, they purchase their computing services from remote providers and pay only for the amount of computing power they actually use (utility computing) or are billed on a monthly or annual subscription basis. The term **on-demand computing** has also been used to describe such services.

Cloud computing has some drawbacks. Unless users make provisions for storing their data locally, the responsibility for data storage and control is in the hands of the provider. Some companies worry about the security risks related to entrusting their critical data and systems to an outside vendor that also works with other companies. Companies expect their systems to be available 24/7 and do not want to suffer any loss of business capability if cloud infrastructures malfunction. Nevertheless, the trend is for companies to shift more of their computer processing and storage to some form of cloud infrastructure. You can find out more about cloud computing in the Learning Tracks for this chapter.

Green Computing

By curbing hardware proliferation and power consumption, virtualization has become one of the principal technologies for promoting green computing. **Green computing** or **green IT**, refers to practices and technologies for designing, manufacturing, using, and disposing of computers, servers, and associated devices such as monitors, printers, storage devices, and networking and communications systems to minimize impact on the environment.

Reducing computer power consumption has been a very high "green" priority. Information technology is responsible for about 2 percent of total U.S. power demand and is believed to contribute about 2 percent of the world's greenhouse gases. Cutting power consumption in data centers has become both a serious business and environmental challenge. The Interactive Session on Technology examines this problem.

INTERACTIVE SESSION: TECHNOLOGY   Green Data Centers: Good for Business?

Computer rooms are becoming too hot to handle. Data-hungry tasks such as watching videos on demand, downloading music, exchanging photos, and maintaining Web sites require more and more power-hungry machines. Power and cooling costs for data centers have skyrocketed.

The heat generated from rooms full of servers is causing equipment to fail. Some organizations spend more money to power and cool their data centers than they spend to lease or purchase their hardware. It's a vicious cycle, as companies must pay to power their servers, and then pay again to keep them cool and operational. Cooling a server requires roughly the same number of kilowatts of energy as running one. All this additional power consumption has a negative impact on the environment and as well as corporate operating costs.

Companies are now looking to green computing for solutions. The standard for measuring data center energy efficiency is Power Usage Effectiveness (PUE). This metric is a ratio of the total annual power consumed by a facility as opposed to how much is used annually by IT equipment. The lower the ratio the better, with a PUE of 1.0 representing a desirable target. (The PUE of traditional data centers has hovered around 2.0.) New data center designs with PUEs of 1.5 or better are emerging. PUE is influenced by many factors, including hardware efficiency, data center size, the types of servers and their uses, the proficiency of monitoring software, building architecture, and the climate outside the facility.

Virtualization is a highly effective tool for cost-effective green computing because it reduces the number of servers and storage resources in the firm's IT infrastructure. Union Pacific, the largest North American railroad, implemented Microsoft Windows Server 2008 virtualization technology to use its computing resources more efficiently. It had been running one application per server, which left many server resources underutilized. By late 2009, Union Pacific had created 380 virtual machines on 40 virtualized host servers. The company is able to put an average of 12 "virtual" machines on a single physical host server, saving over 60 percent in hardware costs for each virtual server it creates. Server virtualization also reduced Union Pacific's energy costs by 10 percent in 2010.

Other tools and techniques are also available to make data centers more energy efficient. Some of the world's most prominent firms are leading the way with innovative programs and technologies for reducing power consumption. Google and Microsoft are building data centers that take advantage of hydroelectric power. Hewlett Packard is working on a series of technologies to reduce the carbon footprint of data centers by 75 percent and along with new software and services to measure energy use and carbon emissions. It reduced its power costs by 20 to 25 percent through consolidation of servers and data centers. Since these companies' technology and processes are more efficient than most other companies, using their online software services in place of in-house software may also count as a green investment.

In April 2011 Facebook publicly posted the specifications for the design of its data centers, including motherboards, power supply, server chassis, server rack, and battery cabinets, as well as data center electrical and mechanical construction specifications. Facebook hardware engineers re-thought the electric design, power distribution, and thermal design of its servers to optimize energy efficiency, reducing power usage by 13 percent. The power supply, which converts alternating current into direct current consumed by the motherboard, operates at 94.5 percent efficiency. Instead of using air conditioning or air ducts, the servers are cooled by evaporative cooling and misting machines, which flow air through grill covered walls. The server racks are taller to provide for bigger heat sinks, and the data center's large fans can move air through the servers more efficiently. Facebook's engineers modified the programming in the servers to work with these larger fans and reduce their reliance on small, individual fans that consume more power.

This data center design, which has a 1.07 PUE rating, was implemented at Facebook's Prineville, Oregon data center. All of these changes have reduced Facebook's energy consumption per unit of computing power by 38 percent and operating costs by nearly 25 percent. The Prineville data center reports its PUE is 1.07, one of the lowest.

PCs typically stay on more than twice the amount of time they are actually being used each day. According to a report by the Alliance to Save Energy, a company with 10,000 personal computer desktops will spend more than \$165,000 per year in electricity bills if these machines are left on all night. The group estimates that this practice is wasting around \$1.7 billion each year in the United States alone.

Although many companies establish default PC power management settings, about 70 percent of employees turn these settings off. PC power management software turns down PC power settings during the evening and automatically powers PCs up right before employees arrive for work in the morning. Boston-based Partners Healthcare, a leading U.S. nonprofit health care provider, deployed Verdiem's SURVEYOR PC power management software on more than 27,000 networked PCs. SURVEYOR enabled Partners to centrally manage and measure PC power consumption without impacting end user productivity, thereby reducing energy costs by 39.5 percent and saving more than $1 million each year.

Experts note that it's important for companies to measure their energy use and inventory and track their information technology assets both before and after they start their green initiatives. And it isn't always necessary to purchase new technologies to achieve "green" goals. Organizations can achieve sizable efficiencies by better managing the computing resources they already have. Unfortunately, many information systems departments still aren't deploying their existing technology resources efficiently or using green measurement tools.

Sources: Kovar, Joseph F. "Data Center Power Consumption Grows Less Than Expected: Report" CRN, August 10, 2011; Kenneth Miller, "The Data Center Balancing Act," *Information Week*, May 16, 2011; Vivian Wagner, "Green Data Centers Are Where It's At," *TechNewsWorld*, April 20, 2011; Bill Kenealy, "Facebook Reveals Its Server Secrets," *Information Management*, April, 11, 2011; Kathleen Lao, "The Green Issue," *Computerworld Canada*, April 2010; www.verdiem.com, accessed May 21, 2011; "Union Pacific Reduces Costs, Boosts IT Responsiveness with Hyper-V," www.microsoft.com, accessed May 21, 2011; and Matthew Sarrell, "Greening Your Data Center: The Real Deal," *eWeek*, January 15, 2010.

CASE STUDY QUESTIONS

1. What business and social problems does data center power consumption cause?

2. What solutions are available for these problems? Are they people, organizational, or technology solutions? Explain your answer.

3. What are the business benefits and costs of these solutions?

4. Should all firms move toward green computing? Why or why not?

MIS IN ACTION

Perform an Internet search on the phrase "green computing" and then answer the following questions:

1. Who are some of the leaders of the green computing movement? Which corporations are leading the way? Which environmental organizations are playing an important role?

2. What are the latest trends in green computing? What kind of impact are they having?

3. What can individuals do to contribute to the green computing movement? Is the movement worthwhile?

High-Performance and Power-Saving Processors

Another way to reduce power requirements and hardware sprawl is to use more efficient and power-saving processors. Contemporary microprocessors now feature multiple processor cores (which perform the reading and execution of computer instructions) on a single chip. A **multicore processor** is an integrated circuit to which two or more processor cores have been attached for enhanced performance, reduced power consumption and more efficient simultaneous processing of multiple tasks. This technology enables two or more processing engines with reduced power requirements and heat dissipation to perform tasks faster than a resource-hungry chip with a single processing core. Today you'll find dual-core and quad-core processors in PCs and servers with 8-, 10-, 12-, and 16-core processors.

Intel and other chip manufacturers are working on microprocessors that minimize power consumption. Low power consumption is essential for prolonging battery life in smartphones, netbooks, and other mobile digital devices. You will now find highly power-efficient microprocessors, such as ARM, Apple's A4 processor, and Intel's Atom in netbooks, digital media players, and smartphones. The A4 processor used in the iPhone and the iPad consumes approximately 500-800 milliwatts of power, about one fiftieth of the power consumption of a laptop dual-core processor.

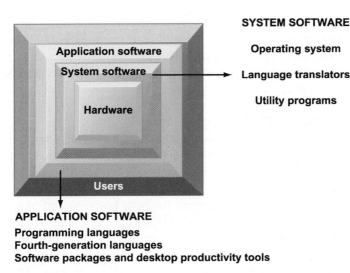

SYSTEM SOFTWARE

Operating system

Language translators

Utility programs

APPLICATION SOFTWARE
Programming languages
Fourth-generation languages
Software packages and desktop productivity tools

Figure 4.7
The Major Types of Software
The relationship between the system software, application software, and users can be illustrated by a series of nested boxes. System software—consisting of operating systems, language translators, and utility programs—controls access to the hardware. Application software, including programming languages and "fourth-generation" languages, must work through the system software to operate. The user interacts primarily with the application software.

Autonomic Computing

With large systems encompassing many thousands of networked devices, computer systems have become so complex today that some experts believe they may not be manageable in the future. One approach to this problem is autonomic computing. **Autonomic computing** is an industry-wide effort to develop systems that can configure themselves, optimize and tune themselves, heal themselves when broken, and protect themselves from outside intruders and self-destruction.

You can glimpse a few of these capabilities in desktop systems. For instance, virus and firewall protection software are able to detect viruses on PCs, automatically defeat the viruses, and alert operators. These programs can be updated automatically as the need arises by connecting to an online virus protection service such as McAfee. IBM and other vendors are starting to build autonomic features into products for large systems.

4.2 IT Infrastructure: Computer Software

In order to use computer hardware, you will need software, which provides the detailed instructions that direct the computer's work. System software and application software are interrelated and can be thought of as a set of nested boxes, each of which must interact closely with the other boxes surrounding it. Figure 4.7 illustrates this relationship. The system software surrounds and controls access to the hardware. Application software must work through the system software in order to operate. End users work primarily with application software. Each type of software must be designed for a specific machine to ensure its compatibility.

OPERATING SYSTEM SOFTWARE

The system software that manages and controls the computer's activities is called the **operating system**. Other system software consists of computer language translation programs that convert programming languages into machine language that can be understood by the computer and utility programs that perform common processing tasks, such as copying, sorting, or computing a square root.

The operating system is the computer system's chief manager, enabling the system to handle many different tasks and users at the same time. The operating system allocates and assigns system resources, schedules the use of computer resources and computer jobs, and monitors computer system activities. The operating system provides locations in primary memory for data and programs, and controls the input and output devices, such as printers, terminals, and telecommunication links. The operating system also coordinates the scheduling of work in various areas of the computer so that different parts of different jobs can be worked on at the same time. Finally, the operating system keeps track of each computer job and may also keep track of who is using the system, of what programs have been run, and of any unauthorized attempts to access the system.

PC, Server, and Mobile Operating Systems

The operating system controls the way users interact with the computer. Contemporary PC operating systems and many types of contemporary application software use a **graphical user interface**, often called a **GUI**, which makes extensive use of icons, buttons, bars, and boxes to perform tasks.

New interface technologies are emerging for both business and home systems. One promising interface technology is **multitouch**, which has been popularized by the iPhone. Multitouch interfaces allow you to use one or more fingers to perform special gestures to manipulate lists or objects on a screen without using a mouse or a keyboard.

Table 4.2 compares leading PC and server operating systems. These include the Windows family of operating systems (Windows 7, Windows 8, Windows Server 2008), UNIX, Linux, and the Macintosh operating system.

The Microsoft Windows family of operating systems has both client and server versions and a streamlined GUI. Windows systems can perform multiple programming tasks simultaneously and have powerful networking capabilities, including the ability to access information from the Internet. At the client level, 90 percent of PCs use some form of Microsoft Windows operating system. Microsoft **Windows 7** has made improvements over earlier Windows operating systems such as Windows Vista and Windows XP, which include enhanced usability, faster performance, a new taskbar, support for multitouch interfaces, and additional security enhancements. There are versions for home, small

TABLE 4.2

Leading PC and Server Operating Systems

Operating System	Features
Windows 8	Most recent Windows operating system.
Windows 7	Recent Windows operating system for end users, with improved usability, taskbar, performance, and security as well as support for multitouch interfaces.
Windows Server 2008	Most recent Windows operating system for servers.
UNIX	Used for PCs, workstations, and network servers. Supports multitasking, multiuser processing, and networking. Is portable to different models of computer hardware.
Linux	Open source, reliable alternative to UNIX and Windows operating systems that runs on many different types of computer hardware and can be modified by software developers.
Mac OS X	Operating system for the Macintosh computer that is stable and reliable, with powerful search capabilities, support for video and image processing, and an elegant user interface. Most recent version is OS X Lion. The iPhone's iOS operating system is derived from OS X.

business, and enterprise users. The latest Windows client version is **Windows 8**. Its user interface is optimized for touch, but works equally well with a mouse and keyboard. The software runs on a wide array of devices including tablets as well as traditional desktops and laptops.

Windows operating systems for servers provide network management functions, including tools for creating and operating Web sites and other Internet services. Windows Server 2008 has multiple versions for small, medium, and large businesses.

Today there is a much greater variety of operating systems than in the past, with new operating systems for computing on handheld mobile digital devices or cloud-connected computers. Google's **Chrome OS** provides a lightweight operating system for cloud computing using a Web-connected computer or mobile device. Programs are not stored on the user's PC but are used over the Internet and accessed through the Chrome Web browser. User data reside on servers across the Internet. **Android** is an open source operating system for mobile devices such as smartphones and tablet computers developed by the Open Handset Alliance led by Google. It has become the most popular smartphone platform worldwide, competing with iOS, Apple's mobile operating system for the iPhone, iPad, and iPod Touch.

UNIX is a multiuser, multitasking operating system developed by Bell Laboratories in 1969 to connect various machines together and is highly supportive of communications and networking. UNIX is often used on workstations and servers, and provides the reliability and scalability for running large systems on high-end servers. UNIX can run on many different kinds of computers and can be easily customized. Application programs that run under UNIX can be ported from one computer to run on a different computer with little modification. Graphical user interfaces have been developed for UNIX. Vendors have developed different versions of UNIX that are incompatible, thereby limiting software portability.

Linux is a UNIX-like operating system that can be downloaded from the Internet free of charge or purchased for a small fee from companies that provide additional tools for the software. It is free, reliable, compactly designed, and capable of running on many different hardware platforms, including servers, handheld computers, and consumer electronics.

Linux has become popular as a robust low-cost alternative to UNIX and the Windows operating systems. For example, E*Trade Financial saves $13 million annually with improved computer performance by running Linux on a series of small inexpensive IBM servers instead of large expensive Sun Microsystems servers running Sun's proprietary version of UNIX.

Linux plays a major role in the back office, running Web servers and local area networks in about 25 percent of the U.S. server market. Its use in desktop computers is growing steadily. IBM, HP, Intel, Dell, and Sun have made Linux a central part of their offerings to corporations, and major software vendors are starting to provide versions of their products that can run on Linux. Both IBM and Sun offer Linux-based office tools for free or a minimal fee.

Linux is an example of **open source software**, which provides all computer users with free access to its program code, so they can modify the code to fix errors or to make improvements. Open source software is not owned by any company or individual. A global network of programmers and users manages and modifies the software, usually without being paid to do so. Open source software is by definition not restricted to any specific operating system or hardware technology, although most open source software is currently based on a Linux or UNIX.

APPLICATION SOFTWARE AND DESKTOP PRODUCTIVITY TOOLS

Today, businesses have access to an array of tools for developing their application software. These include traditional programming languages, fourth-generation languages, application software packages, and desktop productivity tools; software for developing Internet applications; and software for enterprise integration. It is important to know which software tools and programming languages are appropriate for the work your business wants to accomplish.

Application Programming Languages for Business

For business applications, the most important programming languages have been C, C++, Visual Basic, and COBOL. **C** is a powerful and efficient language developed in the early 1970s that combines machine portability with tight control and efficient use of computer resources. C is used primarily by professional programmers to create operating systems and application software, especially for PCs. **C++** is a newer version of C that has all the capabilities of C plus additional features for working with software objects. Unlike traditional programs, which separate data from the actions to be taken on the data, a software **object** combines data and procedures. Chapter 11 describes object-oriented software development in detail. **Visual Basic** is a widely used visual programming tool and environment for creating applications that run on Microsoft Windows operating systems. A **visual programming language** allows users to manipulate graphic or iconic elements to create programs. COBOL (COmmon Business Oriented Language) was developed in the early 1960s for processing large data files with alphanumeric characters (mixed alphabetic and numeric data) and for business reporting. You'll find it today primarily in large legacy business systems.

Fourth-Generation Languages

Fourth-generation languages consist of a variety of software tools that enable end users to develop software applications with minimal or no technical assistance or that enhance professional programmers' productivity. Fourth-generation languages tend to be nonprocedural, or less procedural, than conventional programming languages. Procedural languages require specification of the sequence of steps, or procedures, that tell the computer what to do and how to do it. Nonprocedural languages need only specify what has to be accomplished rather than provide details about how to carry out the task. Some of these nonprocedural languages are *natural languages* that enable users to communicate with the computer using conversational commands resembling human speech.

Table 4.3 describes six categories of fourth-generation languages: PC software tools, query languages, report generators, graphics languages, application generators, and application software packages. The table lists the tools in order of ease of use by nonprogramming end users. End users are most likely to work with PC software tools and query languages. **Query languages** are software tools that provide immediate online answers to requests for information that are not predefined, such as "Who are the highest-performing sales representatives?" Query languages are often tied to data management software (described later in this section) and to database management systems (see Chapter 5).

Software Packages and Desktop Productivity Tools

Much of the software used in businesses today is not custom programmed but consists of application software packages and desktop productivity tools. A **software package** is a prewritten, precoded, commercially available set of programs that eliminates the need for individuals or organizations to write their own software programs for certain functions. There are software packages for system software, but most package software is application software.

Software packages that run on mainframes and larger computers usually require professional programmers for their installation and support. Desktop productivity software packages for word processing, spreadsheets, data management, presentation graphics, and Web browsers are the most widely used software tools among business and consumer users.

Word Processing Software If you work in an office or attend school, you probably use word processing software every day. **Word processing software** stores text data electronically as a computer file rather than on paper. The word processing software allows the user

Table 4.3

Categories of Fourth-Generation Languages

Fourth-Generation Tool	Description	Example	
PC software tools	General-purpose application software packages for PCs	WordPerfect Microsoft Access	**Oriented toward end users**
Query language	Languages for retrieving data stored in databases or files; capable of supporting requests for information that are not predefined	SQL	
Report generator	Extract data from files or databases to create customized reports in a wide range of formats not routinely produced by an information system	Crystal Reports	
Graphics language	Retrieve data from files or databases and display them in graphic format	SAS/Graph Systat	
Application generator	Contain preprogrammed modules that can generate entire applications, including Web sites, can specify what needs to be done, and the application generator will create the appropriate program code for input, validation, update, processing, and reporting	WebFOCUS QuickBase	
Application software package	Software programs sold or leased by commercial vendors that eliminate the need for custom-written, in-house software	Oracle PeopleSoft HCM mySAP ERP	**Oriented toward IS professionals**

to make changes in the document electronically, with formatting options to make changes in line spacing, margins, character size, and column width. Microsoft Word and WordPerfect are popular word processing packages.

Businesses that need to create highly professional looking brochures, manuals, or books will likely use desktop publishing software for this purpose. Desktop publishing software provides more control over the placement of text, graphics, and photos in the layout of a page than does word processing software. Adobe InDesign and QuarkXpress are two professional publishing packages.

Spreadsheet Software Spreadsheets are valuable for applications in which numerous calculations with pieces of data must be related to each other. **Spreadsheet software** organizes data into a grid of columns and rows. When you change a value or values, all other related values on the spreadsheet will be automatically recomputed.

You will often see spreadsheets in applications that require modeling and "what-if" analysis. After the user has constructed a set of mathematical relationships, the spreadsheet can be recalculated instantaneously using a different set of assumptions. Spreadsheet packages include graphics functions to present data in the form of line graphs, bar graphs, or pie charts, and the ability to read and create Web files. The most popular spreadsheet package is Microsoft Excel. Figure 4.8 illustrates the output from a spreadsheet for a break-even analysis and its accompanying graph.

Data Management Software Although spreadsheet programs are powerful tools for manipulating quantitative data, data management software, which we defined earlier in this chapter, is more suitable for creating and manipulating lists and for combining information

Figure 4.8
Spreadsheet
Software
Spreadsheet software organizes data into columns and rows for analysis and manipulation. Contemporary spreadsheet software provides graphing abilities for a clear, visual representation of the data in the spreadsheets. This sample break-even analysis is represented as numbers in a spreadsheet as well as a line graph for easy interpretation.

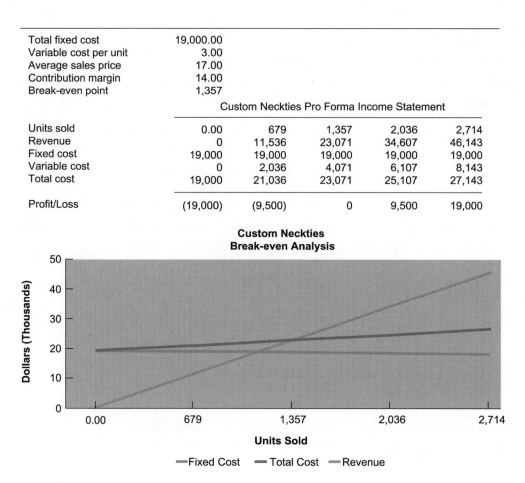

Total fixed cost	19,000.00
Variable cost per unit	3.00
Average sales price	17.00
Contribution margin	14.00
Break-even point	1,357

Custom Neckties Pro Forma Income Statement

Units sold	0.00	679	1,357	2,036	2,714
Revenue	0	11,536	23,071	34,607	46,143
Fixed cost	19,000	19,000	19,000	19,000	19,000
Variable cost	0	2,036	4,071	6,107	8,143
Total cost	19,000	21,036	23,071	25,107	27,143
Profit/Loss	(19,000)	(9,500)	0	9,500	19,000

from different files. PC database management packages have programming features and easy-to-learn menus that enable nonspecialists to build small information systems.

Data management software typically has facilities for creating files and databases and for storing, modifying, and manipulating data for reports and queries. Popular database management software for the personal computer includes Microsoft Access, which has been enhanced to publish data on the Web. We discuss data management software in greater detail in Chapter 5.

Presentation Graphics Users can create professional-quality graphics presentations with presentation graphics software. This software can convert numeric data into charts and other types of graphics and can include multimedia displays of sound, animation, photos, and video clips. The leading presentation graphics packages include capabilities for computer-generated slide shows and translating content for the Web. Microsoft PowerPoint and Lotus Freelance Graphics are popular presentation graphics packages.

Software Suites Typically, the major office productivity tools are bundled together as a software suite. Microsoft Office is an example. There are a number of different versions of Office for home and business users, but the core office tools include Word word processing software, Excel spreadsheet software, Access database software, PowerPoint presentation graphics software, and Outlook, a set of tools for e-mail, scheduling, and contact management. Microsoft **Office 2010** is the latest version of this suite. Microsoft has added a hosted cloud version of its productivity and collaboration tools called Office 365. Its Word and Excel documents can be edited by multiple users at once and viewed on mobile devices.

Competing with Microsoft Office are low-cost office productivity suites such as the open source OpenOffice (which can be downloaded for free over the Internet). However, the real challenge to Microsoft is coming from the cloud. Web-based versions of desktop productivity software are becoming popular because of their convenience, flexibility, and low cost. There are over three million businesses of all sizes using **Google Apps**, which we introduced in our discussion of collaboration tools in Chapter 2. This online suite includes tools for word processing, spreadsheets, presentations, calendar, and e-mail, and is available for free or as a more full-featured Google Apps for Business edition charging businesses $50 per year.

Web Browsers Easy-to-use software tools called **Web browsers** are used for displaying Web pages and for accessing the Web and other Internet resources. Browsers can display or present graphics, audio, and video information, as well as traditional text, and they allow you to click (or touch) on-screen buttons or highlighted words to link to related Web sites. Web browsers have become the primary interface for accessing the Internet or for using networked systems based on Internet technology. The leading Web browsers today are Microsoft Internet Explorer, Mozilla Firefox, Apple Safari, and Google Chrome. Mobile handhelds have their own specialized Web browsers.

SOFTWARE FOR THE WEB: JAVA AND HTML

There are a number of software tools that that businesses use to build Web sites and applications that run on the Web. Java is used for building applications that run on the Web, and HTML is used for creating Web pages.

Java

Java is an operating system-independent, processor-independent, object-oriented programming language that has become a leading interactive programming environment for the Web. Java enables users to work with data on networked systems using Web browsers, reducing the need to write specialized software. At the enterprise level, Java is used for more complex e-commerce and e-business applications that require communication with an organization's back-end transaction processing systems.

Nearly all Web browser software has a Java platform built in. The Java platform has migrated into cell phones, automobiles, music players, game machines, and, finally, into set-top cable television systems serving interactive content.

Java software is designed to run on any computer or computing device, regardless of the specific microprocessor or operating system the device uses. Java achieves this neat trick by using a Java virtual machine built for each type of computer and operating system. The virtual machine enables it to run Java applications. A Macintosh PC, an IBM PC running Windows, a Sun server running UNIX, and even a smart cell phone or PDA can share the same Java application, reducing the costs of software development and creating the same user experience regardless of what kind of computer the user is working with.

In network environments, such as the Internet, Java is used to create miniature programs called *applets* that are designed to reside on centralized network servers. The network delivers to client computers only the applets required for a specific function. With Java applets residing on a network, a user can download only the software functions and data that he or she needs to perform a particular task, such as analyzing the revenue from one sales territory. The user does not need to maintain large software programs or data files on his or her desktop machine.

Hypertext Markup Language (HTML)

Hypertext Markup Language (HTML) is a page description language for specifying how text, graphics, video, and sound are placed on a Web page and for creating dynamic links to other Web pages and objects. Using these links, a user need only point at a highlighted keyword or graphic, click on it, and immediately be transported to another document. Table 4.4 illustrates some sample HTML statements.

HTML programs can be custom written, but they also can be created using the HTML authoring capabilities of Web browsers or of popular word processing, spreadsheet, data management, and presentation graphics software packages. HTML editors, such as Adobe Dreamweaver, are more powerful HTML authoring tool programs for creating Web pages.

TABLE 4.4

Examples of HTML

Plain English	HTML
Subcompact	<TITLE>Automobile</TITLE>
4 passenger	<LI>4 passenger</LI>
$16,800	<LI>$16,800</LI>

HTML5

HTML was originally designed to create and link static documents composed largely of text. Today, however, the Web is much more social and interactive, and many Web pages have multimedia elements-images, audio, and video. Third-party plug-in applications like Flash, Silverlight, and Java have been required to integrate these rich media with Web pages. However, these add-ons require additional programming and put strains on computer processing. This is one reason Apple dropped support for Flash on its mobile devices. The next evolution of HTML, called **HTML5,** solves this problem by making it possible to embed images, audio, video, and other elements directly into a document without processor-intensive add-ons. HTML5 will also make it easier for Web pages to function across different display devices, including mobile devices as well as desktops, and it will support the storage of data offline for apps that run over the Web. Web pages will execute more quickly, and look like smartphone apps.

Although HTML5 is still under development, elements are already being used in a number of Internet tools, including Apple's Safari browsers, Google Chrome, and recent versions of the Firefox Web browser. Google's Gmail and Google Reader have adopted parts of the HTML5 standard as well. Web sites listed as "iPad ready" are making extensive use of HTML5 including CNN, The New York Times, and CBS.

WEB SERVICES

Web services refer to a set of loosely coupled software components that exchange information with each other using universal Web communication standards and languages. They can exchange information between two different systems regardless of the operating systems or programming languages on which the systems are based. They can be used to build open-standard, Web-based applications linking systems of two different organizations, and they can be used to create applications that link disparate systems within a single company. Web services are not tied to any one operating system or programming language, and different applications can use them to communicate with each other in a standard way without time-consuming custom coding.

The foundation technology for Web services is **XML**, which stands for **Extensible Markup Language**. This language was developed in 1996 by the World Wide Web Consortium (W3C, the international body that oversees the development of the Web) as a more powerful and flexible markup language than HTML for Web pages. Whereas HTML is limited to describing how data should be presented in the form of Web pages, XML can perform presentation, communication, and storage of data. In XML, a number is not simply a number; the XML tag specifies whether the number represents a price, a date, or a zip code. Table 4.5 illustrates some sample XML statements.

By tagging selected elements of the content of documents for their meanings, XML makes it possible for computers to manipulate and interpret their data automatically and perform operations on the data without human intervention. Web browsers and computer programs, such as order processing or enterprise resource planning (ERP) software, can

TABLE 4.5	Plain English	XML
Examples of XML	Subcompact	<AUTOMOBILETYPE="Subcompact">
	4 passenger	<PASSENGERUNIT="PASS">4</PASSENGER>
	$16,800	<PRICE CURRENCY="USD">$16,800</PRICE>

follow programmed rules for applying and displaying the data. XML provides a standard format for data exchange, enabling Web services to pass data from one process to another.

Web services communicate through XML messages over standard Web protocols. Companies discover and locate Web services through a directory much as they would locate services in the Yellow Pages of a telephone book. Using Web protocols, a software application can connect freely to other applications without custom programming for each different application with which it wants to communicate. Everyone shares the same standards.

The collection of Web services that are used to build a firm's software systems constitutes what is known as a service-oriented architecture. A **service-oriented architecture (SOA)** is set of self-contained services that communicate with each other to create a working software application. Business tasks are accomplished by executing a series of these services. Software developers reuse these services in other combinations to assemble other applications as needed.

Virtually all major software vendors, such as IBM, Microsoft, Oracle, and HP, provide tools and entire platforms for building and integrating software applications using Web services. IBM includes Web service tools in its WebSphere e-business software platform, and Microsoft has incorporated Web services tools in its Microsoft .NET platform.

Dollar Rent-A-Car's systems use Web services to link its online booking system with the Southwest Airlines Web site. Although both companies' systems are based on different technology platforms, a person booking a flight on Southwest.com can reserve a car from Dollar without leaving the airline's Web site. Instead of struggling to get Dollar's reservation system to share data with Southwest's information systems, Dollar used Microsoft .NET Web services technology as an intermediary. Reservations from Southwest are translated into Web services protocols, which are then translated into formats that can be understood by Dollar's computers.

Other car rental companies have linked their information systems to airline companies' Web sites before. But without Web services, these connections had to be built one at a time. Web services provide a standard way for Dollar's computers to "talk" to other companies' information systems without having to build special links to each one. Dollar is now expanding its use of Web services to link directly to the systems of a small tour operator and a large travel reservation system as well as a wireless Web site for mobile phones and PDAs. It does not have to write new software code for each new partner's information systems or each new wireless device (see Figure 4.9).

SOFTWARE TRENDS

Today there are many more sources for obtaining software and many more capabilities for users to create their own customized software applications. Expanding use of open source software and cloud-based software tools and services exemplify this trend.

Open Source Software
Arguably the most influential software trend is the movement towards open source software. As noted earlier, open source software is developed by a community of programmers

Figure 4.9
How Dollar Rent-A-Car Uses Web Services
Dollar Rent-A-Car uses Web services to provide a standard intermediate layer of software to "talk" to other companies' information systems. Dollar Rent-A-Car can use this set of Web services to link to other companies' information systems without having to build a separate link to each firm's systems.

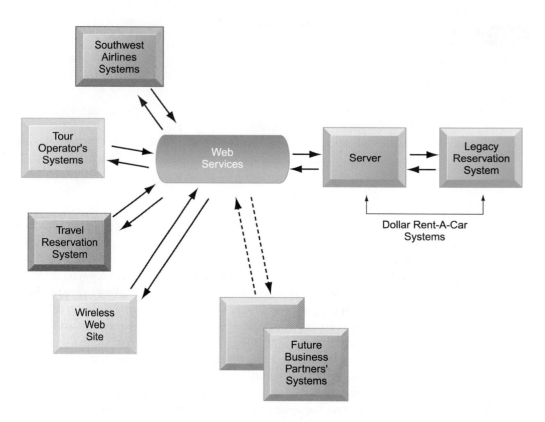

around the world, who make their programs available to users under one of several different licensing schemes. Essentially, users of the software can use the software as is, modify it at will, and even include it in for-profit software applications.

The open source movement started out small in 1983 (when it was called "hippie software"), but it has since grown to be a major part of corporate computing infrastructure, as the foundation for programs such as Linux, and Apache, the most widely used Web server software. Today you can find thousands of open source computer programs to accomplish everything from e-commerce shopping carts and funds clearance to sales force management. Some of the cloud computing applications described in this chapter, such as as Google's Chrome Web browser, are based on open source code.

Cloud-Based Software Services and Tools

In the past, software such as Microsoft Word or Adobe Illustrator came in a box and was designed to operate on a single machine. Today, you're more likely to download the software from the vendor's Web site, or to use the software as a cloud service delivered over the Internet. Services for delivering and providing access to software remotely as a Web-based service are now referred to as **Software as a Service (SaaS)**.

Cloud-based software and the data it uses are hosted on powerful servers in massive data centers, and can be accessed with an Internet connection and standard Web browser. In addition to free or low-cost tools for individuals and small businesses provided by Google or Yahoo!, enterprise software and other complex business functions are available as services from the major commercial software vendors. (See the Chapter 8 Interactive Session on Technology for examples.) Instead of buying and installing software programs, subscribing companies rent the same functions from these services, with users paying either on a subscription or per transaction basis.

Mashups and Apps The software you use for both personal and business tasks may consist of large self-contained programs, or it may be composed of interchangeable components that integrate freely with other applications on the Internet. Individual users and entire companies mix and match these software components to create their own customized applications and to share information with others. The resulting software applications are called **mashups**. The idea is to take different sources and produce a new work that is "greater than" the sum of its parts. You have performed a mashup if you've ever personalized your Facebook profile or your blog with a capability to display videos or slide shows.

Web mashups combine the capabilities of two or more online applications to create a kind of hybrid that provides more customer value than the original sources alone. For instance, Zip Realty uses Google Maps and data provided by online real estate database Zillow.com to display a complete list of multiple listing service (MLS) real estate listings for any zip code specified by the user. Amazon.com uses mashup technolgies to aggregate product descriptions with partner sites and user profiles.

Apps are small pieces of software that run on the Internet, on your computer, or on your mobile phone or tablet and are generally delivered over the Internet. Google refers to its online services as apps, including the Google Apps suite of desktop productivity tools. But when we talk about apps today, most of the attention goes to the apps that have been developed for the mobile digital platform. It is these apps that turn smartphones and other mobile handheld devices into general-purpose computing tools.

Most of these apps are for the iPhone, Android and BlackBerry operating system platforms. Many are free or purchased for a small charge, much less than conventional software. There are already over 500,000 apps for the Apple iPhone and iPad platform and about 100,000 that run on devices using Google's Android operating system. The success of these mobile platforms depends in large part on the quantity and the quality of the apps they provide. Apps tie the customer to a specific hardware platform: As the user adds more and more apps to his or her mobile phone, the cost of switching to a competing mobile platform (for instance from the iPhone to an Android phone) rises.

At the moment, the most commonly downloaded apps are games, music, social networking, news and weather, maps/navigation, and video/movies. But there are also serious apps for business users that make it possible to create and edit documents, connect to corporate systems, schedule and participate in meetings, track shipments, and dictate voice messages (see the Chapter 1 Interactive Session on Organizations). There are also a huge number of e-commerce apps for researching and buying goods and services online.

4.3 Managing Hardware and Software Technology

Selection and use of computer hardware and software technology has a profound impact on business performance. We now describe the most important issues you will face when managing hardware and software technology: capacity planning and scalability; determining the total cost of technology assets; determining whether to own and maintain your own hardware, software, and other infrastructure components or lease them from an external technology service provider; and managing mobile platforms and software localization.

CAPACITY PLANNING AND SCALABILITY

E-commerce and e-business are placing heavy new demands on hardware technology. Much larger processing and storage resources are required to process and store the surging digital transactions flowing between different parts of the firm, and between the firm and its customers and suppliers. Many people using a Web site simultaneously place great strains on a computer system, as does hosting large numbers of interactive Web pages with data-intensive graphics or video.

Managers and information systems specialists now need to pay more attention to hardware capacity planning and scalability than before. From an IT perspective, **capacity planning** is the process of predicting when a computer hardware system becomes saturated. It considers factors such as the maximum number of users that the system can accommodate at one time, the impact of existing and future software applications, and performance measures, such as minimum response time for processing business transactions. Capacity planning ensures that the firm has enough computing power for its current and future needs. For example, the Nasdaq Stock Market performs ongoing capacity planning to identify peaks in the volume of stock trading transactions and to ensure it has enough computing capacity to handle large surges in volume when trading is very heavy.

Although information systems specialists perform capacity planning, input from business managers is essential. Business managers need to determine acceptable levels of computer response time and availability for the firm's mission-critical systems to maintain the level of business performance they expect. New applications, mergers and acquisitions, and changes in business volume all impact computer workload and must be considered when planning hardware capacity.

Scalability refers to the ability of a computer, product, or system to expand to serve a large number of users without breaking down. Electronic commerce and electronic business both call for scalable IT infrastructures that have the capacity to grow with the business as the size of a Web site and number of visitors increase. Organizations must make sure they have sufficient computer processing, storage, and network resources to handle surging volumes of digital transactions and to make such data immediately available online.

TOTAL COST OF OWNERSHIP (TCO) OF TECHNOLOGY ASSETS

When you calculate how much your hardware and software cost, their purchase price is only the beginning. You must also consider ongoing administration costs for hardware and software upgrades, maintenance, technical support, training, and even utility and real estate costs for running and housing the technology. The **total cost of ownership (TCO)** model can be used to analyze these direct and indirect costs to help determine the actual cost of owning a specific technology. Table 4.6 describes the most important TCO components to consider in a TCO analysis.

When all these cost components are considered, the TCO for a PC might run up to three times the original purchase price of the equipment. "Hidden costs" for support staff, downtime, and additional network management can make distributed client/server architectures—especially those incorporating handheld computers and wireless devices—more expensive than centralized mainframe architectures.

Many large firms are saddled with redundant, incompatible hardware and software because of poor planning. These firms could reduce their TCO through greater centralization

TABLE 4.6 TCO Cost Components		
Hardware acquisition		Purchase price of computer hardware equipment, including computers, terminals, storage, and printers
Software acquisition		Purchase or license of software for each user
Installation		Cost to install computers and software
Training		Cost to provide training to information systems specialists and end users
Support		Cost to provide ongoing technical support, help desks, and so forth
Maintenance		Cost to upgrade the hardware and software
Infrastructure		Cost to acquire, maintain, and support related infrastructure, such as networks and specialized equipment (including storage backup units)
Downtime		Lost productivity if hardware or software failures cause the system to be unavailable for processing and user tasks
Space and energy		Real estate and utility costs for housing and providing power for the technology

and standardization of their hardware and software resources. Companies could reduce the size of the information systems staff required to support their infrastructure if the firm minimized the number of different computer models and pieces of software that employees are allowed to use.

USING TECHNOLOGY SERVICE PROVIDERS

Some of the most important questions facing managers are "How should we acquire and maintain our technology assets? Should we build software applications ourselves or outsource them to an external contractor? Should we purchase and run them ourselves or rent them from external service providers?" In the past, most companies ran their own computer facilities and developed their own software. Today, more and more companies are obtaining their hardware and software technology from external service vendors.

Outsourcing

A number of firms are **outsourcing** the maintenance of their IT infrastructures and the development of new systems to external vendors. They may contract with an external service provider to run their computer center and networks, to develop new software, or to manage all of the components of their IT infrastructures. For example, Chrysler Corporation signed a multi-year outsourcing agreement with Computer Sciences Corporation (CSC) in which CSC provides mainframe, server, and storage services for all of Chrysler's worldwide locations.

Specialized Web hosting services are available for companies that lack the financial or technical resources to operate their own Web sites. A **Web hosting service** maintains a large Web server, or a series of servers, and provides fee-paying subscribers with space to maintain their Web sites. The subscribing companies may create their own Web pages or have the hosting service, or a Web design firm, create them. Some services offer *co-location*, in which the firm actually purchases and owns the server computer housing its Web site but locates the server in the physical facility of the hosting service.

Firms often retain control over their hardware resources but outsource custom software development or maintenance to outside firms, frequently firms that operate offshore in low-wage areas of the world. When firms outsource software work outside their national borders, the practice is called **offshore software outsourcing**. Until recently, this type of software development involved lower-level maintenance, data entry, and call center operations, but with the growing sophistication and experience of offshore firms, particularly in India, more and more new program development is taking place offshore. Chapter 11 discusses offshore software outsourcing in greater detail.

In order to manage their relationship with an outsourcer or technology service provider, firms will need a contract that includes a **service level agreement (SLA)**. The SLA is a formal contract between customers and their service providers that defines the specific responsibilities of the service provider and the level of service expected by the customer. SLAs typically specify the nature and level of services provided, criteria for performance measurement, support options, provisions for security and disaster recovery, hardware and software ownership and upgrades, customer support, billing, and conditions for terminating the agreement.

Using Cloud Services

Firms now have the option of maintaining their own IT infrastructures or using cloud-based hardware and software services. There are many factors that go into the decision of whether to keep IT infrastructure in-house or turn it over to an external provider. Companies considering the cloud computing model need to carefully assess the costs and benefits of external services, weighing all people, organizational, and technology issues, including the level of service and performance that is acceptable for the business.

Small businesses that typically lack the resources for maintaining their own hardware and software may find it much easier to "rent" infrastructure from another firm and avoid the expense and difficulty of installing, operating, and maintaining hardware and software

*In order to achieve a
global presence, firms
need to efficiently
translate their online
interfaces to multiple
languages. This process
is called localization.*

© Maurice Savage, 2011, Alamy.

on their own. However, larger businesses often have complex proprietary systems supporting unique business processes, some of which provide strategic advantages. These firms will have to consider whether cloud computing capabilities are sufficiently secure or reliable for their critical systems. The most likely scenario is a hybrid computing model where firms use their own infrastructure for their most essential core activities and adopt public cloud computing for less-critical systems or for additional processing capacity during peak business periods.

In some instances, the cost of renting software adds up to more than purchasing and maintaining an application in-house. Yet there may be benefits to using software as a service (SaaS) if it allows the company to focus on core business issues instead of technology challenges.

MANAGING MOBILE PLATFORMS

Gains in productivity and efficiency from equipping employees with mobile computing devices must be balanced against increased costs from integrating these devices into the firm's IT infrastructure and from providing technical support. Other cost components include fees for wireless airtime, end-user training, help desk support, and software for special applications. Although the cost for a wireless handheld for a corporate employee may run several hundred dollars, the TCO for each device is much higher, ranging from $1,000 to $3,000, according to various consultant estimates.

A large firm may have many thousands of wireless devices to configure and monitor, similar to a desktop environment. Firms will need to inventory all of their mobile devices and develop policies and tools for tracking, updating, and securing them and for controlling the data and applications that run on them. The Interactive Session on People explores these issues.

MANAGING SOFTWARE LOCALIZATION FOR GLOBAL BUSINESS

If you are operating a global company, all of the management issues we have just described will be affected by the need to create systems that can be realistically used by multiple business units in different countries. Although English has become a kind of standard business language, this is truer at higher levels of companies and not throughout the middle and lower ranks. Software may have to be built with local language interfaces before a new information system can be successfully implemented worldwide.

INTERACTIVE SESSION: PEOPLE   Should You Use Your iPhone for Work?

Look around. On the street, at restaurants, sports events, and stores, you'll find many people using their smartphones. By 2013, 1.3 billion people will be able to use their mobile phone to do work on the go, and by 2015, 4.4 billion people, which is more than 60 percent of the world's population, will have access to some form of 4G mobile broadband technology.

If almost everyone has a personal smartphone, why not use it for work? Employees using their own smartphones would allow companies to enjoy all of the same benefits of a mobile workforce without spending their own money on these devices, but IT departments need to overcome several logistical hurdles to make that vision a reality. Using personal devices for business poses difficult problems for companies, including security, inventory management, support, integrating mobile devices into pre-existing IT functions and systems, and measuring return on investment. In other words, it's not that simple.

A significant portion of corporate IT resources is dedicated to managing and maintaining a large number of devices within an organization. In the past, companies tried to limit business smartphone use to a single platform. This made it easier to keep track of each mobile device and to roll out software upgrades or fixes, because all employees were using the same devices, or at the very least, the same operating system. The most popular employer-issued smartphone was Research in Motion's BlackBerry, which is considered the "most secure" mobile platform available. BlackBerry mobile devices access corporate e-mail and data using a proprietary software and networking platform that is company-controlled and protected from outsiders. Today, the mobile digital landscape is much more complicated, with a variety of devices and operating systems on the market that do not have well-developed tools for administration and security.

If employees are allowed to work with more than one type of mobile device and operating system, companies need an effective way to keep track of all the devices employees are using. To access company information, the company's networks must be configured to receive connections from that device. When employees make changes to their personal phone, such as switching cellular carriers, changing their phone number, or buying a new mobile device altogether, companies will need to quickly and flexibly ensure that their employees are still able to remain productive. Firms need an efficient inventory management system that keeps track of which devices employees are using, where the device is located, whether it

is being used, and what software it is equipped with. For unprepared companies, keeping track of who gets access to what data could be a nightmare.

With the variety of phones and operating systems available, providing adequate technical support for every employee could be difficult. When employees are not able to access critical data or encounter other problems with their mobile devices, they will need assistance from the information systems department. Companies that rely on desktop computers tend to have many of the same computers with the same specs and operating systems, making tech support that much easier. Mobility introduces a new layer of variety and complexity to tech support that companies need to be prepared to handle.

A firm's software development teams can benefit from having one person specifically focused on ensuring that new applications will be easily usable and useful on smartphones. Many companies are integrating these "mobility experts" into core IT functions and software development. Unless applications and software can be used on mobile devices to connect to the firm's existing IT platform and company-wide CRM, SCM, and ERP systems, a business smartphone is just a phone, and mobility experts can help a company leverage mobility more effectively.

There are significant concerns with securing company information accessed with mobile devices. If a device is stolen or compromised, companies need ways to ensure that sensitive or confidential information isn't freely available to anyone. Mobility puts assets and data at greater risk than if they were only located within company walls and on company machines. Companies often use technologies that allow them to wipe data from devices remotely, or encrypt data so that if a device is stolen, it cannot be used. You'll find a detailed discussion of mobile security issues in Chapter 7.

A number of software products have emerged to help companies manage diverse mobile platforms. Sybase Afaria, Trellia, Microsoft Systems Center Device Manager, and Odyssey Software Athena have capabilities for configuring devices remotely, enforcing different sets of policies for different users and devices, and managing applications running on all of them.

Novo Nordisk, headquartered in Denmark, manufactures and markets pharmaceutical products and services throughout the world. Its 2,000-member sales force operates in 25 different countries, and uses a diverse assortment of mobile phones, smartphones, and mobile handhelds. To manage all of these devices centrally, Novo Nordisk implemented Sybase Afaria. Using Afaria, the company's internal IT department can deploy new applications to mobile devices quickly and without extensive end-user interaction. A new mobile phone user just needs to answer "yes" to Novo Nordisk's configuration process, and the installation happens automatically. Afaria also has features for enabling individual countries or regions to provide their own local support, a necessity since each Novo Nordisk market has it own data connections, policies and requirements.

Another approach to mobile device management is virtualization. Companies can install software such as Citrix Systems XenDesktop that runs Windows desktops and individual applications on any device, regardless of operating system. Employees then use that software to access their entire desktop on their smartphones and mobile handhelds, and are thus able to use the same programs on the road that they use in the office. The virtualization software has built-in security features that allow corporations to prohibit saving data on local devices, to encrypt all corporate data without touching employees' personal applications and data, and to remotely erase the data in the event of a security breach. Royal Dutch Shell PLC is testing virtualized systems for use with tablets such as the iPad. Placing virtualization software on employees' personal tablets is less expensive than outfitting them with company-purchased laptops.

In order to successfully integrate mobile devices into corporate and IT strategy, companies need to carefully examine their business processes and determine whether or not mobility makes sense for them. Not every firm will benefit from mobility to the same degree. Without a clear idea of how exactly mobile devices fit into the long-term plans for the firm, companies will end up wasting their money on unnecessary devices and mobile initiatives. One of the biggest worries that managers have about mobility is the difficulty of measuring return on investment. Many workers swear by their mobile devices, and the benefits are too significant to ignore, but quantifying how much money is earned or saved by going mobile can be difficult.

Sources: "So You Want to Use Your IPhone for Work: Uh-Oh," *The Wall Street Journal*, April 25, 2011. Samuel Greengard, "Managing Mobility in the Enterprise," *Baseline*, January 28, 2011; Dell Computer, "Management Madness: How to Manage Mobile Devices," mkting.cio.com, accessed July 18, 2011; Dell Computer, "Is Your Infrastructure Mobile-Ready?" www.cio.com, accessed May 21, 2011; and Citrix Systems, "BYO-Rethinking Your Device Strategy," 2010.

CASE STUDY QUESTIONS

1. What are the advantages and disadvantages of allowing employees to use their personal smartphones for work?

2. What people, organization, and technology factors should be addressed when deciding whether to allow employees to use their personal smartphones for work?

3. Allowing employees to use their own smartphones for work will save the company money. Do you agree? Why or why not?

MIS IN ACTION

Visit the Web sites of Sybase and Citrix Systems and review the portion of these Web sites dealing with Sybase's Afaria and Citrix's XenDesktop. If you wanted to use your personal iPhone for work, explain what each of these products could do to help your company manage your mobile device.

These interfaces can be costly and messy to build. Menu bars, commands, error messages, reports, queries, online data entry forms, and system documentation may need to be translated into all the languages of the countries where the system will be used. To be truly useful for enhancing productivity of a global workforce, the software interfaces must be easily understood and mastered quickly. The entire process of converting software to operate in a second language is called *software localization*.

Global systems must also consider differences in local cultures and business processes. Cross-functional systems such as enterprise and supply chain management systems are not always compatible with differences in languages, cultural heritages, and business processes in other countries.

In a global systems environment, all of these factors add to the TCO and will influence decisions about whether to outsource or use technology service providers.

> ### LEARNING TRACKS
>
> The following Learning Tracks provide content relevant to topics covered in this chapter:
>
> 1. How Computer Hardware Works
> 2. How Computer Software Works
> 3. Service Level Agreements
> 4. Cloud Computing
> 5. The Open Source Software Initiative
> 6. Evolution of IT Infrastructure
> 7. Technology Drivers of IT Infrastructure Evolution
> 8. IT Infrastructure; Management Opportunities, Challenges, and Solutions

Review Summary

1 **What are the components of IT infrastructure?** IT infrastructure consists of the shared technology resources that provide the platform for the firm's specific information system applications. Major IT infrastructure components include computer hardware, software, data management technology, networking and telecommunications technology, and technology services.

2 **What are the major computer hardware, data storage, input, and output technologies used in business?** Computers are categorized as mainframes, midrange computers, PCs, workstations, or supercomputers. Mainframes are the largest computers, midrange computers are servers, PCs are desktop or laptop machines, workstations are desktop machines with powerful mathematical and graphic capabilities, and supercomputers are sophisticated, powerful computers that can perform massive and complex computations rapidly. Computing power can be further increased by creating a computational grid that combines the computing power of all the computers on a network. In the client/server model of computing, computer processing is split between "clients" and "servers" connected via a network. The exact division of tasks between client and server depends on the application.

The principal secondary storage technologies are magnetic disk, optical disc, and magnetic tape. Optical CD-ROM and DVD discs can store vast amounts of data compactly and some types are rewritable. Storage area networks (SANs) connect multiple storage devices on a separate high-speed network dedicated to storage. The principal input devices are keyboards, computer mice, touch screens (including those with multitouch), magnetic ink and optical character recognition devices, pen-based instruments, digital scanners, sensors, audio input devices, and radio-frequency identification devices. The principal output devices are display monitors, printers, and audio output devices.

3 **What are the major types of computer software used in business?** The two major types of software are system software and application software. System software coordinates the various parts of the computer system and mediates between application software and computer hardware. Application software is used to develop specific business applications.

The system software that manages and controls the activities of the computer is called the operating system. Leading PC and server operating systems include Windows 8, Windows 7, Windows Server 2008, UNIX, Linux, and the Macintosh operating system.

Linux is a powerful, resilient open source operating system that can run on multiple hardware platforms and is used widely to run Web servers.

The principal programming languages used in business application software include COBOL, C, C++, and Visual Basic. Fourth-generation languages are less procedural than conventional programming languages and enable end users to perform many software tasks that previously required technical specialists. PC and cloud-based productivity tools include word processing, spreadsheet, data management, presentation graphics, and Web browser software. Java is an operating-system- and hardware-independent programming language that is the leading interactive programming environment for the Web. HTML is a page description language for creating Web pages.

Web services are loosely coupled software components based on XML and open Web standards that can work with any application software and operating system. They can be used as components of Web-based applications to link the systems of two different organizations or to link disparate systems of a single company.

4 **What are the most important contemporary hardware and software trends?**
Contemporary hardware trends include the emerging mobile digital platform, nanotechnology, virtualization, cloud computing, green computing, high-performance/ power-saving processors, and autonomic computing. Cloud computing provides computer processing, storage, software, and other services as virtualized resources over a network, primarily the Internet, on an as-needed basis. Software trends include the expanding use of open source software and cloud-based software tools and services (including SaaS).

5 **What are the principal issues in managing hardware and software technology?**
Managers and information systems specialists need to pay special attention to hardware capacity planning and scalability to ensure that the firm has enough computing power for its current and future needs. Businesses also need to balance the costs and benefits of building and maintaining their own hardware and software versus outsourcing or using an on-demand computing model. The total cost of ownership (TCO) of the organization's technology assets includes not only the original cost of computer hardware and software but also costs for hardware and software upgrades, maintenance, technical support, and training, including the costs for managing and maintaining mobile devices. Companies with global operations need to manage software localization.

Key Terms

Android, 125
Application server, 115
Application software, 112
Apps, 133
Autonomic computing, 123
C, 126
C++, 126
Capacity planning, 133
CD-ROM (compact disc read-only memory), 116
Centralized processing, 114
Chrome OS, 125
Client, 114
Client/server computing, 114
Cloud computing, 119
Data center, 111
Data management software, 112
Digital video disc (DVD), 116
Distributed processing, 114

Extensible Markup Language (XML), 130
Fourth-generation languages, 126
Google Apps, 129
Graphical user interface (GUI), 124
Green computing (green IT), 120
Grid computing, 114
HTML5, 130
Hypertext Markup Language (HTML), 129
Input devices, 116
Java, 129
Legacy systems, 113
Linux, 125
Magnetic disk, 000
Magnetic tape, 116
Mainframe, 113

Mashups, 133
Multicore processor, 122
Multitouch, 124
Nanotechnology, 118
N-tier client/server architectures, 114
Object, 126
Office 2010, 128
Offshore software outsourcing, 135
On-demand computing, 120
Open source software, 125
Operating system, 123
Output devices, 116
Outsourcing, 135
Personal computer (PC), 113
Presentation graphics software, 000
Private cloud, 120
Public cloud, 120

Review Questions

1. What are the components of IT infrastructure?
- Define information technology (IT) infrastructure and describe each of its components.

2. What are the major computer hardware, data storage, input, and output technologies used in business?
- List and describes the various type of computers available to businesses today.
- Define the client/server model of computing, and describe the difference between a two-tiered and n-tier client/server architecture.
- List the most important secondary storage media and the strengths and limitations of each.
- List and describe the major computer input and output devices.

3. What are the major types of computer software used in business?
- Distinguish between application software and system software, and explain the role played by the operating system of a computer.
- List and describe the major PC and server operating systems.
- Name and describe each category of fourth-generation software tools, and explain how fourth-generation languages differ from conventional programming languages.
- Name and describe the major desktop productivity software tools.
- Explain how Java and HTML are used in building applications for the Web.
- Define Web services, describe the technologies they use, and explain how Web services benefit businesses.

4. What are the most important contemporary hardware and software trends?
- Define and describe the mobile digital platform, nanotechnology, grid computing, cloud computing, autonomic computing, virtualization, green computing, HTML5, and multicore processing.
- Explain why open source software is so important today and its benefits for business.
- List and describe cloud computing software services, mashups, and apps, and explain how they benefit individuals and businesses.

5. What are the principal issues in managing hardware and software technology?
- Explain why managers need to pay attention to capacity planning and scalability of technology resources.
- Describe the cost components used to calculate the TCO of technology assets.
- Identify the benefits and challenges of using outsourcing, cloud computing services, and mobile platforms.
- Explain why software localization has become an important management issue for global companies.

Discussion Questions

1. Why is selecting computer hardware and software for the organization an important business decision? What people, organization, and technology issues should be considered when selecting computer hardware and software?

2. Should organizations use software service providers (including cloud services) for all their software needs? Why or why not? What people, organization, and technology factors should be considered when making this decision?

3. What are the advantages and disadvantages of cloud computing?

Hands-on MIS Projects

The projects in this section give you hands-on experience in developing solutions for managing IT infrastructures and IT outsourcing, using spreadsheet software to evaluate alternative desktop systems, and using Web research to budget for a sales conference.

MANAGEMENT DECISION PROBLEMS

1. The University of Pittsburgh Medical Center (UPMC) relies on information systems to operate 19 hospitals, a network of other care sites, and international and commercial ventures. Demand for additional servers and storage technology was growing by 20 percent each year. UPMC was setting up a separate server for every application, and its servers and other computers were running a number of different operating systems, including several versions of UNIX and Windows. UPMC had to manage technologies from many different vendors, including Hewlett-Packard (HP), Sun Microsystems, Microsoft, and IBM. Assess the impact of this situation on business performance. What factors and management decisions must be considered when developing a solution to this problem?

2. Qantas Airways, Australia's leading airline, faces cost pressures from high fuel prices and lower levels of global airline traffic. To remain competitive, the airline must find ways to keep costs low while providing a high level of customer service. Qantas had a 30-year-old data center. Management had to decide whether to replace its IT infrastructure with newer technology or outsource it. What factors should be considered by Qantas management when deciding whether to outsource? If Qantas decides to outsource, list and describe points that should be addressed in a service level agreement.

IMPROVING DECISION MAKING: USING A SPREADSHEET TO EVALUATE HARDWARE AND SOFTWARE OPTIONS

Software skills: Spreadsheet formulas
Business skills: Technology pricing

In this exercise, you will use spreadsheet software to calculate the cost of desktop systems, printers, and software.

Use the Internet to obtain pricing information on hardware and software for an office of 30 people. You will need to price 30 PC desktop systems (monitors, computers, and keyboards) manufactured by Lenovo, Dell, and HP/Compaq. (For the purposes of this exercise, ignore the fact that desktop systems usually come with preloaded software packages.) Obtain pricing on 15 desktop printers manufactured by HP, Canon, and Dell.

Each desktop system must satisfy the minimum specifications shown in tables which you can find in MyMISLab. Also obtain pricing on 30 copies of the most recent versions of Microsoft Office, Lotus SmartSuite, and Oracle OpenOffice, and on 30 copies of Microsoft Windows 7 Professional. Each desktop productivity package should contain programs for word processing, spreadsheets, database, and presentations. Prepare a spreadsheet showing your research results for the software and the desktop system, printer, and software combination offering the best performance and pricing per worker. Because every two workers share one printer (15 printers/30 systems), your calculations should assume only half a printer cost per worker.

IMPROVING DECISION MAKING: USING WEB RESEARCH TO BUDGET FOR A SALES CONFERENCE

Software skills: Internet-based software
Business skills: Researching transportation and lodging costs

In this exercise, you'll use software at various online travel sites to obtain pricing for total travel and lodging costs for a sales conference.

The Foremost Composite Materials Company is planning a two-day sales conference for October 19–20, starting with a reception on the evening of October 18. The conference consists of all-day meetings that the entire sales force, numbering 125 sales representatives and their 16 managers, must attend. Each sales representative requires his or her own room, and the company needs two common meeting rooms, one large enough to hold the entire sales force plus a few visitors (200 total) and the other able to hold half the force. Management has set a budget of $135,000 for the representatives' room rentals. The company would like to hold the conference in either Miami or Marco Island, Florida, at a Hilton- or Marriott-owned hotel.

Use the Hilton and Marriott Web sites to select a hotel in whichever of these cities that would enable the company to hold its sales conference within its budget and meet its sales conference requirements. Then locate flights arriving the afternoon prior to the conference. Your attendees will be coming from Los Angeles (54), San Francisco (32), Seattle (22), Chicago (19), and Pittsburgh (14). Determine costs of each airline ticket from these cities. When you are finished, create a budget for the conference. The budget will include the cost of each airline ticket, the room cost, and $60 per attendee per day for food.

Video Cases

Video Cases and Instructional Videos illustrating some of the concepts in this chapter are available. Contact your instructor to access these videos.

Collaboration and Teamwork

Evaluating Server and Mobile Operating Systems

Form a group with three or four of your classmates. Choose server or mobile operating systems to evaluate. You might research and compare the capabilities and costs of Linux versus UNIX or the most recent version of the Windows operating system for servers. Alternatively, you could compare the capabilities of the Android mobile operating system with the Symbian operating system or either of these with the most recent version of the iPhone operating system ((iOS). If possible, use Google Sites to post links to Web pages, team communication announcements, and work assignments; to brainstorm; and to work collaboratively on project documents. Try to use Google Docs to develop a presentation of your findings for the class.

BUSINESS PROBLEM-SOLVING CASE

Should Businesses Move to the Cloud?

Cloud computing has just begun to take off in the business world. The biggest player in the cloud computing marketplace is one you might not expect: Amazon. Under its Web Services (AWS) division, the company has streamlined cloud computing and made it an affordable and sensible option for companies ranging from Internet start-ups like Zynga to established companies like FedEx.

AWS provides subscribing companies with flexible computing power and data storage, as well as data management, messaging, payment, and other services that can be used together or individually as the business requires. Anyone with an Internet connection and a little bit of money can harness the same computing systems that Amazon itself uses to run its $34 billion a year retail business.

Since its launch in March 2006, AWS has continued to grow in popularity, with $750 million in business in 2011 and hundreds of thousands of customers. In fact, Amazon believes that Amazon Web Services will someday become more valuable than its vaunted retail operation. Amazon's sales pitch is that you don't pay a monthly or yearly fee to use their computing resources—instead, you pay for exactly what you use. For many businesses, this is an appealing proposition, because it allows Amazon to handle all of the maintenance and upkeep of IT infrastructures, leaving businesses to spend more time on higher-value work.

Many companies have struggled to handle huge amounts of data required to run their businesses. Web companies used to build dozens of data centers, often up to a half a billion dollars in cost per center. Leading cloud companies such as Amazon, Google, and Microsoft have built software that uses automated methods to spread data across the globe and control thousands of servers, and they have refined data center designs with the goal of increasing efficiency. Now, more than ever, companies are turning to cloud computing providers like these for their computing resources.

Zynga is a good example of a company using cloud computing to improve its business in a new way. Zynga is the developer of the wildly popular Facebook applications FarmVille, Mafia Wars, and many others. With over 280 million monthly active users, Zynga's computing demands are already significant. When Zynga releases a new game, however, it has no way of knowing what amount of computing resources to dedicate to the game. The game might be a mild success, or a smash hit that adds millions of new users. The ability to design applications that can scale up quickly in the number of users is one of Zynga's competitive advantages.

Because of the uncertainty surrounding resource usage for new game launches, Zynga has used Amazon's cloud computing platform to launch new offerings. That way, it pays only for the resources it ends up using, and once game traffic stabilizes and reaches a steady number of users, Zynga moves the game onto its private Z Cloud which is structurally similar to Amazon's cloud, but operates under Zynga's control. This is a twist on the traditional approach of running most of the computing load in-house, and offloading the remainder to a public cloud.

There are a few reasons why Zynga is uniquely suited to use this combination of public and private clouds. The first is its business model, which involves games that have a tendency to be boom-or-bust. Rather than spending on computing resources of its own before the launch of each game, it's much more cost-effective to use Amazon's cloud services until Zynga can more accurately predict the computing power it needs. As a recent start-up, Zynga lacks the accumulated legacy systems and infrastructure typically found in older companies. The more systems a company has, the tougher it is to integrate its applications and data with cloud systems.

When Zynga released its most recent offering, CityVille, it brought in 20 million additional users very quickly, and eventually stabilized at 90 million active users per month. After CityVille's user base stabilized, Zynga moved CityVille's computing resources from Amazon's cloud to its own Z Cloud, which exists in data centers on the East and West coasts. Zynga leases space in these data centers and installs its own servers and software. To streamline the process of moving application data from Amazon to the Z Cloud, Zynga has automated many computing tasks, selecting hardware and chip configurations that are very similar to Amazon's, and making significant use of virtualization.

Although the consequences for server downtime are not as catastrophic for Zynga as they would be for a financial services firm, Zynga still needs 99.9 percent uptime. On its own financial reports, Zynga states that "A significant majority of our game traffic is hosted by a single vendor and any failure or significant interruption in our network could impact our operations and harm our business." Whether Zynga will migrate fully to its own private cloud or its own infrastructure, and move away from Amazon Web Services, is an open issue. In its initial public offering (IPO) document, Zynga said that one of its risk factors is its dependence on Amazon Web Services, which had an outage for several hours in April that made it impossible for users to log into some of Zynga's games.

However, owning data centers also comes with risks. If the demand for Zynga's games were to drop dramatically, as has happened on occasion, Zynga would have too much IT infrastructure on its hands and losses could result. The most likely scenario has Zynga owning part of its data centers and relying on external services such as Amazon for the rest.

InterContinental Hotels has revamped its infrastructure to include both private and public cloud usage. To improve response time for customers, InterContinental moved its core room reservation transaction system onto a private cloud within its own data center, but it moved room availability and pricing Web site applications onto public cloud data centers on the East and West coasts. In fact, InterContinental hopes to put all of its publicly accessible information in these public clouds so that customers receive faster results to site queries. Customers receive data faster if the data are located on a server that is physically close to them, and cloud computing helps InterContinental take advantage of this.

Start-up companies and smaller companies are finding that they no longer need to build a data center. With cloud infrastructures like Amazon's readily available, they have access to technical capability that was formerly only available to much larger businesses. For example, online crafts marketplace Etsy uses Amazon computers to analyze data from the 1 billion monthly views of its Web site. Etsy can then use its findings to create product recommendation systems that allow customers to rank which products they like best and to generate a list of 100 products they might enjoy. Etsy's engineers and managers are both excited about their ability to handle these types of issues on someone else's computer systems.

IBM, Cisco, and other traditional data center giants realize that cloud computing is a threat to their technology infrastructure business. As a solution to rising computing costs, they have been steering their customers toward virtualization software, which allows them to run many more applications on each individual server that they buy. There are also many companies that simply have too much legacy technology to use the cloud effectively. For example, Credit Suisse has 7,000 software applications running on their systems that they have developed over the past 20 years. Ensuring that all of these applications would work the same way in the cloud would be more trouble than it's worth.

Many other companies share Zynga's concern about cloud reliability and security, and this remains a major barrier to widespread cloud adoption. Amazon's cloud experienced significant outages in April and August 2011. Normally, cloud networks are very reliable, and often more so than private networks operated by individual companies. But when a cloud of significant size like Amazon's goes down, it sends ripples across the entire Web.

According to Amazon, a simple network configuration error caused a major multiday service outage in Amazon's East coast region from April 21–24, 2011. Amazingly, the error was most likely a simple error made by a human being during a routine network adjustment. Sites affected included Reddit, Foursquare, Engine Yard, Hootsuite, Quora, Zynga, and many more. Amazon's East coast data center was performing adjustments to prepare for the next morning's activity, where many customers refresh their sites with new content for the next day. Due to the manual error, many pieces of data on Amazon's systems lost contact with their backed-up copies elsewhere on the cloud. Amazon's automated procedures specified that new backups be created, but the total size of the data that lost its connection to its backup was too large. The resulting incident is known as a "mirroring storm", as thousands of volumes of data tried and failed to find new disk space on the cloud to re-create backups. In reality, none of the data was actually lost—the system only thought that it was lost, and that triggered the mirroring storm. In the August 8 outage, cloud services from both Amazon and Microsoft were disrupted after a lightning strike crippled power supplies to their data centers in Dublin, affecting sites mainly in Europe.

The outages were proof that the vision of a cloud with 100 percent uptime is still far from reality. Amazon was praised for its handling of the April outage, compiling a 5,700-word document describing exactly what happened and the series of events leading to the crisis and issuing a credit to customers and a pledge to improve their communications.

Still, cloud computing has finally gone mainstream, and the major cloud providers have the sales numbers to prove it. Amazon, Microsoft, Google, and other cloud providers will have to continue to work to avoid outages, and other companies must decide whether the cloud is right for them, and if so, how to most effectively use the cloud to enhance their businesses.

Sources: Dean Takahashi, " Zynga Planning to Diversify Beyond Amazon, Build Its Own Data Centers,"GamesBeat, July 4, 2011; Charles Babcock, "4 Companies Getting Real Results from Cloud Computing." *Information Week*, January 15, 2011; Ashlee Vance, "The Cloud: Battle of the Tech Titans." *Bloomberg Business Week* (March 3, 2011); Peter Svensson, "Amazon Failure Takes Down Sites Across Internet," Associated Press, April 21, 2011; Steve Lohr, "Amazon's Trouble Raises Cloud Computing Doubts," *New York Time*s, April 22, 2011; Thomas Claburn, "Amazon Web Services Apologizes, Explains Outage," *Information Week*, April 29, 2011; Charles Babcock. "Post Mortem: When Amazon's Cloud Turned on Itself," Information Week, April 29, 2011; Patrick Thibodeau, "Amazon Cloud Outage Was Triggered by Configuration Error, "Computerworld, April 29, 2011; Charles Babcock. "Zynga's Unusual Cloud Strategy is Key To Success," *Information Week*, July 1, 2011.

Case Study Questions

1. What business benefits do cloud computing services provide? What problems do they solve?
2. What are the disadvantages of cloud computing?
3. How do the concepts of capacity planning, scalability, and TCO apply to this case? Apply these concepts both to Amazon and to subscribers of its services.
4. What kinds of businesses are most likely to benefit from using cloud computing? Why?

Foundations of Business Intelligence: Databases and Information Management

CHAPTER 5

STUDENT LEARNING OBJECTIVES

After completing this chapter, you will be able to answer the following questions:

1. How does a relational database organize data, and how does it differ from an object-oriented database?

2. What are the principles of a database management system?

3. What are the principal tools and technologies for accessing information from databases to improve business performance and decision making?

4. What is the role of information policy and data administration in the management of organizational data resources?

5. Why is data quality assurance so important for a business?

Chapter Outline

BANCO DE CREDITO DEL PERU BANKS ON BETTER DATA MANAGEMENT

Banco de Crédito del Perú (BCP) is Peru's largest commercial bank and also offers investment and retail banking services, including bank accounts, insurance policies, credit cards, mortgage loans, mutual funds, and mobile banking services. With 326 offices in Panama, Miami, and Bolivia, BCP employs 15,000 people and generated US $425 million in net income in 2010. Running this firm obviously requires many different pieces of information.

Although BCP has grown and prospered, its business performance had been hampered by outdated information systems that made it difficult to use data efficiently for operational activities and reporting. Over time, different BCP departments had acquired a large number of applications to support processes in administration, human resources, and accounting that were not integrated. These isolated systems were very time-consuming and expensive to update and use. Each kept track of many different pieces of data. The same piece of data, such as customer name, might be found in multiple systems, but use different spellings or formats or be updated at different times.

Accessing the data from these multiple systems was a complicated undertaking, severely hindering reporting procedures and delaying business decision making.

© Andrey Prokhorov, 2011, iStockPhoto LP.

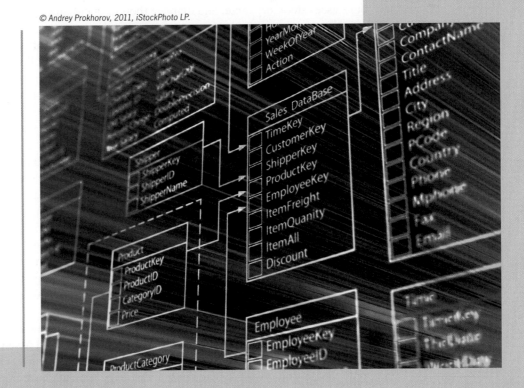

BCP's information systems staff was collecting data from 15 to 16 satellite applications and Microsoft Excel spreadsheets before manually collating and analyzing the data in response to simple queries from managers. The fact that the data were not always accurate and consistent added an extra layer of uncertainty and complexity to any reports that were prepared.

What BCP needed was a single repository for business information that would support a more streamlined set of business applications. The bank decided to replace its legacy systems with an integrated software suite from SAP that included modules for enterprise resource planning (ERP) and a data warehouse supporting enterprise-wide reporting. BCP implemented IBM's DB2 version 9 database management system for Linux, UNIX and Windows to replace its older systems for managing data. DB2 organizes data so that they appear to come from a single source, enabling individual business applications to extract the data they need without having to create separate data files for each application. All of this software runs on IBM Power 595, IBM BladeCenter JS43, and IBM Power 570 servers running the AIX operating system, IBM's version of UNIX.

Combining IBM DB2 and SAP NetWeaver Business Warehouse technology has given Banco de Crédito del Perú comprehensive data management capabilities. The warehouse includes tools for analyzing the data along multiple dimensions. The bank's key decision makers can use real-time enterprise-wide data to keep track of company performance and capitalize on opportunities immediately, boosting responsiveness and agility. Sophisticated business analytics and modeling tools are available.

The new solution has also produced significant cost savings at BCP in terms of data management and storage, while boosting performance. With fewer systems and data files to manage, BCP cut its data management costs in half and lowered data storage costs by 45 percent.

Sources: IBM, "Banco de Crédito del Peru Vaults over the Competition with Help from IBM and SAP," January 20, 2011 and "Banco Credito Del Peru C," www.investing.businessweek.com, accessed April 19, 2011.

The experience of Banco de Crédito del Perú illustrates the importance of data management. Business performance depends on what a firm can or cannot do with its data. The bank had grown its business, but both operational efficiency and management decision making were hampered by fragmented data stored in outdated systems that were difficult to access. How businesses store, organize, and manage their data has an enormous impact on organizational effectiveness.

The chapter-opening diagram calls attention to important points raised by this case and this chapter. Banco de Crédito del Perú's management decided that the firm needed to improve the management of its data. Pieces of data about customers, accounts, and employees had been stored in a bewildering number of systems that made it extremely difficult for the data to be retrieved and analyzed. The data were often redundant and inconsistent, limiting their usefulness. Management was unable to obtain an enterprise-wide view of the company.

In the past, Banco de Crédito del Perú had heavily used manual paper processes to reconcile its inconsistent and redundant data and to assemble data for management reporting. This solution was extremely time-consuming and costly and prevented the bank's information technology department from performing higher-value work. A more appropriate solution was to install new hardware and software to create an enterprise-wide repository for business information that would support a more streamlined set of business applications. Enterprise software was integrated with an up-to-date database management system and a data warehouse that could supply data for enterprise-wide reporting. The bank had to reorganize its data into a standard company-wide format, eliminate redundancies, and establish rules, responsibilities, and procedures for updating and using the data.

A modern database management system and data warehouse helps Banco de Crédito del Perú boost efficiency by making it easier to locate and assemble data for management reporting and for processing day-to-day financial transactions. The data are more accurate and reliable, and costs for managing and storing the data have been reduced considerably.

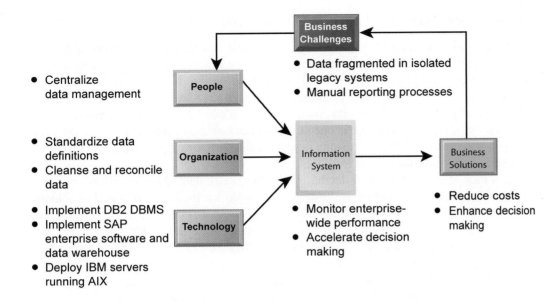

5.1 The Database Approach to Data Management

A **database** is a collection of related files containing records on people, places, or things. One of the most successful databases in modern history is the telephone book. The telephone book is a collection of records on people and businesses who use telephones. The telephone book lists four pieces of information for each phone user: last name, first name, address, and phone number. It also contains information on businesses and business categories, such as auto dealers or plumbing suppliers. The telephone book draws its information from a database with files for customers, business classifications, and area codes and geographic regions.

Prior to the development of digital databases, a business would use large filing cabinets filled with paper files to store information on transactions, customers, suppliers, inventory, and employees. They would also use lists, laboriously collated and typed by hand, to quickly summarize the information in paper files. You can still find paper-based manual databases in most doctors' offices where patient records are stored in thousands of paper files.

Needless to say, paper-based databases are extremely inefficient and costly to maintain, often contain inaccurate data, are slow, and make it difficult to access the data in a timely fashion. Paper-based databases are also extremely inflexible. For instance, it would be nearly impossible for a paper-based doctor's office to combine its files on prescriptions with its files on patients in order to produce a list of all people for whom they had prescribed a specific drug. For a modern computer database, this would be very easy. In fact, a powerful feature of computer databases is the ability to quickly relate one set of files to another.

ENTITIES AND ATTRIBUTES

How do you start thinking about the data for your business and how to manage them? The first step is to identify the data you will need to run your business. Typically, you will be using data on categories of information, such as customers, suppliers, employees, orders, products, shippers, and perhaps parts. Each of these generalized categories representing a person, place, or thing on which we store and maintain information is called an **entity**. Each entity has specific characteristics, called **attributes**. For example, the entity SUPPLIER has specific attributes, such as the supplier's name and address, which would most likely include street, city, state, and zip code. The entity PART typically has attributes such as part description, price of each part (unit price), and supplier who produced the part.

ORGANIZING DATA IN A RELATIONAL DATABASE

If you stored this information in paper files, you would probably have a file on each entity and its attributes. In an information system, a database organizes the data much the same way, grouping related pieces of data together. The **relational database** is the most common type of database today. Relational databases organize data into two-dimensional tables (called *relations*) with columns and rows. Each table contains data on an entity and its attributes. For the most part, there is one table for each business entity. So, at the most basic level, you will have one table for customers, and a table each for suppliers, parts in inventory, employees, and sales transactions.

Let's look at how a relational database would organize data about suppliers and parts. Take the SUPPLIER table, which is illustrated in Figure 5.1. It consists of a grid of columns and rows of data. Each individual element of data about a supplier, such as the supplier name, street, city, state, and zip code, is stored as a separate **field** within the SUPPLIER table. Each field represents an attribute for the entity SUPPLIER. Fields in a relational database are also called *columns*.

The actual information about a single supplier that resides in a table is called a *row*. Rows are commonly referred to as **records**, or, in very technical terms, as **tuples**.

Note that there is a field for Supplier_Number in this table. This field uniquely identifies each record so that the record can be retrieved, updated, or sorted, and it is called a **key field**. Each table in a relational database has one field designated as its **primary key**. This key field is the unique identifier for all the information in any row of the table, and this primary key cannot be duplicated.

We could use the supplier's name as a key field. However, if two different suppliers had the same name (which does happen from time to time), supplier name would not uniquely identify each, so it is necessary to assign a special identifier field for this purpose. For example, if you had two suppliers, both named "CBM," but one was based in Dayton and another in St. Louis, it would be easy to confuse them. However, if each has a unique supplier number, such confusion is prevented.

We also see that the address information has been separated into four separate fields: Supplier_Street, Supplier_City, Supplier_State, and Supplier_Zip. Data are separated into the smallest elements that one would want to access separately to make it easy to select only the rows in the table that match the contents of one field, such as all the suppliers in Ohio (OH). The rows of data can also be sorted by the contents of the Supplier_State field to get a list of suppliers by state regardless of their cities.

So far, the SUPPLIER table does not have any information about the parts that a particular supplier provides for your company. PART is a separate entity from SUPPLIER, and fields with information about parts should be stored in a separate PART table (see Figure 5.2).

Figure 5.1
A Relational Database Table
A relational database organizes data in the form of two-dimensional tables. Illustrated here is a table for the entity SUPPLIER showing how it represents the entity and its attributes. Supplier_Number is the key field.

SUPPLIER   Columns (Attributes, Fields)

Supplier_Number	Supplier_Name	Supplier_Street	Supplier_City	Supplier_State	Supplier_Zip
8259	CBM Inc.	74 5th Avenue	Dayton	OH	45220
8261	B. R. Molds	1277 Gandolly Street	Cleveland	OH	49345
8263	Jackson Composites	8233 Micklin Street	Lexington	KY	56723
8444	Bryant Corporation	4315 Mill Drive	Rochester	NY	11344

Rows (Records, Tuples)

Key Field (Primary Key)

PART

Part_Number	Part_Name	Unit_Price	Supplier_Number
137	Door latch	22.00	8259
145	Side mirror	12.00	8444
150	Door molding	6.00	8263
152	Door lock	31.00	8259
155	Compressor	54.00	8261
178	Door handle	10.00	8259

Primary Key   Foreign Key

Figure 5.2
The PART Table
Data for the entity PART have their own separate table. Part_Number is the primary key and Supplier_Number is the foreign key, enabling users to find related information from the SUPPLIER table about the supplier for each part.

Why not keep information on parts in the same table as suppliers? If we did that, each row of the table would contain the attributes of both PART and SUPPLIER. Because one supplier could supply more than one part, the table would need many extra rows for a single supplier to show all the parts that supplier provided. We would be maintaining a great deal of redundant data about suppliers, and it would be difficult to search for the information on any individual part because you would not know whether this part is the first or fiftieth part in this supplier's record. A separate table, PART, should be created to store these three fields and solve this problem.

The PART table would also have to contain another field, Supplier_Number, so that you would know the supplier for each part. It would not be necessary to keep repeating all the information about a supplier in each PART record because having a Supplier_ Number field in the PART table allows you to "look up" the data in the fields of the SUPPLIER table.

Notice that Supplier_Number appears in both the SUPPLIER and PART tables. In the SUPPLIER table, Supplier_Number is the primary key. When the field Supplier_Number appears in the PART table it is called a **foreign key** and is essentially a look-up field to find data about the supplier of a specific part. Note that the PART table would itself have its own primary key field, Part_Number, to uniquely identify each part. This key is not used to link PART with SUPPLIER but might be used to link PART with a different entity.

As we organize data into tables, it is important to make sure that all the attributes for a particular entity apply only to that entity. If you were to keep the supplier's address with the PART record, that information would not really relate only to PART; it would relate to both PART and SUPPLIER. If the supplier's address were to change, it would be necessary to alter the data in every PART record rather than only once in the SUPPLIER record.

ESTABLISHING RELATIONSHIPS

Now that we've broken down our data into a SUPPLIER table and a PART table, we must make sure we understand the relationship between them. A schematic called an **entity-relationship diagram** is used to clarify table relationships in a relational database. The most important piece of information provided by an entity-relationship diagram is the manner in which two tables are related to each other. Tables in a relational database may have one-to-one, one-to-many, and many-to-many relationships.

An example of a one-to-one relationship might be a situation where a human resources system must store confidential data about employees. It might store data, such as the employee name, date of birth, address, and job position in one table, and confidential data

Figure 5.3
A Simple Entity-Relationship Diagram
This diagram shows the relationship between the entities SUPPLIER and PART.

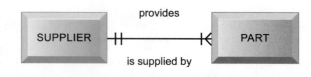

about that employee, such as salary or pension benefits, in another table. These two tables pertaining to a single employee would have a one-to-one relationship because each record in the EMPLOYEE table with basic employee data has only one related record in the table storing confidential data.

The relationship between the SUPPLIER and PART entities in our database is a one-to-many relationship: Each supplier can supply more that one part, but each part has only one supplier. For every record in the SUPPLIER table, there may be many related records in the PART table.

Figure 5.3 illustrates how an entity-relationship diagram would depict this one-to-many relationship. The boxes represent entities. The lines connecting the boxes represent relationships. A line connecting two entities that ends in two short marks designates a one-to-one relationship. A line connecting two entities that ends with a crow's foot preceded by a short mark indicates a one-to-many relationship. Figure 5.3 shows that each part has only one supplier, but many parts can be provided by the same supplier.

We would also see a one-to-many relationship if we wanted to add a table about orders to our database because one supplier services many orders. The ORDER table would contain only the Order_Number and Order_Date fields. Figure 5.4 illustrates a report showing an order of parts from a supplier. If you look at the report, you can see that the information on the top-right portion of the report comes from the ORDER table. The actual line items ordered are listed in the lower portion of the report.

Because one order can be for many parts from a supplier, and a single part can be ordered many times on different orders, this creates a many-to-many relationship between the PART and ORDER tables. Whenever a many-to-many relationship exists between two tables, it is necessary to link these two tables in a table that joins this information. Creating a separate table for a line item in the order would serve this purpose. This table is often called a *join table* or an *intersection relation*. This join table contains only three fields: Order_Number and Part_Number, which are used only to link the ORDER and PART tables, and Part_Quantity.

Figure 5.4
Sample Order Report
The shaded areas show which data came from the ORDER, SUPPLIER, and LINE_ITEM tables. The database does not maintain data on extended price or order total because they can be derived from other data in the tables.

Order Number: 3502
Order Date: 1/15/2012

Supplier Number: 8259
Supplier Name: CBM Inc.
Supplier Address: 74 5th Avenue, Dayton, OH 45220

Order_Number	Part_Number	Part_Quantity	Part_Name	Unit_Price	Extended Price
3502	137	10	Door latch	22.00	$220.00
3502	152	20	Door lock	31.00	620.00
3502	178	5	Door handle	10.00	50.00
			Order Total:		$890.00

If you look at the bottom-left part of the report, this is the information coming from the LINE_ITEM table.

We would thus wind up with a total of four tables in our database. Figure 5.5 illustrates the final set of tables, and Figure 5.6 shows what the entity-relationship diagram for this set of tables would look like. Note that the ORDER table does not contain data on the extended price because that value can be calculated by multiplying Unit_Price by Part_Quantity. This data element can be derived when needed using information that already exists in the PART and LINE_ITEM tables. Order_Total is another derived field calculated by totaling the extended prices for items ordered.

The process of streamlining complex groups of data to minimize redundant data elements and awkward many-to-many relationships, and increase stability and flexibility is called **normalization.** A properly designed and normalized database is easy to maintain, and minimizes duplicate data. The Learning Tracks at the end of this chapter direct you to more detailed discussions of database design, normalization, and entity-relationship diagramming in MyMISLab.

Relational database systems enforce **referential integrity** rules to ensure that relationships between coupled tables remain consistent. When one table has a foreign key that points to another table, you may not add a record to the table with the foreign key unless there is a corresponding record in the linked table. In the database we have just created, the foreign key Supplier_Number links the PART table to the SUPPLIER table. We may not add a new record to the PART table for a part with supplier number 8266 unless there is a corresponding record in the SUPPLIER table for supplier number 8266. We must also delete the corresponding record in the PART table if we delete the record in the SUPPLIER table for supplier number 8266. In other words, we shouldn't have parts from nonexistent suppliers!

The example provided here for parts, orders, and suppliers is a simple one. Even in a very small business, you will have tables for other important entities, such as customers, shippers, and employees. A very large corporation might have databases with thousands of entities (tables) to maintain. What is important for any business, large or small, is to have a good data model that includes all of its entities and the relationships among them, one that is organized to minimize redundancy, maximize accuracy, and make data easily accessible for reporting and analysis.

It cannot be emphasized enough: If the business does not get its data model right, the system will not be able to serve the business properly. The company's systems will not be as effective as they could be because they will have to work with data that may be inaccurate, incomplete, or difficult to retrieve. Understanding the organization's data and how they should be represented in a database is perhaps the most important lesson you can learn from this course.

For example, Famous Footwear, a shoe store chain with more than 1100 locations in 49 states, could not achieve its goal of having "the right style of shoe in the right store for sale at the right price" because its database was not properly designed for a rapidly adjusting store inventory. The company had an Oracle relational database running on an IBM AS/400 midrange computer, but the database was designed primarily for producing standard reports for management rather than for reacting to marketplace changes. Management could not obtain precise data on specific items in inventory in each of its stores. The company had to work around this problem by building a new database where the sales and inventory data could be better organized for analysis and inventory management.

5.2 Database Management Systems

Now that you have started creating the files and identifying the data required by your business, you will need a database management system to help you manage and use the data. A **database management system (DBMS)** is a specific type of software for creating, storing, organizing, and accessing data from a database. Microsoft Access is a DBMS for desktop systems, whereas DB2, Oracle Database, and Microsoft SQL Server are DBMS

PART

Part_Number	Part_Name	Unit_Price	Supplier_Number
137	Door latch	22.00	8259
145	Side mirror	12.00	8444
150	Door molding	6.00	8263
152	Door lock	31.00	8259
155	Compressor	54.00	8261
178	Door handle	10.00	8259

LINE_ITEM

Order_Number	Part_Number	Part_Quantity
3502	137	10
3502	152	20
3502	178	5

ORDER

Order_Number	Order_Date
3502	1/15/2012
3503	1/16/2012
3504	1/17/2012

SUPPLIER

Supplier_Number	Supplier_Name	Supplier_Street	Supplier_City	Supplier_State	Supplier_Zip
8259	CBM Inc.	74 5th Avenue	Dayton	OH	45220
8261	B. R. Molds	1277 Gandolly Street	Cleveland	OH	49345
8263	Jackson Components	8233 Micklin Street	Lexington	KY	56723
8444	Bryant Corporation	4315 Mill Drive	Rochester	NY	11344

Figure 5.5
The Final Database Design with Sample Records
The final design of the database for suppliers, parts, and orders has four tables. The LINE_ITEM table is a join table that eliminates the many-to-many relationship between ORDER and PART.

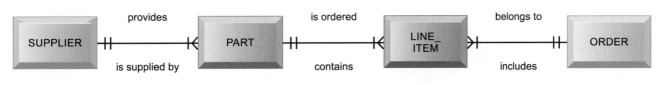

Figure 5.6
Entity-Relationship Diagram for the Database with Four Tables
This diagram shows the relationship between the entities SUPPLIER, PART, LINE_ITEM, and ORDER.

for large mainframes and midrange computers. MySQL is a popular open-source DBMS, and Oracle Database Lite is a DBMS for small handheld computing devices. All of these products are relational DBMS that support a relational database.

The DBMS relieves the end user or programmer from the task of understanding where and how the data are actually stored by separating the logical and physical views of the data. The *logical view* presents data as end users or business specialists would perceive them, whereas the *physical view* shows how data are actually organized and structured on physical storage media, such as a hard disk.

The database management software makes the physical database available for different logical views required by users. For example, for the human resources database illustrated in Figure 5.7, a benefits specialist might require a view consisting of the employee's name, social security number, and health insurance coverage. A payroll department member might need data such as the employee's name, social security number, gross pay, and net pay. The data for all of these views is stored in a single database, where it can be more easily managed by the organization.

OPERATIONS OF A RELATIONAL DBMS

In a relational database, tables can be easily combined to deliver data required by users, provided that any two tables share a common data element. Let's return to the database we set up earlier with PART and SUPPLIER tables illustrated in Figures 5.1 and 5.2.

Suppose we wanted to find in this database the names of suppliers who could provide us with part number 137 or part number 150. We would need information from two tables: the SUPPLIER table and the PART table. Note that these two tables have a shared data element: Supplier_Number.

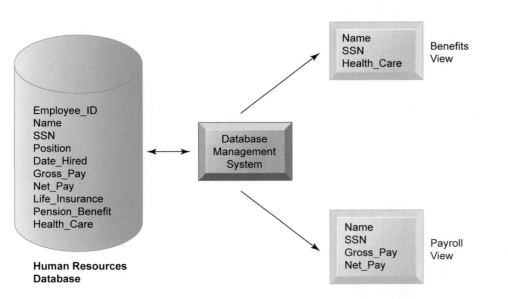

Figure 5.7
Human Resources Database with Multiple Views
A single human resources database provides many different views of data, depending on the information requirements of the user. Illustrated here are two possible views, one of interest to a benefits specialist and one of interest to a member of the company's payroll department.

PART

Part_Number	Part_Name	Unit_Price	Supplier_Number
137	Door latch	22.00	8259
145	Side mirror	12.00	8444
150	Door molding	6.00	8263
152	Door lock	31.00	8259
155	Compressor	54.00	8261
178	Door handle	10.00	8259

Select Part_Number = 137 or 150

SUPPLIER

Supplier_Number	Supplier_Name	Supplier_Street	Supplier_City	Supplier_State	Supplier_Zip
8259	CBM Inc.	74 5th Avenue	Dayton	OH	45220
8261	B. R. Molds	1277 Gandolly Street	Cleveland	OH	49345
8263	Jackson Components	8233 Micklin Street	Lexington	KY	56723
8444	Bryant Corporation	4315 Mill Drive	Rochester	NY	11344

Join by Supplier_Number

Part_Number	Part_Name	Supplier_Number	Supplier_Name
137	Door latch	8259	CBM Inc.
150	Door molding	8263	Jackson Components

Project selected columns

Figure 5.8
The Three Basic Operations of a Relational DBMS
The select, join, and project operations enable data from two different tables to be combined and only selected attributes to be displayed.

In a relational database, three basic operations, as shown in Figure 5.8, are used to develop useful sets of data: select, project, and join. The *select* operation creates a subset consisting of all records in the file that meet stated criteria. Select creates, in other words, a subset of rows that meet certain criteria. In our example, we want to select records (rows) from the PART table where the Part_Number equals 137 or 150. The *join* operation combines relational tables to provide the user with more information than is available in individual tables. In our example, we want to join the now-shortened PART table (only parts 137 or 150 will be presented) and the SUPPLIER table into a single new table.

The *project* operation creates a subset consisting of columns in a table, permitting the user to create new tables that contain only the information required. In our example, we want to extract from the new table only the following columns: Part_Number, Part_Name, Supplier_Number, and Supplier_Name (see Figure 5.8).

CAPABILITIES OF DATABASE MANAGEMENT SYSTEMS

A DBMS includes capabilities and tools for organizing, managing, and accessing the data in the database. The most important are its data definition capability, data dictionary, and data manipulation language.

DBMS have a **data definition** capability to specify the structure of the content of the database. It would be used to create database tables and to define the characteristics of the fields in each table. This information about the database would be documented in a **data dictionary**. A data dictionary is an automated or manual file that stores definitions of data elements and their characteristics. Microsoft Access has a rudimentary data dictionary capability that displays information about the name, description, size, type, format, and other properties of each field in a table (see Figure 5.9). Data dictionaries for large corporate databases may capture additional information, such as usage, ownership (who in the organization is responsible for maintaining the data), authorization, security, and the individuals, business functions, programs, and reports that use each data element.

Querying and Reporting

DBMS include tools for accessing and manipulating information in databases. Most DBMS have a specialized language called a **data manipulation language** that is used to add, change, delete, and retrieve the data in the database. This language contains commands that permit end users and programming specialists to extract data from the database to satisfy information requests and develop applications. The most prominent data manipulation

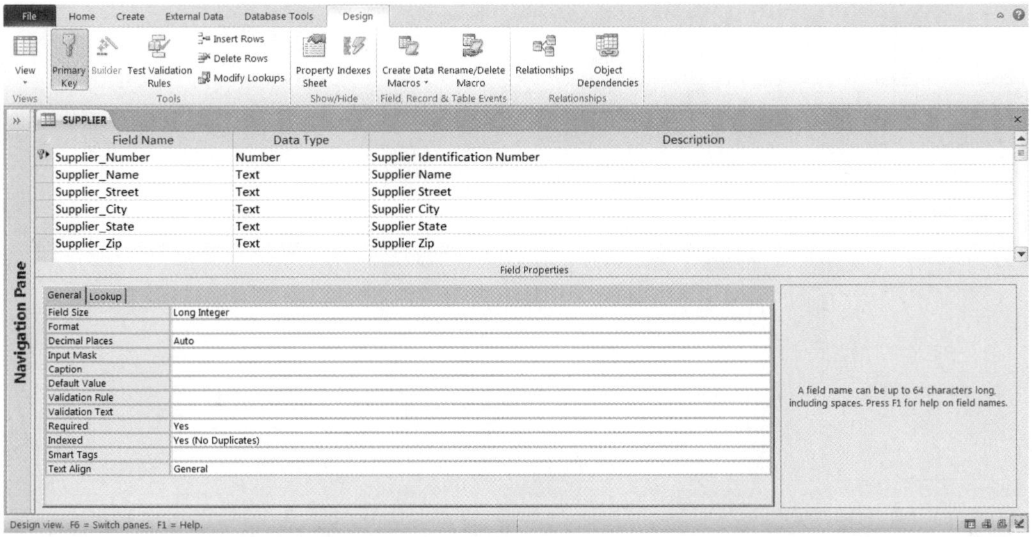

Figure 5.9
Access Data Dictionary Features
Microsoft Access has a rudimentary data dictionary capability that displays information about the size, format, and other characteristics of each field in a database. Displayed here is the information maintained in the SUPPLIER table. The small key icon to the left of Supplier_Number indicates that it is a key field.

Figure 5.10
Example of a SQL Query
Illustrated here are the SQL statements for a query to select suppliers for parts 137 or 150. They produce a list with the same results as Figure 5.8.

```
SELECT PART.Part_Number, PART.Part_Name, SUPPLIER.Supplier_Number,
SUPPLIER.Supplier_Name
FROM PART, SUPPLIER
WHERE PART.Supplier_Number = SUPPLIER.Supplier_Number AND
Part_Number = 137 OR Part_Number = 150;
```

language today is **Structured Query Language**, or **SQL**. Figure 5.10 illustrates the SQL query that would produce the new resultant table in Figure 5.8. You can find out more about how to perform SQL queries in our Learning Tracks for this chapter, which can be found in MyMISLab.

Users of DBMS for large and midrange computers, such as DB2, Oracle, or SQL Server, would employ SQL to retrieve information they needed from the database. Microsoft Access also uses SQL, but it provides its own set of user-friendly tools for querying databases and for organizing data from databases into more polished reports.

Microsoft Access has capabilities to help users create queries by identifying the tables and fields they want and the results, and then selecting the rows from the database that meet particular criteria. These actions in turn are translated into SQL commands. Figure 5.11 illustrates how the SQL query to select parts and suppliers in Figure 5.10 would be constructed using Microsoft Access.

DBMS typically include capabilities for report generation so that the data of interest can be displayed in a more structured and polished format than would be possible just by querying. Crystal Reports is a popular report generator for large corporate DBMS, although it can also be used with Microsoft Access.

Microsoft Access also has capabilities for developing desktop system applications. These include tools for creating data entry screens, reports, and developing the logic for processing transactions. These capabilities are primarily used by information systems specialists.

OBJECT-ORIENTED DATABASES

Many applications today require databases that can store and retrieve not only structured numbers and characters but also drawings, images, photographs, voice, and full-motion

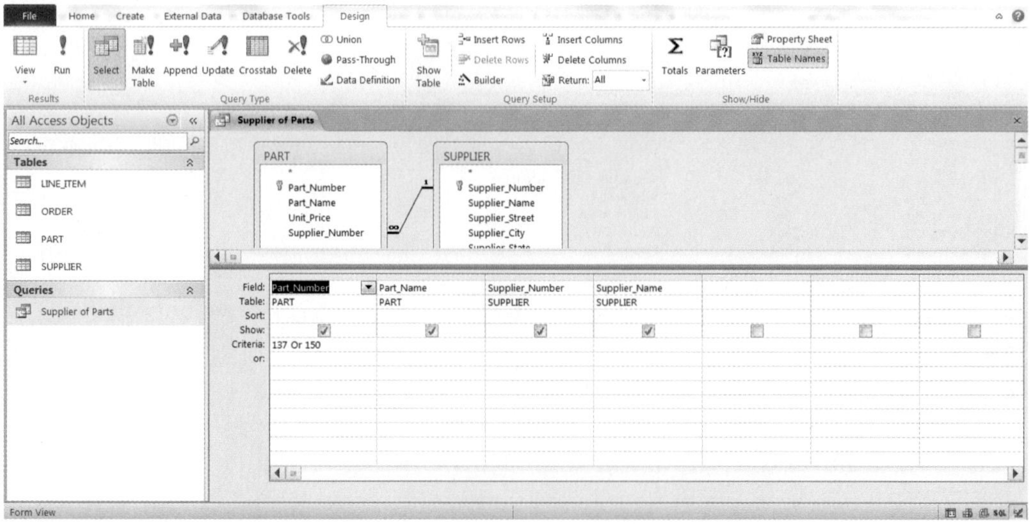

Figure 5.11
An Access Query
Illustrated here is how the query in Figure 5.10 would be constructed using Microsoft Access query-building tools. It shows the tables, fields, and selection criteria used for the query.

video. DBMS designed for organizing structured data into rows and columns are not well suited to handling graphics-based or multimedia applications. Object-oriented databases are better suited for this purpose.

An **object-oriented DBMS** stores the data, and procedures that act on those data, as objects that can be automatically retrieved and shared. Object-oriented database management systems (OODBMS) are becoming popular because they can be used to manage the various multimedia components or Java applets in Web applications, which typically integrate pieces of information from a variety of sources.

Although object-oriented databases can store more complex types of information than relational DBMS, they are relatively slow compared with relational DBMS for processing large numbers of transactions. Hybrid **object-relational DBMS** systems are now available to provide capabilities of both object-oriented and relational DBMS.

DATABASES IN THE CLOUD

Suppose your company wants to use cloud computing services. Is there a way to manage data in the cloud? The answer is a qualified "Yes." Cloud computing providers offer database management services, but these services typically have less functionality than their on-premises counterparts. At the moment, the primary customer base for cloud-based data management consists of Web-focused start-ups or small to medium-size businesses looking for database capabilities at a lower price than a standard relational DBMS.

Amazon Web Services has both a simple non-relational database called SimpleDB and a relational database service. Amazon Relational Database Service (Amazon RDS) offers MySQL or Oracle Database as database engines. Pricing is based on usage. Microsoft SQL Azure Database is a cloud-based relational database service based on Microsoft's SQL Server DBMS hosted by Microsoft in the cloud.

5.3 Using Databases to Improve Business Performance and Decision Making

Businesses use their databases to keep track of basic transactions, such as paying suppliers, processing orders, serving customers, and paying employees. But they also need databases to provide information that will help the company run the business more efficiently, and help managers and employees make better decisions. If a company wants to know which product is the most popular or who is its most profitable customer, the answer lies in the data.

For example, by analyzing data from customer credit card purchases, Louise's Trattoria, a Los Angeles restaurant chain, learned that quality was more important than price for most of its customers, who were college-educated and liked fine wine. Acting on this information, the chain introduced vegetarian dishes, more seafood selections, and more expensive wines, raising sales by more than 10 percent.

In a large company, with large databases or large systems for separate functions, such as manufacturing, sales, and accounting, special capabilities and tools are required for analyzing vast quantities of data and for accessing data from multiple systems. These capabilities include data warehousing, data mining, and tools for accessing internal databases through the Web.

DATA WAREHOUSES

What if you wanted concise, reliable information about current operations, trends, and changes across the entire company? If you worked in a large company, this might be difficult because data are often maintained in separate systems, such as sales, manufacturing, or accounting. Some of the data you needed might be found in the sales system, and other pieces in the manufacturing system. Many of these systems are older legacy systems that use outdated data management technologies or file systems where information is difficult for users to access.

You might have to spend an inordinate amount of time locating and gathering the data you needed, or you would be forced to make your decision based on incomplete knowledge. If you wanted information about trends, you might also have trouble finding data about past events because most firms only make their current data immediately available. Data warehousing addresses these problems.

WHAT IS A DATA WAREHOUSE?

A **data warehouse** is a database that stores current and historical data of potential interest to decision makers throughout the company. The data originate in many core operational transaction systems, such as systems for sales, customer accounts, and manufacturing, and may include data from Web site transactions. The data warehouse consolidates and standardizes information from different operational databases so that the information can be used across the enterprise for management analysis and decision making.

Figure 5.12 illustrates how a data warehouse works. The data warehouse makes the data available for anyone to access as needed, but it cannot be altered. A data warehouse system also provides a range of ad hoc and standardized query tools, analytical tools, and graphical reporting facilities. Many firms use intranet portals to make the data warehouse information widely available throughout the firm.

Catalina Marketing, a global marketing firm for major consumer packaged goods companies and retailers, operates a gigantic data warehouse that includes three years of purchase history for 195 million U.S. customer loyalty program members at supermarkets, pharmacies, and other retailers. It is the largest loyalty database in the world. Catalina's retail store customers analyze this database of customer purchase histories to determine individual customers' buying preferences. When a shopper checks out at the cash register of one of Catalina's retail customers, the purchase is instantly analyzed along with that customer's buying history in the data warehouse to determine what coupons that customer will receive at checkout along with a receipt.

Data Marts

Companies often build enterprise-wide data warehouses, in which a central data warehouse serves the entire organization, or they create smaller, decentralized warehouses called data marts. A **data mart** is a subset of a data warehouse in which a summarized or highly

Figure 5.12
Components of a Data Warehouse
The data warehouse extracts current and historical data from multiple operational systems inside the organization. These data are combined with data from external sources and reorganized into a central database designed for management reporting and analysis. The information directory provides users with information about the data available in the warehouse.

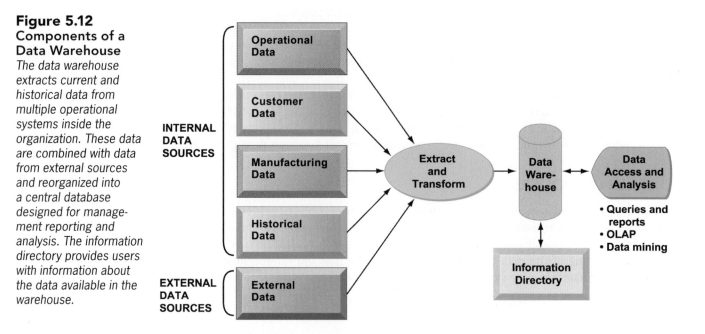

focused portion of the organization's data is placed in a separate database for a specific population of users. For example, a company might develop marketing and sales data marts to deal with customer information. Before implementing an enterprise-wide data warehouse, bookseller Barnes & Noble maintained a series of data marts—one for point-of-sale data in retail stores, another for college bookstore sales, and a third for online sales. A data mart typically focuses on a single subject area or line of business, so it usually can be constructed more rapidly and at lower cost than an enterprise-wide data warehouse.

TOOLS FOR BUSINESS INTELLIGENCE: MULTIDIMENSIONAL DATA ANALYSIS AND DATA MINING

Once data have been captured and organized in data warehouses and data marts, they are available for further analysis using tools for business intelligence, which we introduced briefly in Chapter 2. Business intelligence tools enable users to analyze data to see new patterns, relationships, and insights that are useful for guiding decision making.

Principal tools for business intelligence include software for database querying and reporting, tools for multidimensional data analysis (online analytical processing), and tools for data mining. This section will introduce you to these tools, with more detail about business intelligence analytics and applications in the Chapter 10 discussion of decision making.

Online Analytical Processing (OLAP)

Suppose your company sells four different products—nuts, bolts, washers, and screws—in the East, West, and Central regions. If you wanted to ask a fairly straightforward question, such as how many washers sold during the past quarter, you could easily find the answer by querying your sales database. But what if you wanted to know how many washers sold in each of your sales regions and compare actual results with projected sales?

To obtain the answer, you would need to use **online analytical processing (OLAP)**. OLAP supports multidimensional data analysis, enabling users to view the same data in different ways using multiple dimensions. Each aspect of information—product, pricing, cost, region, or time period—represents a different dimension. So, a product manager could use a multidimensional data analysis tool to learn how many washers were sold in the East in June, how that compares with the previous month and the previous June, and how it compares with the sales forecast. OLAP enables users to obtain online answers to ad hoc questions such as these in a fairly rapid amount of time, even when the data are stored in very large databases, such as sales figures for multiple years.

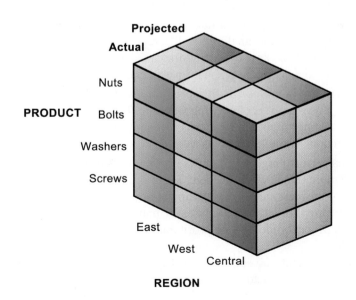

Figure 5.13
Multidimensional Data Model
This view shows product versus region. If you rotate the cube 90 degrees, the face that will show is product versus actual and projected sales. If you rotate the cube 90 degrees again, you will see region versus actual and projected sales. Other views are possible.

Figure 5.13 shows a multidimensional model that could be created to represent products, regions, actual sales, and projected sales. A matrix of actual sales can be stacked on top of a matrix of projected sales to form a cube with six faces.

If you rotate the cube 90 degrees one way, the face showing will be product versus actual and projected sales. If you rotate the cube 90 degrees again, you will see region versus actual and projected sales. If you rotate 180 degrees from the original view, you will see projected sales and product versus region. Cubes can be nested within cubes to build complex views of data. A company would use either a specialized multidimensional database or a tool that creates multidimensional views of data in relational databases.

DATA MINING

Traditional database queries answer such questions as, "How many units of product number 403 were shipped in February 2012?" OLAP, or multidimensional analysis, supports much more complex requests for information, such as, "Compare sales of product 403 relative to plan by quarter and sales region for the past two years." With OLAP and query-oriented data analysis, users need to have a good idea about the information for which they are looking.

Data mining is more discovery driven. Data mining provides insights into corporate data that cannot be obtained with OLAP by finding hidden patterns and relationships in large databases and inferring rules from them to predict future behavior. The patterns and rules are used to guide decision making and forecast the effect of those decisions. The types of information obtainable from data mining include associations, sequences, classifications, clusters, and forecasts.

- *Associations* are occurrences linked to a single event. For instance, a study of supermarket purchasing patterns might reveal that, when corn chips are purchased, a cola drink is purchased 65 percent of the time, but when there is a promotion, cola is purchased 85 percent of the time. This information helps managers make better decisions because they have learned the profitability of a promotion.

- In *sequences*, events are linked over time. We might find, for example, that if a house is purchased, a new refrigerator will be purchased within two weeks 65 percent of the time, and an oven will be bought within one month of the home purchase 45 percent of the time.

- *Classification* recognizes patterns that describe the group to which an item belongs by examining existing items that have been classified and by inferring a set of rules. For example, businesses such as credit card or telephone companies worry about the loss of steady customers. Classification helps discover the characteristics of customers who are likely to leave and can provide a model to help managers predict who those customers are so that the managers can devise special campaigns to retain such customers.

- *Clustering* works in a manner similar to classification when no groups have yet been defined. A data mining tool can discover different groupings within data, such as finding affinity groups for bank cards or partitioning a database into groups of customers based on demographics and types of personal investments.

- Although these applications involve predictions, *forecasting* uses predictions in a different way. It uses a series of existing values to forecast what other values will be. For example, forecasting might find patterns in data to help managers estimate the future value of continuous variables, such as sales figures.

These systems perform high-level analyses of patterns or trends, but they can also drill down to provide more detail when needed. There are data mining applications for all the functional areas of business, and for government and scientific work. One popular use for data mining is to provide detailed analyses of patterns in customer data for one-to-one marketing campaigns or for identifying profitable customers, as described in the Interactive Session on People.

Harrah's Entertainment, the second-largest gambling company in its industry, continually analyzes data about its customers gathered when people play its slot machines or use

INTERACTIVE SESSION: PEOPLE — Asking the Customer by Asking the Database

What's the best way to find out what your customers want? If you're a large business with millions of customers, it's impossible to ask each one face-to-face. But thanks to modern data management and data mining technology, you can "ask" each one by mining your customer database. The results are dazzling.

Customer databases typically contain data such as a customer's name, address, and history of purchases. These databases include records of the company's communication with its own customers or customer "lists" purchased from other organizations, including charity donation forms, application forms for free products or contests, product warranty cards, subscription forms, and credit application forms. Today these databases are starting to include customer data gathered from social media, mobile, Web, and e-mail transactions.

Until fairly recently, large companies, such as Forbes, did not look closely at their own data. Forbes is an American publishing and media company that publishes the bi-weekly *Forbes* business magazine and maintains an extensive Web site. Its worldwide print and online readership numbers over 45 million people. The Forbes business model relies heavily on advertising to supplement revenue from paid subscriptions, so it is constantly looking for ways to help its advertisers reach Forbes readers more effectively.

For many years, the various entities in the Forbes media empire employed third-party research services to analyze their customer data. These services compiled information about Forbes readers by selecting and analyzing subsets of the reader population as a way of learning about the entire readership. Decisions were made on the basis of what could be predicted about the "average" reader. But readers are individuals, and what Forbes and its advertisers really wanted was to find out what each individual customer was doing with Forbes publications.

Enter corporate databases and data mining. Forbes did maintain extensive data on its individual subscribers and Web site visitors from magazine subscriptions and visits to its Web sites. It just needed to make better use of the data. Management realized it could actually learn details about each of its individual readers by examining Forbes's entire reader population, using the data it had already accumulated on a regular basis.

Forbes started to use SAP BusinessObjects software to analyze its own readership data, examining variables of greatest interest to its advertisers. Forbes claims it can now understand each individual who interacts with its brand. Whether that person is a subscriber or registered Web site visitor, Forbes has some knowledge of that individual's demographics, values,

and lifestyle as well as how that person has interacted with Forbes over the years. These details help Forbes's advertisers target their campaigns more precisely and also help Forbes publications increase their circulation.

Allowing customer data to drive marketing decisions helped Eastman Kodak Company successfully transition from making photographic film to becoming a leading provider of imaging technology products and services, including digital photography. Kodak used to make decisions in a top-down manner, with annual budgets for broadcast, print, direct mail, online, e-mail, and other marketing programs based on the previous year's spending. Campaigns were built around fictional customer "personas" that were "more aspirational than real," such as the 25- to 35-year-old suburban soccer mom with two children.

Kodak now relies more heavily on the actual data in its Oracle customer database, which maintains data on 50 million customers compiled from direct purchases and registrations on Kodak's Web site and photo-sharing site, customer-service interactions, product registrations from retail store purchases, and interactions from social networks. Kodak supplements these data with demographic and psychographic information purchased from third-party database vendors. Instead of combining data from numerous spreadsheets, the company has consolidated data on all of its marketing activities, including customer targets, campaign plans, budgets, lists, and results.

Kodak has been able to replace its crude customer "personas" with detailed in-depth profiles of customer groups and buying patterns based on actual data. For example, the profile of buyers of Kodak's C310 multi-function entry-level printer can be differentiated from that of people who purchase Kodak's more advanced (and expensive) ESP Office 6150 printer. Armed with that information, Kodak is able to target each type of customer more precisely with its retail packaging, product descriptions, and advertising placements. Instead of advertising its entire ink-jet printer line in a broad publication, Kodak will target prospective 6150 buyers through a lower-cost combination of print ads in niche magazines, Web banner ads on selected sites, and e-mail lists of small-office or home-office owners.

Kodak can measure the actual effect of promotional offers, customer segmentations, and messaging across all of its channels. For customers that are heavy users of smartphones Kodak tracks what kind of device is used to access an e-mail or Web site and it customizes campaigns for the most popular mobile platforms.

Sources: Doug Henschen, "IT Meets Marketing," *Information Week*, April 11, 2011; "Forbes: SAP BusinessObjects Software Provides New Marketing Insights," www.sap.com, accessed April 21, 2011.

CASE STUDY QUESTIONS

1. Why would a customer database be so useful for a company such as Forbes or Kodak? What would happen if these companies had not kept their customer data in databases?

2. List and describe two entities and several of their attributes that might be found in Kodak's marketing database.

3. How did better data management improve each company's business performance? Give examples of two decisions that were improved by mining these customer databases.

MIS IN ACTION

Go to the Forbes Web site and click on one of the display ads from other companies. Then answer the following questions.

1. What knowledge of Forbes customers does this display ad reflect?

2. What information would this company like to learn about Forbes Web site visitors in order to improve its sales and revenue? How could this company use data about Forbes subscribers and Web site visitors? What pieces of information are most important?

Harrah's casinos and hotels. Harrah's marketing department uses this information to build a detailed gambling profile, based on a particular customer's ongoing value to the company. For instance, data mining lets Harrah's know the favorite gaming experience of a regular customer at one of its Midwest riverboat casinos, along with that person's preferences for room accommodations, restaurants, and entertainment. This information guides management decisions about how to cultivate the most profitable customers, encourage those customers to spend more, and attract more customers with high revenue-generating potential. Business intelligence has improved Harrah's profits so much that it has become the centerpiece of the firm's business strategy.

Predictive analytics use data mining techniques, historical data, and assumptions about future conditions to predict outcomes of events, such as the probability a customer will respond to an offer or purchase a specific product. For example, the U.S. division of The Body Shop International plc used predictive analysis with its database of catalog, Web, and retail store customers to identify customers who were more likely to make catalog purchases. That information helped the company build a more precise and targeted mailing list for its catalogs, improving the response rate for catalog mailings and catalog revenues.

Text Mining and Web Mining

Business intelligence tools deal primarily with data that have been structured in databases and files. However, unstructured data, most in the form of text files, are believed to account for over 80 percent of an organization's useful information. E-mail, memos, call center transcripts, survey responses, legal cases, patent descriptions, and service reports are all valuable for finding patterns and trends that will help employees make better business decisions. **Text mining** tools are now available to help businesses analyze these data. These tools are able to extract key elements from large unstructured data sets, discover patterns and relationships, and summarize the information. Businesses might turn to text mining to analyze transcripts of calls to customer service centers to identify major service and repair issues. You can find examples of business text mining applications in the chapter-ending case study.

The Web is another rich source of valuable information, some of which can now be mined for patterns, trends, and insights into customer behavior. The discovery and analysis of useful patterns and information from the World Wide Web is called **Web mining**. Businesses might turn to Web mining to help them understand customer behavior, evaluate the effectiveness of a particular Web site, or quantify the success of a marketing campaign.

For instance, marketers use Google Trends and Google Insights for Search services, which track the popularity of various words and phrases used in Google search queries, to learn what people are interested in and what they are interested in buying.

Web mining looks for patterns in data through content mining, structure mining, and usage mining. Web content mining is the process of extracting knowledge from the content of Web pages, which may include text, image, audio, and video data. Web structure mining examines data related to the structure of a particular Web site. For example, links pointing to a document indicate the popularity of the document, while links coming out of a document indicate the richness or perhaps the variety of topics covered in the document. Web usage mining examines user interaction data recorded by a Web server whenever requests for a Web site's resources are received. The usage data records the user's behavior when the user browses or performs transactions on the Web site and collects the data in a server log. Analyzing such data helps companies determine the value of particular customers, cross marketing strategies across products, and the effectiveness of promotional campaigns.

DATABASES AND THE WEB

Many companies are using the Web to make some of the information in their internal databases available to customers and business partners. Prospective customers might use a company's Web site to view the company's product catalog or to place an order. The company in turn might use the Web to check inventory availability for that product from its supplier. That supplier in turn may have to check with its own suppliers as well as delivery firms needed to ship the products on time.

These actions involve accessing and (in the case of ordering) updating corporate databases through the Web. Suppose, for example, a customer with a Web browser wants to search an online retailer's database for pricing information. Figure 5.14 illustrates how that customer might access the retailer's internal database over the Web. The user would access the retailer's Web site over the Internet using Web browser software on his or her client PC. The user's Web browser software would request data from the organization's database, using HTML commands to communicate with the Web server.

Because many "back-end" databases cannot interpret commands written in HTML, the Web server would pass these requests for data to software that translates HTML commands into SQL so that they can be processed by the DBMS working with the database. In a client/server environment, the DBMS resides on a dedicated computer called a **database server**. The DBMS receives the SQL requests and provides the required data. The information is transferred from the organization's internal database back to the Web server for delivery in the form of a Web page to the user.

Figure 5.14 shows that the software working between the Web server and the DBMS could be on an application server running on its own dedicated computer (see Chapter 4). The application server software handles all application operations, including transaction processing and data access, between browser-based computers and a company's back-end business applications or databases. The application server takes requests from the Web server, runs the business logic to process transactions based on those requests, and provides connectivity to the organization's back-end systems or databases. Alternatively, the software for handling these operations could be a custom program or a CGI script. A CGI script is a

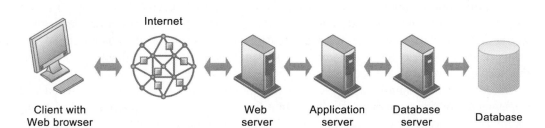

Client with
Web browser

Internet

Web
server

Application
server

Database
server

Database

Figure 5.14
Linking Internal Databases to the Web
Users access an organization's internal database through the Web using their desktop PCs and Web browser software.

compact program using the *Common Gateway Interface (CGI)* specification for processing data on a Web server.

There are a number of advantages to using the Web to access an organization's internal databases. First, everyone knows how to use Web browser software, and employees require much less training than if they used proprietary query tools. Second, the Web interface requires few or no changes to the internal database. Companies leverage their investments in older systems because it costs much less to add a Web interface in front of a legacy system than to redesign and rebuild the system to improve user access. For this reason, most large Fortune 500 firms have back-end legacy databases running on mainframe computers that are linked to "front-end" software that makes the information available in the form of a Web page to users on request.

Accessing corporate databases through the Web is creating new efficiencies and opportunities, and, in some cases, it is even changing the way business is being done. ThomasNet. com provides an up-to-date directory of information from more than 600,000 suppliers of industrial products, such as chemicals, metals, plastics, rubber, and automotive equipment. Formerly called Thomas Register, the company used to send out huge paper catalogs with this information. Now, it provides this information to users online via its Web site and has become a smaller, leaner company.

Other companies have created entirely new businesses based on access to large databases through the Web. One is the social networking service Facebook, which helps users stay connected with each other and meet new people. Facebook features "profiles" with information on more than 800 million active users with information about themselves, including interests, friends, photos, and groups with which they are affiliated. Facebook maintains a massive database to house and manage all of this content.

There are also many Web-enabled databases in the public sector to help consumers and citizens access helpful information. The Interactive Session on Organizations describes one of these databases, which has generated controversy over its methods for providing consumer product safety data.

5.4 Managing Data Resources

Setting up a database is only a start. In order to make sure that the data for your business remain accurate, reliable, and readily available to those who need it, your business will need special policies and procedures for data management.

ESTABLISHING AN INFORMATION POLICY

Every business, large and small, needs an information policy. Your firm's data are an important resource, and you don't want people doing whatever they want with them. You need to have rules on how the data are to be organized and maintained, and who is allowed to view the data or change them.

An **information policy** specifies the organization's rules for sharing, disseminating, acquiring, standardizing, classifying, and inventorying information. Information policies lay out specific procedures and accountabilities, identifying which users and organizational units can share information, where information can be distributed, and who is responsible for updating and maintaining the information. For example, a typical information policy would specify that only selected members of the payroll and human resources department would have the right to change and view sensitive employee data, such as an employee's salary or social security number, and that these departments are responsible for making sure that such employee data are accurate.

If you are in a small business, the information policy would be established and implemented by the owners or managers. In a large organization, managing and planning for information as a corporate resource often requires a formal data administration function.

INTERACTIVE SESSION: ORGANIZATIONS — Controversy Whirls Around the Consumer Product Safety Database

Michele Witte was one of dozens of parents who lost their children because of the defective design of drop-side cribs. In 1997, Witte's 10-month-old son Tyler perished when the drop-side rail on his crib came loose, partially detached, and then trapped his neck between the rail and the headboard. The cribs are now banned. Witte wishes that a public information resource for consumer complaints had been available prior to the death of her child. Reading other parents' horror stories might have dissuaded her from purchasing a drop-side crib.

In March 2011, the U.S. Consumer Product Safety Commission (CPSC) stood poised to meet the needs of parents like Witte by launching an online database, located at www.saferproducts.gov. The database provides the public with access to the full repository of product safety complaints that it has received. Users can submit these complaints online directly into the database. Visitors to the database can search for products, read other complaints, and view safety warnings issued by the CPSC. Complaints in the database include a description of the product, the harm or risk from the product, the name of the manufacturer, contact information, and an affirmation that the submitter is telling the truth. The submitter's name does not appear in the database but can be provided to manufacturers if the submitter agrees.

Consumer advocates such as the Consumer Federation of America are praising the database as a revolutionary resource that will drastically improve the way consumers buy products. However, manufacturing companies and many members of Congress are in opposition. They argue that because any user can submit a complaint, the database will be filled with inaccurate and misleading information—"fictitious slams" against products. It will also be open to abuse from customers with an axe to grind, or trial lawyers seeking to tarnish a product or manufacturer's reputation for personal gain.

The database represents an increase in visibility and authority for the CPSC, which was formed in 1972 by the Consumer Product Safety Act. The role of the CPSC is to regulate thousands of different types of products, with special focus on those that are not regulated by other areas of the government already, like food, firearms, and automobiles. (The CPSC database does not include safety problems with these products.)

The CPSC collects reports on defective products from consumers, health care providers, death certifi-

cates, media accounts, and other sources. It uses that information to make decisions on product recalls and bans, but until recently, very little of that information was accessible to the public. Federal law formerly required the approval of manufacturers to publicize that information, and manufacturers weren't eager to release information about their faulty products. Not only that, but the CPSC had to negotiate directly with manufacturers to determine the terms of product recalls. Because this process usually takes a year or more, consumers continue to buy shoddy and perhaps dangerous products like drop-side cribs in the interim.

Under the new system, complaints filed by consumers are posted online and available to the public within 15 days. Companies are notified within 5 days when complaints are made about their products, and the CPSC gives them 10 days to respond publicly and have their comments published alongside the complaints in the database. Users have the option for their comments to remain confidential if they prefer. Manufacturers can appeal to the CPSC to eliminate false or misleading complaints, and complaints are limited to defects that can cause injury, not reliability or product quality.

At a time when the federal budget is under increased scrutiny, programs like the CPSC database have become targets for cost-cutting, and manufacturers have seized an opportunity to stop the database in its tracks. The law gave CPSC new authority to regulate unsafe products but businesses say it is overly burdensome. A House Energy and Commerce subcommittee is considering draft legislation to restrict who can submit reports to the database, to improve how products are identified, and to resolve claims that reports are inaccurate.

Despite strong opposition from manufacturers and others, in March 2011, the site was launched to generally positive reviews. The CPSC provided additional features, like the ability to attach images to comments. Commenters must provide their name, mailing address, telephone number, and e-mail address, which is expected to curtail the types of anonymous comments that manufacturers fear. Even so, keeping the database free of inaccurate reports is likely to require more time and hours than the CPSC staff will be able to provide.

Since the database went live, there have been more than 305,000 visits to the site and 1.8 million product searches conducted by visitors, according to the CPSC. Despite its growing popularity, it may not survive congressional attempts to take away its funding, in response to pressures to reduce the federal budget as well as criticism from the business community. Time will tell whether saferproducts.gov becomes an indispensable consumer resource.

Sources: Josh Cable, "Democrats Defend Consumer Product Safety Database," *Industry Week*, July 7, 2011; Don Mays, "My Experience With the CPSC Database," blogs.consumerreports.com, March 16, 2011; Andrew Martin, "Child-Product Makers Seek to Soften New Rules," *The New York Times*, February 21, 2011; Lyndsey Layton, "Consumer Product Safety Commission to Launch Public Database of Complaints," *Washington Post*, January 10, 2011; Jayne O'Donnell, "Product-Safety Database Under Multiple Attacks," *USA Today*, April 12, 2011.

CASE STUDY QUESTIONS

1. What is the value of the CPSC database to consumers, businesses, and the U.S. government?

2. What problems are raised by this database? Why is it so controversial? Why is data quality an issue?

3. Name two entities in the CPSC database and describe some of their attributes.

4. When buying a crib, or other consumer product for your family, would you use this database? Why or why not?

MIS IN ACTION

1. There is a precedent for a user-generated database like the proposed CPSC database. The National Highway Traffic Safety Administration operates a Web site (www.safercar.gov) where users can post complaints about cars, tires, child seats, and other automobile-related equipment. Site visitors can search for cars with five-star crash safety ratings, browse the latest product recalls, and more. The CPSC hopes to take this model and extend it to cover a broader variety of products. Visit this site and evaluate the quality of information posted by the public. Does the information posted by consumers appear reasonable to you?

2. Customer reviews are now a common feature of consumer Web sites, most notably, Amazon. How do private sector Web sites keep outrageous and/or malicious comments off their product review pages (or discourage such comments from being posted)? Do a search on "Amazon General Review Creation Guidelines" and consider how these techniques could be used by the CPSC.

Data administration is responsible for the specific policies and procedures through which data can be managed as an organizational resource. These responsibilities include developing information policy, planning for data, overseeing logical database design and data dictionary development, and monitoring how information systems specialists and end-user groups use data.

A large organization will also have a database design and management group within the corporate information systems division that is responsible for defining and organizing the structure and content of the database, and maintaining the database. In close cooperation with users, the design group establishes the physical database, the logical relations among elements, and the access rules and security procedures. The functions it performs are called **database administration**.

ENSURING DATA QUALITY

A well-designed database and information policy will go a long way toward ensuring that the business has the information it needs. However, additional steps must be taken to ensure that the data in organizational databases are accurate and remain reliable.

What would happen if a customer's telephone number or account balance were incorrect? What would be the impact if the database had the wrong price for the product you sold? Data that are inaccurate, untimely, or inconsistent with other sources of information create serious operational and financial problems for businesses. When faulty data go unnoticed, they often lead to incorrect decisions, product recalls, and even financial losses.

Gartner Group consultants reported that more than 25 percent of the critical data in large Fortune 1000 companies' databases is inaccurate or incomplete, including bad product codes and product descriptions, faulty inventory descriptions, erroneous financial data, incorrect supplier information, and incorrect employee data. A Sirius Decisions study titled "The Impact of Bad Data on Demand Creation" found that 10 to 25 percent of customer and prospect records contain critical data errors. Correcting these errors at their source and following best practices for promoting data quality increased the productivity of the sales process and generated a 66 percent increase in revenue (Lager, 2009; Gage and McCormick, 2005).

Some of these data quality problems are caused by redundant and inconsistent data produced by multiple systems feeding a data warehouse. For example, the sales ordering system and the inventory management system might both maintain data on the organization's products. However, the sales ordering system might use the term *Item Number* and the inventory system might call the same attribute *Product Number*. The sales, inventory, or manufacturing systems of a clothing retailer might use different codes to represent values for an attribute. One system might represent clothing size as "extra large," whereas the other system might use the code "XL" for the same purpose. During the design process for the warehouse database, data describing entities, such as a customer, product, or order, should be named and defined consistently for all business areas using the database.

If a database is properly designed and enterprise-wide data standards established, duplicate or inconsistent data elements should be minimal. Most data quality problems, however, such as misspelled names, transposed numbers, or incorrect or missing codes, stem from errors during data input. The incidence of such errors is rising as companies move their businesses to the Web and allow customers and suppliers to enter data into their Web sites that directly update internal systems.

Think of all the times you have received several pieces of the same direct mail advertising on the same day. This is very likely the result of having your name maintained multiple times in a database. Your name may have been misspelled or you used your middle initial on one occasion and not on another or the information was initially entered onto a paper form and not scanned properly into the system. Because of these inconsistencies, the database would treat you as different people! We often receive redundant mail addressed to Laudon, Lavdon, Lauden, or Landon.

Before a new database is in place, organizations need to identify and correct their faulty data and establish better routines for editing data once their database is in operation. Analysis of data quality often begins with a **data quality audit**, which is a structured survey of the accuracy and level of completeness of the data in an information system. Data quality audits can be performed by surveying entire data files, surveying samples from data files, or surveying end users for their perceptions of data quality.

Data cleansing, also known as *data scrubbing*, consists of activities for detecting and correcting data in a database that are incorrect, incomplete, improperly formatted, or redundant. Data cleansing not only corrects data but also enforces consistency among different sets of data that originated in separate information systems. Specialized data-cleansing software is available to automatically survey data files, correct errors in the data, and integrate the data in a consistent company-wide format.

LEARNING TRACKS

The following Learning Tracks provide content relevant to topics covered in this chapter:

1. Database Design, Normalization, and Entity-Relationship Diagramming
2. Introduction to SQL
3. Hierarchical and Network Data Models

Review Summary

1 **How does a relational database organize data, and how does it differ from an object-oriented database?** The relational database is the primary method for organizing and maintaining data today in information system. It organizes data in two-dimensional tables with rows and columns called relations. Each table contains data about an entity and its attributes. Each row represents a record and each column represents an attribute or field. Each table also contains a key field to uniquely identify each record for retrieval or manipulation. An entity-relationship diagram graphically depicts the relationship between entities (tables) in a relational database. The process of breaking down complex groupings of data and streamlining them to minimize redundancy and awkward many-to-many relationships is called normalization. An object-oriented database management system (DBMS) stores data and procedures that act on the data as objects, and it can handle multimedia as well as characters and numbers.

2 **What are the principles of a database management system?** A DBMS consists of software that permits centralization of data and data management so that businesses have a single consistent source for all their data needs. A single database services multiple applications. The DBMS separates the logical and physical views of data so that the user does not have to be concerned with the data's physical location. The principal capabilities of a DBMS includes a data definition capability, a data dictionary capability, and a data manipulation language.

3 **What are the principal tools and technologies for accessing information from databases to improve business performance and decision making?** A data warehouse consolidates current and historical data from many different operational systems in a central database designed for reporting and analysis. Data warehouses support multidimensional data analysis, also known as online analytical processing (OLAP). OLAP represents relationships among data as a multidimensional structure, which can be visualized as cubes of data and cubes within cubes of data. Data mining analyzes large pools of data, including the contents of data warehouses, to find patterns and rules that can be used to predict future behavior and guide decision making. Text mining tools help businesses analyze large unstructured data sets consisting of text. Web mining tools focus on analyzing useful patterns and information fromo the World Wide Web, examining the structure of Web sites, activities of Web site users, and the contents of Web pages. Conventional databases can be linked to the Web or a Web interface to facilitate user access to an organization's internal data.

4 **What is the role of information policy and data administration in the management of organizational data resources?** Developing a database environment requires policies and procedures for managing organizational data as well as a good data model and

database technology. A formal information policy governs the maintenance, distribution, and use of information in the organization. In large corporations, a formal data administration function is responsible for information policy, as well as for data planning, data dictionary development, and monitoring data usage in the firm.

5 **Why is data quality assurance so important for a business?** Data that are inaccurate, incomplete, or inconsistent create serious operational and financial problems for businesses if they lead to inaccurate decisions about the actions that should be taken by the firm. Assuring data quality involves using enterprise-wide data standards, databases designed to minimize inconsistent and redundant data, data quality audits, and data cleansing software.

Key Terms

Attributes, 149	Database management system (DBMS), 153	Object-relational DBMS, 159
Data administration, 168		Online analytical processing (OLAP), 161
Data cleansing, 169	Database server, 165	
Data definition, 157	Entity, 149	Predictive analytics, 164
Data dictionary, 157	Entity-relationship diagram, 151	Primary key, 150
Data manipulation language, 157	Field, 150	Records, 150
Data mart, 160	Foreign key, 151	Referential integrity, 153
Data mining, 162	Information policy, 166	Relational database, 150
Data quality audit, 169	Key field, 150	Structured Query Language (SQL), 158
Data warehouse, 160	Normalization, 153	Text mining, 164
Database, 149	Object-oriented DBMS, 159	Tuples, 150
Database administration, 168		Web mining, 164

Review Questions

1. How does a relational database organize data, and how does it differ from an object-oriented database?
- Define and explain the significance of entities, attributes, and key fields.
- Define a relational database and explain how it organizes and stores information.
- Explain the role of entity-relationship diagrams and normalization in database design.
- Define an object-oriented database and explain how it differs from a relational database.

2. What are the principles of a database management system?
- Define a database management system (DBMS), describe how it works, and explain how it benefit organizations.
- Define and compare the logical and a physical view of data.
- Define and describe the three operations of a relational database management system.
- Name and describe the three major capabilities of a DBMS.

3. What are the principal tools and technologies for accessing information from databases to improve business performance and decision making?
- Define a data warehouse and describe how it works.
- Define business intelligence and explain how it is related to database technology.
- Describe the capabilities of online analytical processing (OLAP).
- Define data mining, describe what types of information can be obtained from it, and explain how does it differs from OLAP.

- Explain how text mining and Web mining differ from conventional data mining.
- Explain how users can access information from a company's internal databases through the Web.

4. What is the role of information policy and data administration in the management of organizational data resources?
- Define information policy and data administration and explain how they help organi-zations manage their data.

5. Why is data quality assurance so important for a business?
- List and describe the most common data quality problems.
- List and describe the most important tools and techniques for assuring data quality.

Discussion Questions

1. It has been said that you do not need database management software to create a database environment. Discuss.

2. To what extent should end users be involved in the selection of a database management system and database design?

3. What are the consequences of an organization not having an information policy?

Hands-on MIS Projects

The projects in this section give you hands-on experience in analyzing data quality problems, establishing company-wide data standards, creating a database for inventory management, and using the Web to search online databases for overseas business resources.

MANAGEMENT DECISION PROBLEMS

1. Emerson Process Management, a global supplier of measurement, analytical, and monitoring instruments and services based in Austin, Texas, had a new data warehouse designed for analyzing customer activity to improve service and marketing. However, the data warehouse was full of inaccurate and redundant data. The data in the warehouse came from numerous transaction processing systems in Europe, Asia, and other locations around the world. The team that designed the warehouse had assumed that sales groups in all these areas would enter customer names and addresses the same way. In fact, companies in different countries were using multiple ways of entering quote, billing, shipping, and other data. Assess the potential business impact of these data quality problems. What decisions have to be made and steps taken to reach a solution?

2. Your industrial supply company wants to create a data warehouse where management can obtain a single corporate-wide view of critical sales information to identify bestselling products, key customers, and sales trends. Your sales and product information are stored in several different systems: a divisional sales system running on a UNIX server and a corporate sales system running on an IBM mainframe. You would like to create a single standard format that consolidates these data from both systems. In MyMISLab, you can review the proposed format, along with sample files from the two systems that would supply the data for the data warehouse. Then anwer the following questions:
- What business problems are created by not having these data in a single standard format?
- How easy would it be to create a database with a single standard format that could store the data from both systems? Identify the problems that would have to be addressed.
- Should the problems be solved by database specialists or general business managers? Explain.

- Who should have the authority to finalize a single company-wide format for this information in the data warehouse?

ACHIEVING OPERATIONAL EXCELLENCE: BUILDING A RELATIONAL DATABASE FOR INVENTORY MANAGEMENT

Software skills: Database design, querying, and reporting
Business skills: Inventory management

In this exercise, you will use database software to design a database for managing inventory for a small business. Sylvester's Bike Shop, located in San Francisco, California, sells road, mountain, hybrid, leisure, and children's bicycles. Currently, Sylvester's purchases bikes from three suppliers, but plans to add new suppliers in the near future. Using the information found in the tables in MyMISLab, build a simple relational database to manage information about Sylvester's suppliers and products. MyMISLab contains more details about the specifications for the database.

Once you have built the database, perform the following activities.

- Prepare a report that identifies the five most expensive bicycles. The report should list the bicycles in descending order from most expensive to least expensive, the quantity on hand for each, and the markup percentage for each.
- Prepare a report that lists each supplier, its products, the quantities on hand, and associated reorder levels. The report should be sorted alphabetically by supplier. Within each supplier category, the products should be sorted alphabetically.
- Prepare a report listing only the bicycles that are low in stock and need to be reordered. The report should provide supplier information for the items identified.
- Write a brief description of how the database could be enhanced to further improve management of the business. What tables or fields should be added? What additional reports would be useful?

IMPROVING DECISION MAKING: SEARCHING ONLINE DATABASES FOR OVERSEAS BUSINESS RESOURCES

Software skills: Online databases
Business skills: Researching services for overseas operations

This project develops skills in searching online Web-enabled databases with information about products and services in faraway locations.

Your company is located in Greensboro, North Carolina, and manufactures office furniture of various types. You are considering opening a facility to manufacture and sell your products in Australia. You would like to contact organizations that offer many services necessary for you to open your Australian office and manufacturing facility, including lawyers, accountants, import-export experts, and telecommunications equipment and support firms. Access the following online databases to locate companies that you would like to meet with during your upcoming trip: Australian Business Register (abr.gov.au), AustraliaTrade Now (australiatradenow.com), and the Nationwide Business Directory of Australia (www.nationwide.com.au). If necessary, use search engines such as Yahoo!and Google.

- List the companies you would contact on your trip to determine whether they can help you with these and any other functions you think are vital to establishing your office.
- Rate the databases you used for accuracy of name, completeness, ease of use, and general helpfulness.

Video Cases

Video Cases and Instructional Videos illustrating some of the concepts in this chapter are available. Contact your instructor to access these videos.

Collaboration and Teamwork

Identifying Entities and Attributes in an Online Database

With a group of two or three of your fellow students, select an online database to explore, such as AOL Music or the Internet Movie Database. Explore these Web sites to see what information they provide. Then list the entities and attributes that they must keep track of in their databases. Diagram the relationship between the entities you have identified. If possible, use Google Sites to post links to Web pages, team communication announcements, and work assignments; to brainstorm; and to work collaboratively on project documents. Try to use Google Docs to develop a presentation of your findings for the class.

BUSINESS PROBLEM-SOLVING CASE

Text Mining For Gold?

Thanks to the explosion of social media and mobile computing, the amount of data consumers are generating is much larger than ever before. What's more, most of the data are unstructured—generated from a variety of different events such as Facebook statuses and posts, tweets, blog posts, call center transcripts, message board posts, e-mails, and phone calls. Companies have found they can learn a great deal from this deluge of unstructured data, and they are now turning to text mining for help.

Text mining has advanced beyond just analyzing consumer sentiment. Law firms are using text mining for "e-discovery," financial analysts are using it to analyze the content of corporate earnings calls and make stock predictions, and text mining software developers are constantly modifying their software to perform newer, more difficult tasks.

In a lawsuit, "discovery" involves finding all of the facts relevant to the suit before trial, which includes reading over documents to determine their relevance to the case. For larger cases, the total number of documents can reach the millions. For example, in 1978, several television studios were involved in an anti-trust lawsuit filed by the Justice Department against CBS. At the request of the Justice Department, the studios had to carefully read over 6 million documents to identify the ones that would be relevant to the case. The total cost of discovery was $2.2 million, the majority of which went to pay lawyers and paralegals at exorbitant hourly rates.

Today, text mining software can perform the task of discovery for a fraction of the time and cost. This special software, known as "e-discovery software," can do more than just find documents with relevant keywords at extremely fast speeds. Advanced e-discovery software is able to analyze the concepts discussed in each document even without the guidance of key terms, and it can also detect and understand deeper patterns to find documents that might even have escaped the notice of lawyers reading through manually. Because this software analyzes concepts rather than specific keywords, a single lawyer can use it to perform work that once required hundreds of lawyers much more time to complete.

For example, the law firm DLA Piper used Clearwell e-discovery software to search through, analyze, and sort 570,000 documents (each of which might have many pages) in two days. On the third day, the firm was able to identify 3,070 documents that were relevant to its court-ordered discovery motion. In January 2011, Blackstone Discovery of Palo Alto, California, helped analyze 1.5 million documents for less than $100,000.

The two major types of e-discovery techniques are the linguistic approach and the sociological approach. The linguistic approach is the traditional approach to text mining, where software searches for specific words and filters documents through an extensive series of synonyms, definitions, and related phrases. For example, searching documents for "dog" returns documents that make mention of "man's best friend" and other related concepts.

The sociological approach is much more advanced. Cutting-edge text mining software companies like Blackstone Discovery and Cataphora have developed software that mines documents for certain types of activities and interactions. Instead of searching for terms, the software attempts to visualize and model chains of events and discussions that cross over into multiple methods of communication. For example, the software can follow the discussion of a certain topic in the workplace across e-mail, instant messages, and telephone calls by detecting commonalities among the conversations between employees.

In order for Blackstone, Cataphora, and other companies to perfect their e-discovery software, they needed a trove of data large enough to test the social algorithms in their products. That data came from an unlikely source: Enron. The government collected over 5 million messages sent by the fallen energy giant's employees as part of its prosecution, and the analysis of those messages has helped text mining software developers better understand how language is used in the workplace, how social networks function, and how e-mail can shed insights on the formation and maintenance of social groups in the workplace.

The software identifies certain types of conversational traits that suggest the possibility of crime, such as when employees demonstrate reluctance to discuss an issue via e-mail or instant messaging, preferring face-to-face interaction instead. The software also detects changes in writing style, such as shifts to more formal language or heightened defensiveness when discussing a sensitive issue. These shifts may also be suggestive of crime. Since Enron was engaged in significant criminal activity, its communications were invaluable to the developers of e-discovery products as they fine-tuned their algorithms to detect increased probabilities of crime.

Could text analytics also do the work of economists? One financial services firm, Boston-based Business Intelligence Advisors (BIA), is using text mining to do just that. BIA provided the relatively commonplace service of filtering through corporate earnings calls to detect warning signs in executive behavior. BIA employees listened individually to those calls at first, but as the service became more popular, the only reasonable way to grow that service was to automate it. A variation of text mining was the best way to accomplish that automation.

BIA developed an algorithm that models the methods used by human beings to judge the content of an earnings call. Its proprietary linguistic pattern-recognition software delves into the content of earnings calls in search of response patterns associated with a wide range of behavioral indicators. The software can detect behavior that indicates uncertainty and a lack of confidence—both bad signs. The algorithm is trained to recognize a variety of warning signs. Evasive language suggests a desire to avoid giving incorrect information and a desire to hide the truth; "protest statements," or statements that convey no useful information, are strong indicators of trouble; and "qualified language," such as "fairly normal" or "pretty typical," suggest that some aspects of the topic being discussed are abnormal or atypical, but that the executive doesn't want to divulge what those things might be. Excessively courteous behavior, delays in answers or refusal to answer, and any mention of religion are among the other warning signs that the program is trained to recognize.

BIA's program assigns each call a grade from 1 to 10, with 10 being the most problematic. Sudden jumps in grades are flagged and reviewed individually. BIA charges a hefty sum for this service, in the low six-figure area on a yearly basis, but research suggests that there is a strong correlation between the rankings provided by BIA's system and future stock performance, so the price may be worth it.

While e-discovery and analyzing corporate calls are newer, creative uses of text analytics, the technology is most frequently used by corporations eager to better understand what its customers are saying about them—a process known as sentiment analysis. Companies like Best Buy, Viacom, Paramount Pictures, Cisco, and Intuit are among the companies that heavily rely on sentiment analysis to guide their advertising efforts and business strategies, and most large companies are using some form of the technology.

Kia Motors used sentiment analysis to determine the effectiveness of its Super Bowl ad in 2011. Kia hoped to "change consumer perception" of its brand, but in order to do that, the Korean automaker needed to know what that perception was. Using software developed by WiseWindow, a California-based text analytics company, Kia was able to monitor the percentage of conversations about automobiles on the Web that pertained to its brand. Before the Super Bowl ad aired, WiseWindow software indicated that approximately 4 percent of auto conversations were about Kias. After the game, that percentage jumped to 9 percent. Those figures allowed the company to determine whether or not the money spent on the ad was a wise investment. In Kia's case, it was.

WiseWindow's flagship product, Mass Opinion Business Intelligence (MOBI), provides a continuous feed of relevant consumer sentiment. The software filters through millions of sites to acquire information, measuring consumer sentiment in real time for just a fraction of the cost of conventional methods, like mass mailings, surveys, and focus groups. The software uses natural language processing, just like BIA's conference call analyzer and e-discovery software, to interpret written conversations and determine whether the opinions expressed are favorable or unfavorable.

Companies are using sentiment analysis more frequently to adjust how they interact with consumers. Gaylord Hotels, a network of upscale meeting-focused resorts, discovered that the majority of customer service complaints pertained to just five separate issues and that the first 20 minutes of each customer's stay were the most important in fostering guest satisfaction. Previously, Gaylord believed that there were 80 things it needed to do to ensure customer satisfaction. The hotel chain promptly fixed the most prominent problems and devoted extra effort to customer service at the start of customers' visits, such as assigning hotel staff to accompany guests to their destinations in its resorts. The company saw an immediate jump in guest satisfaction.

These automated tools for text mining have renewed the debate over the broader social and economic impact of information technology. In the case of the legal profession, the shift from manual document discovery to e-discovery might mean that one lawyer would be able to manage work that once required 500. The newest generation of software, which is able to detect duplicates and locate clusters of documents on a specific topic could reduce head count by another 50 percent. According to David H. Autor, an economics professor at the Massachusetts Institute of Technology, the U.S. economy is being "hollowed out." Automation is putting a brake on the growth of higher and middle-level jobs. New jobs will primarily be generated at the bottom of the economic pyramid. Autor notes that technology may not increase unemployment, but, "the harder question is, does changing technology always lead to better jobs?" Autor doesn't think so.

Sources: Vito J. Racanelli, "Move Over Watson," *Barrons*, March 5, 2011; John Markoff, "Armies of Expensive Lawyers, Replaced by Cheaper Software," *The New York Times*, March 4, 2011; Rachael King, "Sentiment Analysis Gives Companies Insight into Consumer Opinion," *Business Week* March 1, 2011.

Case Study Questions

1. What is the business impact of text mining? What problems does it solve?
2. How does text mining improve operational efficiency and decision making?
3. Is text mining more effective than humans doing the work manually? Explain your answer.
4. What are some of the drawbacks or shortcomings of text mining?

Telecommunications, the Internet, and Wireless Technology

CHAPTER 6

STUDENT LEARNING OBJECTIVES

After completing this chapter, you will be able to answer the following questions:

1. What are the principal components of telecommunications networks and key networking technologies?

2. What are the main telecommunications transmission media and types of networks?

3. How do the Internet and Internet technology work and how do they support communication and e-business?

4. What are the principal technologies and standards for wireless networking, communication, and Internet access?

5. Why are radio frequency identification (RFID) and wireless sensor networks valuable for business?

CHAPTER OUTLINE

HYUNDAI HEAVY INDUSTRIES CREATES A WIRELESS SHIPYARD

What's it like to be the world's largest shipbuilder? Ask Hyundai Heavy Industries (HHI), headquartered in Ulsan, South Korea, which produces 10 percent of the world's ships. HHI produces tankers, bulk carriers, containerships, gas and chemical carriers, ship engines, offshore oil and gas drilling platforms, and undersea pipelines.

Coordinating and optimizing the production of so many different products is obviously a daunting task. The company has already invested nearly $50 million in factory planning software to help manage this effort. But HHI's "factory" encompasses 11 square kilometers (4.2 square miles) stretching over land and sea, including nine drydocks, the largest of which spans more than seven football fields to support construction of four vessels simultaneously. Over 12,000 workers build up to 30 ships at one time, using millions of parts ranging in size from small rivets to five-story buildings.

This production environment proved too large and complex to easily track the movement of parts and inventory in real time as these events were taking place. Without up-to-the-minute data, the efficiencies from enterprise resource planning software are

© Oleksandr Kalinichenko, 2011, iStockPhoto LP.

very limited. To make matters worse, the recent economic downturn hit HHI especially hard, as world trading and shipping plummeted. Orders for new ships in 2009 plunged to 7.9 million compensated gross tons (CGT, a measurement of vessel size), down from 150 million CGT the previous year. In this economic environment, Hyundai Heavy was looking for new ways to reduce expenses and streamline production.

HHI's solution was a high-speed wireless network across the entire shipyard, which was built by KT Corp., South Korea's largest telecommunications firm. It is able to transmit data at a rate of 4 megabits per second, about four times faster than the typical cable modem delivering high-speed Internet service to U.S. households. The company uses radio sensors to track the movement of parts as they move from fabrication shop to the side of a drydock and then onto a ship under construction. Workers on the ship use notebook computers or handheld mobile phones to access plans and engage in two-way video conversations with ship designers in the office, more than a mile away.

In the past, workers who were inside a vessel below ground or below sea level had to climb topside to use a phone or walkie-talkie when they had to talk to someone about a problem. The new wireless network is connected to the electric lines in the ship, which convey digital data to Wi-Fi wireless transmitters placed around the hull during construction. Workers' Internet phones, webcams, and PCs are linked to the Wi-Fi system, so workers can use Skype VoIP to call their colleagues on the surface. Designers in an office building a mile from the construction site use the webcams to investigate problems.

On the shipyard roads, 30 transporter trucks fitted to receivers connected to the wireless network update their location every 20 seconds to a control room. This helps dispatchers match the location of transporters with orders for parts, shortening the trips each truck makes. All of the day's movements are finished by 6 p.m. instead of 8 p.m. By making operations more efficient and reducing labor costs, the wireless technology is expected to save Hyundai Heavy $40 million annually.

Sources: Evan Ramstad, "High-Speed Wireless Transforms a Shipyard," *Wall Street Journal*, March 15, 2010; English. hhi.co.kr, accessed June 3, 2011; and "Hyundai Heavy Plans Wireless Shipyard," *Korea Herald*, March 30, 2010.

Hyundai Heavy Industries's experience illustrates some of the powerful capabilities and opportunities provided by contemporary networking technology. The company used wireless networking technology to connect designers, laborers, ships under construction, and transportation vehicles to accelerate communication and coordination, and cut down on the time, distance, or number of steps required to perform a task.

The chapter-opening diagram calls attention to important points raised by this case and this chapter. Hyundai Heavy Industries produces ships and other products that are very labor-intensive and sensitive to changes in global economic conditions. Its production environment is large, complex, and extremely difficult to coordinate and manage. The company needs to keep operating costs as low as possible. HHI's shipyard extends over a vast area, and it was extremely difficult to monitor and coordinate different projects and work teams.

Management decided that wireless technology provided a solution and arranged for the deployment of a wireless network throughout the entire shipyard. The network also links the yard to designers in HHI's office a mile away. The network made it much easier to track parts and production activities and to optimize the movements of transporter trucks. HHI had to redesign its production and other work processes to take advantage of the new technology.

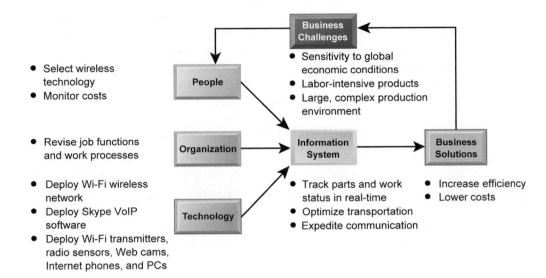

- Select wireless technology
- Monitor costs

- Revise job functions and work processes

- Deploy Wi-Fi wireless network
- Deploy Skype VoIP software
- Deploy Wi-Fi transmitters, radio sensors, Web cams, Internet phones, and PCs

Business Challenges
- Sensitivity to global economic conditions
- Labor-intensive products
- Large, complex production environment

People

Organization

Technology

Information System
- Track parts and work status in real-time
- Optimize transportation
- Expedite communication

Business Solutions
- Increase efficiency
- Lower costs

6.1 Telecommunications and Networking in Today's Business World

If you run or work in a business, you can't do without networks. You need to communicate rapidly with your customers, suppliers, and employees. Until about 1990, businesses used the postal system or telephone system with voice or fax for communication. Today, however, you and your employees use computers, e-mail and messaging, the Internet, cell phones, and mobile computers connected to wireless networks for this purpose. Networking and the Internet are now nearly synonymous with doing business.

NETWORKING AND COMMUNICATION TRENDS

Firms in the past used two fundamentally different types of networks: telephone networks and computer networks. Telephone networks historically handled voice communication, and computer networks handled data traffic. Telephone networks were built by telephone companies throughout the twentieth century using voice transmission technologies (hardware and software), and these companies almost always operated as regulated monopolies throughout the world. Computer networks were originally built by computer companies seeking to transmit data between computers in different locations.

Thanks to continuing telecommunications deregulation and information technology innovation, telephone and computer networks are converging into a single digital network using shared Internet-based standards and equipment. Telecommunications providers today, such as AT&T and Verizon, offer data transmission, Internet access, cellular telephone service, and television programming as well as voice service. (See the Chapter 3 opening case.) Cable companies, such as Cablevision and Comcast, offer voice service and Internet access. Computer networks have expanded to include Internet telephone and video services. Increasingly, all of these voice, video, and data communications are based on Internet technology.

Both voice and data communication networks have also become more powerful (faster), more portable (smaller and mobile), and less expensive. For instance, the typical Internet connection speed in 2000 was 56 kilobits per second, but today more than 68 percent of the 238 million U.S. Internet users have high-speed **broadband** connections provided by telephone and cable TV companies running at 1 to 15 million bits per second. The cost for this service has fallen exponentially, from 25 cents per kilobit in 2000 to a tiny fraction of a cent today.

Increasingly, voice and data communication, as well as Internet access, are taking place over broadband wireless platforms, such as cell phones, mobile handheld devices, and PCs in wireless networks. In a few years, more than half the Internet users in the United States will use smartphones and mobile netbooks to access the Internet. In 2011, 91 million Americans accessed the Internet through mobile devices, and this number is expected to grow to 135 million (half of all Internet users) by 2015. (eMarketer, 2011).

WHAT IS A COMPUTER NETWORK?

If you had to connect the computers for two or more employees together in the same office, you would need a computer network. Exactly what is a network? In its simplest form, a network consists of two or more connected computers. Figure 6.1 illustrates the major hardware, software, and transmission components used in a simple network: a client computer and a dedicated server computer, network interfaces, a connection medium, network operating system software, and either a hub or a switch.

Each computer on the network contains a network interface device to link the computer to the network. The connection medium for linking network components can be a telephone wire, coaxial cable, or radio signal in the case of cell phone and wireless local area networks (Wi-Fi networks).

The **network operating system (NOS)** routes and manages communications on the network and coordinates network resources. It can reside on every computer in the network, or it can reside primarily on a dedicated server computer for all the applications on the network. A server computer is a computer on a network that performs important network functions for client computers, such as serving up Web pages, storing data, and storing the network operating system (and hence controlling the network). Server software such as Microsoft Windows Server, Linux, and Novell Open Enterprise Server are the most widely used network operating systems.

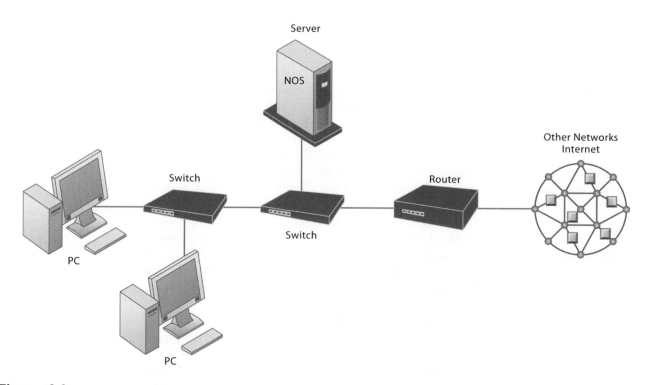

Figure 6.1
Components of a Simple Computer Network
Illustrated here is a very simple computer network, consisting of computers, a network operating system residing on a dedicated server computer, cable (wiring) connecting the devices, switches, and a router.

Most networks also contain a switch or a hub acting as a connection point between the computers. **Hubs** are very simple devices that connect network components, sending a packet of data to all other connected devices. A **switch** has more intelligence than a hub and can filter and forward data to a specified destination on the network.

What if you want to communicate with another network, such as the Internet? You would need a router. A **router** is a communications processor used to route packets of data through different networks, ensuring that the data sent gets to the correct address.

Networks in Large Companies

The network we've just described might be suitable for a small business. But what about large companies with many different locations and thousands of employees? As a firm grows, and collects hundreds of small local area networks, these networks can be tied together into a corporate-wide networking infrastructure. The network infrastructure for a large corporation consists of a large number of these small local area networks linked to other local area networks and to firmwide corporate networks. A number of powerful servers support a corporate Web site, a corporate intranet, and perhaps an extranet. Some of these servers link to other large computers supporting back-end systems.

Figure 6.2 provides an illustration of these more complex, larger scale corporate-wide networks. Here you can see that the corporate network infrastructure supports a mobile sales force using cell phones and smartphones, mobile employees linking to the company Web site, internal company networks using mobile wireless local area networks (Wi-Fi networks), and a videoconferencing system to support managers across the world. In addition to these computer networks, the firm's infrastructure usually includes a separate telephone network that handles most voice data. Many firms are dispensing with their traditional telephone networks and using Internet telephones that run on their existing data networks (described later).

As you can see from this figure, a large corporate network infrastructure uses a wide variety of technologies—everything from ordinary telephone service and corporate data networks to Internet service, wireless Internet, and cell phones. One of the major problems

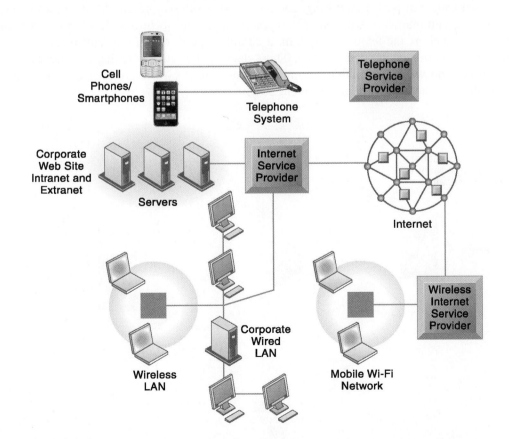

Figure 6.2
Corporate Network Infrastructure
Today's corporate network infrastructure is a collection of many different networks from the public switched telephone network, to the Internet, to corporate local area networks linking workgroups, departments, or office floors.

facing corporations today is how to integrate all the different communication networks and channels into a coherent system that enables information to flow from one part of the corporation to another, and from one system to another. As more and more communication networks become digital, and based on Internet technologies, it will become easier to integrate them.

KEY DIGITAL NETWORKING TECHNOLOGIES

Contemporary digital networks and the Internet are based on three key technologies: client/server computing, the use of packet switching, and the development of widely used communications standards (the most important of which is Transmission Control Protocol/Internet Protocol, or TCP/IP) for linking disparate networks and computers.

Client/Server Computing

Client/server computing, introduced in Chapter 4, is a distributed computing model in which some of the processing power is located within small, inexpensive client computers, and resides literally on desktops, laptops, or in handheld devices. These powerful clients are linked to one another through a network that is controlled by a network server computer. The server sets the rules of communication for the network and provides every client with an address so others can find it on the network.

Client/server computing has largely replaced centralized mainframe computing in which nearly all of the processing takes place on a central large mainframe computer. Client/server computing has extended computing to departments, workgroups, factory floors, and other parts of the business that could not be served by a centralized architecture. The Internet is the largest implementation of client/server computing.

Packet Switching

Packet switching is a method of slicing digital messages into parcels called packets, sending the packets along different communication paths as they become available, and then reassembling the packets once they arrive at their destinations (see Figure 6.3). Prior to the development of packet switching, computer networks used leased, dedicated telephone circuits to communicate with other computers in remote locations. In circuit-switched networks, such as the telephone system, a complete point-to-point circuit is assembled, and then communication can proceed. These dedicated circuit-switching techniques were expensive and wasted available communications capacity—the circuit was maintained regardless of whether any data were being sent.

Figure 6.3
Packed-Switched Networks and Packet Communications
Data are grouped into small packets, which are transmitted independently over various communications channels and reassembled at their final destination.

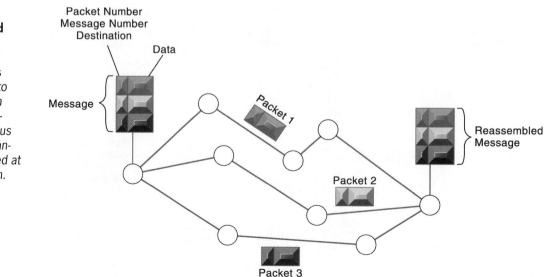

Packet switching makes much more efficient use of the communications capacity of a network. In packet-switched networks, messages are first broken down into small fixed bundles of data called packets. The packets include information for directing the packet to the right address and for checking transmission errors along with the data. The packets are transmitted over various communications channels using routers, each packet traveling independently. Packets of data originating at one source will be routed through many different paths and networks before being reassembled into the original message when they reach their destinations.

TCP/IP and Connectivity

In a typical telecommunications network, diverse hardware and software components need to work together to transmit information. Different components in a network communicate with each other only by adhering to a common set of rules called protocols. A **protocol** is a set of rules and procedures governing transmission of information between two points in a network.

In the past, many diverse proprietary and incompatible protocols often forced business firms to purchase computing and communications equipment from a single vendor. But today, corporate networks are increasingly using a single, common, worldwide standard called **Transmission Control Protocol/ Internet Protocol (TCP/IP).** TCP/IP was developed during the early 1970s to support U.S. Department of Defense Advanced Research Projects Agency (DARPA) efforts to help scientists transmit data among different types of computers over long distances.

TCP/IP uses a suite of protocols, the main ones being TCP and IP. TCP refers to the Transmission Control Protocol, which handles the movement of data between computers. TCP establishes a connection between the computers, sequences the transfer of packets, and acknowledges the packets sent. IP refers to the Internet Protocol (IP), which is responsible for the delivery of packets and includes the disassembling and reassembling of packets during transmission. Figure 6.4 illustrates the four-layered Department of Defense reference model for TCP/IP, and the layers are described as follows:

1. Application layer. The Application layer enables client application programs to access the other layers and defines the protocols that applications use to exchange data. One of these application protocols is the Hypertext Transfer Protocol (HTTP), which is used to transfer Web page files.
2. Transport layer. The Transport layer is responsible for providing the Application layer with communication and packet services. This layer includes TCP and other protocols.
3. Internet layer. The Internet layer is responsible for addressing, routing, and packaging data packets called IP datagrams. The Internet Protocol is one of the protocols used in this layer.

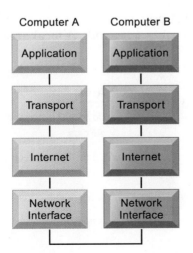

Figure 6.4
The Transmission Control Protocol/ Internet Protocol (TCP/IP) Reference Model
This figure illustrates the four layers of the TCP/IP reference model for communications

4. Network Interface layer. At the bottom of the reference model, the Network Interface layer is responsible for placing packets on and receiving them from the network medium, which could be any networking technology.

Two computers using TCP/IP are able to communicate even if they are based on different hardware and software platforms. Data sent from one computer to the other passes downward through all four layers, starting with the sending computer's Application layer and passing through the Network Interface layer. After the data reach the recipient host computer, they travel up the layers and are reassembled into a format the receiving computer can use. If the receiving computer finds a damaged packet, it asks the sending computer to retransmit it. This process is reversed when the receiving computer responds.

6.2 Communications Networks

Let's look more closely at alternative networking technologies available to businesses.

SIGNALS: DIGITAL VS. ANALOG

There are two ways to communicate a message in a network: either using an analog signal or a digital signal. An *analog signal* is represented by a continuous waveform that passes through a communications medium and has been used for voice communication. The most common analog devices are the telephone handset, the speaker on your computer, or your iPod earphone, all of which create analog waveforms that your ear can hear.

A *digital signal* is a discrete, binary waveform, rather than a continuous waveform. Digital signals communicate information as strings of two discrete states: one bit and zero bits, which are represented as on-off electrical pulses. Computers use digital signals and require a modem to convert these digital signals into analog signals that can be sent over (or received from) telephone lines, cable lines, or wireless media that use analog signals (see Figure 6.5). **Modem** stands for modulator-demodulator. Cable modems connect your computer to the Internet using a cable network. DSL modems connect your computer to the Internet using a telephone company's land line network. Wireless modems perform the same function as traditional modems, connecting your computer to a wireless network that could be a cell phone network, or a Wi-Fi network. Without modems, computers could not communicate with one another using analog networks (which include the telephone system and cable networks).

TYPES OF NETWORKS

There are many different kinds of networks and ways of classifying them. One way of looking at networks is in terms of their geographic scope (see Table 6.1).

Local Area Networks

If you work in a business that uses networking, you are probably connecting to other employees and groups via a local area network. A **local area network (LAN)** is designed

TABLE 6.1

Types of Networks

Type	Area
Local area network (LAN)	Up to 500 meters (half a mile); an office or floor of a building
Campus area network (CAN)	Up to 1,000 meters (a mile); a college campus or corporate facility
Metropolitan area network (MAN)	A city or metropolitan area
Wide area network (WAN)	A transcontinental or global area

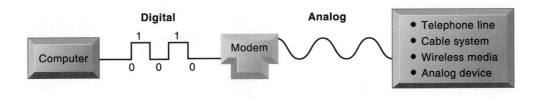

Figure 6.5
Functions of the Modem
A modem is a device that translates digital signals into analog form (and vice versa) so that computers can transmit data over analog networks such as telephone and cable networks.

to connect personal computers and other digital devices within a half-mile or 500-meter radius. LANs typically connect a few computers in a small office, all the computers in one building, or all the computers in several buildings in close proximity. LANs also are used to link to long-distance wide area networks (WANs, described later in this section) and other networks around the world using the Internet.

Review Figure 6.1, which could serve as a model for a small LAN that might be used in an office. One computer is a dedicated network file server, providing users with access to shared computing resources in the network, including software programs and data files.

The server determines who gets access to what and in which sequence. The router connects the LAN to other networks, which could be the Internet or another corporate network, so that the LAN can exchange information with networks external to it. The most common LAN operating systems are Windows, Linux, and Novell. Each of these network operating systems supports TCP/IP as their default networking protocol.

Ethernet is the dominant LAN standard at the physical network level, specifying the physical medium to carry signals between computers, access control rules, and a standardized set of bits used to carry data over the system. Originally, Ethernet supported a data transfer rate of 10 megabits per second (Mbps). Newer versions, such as Fast Ethernet and Gigabit Ethernet, support data transfer rates of 100 Mbps and 1 gigabits per second (Gbps), respectively, and are used in network backbones.

The LAN illustrated in Figure 6.1 uses a client/server architecture where the network operating system resides primarily on a single file server, and the server provides much of the control and resources for the network. Alternatively, LANs may use a **peer-to-peer** architecture. A peer-to-peer network treats all processors equally and is used primarily in small networks with 10 or fewer users. The various computers on the network can exchange data by direct access and can share peripheral devices without going through a separate server.

In LANs using the Windows Server family of operating systems, the peer-to-peer architecture is called the *workgroup network model*, in which a small group of computers can share resources, such as files, folders, and printers, over the network without a dedicated server. The Windows *domain network model*, in contrast, uses a dedicated server to manage the computers in the network.

Larger LANs have many clients and multiple servers, with separate servers for specific services, such as storing and managing files and databases (file servers or database servers), managing printers (print servers), storing and managing e-mail (mail servers), or storing and managing Web pages (Web servers).

Sometimes LANs are described in terms of the way their components are connected together, or their **topology**. There are three major LAN topologies: star, bus, and ring (see Figure 6.6).

In a **star topology**, all devices on the network connect to a single hub. Figure 6.6 illustrates a simple star topology in which all network traffic flows through the hub. In an *extended star network*, multiple layers of hubs are organized into a hierarchy.

In a **bus topology**, one station transmits signals, which travel in both directions along a single transmission segment. All of the signals are broadcast in both directions to the entire network. All machines on the network receive the same signals, and software installed on the client computers enables each client to listen for messages addressed specifically to it. The bus topology is the most common Ethernet topology.

Figure 6.6
Network
Topologies
The three basic network topologies are the star, bus, and ring.

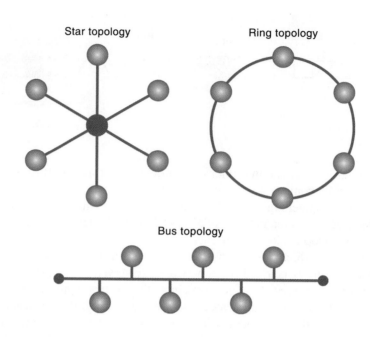

Star topology

Ring topology

Bus topology

A **ring topology** connects network components in a closed loop. Messages pass from computer to computer in only one direction around the loop, and only one station at a time may transmit. The ring topology is primarily found in older LANs using Token Ring networking software.

Metropolitan and Wide Area Networks

Wide area networks (WANs) span broad geographical distances—entire regions, states, continents, or the entire globe. The most universal and powerful WAN is the Internet. Computers connect to a WAN through public networks, such as the telephone system or private cable systems, or through leased lines or satellites. A **metropolitan area network (MAN)** is a network that spans a metropolitan area, usually a city and its major suburbs. Its geographic scope falls between a WAN and a LAN.

PHYSICAL TRANSMISSION MEDIA

Networks use different kinds of physical transmission media, including twisted wire, coaxial cable, fiber optics, and media for wireless transmission. Each has advantages and limitations. A wide range of speeds is possible for any given medium depending on the software and hardware configuration.

Twisted Wire

Twisted wire consists of strands of copper wire twisted in pairs and is an older type of transmission medium. Many of the telephone systems in buildings had twisted wires installed for analog communication, but they can be used for digital communication as well. Although an older physical transmission medium, the twisted wires used in today's LANs, such as CAT5, can obtain speeds up to 1 Gbps. Twisted-pair cabling is limited to a maximum recommended run of 100 meters (328 feet).

Coaxial Cable

Coaxial cable, similar to that used for cable television, consists of thickly insulated copper wire that can transmit a larger volume of data than twisted wire. Cable was used in early LANs and is still used today for longer (more than 100 meters) runs in large buildings. Coaxial has speeds up to 1 Gbps.

Fiber Optics and Optical Networks

Fiber-optic cable consists of bound strands of clear glass fiber, each the thickness of a human hair. Data are transformed into pulses of light, which are sent through the fiber-optic cable by a laser device at rates varying from 500 kilobits to several trillion bits per second in experimental settings. Fiber-optic cable is considerably faster, lighter, and more durable than wire media, and is well suited to systems requiring transfers of large volumes of data. However, fiber-optic cable is more expensive than other physical transmission media and harder to install.

Until recently, fiber-optic cable had been used primarily for the high-speed network backbone, which handles the major traffic. Now telecommunications companies such as Verizon are starting to bring fiber lines into the home for new types of services, such as Verizon's Fiber Optic Services (FiOS) Internet service that provides up 50 Mbps download speeds.

Wireless Transmission Media

Wireless transmission is based on radio signals of various frequencies. There are three kinds of wireless networks used by computers: microwave, cellular, and Wi-Fi. **Microwave** systems, both terrestrial and celestial, transmit high-frequency radio signals through the atmosphere and are widely used for high-volume, long-distance, point-to-point communication. Microwave signals follow a straight line and do not bend with the curvature of the earth. Therefore, long-distance terrestrial transmission systems require that transmission stations be positioned about 37 miles apart. Long-distance transmission is also possible by using communication satellites as relay stations for microwave signals transmitted from terrestrial stations.

Communication satellites use microwave transmission and are typically used for transmission in large, geographically dispersed organizations that would be difficult to network using cabling media or terrestrial microwave, as well as for home Internet service, especially in rural areas. For instance, the global energy company BP p.l.c. uses satellites for real-time data transfer of oil field exploration data gathered from searches of the ocean floor. Using geosynchronous satellites, exploration ships transfer these data to central computing centers in the United States for use by researchers in Houston, Tulsa, and suburban Chicago. Figure 6.7 illustrates how this system works. Satellites are also used for home television and Internet service. The two major satellite Internet providers (Dish Network and DirectTV) have about 1.1 million Internet subscribers, and about 1 percent of all U.S. Internet users access the Internet using satellite services (eMarketer, 2011).

Satellite Internet subscribers are typically in rural areas where cable and DSL lines are not economical. Download speeds via satellite are as high as 2 Mbps.

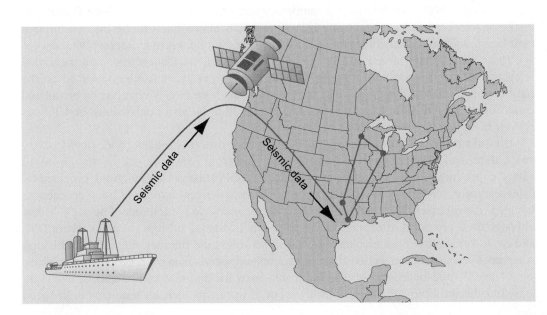

Figure 6.7
BP's Satellite Transmission System
Communication satellites help BP transfer seismic data between oil exploration ships and research centers in the United States.

Cellular systems also use radio waves and a variety of different protocols to communicate with radio antennas (towers) placed within adjacent geographic areas called cells. Communications transmitted from a **cell phone** to a local cell pass from antenna to antenna—cell to cell—until they reach their final destination.

Wireless networks are supplanting traditional wired networks for many applications and creating new applications, services, and business models. In Section 6.4, we provide a detailed description of the applications and technology standards driving the "wireless revolution."

Transmission Speed

The total amount of digital information that can be transmitted through any telecommunications medium is measured in bits per second (bps). One signal change, or cycle, is required to transmit one or several bits; therefore, the transmission capacity of each type of telecommunications medium is a function of its frequency. The number of cycles per second that can be sent through that medium is measured in **hertz**—one hertz is equal to one cycle of the medium.

The range of frequencies that can be accommodated on a particular telecommunications channel is called its **bandwidth**. The bandwidth is the difference between the highest and lowest frequencies that can be accommodated on a single channel. The greater the range of frequencies, the greater the bandwidth and the greater the channel's transmission capacity.

6.3 The Global Internet

We all use the Internet, and many of us can't do without it. It's become an indispensable personal and business tool. But what exactly is the Internet? How does it work, and what does Internet technology have to offer for business? Let's look at the most important Internet features.

WHAT IS THE INTERNET?

The Internet has become the world's most extensive, public communication system that now rivals the global telephone system in reach and range. It's also the world's largest implementation of client/server computing and internetworking, linking millions of individual networks all over the world. This global network of networks began in the early 1970s as a U.S. Department of Defense network to link scientists and university professors around the world.

Most homes and small businesses connect to the Internet by subscribing to an Internet service provider. An **Internet service provider (ISP)** is a commercial organization with a permanent connection to the Internet that sells temporary connections to retail subscribers. EarthLink, NetZero, AT&T, and Time Warner are ISPs. Individuals also connect to the Internet through their business firms, universities, or research centers that have designated Internet domains.

There are a variety of services for ISP Internet connections. Connecting via a traditional telephone line and modem, at a speed of 56.6 kilobits per second (Kbps) used to be the most common form of connection worldwide, but it has been largely replaced by broadband connections. Digital subscriber line (DSL), cable, satellite Internet connections, and T lines provide these broadband services.

Digital subscriber line (DSL) technologies operate over existing telephone lines to carry voice, data, and video at transmission rates ranging from 385 Kbps all the way up to 40 Mbps, depending on usage patterns and distance. **Cable Internet connections** provided by cable television vendors use digital cable coaxial lines to deliver high-speed Internet access to homes and businesses. They can provide high-speed access to the Internet of up to 50 Mbps, although most providers offer service ranging from 1 Mbps to 6 Mbps. In areas where DSL and cable services are unavailable, it is possible to access the Internet via satellite, although some satellite Internet connections have slower upload speeds than other broadband services.

T1 and T3 are international telephone standards for digital communication. They are leased, dedicated lines suitable for businesses or government agencies requiring high-speed guaranteed service levels. **T1 lines** offer guaranteed delivery at 1.54 Mbps, and T3 lines offer delivery at 45 Mbps. The Internet does not provide similar guaranteed service levels, but simply "best effort."

INTERNET ADDRESSING AND ARCHITECTURE

The Internet is based on the TCP/IP networking protocol suite described earlier in this chapter. Every computer on the Internet is assigned a unique **Internet Protocol (IP) address**, which currently is a 32-bit number represented by four strings of numbers ranging from 0 to 255 separated by periods. For instance, the IP address of www.microsoft.com is 207.46.250.119.

When a user sends a message to another user on the Internet, the message is first decomposed into packets using the TCP protocol. Each packet contains its destination address. The packets are then sent from the client to the network server and from there on to as many other servers as necessary to arrive at a specific computer with a known address. At the destination address, the packets are reassembled into the original message.

The Domain Name System

Because it would be incredibly difficult for Internet users to remember strings of 12 numbers, the **Domain Name System (DNS)** converts domain names to IP addresses. The **domain name** is the English-like name that corresponds to the unique 32-bit numeric IP address for each computer connected to the Internet. DNS servers maintain a database containing IP addresses mapped to their corresponding domain names. To access a computer on the Internet, users need only specify its domain name.

DNS has a hierarchical structure (see Figure 6.8). At the top of the DNS hierarchy is the root domain. The child domain of the root is called a top-level domain, and the child domain of a top-level domain is called is a second-level domain. Top-level domains are two-and three-character names you are familiar with from surfing the Web, for example, .com, .edu, .gov, and the various country codes such as .ca for Canada or .it for Italy. Second-level domains have two parts, designating a top-level name and a second-level name—such as buy.com, nyu.edu, or amazon.ca. A host name at the bottom of the hierarchy designates a specific computer on either the Internet or a private network.

The most common domain extensions currently available and officially approved are shown in the following list. Countries also have domain names such as .uk, .au, and .fr (United Kingdom, Australia, and France, respectively), and there is a new class of

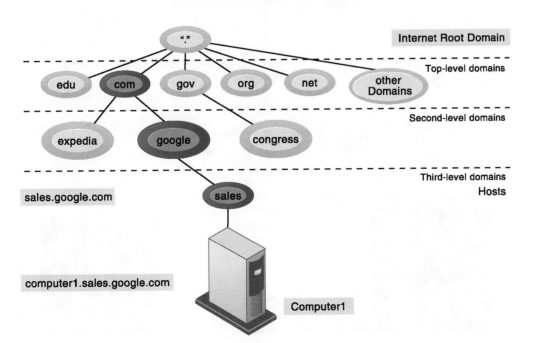

Figure 6.8
The Domain Name System
Domain Name System is a hierarchical system with a root domain, top-level domains, second-level domains, and host computers at the third level.

"internationalized" top-level domains that use non-English characters (ICANN, 2010). In the future, this list will expand to include many more types of organizations and industries.

.com	Commercial organizations/businesses
.edu	Educational institutions
.gov	U.S. government agencies
.mil	U.S. military
.net	Network computers
.org	Nonprofit organizations and foundations
.biz	Business firms
.info	Information providers

Internet Architecture and Governance

Internet data traffic is carried over transcontinental high-speed backbone networks that generally operate in the range of 45 Mbps to 2.5 Gbps (see Figure 6.9). These trunk lines are typically owned by long-distance telephone companies (called *network service providers*) or by national governments. Local connection lines are owned by regional telephone and cable television companies in the United States that connect retail users in homes and businesses to the Internet. The regional networks lease access to ISPs, private companies, and government institutions.

Each organization pays for its own networks and its own local Internet connection services, a part of which is paid to the long-distance trunk line owners. Individual Internet users pay ISPs for using their service, and they generally pay a flat subscription fee, no matter how much or how little they use the Internet. A debate is now raging on whether this arrangement should continue or whether heavy Internet users who download large video and music files should pay more for the bandwidth they consume. The Interactive Session on Organizations explores this topic, by examining the pros and cons of network neutrality.

Figure 6.9
Internet Network Architecture
The Internet backbone connects to regional networks, which in turn provide access to Internet service providers, large firms, and government institutions. Network access points (NAPs) and metropolitan area exchanges (MAEs) are hubs where the backbone intersects regional and local networks and where backbone owners connect with one another.

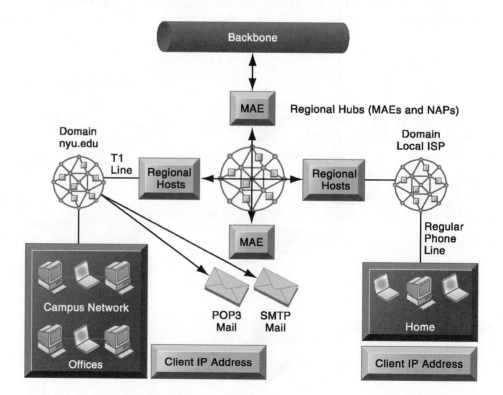

INTERACTIVE SESSION: ORGANIZATIONS The Battle Over Net Neutrality

What kind of Internet user are you? Do you primarily use the Net to do a little e-mail and look up phone numbers? Or are you online all day, watching YouTube videos, downloading music files, or playing online games? If you have a smartphone, do you use it to make calls and check the Web every so often, or do you stream TV shows and movies on a regular basis? If you're a power Internet or smartphone user, you are consuming a great deal of bandwidth, and hundreds of millions of people like you might start to slow the Internet down. YouTube consumed as much bandwidth in 2007 as the entire Internet did in 2000, and AT&T's mobile network will carry more data in the first two months of 2015 than in all of 2010.

If user demand for the Internet overwhelms network capacity, the Internet might not come to a screeching halt, but users would be faced with very sluggish download speeds and slow performance of Netflix, Spotify, YouTube, and other data-heavy services. Heavy use of iPhones in urban areas such as New York and San Francisco has already degraded service on the AT&T wireless network. AT&T reports that 3 percent of its subscriber base accounts for 40 percent of its data traffic.

Some analysts believe that as digital traffic on the Internet grows, even at a rate of 50 percent per year, the technology for handling all this traffic is advancing at an equally rapid pace. But regardless of what happens with Internet infrastructure, costs for Internet providers will continue to increase, and prominent media companies are searching for new revenue streams to meet those costs. One solution is to make Internet users pay for the amount of bandwidth they use. But metering Internet use is not universally accepted, because of an ongoing debate about network neutrality.

Network neutrality is the idea that Internet service providers must allow customers equal access to content and applications, regardless of the source or nature of the content. Presently, the Internet is indeed neutral: all Internet traffic is treated equally on a first-come, first-served basis by Internet backbone owners. However, this arrangement prevents telecommunications and cable companies from charging differentiated prices based on the amount of bandwidth consumed by content being delivered over the Internet. These companies believe that differentiated pricing is "the fairest way" to finance necessary investments in their network infrastructures.

Internet service providers point to the upsurge in piracy of copyrighted materials over the Internet. Comcast, the second largest U.S. Internet service provider, reported that illegal file sharing of copyrighted material was consuming 50 percent of its network capacity. In 2008, the company slowed down transmission of BitTorrent files used extensively for piracy and illegal sharing of copyrighted materials, including video. The Federal Communications Commission (FCC) ruled that Comcast had to stop slowing peer-to-peer traffic in the name of network management. Comcast then filed a lawsuit challenging the FCC's authority to enforce network neutrality. In April 2010, a federal appeals court ruled in favor of Comcast that the FCC did not have the authority to regulate how an Internet provider manages its network. This was a considerable blow to net neutrality. In late 2010, Comcast reportedly began charging Level 3 Communications, which helps stream Netflix's movies, an additional fee for continued normal service. Level 3 asked the FCC to investigate the action.

Groups favoring net neutrality are pushing Congress to find ways to regulate the industry to prevent network providers from adopting Comcast-like practices. The strange alliance of net neutrality advocates includes MoveOn.org, the Christian Coalition, the American Library Association, every major consumer group, and a host of bloggers and small businesses.

Net neutrality advocates argue that the risk of censorship increases when network operators can selectively block or slow access to certain content such as Netflix video streams or access to competing low-cost services such as Skype. Proponents of net neutrality also argue that a neutral Internet encourages everyone to innovate without permission from the phone and cable companies or other authorities, and this level playing field has spawned countless new businesses. Allowing unrestricted information flow becomes essential to free markets and democracy as commerce and society increasingly move online.

Network owners believe regulation to enforce net neutrality will impede U.S. competitiveness by stifling innovation, discouraging capital expenditures for new networks, and curbing their networks' ability to cope with the exploding demand for Internet and wireless traffic. U.S. Internet service lags behind many other nations in overall speed, cost, and quality of service, adding credibility to this argument.

And with enough options for Internet access, regulation would not be essential for promoting net neutrality. Dissatisfied consumers could simply switch to providers who enforce net neutrality and allow unlimited Internet use.

In December 2010, the FCC approved measures that would allow the federal government to regulate Internet traffic. Broadband providers will be required to provide information regarding Internet speeds and service to their subscribers, and they cannot block access to sites or products that compete against their own products. However, the regulations did not officially safeguard net neutrality, and wireless providers may block applications that use too much bandwidth. Wireless providers have already moved to develop tiered plans that charge heavy bandwidth users larger service fees, and online content provid-ers like Amazon and Netflix have increased lobbying efforts to persuade Congress to allow them to do the same. Internet- and content-providers are both pushing hard for tiered systems where those that pay the most get the best service.

Sources: John Eggerton, "Net Neutrality Rules Signed Off On By OMB," *Broadcasting & Cable*, September 13, 2011; Jenna Wortham, "As Networks Speed Up, Data Hits a Wall," *New York Times*, August 14, 2011; "FCC Approves Net Neutrality But With Concessions," *eWeek*, December 22, 2010; Brian Stelter, "Comcast Fee Ignites Fight Over Videos on Internet," *New York Times*, November 30, 2010; Roger Cheng, "AT&T Sees Hope on Web Rules," *Wall Street Journal*, August 12, 2010; Amy Schatz, "New U.S. Push to Regulate Internet Access," *Wall Street Journal*, May 5, 2010; and Claire Cain Miller, "Web Plan is Dividing Companies," *New York Times*, August 11, 2010.

CASE STUDY QUESTIONS

1. What is network neutrality? Why has the Internet operated under net neutrality up to this point in time?

2. Who's in favor of net neutrality? Who's opposed? Why?

3. What would be the impact on individual users, businesses, and government if Internet providers switched to a tiered service model?

4. Are you in favor of legislation enforcing network neutrality? Why or why not?

MIS IN ACTION

1. Visit the Web site of the Open Internet Coalition and select five member organizations. Then visit the Web site of each of these organizations or surf the Web to find out more information about each. Write a short essay explaining why each organization is in favor of network neutrality.

2. Calculate how much bandwidth you consume when using the Internet every day. How many e-mails do you send daily and what is the size of each? (Your e-mail program may have e-mail file size information.) How many music and video clips do you download daily and what is the size of each? If you view YouTube often, surf the Web to find out the size of a typical YouTube file. Add up the number of e-mail, audio, and video files you transmit or receive on a typical day.

No one "owns" the Internet, and it has no formal management. However, worldwide Internet policies are established by a number of professional organizations and govern-ment bodies, including the Internet Architecture Board (IAB), which helps define the overall structure of the Internet; the Internet Corporation for Assigned Names and Numbers (ICANN), which assigns IP addresses; and the World Wide Web Consortium (W3C), which sets Hypertext Markup Language and other programming standards for the Web.

These organizations influence government agencies, network owners, ISPs, and soft-ware developers with the goal of keeping the Internet operating as efficiently as pos-sible. The Internet must also conform to the laws of the sovereign nation-states in which it operates, as well as the technical infrastructures that exist within the nation-states. Although in the early years of the Internet and the Web there was very little legisla-tive or executive interference, this situation is changing as the Internet plays a growing role in the distribution of information and knowledge, including content that some find objectionable.

The Future Internet: IPv6 and Internet2

The Internet was not originally designed to handle the transmission of massive quantities of data and billions of users. Because many corporations and governments have been given large blocks of millions of IP addresses to accommodate current and future workforces, and because of sheer Internet population growth, the world will run out of available IP addresses using the existing addressing convention by 2012 or 2013. The old addressing system is being replaced by a new version of the IP addressing schema called **IPv6** (Internet Protocol version 6), which contains 128-bit addresses (2 to the power of 128), or more than a quadrillion possible unique addresses. IPv6 is not compatible with the existing Internet addressing system, so the transition to the new standard will take years.

Internet2 is an advanced networking consortium representing over 330 U.S. universities, private businesses, and government agencies working with 60,000 institutions across the U.S. and international networking partners from more than 50 countries. To connect these communities, Internet2 developed a high-capacity 100 gigabit-per-second network that serves as a testbed for leading-edge technologies that may eventually migrate to the public Internet, including telemedicine, distance learning, and other advanced applications not possible with consumer-grade Internet services. The fourth generation of this network, which began to be rolled out in 2011, will provide 8.8 terabits of capacity.

INTERNET SERVICES AND COMMUNICATION TOOLS

The Internet is based on client/server technology. Individuals using the Internet control what they do through client applications on their computers, such as Web browser software. The data, including e-mail messages and Web pages, are stored on servers. A client uses the Internet to request information from a particular Web server on a distant computer, and the server sends the requested information back to the client over the Internet. Chapters 4 and 5 describe how Web servers work with application servers and database servers to access information from an organization's internal information systems applications and their associated databases. Client platforms today include not only PCs and other computers but also cell phones, small handheld digital devices, and other information appliances.

Internet Services

A client computer connecting to the Internet has access to a variety of services. These services include e-mail, chatting and instant messaging, electronic discussion groups, **Telnet**, **File Transfer Protocol (FTP)**, and the Web. Table 6.2 provides a brief description of these services.

Capability	Functions Supported
E-mail	Person-to-person messaging; document sharing
Chatting and instant messaging	Interactive conversations
Newsgroups	Discussion groups on electronic bulletin boards
Telnet	Logging on to one computer system and doing work on another
File Transfer Protocol (FTP)	Transferring files from computer to computer
World Wide Web	Retrieving, formatting, and displaying information (including text, audio, graphics, and video) using hypertext links

TABLE 6.2

Major Internet Services

Each Internet service is implemented by one or more software programs. All of the services may run on a single server computer, or different services may be allocated to different machines. Figure 6.10 illustrates one way that these services can be arranged in a multitiered client/server architecture.

E-mail enables messages to be exchanged from computer to computer, with capabilities for routing messages to multiple recipients, forwarding messages, and attaching text documents or multimedia files to messages. Although some organizations operate their own internal electronic mail systems, most e-mail today is sent through the Internet. The costs of e-mail is far lower than equivalent voice, postal, or overnight delivery costs, making the Internet a very inexpensive and rapid communications medium. Most e-mail messages arrive anywhere in the world in a matter of seconds.

Nearly 90 percent of U.S. workplaces have employees communicating interactively using **chat** or instant messaging tools. Chatting enables two or more people who are simultaneously connected to the Internet to hold live, interactive conversations. Chat systems now support voice and video chat as well as written conversations. Many online retail businesses offer chat services on their Web sites to attract visitors, to encourage repeat purchases, and to improve customer service.

Instant messaging is a type of chat service that enables participants to create their own private chat channels. The instant messaging system alerts the user whenever someone on his or her private list is online so that the user can initiate a chat session with other individuals. Instant messaging systems for consumers include Yahoo! Messenger, Google Talk, and Windows Live Messenger. Companies concerned with security use proprietary instant messaging systems such as Lotus Sametime.

Newsgroups are worldwide discussion groups posted on Internet electronic bulletin boards on which people share information and ideas on a defined topic, such as radiology or rock bands. Anyone can post messages on these bulletin boards for others to read. Many thousands of groups exist that discuss almost all conceivable topics.

Employee use of e-mail, instant messaging, and the Internet is supposed to increase worker productivity, but the accompanying Interactive Session on People shows that this may not always be the case. Many company managers now believe they need to monitor and

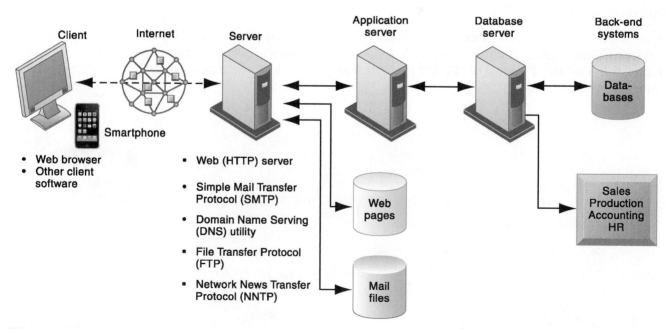

Figure 6.10
Client/Server Computing on the Internet
Client computers running Web browser and other software can access an array of services on servers over the Internet. These services may all run on a single server or on multiple specialized servers.

INTERACTIVE SESSION: PEOPLE   Monitoring Employees on Networks: Unethical or Good Business?

When you were at work, how minutes (or hours) did you spend on Facebook today? Did you send personal e-mail or visit some sports Web sites? If so, you're not alone. According to a Nucleus Research study, 77 percent of workers with Facebook accounts use them during work hours. A Ponemon Institute study reported that the average employee wastes approximately 30 percent of the workday on non-work-related Web browsing, while other studies report as many as 90 percent of employees receive or send personal e-mail at work.

This behavior creates serious business problems. Checking e-mail, responding to instant messages, or sneaking in a brief YouTube video create a series of nonstop interruptions that divert employee attention from the job tasks they are supposed to be performing. According to Basex, a New York City business research company, these distractions result in $650 billion in lost productivity each year!

Many companies have begun monitoring employee use of e-mail and the Internet, sometimes without their knowledge. A 2010 study from Proofpoint Plus found that more than one in three large U.S corporations assign staff to read or analyze employee e-mail. Another recent survey from the American Management Association (AMA) and the ePolicy Institute found that two out of three of the small, medium, and large companies surveyed monitored Web use. Instant-message and text message monitoring are also increasing. Although U.S. companies have the legal right to monitor employee Internet and e-mail activity while they are at work, is such monitoring unethical, or is it simply good business?

Managers worry about the loss of time and employee productivity when employees are focusing on personal rather than company business. Too much time on personal business translates into lost revenue. Some employees may even be billing time they spend pursuing personal interests online to clients, thus overcharging them.

If personal traffic on company networks is too high, it can also clog the company's network so that legitimate business work cannot be performed. Schemmer Associates, an architecture firm in Omaha, Nebraska, and Potomac Hospital in Woodridge, Virginia, found that computing resources were limited by a lack of bandwidth caused by employees using corporate Internet connections to watch and download video files.

When employees use e-mail or the Web (including social networks) at employer facilities or with employer equipment, anything they do, including anything illegal, carries the company's name. Therefore, the employer can be traced and held liable. Management in many firms fear that racist, sexually explicit, or other potentially offensive material accessed or traded by their employees could result in adverse publicity and even lawsuits for the firm. Even if the company is found not to be liable, responding to lawsuits could run up huge legal bills. Symantec's 2011 Social Media Protection Flash Poll found that the average litigation cost for companies with social media incidents ran over $650,000.

Companies also fear leakage of confidential information and trade secrets through e-mail or social networks. Another survey conducted by the American Management Association and the ePolicy Institute found that 14 percent of the employees polled admitted they had sent confidential or potentially embarrassing company e-mails to outsiders.

U.S. companies have the legal right to monitor what employees are doing with company equipment during business hours. The question is whether electronic surveillance is an appropriate tool for maintaining an efficient and positive workplace. Some companies try to ban all personal activities on corporate networks—zero tolerance. Others block employee access to specific Web sites or social sites, closely monitor e-mail messages, or limit personal time on the Web.

For example, Enterprise Rent-A-Car blocks employee access to certain social sites and monitors the Web for employees' online postings about the company. Ajax Boiler in Santa Ana, California, uses software from SpectorSoft Corporation that records all the Web sites employees visit, time spent at each site, and all e-mails sent. Financial services and investment firm Wedbush Securities monitors the daily e-mails, instant messaging, and social networking activity of its 1,000-plus employees. The firm's e-mail monitoring software flags certain types of messages and keywords within messages for further investigation.

A number of firms have fired employees who have stepped out of bounds. The Proofpoint survey found that one in five large U.S. companies fired an employee for violating e-mail policies in the past year. Among managers who fired employees for Internet misuse, the majority did so because the employees' e-mail contained sensitive, confidential, or embarrassing information.

No solution is problem free, but many consultants believe companies should write corporate policies on employee e-mail and Internet use. The policies should include explicit ground rules that state, by position or level, under what circumstances employees can use company facilities for e-mail, blogging, or Web surfing. The policies should also inform employees whether these activities are monitored and explain why.

IBM now has "social computing guidelines" that cover employee activity on sites such as Facebook and Twitter. The guidelines urge employees not to conceal their identities, to remember that they are personally responsible for what they publish, and to refrain from discussing controversial topics that are not related to their IBM role.

The rules should be tailored to specific business needs and organizational cultures. For example, investment firms will need to allow many of their employees access to other investment sites. A company dependent on widespread information sharing, innovation, and independence could very well find that monitoring creates more problems than it solves.

Sources: Jennifer Lawinski, "Social Media Costs Companies Bigtime," *Baseline*, August 29, 2011; Don Reisinger, "March Madness: The Great Productivity Killer," *CIO Insight* March 18, 2011; "Seven Employee Monitoring Tips for Small Business," IT BusinessEdge, May 29, 2011; Catey Hill, "Things Your Boss Won't Tell You," *Smart Money* January 12, 2011; and Joan Goodchild, "Not Safe for Work: What's Acceptable for Office Computer Use," CIO Australia, June 17, 2010.

CASE STUDY QUESTIONS

1. Should managers monitor employee e-mail and Internet usage? Why or why not?

2. Describe an effective e-mail and Web use policy for a company.

3. Should managers inform employees that their Web behavior is being monitored? Or should managers monitor secretly? Why or why not?

MIS IN ACTION

Explore the Web site of online employee monitoring software such as Websense, Barracuda Networks, or SpectorSoft, and answer the following questions.

1. What employee activities does this software track? What can an employer learn about an employee by using this software?

2. How can businesses benefit from using this software?

3. How would you feel if your employer used this software where you work to monitor what you are doing on the job? Explain your response.

even regulate their employees' online activity. But is this ethical? Although there are some strong business reasons why companies may need to monitor their employees' e-mail and Web activities, what does this mean for employee privacy?

Voice over IP

The Internet has also become a popular platform for voice transmission and corporate networking. **Voice over IP (VoIP)** technology delivers voice information in digital form using packet switching, avoiding the tolls charged by local and long-distance telephone networks (see Figure 6.11). Calls that would ordinarily be transmitted over public telephone networks travel over the corporate network based on the Internet Protocol, or the public Internet. Voice calls can be made and received with a computer equipped with a microphone and speakers or with a VoIP-enabled telephone.

Cable firms such as Time Warner and Cablevision provide VoIP service bundled with their high-speed Internet and cable offerings. Skype offers free VoIP worldwide using a peer-to-peer network, and Google has its own free VoIP service.

Although there are up-front investments required for an IP phone system, VoIP can reduce communication and network management costs by 20 to 30 percent. For example, VoIP saves Virgin Entertainment Group $700,000 per year in long-distance bills. In addition to lowering long-distance costs and eliminating monthly fees for private lines, an IP network provides a single voice-data infrastructure for both telecommunications and computing services. Companies no longer have to maintain separate networks or provide support services and personnel for each different type of network.

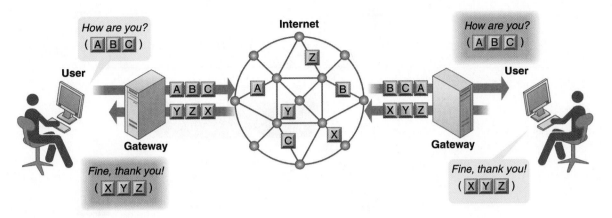

Figure 6.11
How Voice over IP Works
A VoIP phone call digitizes and breaks up a voice message into data packets that may travel along different routes before being reassembled at the final destination. A processor nearest the call's destination, called a gateway, arranges the packets in the proper order and directs them to the telephone number of the receiver or the IP address of the receiving computer.

Another advantage of VoIP is its flexibility. Unlike the traditional telephone network, phones can be added or moved to different offices without rewiring or reconfiguring the network. With VoIP, a conference call is arranged by a simple click-and-drag operation on the computer screen to select the names of the conferees. Voice mail and e-mail can be combined into a single directory.

Unified Communications

In the past, each of the firm's networks for wired and wireless data, voice communications, and videoconferencing operated independently of each other and had to be managed separately by the information systems department. Now, however, firms are able to merge disparate communications modes into a single universally accessible service using unified communications technology. **Unified communications** integrates disparate channels for voice communications, data communications, instant messaging, e-mail, and electronic conferencing into a single experience where users can seamlessly switch back and forth between different communication modes. Presence technology shows whether a person is available to receive a call. Companies will need to examine how work flows and business processes will be altered by this technology in order to gauge its value.

CenterPoint Properties, a major Chicago area industrial real estate company, used unified communications technology to create collaborative Web sites for each of its real estate deals. Each Web site provides a single point for accessing structured and unstructured data. Integrated presence technology lets team members e-mail, instant message, call, or videoconference with one click.

Virtual Private Networks

What if you had a marketing group charged with developing new products and services for your firm with members spread across the United States? You would want to be able to e-mail each other and communicate with the home office without any chance that outsiders could intercept the communications. In the past, one answer to this problem was to work with large private networking firms who offered secure, private, dedicated networks to customers. But this was an expensive solution. A much less-expensive solution is to create a virtual private network within the public Internet.

A **virtual private network (VPN)** is a secure, encrypted, private network that has been configured within a public network to take advantage of the economies of scale and management facilities of large networks, such as the Internet (see Figure 6.12). A VPN provides your firm with secure, encrypted communications at a much lower cost than the

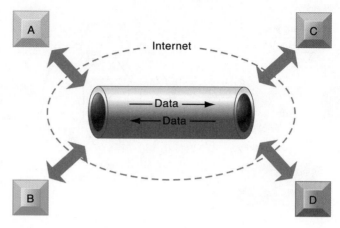

Figure 6.12
A Virtual Private Network Using the Internet
This VPN is a private network of computers linked using a secure "tunnel" connection over the Internet. It protects data transmitted over the public Internet by encoding the data and "wrapping" them within the Internet Protocol (IP). By adding a wrapper around a network message to hide its content, organizations can create a private connection that travels through the public Internet.

same capabilities offered by traditional non-Internet providers who use their private networks to secure communications. VPNs also provide a network infrastructure for combining voice and data networks.

Several competing protocols are used to protect data transmitted over the public Internet, including *Point-to-Point Tunneling Protocol (PPTP)*. In a process called tunneling, packets of data are encrypted and wrapped inside IP packets. By adding this wrapper around a network message to hide its content, business firms create a private connection that travels through the public Internet.

THE WEB

You've probably used the Web to download music, to find information for a term paper, or to obtain news and weather reports. The Web is the most popular Internet service. It's a system with universally accepted standards for storing, retrieving, formatting, and displaying information using a client/server architecture. Web pages are formatted using hypertext with embedded links that connect documents to one another and that also link pages to other objects, such as sound, video, or animation files. When you click a graphic and a video clip plays, you have clicked a hyperlink. A typical **Web site** is a collection of Web pages linked to a home page.

Hypertext

Web pages are based on a standard Hypertext Markup Language (HTML), which formats documents and incorporates dynamic links to other documents and pictures stored in the same or remote computers (see Chapter 4). Web pages are accessible through the Internet because Web browser software operating your computer can request Web pages stored on an Internet host server using the **Hypertext Transfer Protocol (HTTP)**. HTTP is the communications standard used to transfer pages on the Web. For example, when you type a Web address in your browser, such as http://www.sec.gov, your browser sends an HTTP request to the sec.gov server requesting the home page of sec.gov.

HTTP is the first set of letters at the start of every Web address, followed by the domain name, which specifies the organization's server computer that is storing the document. Most companies have a domain name that is the same as or closely related to their official corporate name. The directory path and document name are two more pieces of information within the Web address that help the browser track down the requested page. Together, the address is called a **uniform resource locator (URL)**. When typed into a browser, a URL tells the browser software exactly where to look for the information. For example, in the URL *http://www.megacorp.com/content/features/082610.html,* *http* names the protocol used to display Web pages, www.megacorp.com is the domain name, *content/features* is the directory path that identifies where on the domain Web server the page is stored, and *082610.html* is the document name and the name of the format it is in (it is an HTML page).

Web Servers

A Web server is software for locating and managing stored Web pages. It locates the Web pages requested by a user on the computer where they are stored and delivers the Web pages to the user's computer. Server applications usually run on dedicated computers, although they can all reside on a single computer in small organizations.

The most common Web server in use today is Apache HTTP Server, which controls 59 percent of the market. Apache is an open source product that is free of charge and can be downloaded from the Web. Microsoft Internet Information Services (IIS) is the second most commonly used Web server, with a 21 percent market share.

Searching for Information on the Web

No one knows for sure how many Web pages there really are. The surface Web is the part of the Web that search engines visit and about which information is recorded. For instance, Google visited about 250 billion pages in 2011, and this reflects a large portion of the publicly accessible Web page population. But there is a "deep Web" that contains an estimated 1 trillion additional pages, many of them proprietary (such as the pages of the *Wall Street Journal Online*, which cannot be visited without an access code) or that are stored in protected corporate databases.

Search Engines Obviously, with so many Web pages, finding specific Web pages that can help you or your business, nearly instantly, is an important problem. The question is, how can you find the one or two pages you really want and need out of billions of indexed Web pages? **Search engines** attempt to solve the problem of finding useful information on the Web nearly instantly, and, arguably, they are the "killer app" of the Internet era. Today's search engines can sift through HTML files, files of Microsoft Office applications, PDF files, as well as audio, video, and image files. There are hundreds of different search engines in the world, but the vast majority of search results are supplied by Google, Yahoo!, Baidu, and Microsoft's Bing search engine (see Figure 6.13).

Web search engines started out in the early 1990s as relatively simple software programs that roamed the nascent Web, visiting pages and gathering information about the content

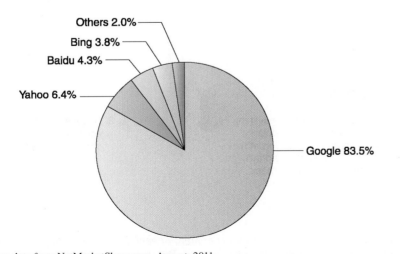

Figure 6.13
Top U.S. Web Search Engines
Google is the most popular search engine, handling 84 percent of Web searches.

Others 2.0%
Bing 3.8%
Baidu 4.3%
Yahoo 6.4%
Google 83.5%

Source: Based on data from NetMarketShare.com, August, 2011.

of each page. The first search engines were simple keyword indexes of all the pages they visited, leaving the user with lists of pages that may not have been truly relevant to their search.

In 1994, Stanford University computer science students David Filo and Jerry Yang created a hand-selected list of their favorite Web pages and called it "Yet Another Hierarchical Officious Oracle," or Yahoo. Yahoo was not initially a search engine but rather an edited selection of Web sites organized by categories the editors found useful, but it has since developed its own search engine capabilities.

In 1998, Larry Page and Sergey Brin, two other Stanford computer science students, released their first version of Google. This search engine was different: Not only did it index each Web page's words but it also ranked search results based on the relevance of each page. Page patented the idea of a page ranking system (called PageRank System), which essentially measures the popularity of a Web page by calculating the number of sites that link to that page as well as the number of pages which it links to. Brin contributed a unique Web crawler program that indexed not only keywords on a page but also combinations of words (such as authors and the titles of their articles). These two ideas became the foundation for the Google search engine. Figure 6.14 illustrates how Google works.

Search engine Web sites are so popular that many people use them as their home page, the page where they start surfing the Web (see Chapter 9). Search engines are also the foundation for the fastest growing form of marketing and advertising, search engine marketing.

Mobile Search With the growth of mobile smartphones and tablet computers, and with about 91 million Americans accessing the Internet via mobile devices, the nature of e-commerce and search is changing. Mobile search now makes up about 15 percent of all searches in

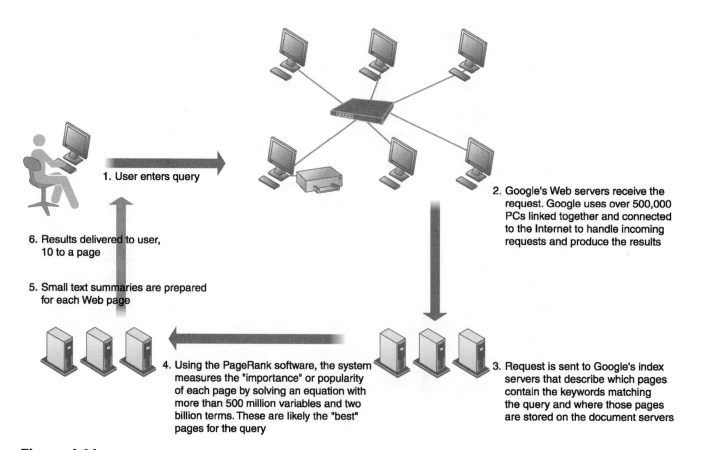

1. User enters query

6. Results delivered to user, 10 to a page

5. Small text summaries are prepared for each Web page

4. Using the PageRank software, the system measures the "importance" or popularity of each page by solving an equation with more than 500 million variables and two billion terms. These are likely the "best" pages for the query

2. Google's Web servers receive the request. Google uses over 500,000 PCs linked together and connected to the Internet to handle incoming requests and produce the results

3. Request is sent to Google's index servers that describe which pages contain the keywords matching the query and where those pages are stored on the document servers

Figure 6.14
How Google Works
The Google search engine is continuously crawling the Web, indexing the content of each page, calculating its popularity, and storing the pages so that it can respond quickly to user requests to see a page. The entire process takes about one-half second.

2011, and will expand to 25 percent in the next few years. Both Google and Yahoo have developed new search interfaces to make searching from smartphones more convenient. Amazon, for instance, sold over $1 billion in goods in 2011 through mobile searches of its store (comScore, 2011).

Search Engine Marketing Search engines have become major shopping tools by offering what is now called **search engine marketing**. When users enter a search term at Google, Bing, Yahoo!, or any of the other sites serviced by these search engines, they receive two types of listings: sponsored links, for which advertisers have paid to be listed (usually at the top of the search results page), and unsponsored "organic" search results. In addition, advertisers can purchase small text boxes on the side of search results pages. The paid, sponsored advertisements are the fastest growing form of Internet advertising and are powerful new marketing tools that precisely match consumer interests with advertising messages at the right moment. Search engine marketing monetizes the value of the search process. In 2011, search engine marketing generated $14.4 billion in revenue, nearly half of all online advertising ($31.3 billion). Ninety-seven percent of Google's annual revenue of $23.6 billion comes from search engine marketing (eMarketer, 2010).

Because search engine marketing is so effective (it has the highest click-through rate and the highest return on ad investment), companies are starting to optimize their Web sites for search engine recognition. The better optimized the page is, the higher a ranking it will achieve in search engine result listings. **Search engine optimization (SEO)** is the process of improving the quality and volume of Web traffic to a Web site by employing a series of techniques that help a Web site achieve a higher ranking with the major search engines when certain keywords and phrases are put in the search field. One technique is to make sure that the keywords used in the Web site description match the keywords likely to be used as search terms by prospective customers. For example, your Web site is more likely to be among the first ranked by search engines if it uses the keyword "lighting" rather than "lamps" if most prospective customers are searching for "lighting." It is also advantageous to link your Web site to as many other Web sites as possible because search engines evaluate such links to determine the popularity of a Web page and how it is linked to other content on the Web. The assumption is the more links there are to a Web site, the more useful the Web site must be.

In general, search engines have been very helpful to small businesses that cannot afford large marketing campaigns. Because shoppers are looking for a specific product or service when they use search engines, they are what marketers call "hot prospects"— people who are looking for information and often intending to buy. Moreover, search engines charge only for click-throughs to a site. Merchants do not have to pay for ads that don't work, only for ads that receive a click. Consumers benefit from search engine marketing because ads for merchants appear only when consumers are looking for a specific product. There are no pop-ups, Flash animations, videos, interstitials, e-mails, or other irrelevant communications to deal with. Thus, search engine marketing saves consumers cognitive energy and reduces search costs (including the cost of transportation needed to physically search for products). In a recent study, the global value of search to both merchants and consumers was estimated to be more than $800 billion, with about 65 percent of the benefit going to consumers in the form of lower search costs and lower prices (McKinsey, 2011).

Social Search One problem with Google and mechanical search engines is that they are so thorough: enter a search for kidney stones and in .10 seconds you will receive 8.2 million results, some of them providing helpful information, others will be suspect. **Social search** is an effort to provide fewer, more relevant, and trustworthy search results based on a person's network of social contacts. In contrast to the top search engines that use a mathematical algorithm to find pages that satisfy your query, a social search Web site would review your friends' recommendations (and their friends'), their past Web visits, and their use of "Like" buttons.

For instance, Google has developed Google +1 as a social layer on top of its existing search engine. Users can place a +1 next to the Web sites they found helpful, and their friends will be notified automatically. Subsequent searches by their friends would list the +1 sites recommended by friends higher up on the page. Facebook's "Like" button is a similar social search tool So far, neither Facebook or Google has fully implemented a social search engine (Efrati, 2011). One problem with social search is that your close friends may not have intimate knowledge of topics you are exploring.

Although search engines were originally built to search text documents, the explosion in online video and images has created a demand for search engines that can quickly find specific videos. The words "dance," "love," "music," and "girl" are all exceedingly popular in titles of YouTube videos, and searching on these keywords produces a flood of responses even though the actual contents of the videos may have nothing to do with the search term. Searching videos is challenging because computers are not very good or quick at recognizing digital images. Some search engines have started indexing movie scripts so it will be possible to search on dialogue to find a movie. Blinkx.com is a popular video search service, and Google has added video search capabilities.

Intelligent Agent Shopping Bots Chapter 10 describes the capabilities of software agents with built-in intelligence that can gather or filter information and perform other tasks to assist users. **Shopping bots** use intelligent agent software for searching the Internet for shopping information. Shopping bots such as MySimon or Google Product Search can help people interested in making a purchase filter and retrieve information about products of interest, evaluate competing products according to criteria the users have established, and negotiate with vendors for price and delivery terms. Many of these shopping agents search the Web for pricing and availability of products specified by the user and return a list of sites that sell the item along with pricing information and a purchase link.

Web 2.0

Today's Web sites don't just contain static content—they enable people to collaborate, share information, and create new services and content online. These second-generation interactive Internet-based services are referred to as **Web 2.0.** If you have shared photos over the Internet at Flickr or another photo site, posted a video to YouTube, created a blog, used Wikipedia, or added an app to your Facebook page, you've used some of these Web 2.0 services.

Web 2.0 has four defining features: interactivity, real-time user control, social participation (sharing), and user-generated content. The technologies and services behind these features include cloud computing, software mashups and apps, blogs, RSS, wikis, and social networks.

Mashups, which we introduced in Chapter 4, are software services that enable users and system developers to mix and match content or software components to create something entirely new. For example, Yahoo's photo storage and sharing site Flickr combines photos with other information about the images provided by users and tools to make it usable within other programming environments. Web 2.0 tools and services have fueled the creation of social networks and other online communities where people can interact with one another in the manner of their choosing.

A **blog**, the popular term for a Weblog, is a personal Web site that typically contains a series of chronological entries (newest to oldest) by its author, and links to related Web pages. The blog may include a *blogroll* (a collection of links to other blogs) and *trackbacks* (a list of entries in other blogs that refer to a post on the first blog). Most blogs allow readers to post comments on the blog entries as well. The act of creating a blog is often referred to as "blogging." Blogs can be hosted by a third-party service such as Blogger.com, TypePad.com, and Xanga.com, and blogging features have been incorporated into social networks such as Facebook and collaboration platforms such as Lotus Notes. **Microblogging**, used in Twitter, is a type of blogging that features very short posts.

Blog pages are usually variations on templates provided by the blogging service or software. Therefore, millions of people without HTML skills of any kind can post their own Web pages and share content with others. The totality of blog-related Web sites is often referred to as the **blogosphere**. Although blogs have become popular personal publishing tools, they also have business uses (see Chapters 2 and 9).

If you're an avid blog reader, you might use RSS to keep up with your favorite blogs without constantly checking them for updates. **RSS**, which stands for Really Simple Syndication or Rich Site Summary, pulls specified content from Web sites and feeds it automatically to users' computers. RSS reader software gathers material from the Web sites or blogs that you tell it to scan and brings new information from those sites to you. RSS readers are available through Web sites such as Google and Yahoo, and they have been incorporated into the major Web browsers and e-mail programs.

Blogs allow visitors to add comments to the original content, but they do not allow visitors to change the original posted material. **Wikis**, in contrast, are collaborative Web sites where visitors can add, delete, or modify content on the site, including the work of previous authors. Wiki comes from the Hawaiian word for "quick."

Wiki software typically provides a template that defines layout and elements common to all pages, displays user-editable software program code, and then renders the content into an HTML-based page for display in a Web browser. Some wiki software allows only basic text formatting, whereas other tools allow the use of tables, images, or even interactive elements, such as polls or games. Most wikis provide capabilities for monitoring the work of other users and correcting mistakes.

Because wikis make information sharing so easy, they have many business uses. The U.S. Department of Homeland Security's National Cyber Security Center (NCSC) deployed a wiki to facilitate collaboration among federal agencies on cybersecurity. NCSC and other agencies use the wiki for real-time information sharing on threats, attacks, and responses and as a repository for technical and standards information. Pixar Wiki is a collaborative community wiki for publicizing the work of Pixar Animation Studios. The wiki format allows anyone to create or edit an article about a Pixar film.

Social networking sites enable users to build communities of friends and professional colleagues. Members typically create a "profile," a Web page for posting photos, videos, MP3 files, and text, and then share these profiles with others on the service identified as their "friends" or contacts. Social networking sites are highly interactive, offer real-time user control, rely on user-generated content, and are broadly based on social participation and sharing of content and opinions. Leading social networking sites include Facebook, Twitter (with 800 million and 100 million active users respectively in 2011), and LinkedIn (for professional contacts).

For many, social networking sites are the defining Web 2.0 application, and one that has radically changed how people spend their time online; how people communicate and with whom; how business people stay in touch with customers, suppliers, and employees; how providers of goods and services learn about their customers; and how advertisers reach potential customers. The large social networking sites are also morphing into application development platforms where members can create and sell software applications to other members of the community. Facebook alone has over 1 million developers who created over 550,000 applications for gaming, video sharing, and communicating with friends and family. We talk more about business applications of social networking in Chapters 2 and 9, and you can find social networking discussions in many other chapters of this book. You can also find a more detailed discussion of Web 2.0 in our Learning Tracks.

Web 3.0: The Future Web

Every day about 120 million Americans enter 630 million queries into search engines. How many of these 630 million queries produce a meaningful result (a useful answer in the first three listings)? Arguably, fewer than half. Google, Yahoo, Microsoft, and Amazon are all trying to increase the odds of people finding meaningful answers to search engine queries. But with over 200 billion Web pages indexed, the means available for finding the information you really want are quite primitive, based on the words used on the pages, and the relative popularity of the page among people who use those same search terms. In other words, it's hit or miss. (eMarketer, 2011).

To a large extent, the future of the Web involves developing techniques to make searching the 200 billion public Web pages more productive and meaningful for ordinary people. Web 1.0 solved the problem of obtaining access to information. Web 2.0 solved the problem of sharing that information with others, and building new Web experiences. **Web 3.0** is the promise of a future Web where all this digital information, all these contacts, can be woven together into a single meaningful experience.

Sometimes this is referred to as the **Semantic Web**. "Semantic" refers to meaning. Most of the Web's content today is designed for humans to read and for computers to display, not for computer programs to analyze and manipulate. Search engines can discover when a particular term or keyword appears in a Web document, but they do not really understand its meaning or how it relates to other information on the Web. You can check this out on Google by entering two searches. First, enter "Paris Hilton". Next, enter "Hilton in Paris". Because Google does not understand ordinary English, it has no idea that you are interested in the Hilton Hotel in Paris in the second search. Because it cannot understand the meaning of pages it has indexed, Google's search engine returns the most popular pages for those queries where "Hilton" and "Paris" appear on the pages.

First described in a 2001 *Scientific American* article, the Semantic Web is a collaborative effort led by the World Wide Web Consortium to add a layer of meaning atop the existing Web to reduce the amount of human involvement in searching for and processing Web information (Berners-Lee et al., 2001).

Views on the future of the Web vary, but they generally focus on ways to make the Web more "intelligent," with machine-facilitated understanding of information promoting a more intuitive and effective user experience. For instance, let's say you want to set up a party with your tennis buddies at a local restaurant Friday night after work. One problem is that you are already scheduled to go to a movie with another friend. In a Semantic Web 3.0 environment, you would be able to coordinate this change in plans with the schedules of your tennis buddies, the schedule of your movie friend, and make a reservation at the restaurant all with a single set of commands issued as text or voice to your handheld smartphone. Right now, this capability is beyond our grasp.

Work proceeds slowly on making the Web a more intelligent experience, in large part because it is difficult to make machines, including software programs, that are truly intelligent like humans. But there are other views of the future Web. Some see a 3-D Web where you can walk through pages in a 3-D environment. Others point to the idea of a pervasive Web that controls everything from the lights in your living room, to your car's rear view mirror, not to mention managing your calendar and appointments.

Other complementary trends leading toward a future Web 3.0 include more widespread use of cloud computing and SaaS business models, ubiquitous connectivity among mobile platforms and Internet access devices, and the transformation of the Web from a network of separate siloed applications and content into a more seamless and interoperable whole. These more modest visions of the future Web 3.0 are more likely to be realized in the near term.

6.4 The Wireless Revolution

Welcome to the wireless revolution! Cell phones, smartphones, tablets, and wireless-enabled personal computers have morphed into portable computing platforms that let you perform many of the computing tasks you used to do at your desk. We introduced **smartphones** in our discussions of the mobile digital platform in Chapters 1 and 4. Smartphones such as the iPhone, Android phones, and BlackBerry combine the functionality of a cell phone with that of a mobile laptop computer with Wi-Fi capability. This makes it possible to combine music, video, Internet access, and telephone service in one device. Smartphones are the fastest growing wireless devices with respect to Internet access. A large part of the future Internet will be mobile, access-anywhere broadband service for the delivery of video, music, and Web search.

CELLULAR SYSTEMS

In 2011, there were over 1 billion cell phones sold worldwide, and cellular telephones are now the largest providers of wireless access to the Internet. Digital cellular service uses several competing standards. In Europe and much of the rest of the world outside the United Sates, the standard is Global System for Mobile Communication (GSM). GSM's strength is its international roaming capability. There are GSM cell phone systems in the United States, including T-Mobile and AT&T Wireless.

The major standard in the United States is Code Division Multiple Access (CDMA), which is the system used by Verizon and Sprint. CDMA was developed by the military during World War II. It transmits over several frequencies, occupies the entire spectrum, and randomly assigns users to a range of frequencies over time.

Earlier generations of cellular systems were designed primarily for voice and limited data transmission in the form of short text messages. Wireless carriers now offer more powerful cellular networks called third-generation or **3G networks**, with transmission speeds ranging from 144 Kbps for mobile users in, say, a car, to more than 2 Mbps for stationary users. This is sufficient transmission capacity for video, graphics, and other rich media, in addition to voice, making 3G networks suitable for wireless broadband Internet access.

High-speed cellular networks are widely used in Japan, South Korea, Taiwan, Hong Kong, Singapore, and parts of northern Europe. U.S. cellular carriers have upgraded their networks to support higher-speed transmission, enabling mobile phones to be used for Web access, music downloads, and other broadband services. PCs equipped with a special card can use these broadband cellular services for anytime, anywhere wireless Internet access.

The next evolution in wireless communication, called **4G networks**, is entirely packet switched and capable of 100 Mbps transmission speed (which can reach 1 Gbps under optimal conditions), with premium quality and high security. Voice, data, and high-quality streaming video are available to users anywhere, anytime. Pre-4G technologies currently include Long Term Evolution (LTE) and the mobile WiMax. (See the discussion of WiMax in the following section.) You can find out more about cellular generations in the Learning Tracks for this chapter.

WIRELESS COMPUTER NETWORKS AND INTERNET ACCESS

If you have a laptop computer or tablet, you might be able to use it to access the Internet as you move from room to room in your dorm, or table to table in your university library. An array of technologies provide high-speed wireless access to the Internet for PCs and other wireless hand-held devices as well as for cell phones. These new high-speed services have extended Internet access to numerous locations that could not be covered by traditional wired Internet services.

Bluetooth

Bluetooth is the popular name for the 802.15 wireless networking standard, which is useful for creating small **personal area networks (PANs)**. It links up to eight devices within a 10-meter area using low-power, radio-based communication and can transmit up to 722 Kbps in the 2.4-GHz band.

Wireless phones, pagers, computers, printers, and computing devices using Bluetooth communicate with each other and even operate each other without direct user intervention (see Figure 6.15). For example, a person could direct a notebook computer to send a document file wirelessly to a printer. Bluetooth connects wireless keyboards and mice to PCs or cell phones to earpieces without wires. Bluetooth has low-power requirements, making it appropriate for battery-powered handheld computers or cell phones.

Although Bluetooth lends itself to personal networking, it has uses in large corporations. For example, FedEx drivers use Bluetooth to transmit the delivery data captured by their handheld PowerPad computers to cellular transmitters, which forward the data to corporate computers. Drivers no longer need to spend time docking their handheld units physically in the transmitters, and Bluetooth has saved FedEx $20 million per year.

Figure 6.15
A Bluetooth
Network (PAN)
Bluetooth enables a
variety of devices,
including cell phones,
smartphones, wireless
keyboards and mice,
PCs, and printers, to
interact wirelessly with
each other within a small
30-foot (10-meter) area.
In addition to the links
shown, Bluetooth can be
used to network similar
devices to send data
from one PC to another,
for example.

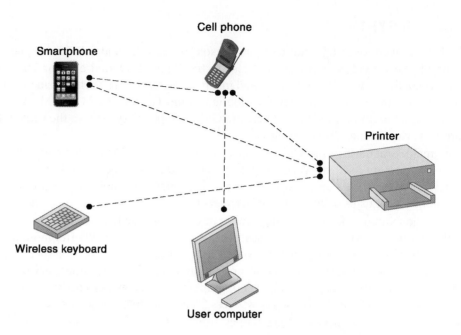

Wi-Fi and Wireless Internet Access

The 802.11 set of standards for wireless LANs and wireless Internet access is also known as **Wi-Fi**. The first of these standards to be widely adopted was 802.11b, which can transmit up to 11 Mbps in the unlicensed 2.4-GHz band and has an effective distance of 30 to 50 meters. The 802.11g standard can transmit up to 54 Mbps in the 2.4-GHz range. 802.11n is capable of transmitting over 100 Mbps. Today's PCs and netbooks have built-in support for Wi-Fi, as do the iPhone, iPad, and other smartphones.

In most Wi-Fi communication, wireless devices communicate with a wired LAN using access points. An access point is a box consisting of a radio receiver/transmitter and antennas that links to a wired network, router, or hub. Mobile access points such as Verizon's Mobile Hotspots use the existing cellular network to create Wi-Fi connections.

Figure 6.16 illustrates an 802.11 wireless LAN that connects a small number of mobile devices to a larger wired LAN and to the Internet. Most wireless devices are client machines. The servers that the mobile client stations need to use are on the wired LAN. The access point controls the wireless stations and acts as a bridge between the main wired LAN and the wireless LAN. (A bridge connects two LANs based on different technologies.) The access point also controls the wireless stations.

The most popular use for Wi-Fi today is for high-speed wireless Internet service. In this instance, the access point plugs into an Internet connection, which could come from a cable TV line or DSL telephone service. Computers within range of the access point use it to link wirelessly to the Internet.

Hotspots typically consist of one or more access points providing wireless Internet access in a public place. Some hotspots are free or do not require any additional software to use; others may require activation and the establishment of a user account by providing a credit card number over the Web.

Businesses of all sizes are using Wi-Fi networks to provide low-cost wireless LANs and Internet access. Wi-Fi hotspots can be found in hotels, airport lounges, libraries, cafes, and college campuses to provide mobile access to the Internet. Dartmouth College is one of many campuses where students now use Wi-Fi for research, course work, and entertainment.

Wi-Fi technology poses several challenges, however. One is Wi-Fi's security features, which make these wireless networks vulnerable to intruders. We provide more detail about Wi-Fi security issues in Chapter 7.

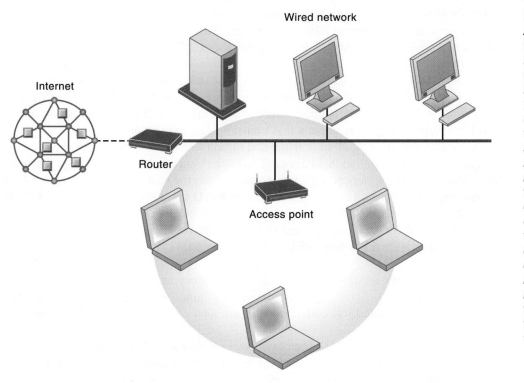

Figure 6.16
An 802.11 Wireless LAN
Mobile laptop computers equipped with network interface cards link to the wired LAN by communicating with the access point. The access point uses radio waves to transmit network signals from the wired network to the client adapters, which convert them into data that the mobile device can understand. The client adapter then transmits the data from the mobile device back to the access point, which forwards the data to the wired network.

Another drawback of Wi-Fi networks is susceptibility to interference from nearby systems operating in the same spectrum, such as wireless phones, microwave ovens, or other wireless LANs. However, wireless networks based on the 802.11n standard are able to solve this problem by using multiple wireless antennas in tandem to transmit and receive data and technology called *MIMO* (multiple input multiple output) to coordinate multiple simultaneous radio signals.

WiMax

A surprisingly large number of areas in the United States and throughout the world do not have access to Wi-Fi or fixed broadband connectivity. The range of Wi-Fi systems is no more than 300 feet from the base station, making it difficult for rural groups that don't have cable or DSL service to find wireless access to the Internet.

The IEEE developed a new family of standards known as WiMax to deal with these problems. **WiMax**, which stands for Worldwide Interoperability for Microwave Access, is the popular term for IEEE Standard 802.16. It has a wireless access range of up to 31 miles and transmission speed of up to 75 Mbps.

WiMax antennas are powerful enough to beam high-speed Internet connections to rooftop antennas of homes and businesses that are miles away. Cellular handsets and laptops with WiMax capabilities are appearing in the marketplace. Mobile WiMax is one of the 4G network technologies we discussed earlier in this chapter.

RFID AND WIRELESS SENSOR NETWORKS

Mobile technologies are creating new efficiencies and ways of working throughout the enterprise. In addition to the wireless systems we have just described, radio frequency identification systems and wireless sensor networks are having a major impact.

Radio Frequency Identification (RFID)

Radio frequency identification (RFID) systems provide a powerful technology for tracking the movement of goods throughout the supply chain. RFID systems use tiny tags with embedded microchips containing data about an item and its location to transmit radio signals over a short distance to RFID readers. The RFID readers then pass the data over a network to a computer for processing. Unlike bar codes, RFID tags do not need line-of-sight contact to be read.

The RFID tag is electronically programmed with information that can uniquely identify an item plus other information about the item, such as its location, where and when it was made, or its status during production. Embedded in the tag is a microchip for storing the data. The rest of the tag is an antenna that transmits data to the reader.

The reader unit consists of an antenna and radio transmitter with a decoding capability attached to a stationary or handheld device. The reader emits radio waves in ranges anywhere from 1 inch to 100 feet, depending on its power output, the radio frequency employed, and surrounding environmental conditions. When an RFID tag comes within the range of the reader, the tag is activated and starts sending data. The reader captures these data, decodes them, and sends them back over a wired or wireless network to a host computer for further processing (see Figure 6.17). Both RFID tags and antennas come in a variety of shapes and sizes.

Active RFID tags are powered by an internal battery and typically enable data to be rewritten and modified. Active tags can transmit for hundreds of feet but may cost several dollars per tag. Automated toll-collection systems such as New York's E-ZPass use active RFID tags.

Passive RFID tags do not have their own power source and obtain their operating power from the radio frequency energy transmitted by the RFID reader. They are smaller, lighter, and less expensive than active tags, but only have a range of several feet.

In inventory control and supply chain management, RFID systems capture and manage more detailed information about items in warehouses or in production than bar coding systems. If a large number of items are shipped together, RFID systems track each pallet, lot, or even unit item in the shipment. This technology may help companies such as Walmart improve receiving and storage operations by improving their ability to "see" exactly what stock is stored in warehouses or on retail store shelves.

Walmart has installed RFID readers at store receiving docks to record the arrival of pallets and cases of goods shipped with RFID tags. The RFID reader reads the tags a second time just as the cases are brought onto the sales floor from backroom storage areas. Software combines sales data from Walmart's point-of-sale systems and the RFID

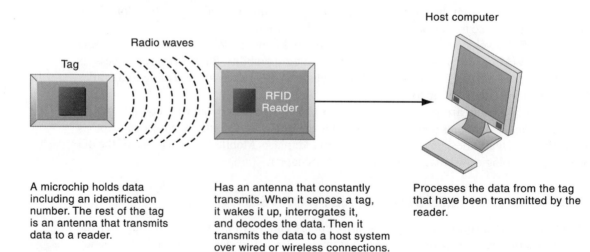

| A microchip holds data including an identification number. The rest of the tag is an antenna that transmits data to a reader. | Has an antenna that constantly transmits. When it senses a tag, it wakes it up, interrogates it, and decodes the data. Then it transmits the data to a host system over wired or wireless connections. | Processes the data from the tag that have been transmitted by the reader. |

Figure 6.17
How RFID Works
RFID uses low-powered radio transmitters to read data stored in a tag at distances ranging from 1 inch to 100 feet. The reader captures the data from the tag and sends them over a network to a host computer for processing.

data regarding the number of cases brought out to the sales floor. The program determines which items will soon be depleted and automatically generates a list of items to pick in the warehouse to replenish store shelves before they run out. This information helps Walmart reduce out-of-stock items, increase sales, and further shrink its costs.

The cost of RFID tags used to be too high for widespread use, but now it starts at 5 cents per passive tag in the United States. As the price decreases, RFID is starting to become cost-effective for some applications.

In addition to installing RFID readers and tagging systems, companies may need to upgrade their hardware and software to process the massive amounts of data produced by RFID systems—transactions that could add up to tens or hundreds of terabytes.

Software is used to filter, aggregate, and prevent RFID data from overloading business networks and system applications. Applications often need to be redesigned to accept large volumes of frequently generated RFID data and to share those data with other applications. Major enterprise software vendors, including SAP and Oracle PeopleSoft, now offer RFID-ready versions of their supply chain management applications.

Wireless Sensor Networks

If your company wanted state-of-the art technology to monitor building security or detect hazardous substances in the air, it might deploy a wireless sensor network. **Wireless sensor networks (WSNs)** are networks of interconnected wireless devices that are embedded into the physical environment to provide measurements of many points over large spaces. These devices have built-in processing, storage, and radio frequency sensors and antennas. They are linked into an interconnected network that routes the data they capture to a computer for analysis.

These networks range from hundreds to thousands of nodes. Because wireless sensor devices are placed in the field for years at a time without any maintenance or human intervention, they must have very low power requirements and batteries capable of lasting for years.

Figure 6.18 illustrates one type of wireless sensor network, with data from individual nodes flowing across the network to a server with greater processing power. The server acts as a gateway to a network based on Internet technology.

Wireless sensor networks are valuable in areas such as monitoring environmental changes, monitoring traffic or military activity, protecting property, efficiently operating and managing machinery and vehicles, establishing security perimeters, monitoring supply chain management, or detecting chemical, biological, or radiological material.

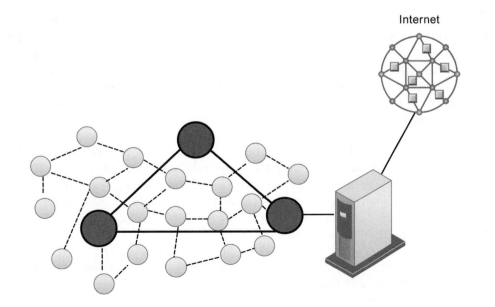

Internet

**Figure 6.18
A Wireless Sensor Network**
The small circles represent lower-level nodes and the larger circles represent high-end nodes. Lower-level nodes forward data to each other or to higher-level nodes, which transmit data more rapidly and speed up network performance.

LEARNING TRACKS

The following Learning Tracks provide content relevant to topics covered in this chapter:

1. Computing and Communications Services Provided by Commercial Communications Vendors

2. Broadband Network Services and Technologies

3. Cellular System Generations

4. Wireless Applications for Customer Relationship Management, Supply Chain Management, and Health care

5. Web 2.0

Review Summary

1 **What are the principal components of telecommunications networks and key networking technologies?** A simple network consists of two or more connected computers. Basic network components include computers, network interfaces, a connection medium, network operating system software, and either a hub or a switch. The networking infrastructure for a large company includes the traditional telephone system, mobile cellular communication, wireless local area networks, videoconferencing systems, a corporate Web site, intranets, extranets, and an array of local and wide area networks, including the Internet.

Contemporary networks have been shaped by the rise of client/server computing, the use of packet switching, and the adoption of Transmission Control Protocol/Internet Protocol (TCP/IP) as a universal communications standard for linking disparate networks and computers, including the Internet. Protocols provide a common set of rules that enable communication among diverse components in a telecommunications network.

2 **What are the main telecommunications transmission media and types of networks?** The principal physical transmission media are twisted copper telephone wire, coaxial copper cable, fiber-optic cable, and wireless transmission. Twisted wire enables companies to use existing wiring for telephone systems for digital communication, although it is relatively slow. Fiber-optic and coaxial cable are used for high-volume transmission but are expensive to install. Microwave and communications satellites are used for wireless communication over long distances.

Local area networks (LANs) connect PCs and other digital devices together within a 500-meter radius and are used today for many corporate computing tasks. Network components may be connected together using a star, bus, or ring topology. Wide area networks (WANs) span broad geographical distances, ranging from several miles to continents, and are private networks that are independently managed. Metropolitan area networks (MANs) span a single urban area.

Digital subscriber line (DSL) technologies, cable Internet connections, and T1 lines are often used for high-capacity Internet connections.

3 **How do the Internet and Internet technology work, and how do they support communication and e-business?** The Internet is a worldwide network of networks that uses the client/server model of computing and the TCP/IP network reference model. Every computer on the Internet is assigned a unique numeric IP address. The Domain Name System (DNS) converts IP addresses to more user-friendly domain names. Worldwide Internet policies are established by organizations and government bodies, such as the Internet Architecture Board (IAB) and the World Wide Web Consortium (W3C).

Major Internet services include e-mail, newsgroups, chatting, instant messaging, Telnet, FTP, and the Web. Web pages are based on Hypertext Markup Language (HTML) and can display text, graphics, video, and audio. Web site directories, search engines, and RSS technology help users locate the information they need on the Web. RSS, blogs, social networking, and wikis are features of Web 2.0.

Firms are also starting to realize economies by using VoIP technology for voice transmission and by using virtual private networks (VPNs) as low-cost alternatives to private WANs.

4 **What are the principal technologies and standards for wireless networking, communication, and Internet access?** Cellular networks are evolving toward high-speed, high-bandwidth, digital packet-switched transmission. Broadband 3G networks are capable of transmitting data at speeds ranging from 144 Kbps to more than 2 Mbps. 4G networks capable of transmission speeds that could reach 1 Gbps are starting to be rolled out.

Major cellular standards include Code Division Multiple Access (CDMA), which is used primarily in the United States, and Global System for Mobile Communications (GSM), which is the standard in Europe and much of the rest of the world.

Standards for wireless computer networks include Bluetooth (802.15) for small personal area networks (PANs), Wi-Fi (802.11) for local area networks (LANs), and WiMax (802.16) for metropolitan area networks (MANs).

5 **Why are radio frequency identification (RFID) and wireless sensor networks valuable for business?** Radio frequency identification (RFID) systems provide a powerful technology for tracking the movement of goods by using tiny tags with embedded data about an item and its location. RFID readers read the radio signals transmitted by these tags and pass the data over a network to a computer for processing. Wireless sensor networks (WSNs) are networks of interconnected wireless sensing and transmitting devices that are embedded into the physical environment to provide measurements of many points over large spaces.

Key Terms

3G networks, 207
4G networks, 207
Bandwidth, 190
Blog, 204
Blogosphere, 204
Bluetooth, 207
Broadband, 182
Bus topology, 187
Cable Internet connections, 190
Cell phone, 190
Chat, 196

Coaxial cable, 188
Digital subscriber line (DSL), 190
Domain name, 191
Domain Name System (DNS), 191
E-mail, 196
Fiber-optic cable, 189
File Transfer Protocol (FTP), 195
Hertz, 190
Hotspots, 208

Hubs, 183
HypertextTransfer Protocol (HTTP), 200
Instant messaging, 196
Internet Protocol (IP) address, 191
Internet service provider (ISP), 190
Internet2, 195
IPv6, 195
Local area network (LAN), 186

Review Questions

1. What are the principal components of telecommunications networks and key networking technologies?
- Describe the features of a simple network and the network infrastructure for a large company.
- Name and describe the principal technologies and trends that have shaped contemporary telecommunications systems.

2. What are the main telecommunications transmission media and types of networks?
- Name the different types of physical transmission media and compare them in terms of speed and cost.
- Define a LAN, and describe its components and the functions of each component.
- Name and describe the principal network topologies.

3. How do the Internet and Internet technology work, and how do they support communication and e-business?
- Define the Internet, describe how it works, and explain how it provides business value.
- Explain how the Domain Name System (DNS) and IP addressing system work.
- List and describe the principal Internet services.
- Define and describe VoIP and virtual private networks, and explain how they provide value to businesses.
- List and describe alternative ways of locating information on the Web.
- Compare Web 2.0 and Web 3.0.

4. What are the principal technologies and standards for wireless networking, communications, and Internet access?
- Define Bluetooth, Wi-Fi, WiMax, 3G, and 4G networks.
- Describe the capabilities of each and for which types of applications each is best suited.

5. Why are RFID and wireless sensor networks (WSNs) valuable for business?
- Define RFID, explain how it works, and describe how it provides value to businesses.
- Define WSNs, explain how they work, and describe the kinds of applications that use them.

Discussion Questions

1. It has been said that within the next few years, smartphones will become the single most important digital device we own. Discuss the implications of this statement.

2. Should all major retailing and manufacturing companies switch to RFID? Why or why not?

3. Compare Wi-Fi and high-speed cellular systems for accessing the Internet. What are the advantages and disadvantages of each?

Hands-on MIS Projects

The projects in this section give you hands-on experience evaluating and selecting communications technology, using spreadsheet software to improve selection of telecommunications services, and using Web search engines for business research.

MANAGEMENT DECISION PROBLEMS

1. Your company supplies ceramic floor tiles to Home Depot, Lowe's, and other home improvement stores. You have been asked to start using radio frequency identification tags on each case of tiles you ship to help your customers improve the management of your products and those of other suppliers in their warehouses. Use the Web to identify the cost of hardware, software, and networking components for an RFID system for your company. What factors should be considered? What are the key decisions that have to be made in determining whether your firm should adopt this technology?

2. BestMed Medical Supplies Corporation sells medical and surgical products and equipment from over 700 different manufacturers to hospitals, health clinics, and medical offices. The company employs 500 people at seven different locations in western and midwestern states, including account managers, customer service and support representatives, and warehouse staff. Employees communicate via traditional telephone voice services, e-mail, instant messaging, and cell phones. Management is inquiring about whether the company should adopt a system for unified communications. What factors should be considered? What are the key decisions that have to be made in determining whether to adopt this technology? Use the Web, if necessary, to find out more about unified communications and its costs.

IMPROVING DECISION MAKING: USING SPREADSHEET SOFTWARE TO EVALUATE WIRELESS SERVICES

Software skills: Spreadsheet formulas, formatting
Business skills: Analyzing telecommunications services and costs

In this project, you'll use the Web to research alternative wireless services and use spreadsheet software to calculate wireless service costs for a sales force.

You would like to equip your sales force of 35 based in Cincinnati, Ohio, with mobile phones that have capabilities for voice transmission, text messaging, and taking and sending photos. Use the Web to select a wireless service provider that provides nationwide service as well as good service in your home area. Examine the features of the mobile handsets offered by each of these vendors. Assume that each of the 35 salespeople will need to spend three hours per weekday between 8 a.m. and 6 p.m. on mobile voice communication, send 30 text messages per weekday, and send five photos per week. Use your spreadsheet software to determine the wireless service and handset that will offer the best pricing per user over a two-year period. For the purposes of this exercise, you do not need to consider corporate discounts.

ACHIEVING OPERATIONAL EXCELLENCE: USING WEB SEARCH ENGINES FOR BUSINESS RESEARCH

Software skills: Web search tools
Business skills: Researching new technologies

This project will help develop your Internet skills in using Web search engines for business research.

Use Google and Bing to obtain information about ethanol as an alternative fuel for motor vehicles. If you wish, try some other search engines as well. Compare the volume and quality of information you find with each search tool. Which tool is the easiest to use? Which produced the best results for your research? Why?

Video Cases

Video Cases and Instructional Videos illustrating some of the concepts in this chapter are available. Contact your instructor to access these videos.

Collaboration and Teamwork

Evaluating Smartphones

Form a group with three or four of your classmates. Compare the capabilities of Apple's iPhone with a smartphone handset from another vendor with similar features. Your analysis should consider the purchase cost of each device, the wireless networks where each device can operate, service plan and handset costs, and the services available for each device.

You should also consider other capabilities of each device, including the ability to integrate with existing corporate or PC applications. Which device would you select? What criteria would you use to guide your selection? If possible, use Google Sites to post links to Web pages, team communication announcements, and work assignments; to brainstorm; and to work collaboratively on project documents. Try to use Google Docs to develop a presentation of your findings for the class.

BUSINESS PROBLEM-SOLVING CASE

Apple, Google, and Microsoft Battle for Your Internet Experience

The three Internet titans—Google, Microsoft, and Apple—are in an epic struggle to dominate your Internet experience, and caught in the crossfire are search, music, books, videos, and other media, the device you use to do all of these things, cloud computing, and a host of other issues that are likely central to your life. The prize is a projected $400 billion e-commerce marketplace by 2015 where the major access device will be a mobile smartphone or tablet computer. Each firm generates extraordinary amounts of cash based on different business models and is using that cash in hopes of being the top dog in the Internet marketplace.

In this triangular fight, at one point or another, each firm has allied with one of their two major foes to team up on the third. Two of the firms—Google and Apple—are determined to prevent Microsoft from expanding its dominance beyond the PC desktop and onto the new mobile platform. So Google and Apple are friends. But when it comes to mobile phones and apps, Google and Apple are enemies: both want to dominate the mobile market. Apple and Microsoft are determined to prevent Google from extending beyond its dominance in search and advertising. So Apple and Microsoft are friends. But when it comes to the mobile marketplace for devices and apps, Apple and Microsoft are enemies. Google and Microsoft are just plain enemies in a variety of battles. Google is trying to weaken Microsoft's PC software dominance, and Microsoft is trying to break into the search advertising market with Bing.

The Internet, along with hardware devices and software applications, is going through a major expansion. Mobile devices with advanced functionality and ubiquitous Internet access are rapidly gaining on traditional desktop computing as the most popular form of computing, changing the basis for competition throughout the industry. Research firm Gartner predicts that by 2013, mobile phones will surpass PCs as the way most people use the Internet. Today, mobile devices account for 5 percent of all searches performed on the Internet; in 2016, they are expected to account for 23.5 percent of searches. These mobile Internet devices are made possible by a growing cloud of computing capacity available to anyone with a smartphone and Internet connectivity. Who needs a desktop PC anymore when you can listen to music and watch videos anytime, anywhere on mobile devices? It's no surprise, then, that today's tech titans are so aggressively battling for control of this brave new mobile world.

Apple, Google, and Microsoft already compete in an assortment of fields. Google has a huge edge in advertising, thanks to its dominance in Internet search.

Microsoft's offering, Bing, has grown to about 15 percent of the search market, and the rest essentially belongs to Google. Apple is the leader in mobile software applications, thanks to the popularity of the App Store on its iPhones. Google and Microsoft have less popular app offerings on the Web. Microsoft is still the leader in PC operating systems, but has struggled with many of its other efforts, including smartphone hardware and software, mobile computing, cloud-based software apps, and its Internet portal. Even though Microsoft's Xbox consoles and games are popular, they contribute less than 5 percent of Microsoft's revenue (the rest of its revenue comes from Windows, Office, and network software). While Windows is still the operating system on 95 percent of the world's 2 billion PCs, Google's Android OS and Apple's iOS are the dominant players in the mobile computing market, and all three of these companies now realize that this market will only increase in size and scope going forward.

Apple has several advantages that will serve it well in the battle for mobile supremacy. It's no coincidence that since the Internet exploded in size and popularity, so too did Apple's revenue, which totaled well over $65 billion in 2010, up from $40 billion the previous year despite an ongoing economic downturn. The iMac, iPod, and iPhone have all contributed to the company's enormous success in the Internet era, and the iPad has followed the trend of profitability set by these previous products. Apple has a loyal user base that has steadily grown and is very likely to buy future product offerings.

Part of the reason for the popularity of the iPhone, and for the optimism surrounding Internet-equipped smartphones in general, has been the success of the App Store. A vibrant selection of applications distinguishes Apple's offerings from its competitors', and gives them a measurable head start in this marketplace. Apple already offers approximately 500,000 applications for their devices, and Apple takes a 30 percent cut of all app sales. Applications greatly enrich the experience of using a mobile device, and without them, the predictions for the future of mobile Internet would not be nearly as bright. Whoever creates the most appealing set of devices and applications will derive a significant competitive advantage over rival companies. Right now, that company is Apple.

But the development of smartphones and mobile Internet is still in its infancy. Google has acted swiftly to enter the battle for mobile supremacy while they can still "win". More and more people are likely to switch to mobile computing as their primary method of using the Internet, so it's no surprise that Google is aggressively following the eyeballs. Google is as strong as the size of its advertising network. With the impending shift towards mobile computing looming, it's not certain that they'll be able to maintain their dominant position in search. That's why the dominant online search company began developing its Android operating system, which is used on roughly 40 percent of mobile phones. Google offers Android for free to manufacturers of handsets that run the operating system. Via Android, Google hopes to control its own destiny in an increasingly mobile world.

Because Google provides Android at no cost to smart-phone manufacturers, competitors have sought to weigh Apple down with patent claims and other lawsuits. That's part of the reason why Google made its biggest acquisition yet in August 2011, buying Motorola Mobility Holdings for $12.5 billion. The deal gives Google 17,000 patents and another 7,000 more in the pipeline that will help the company defend Android from these patent lawsuits. But buying Motorola's phone busi-ness does more than just give Google patents. It also gives Google the ability to make its own cell phones and tablet devices, which would be its most aggressive move against Apple yet.

There is some skepticism whether Google will even try to enter this marketplace, let alone whether it can succeed in doing so. Google would be entering completely new territory. It has never sold devices before, the profit margins will be much tighter than they are for their search business, and it would place Motorola in an awkward position among the smartphone manufacturers that Google works with. But many analysts believe that Google will indeed begin selling products akin to Apple's offerings, fostering renewed competition and lower costs in the mobile marketplace.

Google has been particularly aggressive with moves such as the acquisition of Motorola's phone business because it is concerned about Apple's preference for "closed," proprietary standards on its phones. Apple retains the final say over whether or not users can access various services on the Web, and that includes services provided by Google. Google doesn't want Apple to be able to block it from providing its services on iPhones, or any other smartphone. Apple is reliant on sales of its devices to remain profitable. It has had no problems with this so far, but Google only needs to spread its adver-tising networks onto these devices to make a profit. In fact, some analysts speculate that Google envisions a future where mobile phones cost a fraction of what they do today, or are even free, requiring only the advertising revenue generated by the devices to turn a profit. Apple would struggle to remain competitive in this environ-ment. Apple has kept the garden closed for a simple reason: you need an Apple device to play there.

The struggle between Apple, Google, and Microsoft wouldn't matter much if there wasn't so much potential money at stake. Billions of dollars hang in the balance, and the majority of that money will come from advertising. App sales are another important component, especially for Apple. Apple has the edge in selection and quality of apps, but while sales have been brisk, developers have complained that making money is too difficult. Roughly a quarter of the apps available in the App Store are free, which makes no money for developers or for Apple, but it does bring consumers to the Apple marketplace where they can be sold other apps or entertainment services.

The three-way struggle between Microsoft, Apple, and Google really has no precedent in the history of computing platforms. In early contests it was typically a single firm that rode the crest of a new technology to become the dominant player. Examples include IBM's dominance of the mainframe market, Digital Equipment's dominance of minicomputers, Microsoft's dominance of operating systems and PC productivity applications, and Cisco's dominance of the Internet router market. In the current struggle, three firms are trying to dominate the customer experience on the Internet. Each firm brings certain strengths and weaknesses to the fray. It's too early to tell if a single firm will "win," or if all three can survive the contest for the consumer Internet experience.

Sources: Kopin Tan, "What Google Sees in Motorola, and Beyond," *Barrons*, August 20, 2011; Amir Efrati and Spencer E. Ante, "Google's $12.5 Billion Gamble", *Wall Street Journal*, August 16, 2011; Evelyn M. Rusli, "Google's Big Bet on the Mobile Future," *New York Times*, August 15, 2011; Claire Cain Miller, "Google, a Giant in Mobile Search, Seeks New Ways to Make It Pay," *New York Times*, April 24, 2011; Brad Stone and Miguel Helft, "Apple's Spat with Google Is Getting Personal." *New York Times*, March 12, 2010; Peter Burrows, "Apple vs. Google," *BusinessWeek*, January 14, 2010; Holman W. Jenkins, Jr. "The Microsofting of Apple?" *Wall Street Journal*, February 10, 2010; Jessica E. Vascellaro and Ethan Smith, "Google and Microsoft Crank Up Rivalry," *Wall Street Journal*, October 21, 2009; Jessica E. Vascellaro and Yukari Iwatani Kane, "Apple, Google Rivalry Heats Up," *Wall Street Journal*, December 10, 2009.

Case Study Questions

1. Compare the business models and areas of strength of Apple, Google, and Microsoft.

2. Why is mobile computing so important to these three firms? Evaluate the mobile platform offerings of each firm.

3. What is the significance of mobile applications, app stores, and closed versus open app standards to the success or failure of mobile computing?

4. Which company and business model do you think will prevail in this epic struggle? Explain your answer.

5. What difference would it make to a business or to an individual consumer if Apple, Google, or Microsoft dominated the Internet experience? Explain your answer.

Securing Information Systems

STUDENT LEARNING OBJECTIVES

After completing this chapter, you will be able to answer the following questions:

1. Why are information systems vulnerable to destruction, error, and abuse?

2. What is the business value of security and control?

3. What are the components of an organizational framework for security and control?

4. What are the most important tools and technologies for safeguarding information resources?

CHAPTER OUTLINE

YOU'RE ON FACEBOOK? WATCH OUT!

Facebook is the world's largest online social network, and increasingly, the destination of choice for messaging friends, sharing photos and videos, and collecting "eyeballs" for business advertising and market research. But, watch out! It's also a great place for losing your identity or being attacked by malicious software.

How could that be? Facebook has a security team that works hard to counter threats on that site. It uses up-to-date security technology to protect its Web site. But with 800 million users, it can't police everyone and everything, and Facebook makes an extraordinarily tempting target for both mischief-makers and criminals.

Facebook has a huge worldwide user base, an easy-to-use Web site, and a community of users linked to their friends. Its members are more likely to trust messages they receive from friends, even if this communication is not legitimate. Perhaps for these reasons, research from the Kaspersky Labs security firm shows malicious software on social networking sites such as Facebook and MySpace is 10 times more successful at infecting users than e-mail–based attacks. Even Facebook founder Mark Zuckerberg saw his Facebook fan page hacked in 2011.

© Petrovich9, 2011, iStockPhoto LP.

Here are some examples of what can go wrong:

An Android app called FaceNiff enables an Android smartphone using a Wi-Fi network to detect any unsecured Facebook or Twitter login made on the same Wi-Fi network by a desktop or laptop using a standard Web browser. The app gives hackers access to a user's private contact details and those of all the user's friends. Using the app, hackers are able to collect personal information needed for identity theft.

During an 18-month-long hacker attack in 2009–2010, Facebook users were tricked into revealing their passwords and downloading a rogue program that steals financial data. A legitimate-looking Facebook e-mail notice asked users to provide information to help the social network update its login system. When the user clicked the "update" button in the e-mail, that person was directed to a bogus Facebook login screen where the user's name was filled in and that person was prompted to provide his or her password. Once the user supplied that information, an "Update Tool" installed the Zeus "Trojan horse" rogue software program designed to steal financial and personal data by surreptitiously tracking users' keystrokes as they enter information into their computers. The hackers stole as many as 68,000 login credentials from 2,400 companies and government agencies for online banking, social networking sites, and e-mail.

The Koobface worm targets Microsoft Windows users of Facebook, Twitter, and other social networking Web sites in order to gather sensitive information from the victims such as credit card numbers. Koobface was first detected in December 2008. It spreads by delivering bogus Facebook messages to people who are "friends" of a Facebook user whose computer has already been infected. Upon receipt, the message directs the recipients to a third-party Web site, where they are prompted to download what is purported to be an update of the Adobe Flash player. If they download and execute the file, Koobface is able to infect their system and use the computer for more malicious work.

Recovering from these attacks is time-consuming and costly, especially for business firms. A September 2010 study by Panda Security found that one-third of small and medium businesses it surveyed had been hit by malicious software from social networks, and more than a third of these suffered more than $5,000 in losses.

Sources: Agence France-Presse, "Hackers Hunt Prey on Smartphones, Facebook," April 13, 2011; Ben Rooney, "Mobile Devices and Social Networks Key Malware Targets," *Wall Street Journal*, April 5, 2011; Lance Whitney, "Social-Media Malware Hurting Small Businesses," *CNET News*, September 15, 2010; Raj Dash, "Report: Facebook Served as Primary Distribution Channel for Botnet Army," allfacebook.com, February 18, 2010; Sam Diaz, "Report: Bad Guys Go Social: Facebook Tops Security Risk List," *ZDNet*, February 1, 2010; and Brian Prince, "Social Networks 10 Times as Effective for Hackers, Malware," *eWeek*, May 13, 2009.

The problems created by malicious software on Facebook illustrate some of the reasons why businesses need to pay special attention to information system security. Facebook provides a plethora of benefits to both individuals and businesses. But from a security standpoint, using Facebook is one of the easiest ways to expose a computer system to malicious software—your computer, your friends' computers, and even the computers of Facebook-participating businesses.

The chapter-opening diagram calls attention to important points raised by this case and this chapter. Although Facebook's management has a security policy and security team in place, Facebook has been plagued with many security problems that affect both individuals and businesses. The "social" nature of this site and large number of users make it unusually attractive for criminals and hackers intent on stealing valuable personal and financial information and propagating malicious software. Even though Facebook and its users deploy security technology, they are still vulnerable to new kinds of malicious software attacks and criminal scams. In addition to losses from theft of financial data, the difficulties of eradicating the malicious software or repairing damage caused by identity theft add to operational costs and make both individuals and businesses less effective.

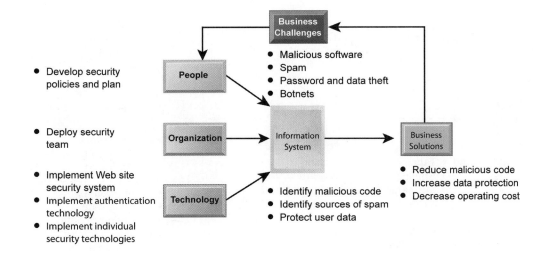

7.1 System Vulnerability and Abuse

Can you imagine what would happen if you tried to link to the Internet without a firewall or antivirus software? Your computer would be disabled in a few seconds, and it might take you many days to recover. If you used the computer to run your business, you might not be able to sell to your customers or place orders with your suppliers while it was down. And you might find that your computer system had been penetrated by outsiders, who perhaps stole or destroyed valuable data, including confidential payment data from your customers. If too much data were destroyed or divulged, your business might never be able to operate!

In short, if you operate a business today, you need to make security and control a top priority. **Security** refers to the policies, procedures, and technical measures used to prevent unauthorized access, alteration, theft, or physical damage to information systems. **Controls** are methods, policies, and organizational procedures that ensure the safety of the organization's assets, the accuracy and reliability of its records, and operational adherence to management standards.

WHY SYSTEMS ARE VULNERABLE

When large amounts of data are stored in electronic form, they are vulnerable to many more kinds of threats than when they existed in manual form. Through communications networks, information systems in different locations are interconnected. The potential for unauthorized access, abuse, or fraud is not limited to a single location but can occur at any access point in the network. Figure 7.1 illustrates the most common threats against contemporary information systems. They can stem from technical, organizational, and environmental factors compounded by poor management decisions. In the multi-tier client/server computing environment illustrated here, vulnerabilities exist at each layer and in the communications between the layers. Users at the client layer can cause harm by introducing errors or by accessing systems without authorization. It is possible to access data flowing over networks, steal valuable data during transmission, or alter messages without authorization. Radiation may disrupt a network at various points as well. Intruders can launch denial-of-service attacks or malicious software to disrupt the operation of Web sites. Those capable of penetrating corporate systems can destroy or alter corporate data stored in databases or files.

Systems malfunction if computer hardware breaks down, is not configured properly, or is damaged by improper use or criminal acts. Errors in programming, improper installation, or unauthorized changes cause computer software to fail. Power failures, floods, fires, or other natural disasters can also disrupt computer systems.

Figure 7.1
Contemporary Security Challenges and Vulnerabilities

The architecture of a Web-based application typically includes a Web client, a server, and corporate information systems linked to databases. Each of these components presents security challenges and vulnerabilities. Floods, fires, power failures, and other electrical problems can cause disruptions at any point in the network.

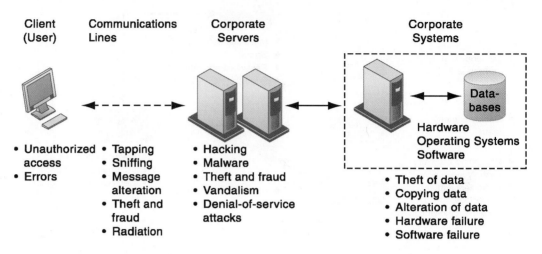

Client (User)

- Unauthorized access
- Errors

Communications Lines

- Tapping
- Sniffing
- Message alteration
- Theft and fraud
- Radiation

Corporate Servers

- Hacking
- Malware
- Theft and fraud
- Vandalism
- Denial-of-service attacks

Corporate Systems

Hardware
Operating Systems
Software

- Theft of data
- Copying data
- Alteration of data
- Hardware failure
- Software failure

Domestic or offshore partnering with another company adds to system vulnerability if valuable information resides on networks and computers outside the organization's control. Without strong safeguards, valuable data could be lost, destroyed, or could fall into the wrong hands, revealing important trade secrets or information that violates personal privacy.

The popularity of handheld mobile devices for business computing adds to these woes. Portability makes cell phones, smartphones, and tablet computers easy to lose or steal. Smartphones share the same security weaknesses as other Internet devices, and are vulnerable to malicious software and penetration from outsiders. Smartphones used by corporate employees often contain sensitive data such as sales figures, customer names, phone numbers, and e-mail addresses. Intruders may be able to access internal corporate systems through these devices.

Internet Vulnerabilities

Large public networks, such as the Internet, are more vulnerable than internal networks because they are virtually open to anyone. The Internet is so huge that when abuses do occur, they can have an enormously widespread impact. When the Internet becomes part of the corporate network, the organization's information systems are even more vulnerable to actions from outsiders.

Computers that are constantly connected to the Internet by cable modems or digital subscriber line (DSL) lines are more open to penetration by outsiders because they use fixed Internet addresses where they can be easily identified. (With dial-up service, a temporary Internet address is assigned for each session.) A fixed Internet address creates a fixed target for hackers.

Telephone service based on Internet technology (see Chapter 6) is more vulnerable than the switched voice network if it does not run over a secure private network. Most Voice over IP (VoIP) traffic over the public Internet is not encrypted, so anyone with a network can listen in on conversations. Hackers can intercept conversations or shut down voice service by flooding servers supporting VoIP with bogus traffic.

Vulnerability has also increased from widespread use of e-mail, instant messaging (IM), and peer-to-peer (P2P) file-sharing programs. E-mail may contain attachments that serve as springboards for malicious software or unauthorized access to internal corporate systems. Employees may use e-mail messages to transmit valuable trade secrets, financial data, or confidential customer information to unauthorized recipients. Popular IM applications for consumers do not use a secure layer for text messages, so they can be intercepted and read by outsiders during transmission over the public Internet. Instant messaging activity over the

Internet can in some cases be used as a back door to an otherwise secure network. Sharing files over P2P networks, such as those for illegal music sharing, may also transmit malicious software or expose information on either individual or corporate computers to outsiders.

Wireless Security Challenges

Is it safe to log onto a wireless network at an airport, library, or other public location? It depends on how vigilant you are. Even the wireless network in your home is vulnerable because radio frequency bands are easy to scan. Both Bluetooth and Wi-Fi networks are susceptible to hacking by eavesdroppers. Local area networks (LANs) using the 802.11 standard can be easily penetrated by outsiders armed with laptops, wireless cards, external antennae, and hacking software. Hackers use these tools to detect unprotected networks, monitor network traffic, and, in some cases, gain access to the Internet or to corporate networks.

Wi-Fi transmission technology was designed to make it easy for stations to find and hear one another. The *service set identifiers (SSIDs)* that identify the access points in a Wi-Fi network are broadcast multiple times and can be picked up fairly easily by intruders' sniffer programs (see Figure 7.2). Wireless networks in many locations do not have basic protections against **war driving**, in which eavesdroppers drive by buildings or park outside and try to intercept wireless network traffic.

An intruder that has associated with an access point by using the correct SSID is capable of accessing other resources on the network. For example, the intruder could use the Windows operating system to determine which other users are connected to the network, access their computer hard drives, and open or copy their files.

Intruders also use the information they have gleaned to set up rogue access points on a different radio channel in physical locations close to users to force a user's radio network interface controller (NIC) to associate with the rogue access point. Once this association occurs, hackers using the rogue access point can capture the names and passwords of unsuspecting users.

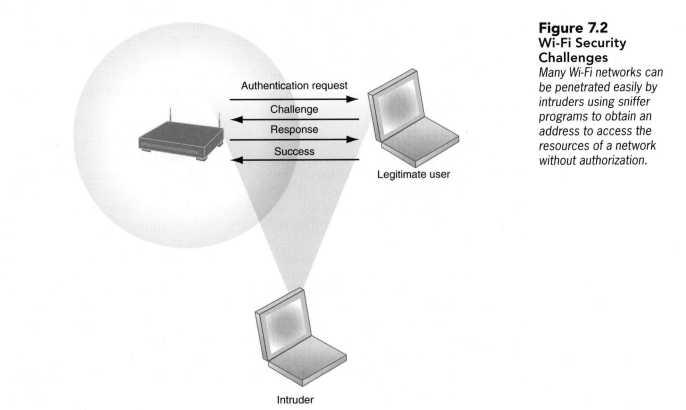

Figure 7.2
Wi-Fi Security Challenges
Many Wi-Fi networks can be penetrated easily by intruders using sniffer programs to obtain an address to access the resources of a network without authorization.

MALICIOUS SOFTWARE: VIRUSES, WORMS, TROJAN HORSES, AND SPYWARE

Malicious software programs are referred to as **malware** and include a variety of threats, such as computer viruses, worms, and Trojan horses. A **computer virus** is a rogue software program that attaches itself to other software programs or data files in order to be executed, usually without user knowledge or permission. Most computer viruses deliver a "payload." The payload may be relatively benign, such as the instructions to display a message or image, or it may be highly destructive—destroying programs or data, clogging computer memory, reformatting a computer's hard drive, or causing programs to run improperly. Viruses typically spread from computer to computer when humans take an action, such as sending an e-mail attachment or copying an infected file.

Most recent attacks have come from **worms**, which are independent computer programs that copy themselves from one computer to other computers over a network. Unlike viruses, worms can operate on their own without attaching to other computer program files and rely less on human behavior in order to spread from computer to computer. This explains why computer worms spread much more rapidly than computer viruses. Worms destroy data and programs as well as disrupt or even halt the operation of computer networks.

Worms and viruses are often spread over the Internet from files of downloaded software, from files attached to e-mail transmissions, or from compromised e-mail messages or instant messaging. Viruses have also invaded computerized information systems from "infected" disks or infected machines.

Hackers can do to a smartphone just about anything they can do to any Internet device: request malicious files without user intervention, delete files, transmit files, install programs running in the background to monitor user actions, and potentially convert the smartphone into a robot in a botnet to send e-mail and text messages to anyone. With smartphones starting to outsell PCs, and smartphones increasingly used as payment devices, they are becoming a major avenue for malware.

Malware targeting mobile devices is not yet as extensive as that targeting larger computers, but nonetheless is spreading using e-mail, text messages, Bluetooth, and file downloads from the Web via Wi-Fi or cellular networks. There are now more than 500 viruses and worms targeting mobile phones. Early attacks, such as the Cabir and Commwarrior worms in 2004 and 2005 caused little damage, but since 2009 the attacks have become more menacing. For example, in September 2010, hackers installed malicious applications on smartphones using the Symbian operating system to help criminals steal money from accounts at a Spanish bank (Richmond, 2011). Mobile device viruses pose serious threats to enterprise computing because so many wireless devices are now linked to corporate information systems.

Blogs, wikis, and social networking sites such as Facebook have emerged as new conduits for malware or spyware. These applications allow users to post software code as part of the permissible content, and such code can be launched automatically as soon as a Web page is viewed. The chapter-opening case study describes other channels for malware targeting Facebook users. On July 4, 2011, hackers broke into the "Fox News Politics" Twitter account, sending fake messages about President Barack Obama. The hackers changed the account's password, preventing Fox from correcting the messages for hours (Sherr, 2011).

Internet security firm Symantec reported in 2011 that it had detected 286 million new and unique threats from malicious software in 2010, or about nine per second, up from 240 million in 2009. Symantec observed that the amount of harmful software in the world passed the amount of beneficial software in 2007, and as many as one of every 10 downloads from the Web includes harmful programs (Drew and Kopytoff, 2011). More malware today is being targeted at small businesses, because it is more difficult for such companies to protect themselves against so many different types of attacks (Fowler and Worthen, 2011). Table 7.1 describes the characteristics of some of the most harmful worms and viruses that have appeared to date.

TABLE 7.1

Examples of Malicious Code

Name	Type	Description
Conficker (aka Downadup, Downup)	Worm	First detected in November 2008. Uses flaws in Windows software to take over machines and link them into a virtual computer that can be commanded remotely. Has more than 5 million computers worldwide under its control. Difficult to eradicate.
Storm	Worm/ Trojan horse	First identified in January 2007. Spreads via e-mail spam with a fake attachment. Infected up to 10 million computers, causing them to join its zombie network of computers engaged in criminal activity.
Sasser.ftp	Worm	First appeared in May 2004. Spread over the Internet by attacking random IP addresses. Causes computers to continually crash and reboot, and infected computers to search for more victims. Affected millions of computers worldwide, disrupting British Airways flight check-ins, operations of British coast guard stations, Hong Kong hospitals, Taiwan post office branches, and Australia's Westpac Bank. Sasser and its variants caused an estimated $14.8 billion to $18.6 billion in damages worldwide.
MyDoom.A	Worm	First appeared on January 26, 2004. Spreads as an e-mail attachment. Sends e-mail to addresses harvested from infected machines, forging the sender's address. At its peak, this worm lowered global Internet performance by 10 percent and Web page loading times by as much as 50 percent. Was programmed to stop spreading after February 12, 2004.
Sobig.F	Worm	First detected on August 19, 2003. Spreads via e-mail attachments and sends massive amounts of mail with forged sender information. Deactivated itself on September 10, 2003, after infecting more than 1 million PCs and doing $5 to $10 billion in damage.
ILOVEYOU	Virus	First detected on May 3, 2000. Script virus written in Visual Basic script and transmitted as an attachment to e-mail with the subject line ILOVEYOU. Overwrites music, image, and other files with a copy of itself and did an estimated $10 billion to $15 billion in damage.
Melissa	Macro virus/ worm	First appeared in March 1999. Word macro script mailing infected Word file to first 50 entries in user's Microsoft Outlook address book. Infected 15 to 29 percent of all business PCs, causing $300 million to $600 million in damage.

A **Trojan horse** is a software program that appears to be benign but then does something other than expected, such as the Zeus Trojan described in the chapter-opening case. The Trojan horse is not itself a virus because it does not replicate, but it is often a way for viruses or other malicious code to be introduced into a computer system. The term *Trojan horse* is based on the huge wooden horse used by the Greeks to trick the Trojans into opening the gates to their fortified city during the Trojan War. Once inside the city walls, Greek soldiers hidden in the horse revealed themselves and captured the city.

At the moment, **SQL injection attacks** are the largest malware threat. SQL injection attacks take advantage of vulnerabilities in poorly coded Web application software to introduce malicious program code into a company's systems and networks. These vulnerabilities occur when a Web application fails to properly validate or filter data entered by a user on a Web page, which might occur when ordering something online. An attacker uses this input validation error to send a rogue SQL query to the underlying database to access the database, plant malicious code, or access other systems on the network. Large Web applications have hundreds of places for inputting user data, each of which creates an opportunity for an SQL injection attack.

A large number of Web-facing applications are believed to have SQL injection vulnerabilities, and tools are available for hackers to check Web applications for these vulnerabilities. Such tools are able to locate a data entry field on a Web page form, enter data into it, and check the response to see if shows vulnerability to a SQL injection.

Some types of spyware also act as malicious software. These small programs install themselves surreptitiously on computers to monitor user Web surfing activity and serve up advertising. Thousands of forms of spyware have been documented.

Many users find such **spyware** annoying and some critics worry about its infringement on computer users' privacy. Some forms of spyware are especially nefarious. **Keyloggers** record every keystroke made on a computer to steal serial numbers for software, to launch Internet attacks, to gain access to e-mail accounts, to obtain passwords to protected computer systems, or to pick up personal information such as credit card numbers. Other spyware programs reset Web browser home pages, redirect search requests, or slow performance by taking up too much memory. The Zeus Trojan described in the chapter-opening case uses keylogging to steal financial information.

HACKERS AND COMPUTER CRIME

A **hacker** is an individual who intends to gain unauthorized access to a computer system. Within the hacking community, the term *cracker* is typically used to denote a hacker with criminal intent, although in the public press, the terms hacker and cracker are used interchangeably. Hackers and crackers gain unauthorized access by finding weaknesses in the security protections employed by Web sites and computer systems, often taking advantage of various features of the Internet that make it an open system and easy to use.

Hacker activities have broadened beyond mere system intrusion to include theft of goods and information, as well as system damage and **cybervandalism**, the intentional disruption, defacement, or even destruction of a Web site or corporate information system. For example, cybervandals have turned many of the MySpace "group" sites, which are dedicated to interests such as home beer brewing or animal welfare, into cyber-graffiti walls, filled with offensive comments and photographs.

Spoofing and Sniffing

Hackers attempting to hide their true identities often spoof, or misrepresent, themselves by using fake e-mail addresses or masquerading as someone else. **Spoofing** also may involve redirecting a Web link to an address different from the intended one, with the site masquerading as the intended destination. For example, if hackers redirect customers to a fake Web site that looks almost exactly like the true site, they can then collect and process orders, effectively stealing business as well as sensitive customer information from the true site. We provide more detail on other forms of spoofing in our discussion of computer crime.

A **sniffer** is a type of eavesdropping program that monitors information traveling over a network. When used legitimately, sniffers help identify potential network trouble spots or criminal activity on networks, but when used for criminal purposes, they can be damaging and very difficult to detect. Sniffers enable hackers to steal proprietary information from anywhere on a network, including e-mail messages, company files, and confidential reports.

Denial-of-Service Attacks

In a **denial-of-service (DoS) attack**, hackers flood a network server or Web server with many thousands of false communications or requests for services to crash the network. The network receives so many queries that it cannot keep up with them and is thus unavailable to service legitimate requests. A **distributed denial-of-service (DDoS)** attack uses numerous computers to inundate and overwhelm the network from numerous launch points.

For example, during the 2009 Iranian election protests, foreign activists trying to help the opposition engaged in DDoS attacks against Iran's government. The official Web site of the Iranian government (ahmadinejad.ir) was rendered inaccessible on several occasions.

Although DoS attacks do not destroy information or access restricted areas of a company's information systems, they often cause a Web site to shut down, making it impossible for legitimate users to access the site. For busy e-commerce sites, these attacks are costly; while the site is shut down, customers cannot make purchases. Especially vulnerable are small and midsize businesses whose networks tend to be less protected than those of large corporations.

Perpetrators of DoS attacks often use thousands of "zombie" PCs infected with malicious software without their owners' knowledge and organized into a **botnet**. Hackers create these botnets by infecting other people's computers with bot malware that opens a back door through which an attacker can give instructions. The infected computer then becomes a slave, or zombie, serving a master computer belonging to someone else. Once hackers infect enough computers, they can use the amassed resources of the botnet to launch DDos attacks, phishing campaigns, or unsolicited "spam" e-mail.

The number of computers that are part of botnets is variously estimated to be from 6 to 24 million, with thousands of botnets operating worldwide. For example, the Mariposa botnet, which started in Spain and spread across the world, had infected and controlled about 12.7 million computers in 2010 in its efforts to steal credit card numbers and online banking passwords.

The Interactive Session on Organizations describes multiple waves of DDoS attacks targeting a number of Web sites of government agencies and other organizations in South Korea and the United States in July 2009. The attacker used a botnet controlling over 65,000 computers, and was able to cripple some of these sites for several days. Most of the botnet originated from China, and North Korea. Botnet attacks thought to have originated in Russia were responsible for crippling the Web sites of the Estonian government in April 2007 and the Georgian government in July 2008.

Computer Crime

Most hacker activities are criminal offenses, and the vulnerabilities of systems we have just described make them targets for other types of **computer crime** as well. In November, 2010, New York resident George Castro was charged with grand larceny for allegedly stealing nearly $4.5 million from Columbia University over the course of two months. Castro had added a TD Bank account belonging to him as a payee in the Columbia University Medical Center's accounts payable system (El-Ghobashy, 2010). Computer crime is defined by the U.S. Department of Justice as "any violations of criminal law that involve a knowledge of computer technology for their perpetration, investigation, or prosecution." Table 7.2 provides examples of the computer as both a target and an instrument of crime.

No one knows the magnitude of the computer crime problem—how many systems are invaded, how many people engage in the practice, or the total economic damage. According to the Ponemon Institute's Second Annual Cost of Cyber Crime Study sponsored by ArcSight, the median annualized cost of cybercrime for the organizations in the study was $5.9 million per year (Ponemon Institute, 2011). Many companies are reluctant to report computer crimes because the crimes may involve employees, or the company fears that publicizing its vulnerability will hurt its reputation. The most economically damaging kinds of computer crime are DoS attacks, introducing viruses, theft of services, and disruption of computer systems.

TABLE 7.2

Examples of Computer Crime

Computers as Targets of Crime
Breaching the confidentiality of protected computerized data
Accessing a computer system without authority
Knowingly accessing a protected computer to commit fraud
Intentionally accessing a protected computer and causing damage, negligently or deliberately
Knowingly transmitting a program, program code, or command that intentionally causes damage to a protected computer
Threatening to cause damage to a protected computer

Computers as Instruments of Crime
Theft of trade secrets
Unauthorized copying of software or copyrighted intellectual property, such as articles, books, music, and video
Schemes to defraud
Using e-mail for threats or harassment
Intentionally attempting to intercept electronic communication
Illegally accessing stored electronic communications, including e-mail and voice mail
Transmitting or possessing child pornography using a computer

Identity Theft

With the growth of the Internet and electronic commerce, identity theft has become especially troubling. **Identity theft** is a crime in which an imposter obtains key pieces of personal information, such as social security identification numbers, driver's license numbers, or credit card numbers, to impersonate someone else. The information may be used to obtain credit, merchandise, or services in the name of the victim or to provide the thief with false credentials.

Identify theft has flourished on the Internet, with credit card files a major target of Web site hackers. Moreover, e-commerce sites are wonderful sources of customer personal information—name, address, and phone number. Armed with this information, criminals are able to assume new identities and establish new credit for their own purposes.

One increasingly popular tactic is a form of spoofing called **phishing**. Phishing involves setting up fake Web sites or sending e-mail messages that look like those of legitimate businesses to ask users for confidential personal data. The e-mail message instructs recipients to update or confirm records by providing social security numbers, bank and credit card information, and other confidential data either by responding to the e-mail message, by entering the information at a bogus Web site, or by calling a telephone number. EBay, PayPal, Amazon.com, Walmart, and a variety of banks are among the top spoofed companies. In a more targeted form of phishing called *spear phishing*, messages appear to come from a trusted source, such as an individual within the recipient's own company or a friend.

Phishing techniques called evil twins and pharming are harder to detect. **Evil twins** are wireless networks that pretend to offer trustworthy Wi-Fi connections to the Internet, such as those in airport lounges, hotels, or coffee shops. The bogus network looks identical to a legitimate public network. Fraudsters try to capture passwords or credit card numbers of unwitting users who log on to the network.

Pharming redirects users to a bogus Web page, even when the individual types the correct Web page address into his or her browser. This is possible if pharming perpetrators gain access to the Internet address information stored by Internet service providers to speed up Web browsing and the ISP companies have flawed software on their servers that allows the fraudsters to hack in and change those addresses.

According to the Ponemon Institute's sixth annual U.S. Cost of a Data Breach Study, data breach incidents cost U.S. companies $214 per compromised customer record in 2010. The average total per-incident cost in 2010 was $7.2 million (George, 2011). Additionally, brand damage can be significant, albeit hard to quantify. Table 7.3 describes the most expensive data breaches that have occurred to date, including the Sony data breach discussed in the chapter-ending case study.

The U.S. Congress addressed the threat of computer crime in 1986 with the Computer Fraud and Abuse Act, which makes it illegal to access a computer system without authorization. Most states have similar laws, and nations in Europe have comparable legislation. Congress passed the National Information Infrastructure Protection Act in 1996 to make malware distribution and hacker attacks to disable Web sites federal crimes.

TABLE 7.3

The Five Most Expensive Data Breaches

Data Breach	Description
U.S. Veterans Affairs Department	In 2006, the names, birth dates, and social security numbers of 17.5 million military veterans and personnel were stolen from a laptop that a Department of Veterans Affairs employee had taken home. The VA spent at least $25 million to run call centers, send out mailings, and pay for a year of a credit-monitoring service for victims.
Heartland Payment Systems	In 2008, criminals led by Miami hacker Albert Gonzales installed spying software on the computer network of Heartland Payment Systems, a payment processor based in Princeton, N.J., and stole the numbers of as many as 100 million credit and debit cards. Gonzales was sentenced in 2010 to 20 years in federal prison, and Heartland paid about $140 million in fines and settlements.
TJX	A 2007 data breach at TJX, the retailer that owns national chains including TJ Maxx and Marshalls, cost at least $250 million. Cyber criminals took more than 45 million credit and debit card numbers, some of which were used later to buy millions of dollars in electronics from Walmart and elsewhere. Albert Gonzales, who played a major role in the Heartland hack, was linked to this cyberattack as well.
Epsilon	In March 2011, hackers stole millions of names and e-mail addresses from the Epsilon e-mail marketing firm, which handles e-mail lists for major retailers and banks like Best Buy, JPMorgan, TiVo, and Walgreens. Costs could range from $100 million to $4 billion, depending on what happens to the stolen data, with most of the costs from losing customers due to a damaged reputation.
Sony	In April 2011, hackers obtained personal information, including credit, debit, and bank account numbers, from over 100 million PlayStation Network users and Sony Online Entertainment users. The breach could cost Sony and credit card issuers up to a total of $2 billion.

U.S. legislation, such as the Wiretap Act, Wire Fraud Act, Economic Espionage Act, Electronic Communications Privacy Act, E-Mail Threats and Harassment Act, and Child Pornography Act, covers computer crimes involving intercepting electronic communication, using electronic communication to defraud, stealing trade secrets, illegally accessing stored electronic communications, using e-mail for threats or harassment, and transmitting or possessing child pornography. A proposed Data Security and Breach Notification Act would mandate organizations that possess personal information to put in place "reasonable" security procedures to keep the data secure and to notify anyone affected by a data breach.

Click Fraud

When you click on an ad displayed by a search engine, the advertiser typically pays a fee for each click, which is supposed to direct potential buyers to its products. **Click fraud** occurs when an individual or computer program fraudulently clicks on an online ad without any intention of learning more about the advertiser or making a purchase. Click fraud has become a serious problem at Google and other Web sites that feature pay-per-click online advertising.

Some companies hire third parties (typically from low-wage countries) to fraudulently click on a competitor's ads to weaken them by driving up their marketing costs. Click fraud can also be perpetrated with software programs doing the clicking, and botnets are often used for this purpose. Search engines such as Google attempt to monitor click fraud but have been reluctant to publicize their efforts to deal with the problem.

Global Threats: Cyberterrorism and Cyberwarfare

The cyber criminal activities we have described-launching malware, denial-of-service attacks, and phishing probes-are borderless. Computer security firm Sophos reported that 40 percent of the malware it identified in early 2011 originated in the United States, while 10 percent came from France, 9 percent from Russia, and 5 percent from China (Sophos, 2011). The global nature of the Internet makes it possible for cybercriminals to operate-and to do harm—anywhere in the world.

Internet vulnerabilities have also turned individuals and even entire nation-states into easy targets for politically motivated hacking to conduct sabotage and espionage. **Cyberwarfare** is a state-sponsored activity designed to cripple and defeat another state or nation by penetrating its computers or networks for the purposes of causing damage and disruption. Cyberwarfare poses a serious threat to the infrastructure of modern societies, since their major financial, health, government, and industrial institutions rely on the Internet for daily operations. Cyberwarfare also involves defending against these types of attacks. The Interactive Session on Organizations describes some recent cyberwarfare attacks and their growing sophistication and severity.

INTERNAL THREATS: EMPLOYEES

We tend to think the security threats to a business originate outside the organization. In fact, company insiders pose serious security problems. Employees have access to privileged information, and in the presence of sloppy internal security procedures, they are often able to roam throughout an organization's systems without leaving a trace.

Studies have found that user lack of knowledge is the single greatest cause of network security breaches. Many employees forget their passwords to access computer systems or allow co-workers to use them, which compromises the system. Malicious intruders seeking system access sometimes trick employees into revealing their passwords by pretending to be legitimate members of the company in need of information. This practice is called **social engineering**.

Both end users and information systems specialists are also a major source of errors introduced into information systems. End users introduce errors by entering faulty data or by not following the proper instructions for processing data and using computer equipment. Information systems specialists may create software errors as they design and develop new software or maintain existing programs.

INTERACTIVE SESSION: ORGANIZATIONS Stuxnet and the Changing Face of Cyberwarfare

In July 2010, reports surfaced about a Stuxnet worm that had been targeting Iran's nuclear facilities. In November of that year, Iran's President Mahmoud Ahmadinejad publicly acknowledged that malicious software had infected the Iranian nuclear facilities and disrupted the nuclear program by disabling the facilities' centrifuges. Stuxnet had earned its place in history as the first visible example of industrial cyberwarfare.

To date, Stuxnet is the most sophisticated cyberweapon ever deployed. Stuxnet's mission was to activate only computers that ran Supervisory Control and Data Acquisition (SCADA) software used in Siemens centrifuges to enrich uranium. The Windows-based worm had a "dual warhead." One part was designed to lay dormant for long periods, then speed up Iran's nuclear centrifuges so that they spun wildly out of control. Another secretly recorded what normal operations at the nuclear plant looked like and then played those recordings back to plant operators so it would appear that the centrifuges were operating normally when they were actually tearing themselves apart.

The worm's sophistication indicated the work of highly skilled professionals. "I view Stuxnet as a weapons delivery system, like the B-2 Bomber," said Michael Assante, president and CEO at the National Board of Information Security Examiners. The software program code was highly modular, so that it could be easily changed to attack different systems. Stuxnet only became active when it encountered a specific configuration of controllers, running a set of processes limited to centrifuge plants.

Over 60 percent of Stuxet-infected computers are in Iran, and digital security company Kaspersky Labs speculates that the worm was launched with nation-state support (probably from Israel and the United States) with the intention of disabling some or all of Iran's uranium enrichment program. Stuxnet wiped out about one-fifth of Iran's nuclear centrifuges. The damage was irreparable and is believed to have delayed Iran's ability to make nuclear arms by as much as five years. And no one is certain that the Stuxnet attacks are over. Some experts who examined the Stuxnet software code believe it contains the seeds for more versions and attacks.

According to a Tofino Security report, Stuxnet is capable of infecting even well-secured computer systems that follow industry best practices. Companies' need for interconnectivity between control systems make it nearly impossible to defend against a well-constructed, multi-pronged attack such as Stuxnet.

In general, cyberwarfare attacks have become much more widespread, sophisticated, and potentially devastating. There are 250,000 probes trying to find their way into U.S. Department of Defense networks every hour, and cyberattacks on U.S. federal agencies have increased 150 percent since 2008.

In July 2009, 27 American and South Korean government agencies and other organizations were hit by a DDoS attack. An estimated 65,000 computers belonging to foreign botnets flooded their Web sites with access requests. Affected sites included those of the White House, the Treasury, the Federal Trade Commission, the Defense Department, the Secret Service, the New York Stock Exchange, and the Washington Post, in addition to the Korean Defense Ministry, National Assembly, and the presidential Blue House. The attacks slowed down most of the U.S. sites and forced several South Korean sites to stop operating. North Korea or pro-North Korean groups were suspected to be behind the attacks.

In March 2011, intruders penetrated the computer system of RSA, which issues SecureID tokens for authenticating users of network resources. The RSA intruders were then able to use the data stolen from RSA to penetrate networks of defense contractors, including Lockheed Martin. The Pentagon reported that about the same time, a foreign intelligence service hacked into the computer system of an unnamed military defense contractor and obtained 24,000 Pentagon files in a single intrusion. Over the years, hackers have stolen plans for missile tracking systems, satellite navigation devices, surveillance drones, and leading-edge jet fighters.

In each cyberwarfare incident, the governments of the countries suspected to be responsible have roundly denied the charges with no repercussions. How could this be possible? The major reason is that tracing identities of specific attackers through cyberspace is next to impossible, making deniability simple.

The real worry for security experts and government officials is an act of cyberwarfare against a critical resource, such as the electric grid, financial system, or communications systems. In April 2009, cyberspies infiltrated the U.S. electrical grid, using weak points where computers on the grid are connected to the Internet, and left behind software programs whose purpose is unclear, but which presumably could be used to disrupt the system.

The U.S. has no clear strategy about how the country would respond to that level of a cyberattack, and the effects of such an attack would likely be devastating. Mike McConnell, the former director of national intelligence, stated that if even a single large American bank were successfully attacked, "it would have an order-of-magnitude greater impact on the global economy" than the World Trade Center attacks, and that "the ability to threaten the U.S. money supply is the equivalent of today's nuclear weapon."

Many security experts believe that U.S. cybersecurity is not well-organized. Several different agencies, including the Pentagon and the National Security Agency (NSA), have their sights on being the leading agency in the ongoing efforts to combat cyberwarfare. The first headquarters designed to coordinate government cybersecurity efforts, called Cybercom, was activated in May 2010 in the hope of resolving this organizational tangle. In May 2011, President

Barack Obama signed executive orders weaving cyber capabilities into U.S. military strategy, but these capabilities are still evolving. Will the U.S. and other nations be ready when the next Stuxnet appears?

Sources: Thom Shanker and Elisabeth Bumiller, "After Suffering Damaging Cyberattack, the Pentagon Takes Defensive Action," *New York Times*, July 15, 2011; Robert Leos, "Secure Best Practices No Proof Against Stuxnet," CSO, March 3, 2011; Lolita C. Baldor, "Pentagon Gets Cyberwar Guidelines," Associated Press, June 22, 2011; William J. Broad, John Markoff, and David E. Sanger, "Israel Tests on Worm Called Crucial in Iran Nuclear Delay," *New York Times*, January 15, 2011; Richard Clarke, "China's Cyberassault on America," *Wall Street Journal*, June 15, 2011; George V. Hulme, "SCADA Insecurity" and Michael S. Mimoso, "Cyberspace Has Gone Offensive," *Information Security's Essential Guide to Threat Management* (June 14, 2011); Sibhan Gorman and Julian A. Barnes, "Cyber Combat: Act of War," *Wall Street Journal*, May 31, 2011; Siobhan Gorman, "U.S. Hampered in Fighting Cyber Attacks, Report Says," *Wall Street Journal*, June, 16, 2010; Sean Gallagher, "New Threats Compel DOD to Rethink Cyber Strategy," *Defense Knowledge Technologies and Net-Enabled Warfare*, January 22, 2010.

CASE STUDY QUESTIONS

1. Is cyberwarfare a serious problem? Why or why not?

2. Assess the people, organizational, and technology factors that have created this problem.

3. What makes Stuxnet different from other cyberwarfare attacks? How serious a threat is this technology?

4. What solutions for have been proposed for this problem? Do you think they will be effective? Why or why not?

MIS IN ACTION

Do an Internet search on cyberwarfare. Select two recent cyberattacks and describe the target of these attacks, the technology used in the attacks, and the impact of the attack. Describe what could have been done to prevent the attacks.

SOFTWARE VULNERABILITY

Software errors pose a constant threat to information systems, causing untold losses in productivity. Growing complexity and size of software programs, coupled with demands for timely delivery to markets, have contributed to an increase in software flaws or vulnerabilities. For example, a database-related software error prevented millions of JPMorgan Chase retail and small-business customers from accessing their online bank accounts for two days in September 2010 (Dash, 2010).

A major problem with software is the presence of hidden **bugs** or program code defects. Studies have shown that it is virtually impossible to eliminate all bugs from large programs. The main source of bugs is the complexity of decision-making code. A relatively small program of several hundred lines will contain tens of decisions leading to hundreds or even thousands of different paths. Important programs within most corporations are usually much larger, containing tens of thousands or even millions of lines of code, each with many times the choices and paths of the smaller programs.

Zero defects cannot be achieved in larger programs. Complete testing simply is not possible. Fully testing programs that contain thousands of choices and millions of paths would require thousands of years. Even with rigorous testing, you would not know for sure that a piece of software was dependable until the product proved itself after much operational use.

Flaws in commercial software not only impede performance but also create security vulnerabilities that open networks to intruders. Each year security firms identify thousands of software vulnerabilities in Internet and PC software. For instance, in 2010, Symantec identified 500 browser vulnerabilities: 191 in Chrome, 119 in Safari, 100 in Firefox, 59 in Internet Explorer, and 31 in Opera. Some of these vulnerabilities were critical (Symantec 2011).

To correct software flaws once they are identified, the software vendor creates small pieces of software called **patches** to repair the flaws without disturbing the proper operation of the software. An example is Microsoft's Windows Vista Service Pack 2, released in April 2009, which includes some security enhancements to counter malware and hackers. It is up to users of the software to track these vulnerabilities, test, and apply all patches. This process is called *patch management.*

Because a company's IT infrastructure is typically laden with multiple business applications, operating system installations, and other system services, maintaining patches on all devices and services used by a company is often time-consuming and costly. Malware is being created so rapidly that companies have very little time to respond between the time a vulnerability and a patch are announced and the time malicious software appears to exploit the vulnerability.

7.2 Business Value of Security and Control

Many firms are reluctant to spend heavily on security because it is not directly related to sales revenue. However, protecting information systems is so critical to the operation of the business that it deserves a second look.

Companies have very valuable information assets to protect. Systems often house confidential information about individuals' taxes, financial assets, medical records, and job performance reviews. They also can contain information on corporate operations, including trade secrets, new product development plans, and marketing strategies. Government systems may store information on weapons systems, intelligence operations, and military targets. These information assets have tremendous value, and the repercussions can be devastating if they are lost, destroyed, or placed in the wrong hands. Systems that are unable to function because of security breaches, disasters, or malfunctioning technology can permanently impact a company's financial health. Some experts believe that 40 percent of all businesses will not recover from application or data losses that are not repaired within three days (Focus Research, 2010).

Inadequate security and control may result in serious legal liability. Businesses must protect not only their own information assets but also those of customers, employees, and business partners. Failure to do so may open the firm to costly litigation for data exposure or theft. An organization can be held liable for needless risk and harm created if the organization fails to take appropriate protective action to prevent loss of confidential information, data corruption, or breach of privacy. For example, BJ's Wholesale Club was sued by the U.S. Federal Trade Commission for allowing hackers to access its systems and steal credit and debit card data for fraudulent purchases. Banks that issued the cards with the stolen data sought $13 million from BJ's to compensate them for reimbursing card holders for the fraudulent purchases. A sound security and control framework that protects business information assets can thus produce a high return on investment. Strong security and control also increase employee productivity and lower operational costs.

LEGAL AND REGULATORY REQUIREMENTS FOR ELECTRONIC RECORDS MANAGEMENT

Recent U.S. government regulations are forcing companies to take security and control more seriously by mandating the protection of data from abuse, exposure, and unauthorized access. Firms face new legal obligations for the retention and storage of electronic records as well as for privacy protection.

If you work in the health care industry, your firm will need to comply with the Health Insurance Portability and Accountability Act (HIPAA) of 1996. **HIPAA** outlines medical security and privacy rules and procedures for simplifying the administration of health care billing and automating the transfer of health care data between health care providers, payers, and plans. It requires members of the health care industry to retain patient information for six years and ensure the confidentiality of those records. It specifies privacy, security, and electronic transaction standards for health care providers handling patient information, providing penalties for breaches of medical privacy, disclosure of patient records by e-mail, or unauthorized network access.

If you work in a firm providing financial services, your firm will need to comply with the Financial Services Modernization Act of 1999, better known as the **Gramm-Leach-Bliley Act** after its congressional sponsors. This act requires financial institutions to ensure the security and confidentiality of customer data. Data must be stored on a secure medium, and special security measures must be enforced to protect such data on storage media and during transmittal.

If you work in a publicly traded company, your company will need to comply with the Public Company Accounting Reform and Investor Protection Act of 2002, better known as the **Sarbanes-Oxley Act** after its sponsors Senator Paul Sarbanes of Maryland and Representative Michael Oxley of Ohio. This Act was designed to protect investors after the financial scandals at Enron, WorldCom, and other public companies. It imposes responsibility on companies and their management to safeguard the accuracy and integrity of financial information that is used internally and released externally. One of the Learning Tracks for this chapter discusses Sarbanes-Oxley in detail.

Sarbanes-Oxley is fundamentally about ensuring that internal controls are in place to govern the creation and documentation of information in financial statements. Because information systems are used to generate, store, and transport such data, the legislation requires firms to consider information systems security and other controls required to ensure the integrity, confidentiality, and accuracy of their data. Each system application that deals with critical financial reporting data requires controls to make sure the data are accurate. Controls to secure the corporate network, prevent unauthorized access to systems and data, and ensure data integrity and availability in the event of disaster or other disruption of service are essential as well.

ELECTRONIC EVIDENCE AND COMPUTER FORENSICS

Security, control, and electronic records management have become essential for responding to legal actions. Much of the evidence today for stock fraud, embezzlement, theft of company trade secrets, computer crime, and many civil cases is in digital form. In addition to information from printed or typewritten pages, legal cases today increasingly rely on evidence represented as digital data stored on portable storage devices, CDs, and computer hard disk drives, as well as in e-mail, instant messages, and e-commerce transactions over the Internet. E-mail is currently the most common type of electronic evidence.

In a legal action, a firm is obligated to respond to a discovery request for access to information that may be used as evidence, and the company is required by law to produce those data. The cost of responding to a discovery request can be enormous if the company has trouble assembling the required data or the data have been corrupted or destroyed. Courts now impose severe financial and even criminal penalties for improper destruction of electronic documents.

An effective electronic document retention policy ensures that electronic documents, e-mail, and other records are well organized, accessible, and neither retained too long nor discarded too soon. It also reflects an awareness of how to preserve potential evidence for computer forensics. **Computer forensics** is the scientific collection, examination, authentication, preservation, and analysis of data held on or retrieved from computer storage media in such a way that the information can be used as evidence in a court of law. It deals with the following problems:

- Recovering data from computers while preserving evidential integrity

- Securely storing and handling recovered electronic data

- Finding significant information in a large volume of electronic data

- Presenting the information to a court of law

Electronic evidence may reside on computer storage media in the form of computer files and as *ambient data*, which are not visible to the average user. An example might be a file that has been deleted on a PC hard drive. Data that a computer user may have deleted on computer storage media can be recovered through various techniques. Computer forensics experts try to recover such hidden data for presentation as evidence.

An awareness of computer forensics should be incorporated into a firm's contingency planning process. The CIO, security specialists, information systems staff, and corporate legal counsel should all work together to have a plan in place that can be executed if a legal need arises. You can find out more about computer forensics in the Learning Tracks for this chapter.

7.3 Establishing a Framework for Security and Control

Even with the best security tools, your information systems won't be reliable and secure unless you know how and where to deploy them. You'll need to know where your company is at risk and what controls you must have in place to protect your information systems. You'll also need to develop a security policy and plans for keeping your business running if your information systems aren't operational.

INFORMATION SYSTEMS CONTROLS

Information systems controls are both manual and automated and consist of general and application controls. **General controls** govern the design, security, and use of computer programs and the security of data files in general throughout the organization's information technology infrastructure. On the whole, general controls apply to all computerized applications and consist of a combination of hardware, software, and manual procedures that create an overall control environment.

General controls include software controls, physical hardware controls, computer operations controls, data security controls, controls over implementation of system processes, and administrative controls. Table 7.4 describes the functions of each of these controls.

Application controls are specific controls unique to each computerized application, such as payroll or order processing. They include both automated and manual procedures that ensure that only authorized data are completely and accurately processed by that application. Application controls can be classified as (1) input controls, (2) processing controls, and (3) output controls.

Input controls check data for accuracy and completeness when they enter the system. There are specific input controls for input authorization, data conversion, data editing, and error handling. *Processing controls* establish that data are complete and accurate during updating. *Output controls* ensure that the results of computer processing are accurate, complete, and properly distributed. You can find more detail about application and general controls in our Learning Tracks.

RISK ASSESSMENT

Before your company commits resources to security and information systems controls, it must know which assets require protection and the extent to which these assets are vulnerable. A risk assessment helps answer these questions and determine the most cost-effective set of controls for protecting assets.

TABLE 7.4

General Controls

Type of General Control	Description
Software controls	Monitor the use of system software and prevent unauthorized access of software programs, system software, and computer programs.
Hardware controls	Ensure that computer hardware is physically secure, and check for equipment malfunction. Organizations that are critically dependent on their computers also must make provisions for backup or continued operation to maintain constant service.
Computer operations controls	Oversee the work of the computer department to ensure that programmed procedures are consistently and correctly applied to the storage and processing of data. They include controls over the setup of computer processing jobs and backup and recovery procedures for processing that ends abnormally.
Data security controls	Ensure that valuable business data files on either disk or tape are not subject to unauthorized access, change, or destruction while they are in use or in storage.
Implementation controls	Audit the systems development process at various points to ensure that the process is properly controlled and managed.
Administrative controls	Formalize standards, rules, procedures, and control disciplines to ensure that the organization's general and application controls are properly executed and enforced.

A **risk assessment** determines the level of risk to the firm if a specific activity or process is not properly controlled. Not all risks can be anticipated and measured, but most businesses will be able to acquire some understanding of the risks they face. Business managers working with information systems specialists should try to determine the value of information assets, points of vulnerability, the likely frequency of a problem, and the potential for damage. For example, if an event is likely to occur no more than once a year, with a maximum of a $1,000 loss to the organization, it is not be wise to spend $20,000 on the design and maintenance of a control to protect against that event. However, if that same event could occur at least once a day, with a potential loss of more than $300,000 a year, $100,000 spent on a control might be entirely appropriate.

Table 7.5 illustrates sample results of a risk assessment for an online order processing system that processes 30,000 orders per day. The likelihood of each exposure occurring over a one-year period is expressed as a percentage. The next column shows the highest and lowest possible loss that could be expected each time the exposure occurred and an average loss calculated by adding the highest and lowest figures together and dividing by two. The expected annual loss for each exposure can be determined by multiplying the average loss by its probability of occurrence.

This risk assessment shows that the probability of a power failure occurring in a one-year period is 30 percent. Loss of order transactions while power is down could range from $5,000 to $200,000 (averaging $102,500) for each occurrence, depending on how long processing is halted. The probability of embezzlement occurring over a yearly period is about 5 percent, with potential losses ranging from $1,000 to $50,000 (and averaging $25,500) for each occurrence. User errors have a 98 percent chance of occurring over a yearly period, with losses ranging from $200 to $40,000 (and averaging $20,100) for each occurrence.

Exposure	Probability of Occurrence (%)	Loss Range/Average ($)	Expected Annual Loss ($)
Power failure	30%	$5,000–$200,000 ($102,500)	$30,750
Embezzlement	5%	$1,000–$50,000 ($25,500)	$1,275
User error	98%	$200–$40,000 ($20,100)	$19,698

TABLE 7.5

Online Order Processing Risk Assessment

Once the risks have been assessed, system builders will concentrate on the control points with the greatest vulnerability and potential for loss. In this case, controls should focus on ways to minimize the risk of power failures and user errors because anticipated annual losses are highest for these areas.

SECURITY POLICY

Once you've identified the main risks to your systems, your company will need to develop a security policy for protecting the company's assets. A **security policy** consists of statements ranking information risks, identifying acceptable security goals, and identifying the mechanisms for achieving these goals. What are the firm's most important information assets? Who generates and controls this information in the firm? What existing security policies are in place to protect the information? What level of risk is management willing to accept for each of these assets? Is it willing, for instance, to lose customer credit data once every 10 years? Or will it build a security system for credit card data that can withstand the once-in-a-hundred-year disaster? Management must estimate how much it will cost to achieve this level of acceptable risk.

The security policy drives other policies determining acceptable use of the firm's information resources and which members of the company have access to its information assets. An **acceptable use policy (AUP)** defines acceptable uses of the firm's information resources and computing equipment, including desktop and laptop computers, wireless devices, telephones, and the Internet. The policy should clarify company policy regarding privacy, user responsibility, and personal use of company equipment and networks. A good AUP defines unacceptable and acceptable actions for every user and specifies consequences for noncompliance. For example, security policy at Unilever, the giant multinational consumer goods company, requires every employee to use a company-specified device and employ a password or other method of identification when logging onto the corporate network.

Security policy also includes provisions for identity management. **Identity management** consists of business processes and software tools for identifying the valid users of a system and controlling their access to system resources. It includes policies for identifying and authorizing different categories of system users, specifying what systems or portions of systems each user is allowed to access, and the processes and technologies for authenticating users and protecting their identities.

Figure 7.3 is one example of how an identity management system might capture the access rules for different levels of users in the human resources function. It specifies what portions of a human resource database each user is permitted to access, based on the information required to perform that person's job. The database contains sensitive personal information such as employees' salaries, benefits, and medical histories.

The access rules illustrated here are for two sets of users. One set of users consists of all employees who perform clerical functions, such as inputting employee data into the system. All individuals with this type of profile can update the system but can neither read nor update sensitive fields, such as salary, medical history, or earnings data. Another profile applies to a

Figure 7.3
Access Rules for a Personnel System
These two examples represent two security profiles or data security patterns that might be found in a personnel system. Depending on the security profile, a user would have certain restrictions on access to various systems, locations, or data in an organization.

SECURITY PROFILE 1	
User: Personnel Dept. Clerk	
Location: Division 1	
Employee Identification Codes with This Profile:	00753, 27834, 37665, 44116

Data Field Restrictions	Type of Access
All employee data for Division 1 only	Read and Update
• Medical history data	None
• Salary	None
• Pensionable earnings	None

SECURITY PROFILE 2	
User: Divisional Personnel Manager	
Location: Division 1	
Employee Identification Codes with This Profile: 27321	

Data Field Restrictions	Type of Access
All employee data for Division 1 only	Read Only

divisional manager, who cannot update the system but who can read all employee data fields for his or her division, including medical history and salary. We provide more detail on the technologies for user authentication later on in this chapter.

DISASTER RECOVERY PLANNING AND BUSINESS CONTINUITY PLANNING

If you run a business, you need to plan for events, such as power outages, floods, earthquakes, or terrorist attacks that will prevent your information systems and your business from operating. **Disaster recovery planning** devises plans for the restoration of computing and communications services after they have been disrupted. Disaster recovery plans focus primarily on the technical issues involved in keeping systems up and running, such as which files to back up and the maintenance of backup computer systems or disaster recovery services.

For example, MasterCard maintains a duplicate computer center in Kansas City, Missouri, to serve as an emergency backup to its primary computer center in St. Louis. Rather than build their own backup facilities, many firms contract with disaster recovery firms, such as Comdisco Disaster Recovery Services in Rosemont, Illinois, and SunGard Availability Services, headquartered in Wayne, Pennsylvania. These disaster recovery firms provide hot sites housing spare computers at locations around the country where subscribing firms can run their critical applications in an emergency. For example, Champion Technologies, which supplies chemicals used in oil and gas operations, is able to switch its enterprise systems from Houston to a SunGard hot site in Scottsdale, Arizona, in two hours.

Business continuity planning focuses on how the company can restore business operations after a disaster strikes. The business continuity plan identifies critical business processes and determines action plans for handling mission-critical functions if systems go down. For example, Deutsche Bank, which provides investment banking and asset management services in 74 different countries, has a well-developed business continuity plan that it continually updates and refines. It maintains full-time teams in Singapore, Hong Kong, Japan, India, and Australia to coordinate plans addressing loss of facilities, personnel, or critical systems so that the company can continue to operate when a catastrophic event occurs. Deutsche Bank's plan distinguishes between processes critical for business survival and those critical to crisis support and is coordinated with the company's disaster recovery planning for its computer centers.

Business managers and information technology specialists need to work together on both types of plans to determine which systems and business processes are most critical to the company. They must conduct a business impact analysis to identify the firm's most critical systems and the impact a systems outage would have on the business. Management must determine the maximum amount of time the business can survive with its systems down and which parts of the business must be restored first.

THE ROLE OF AUDITING

How does management know that information systems security and controls are effective? To answer this question, organizations must conduct comprehensive and systematic audits. An **MIS audit** examines the firm's overall security environment as well as controls governing individual information systems. The auditor should trace the flow of sample transactions through the system and perform tests, using, if appropriate, automated audit software. The MIS audit may also examine data quality.

Security audits review technologies, procedures, documentation, training, and personnel. A thorough audit will even simulate an attack or disaster to test the response of the technology, information systems staff, and business employees.

The audit lists and ranks all control weaknesses and estimates the probability of their occurrence. It then assesses the financial and organizational impact of each threat. Figure 7.4 is a sample auditor's listing of control weaknesses for a loan system. It includes a section for notifying management of such weaknesses and for management's response. Management is expected to devise a plan for countering significant weaknesses in controls.

Function: Loans Location: Peoria, IL	Prepared by: J. Ericson Date: June 16, 2012		Received by: T. Benson Review date: June 28, 2012	
Nature of Weakness and Impact	Chance for Error/Abuse		Notification to Management	
	Yes/ No	Justification	Report date	Management response
User accounts with missing passwords	Yes	Leaves system open to unauthorized outsiders or attackers	5/10/12	Eliminate accounts without passwords
Network configured to allow some sharing of system files	Yes	Exposes critical system files to hostile parties connected to the network	5/10/12	Ensure only required directories are shared and that they are protected with strong passwords
Software patches can update production programs without final approval from Standards and Controls group	No	All production programs require management approval; Standards and Controls group assigns such cases to a temporary production status		

Figure 7.4
Sample Auditor's List of Control Weaknesses
This chart is a sample page from a list of control weaknesses that an auditor might find in a loan system in a local commercial bank. This form helps auditors record and evaluate control weaknesses and shows the results of discussing those weaknesses with management, as well as any corrective actions taken by management.

7.4 Technologies and Tools for Protecting Information Resources

Businesses have an array of technologies for protecting their information resources. They include tools for managing user identities, preventing unauthorized access to systems and data, ensuring system availability, and ensuring software quality.

IDENTITY MANAGEMENT AND AUTHENTICATION

Midsize and large companies have complex IT infrastructures and many different systems, each with its own set of users. Identity management software automates the process of keeping track of all these users and their system privileges, assigning each user a unique digital identity for accessing each system. It also includes tools for authenticating users, protecting user identities, and controlling access to system resources.

To gain access to a system, a user must be authorized and authenticated. **Authentication** refers to the ability to know that a person is who he or she claims to be. Authentication is often established by using **passwords** known only to authorized users. An end user uses a password to log on to a computer system and may also use passwords for accessing specific systems and files. However, users often forget passwords, share them, or choose poor passwords that are easy to guess, which compromises security. Password systems that are too rigorous hinder employee productivity. When employees must change complex passwords frequently, they often take shortcuts, such as choosing passwords that are easy to guess or keeping their passwords at their workstations in plain view. Passwords can also be "sniffed" if transmitted over a network or stolen through social engineering.

New authentication technologies, such as tokens, smart cards, and biometric authentication, overcome some of these problems. A **token** is a physical device, similar to an identification card, that is designed to prove the identity of a single user. Tokens are small gadgets that typically fit on key rings and display passcodes that change frequently. A **smart card** is a device about the size of a credit card that contains a chip formatted with access permission and other data. (Smart cards are also used in electronic payment systems.) A reader device interprets the data on the smart card and allows or denies access.

Biometric authentication uses systems that read and interpret individual human traits, such as fingerprints, irises, and voices, in order to grant or deny access. Biometric

This PC has a biometric fingerprint reader for fast yet secure access to files and networks. New models of PCs are starting to use biometric identification to authenticate users.

authentication is based on the measurement of a physical or behavioral trait that makes each individual unique. It compares a person's unique characteristics, such as the fingerprints, face, or retinal image, against a stored profile of these characteristics to determine whether there are any differences between these characteristics and the stored profile. If the two profiles match, access is granted. Fingerprint and facial recognition technologies are just beginning to be used for security applications, with many PC laptops equipped with fingerprint identification devices and several models with built-in webcams and face recognition software.

FIREWALLS, INTRUSION DETECTION SYSTEMS, AND ANTIVIRUS SOFTWARE

Without protection against malware and intruders, connecting to the Internet would be very dangerous. Firewalls, intrusion detection systems, and antivirus software have become essential business tools.

Firewalls

Firewalls prevent unauthorized users from accessing private networks. A firewall is a combination of hardware and software that controls the flow of incoming and outgoing network traffic. It is generally placed between the organization's private internal networks and distrusted external networks, such as the Internet, although firewalls can also be used to protect one part of a company's network from the rest of the network (see Figure 7.5).

The firewall acts like a gatekeeper who examines each user's credentials before access is granted to a network. The firewall identifies names, IP addresses, applications, and other characteristics of incoming traffic. It checks this information against the access rules that

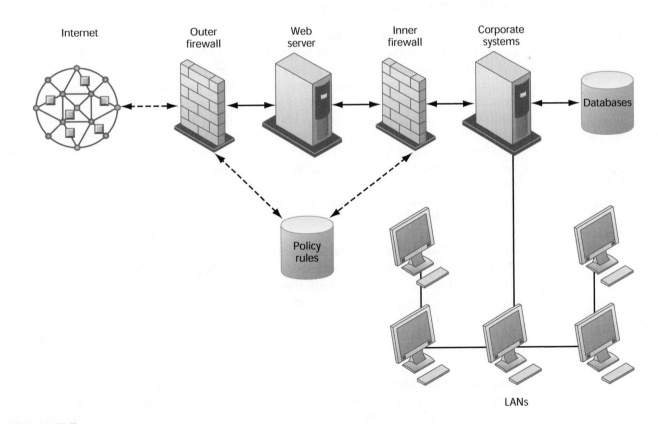

Figure 7.5
A Corporate Firewall
The firewall is placed between the firm's private network and the public Internet or another distrusted network to protect against unauthorized traffic.

have been programmed into the system by the network administrator. The firewall prevents unauthorized communication into and out of the network.

In large organizations, the firewall often resides on a specially designated computer separate from the rest of the network, so no incoming request directly accesses private network resources. There are a number of firewall screening technologies, including static packet filtering, stateful inspection, Network Address Translation, and application proxy filtering. They are frequently used in combination to provide firewall protection.

Packet filtering examines selected fields in the headers of data packets flowing back and forth between the trusted network and the Internet, examining individual packets in isolation. This filtering technology can miss many types of attacks. *Stateful inspection* provides additional security by determining whether packets are part of an ongoing dialogue between a sender and a receiver. It sets up state tables to track information over multiple packets. Packets are accepted or rejected based on whether they are part of an approved conversation or whether they are attempting to establish a legitimate connection.

Network Address Translation (NAT) can provide another layer of protection when static packet filtering and stateful inspection are employed. NAT conceals the IP addresses of the organization's internal host computer(s) to prevent sniffer programs outside the firewall from ascertaining them and using that information to penetrate internal systems.

Application proxy filtering examines the application content of packets. A proxy server stops data packets originating outside the organization, inspects them, and passes a proxy to the other side of the firewall. If a user outside the company wants to communicate with a user inside the organization, the outside user first "talks" to the proxy application and the proxy application communicates with the firm's internal computer. Likewise, a computer user inside the organization goes through the proxy to talk with computers on the outside.

To create a good firewall, an administrator must maintain detailed internal rules identifying the people, applications, or addresses that are allowed or rejected. Firewalls can deter, but not completely prevent, network penetration by outsiders and should be viewed as one element in an overall security plan.

Intrusion Detection Systems

In addition to firewalls, commercial security vendors now provide intrusion detection tools and services to protect against suspicious network traffic and attempts to access files and databases. **Intrusion detection systems** feature full-time monitoring tools placed at the most vulnerable points or "hot spots" of corporate networks to detect and deter intruders continually. The system generates an alarm if it finds a suspicious or anomalous event. Scanning software looks for patterns indicative of known methods of computer attacks, such as bad passwords, checks to see if important files have been removed or modified, and sends warnings of vandalism or system administration errors. Monitoring software examines events as they are happening to discover security attacks in progress. The intrusion detection tool can also be customized to shut down a particularly sensitive part of a network if it receives unauthorized traffic.

Antivirus and Antispyware Software

Defensive technology plans for both individuals and businesses must include anti-malware protection for every computer. **Antivirus software** prevents, detects, and removes malware, including computer viruses, computer worms, Trojan horses, spyware, and adware. However, most antivirus software is effective only against malware already known when the software was written. To remain effective, the antivirus software must be continually updated.

Unified Threat Management Systems

To help businesses reduce costs and improve manageability, security vendors have combined into a single appliance various security tools, including firewalls, virtual private networks, intrusion detection systems, and Web content filtering and antispam software. These comprehensive security management products are called **unified threat management**

(UTM) systems. Although initially aimed at small and medium-sized businesss, UTM products are available for all sizes of networks. Leading UTM vendors include Crossbeam, Fortinent, and Check Point, and networking vendors such as Cisco Systems and Juniper Networks provide some UTM capabilities in their equipment.

SECURING WIRELESS NETWORKS

The initial security standard developed for Wi-Fi, called Wired Equivalent Privacy (WEP), is not very effective because its encryption keys are relatively easy to crack. WEP provides some margin of security, however, if users remember to enable it. Corporations can further improve Wi-Fi security by using it in conjunction with virtual private network (VPN) technology when accessing internal corporate data.

In June 2004, the Wi-Fi Alliance industry trade group finalized the 802.11i specification (also referred to as Wi-Fi Protected Access 2 or WPA2) that replaces WEP with stronger security standards. Instead of the static encryption keys used in WEP, the new standard uses much longer keys that continually change, making them harder to crack. It also employs an encrypted authentication system with a central authentication server to ensure that only authorized users access the network.

ENCRYPTION AND PUBLIC KEY INFRASTRUCTURE

Many businesses use encryption to protect digital information that they store, physically transfer, or send over the Internet. **Encryption** is the process of transforming plain text or data into cipher text that cannot be read by anyone other than the sender and the intended receiver. Data are encrypted by using a secret numerical code, called an encryption key, that transforms plain data into cipher text. The message must be decrypted by the receiver.

Two methods for encrypting network traffic on the Web are SSL and S-HTTP. **Secure Sockets Layer (SSL)** and its successor Transport Layer Security (TLS) enable client and server computers to manage encryption and decryption activities as they communicate with each other during a secure Web session. **Secure Hypertext Transfer Protocol (S-HTTP)** is another protocol used for encrypting data flowing over the Internet, but it is limited to individual messages, whereas SSL and TLS are designed to establish a secure connection between two computers.

The capability to generate secure sessions is built into Internet client browser software and servers. The client and the server negotiate what key and what level of security to use. Once a secure session is established between the client and the server, all messages in that session are encrypted.

There are two alternative methods of encryption: symmetric key encryption and public key encryption. In symmetric key encryption, the sender and receiver establish a secure Internet session by creating a single encryption key and sending it to the receiver so both the sender and receiver share the same key. The strength of the encryption key is measured by its bit length. Today, a typical key will be 128 bits long (a string of 128 binary digits).

The problem with all symmetric encryption schemes is that the key itself must be shared somehow among the senders and receivers, which exposes the key to outsiders who might just be able to intercept and decrypt the key. A more secure form of encryption called **public key encryption** uses two keys: one shared (or public) and one totally private as shown in Figure 7.6. The keys are mathematically related so that data encrypted with one key can be decrypted using only the other key. To send and receive messages, communicators first create separate pairs of private and public keys. The public key is kept in a directory and the private key must be kept secret. The sender encrypts a message with the recipient's public key. On receiving the message, the recipient uses his or her private key to decrypt it.

Digital certificates are data files used to establish the identity of users and electronic assets for protection of online transactions (see Figure 7.7). A digital certificate system uses a trusted third party, known as a certificate authority (CA, or certification authority), to validate a user's identity. There are many CAs in the United States and around the world, including VeriSign, GoDaddy, and Comodo.

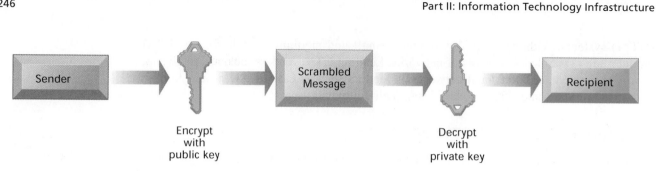

Figure 7.6
Public Key Encryption
A public key encryption system can be viewed as a series of public and private keys that lock data when they are transmitted and unlock the data when they are received. The sender locates the recipient's public key in a directory and uses it to encrypt a message. The message is sent in encrypted form over the Internet or a private network. When the encrypted message arrives, the recipient uses his or her private key to decrypt the data and read the message.

The CA verifies a digital certificate user's identity offline. This information is put into a CA server, which generates an encrypted digital certificate containing owner identification information and a copy of the owner's public key. The certificate authenticates that the public key belongs to the designated owner. The CA makes its own public key available either in print or perhaps on the Internet. The recipient of an encrypted message uses the CA's public key to decode the digital certificate attached to the message, verifies it was issued by the CA, and then obtains the sender's public key and identification information contained in the certificate. Using this information, the recipient can send an encrypted reply. The digital certificate system would enable, for example, a credit card user and a merchant to validate that their digital certificates were issued by an authorized and trusted third party before they exchange data. **Public key infrastructure (PKI)**, the use of public key cryptography working with a CA, is now widely used in e-commerce.

Figure 7.7
Digital Certificates
Digital certificates help establish the identity of people or electronic assets. They protect online transactions by providing secure, encrypted, online communication.

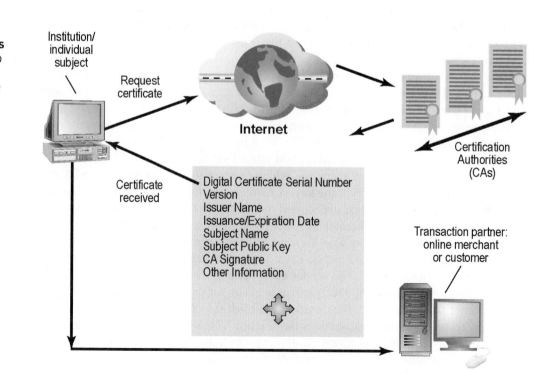

ENSURING SYSTEM AVAILABILITY

As companies increasingly rely on digital networks for revenue and operations, they need to take additional steps to ensure that their systems and applications are always available. Firms such as those in the airline and financial services industries with critical applications requiring online transaction processing have traditionally used fault-tolerant computer systems for many years to ensure 100 percent availability. In **online transaction processing**, transactions entered online are immediately processed by the computer. Multitudinous changes to databases, reporting, and requests for information occur each instant.

Fault-tolerant computer systems contain redundant hardware, software, and power supply components that create an environment that provides continuous, uninterrupted service. Fault-tolerant computers use special software routines or self-checking logic built into their circuitry to detect hardware failures and automatically switch to a backup device. Parts from these computers can be removed and repaired without disruption to the computer system.

Fault tolerance should be distinguished from **high-availability computing**. Both fault tolerance and high-availability computing try to minimize downtime. **Downtime** refers to periods of time in which a system is not operational. However, high-availability computing helps firms recover quickly from a system crash, whereas fault tolerance promises continuous availability and the elimination of recovery time altogether.

High-availability computing environments are a minimum requirement for firms with heavy e-commerce processing or for firms that depend on digital networks for their internal operations. High-availability computing requires backup servers, distribution of processing across multiple servers, high-capacity storage, and good disaster recovery and business continuity plans. The firm's computing platform must be extremely robust with scalable processing power, storage, and bandwidth.

Researchers are exploring ways to make computing systems recover even more rapidly when mishaps occur, an approach called **recovery-oriented computing**. This work includes designing systems that recover quickly, and implementing capabilities and tools to help operators pinpoint the sources of faults in multi-component systems and easily correct their mistakes.

Controlling Network Traffic: Deep Packet Inspection

Have you ever tried to use your campus network and found it was very slow? It may be because your fellow students are using the network to download music or watch YouTube. Bandwith-consuming applications such as file-sharing programs, Internet phone service, and online video are able to clog and slow down corporate networks, degrading performance. For example, Ball State University in Muncie, Indiana, found its network had slowed because a small minority of students were using P2P file-sharing programs to download movies and music.

A technology called **deep packet inspection (DPI)** helps solve this problem. DPI examines data files and sorts out low-priority online material while assigning higher priority to business-critical files. Based on the priorities established by a network's operators, it decides whether a specific data packet can continue to its destination or should be blocked or delayed while more important traffic proceeds. Using a DPI system from Allot Communications, Ball State was able to cap the amount of file-sharing traffic and assign it a much lower priority. Ball State's preferred network traffic speeded up.

Security Outsourcing

Many companies, especially small businesses, lack the resources or expertise to provide a secure high-availability computing environment on their own. They can outsource many security functions to **managed security service providers (MSSPs)** that monitor network activity and perform vulnerability testing and intrusion detection. SecureWorks, BT Managed Security Solutions Group, and Symantec are leading providers of MSSP services.

SECURITY ISSUES FOR CLOUD COMPUTING AND THE MOBILE DIGITAL PLATFORM

Although cloud computing and the emerging mobile digital platform have the potential to deliver powerful benefits, they pose new challenges to system security and reliability. We now describe some of these challenges and how they should be addressed.

Security in the Cloud

When processing takes place in the cloud, accountability and responsibility for protection of sensitive data still reside with the company owning that data. Understanding how the cloud computing provider organizes its services and manages the data is critical.

Cloud computing is highly distributed. Cloud applications reside in large remote data centers and server farms that supply business services and data management for multiple corporate clients. To save money and keep costs low, cloud computing providers often distribute work to data centers around the globe where work can be accomplished most efficiently. When you use the cloud, you may not know precisely where your data are being hosted.

The dispersed nature of cloud computing makes it difficult to track unauthorized activity. Virtually all cloud providers use encryption, such as Secure Sockets Layer, to secure the data they handle while the data are being transmitted. But if the data are stored on devices that also store other companies' data, it's important to ensure these stored data are encrypted as well.

Companies expect their systems to be running 24/7, but cloud providers haven't always been able to provide this level of service. On several occasions over the past few years, the cloud services of Amazon.com and Salesforce.com experienced outages that disrupted business operations for millions of users (see the Chapter 4 ending case study).

Cloud users need to confirm that regardless of where their data are stored, they are protected at a level that meets their corporate requirements. They should stipulate that the cloud provider store and process data in specific jurisdictions according to the privacy rules of those jurisdictions. Cloud clients should find how the cloud provider segregates their corporate data from those of other companies and ask for proof that encryption mechanisms are sound. It's also important to know how the cloud provider will respond if a disaster strikes, whether the provider will be able to completely restore your data, and how long this should take. Cloud users should also ask whether cloud providers will submit to external audits and security certifications. These kinds of controls can be written into the service level agreement (SLA) before to signing with a cloud provider.

Securing Mobile Platforms

If mobile devices are performing many of the functions of computers, they need to be secured like desktops and laptops against malware, theft, accidental loss, unauthorized access, and hacking attempts. The Interactive Session on Technology describes these mobile vulnerabilities in greater detail and their implications for both individuals and businesses.

Mobile devices accessing corporate systems and data require special protection. Companies should make sure that their corporate security policy includes mobile devices, with additional details on how mobile devices should be supported, protected, and used. They will need mobile device management tools to authorize all devices in use; to maintain accurate inventory records on all mobile devices, users, and applications; to control updates to applications; and to lock down or erase lost or stolen devices so they can't be compromised. Firms should develop guidelines stipulating approved mobile platforms and software applications as well as the required software and procedures for remote access of corporate systems.

Companies will need to ensure that all smartphones are up-to-date with the latest security patches and antivirus/antispam software, and they should encrypt communication whenever possible. All mobile device users should be required to use the password feature found in every smartphone. Mobile security products are available from F-Secure, Kaspersky, Lookout, and DroidSecurity.

INTERACTIVE SESSION: TECHNOLOGY   How Secure Is Your Smartphone?

Have you ever purchased antivirus software for your iPhone, Android, or cell phone? Probably not. Many users believe that their iPhones and Androids are unlikely to be hacked into because they think Apple and Google are protecting them from malware apps, and that the carriers like Verizon and AT&T can keep the cellphone network clean from malware just as they do the land phone line system. (Telephone systems are "closed" and therefore not subject to the kinds of the attacks that occur on the open Internet.)

Phishing is also a growing smartphone problem. Mobile users are believed to be three times more likely to fall for scams luring them to bogus Web sites where they reveal personal data: Why? Because mobile devices are activated all the time, and small-screen formatting makes the fraud more difficult to detect.

So far there has not been a major smartphone hack resulting in millions of dollars in losses, or the breach of millions of credit cards, or the breach of national security. But with 74 million smartphone users in the United States, 91 million people accessing the Internet from mobile devices, business firms increasingly switching their employees to the mobile platform, consumers using their phones for financial transactions and even paying bills, the size and richness of the smartphone target for hackers is growing.

In December 2010, one of the first Android botnets, called "Gemini," was discovered. The code was wrapped inside a legitimate Android app whose developers did not realize they were spreading malware. IPhones worldwide were hacked by a worm called "Rick Roll" used to create a botnet for stealing online banking information. In March 2011, Google discovered a botnet called DroidDream, code for which was found in 50 infected apps. Apple iPhones had a known security issue with PDF files. When an iPhone user opened PDF files, there was a possibility the files contained code that could take over the user's iPhone completely.

Apps are one avenue for potential security breaches. Apple, Google, and RIM (BlackBerry) offer over 700,000 apps collectively. Apple claims that it examines each and every app to ensure that it complies with Apple's iTunes rules, but risks remain. In April 2008, Apple pulled a popular game from its iTunes Store when the program was discovered harvesting users' contact lists (names, telephone numbers, e-mail and postal mail addresses) and sending them to the firm's own servers without the user's knowledge. Later, Apple announced it had removed hundreds of other apps because of similar security concerns.

Apple iTunes app rules make some user information available to all app programs by default, including the user's GPS position and name. However, a rogue app could easily do much more. A Swiss researcher named Nicolas Seriot built a test app called "SpyPhone" that was capable of tracking users and all their activities, then transmitting this data to remote servers, all without user knowledge. The app harvested geolocation data, passwords, address book entries, and e-mail account information. Apple removed the app once it was identified. The fact that this proof-of-concept app was accepted by the iTunes staff of reviewers suggests that Apple cannot effectively review new apps prior to their use. Thousands of apps arrive each week. Apple's iPhone does not inform users what information apps are using, but does restrict the information that can be collected by any app.

Security on the Android platform is much less under Google's control because it has an open app model. Google does not review any of the apps for the Android platform, but instead relies on technical hurdles to limit the impact of malicious code, as well as user and security expert feedback. Google apps run in a "sandbox," where they cannot affect one another or manipulate device features without user permission. Android apps can use any personal information found on an Android phone but they must also inform the user what each app is capable of doing, and what personal data it requires. Google removes from its official Android Market any apps that break its rules against malicious activity. One problem: users may not pay attention to permission requests and simply click "Yes" when asked to grant permissions.

Google can perform a remote wipe of offending apps from all Android phones without user intervention. A wonderful capability, but itself a security threat if hackers gain access to the remote wipe capability at Google. Google does take preventive steps to reduce malware apps such as vetting the backgrounds of developers, and requiring developers to register with its Checkout payment service (both to encourage users to pay for apps using their service but also to force developers to reveal their identities and financial information).

Beyond the threat of rogue apps, smartphones of all stripes are susceptible to browser-based malware that takes advantage of vulnerabilities in all browsers. In addition, most smartphones, including the iPhone, permit the manufacturers to remotely download configuration files to update operating systems and security protections. Unfortunately, cryptologists in 2010 discovered a flaw in the public key encryption procedures that permit remote server access to iPhones. The result: "There is absolutely no reason for an iPhone/iPod to trust root Certificate Authorities which are the foundation for public key encryption of files for over-the-air mobile configuration downloads."

So far there have been few publicly identified, large-scale, smartphone security breaches. In 2011, the biggest security danger facing smartphone users is that they will lose their phone. In reality, all of the personal and corporate data stored on the device, as well as access to corporate data on remote servers, are at risk.

For security analysts, large-scale smartphone attacks are just disasters waiting to happen.

Sources: Byron Achoido, "Android, Apple Face Growing Cyberattacks," *USA Today*, June 3, 2011; John Stankey, "AT&T Plans Smartphone Security Service for 2012," AT&T Enterprise CTO, interview May 16, 2011; Brad Reed, "Smartphone Security Follies: A Brief History," *Network World*, April 18, 2011; Jesus Diaz, "Apple Security Breach Gives Complete Access to Your iPhone," Gizmodo.com, August 3, 2010; and Cryptopath.com, "iPhone Certificate Flaws, iPhone PKI Kandling flaws," by Cryptopath.com, January 2010.

CASE STUDY QUESTIONS

1. It has been said that a smartphone is "a microcomputer in your hand." Discuss the security implications of this statement.

2. What people, organizational, and technology issues must be addressed by smartphone security?

3. What problems do smartphone security weaknesses cause for businesses?

4. What steps can individuals and businesses take to make their smartphones more secure?

MIS IN ACTION

Visit two of the following Web sites: Droid Security, F-Secure, Lookout, and Kaspersky and review their capabilities for mobile device security. Compare the capabilities of two of these services. What mobile platforms does each support? What protection does each provide?

Some companies insist that employees use only company-issued smartphones. BlackBerry devices are considered the most secure because they run within their own secure system. But, increasingly, companies are allowing employees to use their own smartphones, including iPhones and Android phones, for work, to make employees more available and productive. Protective software products, such as the tools from Good Technology, are now available for segregating corporate data housed within personally owned mobile devices from the device's personal content.

ENSURING SOFTWARE QUALITY

In addition to implementing effective security and controls, organizations can improve system quality and reliability by employing software metrics and rigorous software testing. Software metrics are objective assessments of the system in the form of quantified measurements. Ongoing use of metrics allows the information systems department and end users to jointly measure the performance of the system and identify problems as they occur. Examples of software metrics include the number of transactions that can be processed in a specified unit of time, online response time, the number of payroll checks printed per hour, and the number of known bugs per hundred lines of program code. For metrics to be successful, they must be carefully designed, formal, objective, and used consistently.

Early, regular, and thorough testing will contribute significantly to system quality. Many view testing as a way to prove the correctness of work they have done. In fact, we know that all sizable software is riddled with errors, and we must test to uncover these errors.

Good testing begins before a software program is even written by using a *walkthrough*— a review of a specification or design document by a small group of people carefully selected based on the skills needed for the particular objectives being tested. Once developers start writing software programs, coding walkthroughs also can be used to review program code.

However, code must be tested by computer runs. When errors are discovered, the source is found and eliminated through a process called *debugging*. You can find out more about the various stages of testing required to put an information system into operation in Chapter 11. Our Learning Tracks also contain descriptions of methodologies for developing software programs that also contribute to software quality.

LEARNING TRACKS

The following Learning Tracks provide content relevant to topics covered in this chapter:

1. The Booming Job Market in IT Security
2. The Sarbanes-Oxley Act
3. Computer Forensics
4. General and Application Controls for Information Systems
5. Management Challenges of Security and Control
6. Software Vulnerability and Reliability

Review Summary

1 **Why are information systems vulnerable to destruction, error, and abuse?** Digital data are vulnerable to destruction, misuse, error, fraud, and hardware or software failures. The Internet is designed to be an open system and makes internal corporate systems more vulnerable to actions from outsiders. Hackers can unleash denial-of-service (DoS) attacks or penetrate corporate networks, causing serious system disruptions. Wi-Fi networks can easily be penetrated by intruders using sniffer programs to obtain an address to access the resources of the network. Computer viruses and worms can disable systems and Web sites. The dispersed nature of cloud computing makes it difficult to track unauthorized activity or to apply controls from afar. Software presents problems because software bugs may be impossible to eliminate and because software vulnerabilities can be exploited by hackers and malicious software. End users often introduce errors.

2 **What is the business value of security and control?** Lack of sound security and control can cause firms relying on computer systems for their core business functions to lose sales and productivity. Information assets, such as confidential employee records, trade secrets, or business plans, lose much of their value if they are revealed to outsiders or if they expose the firm to legal liability. New laws, such as HIPAA, the Sarbanes-Oxley Act, and the Gramm-Leach-Bliley Act, require companies to practice stringent electronic records management and adhere to strict standards for security, privacy, and control. Legal actions requiring electronic evidence and computer forensics also require firms to pay more attention to security and electronic records management.

3 **What are the components of an organizational framework for security and control?** Firms need to establish a good set of both general and application controls for their information systems. A risk assessment evaluates information assets, identifies control points and control weaknesses, and determines the most cost-effective set of controls. Firms must also develop a coherent corporate security policy and plans for continuing business operations in the event of disaster or disruption. The security policy includes policies for acceptable use and identity management. Comprehensive and systematic MIS auditing helps organizations determine the effectiveness of security and controls for their information systems.

4 **What are the most important tools and technologies for safeguarding information resources?** Firewalls prevent unauthorized users from accessing a private network when it is linked to the Internet. Intrusion detection systems monitor private networks from suspicious network traffic and attempts to access corporate systems. Passwords, tokens, smart cards, and biometric authentication are used to authenticate system users. Antivirus software checks computer systems for infections by viruses and worms and often eliminates the malicious software, while antispyware software combats intrusive and harmful spyware programs. Encryption, the coding and scrambling of messages, is a widely used technology for securing electronic transmissions over unprotected networks. Digital certificates combined with public key encryption provide further protection of electronic transactions by authenticating a user's identity. Companies can use fault-tolerant computer systems or create high-availability computing environments to make sure that their information systems are always available. Use of software metrics and rigorous software testing help improve software quality and reliability.

Key Terms

Acceptable use policy (AUP), 239
Antivirus software, 244
Application controls, 237
Authentication, 242
Biometric authentication, 242
Botnet, 229
Bugs, 234
Business continuity planning, 240
Click fraud, 232
Computer crime, 229
Computer forensics, 236
Computer virus, 226
Controls, 223
Cybervandalism, 228
Cyberwarfare, 232
Deep packet inspection (DPI), 247
Denial-of-service (DoS) attack, 229
Digital certificates, 245
Disaster recovery planning, 240
Distributed denial-of-service (DDoS) attack, 229
Downtime, 247

Encryption, 245
Evil twin, 230
Fault-tolerant computer systems, 247
Firewall, 243
General controls, 237
Gramm-Leach-Bliley Act, 236
Hacker, 228
High-availability computing, 247
HIPAA, 236
Identity management, 239
Identity theft, 230
Intrusion detection systems, 244
Keyloggers, 228
Malware, 226
Managed security service providers (MSSPs), 247
MIS audit, 241
Online transaction processing, 247
Password, 242
Patches, 235
Pharming, 231
Phishing, 230

Public key encryption, 245
Public key infrastructure (PKI), 246
Recovery-oriented computing, 247
Risk assessment, 238
Sarbanes-Oxley Act, 236
Secure Hypertext Transfer Protocol (S-HTTP), 245
Secure Sockets Layer (SSL), 245
Security, 223
Security policy, 239
Smart card, 242
Sniffer, 228
Social engineering, 232
Spoofing, 228
Spyware, 228
SQL injection attack, 228
Token, 242
Trojan horse, 227
Unified threat management (UTM), 244
War driving, 225
Worms, 226

Review Questions

1. Why are information systems vulnerable to destruction, error, and abuse?
- List and describe the most common threats against contemporary information systems.
- Define malware and distinguish among a virus, a worm, and a Trojan horse.
- Define a hacker and explain how hackers create security problems and damage systems.
- Define computer crime. Provide two examples of crime in which computers are targets and two examples in which computers are used as instruments of crime.

- Define identity theft and phishing and explain why identity theft is such a big problem today.
- Describe the security and system reliability problems created by employees.
- Explain how software defects affect system reliability and security.

2. What is the business value of security and control?
- Explain how security and control provide value for businesses.
- Describe the relationship between security and control and recent U.S. government regulatory requirements and computer forensics.

3. What are the components of an organizational framework for security and control?
- Define general controls and describe each type of general control.
- Define application controls and describe each type of application control.
- Describe the function of risk assessment and explain how it is conducted for information systems.
- Define and describe the following: security policy, acceptable use policy, and identity management.
- Explain how MIS auditing promotes security and control.

4. What are the most important tools and technologies for safeguarding information resources?
- Name and describe three authentication methods.
- Describe the roles of firewalls, intrusion detection systems, and antivirus software in promoting security.
- Explain how encryption protects information.
- Describe the role of encryption and digital certificates in a public key infrastructure.
- Distinguish between fault tolerance and high-availability computing, and between disaster recovery planning and business continuity planning.
- Identify and describe the security problems posed by cloud computing.
- Describe measures for improving software quality and reliability.

Discussion Questions

1. Security isn't simply a technology issue, it's a business issue. Discuss.

2. If you were developing a business continuity plan for your company, where would you start? What aspects of the business would the plan address?

3. Suppose your business had an e-commerce Web site where it sold goods and accepted credit card payments. Discuss the major security threats to this Web site and their potential impact. What can be done to minimize these threats?

Hands-on MIS Projects

The projects in this section give you hands-on experience analyzing security vulnerabilities, using spreadsheet software for risk analysis, and using Web tools to research security outsourcing services.

MANAGEMENT DECISION PROBLEMS

1. K2 Network operates online game sites used by about 16 million people in over 100 countries. Players are allowed to enter a game for free, but must buy digital "assets" from K2, such as swords to fight dragons, if they want to be deeply involved. The

games can accommodate millions of players at once and are played simultaneously by people all over the world. Prepare a security analysis for this Internet-based business. What kinds of threats should it anticipate? What would be their impact on the business? What steps can it take to prevent damage to its Web sites and continuing operations?

2. A survey of your firm's IT infastructure has identified a number of security vulnerabilities. Review the data on these vulnerabilities, which can be found in a table in MyMISLab. Use the table to answer the following questions:

- Calculate the total number of vulnerabilities for each platform. What is the potential impact of the security problems for each computing platform on the organization?
- If you only have one information systems specialist in charge of security, which platforms should you address first in trying to eliminate these vulnerabilities? Second? Third? Last? Why?
- Identify the types of control problems illustrated by these vulnerabilities and explain the measures that should be taken to solve them.
- What does your firm risk by ignoring the security vulnerabilities identified?

IMPROVING DECISION MAKING: USING SPREADSHEET SOFTWARE TO PERFORM A SECURITY RISK ASSESSMENT

Software skills: Spreadsheet formulas and charts
Business skills: Risk assessment

This project uses spreadsheet software to calculate anticipated annual losses from various security threats identified for a small company.

Mercer Paints is a paint manufacturing company located in Alabama that uses a network to link its business operations. A security risk assessment requested by management identified a number of potential exposures. These exposures, their associated probabilities, and average losses are summarized in a table, which can be found in MyMISLab. Use the table to answer the following questions:
- In addition to the potential exposures listed, identify at least three other potential threats to Mercer Paints, assign probabilities, and estimate a loss range.
- Use spreadsheet software and the risk assessment data to calculate the expected annual loss for each exposure.
- Present your findings in the form of a chart. Which control points have the greatest vulnerability? What recommendations would you make to Mercer Paints? Prepare a written report that summarizes your findings and recommendations.

IMPROVING DECISION MAKING: EVALUATING SECURITY OUTSOURCING SERVICES

Software skills: Web browser and presentation software
Business skills: Evaluating business outsourcing services

This project will help develop your Internet skills in using the Web to research and evaluate security outsourcing services.

You have been asked to help your company's management decide whether to outsource security or keep the security function within the firm. Search the Web to find information to help you decide whether to outsource security and to locate security outsourcing services.
- Present a brief summary of the arguments for and against outsourcing computer security for your company.
- Select two firms that offer computer security outsourcing services, and compare them and their services.

- Prepare an electronic presentation for management summarizing your findings. Your presentation should make the case on whether or not your company should outsource computer security. If you believe your company should outsource, the presentation should identify which security outsourcing service you selected and justify your decision.

Video Cases

Video Cases and Instructional Videos illustrating some of the concepts in this chapter are available. Contact your instructor to access these videos.

Collaboration and Teamwork

Evaluating Security Software Tools

With a group of three or four students, use the Web to research and evaluate security products from two competing vendors, such as antivirus software, firewalls, or antispyware software. For each product, describe its capabilities, for what types of businesses it is best suited, and its cost to purchase and install. Which is the best product? Why? If possible, use Google Sites to post links to Web pages, team communication announcements, and work assignments; to brainstorm; and to work collaboratively on project documents. Try to use Google Docs to develop a presentation of your findings for the class.

BUSINESS PROBLEM-SOLVING CASE

Sony: The World's Largest Data Breach?

On April 19, 2011, system administrators at Sony's online gaming service PlayStation Network (PSN), with over 77 million users, began to notice suspicious activity on some of its 130 servers spread across the globe and 50 software programs. The PlayStation Network is used by Sony game machine owners to play against one another, chat online, and watch video streamed over the Internet. The largest single data breach in Internet history was taking place.

On April 20, Sony engineers discovered that some data had likely been transferred from its servers to outside computers. The nature of the data transferred was not yet known but it could have included credit card and personal information of PlayStation customers. Because of the uncertainty of the data loss, Sony shut down its entire global PlayStation network when it realized it no longer controlled the personal information contained on these servers.

On April 22, Sony informed the FBI of the potential massive data leakage. On April 26, Sony notified the 40 states that have legislation requiring corporations to announce their data breaches (there is no similar federal law at this time), and made a public announcement that hackers had stolen some personal information from all 77 million users, and possibly credit card information from 12 million users. Sony did not know exactly what personal information had been stolen.

The hackers corrupted Sony's servers, causing them to mysteriously reboot. The rogue program deleted all log files to hide its operation. Once inside Sony's servers, the rogue software transferred personal and credit card information on millions of PlayStation users. On May 2, Sony shut down a second service, Sony Online Entertainment, a San Diego-based subsidiary that makes multiplayer games for personal computers. Sony believed hackers had transferred personal customer information such as names, birth dates, and addresses from these servers as well. This was not the result of a second attack but rather part of the earlier attack not immediately discovered. On June 1, Sony Pictures Entertainment's Web site was also hacked, and drained of personal information on its several million customers, in addition to 75,000 "music codes" and 3.5 million coupons.

The total Sony data breach now numbers over 100 million customers. In a normal year, the reported total losses of personal information from online systems in the United States involves about 100 million people. Sony exceeded this in a single attack.

The Sony data breach was apparently the result of a "revenge hacking," the use of the Internet to destroy or disrupt political opponents, or to punish organizations for their public behavior. Currently, it is not clear that any credit card information has actually been abused by hackers. According to Sony, hackers left a text file named Anonymous on Sony's server with the words "We are legion." Anonymous is the name of an Internet collective of hackers and vigilantes whose motto is "We are Anonymous. We are Legion. We do not forgive. We do not forget. Expect us." Anonymous in December 2010 had attacked MasterCard and other company servers in retaliation for cutting their financial relationships with WikiLeaks, a Web site devoted to releasing secret American government files.

Sony and others believe the hacker attack, which followed weeks of a denial-of-service attack on the same Sony servers, was retaliation by Anonymous for Sony's civil suit against George Hotz, one of the world's best known hackers. Holtz cracked the iPhone operating system in 2008, and in 2010 cracked the Sony PlayStation client operating system and later published the procedures on his Web site. Anonymous denied that as an organization it stole credit cards, but the statement is unclear about whether its members as individuals participated in the attack. Anonymous claims Sony is simply trying to discredit Anonymous instead of admitting its own incompetence in computer security.

Sony's Board Chairman apologized to its users and critics in the United States Congress for the security breakdown. Nevertheless, governments around the world reacted harshly to the lapse in security at Sony. The U.S. House Committee on Commerce, Manufacturing and Trading, criticized Sony for not knowing what data had been transferred and for failing to inform customers immediately rather than waiting a week before going public. In a letter to Sony Board Chairman Kazuo Hirai, the committee demanded specifics on the kind of information the hackers stole and assurances that no credit card data were swiped. Representative Edward J. Markey (D-Mass.) said, "Hackers and thieves shouldn't be playing 'Grand Theft Auto' with millions of addresses, emails and other sensitive information." In a letter of

apology to the Committee and Sony customers, Chairman Hirai said "Sony has been the victim of a very carefully planned, very professional, highly sophisticated criminal cyber attack designed to steal personal and credit card information for illegal purposes."

This is the "Darth Vader" defense that many organizations use when they experience a gross breach of security: whatever it was, they believe it was extremely sophisticated, totally unprecedented, and could not possibly have been anticipated.

Many experts in computer security did not buy Sony's explanation. In fact, most computer security breaches are the result of fairly simple tactics, management failure to anticipate well-known security risks, unwillingness to spend resources on expensive security measures, sloppy procedures, lack of training, carelessness, and outdated software. Many hacking attacks use simple, well-known approaches that seem obvious. The hack of Google's computers in late 2010 resulted from a single employee responding to a phishing email from what he thought was Google's human resources department.

Appearing before the House Energy and Commerce Committee, Eugene Spafford, the executive director of the Purdue University Center for Education and Research in Information Assurance and Security (CERIAS), said the problem at Sony was that the PlayStation Network was using an older version of Apache Web server software, which has well-known security issues. In addition, Sony's Web site had very poor firewall protection. He said the problem was reported on an open forum months before the incident. A U.S. Secret Service agent told the committee that "the vast majority of attacks on databases were not highly difficult." Moreover, once hackers are on the inside, critical personal information and credit information are usually not encrypted. If such information were encrypted, hackers would not be able to read the data. The reason most personal data are not encrypted in large-scale private databases is cost, and to a lesser extent speed. Data encryption of the sort needed for an operation like Sony's could easily require a doubling of computing capacity at Sony. This would significantly eat into profits for an Internet-based enterprise like Sony simply because IT is such a huge part of its cost structure.

A group calling itself LulzSec claimed responsibility for the later attack on Sony Pictures. Rather than announcing new powerful methods of hacking sites, the group claimed Sony's lax security allowed it to perform a standard SQL injection attack on a primitive security hole that enabled it to access whatever information it wanted.

Sony notified its customers of the data breach by posting a press release on its blog. It did not e-mail customers. Since the data breach, Sony has offered customers free games and privacy protection ("AllClear ID Plus") offered by a private security firm at Sony's expense for customers concerned about protecting their online identity. This offer is distributed to user e-mail accounts. The privacy protection plan does not offer an insurance policy against potential losses, but does help individuals monitor the use of their personal information by others. The company anticipated that it would have to pay $170 million in the 2011 financial year for these measures, plus associated legal costs.

It took Sony four weeks to restore partial PlayStation service, and by May 31, the company had restored service to the United Sates, Europe, and Asia except for Japan. So far, no law enforcement agency has reported illegal use of credit cards stolen in the Sony affair.

According to Frank Kenney, vice president of global security at Ipswitch, a company specializing in transferring files securely online, the fact that dozens of Sony Web sites and servers had been breached are a sure signs of a company-wide problem. Any type of environment can be breached, but Sony has to devise a plan that not only protects its infrastructure but also convinces customers that their credit card and personal information are safe. Sony's "brand is at stake," he said. Sony's security problems could take years to fix.

The Sony data breach follows a string of recent breaches that are larger and broader in scope than ever before. The Privacy Rights Clearinghouse keeps a database of known data breaches. Prior to the Sony debacle, the largest data breach in 2011 occurred at Epsilon, the world's largest permission-based e-mail marketing services company with more than 2,500 corporate customers, including many major banks and brokerage firms, TiVo, Walgreens, and major universities. Epsilon sends out 40 billion e-mail messages a year for its clients. In April 2011, Epsilon announced a security breach in which millions of e-mail addresses were transferred to outside servers. One result of this breach was millions of phishing e-mails to customers and the potential for the loss of financial assets.

As data breaches rise in significance and frequency, the Obama administration and Congress are proposing new legislation that would require firms to report data breaches within specific time frames, and sets standards for data security. The Data Accountability and Trust Act of 2011 being considered by Congress requires firms to establish security requirements and policies, notify potential victims of a data loss "without unreasonable delay," and notify a major media outlet and all major credit reporting agencies within 60 days if the credit card data on more than 5,000 individuals are at risk. Currently, 46 states have such legislation. In the past, many organizations failed to report data breaches for fear of harming their brand images. It is unclear if the proposed legislation would reduce the incidence of data breaches.

Sources: Riva Richmond, "Hacker Group Claims Responsibility for New Sony Break-In," *New York Times*, June 2, 2011; Ian Sherr and Amy Schatz, "Sony Details Hacker Attack," *Wall Street Journal*, May 5, 2011; Jesse Emspak, "Expert: Sony Had Outdated Software, Lax Security," IBtimes.com, May 5, 2011; Eugene Spafford, "Testimony before the House Energy and Commerce Subcommittee on Commerce, Manufacturing, and Trade, Hearing on "The Threat of Data Theft to American Consumers" May 5, 2011; "Data Accountability and Trust Act" 112th Congress, H.R. 1707, May 4, 2011; Martyn Williams, "PlayStation Network Hack Will Cost Sony $170M," *PC World*, May 23, 2011; Nick Bilton, "Sony's Security Problems Could Take Years to Fix," *New York Times*, June 6, 2011; "Letter to Honorable Mary Bono Black and Ranking Member Butterfield, Sub Committee on Commerce, Manufacturing, and Trade, United States Congress," by Kazuo Jirai, Chairman of the Board, Sony Corporation, May 3, 2011; Ian Sherr "Hackers Breach Second Sony Service," *Wall Street Journal*, May 2, 2011; "International Strategy for Cyberspace," Office of the President, May 2011; "Epsilon Notifies Clients of Unauthorized Entry into Email System," Press Release, Epsilon Corporation, April 1, 2011.

Case Study Questions

1. List and describe the security and control weaknesses at Sony that are discussed in this case.

2. What people, organizational, and technology factors contributed to these problems?

3. What was the business impact of the Sony data losses on Sony and its customers?

4. What solutions would you suggest to prevent these problems?

Key System Applications for the Digital Age

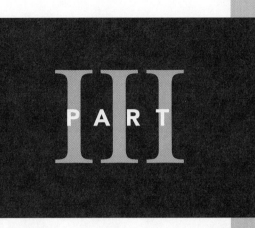

PART III

Part III examines the core information system applications businesses are using today to improve operational excellence and decision making. These applications include enterprise systems; systems for supply chain management, customer relationship management, and knowledge management; e-commerce applications; and business intelligence systems to enhance decision making. This part answers questions such as these: How can enterprise applications improve business performance? How do firms use e-commerce to extend the reach of their businesses? How can systems improve decision making and help companies make better use of their knowledge assets?

Achieving Operational Excellence and Customer Intimacy: Enterprise Applications

CHAPTER 8

STUDENT LEARNING OBJECTIVES

After completing this chapter, you will be able to answer the following questions:

1. How do enterprise systems help businesses achieve operational excellence?

2. How do supply chain management systems coordinate planning, production, and logistics with suppliers?

3. How do customer relationship management systems help firms achieve customer intimacy?

4. What are the challenges posed by enterprise applications?

5. How are enterprise applications taking advantage of new technologies?

CHAPTER OUTLINE

CANNONDALE LEARNS TO MANAGE A GLOBAL SUPPLY CHAIN

If you enjoy cycling, you may very well be using a Cannondale bicycle. Cannondale, headquartered in Bethel, Connecticut, is world-leading manufacturer of high-end bicycles, apparel, footwear, and accessories, with dealers and distributors in more than 66 countries. Cannondale's supply and distribution chains span the globe, and the company must coordinate manufacturing, assembly, and sales/distribution sites in many different countries. Cannondale produces more than 100 different bicycle models each year; 60 percent of these are newly introduced to meet ever-changing customer preferences.

Cannondale offers both make-to-stock and make-to-order models. A typical bicycle requires a 150-day lead time and a four-week manufacturing window, and some models have bills of materials with over 150 parts. (A bill of materials specifies the raw materials, assemblies, components, parts, and the quantities of each needed to manufacture a final product.) Cannondale must manage more than 1 million of these bills of materials and more than 200,000 individual parts. Some of these parts come from specialty vendors with even longer lead times and limited production capacity.

Obviously, managing parts availability in a constantly changing product line impacted by volatile customer demand requires a great deal of manufacturing flexibility.

© P_Wei, 2011, iStockPhoto LP.

Until recently, that flexibility was missing. Cannondale had an antiquated legacy material requirements planning system for planning production, controlling inventory, and managing manufacturing processes that could only produce reports on a weekly basis. By Tuesday afternoon, Monday's reports were already out of date. The company was forced to substitute parts in order to meet demand, and sometimes it lost sales. Cannondale needed a solution that could track the flow of parts more accurately, support its need for flexibility, and work with its existing business systems, all within a restricted budget.

Cannondale selected the Kinaxis RapidResponse on-demand software service as a solution. RapidResponse furnishes accurate and detailed supply chain information via an easy-to-use spreadsheet interface, using data supplied automatically from Cannondale's existing manufacturing systems. Data from operations at multiple sites are assembled in a single place for analysis and decision making. Supply chain participants from different locations are able to model manufacturing and inventory data in "what-if" scenarios to see the impact of alternative actions across the entire supply chain. Old forecasts can be compared to new ones, and the system can evaluate the constraints of a new plan.

Cannondale buyers, planners, master schedulers, sourcers, product managers, and customer service and finance personnel use RapidResponse for sales reporting, forecasting, monitoring daily inventory availability, and feeding production schedule information to Cannondale's manufacturing and order processing systems. Users are able to see up-to-date information for all sites. Management uses the system daily to examine areas where there are backlogs.

The improved supply chain information from RapidResponse enables Cannondale to respond to customer orders much more rapidly with lower levels of inventory and safety stock. Cycle times and lead times for producing products have also been reduced. The company's dates for promising deliveries are more reliable and accurate.

Sources: Kinaxis Corp., "Cannondale Improves Customer Response Times While Reducing Inventory Using RapidResponse," 2011; www.kinaxis.com, accessed June 21, 2011; and www.cannondale.com, accessed June 21, 2011.

Cannondale's problems with its supply chain illustrate the critical role of supply chain management systems in business. Cannondale's business performance was impeded because it could not coordinate its sourcing, manufacturing, and distribution processes. Costs were unnecessarily high because the company was unable to accurately determine the exact amount of each product it needed to fulfill orders and hold just that amount in inventory. Instead, the company resorted to keeping extra "safety stock" on hand "just in case." When products were not available when the customer wanted them, Cannondale lost sales.

The chapter-opening diagram calls attention to important points raised by this case and this chapter. Like many other firms, Cannondale had a complex supply chain and manufacturing processes to coordinate in many different locations. The company had to deal with hundreds and perhaps thousands of suppliers of parts and raw materials. It was not always possible to have just the right amount of each part or component available when it was needed because the company lacked accurate, up-to-date information about parts in inventory and what manufacturing processes needed those parts.

An on-demand supply chain management software service from Kinaxis helped solve this problem. The Kinaxis RapidResponse software takes in data from Cannondale's existing manufacturing systems and assembles data from multiple sites to furnish a single view of Cannondale's supply chain based on up-to-date information. Cannondale staff are able to see exactly what parts are available or on order as well as the status of bikes in production. With better tools for planning, users are able to see the impact of changes in supply and demand so that they can make better decisions about how to respond to these changes. The system has greatly enhanced operational efficiency and decision making.

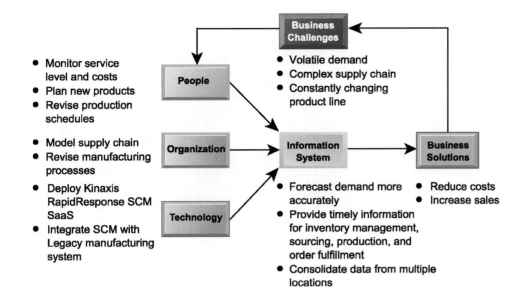

8.1 Enterprise Systems

Around the globe, companies are increasingly becoming more connected, both internally and with other companies. If you run a business, you'll want to be able to react instantaneously when a customer places a large order or when a shipment from a supplier is delayed. You may also want to know the impact of these events on every part of the business and how the business is performing at any point in time, especially if you're running a large company. Enterprise systems provide the integration to make this possible. Let's look at how they work and what they can do for the firm.

WHAT ARE ENTERPRISE SYSTEMS?

Imagine that you had to run a business based on information from tens or even hundreds of different databases and systems, none of which could speak to one another? Imagine your company had 10 different major product lines, each produced in separate factories, and each with separate and incompatible sets of systems controlling production, warehousing, and distribution.

At the very least, your decision making would often be based on manual hard copy reports, often out of date, and it would be difficult to really understand what is happening in the business as whole. Sales personnel might not be able to tell at the time they place an order whether the ordered items are in inventory, and manufacturing could not easily use sales data to plan for new production. You now have a good idea of why firms need a special enterprise system to integrate information.

Chapter 2 introduced enterprise systems, also known as enterprise resource planning (ERP) systems, which are based on a suite of integrated software modules and a common central database. The database collects data from many different divisions and departments in a firm, and from a large number of key business processes in manufacturing and production, finance and accounting, sales and marketing, and human resources, making the data available for applications that support nearly all of an organization's internal business activities. When new information is entered by one process, the information is made immediately available to other business processes (see Figure 8.1).

If a sales representative places an order for tire rims, for example, the system verifies the customer's credit limit, schedules the shipment, identifies the best shipping route, and reserves the necessary items from inventory. If inventory stock were insufficient to fill the order, the system schedules the manufacture of more rims, ordering the needed materials and components from suppliers. Sales and production forecasts are immediately updated.

Figure 8.1
How Enterprise Systems Work
Enterprise systems feature a set of integrated software modules and a central database that enables data to be shared by many different business processes and functional areas throughout the enterprise.

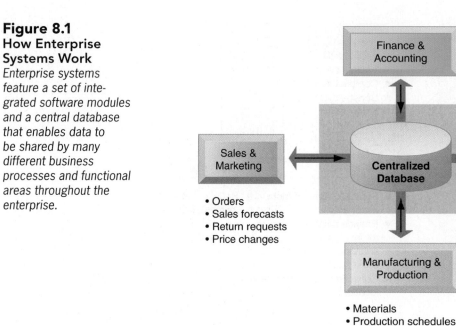

General ledger and corporate cash levels are automatically updated with the revenue and cost information from the order. Users could tap into the system and find out where that particular order was at any minute. Management could obtain information at any point in time about how the business was operating. The system could also generate enterprise-wide data for management analyses of product cost and profitability.

ENTERPRISE SOFTWARE

Enterprise software is built around thousands of predefined business processes that reflect best practices. Table 8.1 describes some of the major business processes supported by enterprise software.

Companies implementing this software would have to first select the functions of the system they wished to use and then map their business processes to the predefined business processes in the software. (One of our Learning Tracks shows how SAP enterprise software handles the procurement process for a new piece of equipment.) To implement a new enterprise system, Tasty Baking Company, identified its existing business processes and then translated them into the business processes built into the SAP ERP software it had selected. A firm would use configuration tables provided by the software to tailor a particular aspect of the system to the way it does business. For example, the firm could use these tables to select whether it wants to track revenue by product line, geographical unit, or distribution channel.

If the enterprise software does not support the way the organization does business, companies can rewrite some of the software to support the way their business processes work. However, enterprise software is unusually complex, and extensive customization may degrade system performance, compromising the information and process integration that are the main benefits of the system. If companies want to reap the maximum benefits from enterprise software, they must change the way they work to conform to the business processes in the software. To implement a new enterprise system, Tasty Baking Company identified its existing business processes and then translated them into the business processes built into the SAP ERP software it had selected. To ensure it obtained the maximum benefits from the enterprise software, Tasty Baking Company deliberately planned for customizing less than 5 percent of the system and made very few changes to the SAP software itself. It used as many tools and

TABLE 8.1

Business Processes Supported by Enterprise Systems

Financial and accounting processes, including general ledger, accounts payable, accounts receivable, fixed assets, cash management and forecasting, product-cost accounting, cost-center accounting, asset accounting, tax accounting, credit management, and financial reporting.

Human resources processes, including personnel administration, time accounting, payroll, personnel planning and development, benefits accounting, applicant tracking, time management, compensation, workforce planning, performance management, and travel expense reporting.

Manufacturing and production processes, including procurement, inventory management, purchasing, shipping, production planning, production scheduling, material requirements planning, quality control, distribution, transportation execution, and plant and equipment maintenance.

Sales and marketing processes, including order processing, quotations, contracts, product configuration, pricing, billing, credit checking, incentive and commission management, and sales planning.

features that were already built into the SAP software as it could. SAP has more than 3,000 configuration tables for its enterprise software.

Leading enterprise software vendors include SAP, Oracle, IBM, Infor Global Solutions, and Microsoft. There are versions of enterprise software packages designed for small businesses and on-demand versions, including software services delivered over the Web (see Section 8.4). Although initially designed to automate the firm's internal "back-office" business processes, enterprise systems have become more externally oriented and capable of communicating with customers, suppliers, and other entities.

BUSINESS VALUE OF ENTERPRISE SYSTEMS

Enterprise systems provide value both by increasing operational efficiency and by providing firmwide information to help managers make better decisions. Large companies with many operating units in different locations have used enterprise systems to enforce standard practices and data so that everyone does business the same way worldwide.

Coca-Cola, for instance, implemented a SAP enterprise system to standardize and coordinate important business processes in 200 countries. Lack of standard, company-wide business processes prevented the company from leveraging its worldwide buying power to obtain lower prices for raw materials and from reacting rapidly to market changes.

Enterprise systems help firms respond rapidly to customer requests for information or products. Because the system integrates order, manufacturing, and delivery data, manufacturing is better informed about producing only what customers have ordered, procuring exactly the right amount of components or raw materials to fill actual orders, staging production, and minimizing the time that components or finished products are in inventory.

Alcoa, the world's leading producer of aluminum and aluminum products with operations spanning 41 countries and 500 locations, had initially been organized around lines of business, each of which had its own set of information systems. Many of these systems were redundant and inefficient. Alcoa's costs for executing requisition-to-pay and financial processes were much higher and its cycle times were longer than those of other companies in its industry. (Cycle time refers to the total elapsed time from the beginning to the end of a process.) The company could not operate as a single worldwide entity.

After implementing enterprise software from Oracle, Alcoa eliminated many redundant processes and systems. The enterprise system helped Alcoa reduce requisition-to-pay cycle time by verifying receipt of goods and automatically generating receipts for payment. Alcoa's accounts payable transaction processing dropped 89 percent. Alcoa was able to centralize financial and procurement activities, which helped the company reduce nearly 20 percent of its worldwide costs.

Enterprise systems provide much valuable information for improving management decision making. Corporate headquarters has access to up-to-the-minute data on sales, inventory, and production and uses this information to create more accurate sales and production forecasts. Enterprise software includes analytical tools for using data captured by the system to evaluate overall organizational performance. Enterprise system data have common standardized definitions and formats that are accepted by the entire organization. Performance figures mean the same thing across the company. Enterprise systems allow senior management to easily find out at any moment how a particular organizational unit is performing, determine which products are most or least profitable, and calculate costs for the company as a whole.

For example, Alcoa's enterprise system includes functionality for global human resources management that shows correlations between investment in employee training and quality, measures the company-wide costs of delivering services to employees, and measures the effectiveness of employee recruitment, compensation, and training.

8.2 Supply Chain Management Systems

If you manage a small firm that makes a few products or sells a few services, chances are you will have a small number of suppliers. You could coordinate your supplier orders and deliveries using a telephone and fax machine. But if you manage a firm that produces more complex products and services, then you will have hundreds of suppliers, and your suppliers will each have their own set of suppliers. Suddenly, you are in a situation where you will need to coordinate the activities of hundreds or even thousands of other firms in order to produce your products and services. Supply chain management (SCM) systems, which we introduced in Chapter 2, are an answer to these problems of supply chain complexity and scale.

THE SUPPLY CHAIN

A firm's **supply chain** is a network of organizations and business processes for procuring raw materials, transforming these materials into intermediate and finished products, and distributing the finished products to customers. It links suppliers, manufacturing plants, distribution centers, retail outlets, and customers to supply goods and services from source through consumption. Materials, information, and payments flow through the supply chain in both directions.

Goods start out as raw materials and, as they move through the supply chain, are transformed into intermediate products (also referred to as components or parts), and finally, into finished products. The finished products are shipped to distribution centers and from there to retailers and customers. Returned items flow in the reverse direction from the buyer back to the seller.

Let's look at the supply chain for Nike sneakers as an example. Nike designs, markets, and sells sneakers, socks, athletic clothing, and accessories throughout the world. Its primary suppliers are contract manufacturers with factories in China, Thailand, Indonesia, Brazil, and other countries. These companies fashion Nike's finished products.

Nike's contract suppliers do not manufacture sneakers from scratch. They obtain components for the sneakers—the laces, eyelets, uppers, and soles—from other suppliers and then assemble them into finished sneakers. These suppliers in turn have their own suppliers. For example, the suppliers of soles have suppliers for synthetic rubber, suppliers for chemicals used to melt the rubber for molding, and suppliers for the molds into which to pour the rubber. Suppliers of laces have suppliers for their thread, for dyes, and for the plastic lace tips.

Figure 8.2 provides a simplified illustration of Nike's supply chain for sneakers; it shows the flow of information and materials among suppliers, Nike, Nike's distributors, retailers, and customers. Nike's contract manufacturers are its primary suppliers. The suppliers of soles, eyelets, uppers, and laces are the secondary (Tier 2) suppliers. Suppliers to these suppliers are the tertiary (Tier 3) suppliers.

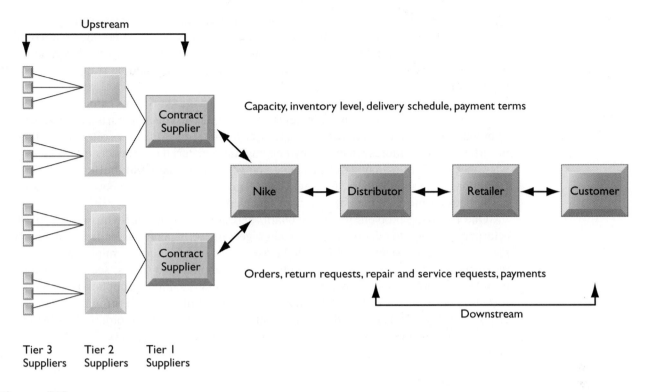

Figure 8.2
Nike's Supply Chain
This figure illustrates the major entities in Nike's supply chain and the flow of information upstream and downstream to coordinate the activities involved in buying, making, and moving a product. Shown here is a simplified supply chain, with the upstream portion focusing only on the suppliers for sneakers and sneaker soles.

The *upstream* portion of the supply chain includes the company's suppliers, the suppliers' suppliers, and the processes for managing relationships with them. The *downstream* portion consists of the organizations and processes for distributing and delivering products to the final customers. Companies doing manufacturing, such as Nike's contract suppliers of sneakers, also manage their own *internal supply chain* processes for transforming materials, components, and services furnished by their suppliers into finished products or intermediate products (components or parts) for their customers and for managing materials and inventory.

The supply chain illustrated in Figure 8.2 has been simplified. It only shows two contract manufacturers for sneakers and only the upstream supply chain for sneaker soles. Nike has hundreds of contract manufacturers turning out finished sneakers, socks, and athletic clothing, each with its own set of suppliers. The upstream portion of Nike's supply chain would actually comprise thousands of entities. Nike also has numerous distributors and many thousands of retail stores where its shoes are sold, so the downstream portion of its supply chain is also large and complex.

INFORMATION SYSTEMS AND SUPPLY CHAIN MANAGEMENT

Inefficiencies in the supply chain, such as parts shortages, underutilized plant capacity, excessive finished goods inventory, or high transportation costs, are caused by inaccurate or untimely information. For example, manufacturers may keep too many parts in inventory because they do not know exactly when they will receive their next shipments from their suppliers. Suppliers may order too few raw materials because they do not have precise information on demand. These supply chain inefficiencies waste as much as 25 percent of a company's operating costs.

If a manufacturer had perfect information about exactly how many units of product customers wanted, when they wanted them, and when they could be produced, it would be possible to implement a highly efficient **just-in-time strategy**. Components would arrive exactly at the moment they were needed and finished goods would be shipped as they left the assembly line.

In a supply chain, however, uncertainties arise because many events cannot be foreseen—uncertain product demand, late shipments from suppliers, defective parts or raw materials, or production process breakdowns. To satisfy customers, manufacturers often deal with such uncertainties and unforeseen events by keeping more material or products in inventory than what they think they may actually need. The *safety stock* acts as a buffer for the lack of flexibility in the supply chain. Although excess inventory is expensive, low fill rates are also costly because business may be lost from canceled orders.

One recurring problem in supply chain management is the **bullwhip effect**, in which information about the demand for a product gets distorted as it passes from one entity to the next across the supply chain. A slight rise in demand for an item might cause different members in the supply chain—distributors, manufacturers, suppliers, secondary suppliers (suppliers' suppliers), and tertiary suppliers (suppliers' suppliers' suppliers)—to stockpile inventory so each has enough "just in case." These changes ripple throughout the supply chain, magnifying what started out as a small change from planned orders, creating excess inventory, production, warehousing, and shipping costs (see Figure 8.3).

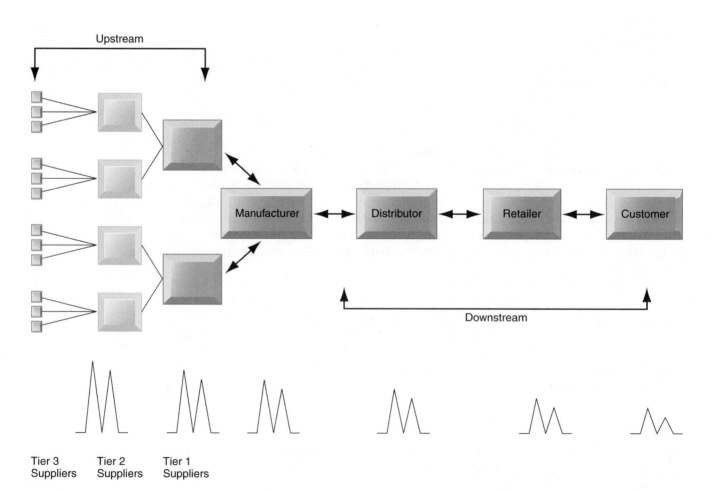

Figure 8.3
The Bullwhip Effect
Inaccurate information can cause minor fluctuations in demand for a product to be amplified as one moves further back in the supply chain. Minor fluctuations in retail sales for a product can create excess inventory for distributors, manufacturers, and suppliers.

For example, Procter & Gamble (P&G) found it had excessively high inventories of its Pampers disposable diapers at various points along its supply chain because of such distorted information. Although customer purchases in stores were fairly stable, orders from distributors would spike when P&G offered aggressive price promotions. Pampers and Pampers' components accumulated in warehouses along the supply chain to meet demand that did not actually exist. To eliminate this problem, P&G revised its marketing, sales, and supply chain processes and used more accurate demand forecasting.

The bullwhip is tamed by reducing uncertainties about demand and supply when all members of the supply chain have accurate and up-to-date information. If all supply chain members share dynamic information about inventory levels, schedules, forecasts, and shipments, they have more precise knowledge about how to adjust their sourcing, manufacturing, and distribution plans. Supply chain management systems provide the kind of information that helps members of the supply chain make better purchasing and scheduling decisions.

SUPPLY CHAIN MANAGEMENT SOFTWARE

Supply chain software is classified as either software to help businesses plan their supply chains (supply chain planning) or software to help them execute the supply chain steps (supply chain execution). **Supply chain planning systems** enable the firm to model its existing supply chain, generate demand forecasts for products, and develop optimal sourcing and manufacturing plans. Such systems help companies make better decisions such as determining how much of a specific product to manufacture in a given time period; establishing inventory levels for raw materials, intermediate products, and finished goods; determining where to store finished goods; and identifying the transportation mode to use for product delivery.

For example, if a large customer places a larger order than usual or changes that order on short notice, it can have a widespread impact throughout the supply chain. Additional raw materials or a different mix of raw materials may need to be ordered from suppliers. Manufacturing may have to change job scheduling. A transportation carrier may have to reschedule deliveries. Supply chain planning software makes the necessary adjustments to production and distribution plans. Information about changes is shared among the relevant supply chain members so that their work can be coordinated. One of the most important—and complex—supply chain planning functions is **demand planning**, which determines how much product a business needs to make to satisfy all of its customers' demands. JDA Software, SAP, and Oracle all offer supply chain management solutions.

Whirlpool Corporation, which produces washing; machines, dryers, refrigerators, ovens, and other home appliances, uses supply chain planning systems to make sure what it produces matches customer demand. The company uses JDA supply chain planning software, which includes modules for master scheduling, deployment planning, and inventory planning. Whirlpool also installed JDA's Web-based tool for Collaborative Planning, Forecasting, and Replenishment (CPFR) for sharing and combining its sales forecasts with those of its major sales partners. Improvements in supply chain planning combined with new state-of-the-art distribution centers helped Whirlpool increase availability of products in stock when customers needed them to 97 percent, while reducing the number of excess finished goods in inventory by 20 percent and forecasting errors by 50 percent (Barrett, 2009).

Supply chain execution systems manage the flow of products through distribution centers and warehouses to ensure that products are delivered to the right locations in the most efficient manner. They track the physical status of goods, the management of materials, warehouse and transportation operations, and financial information involving all parties. Haworth Incorporated's Warehouse Management System (WMS) is an example. Haworth is a world-leading manufacturer and designer of office furniture, with distribution centers in four different states. The WMS tracks and controls the flow of finished goods from Haworth's distribution centers to its customers. Acting on shipping plans for customer orders, the WMS directs the movement of goods based on immediate conditions for space, equipment, inventory, and personnel.

The Interactive Session on Organizations describes how supply chain management software improved decision making and operational performance at Southwest Airlines. This company maintains a competitive edge by combining superb customer service with low costs. Effectively managing its parts inventory is crucial to achieving these goals.

GLOBAL SUPPLY CHAINS AND THE INTERNET

Before the Internet, supply chain coordination was hampered by the difficulties of making information flow smoothly among disparate internal supply chain systems for purchasing, materials management, manufacturing, and distribution. It was also difficult to share information with external supply chain partners because the systems of suppliers, distributors, or logistics providers were based on incompatible technology platforms and standards. Enterprise and supply chain management systems enhanced with Internet technology supply some of this integration.

A manager uses a Web interface to tap into suppliers' systems to determine whether inventory and production capabilities match demand for the firm's products. Business partners use Web-based supply chain management tools to collaborate online on forecasts. Sales representatives access suppliers' production schedules and logistics information to monitor customers' order status.

Global Supply Chain Issues

More and more companies are entering international markets, outsourcing manufacturing operations, and obtaining supplies from other countries as well as selling abroad. Their supply chains extend across multiple countries and regions. There are additional complexities and challenges to managing a global supply chain.

Global supply chains typically span greater geographic distances and time differences than domestic supply chains and have participants from a number of different countries. Performance standards may vary from region to region or from nation to nation. Supply chain management may need to reflect foreign government regulations and cultural differences.

The Internet helps companies manage many aspects of their global supply chains, including sourcing, transportation, communications, and international finance. Today's apparel industry, for example, relies heavily on outsourcing to contract manufacturers in China and other low-wage countries. Apparel companies are starting to use the Web to manage their global supply chain and production issues. (Review the discussion of Li & Fung in Chapter 3.)

In addition to contract manufacturing, globalization has encouraged outsourcing warehouse management, transportation management, and related operations to third-party logistics providers, such as UPS Supply Chain Solutions and Schneider Logistics Services. These logistics services offer Web-based software to give their customers a better view of their global supply chains. Customers are able to check a secure Web site to monitor inventory and shipments, helping them run their global supply chains more efficiently.

Demand-Driven Supply Chains: From Push to Pull Manufacturing and Efficient Customer Response

In addition to reducing costs, supply chain management systems facilitate efficient customer response, enabling the workings of the business to be driven more by customer demand. (We introduced efficient customer response systems in Chapter 3.)

Earlier supply chain management systems were driven by a push-based model (also known as build-to-stock). In a **push-based model**, production master schedules are based on forecasts or best guesses of demand for products, and products are "pushed" to customers. With new flows of information made possible by Web-based tools, supply chain management more easily follows a pull-based model. In a **pull-based model**, also known as a demand-driven or build-to-order model, actual customer orders or purchases trigger events

"Weather at our destination is 50 degrees with some broken clouds, but they'll try to have them fixed before we arrive. Thank you, and remember, nobody loves you or your money more than Southwest Airlines."

Crew humor at 30,000 feet? Must be Southwest Airlines. Southwest Airlines is the largest low-fare, high-frequency, point-to-point airline in the world, and the largest overall measured by number of passengers per year. Founded in 1971 with four planes serving three cities, in 2011, the company operates over 500 aircraft in 72 aiports, with revenues surpassing $12.6 billion. Southwest was known for the best customer service record among major airlines, the lowest cost structure, and low fares. The stock symbol is LUV (for Dallas's Love Field where the company is headquartered), and love is the major theme of Southwest's employee and customer relationships. The company has made a profit every year since 1973, one of the few airlines that can make that claim.

Despite a freewheeling, innovative corporate culture, even Southwest needs to get serious about its information systems to maintain profitability. Southwest is just like any other company that needs to manage its supply chain and inventory efficiently. The airline's success has led to continued expansion, and as the company has grown, its legacy information systems have been unable to keep up with the increasingly large amount of data being generated.

One of the biggest problems with Southwest's legacy systems was lack of information visibility. Often, the data that Southwest's managers needed were safely stored on their systems, but weren't 'visible', or readily available for viewing or use in other systems. Information about what replacement parts were available at a given time was difficult or impossible to acquire, and that affected response times for everything from mechanical problems to part fulfillment.

For Southwest, which prides itself on its excellent customer service, getting passengers from one location to another with minimal delay is critically important. Repairing aircraft quickly is an important part of accomplishing that goal. The company had $325 million in service parts inventory, so any solution that more efficiently handled that inventory and reduced aircraft groundings would have a strong impact on the airline's bottom line. Richard Zimmerman, Southwest's Manager of Inventory Management, stated that "there's a significant cost when we have to ground aircraft because we ran

out of a part. The long-term, cost-effective way to solve that problem was to increase productivity and to ensure that our maintenance crews were supported with the right spare parts, through the right software application."

Southwest's management started looking for a better inventory management solution, and a vendor that was capable of working within the airline's unique corporate culture. After an extensive search, Southwest eventually chose i2 Technologies, a leading supply chain management software and services company that's now part of JDA Software. Southwest implemented the i2 Demand Planner, i2 Service Parts Planner, and i2 Service Budget Optimizer to overhaul its supply chain management and improve data visibility.

Demand Planner improves Southwest's forecasts for all of the part location combinations in its system, and provides better visibility into demand for each part. Planners are able to differentiate among individual parts based on criticality and other dimensions such as demand volume, demand variability, and dollar usage.

Service Parts Planner helps Southwest replenish its store of parts and ensures that "the right parts are in the right location at the right time." The software can recommend the best mix of parts for each location that will satisfy the customer service requirements of that location at the lowest cost. If excess inventory builds up in certain service locations, the software will recommend the most cost-efficient way to transfer that excess inventory to locations with parts deficits. The Service Budget Optimizer helps Southwest use its historical data of parts usage to generate forecasts of future parts usage.

Together, these solutions gather data from Southwest's legacy systems and provide useful information to Southwest's managers. Most importantly, Southwest can recognize demand shortages before they become problems thanks to the visibility provided by JDA's solutions. Thanks to new software, Southwest's managers now have a clear and unobstructed view of all of the data up and down the company's supply chain.

By using what-if analysis, planners can quantify the cost to the company of operating at different levels of service. Zimmerman added that the JDA software "will help us lower inventory costs and keep our cost per air seat mile down to the lowest in the industry. Also, the solutions will help us ensure that the maintenance team can quickly repair the aircraft so that our customers experience minimal delays." The results of the software implementation were increased availability of parts, increased speed and intelligence of decision making, reduced parts inventory by 15 percent, savings of over $30 million, and increased service levels from 92 percent

prior to the implementation to over 95 percent afterwards.

Sources: JDA Software Group, "Ensuring Optimal Parts Inventory at Southwest Airlines," and "Service Parts Management," www.jda.com, accessed June 5, 2011; Scott McCartney, "Can't Call Southwest a Discount Airline These Days," *Wall Street Journal*, June 2, 2011,; and www.southwest.com, accessed June 5, 2011.

CASE STUDY QUESTIONS

1. Why is parts inventory management so important at Southwest Airlines? What business processes are affected by the airlines' ability or inability to have required parts on hand?

2. What people, organization, and technology factors were responsible for Southwest's problems with inventory management?

3. How did implementing the i2 software change the way Southwest ran its business?

4. Describe two decisions that were improved by implementing the i2 system.

MIS IN ACTION

Visit JDA's Web site (www.jda.com) and learn more about some of the other companies using its supply chain software. Pick one of these companies, then answer the following questions:

1. What problem did the company need to address with JDA's software?

2. Why did the company select JDA as its software vendor?

3. What were the gains that the company realized as a result of the software implementation?

---

in the supply chain. Transactions to produce and deliver only what customers have ordered move up the supply chain from retailers to distributors to manufacturers and eventually to suppliers. Only products to fulfill these orders move back down the supply chain to the retailer. Manufacturers use only actual order demand information to drive their production schedules and the procurement of components or raw materials, as illustrated in Figure 8.4. Walmart's continuous replenishment system described in Chapter 3 is an example of the pull-based model.

The Internet and Internet technology make it possible to move from sequential supply chains, where information and materials flow sequentially from company to company,

Figure 8.4
Push- Versus Pull-Based Supply Chain Models
The difference between push- and pull-based models is summarized by the slogan "Make what we sell, not sell what we make."

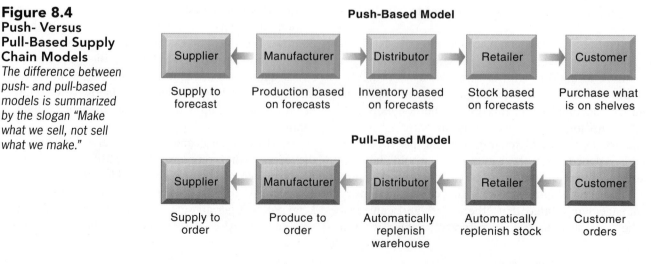

to concurrent supply chains, where information flows in many directions simultaneously among members of a supply chain network. Complex supply networks of manufacturers, logistics suppliers, outsourced manufacturers, retailers, and distributors are able to adjust immediately to changes in schedules or orders. Ultimately, the Internet could create a "digital logistics nervous system" throughout the supply chain (see Figure 8.5).

BUSINESS VALUE OF SUPPLY CHAIN MANAGEMENT SYSTEMS

You have just seen how supply chain management systems enable firms to streamline both their internal and external supply chain processes and provide management with more accurate information about what to produce, store, and move. By implementing a networked and integrated supply chain management system, companies match supply to demand, reduce inventory levels, improve delivery service, speed product time to market, and use assets more effectively.

Total supply chain costs represent the majority of operating expenses for many businesses and in some industries approach 75 percent of the total operating budget. Reducing supply chain costs may have a major impact on firm profitability.

In addition to reducing costs, supply chain management systems help increase sales. If a product is not available when a customer wants it, customers often try to purchase it from someone else. More precise control of the supply chain enhances the firm's ability to have the right product available for customer purchases at the right time.

8.3 Customer Relationship Management Systems

You've probably heard phrases such as "the customer is always right" or "the customer comes first." Today these words ring more true than ever. Because competitive advantage based on an innovative new product or service is often very short lived, companies are realizing that their only enduring competitive strength may be their relationships with their customers. Some say that the basis of competition has switched from who sells the most products and services to who "owns" the customer, and that customer relationships represent a firm's most valuable asset.

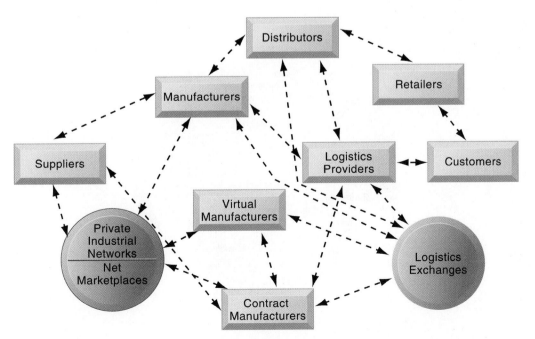

Figure 8.5
The Future Internet-Driven Supply Chain
The future Internet-driven supply chain operates like a digital logistics nervous system. It provides multidirectional communication among firms, networks of firms, and e-marketplaces so that entire networks of supply chain partners can immediately adjust inventories, orders, and capacities.

WHAT IS CUSTOMER RELATIONSHIP MANAGEMENT?

What kinds of information would you need to build and nurture strong, long-lasting relationships with customers? You'd want to know exactly who your customers are, how to contact them, whether they are costly to service and sell to, what kinds of products and services they are interested in, and how much money they spend on your company. If you could, you'd want to make sure you knew each of your customers well, as if you were running a small-town store. And you'd want to make your good customers feel special.

In a small business operating in a neighborhood, it is possible for business owners and managers to really know their customers on a personal, face-to-face basis. But in a large business operating on a metropolitan, regional, national, or even global basis, it is impossible to "know your customer" in this intimate way. In these kinds of businesses there are too many customers and too many different ways that customers interact with the firm (over the Web, the phone, e-mail, blogs, and in person). It becomes especially difficult to integrate information from all theses sources and to deal with the large numbers of customers.

A large business's processes for sales, service, and marketing tend to be highly compartmentalized, and these departments do not share much essential customer information. Some information on a specific customer might be stored and organized in terms of that person's account with the company. Other pieces of information about the same customer might be organized by products that were purchased. There is no way to consolidate all of this information to provide a unified view of a customer across the company.

This is where customer relationship management systems help. Customer relationship management (CRM) systems, which we introduced in Chapter 2, capture and integrate customer data from all over the organization, consolidate the data, analyze the data, and then distribute the results to various systems and customer touch points across the enterprise. A **touch point** (also known as a contact point) is a method of interaction with the customer, such as telephone, e-mail, customer service desk, conventional mail, Facebook, Twitter, Web site, wireless device, or retail store. Well-designed CRM systems provide a single enterprise view of customers that is useful for improving both sales and customer service. (See Figure 8.6.)

Good CRM systems provide data and analytical tools for answering questions such as these: "What is the value of a particular customer to the firm over his or her lifetime?" "Who are our most loyal customers?" (It can cost six times more to sell to a new customer than to an existing customer.) "Who are our most profitable customers?" and "What do these profitable customers want to buy?" Firms use the answers to these questions to acquire

Figure 8.6
Customer Relationship Management (CRM)
CRM systems examine customers from a multi-faceted perspective. These systems use a set of integrated applications to address all aspects of the customer relationship, including customer service, sales, and marketing.

new customers, provide better service and support to existing customers, customize their offerings more precisely to customer preferences, and provide ongoing value to retain profitable customers.

CUSTOMER RELATIONSHIP MANAGEMENT SOFTWARE

Commercial CRM software packages range from niche tools that perform limited functions, such as personalizing Web sites for specific customers, to large-scale enterprise applications that capture myriad interactions with customers, analyze them with sophisticated reporting tools, and link to other major enterprise applications, such as supply chain management and enterprise systems. The more comprehensive CRM packages contain modules for **partner relationship management (PRM)** and **employee relationship management (ERM)**.

PRM uses many of the same data, tools, and systems as customer relationship management to enhance collaboration between a company and its selling partners. If a company does not sell directly to customers but rather works through distributors or retailers, PRM helps these channels sell to customers directly. It provides a company and its selling partners with the ability to trade information and distribute leads and data about customers, integrating lead generation, pricing, promotions, order configurations, and availability. It also provides a firm with tools to assess its partners' performances so it can make sure its best partners receive the support they need to close more business.

ERM software deals with employee issues that are closely related to CRM, such as setting objectives, employee performance management, performance-based compensation, and employee training. Major CRM application software vendors include Oracle, SAP, Salesforce.com, and Microsoft Dynamics CRM.

Customer relationship management systems typically provide software and online tools for sales, customer service, and marketing. We briefly describe some of these capabilities.

Sales Force Automation (SFA)

Sales force automation modules in CRM systems help sales staff increase their productivity by focusing sales efforts on the most profitable customers, those who are good candidates for sales and services. CRM systems provide sales prospect and contact information, product information, product configuration capabilities, and sales quote generation capabilities. Such software can assemble information about a particular customer's past purchases to help the salesperson make personalized recommendations. CRM software enables sales, marketing, and delivery departments to easily share customer and prospect information. It increases each salesperson's efficiency in reducing the cost per sale as well as the cost of acquiring new customers and retaining old ones. CRM software also has capabilities for sales forecasting, territory management, and team selling.

Customer Service

Customer service modules in CRM systems provide information and tools to increase the efficiency of call centers, help desks, and customer support staff. They have capabilities for assigning and managing customer service requests.

One such capability is an appointment or advice telephone line: When a customer calls a standard phone number, the system routes the call to the correct service person, who inputs information about that customer into the system only once. Once the customer's data are in the system, any service representative can handle the customer relationship. Improved access to consistent and accurate customer information helps call centers handle more calls per day and decrease the duration of each call. Thus, call centers and customer service groups achieve greater productivity, reduced transaction time, and higher quality of service at lower cost. The customer is happier because he or she spends less time on the phone restating his or her problem to customer service representatives.

CRM systems may also include Web-based self-service capabilities: The company Web site can be set up to provide inquiring customers personalized support information as well as the option to contact customer service staff by phone for additional assistance.

Marketing

CRM systems support direct-marketing campaigns by providing capabilities for capturing prospect and customer data, for providing product and service information, for qualifying leads for targeted marketing, and for scheduling and tracking direct-marketing mailings or e-mail (see Figure 8.7). Marketing modules also include tools for analyzing marketing and customer data, identifying profitable and unprofitable customers, designing products and services to satisfy specific customer needs and interests, and identifying opportunities for cross-selling.

Cross-selling is the marketing of complementary products to customers. (For example, in financial services, a customer with a checking account might be sold a money market account or a home improvement loan.) CRM tools also help firms manage and execute marketing campaigns at all stages, from planning to determining the rate of success for each campaign.

Figure 8.8 illustrates the most important capabilities for sales, service, and marketing processes that would be found in major CRM software products. Like enterprise software, this software is business-process driven, incorporating hundreds of business processes thought to represent best practices in each of these areas. To achieve maximum benefit, companies need to revise and model their business processes to conform to the best-practice business processes in the CRM software.

Figure 8.9 illustrates how a best practice for increasing customer loyalty through customer service might be modeled by CRM software. Directly servicing customers provides firms with opportunities to increase customer retention by singling out profitable long-term customers for preferential treatment. CRM software can assign each customer a score based on that person's value and loyalty to the company and provide that information to help call centers route each customer's service request to agents who can best handle that customer's needs. The system would automatically provide the service agent with a detailed profile of that customer that includes his or her score for value and loyalty. The service agent would use this information to present special offers or additional service to the customer to encourage the customer to keep transacting business with the company. You will find more information on other best-practice business processes in CRM systems in our Learning Tracks.

Figure 8.7
How CRM Systems Support Marketing
Customer relationship management software provides a single point for users to manage and evaluate marketing campaigns across multiple channels, including e-mail, direct mail, telephone, the Web, and wireless messages.

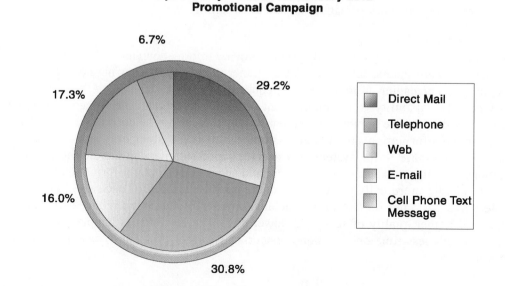

Responses by Channel for January 2012 Promotional Campaign

6.7%
29.2%
17.3%
16.0%
30.8%

Direct Mail
Telephone
Web
E-mail
Cell Phone Text Message

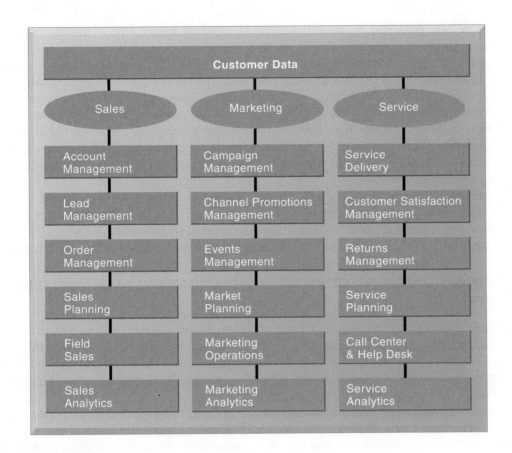

Figure 8.8
CRM Software Capabilities
The major CRM software products support business processes in sales, service, and marketing, integrating customer information from many different sources. Included are support for both the operational and analytical aspects of CRM.

OPERATIONAL AND ANALYTICAL CRM

All of the applications we have just described support either the operational or analytical aspects of customer relationship management. **Operational CRM** includes customer-facing applications, such as tools for sales force automation, call center and customer service support, and marketing automation. **Analytical CRM** includes applications that analyze

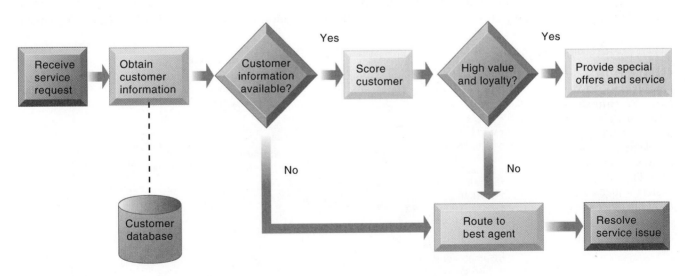

Figure 8.9
Customer Loyalty Management Process Map
This process map shows how a best practice for promoting customer loyalty through customer service would be modeled by customer relationship management software. The CRM software helps firms identify high-value customers for preferential treatment.

customer data generated by operational CRM applications to provide information for improving business performance.

Analytical CRM applications are based on data warehouses that consolidate the data from operational CRM systems and customer touch points for use with online analytical processing (OLAP), data mining, and other data analysis techniques (see Chapter 6). Customer data collected by the organization might be combined with data from other sources, such as customer lists for direct-marketing campaigns purchased from other companies or demographic data. Such data are analyzed to identify buying patterns, to create segments for targeted marketing, and to pinpoint profitable and unprofitable customers (see Figure 8.10).

Another important output of analytical CRM is the customer's lifetime value to the firm. **Customer lifetime value (CLTV)** is based on the relationship between the revenue produced by a specific customer, the expenses incurred in acquiring and servicing that customer, and the expected life of the relationship between the customer and the company.

BUSINESS VALUE OF CUSTOMER RELATIONSHIP MANAGEMENT SYSTEMS

Companies with effective customer relationship management systems realize many benefits, including increased customer satisfaction, reduced direct-marketing costs, more effective marketing, and lower costs for customer acquisition and retention. Information from CRM systems increases sales revenue by identifying the most profitable customers and segments for focused marketing and cross-selling.

Customer churn is reduced as sales, service, and marketing better respond to customer needs. The **churn rate** measures the number of customers who stop using or purchasing products or services from a company. It is an important indicator of the growth or decline of a firm's customer base.

8.4 Enterprise Applications: New Opportunities and Challenges

Many firms have implemented enterprise systems and systems for supply chain management and customer relationship because they are such powerful instruments for achieving operational excellence and enhancing decision making. But precisely because they are so powerful in changing the way the organization works, they are challenging to implement.

Figure 8.10
Analytical CRM
Data Warehouse
Analytical CRM uses a customer data warehouse and tools to analyze customer data collected from the firm's customer touch points and from other sources.

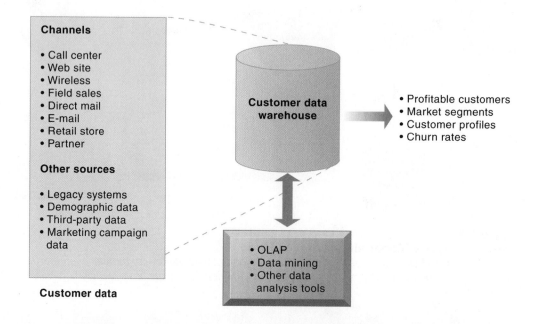

Let's briefly examine some of these challenges, as well as new ways of obtaining value from these systems.

ENTERPRISE APPLICATION CHALLENGES

Promises of dramatic reductions in inventory costs, order-to-delivery time, as well as more efficient customer response and higher product and customer profitability make enterprise systems and systems for supply chain management and customer relationship management very alluring. But to obtain this value, you must clearly understand how your business has to change to use these systems effectively.

Enterprise applications involve complex pieces of software that are very expensive to purchase and implement. It might take a large Fortune 500 company several years to complete a large-scale implementation of an enterprise system or a system for SCM or CRM. The total cost for an average large system implementation based on SAP or Oracle software, including software, database tools, consulting fees, personnel costs, training, and perhaps hardware costs, runs over $12 million. The implementation cost of an enterprise system for a small or mid-sized company based on software from a "Tier II" vendor such as Epicor or Lawson averages $3.5 million (Wailgum, 2009).

Enterprise applications require not only deep-seated technological changes but also fundamental changes in the way the business operates. Companies must make sweeping changes to their business processes to work with the software. Employees must accept new job functions and responsibilities. They must learn how to perform a new set of work activities and understand how the information they enter into the system can affect other parts of the company. This requires new organizational learning.

Supply chain management systems require multiple organizations to share information and business processes. Each participant in the system may have to change some of its processes and the way it uses information to create a system that best serves the supply chain as a whole.

Some firms experienced enormous operating problems and losses when they first implemented enterprise applications because they didn't understand how much organizational change was required. For example, Kmart had trouble getting products to store shelves when it first implemented i2 Technologies supply chain management software in July 2000. The i2 software did not work well with Kmart's promotion-driven business model, which created sharp downward spikes in demand for products. Overstock.com's order tracking system went down for a full week in October 2005 when the company replaced a homegrown system with an Oracle enterprise system. The company rushed to implement the software, and did not properly synchronize the Oracle software's process for recording customer refunds with its accounts receivable system. These problems contributed to a third-quarter loss of $14.5 million that year.

Enterprise applications also introduce "switching costs." Once you adopt an enterprise application from a single vendor, such as SAP, Oracle, or others, it is very costly to switch vendors, and your firm becomes dependent on the vendor to upgrade its product and maintain your installation.

Enterprise applications are based on organization-wide definitions of data. You'll need to understand exactly how your business uses its data and how the data would be organized in a customer relationship management, supply chain management, or enterprise system. CRM systems typically require some data cleansing work.

Enterprise software vendors are addressing these problems by offering pared-down versions of their software and "fast-start" programs for small and medium-sized businesses and best-practice guidelines for larger companies. The Interactive Session on Technology describes how on-demand and cloud-based tools deal with this problem as well.

Companies adopting enterprise applications can also save time and money by keeping customizations to the minimum. For example, Kennametal, a $2 billion metal-cutting tools company in Pennsylvania, had spent $10 million over 13 years maintaining an ERP system with over 6,400 customizations. The company is now replacing it with a "plain vanilla," non-customized-version of SAP enterprise software and changing its business processes to conform to the software (Johnson, 2010).

NEXT-GENERATION ENTERPRISE APPLICATIONS

Today, enterprise application vendors are delivering more value by becoming more flexible, Web-enabled, and capable of integration with other systems. Stand-alone enterprise systems, customer relationship management systems, and supply chain management systems are becoming a thing of the past. The major enterprise software vendors have created what they call *enterprise solutions*, *enterprise suites*, or *e-business* suites to make their customer relationship management, supply chain management, and enterprise systems work closely with each other, and link to systems of customers and suppliers. SAP Business Suite, Oracle e-Business Suite, and Microsoft Dynamics suite (aimed at mid-sized companies) are examples, and they now utilize Web services and service-oriented architecture (SOA) (See Chapter 4).

SAP's next-generation enterprise applications incorporate SOA standards and use the NetWeaver tool as an integration platform linking SAP's own applications and Web services developed by independent software vendors. Oracle also has included SOA and business process management capabilities into its Fusion middleware products. Businesses are able to use these tools to create *service platforms* for new or improved business processes that integrate information from multiple applications. You can find out more about service platforms in the Learning Tracks for this chapter.

Next-generation enterprise applications also include open source and on-demand solutions, as well as more functionality available on mobile platforms. Compared to commercial enterprise application software, open source products such as Compiere, Apache Open for Business (OFBiz), and Openbravo are not as mature, nor do they include as much support. However, companies such as small manufacturers are choosing this option because there are no software licensing fees, and fees are based on usage.

SAP now offers an on-demand enterprise software solution called Business ByDesign for small and medium businesses in select countries. SAP is also working with cloud services providers such as HP and Dell to deploy its applications on their cloud platforms.

Software as a service (SaaS) and cloud-based versions of enterprise systems are starting to be offered by vendors such as NetSuite and Plex Online. Compiere sells both cloud and on-premise versions of its ERP systems. The Interactive Session on Technology describes some of the cloud-based systems for CRM.

Social CRM and Business Intelligence

CRM software vendors are enhancing their products to take advantage of social networking technologies. These social enhancements help firms identify new ideas more rapidly, improve team productivity, and deepen interactions with customers. For example, Salesforce IdeaExchange enables subscribers to harness the "wisdom of crowds" by allowing their customers to submit and discuss new ideas. Dell Computer deployed this technology to encourage its customers to suggest and vote on new concepts and feature changes in Dell products. A collaboration tool called Chatter enables Salesforce users to create Facebook-like profiles and receive real-time news feeds about co-workers, projects, and customers. Users can also form groups and post messages on each other's profiles to collaborate on projects.

Employees who interact with customers via social networking sites such as Facebook and Twitter are often able to provide customer service functions much faster and at lower cost than by using telephone conversations or e-mail. Customers who are active social media users increasingly want—and expect—businesses to respond to their questions and complaints through this channel.

Social CRM tools enable a business to connect customer conversations and relationships from social networking sites to CRM processes. The leading CRM vendors now offer such tools to link data from social networks into their CRM software. Salesforce.com and Oracle CRM products are incorporating technology to monitor, track, and analyze social media activity in Facebook, LinkedIn, Twitter, YouTube, and other sites.

Salesforce recently acquired social media monitoring company Radian6, which helps companies such as Dell, GE, Kodak, and UPS monitor, analyze, and engage in hundreds of millions of social media conversations. Salesforce plans to add these capabilities to

INTERACTIVE SESSION: TECHNOLOGY — Customer Relationship Management Heads to the Cloud

Salesforce.com is the most successful enterprise-scale software as a service (SaaS) and the undisputed global leader in cloud-based customer relationship management systems. Users can access Salesforce applications anywhere through an Internet-enabled mobile device or any online computer. Subscriptions start as low as $15 per user per month for the pared-down Group version for small sales and marketing teams, with monthly subscriptions for large enterprises starting around $65 per user.

Salesforce has over 92,000 corporate customers. Small businesses find the on-demand model especially appealing because there are no large up-front hardware and software investments or lengthy implementations on corporate computer systems. Fireclay Tile, a small sustainable tile manufacturer that converts recycled materials into handmade ceramic tile, adopted Salesforce and realized multiple benefits. Salesforce's e-mail and Web-to-lead capabilities helped the company quadruple new sales leads. (Web-to-lead automatically adds leads collected from the Web to the company's master database.) A task feature automatically generates specific tasks based on the type of lead (architect, contractor, dealer, or homeowner) and the stage in the sales process. The system automates customer service functions including order confirmations, follow-up customer satisfaction surveys, and shipping notifications. Customer satisfaction and productivity have soared.

But Salesforce.com also appeals to large companies. Dr. Pepper Snapple Group adopted Salesforce CRM to replace an outmoded Excel application that required extensive manual data input to compile reports on more than 50 beverage brands and to track sales performance against objectives in real time. The system now tracks field activities for more than 10,000 accounts, with automated reports and dashboards monitoring key performance indicators, sales calls, and sales volume. Siemens, the Wall Street Journal, Pitney Bowes, and Starbucks and are among Salesforce's other large corporate CRM users.

Not to be outdone, established enterprise software companies such as Oracle have moved into cloud software services. Pricing starts at $70 per month per user. Oracle's CRM on Demand system has many capabilities, including embedded tools for forecasting, and analytics and interactive dashboards. Subscribers are able to use these tools to answer questions such as "How efficient is your sales effort?" or "How much are your customers spending?"

Bryant & Stratton College, a pioneer in career education, used Oracle CRM on Demand to create more successful marketing campaigns. Bryant &

Stratton analyzed past campaigns for tech-savvy recent high school graduates, as well as older, non-traditional students returning to school later in life. Oracle CRM on Demand tracked advertising to prospective students and determined accurate costs for each lead, admissions application, and registered attending student. This information helped the school determine the true value of each type of marketing program.

While traditional enterprise software vendors like Oracle are using their well-established position to penetrate the cloud-based application market, newcomers like RightNow and SugarCRM have found success, even among larger companies. For example, camera manufacturer Nikon decided to go with a cloud-based solution as it attempted to merge customer data from 25 disparate sources and applications into a single system. Company officials were hoping to eliminate maintenance and administrative costs, but not at the expense of a storage system that met their requirements, was never out of service, and worked perfectly.

Nikon found its solution with RightNow, a cloud-based CRM provider located in Bozeman, Montana. RightNow has attracted firms intrigued by its customizable applications, impeccable customer service, and robust infrastructure. Prices start at $110 per user per month, and the average deployment time is 45 days.

Nikon had been using several different systems to perform business functions, and was struggling to merge customer data located on a variety of legacy systems. While looking for vendors to help implement a Web-based FAQ system to answer customer questions and provide support on the basis of these data, the company came across RightNow. Nikon found that not only did RightNow have the capability to implement that system, it also had an array of other useful services. When Nikon discovered that it could combine outbound e-mail, contact management, and customer records into a single system in RightNow's cloud, it made the move, expecting to receive a solid return on the investment (ROI).

What Nikon got was far more than expected: a 3,200 percent return on investment (ROI), equivalent to a savings of $14 million after three years. The FAQ system reduced the number of incoming calls to Nikon's customer service staff. More customers found the information they needed on the Web, call response times dropped by 50 percent, and incoming e-mail dropped by 70 percent. While Nikon still hosts its SAP ERP system internally due to its complexity, Nikon switched its entire CRM system to RightNow.

Not all companies experience gains of that magnitude, and cloud computing does have drawbacks.

Many companies are concerned about maintaining control of their data and security. Although cloud computing companies are prepared to handle these issues, availability assurances and service level agreements are not always available. Companies that manage their CRM apps with a cloud infrastructure have no guar- antees that their data will be available at all times, or even that the provider will still exist in the future.

Sources: Brittany Farb, "SaaS Deployments Fuel Competiton," *CRM Magazine*, June 2, 2011; www.salesforce.com, accessed June 9, 2011; www.rightnow. com, accessed June 9, 2011; Marta Bright, "Know Who. Know How" *Oracle Magazine*, January/February 2010; and Brad Stone, "Companies Slowly Join Cloud-Computing," *New York Times*, April 28, 2010.

CASE STUDY QUESTIONS

1. What types of companies are most likely to adopt cloud-based CRM software services? Why? What companies might not be well-suited for this type of software?

2. What are the advantages and disadvantages of using cloud-based enterprise applications?

3. What people, organization, and technology issues should be addressed in deciding whether to use a conventional CRM system versus a cloud-based version?

MIS IN ACTION

Visit the Webs site of Salesforce.com, RightNow, or another competing company offering a cloud-based version of CRM. Then answer the following questions:

1. What CRM capabilities does the company offer? Describe some of the features.

2. Toward what types of companies is the company marketing its services?

3. What other services does the company offer?

its software. Oracle partnered with Buzzient, which provides tools for integrating social media with enterprise applications. The Buzzient platform automatically collects information from a huge number of online sources in real time and analyzes the content based on users' specifications. Buzzient supplies this information to CRM systems to help companies uncover sales leads and identify customer support issues.

Business Intelligence in Enterprise Applications Enterprise application vendors have added business intelligence features to help managers obtain more meaningful information from the massive amounts of data generated by these systems. Included are tools for flexible reporting, ad hoc analysis, interactive dashboards, "what-if" scenario analysis, and data visualization (see Chapter 10 and the Chapter 11 Interactive Session on People). Rather than requiring users to leave an application and launch separate reporting and analytics tools, the vendors are starting to embed analytics within the context of the application itself. They are also offering complementary standalone analytics products, such as SAP Business Objects and Oracle Business Intelligence Enterprise Edition.

The major enterprise application vendors also offer portions of their products that work on mobile handhelds. You can find out more about this topic in our Learning Track on Wireless Applications for Customer Relationship Management, Supply Chain Management, and Healthcare.

LEARNING TRACKS

The following Learning Tracks provide content relevant to topics covered in this chapter:

1. SAP Business Process Map
2. Business Processes in Supply Chain Management and Supply Chain Metrics
3. Best-Practice Business Processes in CRM Software
4. Service Platforms

Review Summary

1 **How do enterprise systems help businesses achieve operational excellence?** Enterprise software is based on a suite of integrated software modules and a common central database. The database collects data from and feeds the data into numerous applications that can support nearly all of an organization's internal business activities. When new information is entered by one process, the information is made available immediately to other business processes.

Enterprise systems support organizational centralization by enforcing uniform data standards and business processes throughout the company and a single unified technology platform. The firmwide data generated by enterprise systems helps managers evaluate organizational performance.

2 **How do supply chain management systems coordinate planning, production, and logistics with suppliers?** Supply chain management systems automate the flow of information among members of the supply chain so they can use it to make better decisions about when and how much to purchase, produce, or ship. More accurate information from supply chain management systems reduces uncertainty and the impact of the bullwhip effect.

Supply chain management software includes software for supply chain planning and for supply chain execution. Internet technology facilitates the management of global supply chains by providing the connectivity for organizations in different countries to share supply chain information. Improved communication among supply chain members also facilitates efficient customer response and movement toward a demand-driven model.

3 **How do customer relationship management systems help firms achieve customer intimacy?** Customer relationship management (CRM) systems integrate and automate customer-facing processes in sales, marketing, and customer service, providing an enterprise-wide view of customers. Companies can use this customer knowledge when they interact with customers to provide them with better service or to sell new products and services. These systems also identify profitable or nonprofitable customers or opportunities to reduce the churn rate.

The major customer relationship management software packages provide capabilities for both operational CRM and analytical CRM. They often include modules for managing relationships with selling partners (partner relationship management) and for employee relationship management.

4 **What are the challenges posed by enterprise applications?** Enterprise applications are difficult to implement. They require extensive organizational change, large new software investments, and careful assessment of how these systems will enhance organizational performance. Enterprise applications cannot provide value if they are implemented atop flawed processes or if firms do not know how to use these systems to measure performance improvements. Employees require training to prepare for new procedures and roles. Attention to data management is essential.

5 **How are enterprise applications taking advantage of new technologies?** Enterprise applications are now more flexible, Web-enabled, and capable of integration with other systems, using Web services and service-oriented architecture (SOA). They also have open source and on-demand versions and are able to run in cloud infrastructures or on mobile platforms. CRM software has added social networking capabilities to enhance internal collaboration, deepen interactions with customers, and utilize data from social networking sites.

Key Terms

Analytical CRM, 277
Bullwhip effect, 268
Churn rate, 278
Cross-selling, 276
Customer lifetime value
  (CLTV), 278
Demand planning, 269
Employee relationship
  management (ERM), 275

Enterprise software, 264
Just-in-time strategy, 268
Operational CRM, 277
Partner relationship
  management (PRM), 275
Pull-based model, 270
Push-based model, 270
Social CRM, 280

Supply chain, 266
Supply chain execution
  systems, 269
Supply chain planning
  systems, 269
Touch point, 274

Review Questions

1. How do enterprise systems help businesses achieve operational excellence?
- Define an enterprise system and explain how enterprise software works.
- Describe how enterprise systems provide value for a business.

2. How do supply chain management systems coordinate planning, production, and logistics with suppliers?
- Define a supply chain and identify each of its components.
- Explain how supply chain management systems help reduce the bullwhip effect and how they provide value for a business.
- Define and compare supply chain planning systems and supply chain execution systems.
- Describe the challenges of global supply chains and how Internet technology can help companies manage them better.
- Distinguish between a push-based and a pull-based model of supply chain management and explain how contemporary supply chain management systems facilitate a pull-based model.

3. How do customer relationship management systems help firms achieve customer intimacy?
- Define customer relationship management and explain why customer relationships are so important today.
- Describe how partner relationship management (PRM) and employee relationship management (ERM) are related to customer relationship management (CRM).
- Describe the tools and capabilities of customer relationship management software for sales, marketing, and customer service.
- Distinguish between operational and analytical CRM.

4. What are the challenges posed by enterprise applications?
- List and describe the challenges posed by enterprise applications.
- Explain how these challenges can be addressed.

5. How are enterprise applications taking advantage of new technologies?
- How are enterprise applications taking advantage of SOA, Web services, open source software, and wireless technology?
- Define social CRM and explain how customer relationship management systems are using social networking.

Discussion Questions

1. Supply chain management is less about managing the physical movement of goods and more about managing information. Discuss the implications of this statement.

2. If a company wants to implement an enterprise application, it had better do its homework. Discuss the implications of this statement.

3. Which enterprise application should a business install first: ERP, SCM, or CRM? Explain your answer.

Hands-on MIS Projects

The projects in this section give you hands-on experience analyzing business process integration, suggesting supply chain management and customer relationship management applications, using database software to manage customer service requests, and evaluating supply chain management business services.

MANAGEMENT DECISION PROBLEMS

1. Toronto-based Mercedes-Benz Canada, with a network of 55 dealers, did not know enough about its customers. Dealers provided customer data to the company on an ad hoc basis. Mercedes did not force dealers to report this information. There was no real incentive for dealers to share information with the company. How could CRM and PRM systems help solve this problem?
2. Office Depot sells a wide range of office supply products and services in the United States and internationally. The company tries to offer a wider range of office supplies at lower cost than other retailers by using just-in-time replenishment and tight inventory control systems. It uses information from a demand forecasting system and point-of-sale data to replenish its inventory in its 1,600 retail stores. Explain how these systems help Office Depot minimize costs and any other benefits they provide. Identify and describe other supply chain management applications that would be especially helpful to Office Depot.

IMPROVING DECISION MAKING: USING DATABASE SOFTWARE TO MANAGE CUSTOMER SERVICE REQUESTS

Software skills: Database design; querying and reporting
Business skills: Customer service analysis

In this exercise, you'll use database software to develop an application that tracks customer service requests and analyzes customer data to identify customers meriting priority treatment.

Prime Service is a large service company that provides maintenance and repair services for close to 1,200 commercial businesses in New York, New Jersey, and Connecticut. Its customers include businesses of all sizes. Customers with service needs call into its customer service department with requests for repairing heating ducts, broken windows, leaky roofs, broken water pipes, and other problems. The company assigns each request a number and writes down the service request number, identification number of the customer account, the date of the request, the type of equipment requiring repair, and a brief description of the problem. The service requests are handled on a first-come-first-served basis. After the service work has been completed, Prime calculates the cost of the work, enters the price on the service request form, and bills the client. This arrangement treats the most important and profitable clients—those with accounts of more than $70,000—no differently from its clients with small accounts. Managment would like to find a way to provide its best customers with better service. Management would also like to know which types of service problems occur most frequently so that it can make sure it has adequate resources to address them.

Prime Service has a small database with client account information, which can be found in MyMISLab. Use database software to design a solution that would enable Prime's customer service representatives to identify the most important customers so that they could receive priority service. Your solution will require more than one table. Populate your database with at least 10 service requests. Create several reports that would be of interest to management, such as a list of the highest—and lowest— priority accounts and a report showing the most frequently occurring service problems. Create a report listing service calls that customer service representatives should respond to first on a specific date.

ACHIEVING OPERATIONAL EXCELLENCE: EVALUATING SUPPLY CHAIN MANAGEMENT SERVICES

Software skills: Web browser and presentation software
Business skills: Evaluating supply chain management services

In addition to carrying goods from one place to another, some trucking companies provide supply chain management services and help their customers manage their information. In this project, you'll use the Web to research and evaluate two of these business services. Investigate the Web sites of two companies, UPS Logistics and Schneider Logistics, to see how these companies' services can be used for supply chain management. Then respond to the following questions:

- What supply chain processes can each of these companies support for their clients?
- How can customers use the Web sites of each company to help them with supply chain management?
- Compare the supply chain management services provided by these companies. Which company would you select to help your firm manage its supply chain? Why?

Video Cases

Video Cases and Instructional Videos illustrating some of the concepts in this chapter are available. Contact your instructor to access these videos.

Collaboration and Teamwork

Analyzing Enterprise Application Vendors

With a group of three or four students, use the Web to research and evaluate the products of two vendors of enterprise application software. You could compare, for example, the SAP and Oracle enterprise systems, the supply chain management systems from JDA Software and SAP, or the customer relationship management systems of Oracle and Salesforce.com. Use what you have learned from these companies' Web sites to compare the software packages you have selected in terms of business functions supported, technology platforms, cost, and ease of use. Which vendor would you select? Why? Would you select the same vendor for a small business as well as a large one? If possible, use Google Sites to post links to Web pages, team communication announcements, and work assignments; to brainstorm; and to work collaboratively on project documents. Try to use Google Docs to develop a presentation of your findings for the class.

BUSINESS PROBLEM-SOLVING CASE

Summit Electric Lights Up with a New ERP System

Summit Electric Supply is one of the top wholesale distributors of industrial electrical equipment and supplies in the United States, with 500 employees and nearly $302 million in 2010 sales. Summit operates in four states and has a global export division based in Houston, a marine division based in New Orleans, and a sales office in Dubai.

Summit distributes products that include motor controls, wire and cable, cords, lighting, conduit and fittings, wiring devices, support systems and fasteners, outlet boxes and enclosures, and transformers and power protection equipment. The company obtains finished goods from manufacturers and then sells them to electrical contractors working on projects ranging from small construction jobs to sophisticated industrial projects. As a distributor, Summit Electric Supply is a "middle man" on the supply chain, and must be able to rapidly handle a high volume of transactions and swift inventory turnover.

Since its founding in 1977 in Albuquerque, New Mexico, Summit has grown very quickly. Unfortunately, its homegrown legacy information systems built in the 1980s could not keep up with the business. One legacy system was for sales entries and purchase orders and another was for back-end reporting. Integration between the two systems was done manually in batches. The systems could only handle a fixed number of locations and limited the range of numbers that could be used on documents. This meant that Summit's information systems department had to use the same range of document numbers over again every few months. Once the company found it could no longer process its nightly inventory and financial updates in the amount of time that was available, the systems had reached their breaking point. A new solution was in order.

Summit started looking for a new enterprise resource planning (ERP) system. This would prove to be challenging, because the company's legacy systems were so old that the business had built many of its processes around them. A new system would require changes to business processes and the way people worked.

Summit also found that most of the available ERP software on the market had been designed for manufacturing or retailing businesses, and did not address some of the unique processes and priorities of the distribution industry. Summit needed a system that could handle a very large number of SKUs (stock-keeping units, which

are numbers or codes for identifying each unique product or item for sale) and transactions, very short lead times for order processing, inventory distributed in various models, products sold in one quantity that could be sold in another; and no-touch inventory. Summit handles some products that are shipped directly from the manufacturer to the customer's job site.

Scalability and inventory visibility were Summit's top requirements. The company needed a system that would handle orders and inventory as it continued its rapid pace of growth. In the distribution business, the lead times for fulfilling an order can be only minutes: a Summit customer might call to place an order while driving to pick up the order, so the company has to know immediately what product is available at what location.

After extensively reviewing ERP vendors, Summit selected ERP software from SAP because of its functionality in sales and distribution, materials management, and financials, and its knowledge of the distribution business. Summit visited other electrical distributors using SAP, including some of its competitors, to make sure the software would work in its line of business. Summit was able to go live with its new ERP system across 19 locations in January 2007.

Nevertheless, Summit still had to customize its SAP software to meet its unique business requirements. Most SAP delivery and material scheduling functions were designed for overnight processing, because many industries have longer lead times for order fulfillment. Waiting for overnight inventory updates would significantly delay Summit's sales. Summit found it could solve this problem by running smaller, more frequent updates for just the material received during the day, rather than running big inventory updates less often. This provided more timely and accurate snapshots of what was actually available in inventory so that orders could be rapidly processed.

Wire and cable are one of Summit's most popular product categories. Summit buys these products by the reel in lengths up to 5,000 feet and then cuts them into various lengths to sell to customers. This makes it difficult to determine how much of this type of inventory has been sold and when it is time to replenish. To address this issue, Summit used a "batch management" solution in SAP's ERP materials management software that treats a wire reel as a "batch" rather than as a single product. Every time a customer buys a length of wire, the length can be entered into the system to track how much of the "batch" was sold. Summit is able to use this capability to find which other customers bought wire from the same reel and trace the wire back to the manufacturer.

To accommodate large customers with long-term job sites, Summit sets up temporary warehouses on-site to supply these customers with its electrical products. Summit still owns the inventory, but it's dedicated to these customers and can't be treated as standard inventory in the ERP system. SAP's ERP software didn't support that way of doing business. Summit used some of the standard functionality in the SAP software to change how it allocated materials into temporary storage locations by creating a parent-child warehouse relationship. If, for instance, Summit's Houston office has several temporary on-site warehouses, the warehouses are managed as subparts of its main warehouse. That prevents someone from selling the consigned inventory in the warehouse.

Summit's old legacy systems used separate systems for orders and financials, so the data could not be easily combined for business intelligence reporting and analysis. In 2010, Summit implemented SAP's NetWeaver BW data warehouse and business intelligence solution to make better use of the data in its ERP system. These tools have helped the company evaluate the profitability of its sales channels, using what-if scenarios. For instance, Summit is now able to analyze profitability by sales person, manufacturer, customer, or branch. Business intelligence findings have encouraged Summit to focus more attention to areas such as sales order quotations and to supplier performance and delivery times. Management has much greater visibility into how the organization is operating and is able to make better decisions.

Summit's SAP software also produced a significant return on investment (ROI) from automating sales tax processing and chargebacks. In the distribution industry, chargebacks occur when a supplier sells a product at a higher wholesale price to the distributor than the price the distributor has set with a retail customer. A chargeback agreement allows the distributor to bill the manufacturer an additional contracted amount in order to make some profit on the deal.

Processing chargebacks requires a very close comparison of sales to contracts, and a distributor can have hundreds or thousands of different chargeback contracts. The distributor must not only be able to identify chargeback deals but also provide the manufacturer with sufficient documentation of the specific chargeback contract that is being invoked. Chargeback management is a large part of any wholesale distributor's

profit model, and Summit was losing revenue opportunities because its chargeback process was flawed.

Before 2007, Summit's outdated legacy system was not able to handle the volume and complexity of the company's chargeback agreements, and reporting capabilities were limited. Processing chargebacks required a great deal of manual work. Summit employees had to pore through customer invoices for specific manufacturers to identify which chargebacks Summit could claim. They would then input the data they had found manually into a Microsoft Excel spreadsheet. Gathering and reviewing invoices sometimes took an entire month, and each month the paper copies of the invoices to give to Summit's vendors consumed an entire case of paper. By the time Summit's vendors responded to the chargeback invoices, the invoices were two or three months old. This cumbersome process inevitably missed some chargebacks for which Summit was eligible, resulting in lost revenue opportunities.

As part of its ERP solution, Summit implemented the SAP Paybacks and Chargebacks application, which was developed specifically for the distribution industry. At the end of each business day, this application automatically reviews Summit's billing activity for that day and compares it to all chargeback agreements loaded in the SAP system. (Summit's system automatically keeps track of 35 vendors with whom it has more than 6,600 chargeback agreements.) Where there is a match, a chargeback can be claimed, and the application creates a separate chargeback document outside of the customer invoice. Depending on the type of vendor, the application consolidates identified chargebacks by vendor daily or monthly, and automatically submits the information to the vendor along with the chargeback document. The vendor can then approve the chargeback or make changes, which are reconciled against individual chargeback documents.

The new system processes chargebacks much more quickly and also makes it possible for Summit to review them more frequently. Where vendors are exchanging data with Summit electronically, Summit is able to make a chargeback claim and obtain vendor approval the same day. By fully automating the chargeback process, the company has increased its chargeback claims by 118 percent over its legacy systems, thereby boosting chargeback revenue as a percentage of sales. Summit is now able to see which vendors, customers, and products are producing the most chargeback revenue.

A key lesson from Summit's ERP implementation was not to force the new system to look like the legacy system. Not only is such customization expensive to set up and maintain, it can perpetuate outdated ways of doing business. According to Summit's CIO David Wascom, "We've done a lot to maintain flexibility (for our users), but still run within a standard SAP business flow."

Sources: David Hannon, "Bringing More Revenue to the Table," SAP InsiderPROFILES, April–June 2011 and "Finding the Right ERP Fit," SAP InsiderPROFILES, January–March 2011; "Summit Electric Supply Drives Business Transformation Through SAP and ASUG," SAPInsider (October–December 2010), http://summit.com, accessed August 22, 2011; and Neetin Datar, "Summit Electric Improves Chargebacks," SAP.info, June 18, 2009.

Case Study Questions

1. Which businesses processes are the most important at Summit Electric Supply? Why?

2. What problems did Summit have with its old systems? What was the business impact of those problems?

3. How did Summit's ERP system improve operational efficiency and decision making? Give several examples.

4. Describe two ways in which Summit's customers benefit from the new ERP system.

5. Diagram Summit's old and new process for handling chargebacks.

E-commerce: Digital Markets, Digital Goods

STUDENT LEARNING OBJECTIVES

After completing this chapter, you will be able to answer the following questions:

1. What are the unique features of e-commerce, digital markets, and digital goods?

2. What are the principal e-commerce business and revenue models?

3. How has e-commerce transformed marketing?

4. How has e-commerce affected business-to-business transactions?

5. What is the role of m-commerce in business and what are the most important m-commerce applications?

6. What issues must be addressed when building an e-commerce presence?

CHAPTER OUTLINE

GROUPON'S BUSINESS MODEL: SOCIAL AND LOCAL

Groupon is a business that offers subscribers daily deals from local merchants. The catch: a group of people (usually at least 25) has to purchase the discounted coupon (a "Groupon"). If you really want to go to that Italian restaurant in your area with a 50 percent discount coupon, you will need to message your friends to pay for the coupon as well. As soon as the minimum number of coupons is sold, the offer is open to everyone.

Here's how it works: Most Groupon deals give the customer 50 percent off the retail price of a product or service offered by a local merchant. For example, a $50 hairstyling is offered at $25. The Groupon offer is e-mailed to thousands of potential customers within driving distance of the retailer. If enough people use their PCs or smartphones to sign up and buy the Groupon, the deal is on, and the customer receives a Groupon by e-mail. Groupon takes a 50 percent cut of the revenue ($12.50), leaving the merchant with $12.50. In other words, the merchant takes a haircut of 75 percent! Instead of generating $50 in revenue for hair styling, the merchant receives only $12.50.

Who wins here? The customer gets a hairstyling for half price. Groupon gets a hefty percentage of the Groupon's face value. The merchant receives many (sometimes too many) customers. Although merchants may lose money on these single offers, they are

© Lee Rogers, 2011, iStockPhoto LP.

hoping to generate repeat purchases, loyal customers, and a larger customer base. Moreover, the deals are short term, often good for only a day. The hope: lose money on a single day, make money on all the other days when regular prices are in effect. It's a customer acquisition cost.

Founded in 2008 by Andrew Mason, in 30 months, Groupon has rocketed to more than 83 million customers, operates in 43 countries, has sold over 70 million Groupons, and generated $644 million in the first quarter of 2011. Groupon is often called the fastest growing company in history.

Nevertheless, Groupon, like many social network sites, is struggling to show a profit. In 2010, it lost $450 million on $315 million in revenue. Its biggest expense is customer acquisition. Groupon clearly believes that the new customers are worth it: Groupon spent $432 million to attract 65 million subscribers in the first half of 2011, and these new customers generated $688 million in revenue.

The question is whether Groupon's business model can work in the long run. Critics point out that Groupon's revenue per customer is falling, the conversion rate of customers into subscribers is slowing down, the tens of millions of e-mails Groupon uses to inform users of deals are poorly targeted, there are increasingly fewer Groupons sold per customer, and the revenue per Groupon is falling. The solution, according to the company, is scale: get big really quick, and develop the brand so that competitors will never be able to find an audience. With enough customers and fast enough growth, Groupon may still turn out to be profitable.

No one knows if this business strategy will work. Many merchants report that the Groupon deals are not creating a larger group of repeat customers. Instead, only the most price-sensitive customers show up at the door, and then never return when prices go back to normal levels. Competitors are springing up everywhere around the globe, including Google Offers and Loopt.

Groupon may overcome some of the hurdles it faces by virtue of its brand and scale. But investors will want a return someday, and Groupon's biggest challenge will be showing a profit of any kind in the next few years.

Sources: Chunka Moi, "Google Offers a Two-Pronged Attack on Groupon's Business Model," *Forbes*, June 29, 2011; Jenna Wortham, "Loopt Flips Daily Deal Model Upside Down With U-Deal," *New York Times*, June 23, 2011; Don Dodge, "How Does Groupon Work? Is Its Business Model Sustainable?" Dondodge.wordpad.com, June 11, 2011; Michel de la Merced, "Is Groupon's Business Model Sustainable?" *New York Times*, June 8, 2011; Utpal M. Dholakia, "How Effective are Groupon Promotions for Businesses?" Rice University, March 12, 2011; Utpal Dholakia, "Google Beware: Groupon Is No YouTube," *Harvard Business Review Blog*, December 3, 2010.

Groupon combines two of the major new trends in e-commerce: localization and social networks. Selling goods and services on the Internet is increasingly based on social networking—friends recommending friends, as is the case with Groupon, and companies targeting individuals and their friends who are members of social networking communities such as Facebook and Twitter. E-commece is also becoming increasingly localized, as companies armed with detailed knowledge of customer locations target special offers of location-based goods and services. There are mobile apps for Groupon as well as for many other companies who are increasingly pitching and selling over mobile platforms, and e-commerce is becoming more mobile as well.

The chapter-opening diagram calls attention to important points raised by this case and this chapter. The business challenge facing Groupon is how to create a profitable business that can take advantage of Internet technology and social networking tools in the face of powerful competitors. Groupon's management decided to base its business model on localization and social technology. The business earns revenue by asking people to recruit their friends and acquaintances to sign up for discount coupons to create a "critical mass" of potential customers for a local product or service. Participating merchants sign up with the expectation of attracting large numbers of new customers. But Groupon has serious competition, participating merchants do not always reap benefits, and it is unclear whether the business model is solid and profitable.

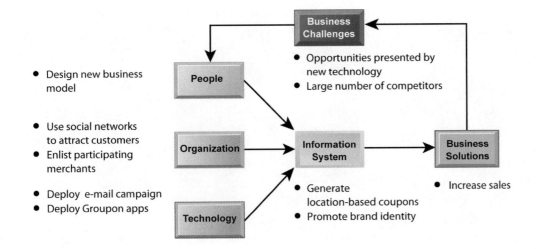

Design new business model

Use social networks to attract customers
Enlist participating merchants

Deploy e-mail campaign
Deploy Groupon apps

9.1 E-commerce and the Internet

Bought an iTunes track lately, streamed a Netflix movie to your home TV, purchased a book at Amazon, or a diamond at Blue Nile? If so you've engaged in e-commerce. In 2011, 148 million adult Americans bought something online, as did millions of others worldwide. And although most purchases still take place through traditional channels, e-commerce continues to grow rapidly and to transform the way many companies do business. In 2011, e-commerce represents about 6 percent of all retail sales in the United States, and is growing at 14 percent annually (eMarketer, 2011a). In just the past two years, e-commerce has expanded from the desktop and home computer to mobile devices, from an isolated activity to a new social commerce, and from a Fortune 1000 commerce with a national audience to local merchants and consumers whose location is known to mobile devices. The key words for understanding this new e-commerce in 2011–2012 are "social, mobile, local."

E-COMMERCE TODAY

E-commerce refers to the use of the Internet and the Web to transact business. More formally, e-commerce is about digitally enabled commercial transactions between and among organizations and individuals. For the most part, this means transactions that occur over the Internet and the Web. Commercial transactions involve the exchange of value (e.g., money) across organizational or individual boundaries in return for products and services.

E-commerce began in 1995 when one of the first Internet portals, Netscape.com, accepted the first ads from major corporations and popularized the idea that the Web could be used as a new medium for advertising and sales. No one envisioned at the time what would turn out to be an exponential growth curve for e-commerce retail sales, which doubled and tripled in the early years. E-commerce grew at double-digit rates until the recession of 2008–2009 when growth slowed to a crawl. In 2009, e-commerce revenues were flat (Figure 9.1), not bad considering that traditional retail sales were shrinking by 5 percent annually. In fact, e-commerce during the recession was the only stable segment in retail. Some online retailers forged ahead at a record pace: Amazon's 2009 revenues were up 25 percent over 2008 sales. Despite the recession, in 2011, the number of online buyers increased by 5 percent to 133 million, and the average annual purchase is up 8 percent to $1,270. Amazon's sales grew by an incredible 30% percent in the year.

Mirroring the history of many technological innovations, such as the telephone, radio, and television, the very rapid growth in e-commerce in the early years created a market bubble in e-commerce stocks. Like all bubbles, the "dot-com" bubble burst (in March 2001). A large number of e-commerce companies failed during this process. Yet for many others, such as Amazon, eBay, Expedia, and Google, the results have been more positive: soaring

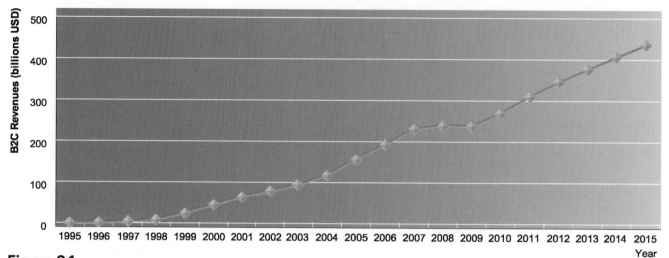

Figure 9.1
The Growth of E-commerce

Retail e-commerce revenues grew 15–25 percent per year until the recession of 2008–2009, when they slowed measurably. In 2011, e-commerce revenues are growing again at an estimated 14 percent annually.

revenues, fine-tuned business models that produce profits, and rising stock prices. By 2006, e-commerce revenues returned to solid growth, and have continued to be the fastest growing form of retail trade in the United States, Europe, and Asia.

- Online consumer sales grew to an estimated $309 billion in 2011, an increase of more than 14 percent over 2010 (including travel services and digital downloads), with 148 million people purchasing online and 178 million shopping and gathering information but not necessarily purchasing (eMarketer, 2011a).

- The number of individuals of all ages online in the United States expanded to 232 million in 2011, up from 147 million in 2004. In the world, over 2.1 billion people are now connected to the Internet. Growth in the overall Internet population has spurred growth in e-commerce (eMarketer, 2011b).

- Approximately 82.5 million households have broadband access to the Internet in 2011, representing about 68 percent of all households (96% of all Internet households).

- About 83 million Americans now access the Internet using a smartphone such as an iPhone, Droid, or BlackBerry. Mobile e-commerce has begun a rapid growth based on apps, ring tones, downloaded entertainment, and location-based services. Mobile commerce will add up to about $5.3 billion in 2011. Amazon sold $1 billion in retail goods to mobile users in 2010. In a few years, mobile phones will be the most common Internet access device.

- On an average day, an estimated 176 million adult U.S. Internet users go online. About 141 million send e-mail, 114 million use a search engine, and 95 million get news. Around 85 million use a social network, 60 million do online banking, 53 million watch an online video, and 39 million look for information on Wikipedia (Pew Internet & American Life Project, 2011).

- B2B e-commerce-use of the Internet for business-to-business commerce and collaboration among business partners expanded to more than $3.2 trillion.

The e-commerce revolution is still unfolding. Individuals and businesses will increasingly use the Internet to conduct commerce as more products and services come online and households switch to broadband telecommunications. More industries will be transformed by e-commerce, including travel reservations, music and entertainment, news, software, education, and finance. Table 9.1 highlights these new e-commerce developments.

TABLE 9.1

The Growth of E-commerce

Business Transformation

- E-commerce remains the fastest growing form of commerce when compared to physical retail stores, services, and entertainment.

- Social, mobile, and local commerce have become the fastest growing forms of e-commerce.

- The first wave of e-commerce transformed the business world of books, music, and air travel. In the second wave, nine new industries are facing a similar transformation scenario: marketing and advertising, telecommunications, movies, television, jewelry and luxury goods, real estate, online travel, bill payments, and software.

- The breadth of e-commerce offerings grows, especially in the services economy of social networking, travel, information clearinghouses, entertainment, retail apparel, appliances, and home furnishings.

- The online demographics of shoppers broaden to match that of ordinary shoppers.

- Pure e-commerce business models are refined further to achieve higher levels of profitability, whereas traditional retail brands, such as Sears, JCPenney, L.L.Bean, and Walmart, use e-commerce to retain their dominant retail positions.

- Small businesses and entrepreneurs continue to flood the e-commerce marketplace, often riding on the infrastructures created by industry giants, such as Amazon, Apple, and Google, and increasingly taking advantage of cloud-based computing resources.

- Mobile e-commerce begins to take off in the United States with location-based services and entertainment downloads including e-books.

Technology Foundations

- Wireless Internet connections (Wi-Fi, WiMax, and 3G/4G smartphones) grow rapidly.

- Powerful handheld mobile devices support music, Web surfing, and entertainment as well as voice communication. Podcasting and streaming take off as mediums for distribution of video, radio, and user-generated content.

- The Internet broadband foundation becomes stronger in households and businesses as transmission prices fall. More than 80 million households had broadband cable or DSL access to the Internet in 2011, about 68 percent of all households in the United States (eMarketer, 2011a).

- Social networking software and sites such as Facebook, MySpace, Twitter, LinkedIn, and thousands of others become a major new platform for e-commerce, marketing, and advertising. Facebook hits 800 million users worldwide, and 225 million in the United States (comScore, 2011).

- New Internet-based models of computing, such as smartphone apps, cloud computing, software as a service (SaaS), and Web 2.0 software greatly reduce the cost of e-commerce Web sites.

New Business Models Emerge

- More than half the Internet user population have joined an online social network, contribute to social bookmarking sites, create blogs, and share photos. Together these sites create a massive online audience as large as television that is attractive to marketers. In 2011, social networking accounts for an estimated 25 percent of online time.

- The traditional advertising industry is disrupted as online advertising grows twice as fast as TV and print advertising; Google, Yahoo!, and Facebook display nearly 1 trillion ads a year.

- Newspapers and other traditional media adopt online, interactive models but are losing advertising revenues to the online players despite gaining online readers. The New York Times adopts a paywall.

- Online entertainment business models offering television, movies, music, sports, and e-books surge, with cooperation among the major copyright owners in Hollywood and New York with the Internet distributors like Apple, Amazon, Google, YouTube, and Facebook.

WHY E-COMMERCE IS DIFFERENT

Why has e-commerce grown so rapidly? The answer lies in the unique nature of the Internet and the Web. Simply put, the Internet and e-commerce technologies are much more rich and powerful than previous technology revolutions like radio, television, and the telephone. Table 9.2 describes the unique features of the Internet and Web as a commercial medium. Let's explore each of these unique features in more detail.

Ubiquity

In traditional commerce, a marketplace is a physical place, such as a retail store, that you visit to transact business. E-commerce is ubiquitous, meaning that is it available just about everywhere, at all times. It makes it possible to shop from your desktop, at home, at work, or even from your car, using mobile commerce. The result is called a **marketspace**—a marketplace extended beyond traditional boundaries and removed from a temporal and geographic location.

TABLE 9.2

Eight Unique Features
of E-commerce
Technology

E-commerce Technology Dimension	Business Significance
Ubiquity. Internet/Web technology is available everywhere: at work, at home, and elsewhere via mobile devices. Mobile devices extend service to local areas and merchants.	The marketplace is extended beyond traditional boundaries and is removed from a temporal and geographic location. "Marketspace" anytime, is created; shopping can take place anywhere. Customer convenience is enhanced, and shopping costs are reduced.
Global reach. The technology reaches across national boundaries, around the Earth.	Commerce is enabled across cultural and national boundaries seamlessly and without modification. The marketspace includes, potentially, billions of consumers and millions of businesses worldwide.
Universal Standards. There is one set of technology standards, namely Internet standards.	With one set of technical standards across the globe, disparate computer systems can easily communicate with each other.
Richness. Video, audio, and text messages are possible.	Video, audio, and text marketing messages are integrated into a single marketing message and consumer experience.
Interactivity. The technology works through interaction with the user.	Consumers are engaged in a dialog that dynamically adjusts the experience to the individual, and makes the consumer a co-participant in the process of delivering goods to the market.
Information Density. The technology reduces information costs and raises quality.	Information processing, storage, and communication costs drop dramatically, whereas currency, accuracy, and timeliness improve greatly. Information becomes plentiful, cheap, and more accurate.
Personalization/Customization. The technology allows personalized messages to be delivered to individuals as well as groups.	Personalization of marketing messages and customization of products and services are based on individual characteristics.
Social Technology. User content generation and social networking.	New Internet social and business models enable user content creation and distribution, and support social networks.

From a consumer point of view, ubiquity reduces **transaction costs**—the costs of participating in a market. To transact business, it is no longer necessary that you spend time or money traveling to a market, and much less mental effort is required to make a purchase.

Global Reach

E-commerce technology permits commercial transactions to cross cultural and national boundaries far more conveniently and cost effectively than is true in traditional commerce. As a result, the potential market size for e-commerce merchants is roughly equal to the size of the world's online population (estimated to be more than 2 billion, and growing rapidly).

In contrast, most traditional commerce is local or regional—it involves local merchants or national merchants with local outlets. Television and radio stations and newspapers, for instance, are primarily local and regional institutions with limited, but powerful, national networks that can attract a national audience but not easily cross national boundaries to a global audience.

Universal Standards

One strikingly unusual feature of e-commerce technologies is that the technical standards of the Internet and, therefore, the technical standards for conducting e-commerce are universal standards. They are shared by all nations around the world and enable any computer to link with any other computer regardless of the technology platform each is using. In contrast, most traditional commerce technologies differ from one nation to the next. For instance, television and radio standards differ around the world, as does cell telephone technology.

The universal technical standards of the Internet and e-commerce greatly lower **market entry costs**—the cost merchants must pay simply to bring their goods to market. At the same time, for consumers, universal standards reduce **search costs**—the effort required to find suitable products.

Richness

Information **richness** refers to the complexity and content of a message. Traditional markets, national sales forces, and small retail stores have great richness: They are able to provide personal, face-to-face service using aural and visual cues when making a sale. The richness of traditional markets makes them powerful selling or commercial environments. Prior to the development of the Web, there was a trade-off between richness and reach: The larger the audience reached, the less rich the message. The Web makes it possible to deliver rich messages with text, audio, and video simultaneously to large numbers of people.

Interactivity

Unlike any of the commercial technologies of the twentieth century, with the possible exception of the telephone, e-commerce technologies are interactive, meaning they allow for two-way communication between merchant and consumer. Television, for instance, cannot ask viewers any questions or enter into conversations with them, and it cannot request that customer information be entered into a form. In contrast, all of these activities are possible on an e-commerce Web site. Interactivity allows an online merchant to engage a consumer in ways similar to a face-to-face experience but on a massive, global scale.

Information Density

The Internet and the Web vastly increase **information density**—the total amount and quality of information available to all market participants, consumers, and merchants alike. E-commerce technologies reduce information collection, storage, processing, and communication costs while greatly increasing the currency, accuracy, and timeliness of information.

Information density in e-commerce markets make prices and costs more transparent. **Price transparency** refers to the ease with which consumers can find out the variety of prices in a market; **cost transparency** refers to the ability of consumers to discover the actual costs merchants pay for products.

There are advantages for merchants as well. Online merchants can discover much more about consumers than in the past. This allows merchants to segment the market into groups that are willing to pay different prices and permits the merchants to engage in **price discrimination**—selling the same goods, or nearly the same goods, to different targeted groups at different prices. For instance, an online merchant can discover a consumer's avid interest in expensive, exotic vacations and then pitch high-end vacation plans to that consumer at a premium price, knowing this person is willing to pay extra for such a vacation. At the same time, the online merchant can pitch the same vacation plan at a lower price to a more price-sensitive consumer. Information density also helps merchants differentiate their products in terms of cost, brand, and quality.

Personalization/Customization

E-commerce technologies permit **personalization**: Merchants can target their marketing messages to specific individuals by adjusting the message to a person's click stream behavior, name, interests, and past purchases. The technology also permits **customization**—changing the delivered product or service based on a user's preferences or prior behavior. Given the interactive nature of e-commerce technology, much information about the consumer can be gathered in the marketplace at the moment of purchase. With the increase in information density, a great deal of information about the consumer's past purchases and behavior can be stored and used by online merchants.

The result is a level of personalization and customization unthinkable with traditional commerce technologies. For instance, you may be able to shape what you see on television by selecting a channel, but you cannot change the content of the channel you have chosen. In contrast, the *Wall Street Journal* Online allows you to select the type of news stories you want to see first and gives you the opportunity to be alerted when certain events happen.

Social Technology: User Content Generation and Social Networking

In contrast to previous technologies, the Internet and e-commerce technologies have evolved to be much more social by allowing users to create and share with their personal friends (and a larger worldwide community) content in the form of text, videos, music, or photos. Using these forms of communication, users are able to create new social networks and strengthen existing ones.

All previous mass media in modern history, including the printing press, use a broadcast model (one-to-many) where content is created in a central location by experts (professional writers, editors, directors, and producers) and audiences are concentrated in huge numbers to consume a standardized product. The new Internet and e-commerce empower users to create and distribute content on a large scale, and permit users to program their own content consumption. The Internet provides a unique many-to-many model of mass communications.

KEY CONCEPTS IN E-COMMERCE: DIGITAL MARKETS AND DIGITAL GOODS IN A GLOBAL MARKETPLACE

The location, timing, and revenue models of business are based in some part on the cost and distribution of information. The Internet has created a digital marketplace where millions of people all over the world are able to exchange massive amounts of information directly, instantly, and for free. As a result, the Internet has changed the way companies conduct business and increased their global reach.

The Internet reduces information asymmetry. An **information asymmetry** exists when one party in a transaction has more information that is important for the transaction than the other party. That information helps determine their relative bargaining power. In digital markets, consumers and suppliers can "see" the prices being charged for goods, and in that sense digital markets are said to be more "transparent" than traditional markets.

For example, before auto retailing sites appeared on the Web, there was a significant information asymmetry between auto dealers and customers. Only the auto dealers knew the manufacturers' prices, and it was difficult for consumers to shop around for the best price. Auto dealers' profit margins depended on this asymmetry of information. Today's consumers have access to a legion of Web sites providing competitive pricing information, and three-fourths of U.S. auto buyers use the Internet to shop around for the best deal. Thus, the Web has reduced the information asymmetry surrounding an auto purchase. The Internet has also helped businesses seeking to purchase from other businesses reduce information asymmetries and locate better prices and terms.

Digital markets are very flexible and efficient because they operate with reduced search and transaction costs, lower **menu costs** (merchants' costs of changing prices), greater price discrimination, and the ability to change prices dynamically based on market conditions. In **dynamic pricing**, the price of a product varies depending on the demand characteristics of the customer or the supply situation of the seller.

These new digital markets may either reduce or increase switching costs, depending on the nature of the product or service being sold, and they may cause some extra delay in gratification. Unlike a physical market, you can't immediately consume a product such as clothing purchased over the Web (although immediate consumption is possible with digital music downloads and other digital products.)

Digital markets provide many opportunities to sell directly to the consumer, bypassing intermediaries, such as distributors or retail outlets. Eliminating intermediaries in the distribution channel can significantly lower purchase transaction costs. To pay for all the steps in a traditional distribution channel, a product may have to be priced as high as 135 percent of its original cost to manufacture.

Figure 9.2 illustrates how much savings result from eliminating each of these layers in the distribution process. By selling directly to consumers or reducing the number of intermediaries, companies are able to raise profits while charging lower prices. The removal of organizations or business process layers responsible for intermediary steps in a value chain is called **disintermediation**.

Disintermediation is affecting the market for services. Airlines and hotels operating their own reservation sites online earn more per ticket because they have eliminated travel agents as intermediaries. Table 9.3 summarizes the differences between digital markets and traditional markets.

Digital Goods

The Internet digital marketplace has greatly expanded sales of digital goods. **Digital goods** are goods that can be delivered over a digital network. Music tracks, video, Hollywood movies, software, newspapers, magazines, and books can all be expressed, stored, delivered, and sold as purely digital products. Today all these products are delivered as digital streams or downloads, while their physical counterparts decline in sales.

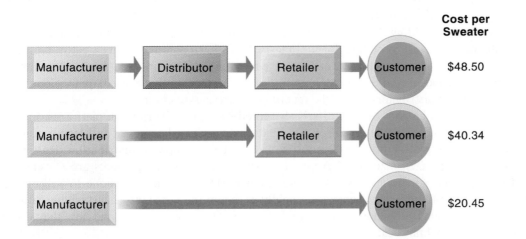

Cost per Sweater

Manufacturer → Distributor → Retailer → Customer $48.50

Manufacturer → Retailer → Customer $40.34

Manufacturer → Customer $20.45

Figure 9.2
The Benefits of Disintermediation to the Consumer
The typical distribution channel has several intermediary layers, each of which adds to the final cost of a product, such as a sweater. Removing layers lowers the final cost to the consumer.

	Digital Markets	**Traditional Market**
Information asymmetry	Asymmetry reduced	Asymmetry high
Search costs	Low	High
Transaction costs	Low (sometimes virtually nothing)	High (time, travel)
Delayed gratification	High (or lower in the case of a digital good)	Lower: purchase now
Menu costs	Low	High
Dynamic pricing	Low cost, instant	High cost, delayed
Price discrimination	Low cost, instant	High cost, delayed
Market segmentation	Low cost, moderate precision	High cost, less precision
Switching costs	Higher/lower (depending on product characteristics)	High
Network effects	Strong	Weaker
Disintermediation	More possible/likely	Less possible/unlikely

In general, for digital goods, the marginal cost of producing another unit is about zero (it costs nothing to make a copy of a music file). However, the cost of producing the original first unit is relatively high—in fact, it is nearly the total cost of the product because there are few other costs of inventory and distribution. Costs of delivery over the Internet are very low, marketing costs often remain the same, and pricing can be highly variable. (On the Internet, the merchant can change prices as often as desired because of low menu costs.)

The impact of the Internet on the market for these kinds of digital goods is nothing short of revolutionary, and we see the results around us every day. Businesses dependent on physical products for sales—such as bookstores, music stores, book publishers, music labels, and film studios—face the possibility of declining sales and even destruction of their businesses. Newspapers and magazines subscriptions to hard copies are declining, while online readership and subscriptions are expanding.

Total record label industry revenues have fallen by one-half since 2000, from $14.6 billion to $6.3 billion, due almost entirely to digital piracy (which accounts for 80 percent of all downloaded music in the United States) and the resulting decline in the CD sales. On the plus side, the Apple iTunes store has sold 15 billion songs for 99 cents each since opening in 2001, providing the industry with a digital distribution model that has restored some of the revenues lost to piracy. Since iTunes, illegal downloading has been cut in half, and legitimate online music sales are estimated to be over $4 billion in 2012. As cloud streaming services expand, illegal downloading will decline further. In that sense, Apple, along with other Internet distributors, saved the record labels from extinction.

Hollywood has not been similarly disrupted by digital distribution platforms, in part because it is more difficult to download high quality, pirated copies of full length movies. To avoid the fate of the music industry, it has struck lucrative distribution deals with Netflix, Google, Amazon, and Apple. Nevertheless, these arrangements are not enough to compensate for the loss in DVD sales (down 20 percent in 2011 alone to $28 billion worldwide), although this is changing rapidly as the online distributors start paying billions for high quality Hollywood content. Table 9.4 describes digital goods and how they differ from traditional physical goods.

	Digital Goods	Traditional Goods
Marginal cost/unit	Zero	Greater than zero , high
Cost of production	High (most of the cost)	Variable
Copying cost	Approximately zero	Greater than zero, high
Distributed delivery cost	Low	High
Inventory cost	Low	High
Marketing cost	Variable	Variable
Pricing	More variable (bundling, random pricing games)	Fixed, based on unit costs

TABLE 9.4

How the Internet Changes the Markets for Digital Goods

9.2 E-commerce: Business and Technology

E-commerce has grown from a few advertisements on early Web portals in 1995, to over 6 percent of all retail sales in 2010 (an estimated $309 billion), surpassing the mail order catalog business. E-commerce is a fascinating combination of business models and new information technologies. Let's start with a basic understanding of the types of e-commerce, and then describe e-commerce business and revenue models. We'll also cover new technologies that help companies reach over 232 million online consumers in the United States, and an estimated 2 billion more worldwide.

TYPES OF E-COMMERCE

There are many ways to classify electronic commerce transactions. One is by looking at the nature of the participants in the electronic commerce transaction. The three major electronic commerce categories are business-to-consumer (B2C) e-commerce, business-to-business (B2B) e-commerce, and consumer-to-consumer (C2C) e-commerce.

- **Business-to-consumer (B2C)** electronic commerce involves retailing products and services to individual shoppers. BarnesandNoble.com, which sells books, software, and music to individual consumers, is an example of B2C e-commerce.

- **Business-to-business (B2B)** electronic commerce involves sales of goods and services among businesses. ChemConnect's Web site for buying and selling chemicals and plastics is an example of B2B e-commerce.

- **Consumer-to-consumer (C2C)** electronic commerce involves consumers selling directly to consumers. For example, eBay, the giant Web auction site, enables people to sell their goods to other consumers by auctioning their merchandise off to the highest bidder, or for a fixed price. Craigslist is the most widely used platform used by consumers to buy from and sell directly to others.

Another way of classifying electronic commerce transactions is in terms of the platforms used by participants in a transaction. Until recently, most e-commerce transactions took place using a personal computer connected to the Internet over wired networks. Two wireless mobile alternatives have emerged: smartphones, tablet computers like iPads, and dedicated e-readers like the Kindle using cellular networks, and smartphones and small tablet computers using Wi-Fi wireless networks. The use of handheld wireless devices for purchasing goods and services from any location is termed **mobile commerce** or **m-commerce**. Both business-to-business and business-to-consumer e-commerce transactions can take place using m-commerce technology, which we discuss in detail in Section 9.3.

E-COMMERCE BUSINESS MODELS

Changes in the economics of information described earlier have created the conditions for entirely new business models to appear, while destroying older business models. Table 9.5 describes some of the most important Internet business models that have emerged. All, in one way or another, use the Internet to add extra value to existing products and services or to provide the foundation for new products and services.

Portal

Portals such as Google, Bing, Yahoo, MSN, and AOL offer powerful Web search tools as well as an integrated package of content and services, such as news, e-mail, instant messaging, maps, calendars, shopping, music downloads, video streaming, and more, all in one place. Initially, portals were primarily "gateways" to the Internet. Today, however, the portal business model provides a destination site where users start their Web searching and linger to read news, find entertainment, and meet other people, and be exposed to advertising. Portals generate revenue primarily by attracting very large audiences, charging advertisers for ad placement, collecting referral fees for steering customers to other sites, and charging for premium services. In 2011, portals generated an estimated $20 billion in revenues. Although there are hundreds of portal/search engine sites, the top five sites (Google, Yahoo, MSN/Bing, AOL, and Ask.com) gather more than 95 percent of the Internet traffic because of their superior brand recognition (eMarketer, 2011).

TABLE 9.5

Internet Business Models

Category	Description	Examples
E-tailer	Sells physical products directly to consumers or to individual businesses.	Amazon RedEnvelope.com
Transaction broker	Saves users money and time by processing online sales transactions and generating a fee each time a transaction occurs.	ETrade.com Expedia
Market creator	Provides a digital environment where buyers and sellers can meet, search for products, display products, and establish prices for those products. Can serve consumers or B2B e-commerce, generating revenue from transaction fees.	eBay Priceline.com
Content provider	Creates revenue by providing digital content, such as news, music, photos, or video, over the Web. The customer may pay to access the content, or revenue may be generated by selling advertising space.	WSJ.com GettyImages.com iTunes.com Games.com
Community provider	Provides an online meeting place where people with similar interests can communicate and find useful information.	Facebook Google+ iVillage, Twitter
Portal	Provides initial point of entry to the Web along with specialized content and other services.	Yahoo Bing Google
Service Provider	Provides Web 2.0 applications such as photo sharing, video sharing, and user-generated content as services. Provides other services such as online data storage and backup.	Google Apps Photobucket.com Box.net

E-tailer

Online retail stores, often called **e-tailers**, come in all sizes, from giant Amazon with 2011 revenues of more than $49 billion, to tiny local stores that have Web sites. An e-tailer is similar to the typical bricks-and-mortar storefront, except that customers only need to connect to the Internet to check their inventory and place an order. Altogether, online retail will generate about $188 billion in revenues for 2011. The value proposition of e-tailers is to provide convenient, low-cost shopping 24/7, offering large selections and consumer choice. Some e-tailers, such as Walmart.com or Staples.com, referred to as "bricks-and-clicks," are subsidiaries or divisions of existing physical stores and carry the same products. Others, however, operate only in the virtual world, without any ties to physical locations. Amazon, BlueNile.com, and Drugstore.com are examples of this type of e-tailer. Several other variations of e-tailers—such as online versions of direct mail catalogs, online malls, and manufacturer-direct online sales—also exist.

Content Provider

While e-commerce began as a retail product channel, it has increasingly turned into a global content channel. "Content" is defined broadly to include all forms of intellectual property. **Intellectual property** refers to all forms of human expression that can be put into a tangible medium such as text, CDs, DVDs, or stored on any digital (or other) media, including the Web. Content providers distribute information content, such as digital video, music, photos, text, and artwork, over the Web. The value proposition of online content providers is that consumers can find a wide range of content online, conveniently, and purchase this content inexpensively, to be played, or viewed, on multiple computer devices or smartphones.

Providers do not have to be the creators of the content (although sometimes they are, like Disney.com), and are more likely to be Internet-based distributors of content produced and created by others. For example, Apple sells music tracks at its iTunes Store, but it does not create or commission new music.

The phenomenal popularity of the iTunes Store, and Apple's Internet-connected devices like the iPhone, iPod, and iPad, have enabled new forms of digital content delivery from podcasting to mobile streaming. **Podcasting** is a method of publishing audio or video broadcasts via the Internet, allowing subscribing users to download audio or video files onto their personal computers or portable music players. **Streaming** is a publishing method for music and video files that flows a continuous stream of content to a user's device without being stored locally on the device.

Estimates vary, but total download, streaming, and subscription media revenues for 2011 are estimated at $14.2 billion annually. They are the fastest growing segment within e-commerce, growing at an estimated 20 percent annual rate (eMarketer, 2011).

Transaction Broker

Sites that process transactions for consumers normally handled in person, by phone, or by mail are transaction brokers. The largest industries using this model are financial services and travel services. The online transaction broker's primary value propositions are savings of money and time, as well as providing an extraordinary inventory of financial products and travel packages, in a single location. Online stock brokers and travel booking services charge fees that are considerably less than traditional versions of these services.

Market Creator

Market creators build a digital environment in which buyers and sellers can meet, display products, search for products, and establish prices. The value proposition of online market creators is that they provide a platform where sellers can easily display their wares and where purchasers can buy directly from sellers. Online auction markets like eBay and Priceline are good examples of the market creator business model. Another example is Amazon's Merchants platform (and similar programs at eBay) where merchants are allowed to set up stores on Amazon's Web site and sell goods at fixed prices to consumers. This is reminiscent of open air markets where the market creator operates a facility (a town square) where merchants and consumers meet. Online market creators will generate about $18 billion in revenues for 2011.

Service Provider

While e-tailers sell products online, service providers offer services online. There's been an explosion in online services. Web 2.0 applications, photo sharing, and online sites for data backup and storage all use a service provider business model. Software is no longer a physical product with a CD in a box, but increasingly software as a service (SaaS) that you subscribe to online rather than purchase from a retailer. Google has led the way in developing online software service applications such as Google Apps, Google Sites, Gmail, and online data storage services.

Community Provider

Community providers are sites that create a digital online environment where people with similar interests can transact (buy and sell goods); share interests, photos, videos; communicate with like-minded people; receive interest-related information; and even play out fantasies by adopting online personalities called avatars. The social networking sites Facebook, Google+, Tumblr, LinkedIn, and Twitter; online communities such as iVillage; and hundreds of other smaller, niche sites such as Doostang and Sportsvite all offer users community-building tools and services. Social networking sites have been the fastest growing Web sites in recent years, often doubling their audience size in a year. However, they are struggling to achieve profitability.

Finding and solidifying the right Internet business model is not always easy. The Interactive Session on Organizations describes how three retail giants-Walmart, Amazon, and eBay, are trying to refine their e-commerce business models as they compete with each other to dominate online retailing.

E-COMMERCE REVENUE MODELS

A firm's **revenue model** describes how the firm will earn revenue, generate profits, and produce a superior return on investment. Although there are many different e-commerce revenue models that have been developed, most companies rely on one, or some combination, of the following six revenue models: advertising, sales, subscription, free/freemium, transaction fee, and affiliate.

Advertising Revenue Model

In the **advertising revenue model**, a Web site generates revenue by attracting a large audience of visitors who can then be exposed to advertisements. The advertising model is the most widely used revenue model in e-commerce, and arguably, without advertising revenues, the Web would be a vastly different experience from what it is now. Content on the Web—everything from news to videos and opinions—is "free" to visitors because advertisers pay the production and distribution costs in return for the right to expose visitors to ads. Companies will spend an estimated $157 billion on advertising in 2011, and an estimated $31 billion of that amount on online advertising (in the form of a paid message on a Web site, paid search listing, video, app, game, or other online medium, such as instant messaging). In the last five years, advertisers have increased online spending and cut outlays on traditional channels such as radio and newspapers. Television advertising has expanded along with online advertising revenues.

Web sites with the largest viewership or that attract a highly specialized, differentiated viewership and are able to retain user attention ("stickiness") are able to charge higher advertising rates. Yahoo, for instance, derives nearly all its revenue from display ads (banner ads) and to a lesser extent search engine text ads. Ninety-eight percent of Google's revenue derives from selling keywords to advertisers in an auction-like market (the AdSense program). Facebook will display one-third of the trillion display ads shown on all sites in

INTERACTIVE SESSION: ORGANIZATIONS   Walmart, Amazon, and EBay: Who Will Dominate Internet Retailing?

Who's the leader in retail e-commerce? Of course, it's Amazon.com. Since the early 1990s, Amazon has grown from a small online bookseller to one of the largest retailing companies in the world, and easily the largest e-commerce retailer. Its constantly growing selection of goods (including books, electronics, clothing, and toys) and competitive prices have led many to refer to Amazon as "The Walmart of the Web."

In 2010, another company emerged as a serious challenger for that title: Walmart. Although Walmart is an e-commerce late-comer, the world's largest retailer has taken on Amazon in a battle for online e-tailing supremacy. Walmart has waged an all-out attack on Amazon in nearly every area of its business.

In 2011, eBay entered the retail e-commerce battle. EBay is the most successful Internet auction business, and a gigantic electronic marketplace hosting thousands of online storefronts all over the world. Founded in 1995, the company sells a staggeringly diverse array of goods and is one of the world's most easily recognizable Web sites. However, CEO John Donahoe and the rest of eBay's management have realized that e-commerce on the Web is increasingly shifting towards fixed prices and away from auctions and other alternative approaches, and the company has changed its business model and growth strategies accordingly.

In contrast with Amazon, Walmart was founded as a traditional, off-line, physical store, and has grown from a single general store managed by founder Sam Walton to thousands of stores worldwide. Based in Bentonville, Arkansas, Walmart earned $426 billion in revenues in 2010, which is about 12 times as much as Amazon's revenues over the same period.

Although Amazon and eBay are gnats compared to Walmart in terms of retail sales revenue, the battle for retail e-commerce on the Web gives them several advantages. Amazon and eBay have created recognizable and highly successful brands in online retailing. Amazon has developed extensive warehousing facilities, a powerful technology platform, and an extremely efficient distribution network specifically designed for Web shopping. EBay has a vast network of dedicated buyers and sellers, including nearly 100 million active auction users. When people think of online shopping, Amazon and eBay are the companies that come to mind, not Walmart.

However, Walmart has a powerful brand as a low-price retailer. Walmart has the flexibility to offer the lowest price on any given item because of its size. The company can lose money selling a hot product at extremely low margins and expect to make money on the strength of large quantities of other items it sells. Walmart's efficiency, flexibility, and ability to fine-tune its inventory to carry exactly what customers want have been enduring sources of competitive advantage. Walmart also has a significant physical presence, with stores all across the United States, and its stores provide the instant gratification of shopping, buying an item, and taking it home immediately, as opposed to waiting for a shipment when ordering from Amazon. (In a nod to Amazon, Walmart is testing home delivery of groceries and household supplies in local markets such as San Jose, California.)

Nevertheless, these advantages are less pronounced on the Web. In late 2009, Walmart.com began aggressively lowering prices on a wide variety of popular items, including books, electronics, and toys, making sure in each instance to undercut Amazon's price. Though Walmart's aggressive strategy is not sustainable over the long term, Walmart sees highly competitive price cuts as a way to gain market share quickly as it enters the online marketplace.

While Walmart looks to first attract site traffic with deep discounts and gradually increase its online audience, Amazon is working on expanding its selection of goods to be as exhaustive as Walmart's. Amazon has allowed third-party sellers to sell goods through its site, and it has beefed up its product selection via acquisitions like their 2009 purchase of online shoe shopping site Zappos.com, giving it an edge in footwear.

Amazon is spending much of its cash building more fulfillment centers, expanding its technology offerings, and building data centers. Amazon has continued to move beyond its traditional business of selling goods online in order to compete with Apple and Google in cloud computing services (see the Chapter 4 ending case) and digital entertainment. Amazon is confident that its investments will soon pay off.

EBay made a significant move towards retail e-commerce relevance in March 2011 with the acquisition of GSI Commerce, an online services company, for $2.4 billion. GSI manages the Web sites and online marketing campaigns for more than 180 top brands and large Web retailers, including Toys"R"Us, Aeropostale, Kenneth Cole, and many others. The acquisition demonstrated eBay's desire to grow beyond its network of individual sellers and create a retail e-commerce infrastructure that will allow it to keep pace with Amazon.

EBay further strengthened its e-commerce position in July 2011 by acquiring Zong, Inc., which allows people to charge online purchases to their mobile phone bills. This acquisition enables eBay's electronic payments unit PayPal to offer its users the option of paying for purchase using their mobile phone.

As more consumers shop online at retail sites instead of auctions, eBay has traditionally avoided stocking merchandise, shipping, and processing returns, but the acquisition of GSI will allow the company to manage orders for large retailers and to offer fulfillment services for small businesses, areas that have helped Amazon expand its product variety and earn loyal customers. GSI has seven warehouses that can stock merchandise, ship products, and track items as they travel. Rather than develop these capabilities from scratch, eBay wisely opted to acquire a company with significant expertise in the retail e-commerce sector. EBay would be able to boost its

already significant profits from its PayPal service on the sites of retailers that use GSI.

Amazon CEO Jeff Bezos is fond of describing the U.S. retail market as having "room for many winners", and this is likely to hold true for Walmart, Amazon, and eBay. Walmart and eBay may end up just enlarging the online retail market space, helping Amazon grow in the process. In the end, the real winners are likely to be American consumers.

Sources: Scott Morrison and Geoffrey A. Fowler, "Ebay Pushes into Amazon Turf," *Wall Street Journal*, March 29, 2011; Tess Stynes and Stu Woo, "EBay Set to Buy Payments Firm," *Wall Street Journal*, July 8, 2011; "Evelyn M. Rusli and Verne G. Kopytoff, "With GSI Deal, Ebay Shifts to Big Retail," *New York Times*, March 28, 2011; "Walmart Testing Home Delivery in California" Associated Press, April 24, 2011; May Martin Peers, "Rivals Explore Amazon's Territory," *Wall Street Journal*, January 7, 2010; and Brad Stone, "Can Amazon Be the Walmart of the Web?" September 20, 2009.

CASE STUDY QUESTIONS

1. Analyze each of these companies using the value chain and competitive forces models.

2. Compare the three companies' e-commerce business models. Which is the strongest? Explain your answer.

3. Which company is likely to have the strongest retail e-commerce growth in the future? Why?

MIS IN ACTION

Visit the Web sites of Amazon, Walmart, and eBay, then answer the following questions.

1. Compare the range of items offered for sale and the steps required to purchase an item of your choice at each of these sites. (Do not include eBay auctions, just goods available at a fixed price.) Which site has the greatest selection? Which site has the best prices, and which is easiest to use? What options are available for shipping or picking up your merchandise?

2. Which site would you use for your online shopping? Why?

2011. Facebook's users spend an average of over 8 hours a week on the site, far longer than other portal sites.

Sales Revenue Model
In the **sales revenue model**, companies derive revenue by selling goods, information, or services to customers. Companies such as Amazon (which sells books, music, and other products), LLBean.com, and Gap.com, all have sales revenue models. Content providers make money by charging for downloads of entire files such as music tracks (iTunes Store) or books, or for downloading music and/or video streams (Hulu.com TV shows). Apple has pioneered and strengthened the acceptance of micropayments. **Micropayment systems** provide content providers with a cost-effective method for processing high volumes of very small monetary transactions (anywhere from $.25 to $5.00 per transaction). MyMISLab has a Learning Track with more detail on micropayment and other e-commerce payment systems.

Subscription Revenue Model
In the **subscription revenue model**, a Web site offering content or services charges a subscription fee for access to some or all of its offerings on an ongoing basis. Content providers

often use this revenue model. For instance, the online version of *Consumer Reports* provides access to premium content, such as detailed ratings, reviews, and recommendations, only to subscribers, who have a choice of paying a $5.95 monthly subscription fee or a $26.00 annual fee. Netflix is one of the most successful subscriber sites with more that 24 million subscribers in September 2011. The Wall Street Journal has the largest online subscription newspaper with more than 1 million online subscribers. To be successful, the subscription model requires that the content be perceived as a having high added value, differentiated, and not readily available elsewhere nor easily replicated. Companies successfully offering content or services online on a subscription basis include Match.com and eHarmony (dating services), Ancestry.com and Genealogy.com (genealogy research), Microsoft's Xboxlive. com (video games), and Rhapsody.com (music).

Free/Fremium Revenue Model

In the **free/freemium revenue model**, firms offer basic services or content for free, while charging a premium for advanced or special features. For example, Google offers free applications, but charges for premium services. Pandora, the subscription radio service, offers a free service with limited play time, and a premium service with unlimited play. The Flickr photo-sharing service offers free basic services for sharing photos with friends and family, and also sells a $24.95 "premium" package that provides users unlimited storage, high-definition video storage and playback, and freedom from display advertising. The idea is to attract very large audiences with free services, and then to convert some of this audience to pay a subscription for premium services. One problem with this model is converting people from being "free loaders" into paying customers. "Free" can be a powerful model for losing money.

Transaction Fee Revenue Model

In the **transaction fee revenue model**, a company receives a fee for enabling or executing a transaction. For example, eBay provides an online auction marketplace and receives a small transaction fee from a seller if the seller is successful in selling an item. E*Trade, an online stockbroker, receives transaction fees each time it executes a stock transaction on behalf of a customer. The transaction revenue model enjoys wide acceptance in part because the true cost of using the platform is not immediately apparent to the user.

Affiliate Revenue Model

In the **affiliate revenue model**, Web sites (called "affiliate Web sites") send visitors to other Web sites in return for a referral fee or percentage of the revenue from any resulting sales. For example, MyPoints makes money by connecting companies to potential customers by offering special deals to its members. When members take advantage of an offer and make a purchase, they earn "points" they can redeem for free products and services, and MyPoints receives a referral fee. Community feedback sites such as Epinions and Yelp receive much of their revenue from steering potential customers to Web sites where they make a purchase. Amazon uses affiliates who steer business to the Amazon Web site by placing the Amazon logo on their blogs. Personal blogs may be involved in affiliate marketing. Some bloggers are paid directly by manufacturers, or receive free products, for speaking highly of products and providing links to sales channels.

WEB 2.0, SOCIAL NETWORKING AND THE WISDOM OF CROWDS

One of the fastest growing areas of e-commerce revenues are Web 2.0 online services, which we described in Chapter 6. The most popular Web 2.0 service is social networking, online meeting places where people can meet their friends and their friends' friends. Every day over 60 million Internet users in the United States visit a social networking site like Facebook, Google+, Tumblr, MySpace, LinkedIn, and hundreds of others.

Social networking sites link people through their mutual business or personal connections, enabling them to mine their friends (and their friends' friends) for sales leads, job-hunting tips, or new friends. Google+, MySpace, Facebook, and Friendster appeal to people who are primarily interested in extending their friendships, while LinkedIn focuses on job networking for professionals.

At **social shopping** sites like Kaboodle, ThisNext, and Stylehive, you can swap shopping ideas with friends. Facebook offers this same service on a voluntary basis. Online communities are also ideal venues to employ viral marketing techniques. Online viral marketing is like traditional word-of-mouth marketing except that the word can spread across an online community at the speed of light, and go much further geographically than a small network of friends.

The Wisdom of Crowds

Creating sites where thousands, even millions, of people can interact offers business firms new ways to market and advertise, to discover who likes (or hates) their products. In a phenomenon called "the **wisdom of crowds**," some argue that large numbers of people can make better decisions about a wide range of topics or products than a single person or even a small committee of experts (Surowiecki, 2004).

Obviously this is not always the case, but it can happen in interesting ways. In marketing, the wisdom of crowds concept suggests that firms should consult with thousands of their customers first as a way of establishing a relationship with them, and second, to better understand how their products and services are used and appreciated (or rejected). Actively soliciting the comments of your customers builds trust and sends the message to your customers that you care what they are thinking, and that you need their advice.

Beyond merely soliciting advice, firms can be actively helped in solving some business problems using what is called **crowdsourcing**. For instance, in 2006, Netflix announced a contest in which it offered to pay $1 million to the person or team who comes up with a method for improving by 10 percent Netflix's prediction of what movies customers would like as measured against their actual choices. By 2009, Netflix received 44,014 entries from 5,169 teams in 186 countries. The winning team improved a key part of Netflix's business: a recommender system that recommends to its customers what new movies to order based on their personal past movie choices and the choices of millions of other customers who are like them (Howe, 2008; Resnick and Varian, 1997).

Firms can also use the wisdom of crowds in the form of prediction markets. **Prediction markets** are established as peer-to-peer betting markets where participants make bets on specific outcomes of, say, quarterly sales of a new product, designs for new products, or political elections. The world's largest commercial prediction market is Betfair, founded in 2000, where you bet for or against specific outcomes on football games, horse races, and whether or not the Dow Jones will go up or down in a single day. Iowa Electronic Markets (IEM) is an academic market focused on elections. You can place bets on the outcome of local and national elections.

E-COMMERCE MARKETING

While e-commerce and the Internet have changed entire industries and enabled new business models, no industry has been more affected than marketing and marketing communications. The Internet provides marketers with new ways of identifying and communicating with millions of potential customers at costs far lower than traditional media, including search engine marketing, data mining, recommender systems, and targeted e-mail. The Internet enables **long tail marketing**. Before the Internet, reaching a large audience was very expensive, and marketers had to focus on attracting the largest number of consumers with popular hit products, whether music, Hollywood movies, books, or cars. In contrast, the Internet allows marketers to inexpensively find potential customers for which demand is very low, people on the far ends of the bell (normal) curve. For instance, the Internet makes it possible to sell independent music profitably to very small audiences. There's always some demand for almost any product. Put a string of such long tail sales together and you have a profitable business.

The Internet also provides new ways—often instantaneous and spontaneous—to gather information from customers, adjust product offerings, and increase customer value. Table 9.6 describes the leading marketing and advertising formats used in e-commerce.

Many e-commerce marketing firms use behavioral targeting techniques to increase the effectiveness of banner, rich media, and video ads. **Behavioral targeting** refers to tracking the clickstreams (history of clicking behavior) of individuals on thousands of Web sites for the purpose of understanding their interests and intentions, and exposing them to advertisements that are uniquely suited to their behavior. Proponents believe this more precise understanding of the customer leads to more efficient marketing (the firm pays for ads only to those shoppers who are most interested in their products) and larger sales and revenues. Unfortunately, behavioral targeting of millions of Web users also leads to the invasion of personal privacy without user consent. When consumers lose trust in their Web experience, they tend not to purchase anything.

Behavioral targeting takes place at two levels: at individual Web sites and on various advertising networks that track users across thousands of Web sites. All Web sites collect data on visitor browser activity and store it in a database. They have tools to record the site that users visited prior to coming to the Web site, where these users go when they leave that site, the type of operating system they use, browser information, and even some location data. They also record the specific pages visited on the particular site, the time spent on each page of the site, the types of pages visited, and what the visitors purchased (see Figure 9.3). Firms analyze this information about customer interests and behavior to develop precise profiles of existing and potential customers. In addition, most major Web sites have hundreds of tracking programs on their home pages, which track your clickstream behavior across the Web by following you from site to site.

Marketing Format	2011 Revenue	Description
Search engine	$14.3	Text ads targeted at precisely what the customer is looking for at the moment of shopping and purchasing. Sales oriented.
Display ads	$7.6	Banner ads (pop-ups and leave-behinds) with interactive features; increasingly behaviorally targeted to individual Web activity. Brand development and sales.
Classified	$3.0	Job, real estate, and services ads; interactive, rich media, and personalized to user searches. Sales and branding.
Video	$2.2	Fastest growing format, engaging and entertaining; behaviorally targeted, interactive. Branding and sales.
Rich media	$1.66	Animations, games, and puzzles. Interactive, targeted, and entertaining. Branding orientation.
Affiliate and blog marketing	$1.42	Blog and Web site marketing steers customers to parent sites; interactive, personal, and often with video. Sales orientation.
Sponsorships	$.91	Online games, puzzles, contests, and coupon sites sponsored by firms to promote products. Sales orientation.
E-mail	$.16	Effective, targeted marketing tool with interactive and rich media potential. Sales oriented.

TABLE 9.6

Online Marketing and Advertising Formats Revenue (Billions)

Figure 9.3
Web Site Visitor Tracking
E-commerce Web sites have tools to track a shopper's every step through an online store and then across the Web as shoppers move from site to site. Close examination of customer behavior at a Web site selling women's clothing shows what the store might learn at each step and what actions it could take to increase sales.

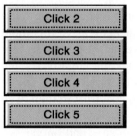

The shopper clicks on the home page. The store can tell that the shopper arrived from the Yahoo! portal at 2:30 PM (which might help determine staffing for customer service centers) and how long she lingered on the home page (which might indicate trouble navigating the site). Tracking beacons load cookies on the shopper's browser to follow her across the Web.

The shopper clicks on blouses, clicks to select a woman's white blouse, then clicks to view the same item in pink. The shopper clicks to select this item in a size 10 in pink and clicks to place it in her shopping cart. This information can help the store determine which sizes and colors are most popular. If the visitor moves to a different site, ads for pink blouses will appear from the same or different vendor.

From the shopping cart page, the shopper clicks to close the browser to leave the Web site without purchasing the blouse. This action could indicate the shopper changed her mind or that she had a problem with the Web site's checkout and payment process. Such behavior might signal that the Web site was not well designed.

This information enables firms to understand how well their Web site is working, create unique personalized Web pages that display content or ads for products or services of special interest to each user, improve the customer's experience, and create additional value through a better understanding of the shopper (see Figure 9.4). By using personalization technology to modify the Web pages presented to each customer, marketers achieve some of the benefits of using individual salespeople at dramatically lower costs. For instance, General Motors will show a Chevrolet banner ad to women emphasizing safety and utility, while men will receive different ads emphasizing power and ruggedness.

Figure 9.4
Web Site Personalization
Firms can create unique personalized Web pages that display content or ads for products or services of special interest to individual users, improving the customer experience and creating additional value.

What if you are a large national advertising company with many different clients trying to reach millions of consumers? What if you were a large global manufacturer trying to reach potential consumers for your products? With millions of Web sites, working with each one would be impractical. Advertising networks solve this problem by creating a network of several thousand of the most popular Web sites visited by millions of people, tracking the behavior of these users across the entire network, building profiles of each user, and then selling these profiles to advertisers. Popular Web sites download dozens of Web tracking cookies, bugs, and beacons, which report user online behavior to remote servers without the users' knowledge. Looking for young, single consumers, with college degrees, living in the Northeast, in the 18–34 age range who are interested purchasing a European car? Not a problem. Advertising networks can identify and deliver hundreds of thousands of people who fit this profile and expose them to ads for European cars as they move from one Web site to another. Estimates vary, but behaviorally targeted ads are 10 times more likely to produce a consumer response than a randomly chosen banner or video ad (see Figure 9.5). So-called advertising exchanges use this same technology to auction access to people with very specific profiles to advertisers in a few milliseconds. In 2011, about 20 percent of display ads are targeted, and the rest depend on the context of the pages shoppers visit or the estimated demographics of visitors.

Social E-commerce and Social Network Marketing

Social e-commerce is commerce based on the idea of the digital **social graph**. The digital social graph is a mapping of all significant online social relationships. The social graph is synonymous with the idea of a "social network" used to describe offline relationships. You can map your own social graph (network) by drawing lines from yourself to the 10 closest people you know. If they know one another, draw lines between these people. If you are ambitious, ask these 10 friends to list and draw in the names of the 10 people closest to them. What emerges from this exercise is a preliminary map of your social network. Now imagine if everyone on the Internet did the same, and posted the results to a very large database with a Web site. Ultimately, you would end up with Facebook or a site like it. The collection of all these personal social networks is called "the social graph."

According to small world theory, you are only six links away from any other person on earth. If you entered your personal address book, say 100 names, on to a list and sent it to your friends, and they in turn entered 50 new names of their friends, and so on, six times, the social network created would encompass 31 billion people! The social graph is therefore

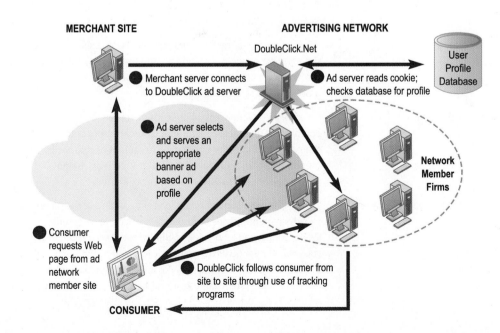

MERCHANT SITE

ADVERTISING NETWORK

DoubleClick.Net

- Merchant server connects to DoubleClick ad server
- Ad server reads cookie; checks database for profile

User Profile Database

- Ad server selects and serves an appropriate banner ad based on profile

Network Member Firms

- Consumer requests Web page from ad network member site

- DoubleClick follows consumer from site to site through use of tracking programs

CONSUMER

Figure 9.5
How an Advertising Network such as DoubleClick Works
Advertising networks and their use of tracking programs have become controversial among privacy advocates because of their ability to track individual consumers across the Internet.

a collection of millions of personal social graphs (and all the people in them). So it's a small world indeed, and we are all more closely linked than we ever thought.

Ultimately, you will find that you are directly connected to many friends and relatives, and indirectly connected to an even larger universe of indirect friends and relatives (your distant second and third cousins, and their friends). Theoretically, it takes six links for anyone person to find another person anywhere on earth.

If you understand the inter-connectedness of people, you will see just how important this concept is to e-commerce: the products and services you buy will influence the decisions of your friends, and their decisions will in turn influence you. If you are a marketer trying to build and strengthen a brand the implication is clear: take advantage of the fact that people are enmeshed in social networks, share interests and values, and communicate and influence one another. As a marketer your target audience is not a million isolated people watching a TV show, but the social network of people who watch the show, and the viewers' personal networks. Table 9.7 describes four features of social commerce that are driving its growth.

In 2011 and 2012, one of the fastest growing media for branding and marketing is social media. Expenditures for social media marketing are much smaller than television, magazines, and even newspapers, but this will change in the future. Social networks in the offline world are collections of people who voluntarily communicate with one another over an extended period of time. Online social networks, such as Facebook, MySpace, LinkedIn, Twitter, Tumblr, and Google's new Google+, along with tens of other sites with social components, are Web sites that enable users to communicate with one another, form group and individual relationships, and share interests, values, and ideas. Individuals establish online profiles with text and photos, creating an online profile of how they want others to see them, and then invite their friends to link to their profile. The network grows by word of mouth and through e-mail links. One of the most ubiquitous graphical elements on Web sites in 2011 is Facebook's "Like" button, which allows users to tell their friends they like a product, service, or content.

TABLE 9.7

Features of Social Commerce

Social Commerce Feature	Description
Social sign-on	Web sites allow users to sign into their sites through their social network pages on Facebook or another social site. This allows Web sites to receive valuable social profile information from Facebook and use it in their own marketing efforts.
Collaborative shopping	Creating an environment where consumers can share their shopping experiences with one another by viewing products, chatting, or texting. Friends can chat online about brands, products, and services.
Network notification	Creating an environment where consumers can share their approval (or disapproval) of products, services, or content, or share their geo-location, perhaps a restaurant or club, with friends. Facebook's ubiquitous "Like" button is an example. Twitter tweets and followers are another example.
Social search (recommendations)	Enabling an environment where consumers can ask their friends for advice on purchases of products, services, and content. While Google can help you find things, social search can help you evaluate the quality of things by listening to the evaluations of your friends, or their friends. For instance, Amazon's social recommender system can use your Facebook social profile to recommend products.

While Facebook with 162 million U.S. monthly visitors receives most of the public attention given to social networking, the other top four social sites are growing very rapidly with the exception of MySpace. LinkedIn has grown 58 percent in 2011 to reach 34 million; Twitter grew 13 percent in 2011 to reach 27 million; and the social blogging site Tumblr reached 10 million people a month, growing 166 percent that year. MySpace, in contrast, has been shrinking but nevertheless attracted 40 million visitors a month in 2011. According to ComScore, about 16 percent of the total time spent online in the United States was spent on social network sites, up from around 8 percent in 2007 (ComScore, 2011). The fastest growing smartphone applications are social network apps: about 30 percent of smartphone users use their phones to visit social sites.

Marketers cannot ignore these huge audiences which rival television and radio in size. Eighty percent of U.S. business firms now have Facebook pages, and a presence on many other social network sites. Marketers will spend over $3 billion on social network marketing in 2011 (twice the level of 2010), about 10 percent of all online marketing. (eMarketer Inc., 2011).

Marketing with social media is still in its very early stages, and companies are experimenting in hopes of finding a winning formula. Social interactions and customer sentiment are not always easy to manage, presenting new challenges for companies eager to protect their brands. The Interactive Session on People provides specific examples of companies' social marketing efforts using Facebook and Twitter.

B2B E-COMMERCE: NEW EFFICIENCIES AND RELATIONSHIPS

The trade between business firms (business-to-business commerce or B2B) represents a huge marketplace. The total amount of B2B trade in the United States in 2010 was about $16 trillion, with B2B e-commerce (online B2B) contributing about $3.3 trillion of that amount (U.S. Census Bureau, 2011; authors' estimates). By 2016, B2B e-commerce should grow to about $4.4 trillion in the United States. The process of conducting trade among business firms is complex and requires significant human intervention, and therefore, it consumes significant resources. Some firms estimate that each corporate purchase order for support products costs them, on average, at least $100 in administrative overhead. Administrative overhead includes processing paper, approving purchase decisions, spending time using the telephone and fax machines to search for products and arrange for purchases, arranging for shipping, and receiving the goods. Across the economy, this adds up to trillions of dollars annually being spent for procurement processes that could potentially be automated. If even just a portion of inter-firm trade were automated, and parts of the entire procurement process assisted by the Internet, literally trillions of dollars might be released for more productive uses, consumer prices potentially would fall, productivity would increase, and the economic wealth of the nation would expand. This is the promise of B2B e-commerce. The challenge of B2B e-commerce is changing existing patterns and systems of procurement, and designing and implementing new Internet-based B2B solutions.

Business-to-business e-commerce refers to the commercial transactions that occur among business firms. Increasingly, these transactions are flowing through a variety of different Internet-enabled mechanisms. About 80 percent of online B2B e-commerce is still based on proprietary systems for **electronic data interchange (EDI)**. Electronic data interchange enables the computer-to-computer exchange between two organizations of standard transactions such as invoices, bills of lading, shipment schedules, or purchase orders. Transactions are automatically transmitted from one information system to another through a network, eliminating the printing and handling of paper at one end and the inputting of data at the other. Each major industry in the United States and much of the rest of the world has EDI standards that define the structure and information fields of electronic documents for that industry.

EDI originally automated the exchange of documents such as purchase orders, invoices, and shipping notices. Although some companies still use EDI for document automation,

INTERACTIVE SESSION: PEOPLE   Social Commerce Creates New Customer Relationships

To most people, Facebook and Twitter are ways to keep in touch with friends and to let them know what they are doing. For companies of all shapes and sizes, however, Facebook and Twitter have become powerful tools for engaging customers. Location-based businesses like gourmet food trucks can tweet their current location to loyal followers and fans. Appointment-based businesses can easily tweet or post cancellations and unexpected openings. Larger companies run sweepstakes and promotions. And companies of all sizes have an opportunity to shape the perception of their brands and to solidify relationships with their customers.

Companies are rolling out ads that capitalize on the social media features of Facebook to achieve greater visibility. For example, many Facebook ads feature the ability to "Like" a brand, send a virtual gift, answer a poll question, or instantly stream information to your news feed. Twitter has developed many new offerings to interested advertisers, like Promoted Tweets and Promoted Trends. These features give advertisers the ability to have their tweets displayed more prominently when Twitter users search for certain keywords.

Levi's was one of the first national brands to use Facebook and Twitter to allow consumers to socialize and share their purchases with friends. The Levi's Facebook page has posted 500,000 "Like" messages posted by friends sharing their favorite jeans. Within the first week of its share campaign, Levis received 4,000 "Likes." The company began using Twitter in 2010 by creating a "Levi's Guy," 23-year-old USC graduate Gareth, to interest customers. He has over 6,000 followers and is responsible for responding to queries and engaging in conversations about the Levi's brand on Twitter. In 2011, the company created a personalized Friends Store where shoppers can see what their friends "Liked" and bought.

Ben and Jerry's contracted with Facebook to run a promotion in tandem with an ice cream giveaway at their physical stores. The ice cream chain made 250,000 virtual ice cream cones available to Facebook users from the company page. Fans quickly scooped them up, so Ben and Jerry's bought another 250,000 virtual cones, and by day's end, those were gone too. Ben and Jerry's Web site saw a marked increase in traffic and in participation in their free cone day. The viral ad campaign went exactly as planned and was a great success.

The all-purpose electronics retailer Best Buy has 4.6 million fans on Facebook and 200,000 followers on Twitter. Best Buy uses a dedicated team of Twitter responders, called the "Twelp Force," to answer user questions and respond to complaints. Because Best Buy has so many social media followers who generate feedback on social networks and related sites, the company uses text mining to gather these data and convert them to useful information. Best Buy has a central analytical platform that can analyze any kind of unstructured data it supplies. The company uses that information to gauge the success of promotions, which products are hot and which are duds, and the impact of advertising campaigns.

Rosetta Stone has used Facebook's targeting capabilities to determine which types of people respond to the various ads it has created. Rosetta Stone designed a series of advertisements for its language-learning products with Webtrends, Inc., and launched the ads on Facebook. Using Facebook analytics, Rosetta Stone found that some of its ads were much more successful among particular kinds of users. For example, the company found that its ads featuring pictures of a brain appealed to Facebook users interested in Mensa, the high IQ society and other intellectual pursuits. By serving Facebook ads only to the groups of people to whom they were most attractive, Rosetta Stone experienced a tripling in advertisement performance compared to previous campaigns.

Many companies are running online ads that focus less on pitching their products than on promoting their Facebook pages and Twitter accounts. The ads feature menu tabs and allow users to click within the ad to see a brand's Twitter messages or Facebook wall posts in real time, or to watch a brand's video content from YouTube—all within the Web page where the ad appears. Incorporating live content from Facebook and Twitter makes online ads appear less "static" and more current than other content.

For example, a recent online ad for the Mrs. Meyers cleaning brand stating "Clean should smell better" instructed users to "hover to expand." When a cursor was placed over the ad, it exposed an area that displayed Facebook wall posts, Twitter postings about Mrs. Meyers, or a company video, all without leaving the Web page being visited. Consumers spent an average of 30 seconds interacting with the ad, compared to 11 seconds for other types of online ads, according to Google. Consumers were also more likely to click on a "learn more" button to go to Mrs. Meyers' own Web site, with 35 of every 1,000 users clicking through, compared with an average of just one in 1,000 for traditional online ads.

Even if the Facebook or Twitter postings in ads show brands apologizing about missteps or customer complaints, advertisers may still benefit. Today, the more honest and human companies appear, the more likely consumers are to like them and stick with them. Still, the results can be unpredictable, and not always beneficial, as Starbucks learned. Starbucks runs contests on Twitter regularly and uses the service to spread free product samples. In 2009, Starbucks launched a social media contest, which was essentially a scavenger hunt for advertising posters. Users who found the posters and posted photos of them on Twitter would win a prize. The campaign backfired. At the urging of anti-Starbucks protesters, users flooded Starbucks' Twitter feed with pictures of employees and protesters holding signs criticizing Starbucks' labor practices.

Sources: Andrew Adam Newman, "Brands Now Direct Their Followers to Social Media," *New York Times*, August 3, 2011; Geoffrey A. Fowler, "Are You Talking to Me?" *Wall Street Journal*, April 25, 2011; Amir Efrati, "Twitter Tests New Ad Types," *Wall Street Journal*, July 29, 2011; "In a Few Words, Growth," *Wall Street Journal*, June 6, 2011; "Starbucks and Twitter: Hash Tag Hell," Viva Visibility, vivavisibilityblog.com/hash-tag-hell/; and "Anti-Starbucks Filmmakers Hijack the Coffee Company's Own Twitter Marketing Campaign," bloggasm.com, May 21, 2009.

CASE STUDY QUESTIONS

1. Assess the people, organization, and technology issues for using social media to engage with customers.

2. What are the advantages and disadvantages of using social media for advertising, brand building, market research, and customer service?

3. Should all companies use Facebook and Twitter for customer service and advertising? Why or why not? What kinds of companies are best suited to use these platforms?

MIS IN ACTION

Visit the Facebook and Twitter pages of Levi's, Starbucks, or another company of your choice. Describe all of the ways the company is using its presence at these sites for engaging with customers, and their business benefits.

firms engaged in just-in-time inventory replenishment and continuous production use EDI as a system for continuous replenishment. Suppliers have online access to selected parts of the purchasing firm's production and delivery schedules and automatically ship materials and goods to meet prespecified targets without intervention by firm purchasing agents (see Figure 9.6).

Although many organizations still use private networks for EDI, they are increasingly Web-enabled because Internet technology provides a much more flexible and low-cost platform for linking to other firms. Businesses are able to extend digital technology to a wider range of activities and broaden their circle of trading partners.

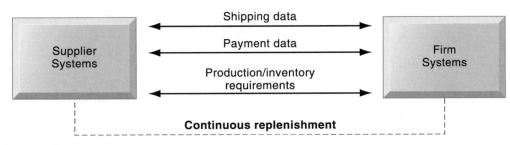

Figure 9.6
Electronic Data Interchange (EDI)

Companies use EDI to automate transactions for B2B e-commerce and continuous inventory replenishment. Suppliers can automatically send data about shipments to purchasing firms. The purchasing firms can use EDI to provide production and inventory requirements and payment data to suppliers.

Take procurement, for example. Procurement involves not only purchasing goods and materials but also sourcing, negotiating with suppliers, paying for goods, and making delivery arrangements. Businesses can now use the Internet to locate the lowest-cost supplier, search online catalogs of supplier products, negotiate with suppliers, place orders, make payments, and arrange transportation. They are not limited to partners linked by traditional EDI networks.

The Internet and Web technology enable businesses to create new electronic storefronts for selling to other businesses with multimedia graphic displays and interactive features similar to those for B2C commerce. Alternatively, businesses can use Internet technology to create extranets or electronic marketplaces for linking to other businesses for purchase and sale transactions.

Private industrial networks typically consist of a large firm using a secure Web site to link to its suppliers and other key business partners (see Figure 9.7). The network is owned by the buyer, and it permits the firm and designated suppliers, distributors, and other business partners to share product design and development, marketing, production scheduling, inventory management, and unstructured communication, including graphics and e-mail. Another term for a private industrial network is a **private exchange.**

An example is VW Group Supply, which links the Volkswagen Group and its suppliers. VW Group Supply handles 90 percent of all global purchasing for Volkswagen, including all automotive and parts components.

Net marketplaces, which are sometimes called e-hubs, provide a single, digital marketplace based on Internet technology for many different buyers and sellers (see Figure 9.8). They are industry owned or operate as independent intermediaries between buyers and sellers. Net marketplaces generate revenue from purchase and sale transactions and other services provided to clients. Participants in Net marketplaces can establish prices through online negotiations, auctions, or requests for quotations, or they can use fixed prices.

There are many different types of Net marketplaces and ways of classifying them. Some Net marketplaces sell direct goods and some sell indirect goods. *Direct goods* are goods used in a production process, such as sheet steel for auto body production. *Indirect goods* are all other goods not directly involved in the production process, such as office supplies or products for maintenance and repair. Some Net marketplaces support contractual purchasing based on long-term relationships with designated suppliers, and others support short-term spot purchasing, where goods are purchased based on immediate needs, often from many different suppliers.

Figure 9.7
A Private Industrial Network
A private industrial network, also known as a private exchange, links a firm to its suppliers, distributors, and other key business partners for efficient supply chain management and other collaborative commerce activities.

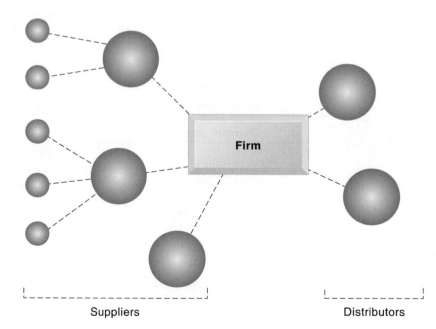

Suppliers   Distributors

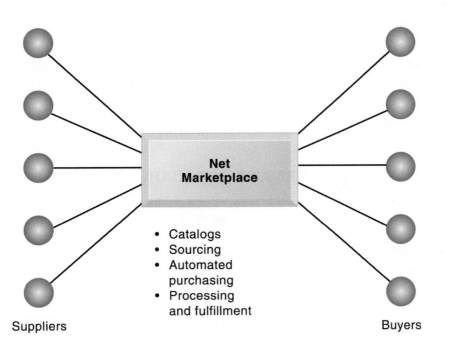

Figure 9.8
A Net Marketplace
Net marketplaces are online marketplaces where multiple buyers can purchase from multiple sellers.

Net
Marketplace

- Catalogs
- Sourcing
- Automated purchasing
- Processing and fulfillment

Suppliers   Buyers

Some Net marketplaces serve vertical markets for specific industries, such as automobiles, telecommunications, or machine tools, whereas others serve horizontal markets for goods and services that can be found in many different industries, such as office equipment or transportation.

Exostar is an example of an industry-owned Net marketplace, focusing on long-term contract purchasing relationships and on providing common networks and computing platforms for reducing supply chain inefficiencies. This aerospace and defense industry-sponsored Net marketplace was founded jointly by BAE Systems, Boeing, Lockheed Martin, Raytheon, and Rolls-Royce plc to connect these companies to their suppliers and facilitate collaboration. More than 70,000 trading partners in the commercial, military, and government sectors use Exostar's sourcing, e-procurement, and collaboration tools for both direct and indirect goods.

Exchanges are independently owned third-party Net marketplaces that connect thousands of suppliers and buyers for spot purchasing. Many exchanges provide vertical markets for a single industry, such as food, electronics, or industrial equipment, and they primarily deal with direct inputs. For example, Go2Paper enables a spot market for paper, board, and kraft among buyers and sellers in the paper industries from over 75 countries.

Exchanges proliferated during the early years of e-commerce but many have failed. Suppliers were reluctant to participate because the exchanges encouraged competitive bidding that drove prices down and did not offer any long-term relationships with buyers or services to make lowering prices worthwhile. Many essential direct purchases are not conducted on a spot basis because they require contracts and consideration of issues such as delivery timing, customization, and quality of products..

9.3 The Mobile Digital Platform and Mobile E-commerce

Walk down the street in any major metropolitan area and count how many people are pecking away at their iPhones or BlackBerrys. Ride the trains, fly the planes, and you'll see your fellow travelers reading an online newspaper, watching a video on their phone, or reading a novel on their Kindle. In five years, the majority of Internet users in the United States will rely on mobile devices as their primary device for accessing the Internet. M-commerce has taken off.

In 2011, m-commerce represented less than 10 percent of all e-commerce, with about $5.3 billion in annual revenues generated by selling music, videos, ring tones, applications, movies, television, and location-based services like local restaurant locators and traffic updates. However, m-commerce is the fastest growing form of e-commerce, with some areas expanding at a rate of 50 percent or more per year, and is estimated to grow to $19 billion in 2014 (see Figure 9.9). In 2010, there were an estimated 5 billion cell phone subscribers worldwide, with over 855 million in China and 300 million in the United States (eMarketer, 2010d).

M-COMMERCE SERVICES AND APPLICATIONS

The main areas of growth in mobile e-commerce are location-based services, about $215 million in revenue in 2010; software application sales at stores such as iTunes (about $1.8 billion); entertainment downloads of ring tones, music, video, and TV shows (about $1 billion); mobile display advertising ($784 million); direct shopping services such as Slifter ($200 million); and e-book sales ($338 million).

M-commerce applications have taken off for services that are time-critical, that appeal to people on the move, or that accomplish a task more efficiently than other methods. They are especially popular in Europe, Japan, South Korea, and other countries with strong wireless broadband infrastructures. The following sections describe some examples.

Location-Based Services

Wikitude.me provides a special kind of browser for smartphones equipped with a built-in global positioning system (GPS) and compass that can identify your precise location and where the phone is pointed. Using information from over 800,000 points of interest available on Wikipedia, plus thousands of other local sites, the browser overlays information about points of interest you are viewing, and displays that information on your smartphone screen, superimposed on a map or photograph that you just snapped. For example, users can point their smartphone cameras towards mountains from a tour bus and see the names and heights of the mountains displayed on the screen. Wikitude.me also allows users to geo-tag the world around them, and then submit the tags to Wikitude in order to share content with other users. In 2010, both Facebook and Twitter launched a Places feature that allows users to let their friends know where they are. These services compete with Foursquare and Gowalla, which allow users to check in at places and broadcast their location to friends.

Loopt is a free social networking application that allows you to share your status and track the location of friends via smartphones such as the iPhone, Android, or BlackBerry, and over 100 other mobile devices. Users also have the ability to integrate Loopt with other social networks, including Facebook and Twitter. Loopt has 5 million users in 2011.

Figure 9.9
Consolidated Mobile Commerce Revenues
Mobile e-commerce is the fastest growing type of B2C e-commerce although it represents only a small part of all e-commerce in 2011.

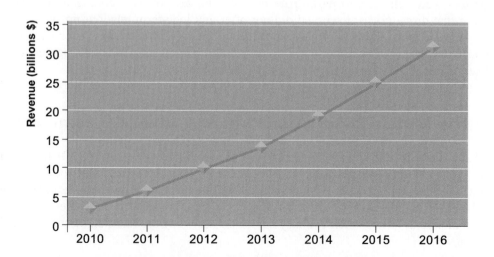

The service doesn't sell information to advertisers, but does post ads based on user location. Loopt's target is to deal with advertisers at the walking level (within 200 to 250 meters).

Foursquare provides a similar location-based social networking service to 10 million registered users, who may connect with friends and update their location. Points are awarded for "checking in" at designated venues. Users choose to have their check-ins posted on their accounts on Twitter, Facebook, or both. Users also earn badges by checking in at locations with certain tags, for check-in frequency, or for the time of check-in. More than 500,000 local merchants worldwide use the merchant platform for marketing.

Banking and Financial Services

Banks and credit card companies are rolling out services that let customers manage their accounts from their mobile devices. JPMorgan Chase and Bank of America customers can use their cell phones to check account balances, transfer funds, and pay bills. An estimated 134 million people bank online at least once a month.

Mobile Advertising and Retailing

Although the mobile advertising market is currently small ($1.1 billion), it is rapidly growing (up 44 percent from last year and expected to grow to over $4.3 billion by 2014), as more and more companies seek ways to exploit new databases of location-specific information (eMarketer, 2011). The largest providers of mobile advertising are Apple's iAd platform and Google's AdMob platform (both with a 21 percent market share). Alcatel-Lucent offers a new service to be managed by Placecast that will identify cell phone users within a specified distance of an advertiser's nearest outlet and notify them about the outlet's address and phone number, perhaps including a link to a coupon or other promotion. Placecast's clients include Hyatt, FedEx, and Avis Rent A Car.

Yahoo displays ads on its mobile home page for companies such as Pepsi, Procter & Gamble, Hilton, Nissan, and Intel. Google is displaying ads linked to cell phone searches by users of the mobile version of its search engine, while Microsoft offers banner and text advertising on its MSN Mobile portal in the United States. Ads are embedded in games, videos, and other mobile applications.

Shopkick is a mobile application that enables retailers such as Best Buy, Sports Authority, and Macy's to offer coupons to people when they walk into their stores. The Shopkick app automatically recognizes when the user has entered a partner retail store and offers a new virtual currency called "kickbucks," which can be redeemed for Facebook credits, iTunes Gift Cards, travel vouchers, DVDs, or immediate cash-back rewards at any of the partner stores.

In 2011, shoppers ordered about $5.3 billion of goods and services goods from Web sites via smartphones (over 1 billion of that at Amazon alone). Forty percent of online retailers now have m-commerce Web sites—simplified versions of their Web sites that make it possible for shoppers to use cell phones to place orders. Clothing retailers Lilly Pulitzer and Armani Exchange, Home Depot, and 1–800 Flowers are among those companies with specialized apps for m-commerce sales.

Games and Entertainment

Smartphones and tablets have developed into portable entertainment platforms. Smartphones like the iPhone and Droid offer downloadable and streaming digital games, movies, TV shows, music, and ringtones.

Users of broadband services from the major wireless vendors can stream on-demand video clips, news clips, and weather reports. MobiTV, offered by Verizon Wireless, AT&T Wireless, and other mobile carriers, features live TV programs, including MSNBC and Fox Sports. Film companies are starting to produce short films explicitly designed to play on mobile phones. User-generated content is also appearing in mobile form. Facebook, MySpace, YouTube, and other social networking sites have versions for mobile devices. In 2011, the top 10 most popular apps on Facebook are games, led by FarmVille and CityVille, each with about 15 million daily users.

9.4 Building an E-commerce Presence

Building a successful e-commerce presence requires a keen understanding of business, technology, and social issues, as well as a systematic approach. In 2011, an e-commerce presence is not just a corporate Web site, but may also include a social network site on Facebook, a Twitter company feed, and smartphone apps where customers can access your services. Developing and coordinating all these different customer venues can be difficult. A complete treatment of the topic is beyond the scope of this text, and students should consult books devoted to just this topic (Laudon and Traver, 2012). The two most important management challenges in building a successful e-commerce presence are (1) developing a clear understanding of your business objectives and (2) knowing how to choose the right technology to achieve those objectives.

PIECES OF THE SITE-BUILDING PUZZLE

Let's assume you are a manager for a medium-sized, industrial parts firm of around 10,000 employees worldwide, operating in eight countries in Europe, Asia, and North America. Senior management has given you a budget of $1 million to build an e-commerce site within one year. The purpose of this site will be to sell and service the firm's 20,000 customers, who are mostly small machine and metal fabricating shops around the world. Where do you start?

First, you must be aware of the main areas where you will need to make decisions. On the organizational and human resources fronts, you will have to bring together a team of individuals who possess the skill sets needed to build and manage a successful e-commerce site. This team will make the key decisions about technology, site design, and social and information policies that will be applied at your site. The entire site development effort must be closely managed if you hope to avoid the disasters that have occurred at some firms.

You will also need to make decisions about your site's hardware, software, and telecommunications infrastructure. The demands of your customers should drive your choices of technology. Your customers will want technology that enables them to find what they want easily, view the product, purchase the product, and then receive the product from your warehouses quickly. You will also have to carefully consider your site's design. Once you have identified the key decision areas, you will need to think about a plan for the project.

BUSINESS OBJECTIVES, SYSTEM FUNCTIONALITY, AND INFORMATION REQUIREMENTS

In planning your Web site you need to answer the question, "What do we want the e-commerce site to do for our business?" The key lesson to be learned here is to let the business decisions drive the technology, not the reverse. This will ensure that your technology platform is aligned with your business. We will assume here that you have identified a business strategy and chosen a business model to achieve your strategic objectives. But how do you translate your strategies, business models, and ideas into a working e-commerce site?

Your planning should identify the specific business objectives for your site, and then develop a list of system functionalities and information requirements. Business objectives are simply capabilities you want your site to have. System functionalities are types of information systems capabilities you will need to achieve your business objectives. The information requirements for a system are the information elements that the system must produce in order to achieve the business objectives.

Table 9.8 describes some basic business objectives, system functionalities, and information requirements for a typical e-commerce site. The objectives must be translated into a description of system functionalities and ultimately into a set of precise information requirements. The specific information requirements for a system typically are defined in much greater detail than Table 9.8 indicates. The business objectives of an e-commerce site are similar to those of a physical retail store, but they must be provided entirely in digital form, 24 hours a day, 7 days a week.

Business Objective	System Functionality	Information Requirements
Display goods	Digital catalog	Dynamic text and graphics catalog
Provide product information (content)	Product database	Product description, stocking numbers, inventory levels
Personalize/customize product	Customer on-site tracking	Site log for every customer visit; data mining capability to identify common customer paths and appropriate responses
Execute a transaction payment	Shopping cart/payment system	Secure credit card clearing; multiple options
Accumulate customer information	Customer database	Name, address, phone, and e-mail for all customers; online customer registration
Provide after-sale customer support	Sales database and customer relationship management system (CRM)	Customer ID, product, date, payment, shipment date
Coordinate marketing/ advertising	Ad server, e-mail server, e-mail, campaign manager, ad banner manager	Site behavior log of prospects and customers linked to e-mail and banner ad campaigns
Understand marketing effectiveness	Site tracking and reporting system	Number of unique visitors, pages visited, products purchased, identified by marketing campaign
Provide production and supplier links	Inventory management system	Product and inventory levels, supplier ID and contact, order quantity data by product

TABLE 9.8

System Analysis: Business Objectives, System Functionality, and Information Requirements for a Typical E-commerce Site

BUILDING THE WEB SITE: IN-HOUSE VERSUS OUTSOURCING

There are many choices for building and maintaining Web sites. Much depends on how much money you are willing to spend. Choices range from outsourcing the entire Web site development to an external vendor to building everything yourself (in-house). You also have a second decision to make: will you host (operate) the site on your firm's own servers or will you outsource the hosting to a Web host provider? There are some vendors who will design,

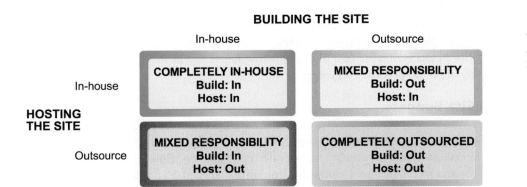

BUILDING THE SITE

Figure 9.10
Choices in Building and Hosting Web Sites
You have a number of alternatives to consider when building and hosting an e-commerce site.

build, and host your site, while others will either build or host (but not both). Figure 9.10 illustrates the alternatives.

The Building Decision

If you elect to build your own site, there are a range of options. Unless you are fairly skilled, you should use a pre-built template to create the Web site. For example, Yahoo Merchant Solutions, Amazon Stores, and eBay all provide templates that merely require you to input text, graphics, and other data, as well as the infrastructure to run the Web site once it has been created. This is the least costly and simplest solution, but you will be limited to the "look and feel" and functionality provided by the template and infrastructure.

If you have some experience with computers, you might decide to build the site yourself. There is a broad variety of tools, ranging from those that help you build everything truly "from scratch," such as Adobe Dreamweaver, Adobe InDesign, and Microsoft Expression, to top-of-the-line prepackaged site-building tools that can create sophisticated sites customized to your needs.

The decision to build a Web site on your own has a number of risks. Given the complexity of features such as shopping carts, credit card authentication and processing, inventory management, and order processing, development costs are high, as are the risks of doing a poor job. You will be reinventing what other specialized firms have already built, and your staff may face a long, difficult learning curve, delaying your entry to market. Your efforts could fail. On the positive side, you may able to build a site that does exactly what you want, and develop the in-house knowledge to revise the site rapidly if necessitated by a changing business environment.

If you choose more expensive site-building packages, you will be purchasing state-of-the-art software that is well tested. You could get to market sooner. However, to make a sound decision, you will have to evaluate many different software packages and this can take a long time. You may have to modify the packages to fit your business needs and perhaps hire additional outside consultants to do the modifications. Costs rise rapidly as modifications mount. A $4,000 package can easily become a $40,000 to $60,000 development project simply because of all the changes in code required.

The Hosting Decision

Now let's look at the hosting decision. Most businesses choose to outsource hosting and pay a company to host their Web site, which means that the hosting company is responsible for ensuring the site is "live" or accessible, 24 hours a day. By agreeing to a monthly fee, the business need not concern itself with technical aspects of setting up and maintaining a Web server, telecommunications links, or specialized staffing.

With a **co-location** agreement, your firm purchases or leases a Web server (and has total control over its operation) but locates the server in a vendor's physical facility. The vendor maintains the facility, communications lines, and the machinery. In the age of cloud computing, it is much less expensive to host your Web site in virtualized computing facilities. In this case, you do not purchase the server, but rent the capabilities of a cloud computing center such as Rackspace (a popular hosting site). There is an extraordinary range of prices for cloud hosting, ranging from $4.95 a month, to several hundred thousands of dollars per month depending on the size of the Web site, bandwidth, storage, and support requirements. Very large providers (such as IBM, HP, and Oracle) achieve large economies of scale by establishing huge "server farms" located strategically around the country and the globe. What this means is that the cost of pure hosting has fallen as fast as the fall in server prices, dropping about 50 percent every year.

Web Site Budgets

Simple Web sites can be built and hosted with a first-year cost of $5,000 or less. The Web sites of large firms with high levels of interactivity and linkage to corporate systems cost several million dollars a year to create and operate. For instance, Bluefly, which sells discounted women's and men's designer clothes online, invested over $5.3 million in connection with

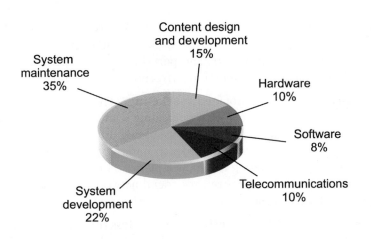

Figure 9.11
Components of a
Web Site Budget

the redevelopment of its Web site. In 2011, Bluefly had online sales of $88 million, and is growing revenues at 10 percent a year. Its e-commerce technology budget is over $8 million a year, roughly 10 percent of its total revenues (Bluefly, Inc., 2011).

Figure 9.11 provides some idea of the relative size of various Web site cost components. In general, the cost of hardware, software, and telecommunications for building and operating a Web site has fallen dramatically (by over 50 percent) since 2000, making it possible for very small entrepreneurs to create fairly sophisticated sites. At the same time, the costs of system maintenance and content creation have risen to make up more than half of typical Web site budgets. Providing content and smooth 24/7 operations are both labor-intensive.

LEARNING TRACKS

The following Learning Tracks provide content relevant to topics covered in this chapter:

1. Building a Web Page
2. E-commerce Challenges: The Story of Online Groceries
3. Build an E-commerce Business Plan
4. Hot New Careers in E-commerce

Review Summary

1 **What are the unique features of e-commerce, digital markets, and digital goods?**
E-commerce involves digitally enabled commercial transactions between and among organizations and individuals. Unique features of e-commerce technology include ubiquity, global reach, universal technology standards, richness, interactivity, information density, capabilities for personalization and customization, and social technology.

Digital markets are said to be more "transparent" than traditional markets, with reduced information asymmetry, search costs, transaction costs, and menu costs, along with the ability to change prices dynamically based on market conditions. Digital goods, such as music, video, software, and books, can be delivered over a digital network. Once a digital product has been produced, the cost of delivering that product digitally is extremely low.

2 **What are the principal e-commerce business and revenue models?** E-commerce business models are e-tailers, transaction brokers, market creators, content providers, community providers, service providers, and portals. The principal e-commerce revenue models are advertising, sales, subscription, free/freemium, transaction fee, and affiliate.

3 **How has e-commerce transformed marketing?** The Internet provides marketers with new ways of identifying and communicating with millions of potential customers at costs far lower than traditional media. Crowdsourcing utilizing the "wisdom of crowds" helps companies learn from customers in order to improve product offerings and increase customer value. Behavioral targeting techniques increase the effectiveness of banner, rich media, and video ads. Social commerce uses social networks and social network sites to improve targeting of products and services.

4 **How has e-commerce affected business-to-business transactions?** B2B e-commerce generates efficiencies by enabling companies to locate suppliers, solicit bids, place orders, and track shipments in transit electronically. Net marketplaces provide a single, digital marketplace for many buyers and sellers. Private industrial networks link a firm with its suppliers and other strategic business partners to develop highly efficient and responsive supply chains.

5 **What is the role of m-commerce in business, and what are the most important m-commerce applications?** M-commerce is especially well-suited for location-based applications, such as finding local hotels and restaurants, monitoring local traffic and weather, and providing personalized location-based marketing. Mobile phones and handhelds are being used for mobile bill payment, banking, securities trading, transportation schedule updates, and downloads of digital content, such as music, games, and video clips. M-commerce requires wireless portals and special digital payment systems that can handle micropayments.

6 **What issues must be addressed when building an e-commerce presence?** Building a successful e-commerce site requires a clear understanding of the business objectives to be achieved by the site and selection of the right technology to achieve those objectives. E-commerce sites can be built and hosted in-house or partially or fully outsourced to external service providers.

Key Terms

Review Questions

1. What are the unique features of e-commerce, digital markets, and digital goods?
- Name and describe four business trends and three technology trends shaping e-commerce today.
- List and describe the eight unique features of e-commerce.
- Define a digital market and digital goods and describe their distinguishing features.

2. What are the principal e-commerce business and revenue models?
- Name and describe the principal e-commerce business models.
- Name and describe the e-commerce revenue models.

3. How has e-commerce transformed marketing?
- Explain how social networking and the "wisdom of crowds" help companies improve their marketing.
- Define behavioral targeting and explain how it works at individual Web sites and on advertising networks.
- Define the social graph and explain how it is used in e-commerce marketing.

4. How has e-commerce affected business-to-business transactions?
- Explain how Internet technology supports business-to-business electronic commerce.
- Define and describe Net marketplaces and explain how they differ from private industrial networks (private exchanges).

5. What is the role of m-commerce in business, and what are the most important m-commerce applications?
- List and describe important types of m-commerce services and applications.
- Describe some of the barriers to m-commerce.

6. What issues must be addressed when building an e-commerce presence?
- List and describe each of the factors that go into the building of an e-commerce Web site.
- List and describe four business objectives, four system functionalities, and four information requirements of a typical e-commerce Web site.
- List and describe each of the options for building and hosting e-commerce Web sites.

Discussion Questions

1. How does the Internet change consumer and supplier relationships?

2. The Internet may not make corporations obsolete, but the corporations will have to change their business models. Do you agree? Why or why not?

3. How have social technologies changed e-commerce?

Hands-On MIS Projects

The projects in this section give you hands-on experience developing e-commerce strategies for businesses, using spreadsheet software to research the profitability of an e-commerce company, and using Web tools to research and evaluate e-commerce hosting services.

MANAGEMENT DECISION PROBLEMS

1. Columbiana is a small, independent island in the Caribbean that has many historical buildings, forts, and other sites, along with rain forests and striking mountains. A few first-class hotels and several dozen less-expensive accommodations can be found along its beautiful white sand beaches. The major airlines have regular flights to Columbiana, as do several small airlines. Columbiana's government wants to increase tourism and develop new markets for the country's tropical agricultural products. How can a Web presence help? What Internet business model would be appropriate? What functions should the Web site perform?

2. Explore the Web sites of the following companies: Blue Nile, J.Crew, Lowe's, and Priceline. Determine which of these Web sites would benefit most from adding a company-sponsored blog to the Web site. List the business benefits of the blog. Specify the intended audience for the blog. Decide who in the company should author the blog, and select some topics for the blog.

IMPROVING DECISION MAKING: USING SPREADSHEET SOFTWARE TO ANALYZE A DOT-COM BUSINESS

Software skills: Spreadsheet downloading, formatting, and formulas
Business skills: Financial statement analysis

Pick one e-commerce company on the Internet, for example, Ashford, Buy.com, Yahoo, or Priceline. Study the Web pages that describe the company and explain its purpose and structure. Use the Web to find articles that comment on the company. Then visit the Securities and Exchange Commission's Web site at www.sec.gov and select Filings & Forms to access the company's 10-K (annual report) form showing income statements and balance sheets. Select only the sections of the 10-K form containing the desired portions of financial statements that you need to examine, and download them into your spreadsheet. (MyMISLab provides more detailed instructions on how to download this 10-K data into a spreadsheet.) Create simplified spreadsheets of the company's balance sheets and income statements for the past three years.

- Is the company a dot-com success, borderline business, or failure? What information provides the basis of your decision? Why? When answering these questions, pay special attention to the company's three-year trends in revenues, costs of sales, gross margins, operating expenses, and net margins.
- Prepare an overhead presentation (with a minimum of five slides), including appropriate spreadsheets or charts, and present your work to your professor and classmates.

ACHIEVING OPERATIONAL EXCELLENCE: EVALUATING E-COMMERCE HOSTING SERVICES

Software skills: Web browser software
Business skills: Evaluating e-commerce hosting services

This project will help develop your Internet skills in commercial services for hosting an e-commerce site for a small start-up company.

You would like to set up a Web site to sell towels, linens, pottery, and tableware from Portugal and are examining services for hosting small business Internet storefronts. Your

Web site should be able to take secure credit card payments and to calculate shipping costs and taxes. Initially, you would like to display photos and descriptions of 40 different products. Visit Yahoo! Small Business, GoDaddy, and Comcast and compare the range of e-commerce hosting services they offer to small businesses, their capabilities, and costs. Also examine the tools they provide for creating an e-commerce site. Compare these services and decide which you would use if you were actually establishing a Web store. Write a brief report indicating your choice and explaining the strengths and weaknesses of each.

Video Cases

Video Cases and Instructional Videos illustrating some of the concepts in this chapter are available. Contact your instructor to access these videos.

Collaboration and Teamwork

Performing a Competitive Analysis of E-commerce Sites

Form a group with three or four of your classmates. Select two businesses that are competitors in the same industry and that use their Web sites for electronic commerce. Visit these Web sites. You might compare, for example, the Web sites for iTunes and Napster, Amazon and BarnesandNoble.com, or E*Trade and Scottrade. Prepare an evaluation of each business's Web site in terms of its functions, user friendliness, and ability to support the company's business strategy. Which Web site does a better job? Why? Can you make some recommendations to improve these Web sites? If possible, use Google Sites to post links to Web pages, team communication announcements, and work assignments; to brainstorm; and to work collaboratively on project documents. Try to use Google Docs to develop a presentation of your findings for the class.

BUSINESS PROBLEM-SOLVING CASE

To Pay or Not To Pay: Zagat's Dilemma

Founded by Tim and Nina Zagat, the Zagat Survey has collected and published ratings of restaurants by diners since 1979. Zagat publishes surveys for restaurants, hotels, and nightlife in 70 major cities. Today, as more people use their smartphones for information on the go, Zagat is moving its content online and onto the mobile platform. It has been a struggle.

Zagat has come a long way from its roots in the early 1980s, when the food-loving Zagats started compiling lists of their favorite restaurants for personal use and to share with their closest friends. To generate the first survey, the Zagats polled 200 people, and increased that number over time. Executives, tourists, and New York foodies alike found the list to be indispensable.

Spurred by this success, the Zagats decided to publish a book with their survey themselves. The few booksellers that took a risk in stocking the book were rewarded with sales so robust that the Zagat Surveys became best sellers.

The pair also published similar lists for other major cities, including Chicago, San Francisco, and Washington, D.C. In addition to print books, Zagat opened a unit that creates custom guides for corporate clients, like the ones at Citibank. For a long time, this business model was sufficient to ensure that Zagat Survey was successful and profitable.

When the dot-com bubble came along, venture capitalists were attracted to Zagat for its brand recognition—the Zagat name is instantly recognizable to food-lovers, travelers, and restaurateurs alike. Zagat was one of the first companies to popularize user-generated content, collecting restaurant reviews from its readers, aggregating those reviews, and computing ratings. In addition to numeric rating scores, the survey also includes a short descriptive paragraph that incorporates selected quotations from several reviewers' comments about each restaurant or service. Venture capitalists saw that Zagat had a golden opportunity to migrate its content from offline to online, Web, and mobile.

Of the many decisions the Zagats faced in bringing their content to the Web, perhaps the most important-was how much to charge for various types of content. They ultimately decided to place all of their content behind a pay wall, relying on the Zagat brand to entice customers to purchase full online access. `One of the most prominent members of the investment group was Nathan Myhrvold, formerly the chief technology officer at Microsoft. Myhrvold supported the Zagats' decision to use a pay wall for their content and maintained that putting all of their content online for free would have undermined their book sales.

Although Myhrvold and the Zagats themselves favored the pay wall, other Zagat investors argued that placing content online for free allows companies like Yelp to get its results on the first page of Google search results, which is critical for maintaining the strength of a brand in today's advertising environment. By not taking this approach, Zagat left itself open to be surpassed by Yelp, Groupon, Google Places, and other similar services offering free content supported by advertising from local businesses.

In 2008, the Zagats tried to sell their company. They failed to do so, partially due to Yelp's growing popularity. The Zagats' failure to sell the company in 2008 highlighted their failure to effectively go digital. Food blogs and similar sites abound on the Web nowadays, but Zagat was in a unique position to get there first and establish itself as a market leader, and it failed to do so.

For much of 2011, Zagat trailed Yelp and other free review sites in the battle for eyeballs. Yelp drew much greater traffic than Zagat.com. In January 2011, according to comScore, Zagat.com had only 269,000 visitors, while Yelp had 26 million. The Zagat Web site claims it has more users, but the disparity is still significant.

A quick visit to the two sites highlights some of the differences. Zagat.com's home page is streamlined, with a minimal number of search boxes and links immediately available. Restaurant reviews are organized by several major "hub" cities as well as popular lists of the top restaurants of a certain type. Clicking on a restaurant shows visitors only a portion of the data Zagat maintains on that restaurant. For example, the site now shows the percentage of users that "like" the restaurant, and several featured reviews. However, individual ratings for food, décor, service, and cost are all behind the pay wall. The site also features a store where users can buy any of the Zagat surveys, Zagat-rated wine, and even Zagat t-shirts.

Yelp's front page is much busier and less streamlined than Zagat's, but has a great deal more content available

immediately. The front page has lists of the most popular restaurants, retail outlets, bars and clubs, and many other categories, all free to the user. Looking for a dentist in New York City? Yelp has reviews of doctors and dentists that include videos put together by the practices to give visitors more information. Like Zagat.com, Yelp's reviews are organized into a similar list of larger cities, but reviews exist for almost any location you can think of, including less prominent cities and towns.

As of July 2011, Yelp had 20 million reviews and estimated that users would write another 5 million reviews by the end of the year. In contrast with Zagat's online offerings, which are primarily restaurant reviews, only 25 percent of Yelp's reviews are for restaurants, with another 25 percent coming from shopping and 10 percent apiece from local entertainment, services, and health and beauty. Yelp has already launched a check-in service to allow mobile users to tell their friends where they've been dining, and Yelp's mobile app has well over 3 million unique users.

Yelp's strategy is to sell local advertisements wherever businesses exist and to provide free content funded by these sales. Yelp has also relied more on individual reviewers. Instead of distilling reviews into one coherent whole, as Zagat's does, Yelp allows its reviewers to post full, unaltered reviews, which allows top reviewers to gain followings and even receive invitations to special events. The drawback of this approach is that many reviews are far longer than necessary and individual reviews may contain distortions or false claims designed to damage reputations. Zagat reviews give a clearer and more concise impression of a restaurant than most Yelp reviews and they are aggregated and given a score.

Investors believe that Yelp is on "a different trajectory" because of its unique business model. Zagat sells content to consumers and corporations; Yelp sells advertising to local businesses. Many analysts believe that there is much more potential for growth with Yelp's business model than with Zagat's, because it is a useful advertising vehicle for small businesses everywhere, not just major cities. Zagat may also have hurt itself with its slow response to the emergence of the mobile digital platform.

Most analysts agree that Zagat could have avoided this state of affairs by making a more aggressive effort to go digital, but migrating Zagat's content from offline to online and mobile has not been as easy or lucrative as envisioned by investors. Their choice to use a pay wall may be the biggest culprit. But is it necessarily hurting their bottom line? The company remains profitable, according to Tim and Nina Zagat. Its book revenue is still strong—the New York survey is still on the New York nonfiction best-seller list, and its corporate custom guide unit is very profitable. The Zagats also counter criticisms of the pay wall by noting that Time.com, The NYTimes.com, and other sites have recently begun instituting pay walls, and that more companies are beginning to view their Web strategy as the right one. But it's possible that going with a pay wall before establishing a loyal online audience may not be the right time to make the move towards a paid model.

Perhaps realizing this, in February 2011, Zagat Survey re-launched its Web site featuring more free content in response to the rising popularity of Yelp and similar sites. The site features revamped search tools that allow users to find restaurants in particular neighborhoods or near prominent landmarks. Members receive more recognition for being active and respected reviewers, including their own quotes in Zagat's previously anonymous reviews. Users can now "like" reviews similarly to Facebook, and they can also upload their own photos to the site. Full access to the site, however, still costs $24.95 per year.

Zagat is also doing more of the right things to compete in the mobile landscape. It developed a smartphone app that runs on Android, Apple, BlackBerry, Windows Mobile, and Palm platforms. Zagat is optimistic that more mobile users will pay $9.99 for its smartphone application than the few Web users that have paid for full access to its Web site. Zagat was on Android phones nearly a year before competitors and embraced other emerging firms like Foursquare and Foodspotting early as well, so it has already made strong progress in the mobile marketplace.

Zagat's mobile app features access to Zagat premium ratings and reviews and the ability to find nearby restaurants using geolocation. The latest version, released in early 2011, includes a full visual overhaul to increase ease of use and integration with Foodspotting and Foursquare and to provide photos of dishes and meal tips based on diners with tastes similar to the user's own. These changes are intended to make the application more social. Another compelling feature of Zagat's app is the ability to download its guides directly to phones. That way, users can access the information even if the Internet is unavailable or if they are outside the United States.

Zagat was bought by Google in September, 2011. The acquisition strengthens Google's position in mobile and local search, helping it to compete against Yelp for high-volume searches for restaurants and hotels. It also means that Google will own some of the media content it serves up for searches, and the content will be of higher quality than in the past. There is less potential for inaccurate or biased reviews or abuse, because Zagat surveys the crowd and then aggregates its opinions rather than posting unfiltered individual reviewer comments. As of this writing, Zagat had no post-acquisition plans to change its content pricing. Will the marriage of Google and Zagat turn both into stronger companies?

Sources: Tim Carmody, "Google Buys Zagat to Reinvent Mobile Search Engine," *Wired*, September 10, 2011; Adam Clark Estes, "Google Buying Zagat Makes Instant Sense," *Atlantic Wire*, September 8, 2011; Leena Rao, "Zagat.com Relaunches With More Free Content, Including Maps, Lists, Third-Party Reviews," *TechCrunch*, February 21, 2011; Erik Berte, "As Online Competition Grows, Zagat. com Relaunches With More Free Features," FoxBusiness.com, February 21, 2011; Ben Parr, "Yelp's Growth is Accelerating, Despite Increased Competition From Groupon & Google," Mashable.com, February 17, 2011; "ZAGAT for Android Features Foodspotting Photos, Foursquare Tips and In-App Review Capabilities," PR Newswire, February 7, 2011; Ron Lieber, "Zagat Survey Aims to Regain Its Online Balance," *New York Times*, November 13, 2010. "Zagat Closes the Book on Sale Effort," Dealbook, *New York Times*, June 5, 2008.

Case Study Questions

1. Evaluate Zagat using the competitive forces and value chain models.
2. Compare Zagat's and Yelp's e-commerce business models. How have those models affected each company's Web strategy?
3. Why was Zagat's content well suited for the Web and for the mobile digital platform?
4. Do you think Zagat's decision to use a pay wall for its Web site was a mistake? Why or why not?
5. Why has Zagat's focused on adding social features to their Android app?

Improving Decision Making and Managing Knowledge

CHAPTER 10

STUDENT LEARNING OBJECTIVES

After completing this chapter, you will be able to answer the following questions:

1. What are the different types of decisions, and how does the decision-making process work?

2. How do business intelligence and business analytics support decision making?

3. How do information systems help people working in a group make decisions more efficiently?

4. What are the business benefits of using intelligent techniques in decision making and knowledge management?

5. What types of systems are used for enterprise-wide knowledge management and knowledge work, and how do they provide value for businesses?

CHAPTER OUTLINE

WHAT TO SELL? WHAT PRICE TO CHARGE? ASK THE DATA

What's the best way to get a discount on your morning coffee at Starbucks? If you live in Manhattan, you could get up an hour early and take the subway downtown to Brooklyn. A single expresso is 10 cents cheaper than in your neighborhood, as are a caffè latte and slice of lemon pound cake. But a muffin runs 10 cents more uptown in Marble Hill, and all Pike Place Roast cost $1.70 no matter where you live.

Starbucks is one of many retailers using sophisticated software to analyze—store by store and item by item—how demand responds to changes in price. What customers are willing to pay for certain items depends very much on the neighborhood or even the region of the country where they live. Shoppers in certain locations are willing to pay more.

The Duane Reade drugstore chain, recently purchased by Walgreens, is also adept at adjusting prices. Software analyzing sales patterns found that parents of newborn babies are not as price-sensitive as those with toddlers, so the company was able to raise prices on diapers for newborn infants without losing sales. The chain's information

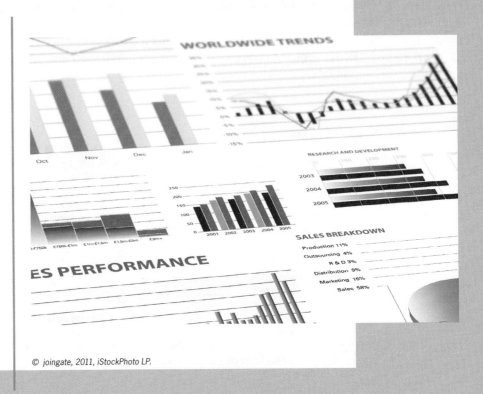

systems also showed how to adjust pricing based on location. Shoppers at the Duane Reade store near 86th Street and Lexington Avenue pay 20 cents more for a box of Kleenex and 50 cents more for a bottle of Pepto-Bismol than customers in Harlem.

Business analytics software such as that used by Duane Reade typically analyzes patterns in sales data to create a "pricing profile." How much of a difference does this knowledge make? Lots. 1-800-Flowers, which sells flowers and gift baskets online, has used analytics software from SAS Inc. to tweak its online storefront and marketing activities. The software helped the company quickly record and analyze buyer profiles to help improve targeting of its product, determine what "specials" to offer, and plan sales and marketing strategies based on an understanding of real customer needs. The company is able to quickly change prices and offerings on its Web site, often every hour. In the first half of 2010, 1-800-Flowers used more finely targeted Web pages and e-mail promotions to improve the conversion rate of Web site browsers to buyers by 20 percent.

Sources: "1-800 Flowers.com Customer Connection Blooms with SAS Business Analytics," http://www.sas.com, accessed April 17, 2011; Anne Kadet, "Price-Point Politics," *Wall Street Journal*, July 24, 2010; Steve Lohr, "A Data Explosion Remakes Retailing," *Wall Street Journal*, July 28, 2010.

The experiences of Starbucks, Duane Reade, and 1-800-Flowers are powerful illustrations of how information systems improve decision making. Managers at these retail chains were unable to make good decisions about what prices to charge to improve profitability and what items to sell to maximize sales at different locations and different time periods. They had access to customer purchase data, but they were unable to analyze millions of pieces of data on their own. Bad decisions about how much to charge and how to stock stores lowered sales revenue and prevented these companies from responding quickly to customer needs.

The chapter-opening diagram calls attention to important points raised by this case and this chapter. Starbucks, Duane Reade, and 1-800-Flowers started using business intelligence software, which is able to find patterns and trends in massive quantities of data. Information from these business intelligence systems helps managers at these companies make better decisions about pricing, shelf-stocking. and product offerings. They are able to see where they can charge a higher price or where they must lower prices to maximize sales revenue, as well as what items to stock and when to change their merchandise mix. Better decision making using business intelligence has made all of these companies more profitable.

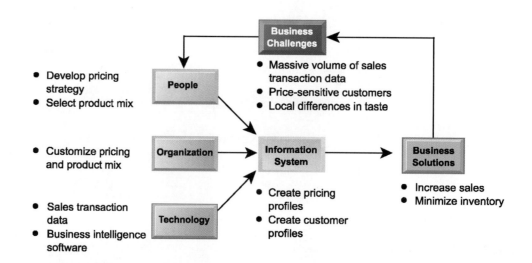

10.1 Decision Making and Information Systems

One of the main contributions of information systems has been to improve decision making, both for individuals and groups. Decision making in businesses used to be limited to management. Today, lower-level employees are responsible for some of these decisions, as information systems make information available to lower levels of the business. But what do we mean by better decision making? How does decision making take place in businesses and other organizations? Let's take a closer look.

BUSINESS VALUE OF IMPROVED DECISION MAKING

What does it mean to the business to be able to make a better decision? What is the monetary value to the business of better, improved decision making? Table 10.1 attempts to measure the monetary value of improved decision making for a small U.S. manufacturing firm with $280 million in annual revenue and 140 employees. The firm has identified a number of key decisions where new system investments might improve the quality of decision making. The table provides selected estimates of annual value (in the form of cost savings or increased revenue) from improved decision making in selected areas of the business.

We can see from Table 10.1 that decisions are made at all levels of the firm, and that some of these decisions are common, routine, and numerous. Although the value of improving any single decision may be small, improving hundreds of thousands of "small" decisions adds up to a large annual value for the business.

TYPES OF DECISIONS

Chapter 2 showed that there are different levels in an organization. Each of these levels has different information requirements for decision support and responsibility for different types of decisions (see Figure 10.1). Decisions are classified as structured, semistructured, and unstructured.

Unstructured decisions are those in which the decision maker must provide judgment, evaluation, and insight to solve the problem. Each of these decisions is novel, important, and nonroutine, and there is no well-understood or agreed-on procedure for making them.

TABLE 10.1

Business Value of Enhanced Decision Making

Example Decision Value	Decision Maker	Number of Annual Decisions	Estimated Value to Firm of a Single Improved Decision	Annual
Allocate support to most-valuable customers	Accounts manager	12	$100,000	$1,200,000
Predict call center daily demand	Call Center management	4	150,000	600,000
Decide parts inventory levels daily	Inventory manager	365	5,000	1,825,000
Identify competitive bids from major suppliers	Senior management	1	2,000,000	2,000,000
Schedule production to fill orders	Manufacturing manager	150	10,000	1,500,000
Allocate labor to complete a job	Production floor manager	100	4,000	400,000

Figure 10.1
Information Requirements of Key Decision-Making Groups in a Firm
Senior managers, middle managers, operational managers, and employees make different types of decisions and information requirements.

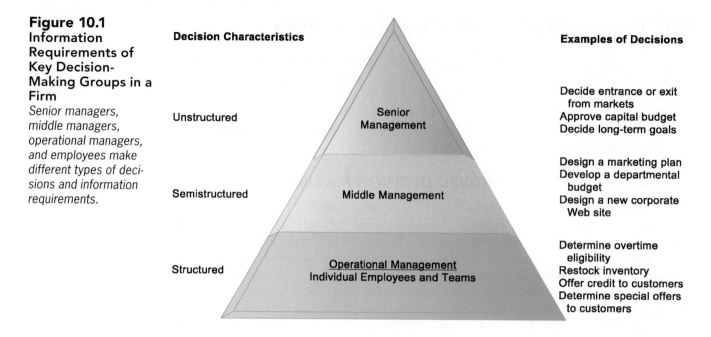

Decision Characteristics

Unstructured — Senior Management

Semistructured — Middle Management

Structured — Operational Management
Individual Employees and Teams

Examples of Decisions

Decide entrance or exit from markets
Approve capital budget
Decide long-term goals

Design a marketing plan
Develop a departmental budget
Design a new corporate Web site

Determine overtime eligibility
Restock inventory
Offer credit to customers
Determine special offers to customers

Structured decisions, by contrast, are repetitive and routine, and they involve a definite procedure for handling them so that they do not have to be treated each time as if they were new. Many decisions have elements of both types and are **semistructured decisions**, where only part of the problem has a clear-cut answer provided by an accepted procedure. In general, structured decisions are more prevalent at lower organizational levels, whereas unstructured problems are more common at higher levels of the firm.

Senior executives face many unstructured decision situations, such as establishing the firm's 5- or 10-year goals or deciding new markets to enter. Answering the question "Should we enter a new market?" would require access to news, government reports, and industry views, as well as high-level summaries of firm performance. However, the answer would also require senior managers to use their own best judgment and poll other managers for their opinions.

Middle management faces more structured decision scenarios, but their decisions may include unstructured components. A typical middle-level management decision might be "Why is the reported order fulfillment showing a decline over the past six months at a distribution center in Minneapolis?" This middle manager could obtain a report from the firm's enterprise system or distribution management system on order activity and operational efficiency at the Minneapolis distribution center. This is the structured part of the decision. But before arriving at an answer, this middle manager will have to interview employees and gather more unstructured information from external sources about local economic conditions or sales trends.

Operational management and rank-and-file employees tend to make more structured decisions. For example, a supervisor on an assembly line has to decide whether an hourly paid worker is entitled to overtime pay. If the employee worked more than eight hours on a particular day, the supervisor would routinely grant overtime pay for any time beyond eight hours that was clocked on that day.

A sales account representative often has to make decisions about extending credit to customers by consulting the firm's customer database that contains credit information. If the customer met the firm's prespecified criteria for granting credit, the account representative would grant that customer credit to make a purchase. In both instances, the decisions are highly structured and are routinely made thousands of times each day in most large firms. The answer has been preprogrammed into the firm's payroll and accounts receivable systems.

THE DECISION-MAKING PROCESS

Making a decision is a multistep process. Simon (1960) described four different stages in decision making: intelligence, design, choice, and implementation (see Figure 10.2). These stages correspond to the four steps in problem-solving used throughout this book.

Intelligence consists of discovering, identifying, and understanding the problems occurring in the organization—why the problem exists, where, and what effects it is having on the firm. **Design** involves identifying and exploring various solutions to the problem. **Choice** consists of choosing among solution alternatives. **Implementation** involves making the chosen alternative work and continuing to monitor how well the solution is working.

What happens if the solution you have chosen does not work? Figure 10.2 shows that you can return to an earlier stage in the decision-making process and repeat it, if necessary. For instance, in the face of declining sales, a sales management team may decide to pay the sales force a higher commission for making more sales to spur on the sales effort. If this does not increase sales, managers would need to investigate whether the problem stems from poor product design, inadequate customer support, or a host of other causes that call for a different solution.

High Velocity Automated Decision Making Today, many decisions made by organizations are not made by managers or any humans. For instance, when you enter a query into Google's search engine, Google's computer system has to decide which URLs to display in about half a second on average (500 milliseconds). High-frequency trading programs at electronic stock exchanges in the United States execute their trades in under 30 milliseconds. Humans are eliminated from the decision chain because they are too slow.

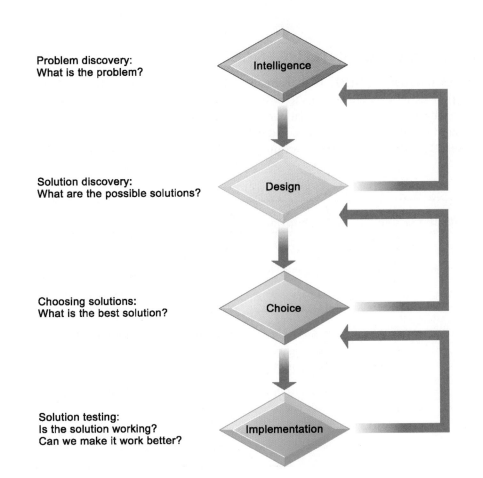

Problem discovery:
What is the problem?

Intelligence

Solution discovery:
What are the possible solutions?

Design

Choosing solutions:
What is the best solution?

Choice

Solution testing:
Is the solution working?
Can we make it work better?

Implementation

**Figure 10.2
Stages in Decision Making**
The decision-making process can be broken down into four stages.

In these high-speed automated decisions, the intelligence, design, choice, and implementation parts of the decision-making process are captured by computer algorithms that precisely define the steps to be followed to produce a decision. The people who wrote the software identified the problem, designed a method for finding a solution, defined a range of acceptable solutions, and implemented the solution. In these situations, organizations are making decisions faster than what managers can monitor or control, and great care needs to be taken to ensure the proper operation of these systems to prevent significant harm.

QUALITY OF DECISIONS AND DECISION MAKING

How can you tell if a decision has become "better" or the decision-making process "improved"? Accuracy is one important dimension of quality: In general, we think decisions are "better" if they accurately reflect the real-world data. Speed is another dimension: We tend to think that the decision-making process should be efficient, even speedy. For instance, when you apply for car insurance, you want the insurance firm to make a fast and accurate decision. But there are many other dimensions of quality in decisions and the decision-making process to consider. Which is important for you will depend on the business firm where you work, the various parties involved in the decision, and your own personal values. Table 10.2 describes some quality dimensions for decision making. When we describe how systems "improve decisions and the decision-making process" in this chapter, we are referencing the dimensions in this table.

10.2 Business Intelligence in the Enterprise

Chapter 2 introduced you to different kinds of systems for supporting the levels and types of decisions we have just described. The foundation for all of these systems is a business intelligence and business analytics infrastructure that supplies data and the analytic tools for supporting decision making.

WHAT IS BUSINESS INTELLIGENCE?

"Business intelligence" (BI) is a term used by hardware and software vendors and information technology consultants to describe the infrastructure for warehousing, integrating, reporting and analyzing data that come from the business environment. The foundation infrastructure collects, stores, cleans, and makes available relevant data to managers. Think databases, data warehouses, and data marts described in Chapter 5. "Business analytics"

TABLE 10.2

Qualities of Decisions and the Decision-Making Process

Quality Dimension	Description
Accuracy	Decision reflects reality
Comprehensiveness	Decision reflects a full consideration of the facts and circumstances
Fairness	Decision faithfully reflects the concerns and interests of affected parties
Speed (efficiency)	Decision making is efficient with respect to time and other resources, including the time and resources of affected parties, such as customers
Coherence	Decision reflects a rational process that can be explained to others and made understandable
Due process	Decision is the result of a known process and can be appealed to a higher authority

(BA) is also a vendor-defined term that focuses more on tools and techniques for analyzing and understanding data. Think OLAP, statistics, models, and data mining, which we also introduced in Chapter 5.

Business intelligence and analytics are essentially about integrating all the information streams produced by a firm into a single, coherent enterprise wide set of data, and then using modeling, statistical analysis and data mining tools to make sense out of all these data so managers can make better decisions and better plans. The companies described in the chapter-opening case are using business intelligence applications to make some very fine-grained decisions about what items to sell and what prices to charge for these items based on customer demographics and geographic location, as well as how to target sales and marketing campaigns to individual customers.

It is important to remember that business intelligence and analytics are products defined by technology vendors and consulting firms. They consist of hardware and software suites sold primarily by large system vendors to very large Fortune 500 firms. The largest five providers of these products are SAP, Oracle, IBM, SAS Institute, and Microsoft. The size of the BI and BA marketplace reached $10.5 billion in 2010 and is expected to grow at over 20 percent annually, making business intelligence one of the fastest growing segments of the U.S. software market (Gartner, 2011).

THE BUSINESS INTELLIGENCE ENVIRONMENT

Figure 10.3 gives an overview of a business intelligence environment, highlighting the kinds of hardware, software, and management capabilities that the major vendors offer and that firms develop over time. There are six elements in this business intelligence environment:

Data from the business environment: Businesses must deal with both structured and unstructured data from many different sources, including mobile devices and the Internet. The data need to be integrated and organized so that they can be analyzed and used by human decision makers.

Business intelligence infrastructure: The underlying foundation of business intelligence is a powerful database system that captures all the relevant data to operate the business. The data may be stored in transactional databases or combined and integrated into an enterprise-data warehouse or series of interrelated data marts.

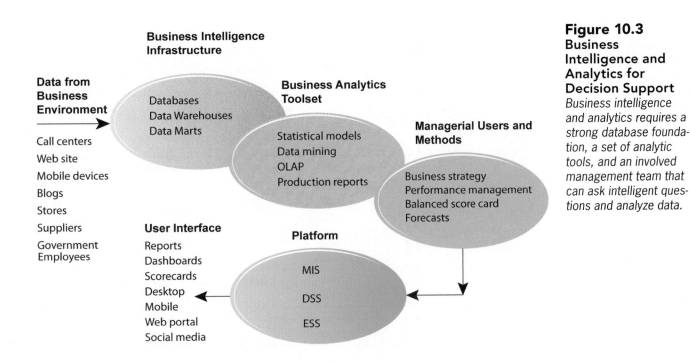

Figure 10.3
Business Intelligence and Analytics for Decision Support
Business intelligence and analytics requires a strong database foundation, a set of analytic tools, and an involved management team that can ask intelligent questions and analyze data.

Business analytics toolset: A set of software tools are used to analyze data and produce reports, respond to questions posed by managers, and track the progress of the business using key indicators of performance.

Managerial users and methods: Business intelligence hardware and software are only as intelligent as the human beings who use them. Managers impose order on the analysis of data using a variety of managerial methods that define strategic business goals and specify how progress will be measured. These include business performance management and balanced scorecard approaches that focus on key performance indicators, with special attention to competitors.

Delivery platform—MIS, DSS, ESS: The results from business intelligence and analytics are delivered to managers and employees in a variety of ways, depending on what they need to know to perform their job. MIS, DSS, and ESS, which we introduced in Chapter 2, deliver information and knowledge to different people and levels in the firm—operational employees, middle managers, and senior executives. In the past, all these systems could not share data and operated as independent systems. Today, one suite of hardware and software tools in the form of a business intelligence and analytics package is able to integrate all this information and bring it to managers' desktop or mobile platforms.

User Interface: Business people are no longer tied to their desks and desktops. They often learn quicker from a visual representation of data than from a dry report with columns and rows of information. Today's business analytics software suites emphasize visual techniques such as dashboards and scorecards. They also are able to deliver reports on BlackBerrys, iPhones, and other mobile handhelds as well as on the firm's Web portal. BA software is adding capabilities to post information on Twitter, Facebook, or internal social media to support decision making in an online, group setting rather than in a face-to-face meeting.

BUSINESS INTELLIGENCE AND ANALYTICS CAPABILITIES

Business intelligence and analytics promise to deliver correct, nearly real-time information to decision makers, and the analytic tools help them quickly understand the information and take action. There are five analytic functionalities that BI systems deliver to achieve these ends:

Production reports: These are pre-defined reports based on industry-specific requirements (see Table 10.3).

TABLE 10.3

Examples of Business Intelligence Pre-Defined Production Reports

Business Functional Area	Production Reports
Sales	Sales forecasts, sales team performance, cross selling, sales cycle times
Service/Call Center	Customer satisfaction, service cost, resolution rates, churn rates
Marketing	Campaign effectiveness, loyalty and attrition, market basket analysis
Procurement and Support	Direct and indirect spending, off-contract purchases, supplier performance
Supply Chain	Backlog, fulfillment status, order cycle time, bill of materials analysis
Financials	General ledger, accounts receivable and payable, cash flow, profitability
Human Resources	Employee productivity, compensation, workforce demographics, retention

Parameterized reports: Users enter several parameters as in a pivot table to filter data and isolate impacts of parameters. For instance, you might want to enter region and time of day to understand how sales of a product vary by region and time. If you were Starbucks, you might find that customers in the eastern United States buy most of their coffee in the morning, whereas in the northwest customers buy coffee throughout the day. This finding might lead to different marketing and ad campaigns in each region. (See the discussion of pivot tables later in this section.)

Dashboards/Scorecards: These are visual tools for presenting performance data defined by users.

Ad hoc query/search/ report creation: These allow users to create their own reports based on queries and searches.

Drill down: This is the ability to move from a high level summary to a more detailed view.

Forecasts, scenarios, models: These include capabilities for linear forecasting, "what if" scenario analysis, and analyzing data using standard statistical tools.

Production Reports

The most widely used output of a BI suite of tools is pre-packaged production reports. Table 10.3 illustrates some common pre-defined reports from Oracle's BI suite of tools.

Predictive Analytics

Predictive analytics, which we introduced in Chapter 5, are being built into business intelligence applications for sales, marketing, finance, fraud detection, and health care. Predictive analytics use statistical analysis and other techniques to extract information from data and use it to predict future trends and behavior patterns.

One of the most established business applications of predictive analytics is predicting response to direct marketing campaigns. By identifying customers less likely to respond, companies are able to lower their marketing and sales costs by bypassing this group and focusing their resources on customers who have been identified as more promising. For example, Capital One conducts more than 30,000 experiments each year using different interest rates, incentives, direct mail packaging, and other variables to identify the best potential customers for targeting its credit card offers. These people are most likely to sign up for credit cards and to pay back Capital One for the balances they ring up in their credit card accounts. Predictive analytics have also helped credit card companies identify customers who are at risk for leaving, and churn modeling is another popular predictive analytics application.

Predictive analytics are helping companies understand other customer-related behaviors. FedEx is using SAS Institute's Enterprise Miner and predictive analytic tools to develop models that predict how customers will respond to price changes and new services, which customers are most at risk of switching to competitors, and how much revenue will be generated by new storefront or drop-box locations. The accuracy rate of the predictive analytics system ranges from 65 to 90 percent. FedEx is now starting to use predictive analytics in call centers to help customer service representatives identify customers with the highest levels of dissatisfaction and take the necessary steps to make them happy.

Data Visualization, Visual Analytics, and Geographic Information Systems

By presenting data in visual form, **data visualization** and visual analytics tools help users see patterns and relationships in large amounts of data that would be difficult to discern if the data were presented as traditional lists of text or numbers. Data are presented in the form of rich graphs, charts, dashboards, and maps. People become more engaged when they can filter information that is presented visually and develop insights on their own.

Geographic information systems (GIS) are a special category of tools for helping decision makers visualize problems requiring knowledge about the geographic distribution of people or other resources. Their software ties location data to points, lines, and areas on a map. Some GIS have modeling capabilities for changing the data and automatically revising business scenarios. GIS might be used to help state and local governments calculate

Clearwater, Florida developed an interactive mapping Web-based GIS based on ESRI software. Data used in this program represent various types of calls for police service, such as armed robbery, assault, drug calls, criminal mischief, and weapons violations. The system provides information that helps law enforcement personnel pinpoint areas of crime activity.

response times to natural disasters and other emergencies or to help banks identify the best location for installing new branches or ATM terminals.

For example, Columbia, South Carolina-based First Citizens Bank uses GIS software from MapInfo to determine which markets to focus on for retaining customers and which to focus on for acquiring new customers. MapInfo also lets the bank drill down into details at the individual branch level and individualize goals for each branch. Each branch is able to see whether the greatest revenue opportunities are from mining its database of existing customers or from finding new customers.

BUSINESS INTELLIGENCE USERS

Figure 10.4 shows that over 80 percent of the audience for BI consists of casual users. Senior executives tend use BI to monitor firm activities using visual interfaces like dashboards and scorecards. Middle managers and analysts are much more likely to be immersed in the data and software, entering queries and slicing and dicing the data along different dimensions. Operational employees will, along with customers and suppliers, be looking mostly at pre-packaged reports.

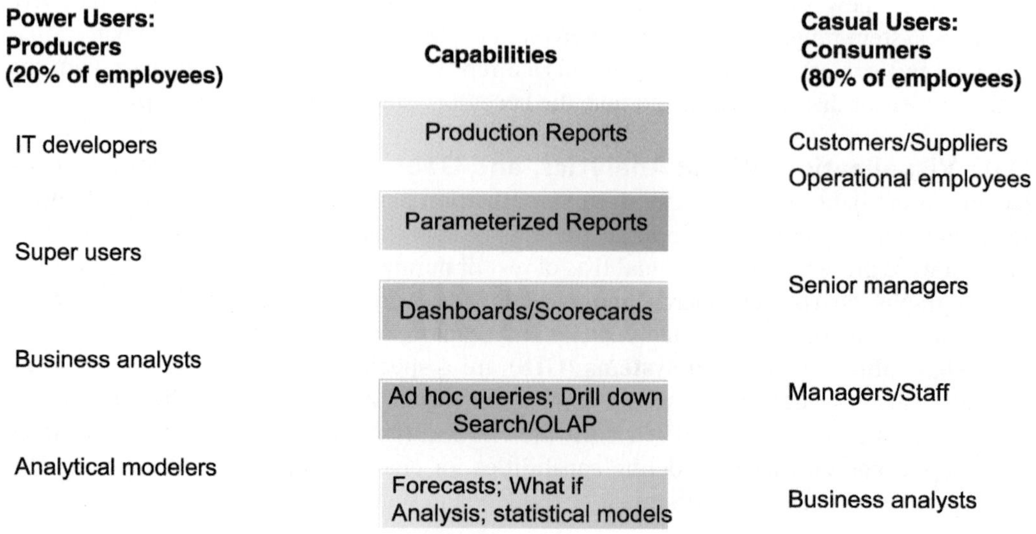

Figure 10.4
Business Intelligence Users
Casual users are consumers of BI output, while intense power users are the producers of reports, new analyses, models, and forecasts.

Power Users: Producers (20% of employees)	Capabilities	Casual Users: Consumers (80% of employees)
IT developers	Production Reports	Customers/Suppliers / Operational employees
Super users	Parameterized Reports	
	Dashboards/Scorecards	Senior managers
Business analysts	Ad hoc queries; Drill down Search/OLAP	Managers/Staff
Analytical modelers	Forecasts; What if Analysis; statistical models	Business analysts

Support for Semistructured Decisions

Many BI pre-packaged production reports are MIS reports supporting structured decision making for operational and middle managers. We described operational and middle management, and the systems they use, in Chapter 2. However, some managers are "super users" and keen business analysts who want to create their own reports, and use more sophisticated analytics and models to find patterns in data, to model alternative business scenarios, or to test specific hypotheses. Decision-support systems (DSS) are the BI delivery platform for this category of users, with the ability to support semistructured decision making.

DSS rely more heavily on modeling than MIS, using mathematical or analytical models to perform what-if or other kinds of analysis. What-if analysis, working forward from known or assumed conditions, allows the user to vary certain values to test results to predict outcomes if changes occur in those values. What happens if we raise product prices by 5 percent or increase the advertising budget by $1 million? **Sensitivity analysis** models ask what-if questions repeatedly to predict a range of outcomes when one or more variables are changed multiple times (see Figure 10.5). Backward sensitivity analysis helps decision makers with goal seeking: If I want to sell 1 million product units next year, how much must I reduce the price of the product?

Chapter 5 described multidimensional data analysis and OLAP as one of the key business intelligence technologies. Spreadsheets have a similar feature for multidimensional analysis called a **pivot table**, which "super user" managers and analysts employ to identify and understand patterns in business information that may be useful for semistructured decision making.

Figure 10.6 illustrates a Microsoft Excel pivot table that examines a large list of order transactions for a company selling online management training videos and books. It shows the relationship between two dimensions: the sales region and the source of contact (Web banner ad or e-mail) for each customer order. It answers the question: does the source of the customer make a difference in addition to region? The pivot table in this figure shows that most customers come from the West and that banner advertising produces most of the customers in all the regions.

One of the Hands-on MIS projects for this chapter asks you to use a pivot table to find answers to a number of other questions using the same list of transactions for the online training company as we used in this discussion. The complete Excel file for these transactions is available in MyMISLab. We have a Learning Track on creating pivot tables using Excel.

In the past, much of this modeling was done with spreadsheets and small stand-alone databases. Today these capabilities are incorporated into large enterprise BI systems, and they are able to analyze data from large corporate databases. BI analytics include tools for intensive modeling, some of which we described earlier. Such capabilities help Progressive Insurance identify the best customers for its products. Using widely available insurance industry data, Progressive defines small groups of customers, or "cells," such as motorcycle riders aged 30 or above with college educations, credit scores over a certain level, and no

Total fixed costs	19000					
Variable cost per unit	3					
Average sales price	17					
Contribution margin	14					
Break-even point	1357					
			Variable Cost per Unit			
Sales	1357	2	3	4	5	6
Price	14	1583	1727	1900	2111	2375
	15	1462	1583	1727	1900	2111
	16	1357	1462	1583	1727	1900
	17	1267	1357	1462	1583	1727
	18	1188	1267	1357	1462	1583

Figure 10.5
Sensitivity Analysis
This table displays the results of a sensitivity analysis of the effect of changing the sales price of a necktie and the cost per unit on the product's break-even point. It answers the question, "What happens to the break-even point if the sales price and the cost to make each unit increase or decrease?"

Figure 10.6
A Pivot Table that Examines Customer Regional Distribution and Advertising Source
In this pivot table, we are able to examine where an online training company's customers come from in terms of region and advertising source.

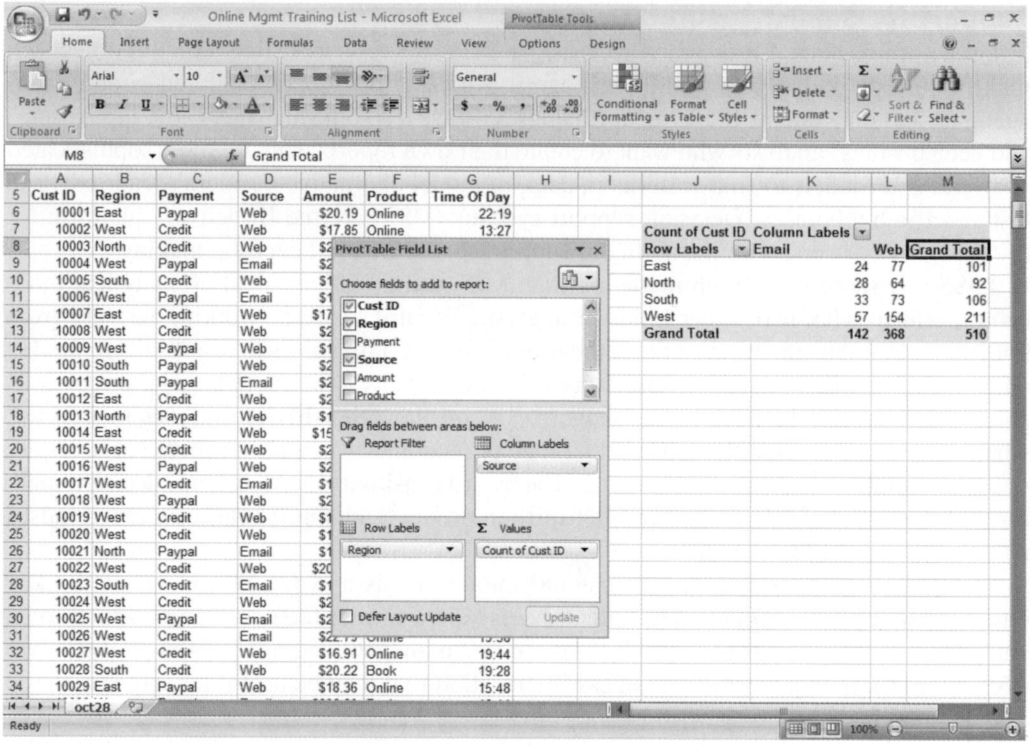

accidents. For each "cell," Progressive performs a regression analysis to identify factors most closely correlated with the insurance losses that are typical for this group. It then sets prices for each cell, and uses simulation software to test whether this pricing arrangement will enable the company to make a profit. These analytic techniques make it possible for Progressive to profitably insure customers in traditionally high-risk categories that other insurers would have rejected.

Decision Support for Senior Management: The Balanced Scorecard and Enterprise Performance Management

Business intelligence delivered in the form of executive support systems (ESS) helps senior executives focus on the really important performance information that affects the overall profitability and success of the firm. Currently, the leading methodology for understanding the most important information needed by a firm's executives is called the **balanced scorecard method** (Kaplan and Norton, 2004; Kaplan and Norton, 1992). The balanced score card is a framework for operationalizing a firm's strategic plan by focusing on measurable outcomes on four dimensions of firm performance: financial, business process, customer, and learning and growth (see Figure 10.7).

Performance on each dimension is measured using **key performance indicators (KPIs)**, which are the measures proposed by senior management for understanding how well the firm is performing along any given dimension. For instance, one key indicator of how well an online retail firm is meeting its customer performance objectives is the average length of time required to deliver a package to a consumer. If your firm is a bank, one KPI of business process performance is the length of time required to perform a basic function like creating a new customer account.

The balanced scorecard framework is thought to be "balanced" because it causes managers to focus on more than just financial performance. In this view, financial performance is past history—the result of past actions—and managers should focus on the things they are able to influence today, such as business process efficiency, customer satisfaction, and employee training. Once a scorecard is developed by consultants and senior

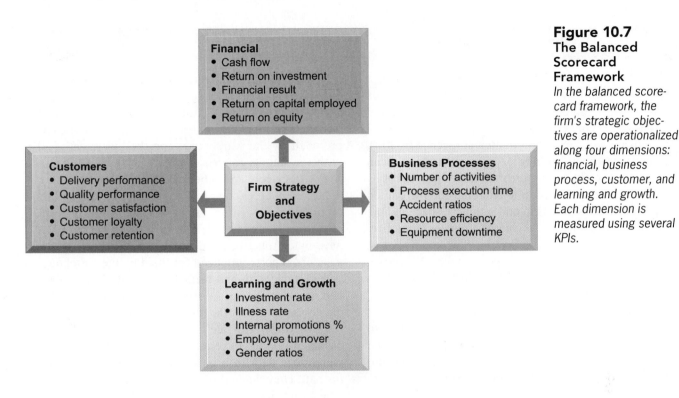

Figure 10.7
The Balanced Scorecard Framework
In the balanced scorecard framework, the firm's strategic objectives are operationalized along four dimensions: financial, business process, customer, and learning and growth. Each dimension is measured using several KPIs.

executives, the next step is automating a flow of information to executives and other managers for each of the key performance indicators.

Another closely related management methodology is **business performance management (BPM)**. Originally defined by an industry group in 2004 (led by the same companies that sell enterprise and database systems like Oracle, SAP, and IBM), BPM attempts to systematically translate a firm's strategies (e.g., differentiation, low-cost producer, market share growth, and scope of operation) into operational targets. Once the strategies and targets are identified, a set of key performance indicators are developed to measure progress toward the targets. The firm's performance is then measured with information drawn from the firm's enterprise database systems. (BPM Working Group, 2004).

Corporate data for contemporary ESS are supplied by the firm's existing enterprise applications (enterprise resource planning, supply chain management, and customer relationship management). ESS also provide access to news services, financial market databases, economic information, and whatever other external data senior executives require. ESS have significant **drill-down** capabilities if managers need more detailed views of data.

Well-designed ESS help senior executives monitor organizational performance, track activities of competitors, recognize changing market conditions, and identify problems and opportunities. Employees lower down in the corporate hierarchy also use these systems to monitor and measure business performance in their areas of responsibility. For these and other business intelligence systems to be truly useful, the information must be "actionable"—it must be readily available and also easy to use when making decisions. If users have difficulty identifying critical metrics within the reports they receive, employee productivity and business performance will suffer. The Interactive Session on People shows how Colgate-Palmolive addressed this problem and helped its managers make more data-driven, actionable decisions.

GROUP DECISION-SUPPORT SYSTEMS

The systems we have just described focus primarily on helping you make a decision acting alone. But what if you are part of a team and need to make a decision as a group? You would use a special category of systems called group decision-support systems (GDSS) for this purpose.

INTERACTIVE SESSION: PEOPLE   Colgate-Palmolive Keeps Managers Smiling with Executive Dashboards

Colgate-Palmolive Company is the second largest consumer products company in the world, and its products are marketed in over 200 countries and territories. The company had 39,000 employees worldwide and $16 billion in annual revenue in 2010. Colgate has been keeping people smiling and clean around the world, with more than three-quarters of its sales in recent years coming from outside the United States. Colgate's brands in oral products, soap, and pet food, are global names, including Colgate, Palmolive, Mennen, Softsoap, Irish Spring, Sorriso, Kolynos, Elmex, Tom's of Maine, Ajax, Axion, Fabuloso, Soupline, and Suavitel, as well as Hill's Science Diet and Hill's Prescription Diet.

The secret to continued growth and stability for the past two decades has been Colgate's ability to move its brands offshore to Latin America, Europe and Asia. In the past, Colgate divided the world into geographic regions: Latin American, Europe, Asia, and North America. Each region had its own information systems. As long as the regions did not need to share resources or information, this patchwork system worked, more or less. This all changed as global operations became more integrated and senior management needed to oversee and coordinate these operations more closely.

Colgate had been a global SAP user since the early 1990s, but it was running five separate ERP systems to serve its different geographic regions. Over a period of time, disparities in the data developed between different geographic regions, and between the data used at the corporate level and the data used by an individual region or business unit. The data were constantly changing. For example, every time a sales report was run, it showed different numbers for orders and shipments. Colgate wanted more usable data to drive business decisions and all of its managers and business units worldwide to work with the same version of the data.

Colgate chose to solve this problem by creating a single global data repository using SAP NetWeaver Business Warehouse, SAP's analytical, reporting and data warehousing solution. Colgate's regional ERP systems feed their data to the warehouse, where the data are standardized and formatted for enterprise-wide reporting and analysis. This eliminates differences in data across the enterprise.

One of the outputs of the warehouse for senior managers is a daily HTML table showing a series of financial and operational metrics for the day compared to the previous month and quarter. The data the executives see are exactly the same as what their peers in all Colgate regions and business units see.

However, the data were not being used by enough employees in their decision making to have an impact on business benefits. Colgate's power users had no trouble using the reporting and analytical tools provided by the warehouse, and they were satisfied with the matrix reports from the system. Colgate's senior managers and other casual users, on the other hand, did not feel comfortable running ad hoc reports or drilling down into the layers of data to answer questions the data brought to light. They did not have much time to spend developing reports, and the standard reports produced for them by the warehouse lacked navigation and drill-down capabilities. Tables had no color coding, so users could only interpret the data by scrutinizing the numbers in the table.

Eventually Colgate's senior managers and other casual users began requesting deeper access to the warehouse data in a more timely and user-friendly format. They wanted reports that were easier to run where the data could be interpreted faster. Senior management requested customizable, real-time dashboards that could be more easily used to drive performance improvement.

Colgate's information systems specialists then implemented SAP NetWeaver BW Accelerator to speed up data loads and improve user perception and adoption, and they implemented SAP Business Objects Web Intelligence to build customized reports. SAP Business Objects Web Intelligence provides a powerful, intuitive interface that enables business analysts and non-technical business professionals to ask spontaneous questions about their data. Casual business users can use simple drag-and-drop techniques to access data sources and create interactive reports that drill, slice, and format information based on their needs. Tools for cutting-edge visualization allow end users to view two- and three-dimensional charts and hone in on specific areas of focus.

Colgate started using SAP's Business Objects tools to build user-friendly dashboards, and quickly created dashboard prototypes for management to review. Using drop-down menus, sliders, and editable labels and colors, the information systems staff was able to create customized dashboards that simplified the presentation of complex business data to suit different types of employees. Once management approved the dashboard design, the dashboards were populated with production data. Now Colgate's senior managers are running the dashboards to monitor the business from a high level.

Employee training was essential to the dashboards' success. Members of Colgate's global information systems development team created customized courses for Colgate's 65 business intelligence experts and ran the classroom training. The training identified people who could be used as resources for developing the reporting tools. When word spread about the dashboards' capabilities, Colgate's power users signed up for the classes as well.

For Colgate, better reporting tools that can support different kinds of users have greatly expanded the use of business intelligence throughout the company. Currently, about 4,000 users interact with Colgate's SAP systems daily, but this number is expected to expand to 15,000 or 20,000 users in the future. People who are accustomed to seeing reports stuffed with numbers are finding that they can use the information presented in dashboards to make faster decisions. For example, managers can determine positive or negative financial conditions by simply looking for where dashboard reports use the color green, which reflects improvements in Colgate's financial position. Executives who formerly relied on other people to obtain their custom reports and data are able to access the information on their own. They can see real data from the system much more easily and quickly.

Sources: David Hannon, "Colgate-Palmolive Empowers Senior Leaders with Executive Dashboards," SAP InsiderPROFILES, April-June 2011; "See Your Business Clearly," SAP, 2010; and "Placing Relevant Business Content within Business User Reach," SAP, 2011.

CASE STUDY QUESTIONS

1. Describe the different types of business intelligence users at Colgate-Palmolive.

2. Describe the "people" issues that were affecting Colgate's ability to use business intelligence.

3. What people, organization, and technology factors had to be addressed in providing business intelligence capabilities for each type of user?

4. What kind of decisions does Colgate's new business intelligence capability support? Give three examples. What is their potential business impact?

MIS IN ACTION

Visit Colgate-Palmolive's Web site to access its annual report. Based on this report, describe two or three dashboards that might be appropriate for senior management.

A **group decision-support system (GDSS)** is an interactive computer-based system for facilitating the solution of unstructured problems by a set of decision makers working together as a group in the same location or in different locations. Groupware and Web-based tools for videoconferencing and electronic meetings described earlier in this text support some group decision processes, but their focus is primarily on communication. GDSS, however, provide tools and technologies geared explicitly toward group decision making.

GDSS-guided meetings take place in conference rooms with special hardware and software tools to facilitate group decision making. The hardware includes computer and networking equipment, overhead projectors, and display screens. Special electronic meeting software collects, documents, ranks, edits, and stores the ideas offered in a decision-making meeting. The more elaborate GDSS use a professional facilitator and support staff. The facilitator selects the software tools and helps organize and run the meeting.

A sophisticated GDSS provides each attendee with a dedicated desktop computer under that person's individual control. No one will be able to see what individuals do on their computers until those participants are ready to share information. Their input is transmitted over a network to a central server that stores information generated by the meeting and makes it available to all on the meeting network. Data can also be projected on a large screen in the meeting room.

GDSS make it possible to increase meeting size while at the same time increasing productivity because individuals contribute simultaneously rather than one at a time. A GDSS promotes a collaborative atmosphere by guaranteeing contributors' anonymity so that attendees can focus on evaluating the ideas themselves without fear of personally being criticized or of having their ideas rejected based on the contributor. GDSS software tools follow structured methods for organizing and evaluating ideas and for preserving the results of meetings, enabling nonattendees to locate needed information after the meeting. The effectiveness of GDSS depends on the nature of the problem and the group and on how well a meeting is planned and conducted.

10.3 Intelligent Systems for Decision Support

Decision making is also enhanced by intelligent techniques and knowledge management systems. **Intelligent techniques** consist of expert systems, case-based reasoning, genetic algorithms, neural networks, fuzzy logic, and intelligent agents. These techniques are based on **artificial intelligence (AI)** technology, which consists of computer-based systems (both hardware and software) that attempt to emulate human behavior and thought patterns. Intelligent techniques aid decision makers by capturing individual and collective knowledge, discovering patterns and behaviors in very large quantities of data, and generating solutions to problems that are too large and complex for human beings to solve on their own.

Knowledge management systems, which we introduced in Chapter 2, and knowledge work systems provide tools for knowledge discovery, communication, and collaboration that make knowledge more easily available to decision makers and integrate it into the business processes of the firm.

EXPERT SYSTEMS

What if employees in your firm had to make decisions that required some special knowledge, such as how to formulate a fast-drying sealing compound or how to diagnose and repair a malfunctioning diesel engine, but all the people with that expertise had left the firm? Expert systems are one type of decision-making aid that could help you out. An **expert system** captures human expertise in a limited domain of knowledge as a set of rules in a software system that can be used by others in the organization. These systems typically perform a limited number of tasks that can be performed by professionals in a few minutes or hours, such as diagnosing a malfunctioning machine or determining whether to grant credit for a loan. They are useful in decision-making situations where expertise is expensive or in short supply.

How Expert Systems Work

Human knowledge must be modeled or represented in a form that a computer can process. Expert systems model human knowledge as a set of rules that collectively are called the **knowledge base**. Expert systems can have from 200 to as many as 10,000 of these rules, depending on the complexity of the decision-making problem. These rules are much more interconnected and nested than in a traditional software program (see Figure 10.8).

The strategy used to search through the collection of rules and formulate conclusions is called the **inference engine**. The inference engine works by searching through the rules and "firing" those rules that are triggered by facts gathered and entered by the user.

Expert systems provide businesses with an array of benefits, including improved decisions, reduced errors, reduced costs, reduced training time, and improved quality and service. For example, Con-Way Transportation built an expert system called Line-haul to automate and optimize planning of overnight shipment routes for its nationwide freight-trucking business. The expert system captures the business rules that dispatchers follow when assigning drivers, trucks, and trailers to transport 50,000 shipments of heavy freight each night across 25 U.S. states and Canada and when plotting their routes.

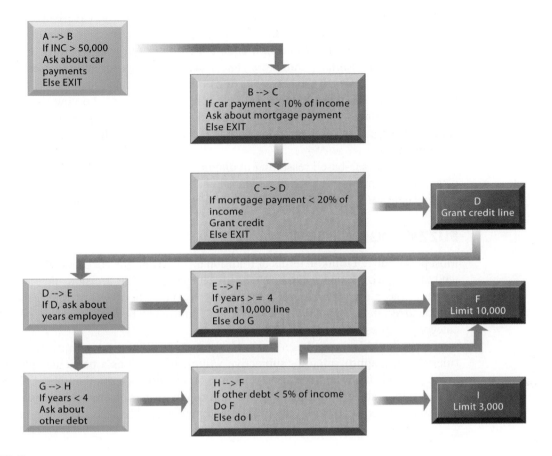

Figure 10.8
Rules in an Expert System
An expert system contains a set of rules to be followed when used. The rules are interconnected, the number of outcomes is known in advance and is limited, there are multiple paths to the same outcome, and the system can consider multiple rules at a single time. The rules illustrated are for a simple credit-granting expert system.

Line-haul runs on a Sun platform and uses data on daily customer shipment requests, available drivers, trucks, trailer space, and weight stored in an Oracle database. The expert system uses thousands of rules and 100,000 lines of program code written in C++ to crunch the numbers and create optimum routing plans for 95 percent of daily freight shipments. Con-Way dispatchers tweak the routing plan provided by the expert system and relay final routing specifications to field personnel responsible for packing the trailers for their nighttime runs. Con-Way recouped its $3 million investment in the system within two years by reducing the number of drivers, packing more freight per trailer, and reducing damage from rehandling. The system also reduces dispatchers' arduous nightly tasks.

Although expert systems lack the robust and general intelligence of human beings, they can provide benefits to organizations if their limitations are well understood. Only certain classes of problems can be solved using expert systems. Virtually all successful expert systems deal with problems of classification in which there are relatively few alternative outcomes and in which these possible outcomes are all known in advance. Expert systems are much less useful for dealing with unstructured problems typically encountered by managers.

CASE-BASED REASONING

Expert systems primarily capture the knowledge of individual experts, but organizations also have collective knowledge and expertise that they have built up over the years. This organizational knowledge can be captured and stored using case-based reasoning. In **case-based reasoning (CBR)**, knowledge and past experiences of human specialists are represented as cases and stored in a database for later retrieval when the user encounters a new case with similar parameters. The system searches for stored cases with problem characteristics similar to the new one, finds the closest fit, and applies the solutions of the old case to the new case. Successful solutions are tagged to the new case and both are stored together with the other cases in the knowledge base. Unsuccessful solutions also are appended to the case database along with explanations as to why the solutions did not work (see Figure 10.9).

You'll find case-based reasoning in diagnostic systems in medicine or customer support where users can retrieve past cases whose characteristics are similar to the new case. The system suggests a solution or diagnosis based on the best-matching retrieved case.

FUZZY LOGIC SYSTEMS

Most people do not think in terms of traditional IF-THEN rules or precise numbers. Humans tend to categorize things imprecisely, using rules for making decisions that may have many shades of meaning. For example, a man or a woman may be *strong* or *intelligent*. A company may be *large, medium*, or *small* in size. Temperature may be *hot, cold, cool*, or *warm*. These categories represent a range of values.

Fuzzy logic is a rule-based technology that represents such imprecision by creating rules that use approximate or subjective values. It describes a particular phenomenon or process linguistically and then represents that description in a small number of flexible rules.

Let's look at the way fuzzy logic would represent various temperatures in a computer application to control room temperature automatically. The terms (known as *membership*

Figure 10.9
How Case-Based Reasoning Works
Case-based reasoning represents knowledge as a database of past cases and their solutions. The system uses a six-step process to generate solutions to new problems encountered by the user.

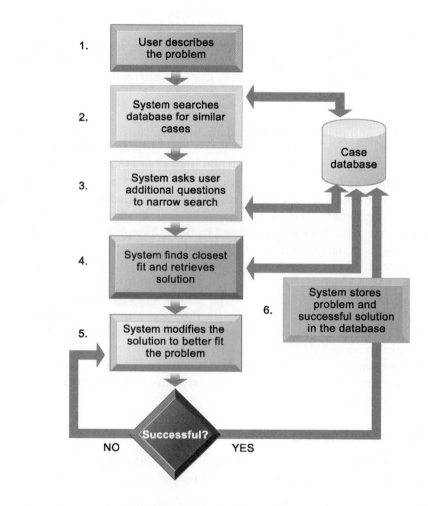

functions) are imprecisely defined so that, for example, in Figure 10.10, cool is between 45 degrees and 70 degrees, although the temperature is most clearly cool between about 60 degrees and 67 degrees. Note that *cool* is overlapped by *cold* or *norm*. To control the room environment using this logic, the programmer would develop similarly imprecise definitions for humidity and other factors, such as outdoor wind and temperature. The rules might include one that says, "If the temperature is *cool* or *cold* and the humidity is low while the outdoor wind is high and the outdoor temperature is low, raise the heat and humidity in the room." The computer would combine the membership function readings in a weighted manner and, using all the rules, raise and lower the temperature and humidity.

Fuzzy logic provides solutions to problems requiring expertise that is difficult to represent in the form of crisp IF-THEN rules. In Japan, Sendai's subway system uses fuzzy logic controls to accelerate so smoothly that standing passengers need not hold on. Fuzzy logic allows incremental changes in inputs to produce smooth changes in outputs instead of discontinuous ones, making it useful for consumer electronics and engineering applications.

NEURAL NETWORKS

Neural networks are used for solving complex, poorly understood problems for which large amounts of data have been collected. They find patterns and relationships in massive amounts of data that would be too complicated and difficult for a human being to analyze. Neural networks discover this knowledge by using hardware and software that parallel the processing patterns of the biological or human brain. Neural networks "learn" patterns from large quantities of data by sifting through data, searching for relationships, building models, and correcting over and over again the model's own mistakes.

A neural network has a large number of sensing and processing nodes that continuously interact with each other. Figure 10.11 represents one type of neural network comprising an input layer, a hidden processing layer, and an output layer. Humans "train" the network by feeding it a set of training data for which the inputs produce a known set of outputs or conclusions. This helps the computer learn the correct solution by example. As the computer is fed more data, each case is compared with the known outcome. If it differs, a correction is calculated and applied to the nodes in the hidden processing layer. These steps are repeated until a condition, such as corrections being less than a certain amount, is reached. The neural network in Figure 10.11 has learned how to identify a fraudulent credit card purchase.

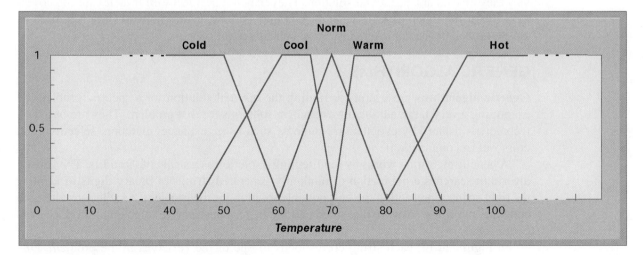

Figure 10.10
Fuzzy Logic for Temperature Control
The membership functions for the input called "temperature" are in the logic of the thermostat to control the room temperature. Membership functions help translate linguistic expressions, such as warm, into numbers that the computer can manipulate.

Figure 10.11
How a Neural Network Works
A neural network uses rules it "learns" from patterns in data to construct a hidden layer of logic. The hidden layer then processes inputs, classifying them based on the experience of the model. In this example, the neural network has been trained to distinguish between valid and fraudulent credit card purchases.

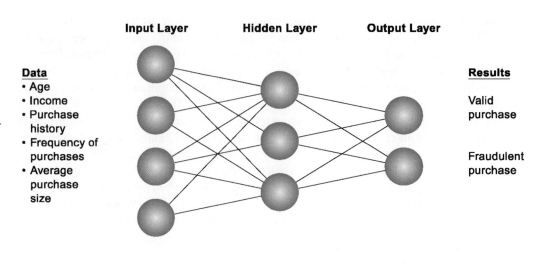

Also, self-organizing neural networks can be trained by exposing them to large amounts of data and allowing them to discover the patterns and relationships in the data.

Whereas expert systems seek to emulate or model a human expert's way of solving problems, neural network builders claim that they do not program solutions and do not aim to solve specific problems. Instead, neural network designers seek to put intelligence into the hardware in the form of a generalized capability to learn. In contrast, the expert system is highly specific to a given problem and cannot be retrained easily.

Neural network applications in medicine, science, and business address problems in pattern classification, prediction, financial analysis, and control and optimization. In medicine, neural network applications are used for screening patients for coronary artery disease, for diagnosing patients with epilepsy and Alzheimer's disease, and for performing pattern recognition of pathology images. The financial industry uses neural networks to discern patterns in vast pools of data that might help investment firms predict the performance of equities, corporate bond ratings, or corporate bankruptcies. Visa International uses a neural network to help detect credit card fraud by monitoring all Visa transactions for sudden changes in the buying patterns of cardholders.

There are many puzzling aspects of neural networks. Unlike expert systems, which typically provide explanations for their solutions, neural networks cannot always explain why they arrived at a particular solution. They may not perform well if their training covers too little or too much data. In most current applications, neural networks are best used as aids to human decision makers instead of substitutes for them.

GENETIC ALGORITHMS

Genetic algorithms are useful for finding the optimal solution for a specific problem by examining a very large number of alternative solutions for that problem. They are based on techniques inspired by evolutionary biology, such as inheritance, mutation, selection, and crossover (recombination).

A genetic algorithm works by representing a solution as a string of 0s and 1s. The genetic algorithm searches a population of randomly generated strings of binary digits to identify the right string representing the best possible solution for the problem. As solutions alter and combine, the worst ones are discarded and the better ones survive to go on to produce even better solutions.

In Figure 10.12, each string corresponds to one of the variables in the problem. One applies a test for fitness, ranking the strings in the population according to their level of desirability as possible solutions. After the initial population is evaluated for fitness, the algorithm then produces the next generation of strings, consisting of strings that survived the fitness test plus offspring strings produced from mating pairs of strings, and tests their fitness. The process continues until a solution is reached.

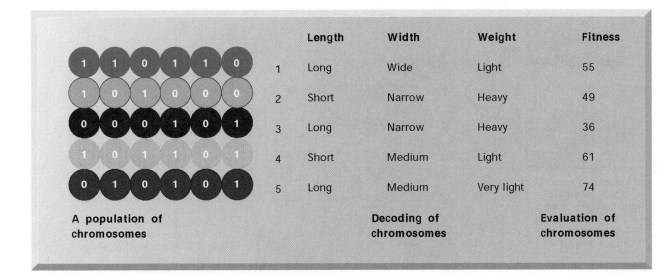

		Length	Width	Weight	Fitness
	1	Long	Wide	Light	55
	2	Short	Narrow	Heavy	49
	3	Long	Narrow	Heavy	36
	4	Short	Medium	Light	61
	5	Long	Medium	Very light	74
A population of chromosomes			Decoding of chromosomes		Evaluation of chromosomes

Figure 10.12
The Components of a Genetic Algorithm
This example illustrates an initial population of "chromosomes," each representing a different solution. The genetic algorithm uses an iterative process to refine the initial solutions so that the better ones, those with the higher fitness, are more likely to emerge as the best solution.

Genetic algorithms are used to solve complex problems that are very dynamic and complex, involving hundreds or thousands of variables or formulas. The problem must be one where the range of possible solutions can be represented genetically and criteria can be established for evaluating fitness. Genetic algorithms expedite the solution because they can evaluate many solution alternatives quickly to find the best one. For example, General Electric engineers used genetic algorithms to help optimize the design for jet turbine aircraft engines, where each design change required changes in up to 100 variables. The supply chain management software from i2 Technologies uses genetic algorithms to optimize production-scheduling models, incorporating hundreds of thousands of details about customer orders, material and resource availability, manufacturing and distribution capability, and delivery dates.

INTELLIGENT AGENTS

Intelligent agent technology helps businesses and decision makers navigate through large amounts of data to locate and act on information that is considered important. **Intelligent agents** are software programs that work in the background without direct human intervention to carry out specific, repetitive, and predictable tasks for an individual user, business process, or software application. The agent uses a limited built-in or learned knowledge base to accomplish tasks or make decisions on the user's behalf, such as deleting junk e-mail, scheduling appointments, or finding the cheapest airfare to California.

There are many intelligent agent applications today in operating systems, application software, e-mail systems, mobile computing software, and network tools. Of special interest to business are intelligent agents that search for information on the Internet. Chapter 6 describes how shopping bots help consumers find products they want and assists them in comparing prices and other features.

Procter & Gamble (P&G) used intelligent agent technology to make its supply chain more efficient (see Figure 10.13). It modeled a complex supply chain as a group of semiautonomous "agents" representing individual supply chain components, such as trucks, production facilities, distributors, and retail stores. The behavior of each agent is programmed to follow rules that mimic actual behavior, such as "order an item when it is out of stock."

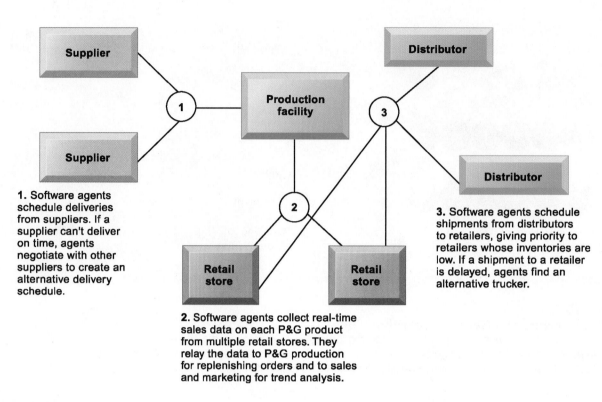

Figure 10.13
Intelligent Agents in P&G's Supply Chain Network
Intelligent agents are helping Procter & Gamble shorten the replenishment cycles for products, such as a box of Tide.

Simulations using the agents enable the company to perform what-if analyses on inventory levels, in-store stockouts, and transportation costs.

Using intelligent agent models, P&G discovered that trucks should often be dispatched before being fully loaded. Although transportation costs would be higher using partially loaded trucks, the simulation showed that retail store stockouts would occur less often, thus reducing the amount of lost sales, which would more than make up for the higher distribution costs. Agent-based modeling has saved P&G $300 million annually on an investment of less than 1 percent of that amount.

Although artificial intelligence technology plays an important role in contemporary knowledge management, it still does not exhibit the breadth, complexity, and originality of human intelligence. Computer scientists and neurologists alike have come to realize how sophisticated our brains actually are, and how complicated certain tasks like recognizing language, identifying objects, and making informed decisions can be for computers.

Solving what's known as the "Paris Hilton problem"—determining whether the phrase "Paris Hilton" refers to the celebrity socialite or a hotel in Paris—has been one of the toughest problems for developers of AI systems. Human beings solve ambiguities like this using context, but computers don't have that option. The Interactive Session on Technology shows how IBM scientists moved closer to a solution with a computer named Watson built to play the popular game show Jeopardy!

10.4 Systems for Managing Knowledge

Systems for knowledge management improve the quality and utilization of knowledge used in the decision-making process. **Knowledge management** refers to the set of business processes developed in an organization to create, store, transfer, and apply knowledge.

INTERACTIVE SESSION: TECHNOLOGY   IBM's Watson: Can Computers Replace Humans?

In February 2011, an IBM computer named Watson took on the two most-decorated champions of the game show Jeopardy, Ken Jennings and Brad Rutter. Watson, which was named after IBM's founder, Thomas J. Watson, won handily.

Watson's achievement represents a milestone in the ability of computers to process and interpret human language. The goal of the IBM team, a group of 25 researchers led by Dr. David Ferrucci, was to develop a more effective set of techniques that computers can use to process "natural language"—language that human beings instinctively use, not language specially formatted to be understood by computers. Watson had to go far beyond responding to simple commands, or receiving only specific, pre-defined inputs. Jeopardy questions are renowned for their wordplay, hidden meanings, and tricky puns, and can deal with practically any subject matter. For computers, language processing doesn't get much harder.

Watson's performance on the show was far from perfect. The computer blundered on a Final Jeopardy question with the category "U.S. Cities," where it selected Toronto as its response. Sometimes, the answers in a category do not directly correspond with the title of the category, so Watson didn't assume, as the human players did, that the answer had to be a city in the United States. Nevertheless, Watson overcame that flub to win convincingly, finishing with over $77,000 to about $20,000 apiece for its human opponents.

The hardware required for Watson to work so quickly and accurately was staggeringly powerful. Watson consists of 10 racks of IBM POWER 750 servers running Linux, uses 15 terabytes of RAM and 2,880 processor cores (equivalent to 6,000 top-end home computers), and operates at 80 teraflops. Watson needed this amount of power to quickly scan its enormous database of information, including information from the Internet. The team downloaded over 10 million documents, including encyclopedias and Wikipedia, the Internet Movie Database (IMDB), and the entire archive of the *New York Times*. All of the data sat in Watson's primary memory, as opposed to a much slower hard drive, so that Watson could find the data it needed within three seconds. The Watson project took 20 IBM engineers three years to build at an $18 million labor cost, and an estimated $1 million in equipment.

Watson is able to learn from its mistakes as well as its successes. To solve a typical problem, Watson tries many of the thousands of algorithms that the team has programmed it to use. The algorithms evaluate the language used in each clue, gather information about the important people and places mentioned in the clue, and generate hundreds of solutions. Human beings don't need to take such a formal approach to generate the solutions that fit a question best, but Watson compensates for this with superior computing power and speed. If a certain algorithm works to solve a problem, Watson remembers what type of question it was and the algorithm it used to get the right answer. In this way, Watson improves at answering questions over time. Watson also learns another way—the team gave Watson thousands of old Jeopardy questions to process. Watson analyzed both questions and answers to determine patterns or similarities between clues, and using these patterns, it assigns varying degrees of confidence to the answers it gives.

Watson was able to correctly answer only a small fraction of the questions it was given at first, but machine learning allowed Watson to continue improving, first growing closer to Jeopardy contestant level, and then finally reaching the Jeopardy champion level of Jennings and Rutter. Similar machine learning techniques are used in computer models that predict weather, likes and dislikes from online retailers like Amazon.com, and speech recognition to develop more accurate predictions, recommendations, and speech processing.

IBM believes future applications for Watson are numerous and wide-ranging in medicine, financial services, or any industry where sifting through large amounts of data to answer questions is important. In September 2011, health insurer WellPoint Inc., with 34.2 million members, enlisted Watson to help it choose among treatment options and medicines. The WellPoint application will combine data from three sources: a patient's chart and electronic records maintained by a physician or hospital, the insurance company's history of medicines and treatments, and Watson's huge library of textbooks and medical journals. Watson should be able to process all of the data and answer a question in moments, providing several possible diagnoses or treatments, ranked in order of the computer's confidence, along with the basis for its answer.

It's unclear how effective Watson will actually be in this field, where the information available in medical journals and other sources is highly disorganized, often contradictory, and littered with typos and inconsistent naming conventions. When human doctors apply their understanding of disease to our bodies, it is based on knowledge of the literature, but also based on prior experience and good guesses. There's no guarantee that Watson can overcome these obstacles, but if it can, it could dramatically increase efficiency and accuracy of medical diagnoses.

Watson's ability to process natural language allows it to perform many jobs requiring factual knowledge and expertise. Jobs that involve answering questions or conducting transactions on the telephone are likely candidates for replacement. While hundreds of thousands of people who perform these jobs could be unemployed, many businesses could use Watson's technology to increase efficiency and improve their bottom lines.

But does Watson really understand language or the answers it's giving? Skeptics of artificial intelligence insist that it doesn't. The IBM researchers who designed the system don't disagree. But to the IBM team, that's less important than the fact that Watson can even answer questions correctly as frequently as it does.

Let's ask Watson: Take a stab at predicting your future impact! Watson is silent on this and other topics. As it turns out, Watson was not programmed to look into the future, or to have intentions, objectives, or feelings about the experience of being Watson.

Sources: Anna Wilde Mathews, "Wellpoint's New Hire. What Is Watson?" *Wall Street Journal*, September 12, 2011; John Markoff, "A Fight to Win the Future: Computers vs. Humans," *New York Times*, February 14, 2011; John Markoff, "Computer Wins on 'Jeopardy!': Trivial, It's Not," *New York Times*, February 16, 2011; "IBM's Watson Heads From 'Jeopardy!' To Columbia University Medical Center," CBSNewYork.com, February 17, 2011; Stanley Fish, "What Did Watson the Computer Do?" *New York Times*, February 21, 2011; Charles Babcock, "Watson's Jeopardy Win a Victory For Mankind," InformationWeek, February 24, 2011; Greg Lindsay,"Changing The Game: 'How I Beat Watson and Came Out a Different Player" and Stephen Baker, "The Programmer's Dilemma: Building a Jeopardy! Champion," McKinsey Quarterly, February 2011.

CASE STUDY QUESTIONS

1. How powerful is Watson? Describe its technology. Why does it require so much powerful hardware?

2. How "intelligent" is Watson? What can it do? What can't it do?

3. What kinds of problems is Watson able to solve?

4. Do you think Watson will be as useful in other disciplines as IBM hopes? Will it be beneficial to everyone? Explain your answer.

MIS IN ACTION

Visit the IBM Web site and search for information on Watson. Then answer the following questions:

1. Which industries or disciplines is IBM targeting with Watson?

2. What improvements is IBM hoping to make in Watson's basic functionality?

3. Try to find video of Watson playing Jeopardy. What kinds of questions does it get wrong?

Knowledge management increases the ability of the organization to learn from its environment and to incorporate knowledge into its business processes and decision making.

Knowledge that is not shared and applied to the problems facing firms and managers does not add any value to the business. Knowing how to do things effectively and efficiently in ways that other organizations cannot duplicate is a major source of profit and competitive advantage. Why? Because the knowledge you generate about your own production processes, and about your customers, usually stays within your firm and cannot be sold or purchased on the open market. In this sense, self-generated business knowledge is a strategic resource and can provide strategic advantage. Businesses will operate less effectively and efficiently if this unique knowledge is not available for decision making and ongoing operations. There are two major types of knowledge management systems: enterprise-wide knowledge management systems and knowledge work systems.

ENTERPRISE-WIDE KNOWLEDGE MANAGEMENT SYSTEMS

Firms must deal with at least three kinds of knowledge. Some knowledge exists within the firm in the form of structured text documents (reports and presentations). Decision makers also need knowledge that is semistructured, such as e-mail, voice mail, chat room exchanges, videos, digital pictures, brochures, or bulletin board postings. In still other cases, there is no formal or digital information of any kind, and the knowledge resides in the heads of employees. Much of this knowledge is **tacit knowledge** and is rarely written down.

Enterprise-wide knowledge management systems deal with all three types of knowledge. Enterprise-wide knowledge management systems are general-purpose, firmwide systems that collect, store, distribute, and apply digital content and knowledge. These systems include capabilities for searching for information, storing both structured and unstructured data, and locating employee expertise within the firm. They also include supporting technologies such as portals, search engines, collaboration tools, and learning management systems.

Enterprise Content Management Systems

Businesses today need to organize and manage both structured and semistructured knowledge assets. **Structured knowledge** is explicit knowledge that exists in formal documents, as well as in formal rules that organizations derive by observing experts and their decision-making behaviors. But, according to experts, at least 80 percent of an organization's business content is semistructured or unstructured—information in folders, messages, memos, proposals, e-mails, graphics, electronic slide presentations, and even videos created in different formats and stored in many locations.

Enterprise content management systems help organizations manage both types of information. They have capabilities for knowledge capture, storage, retrieval, distribution, and preservation to help firms improve their business processes and decisions. Such systems include corporate repositories of documents, reports, presentations, and best practices, as well as capabilities for collecting and organizing semistructured knowledge such as e-mail (see Figure 10.14). Major enterprise content management systems also enable users to access external sources of information, such as news feeds and research, and to communicate via e-mail, chat/instant messaging, discussion groups, and videoconferencing.

A key problem in managing knowledge is the creation of an appropriate classification scheme to organize information into meaningful categories. Once the categories for classifying knowledge have been created, each knowledge object needs to be "tagged," or classified, so that it can be easily retrieved. Enterprise content management systems have capabilities for tagging, interfacing with corporate databases where the documents are stored, and creating an enterprise portal environment for employees to use when searching for corporate knowledge. Open Text, EMC Documentum, IBM, and Oracle are leading vendors of enterprise content management software.

Barrick Gold, the world's leading gold producer, uses Open Text LiveLink Enterprise Content Management tools to manage the massive amounts of information required for building mines. The system organizes and stores both structured and unstructured content, including computer-aided design (CAD) drawings, contracts, engineering data, and production reports. If an operational team needs to refer back to the original document, that

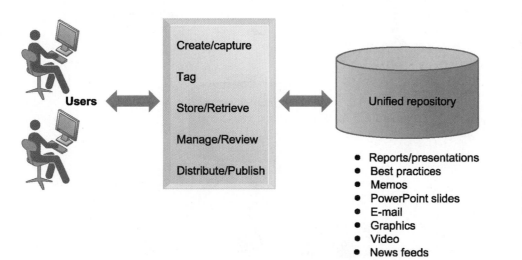

Figure 10.14
An Enterprise Content Management System
An enterprise content management system has capabilities for classifying, organizing, and managing structured and semistructured knowledge and making it available throughout the enterprise.

document is in a single digital repository as opposed to being scattered over multiple systems. Barrick's electronic content management system reduces the amount of time required to search for documents, shortening project schedules, improving the quality of decisions, and minimizing rework (Open Text, 2011).

Firms in publishing, advertising, broadcasting, and entertainment have special needs for storing and managing unstructured digital data such as photographs, graphic images, video, and audio content. **Digital asset management systems** help them classify, store, and distribute these digital objects.

Knowledge Network Systems

Knowledge network systems, also known as *expertise location and management systems*, address the problem that arises when the appropriate knowledge is not in the form of a digital document but instead resides in the memory of expert individuals in the firm. Knowledge network systems provide an online directory of corporate experts in well-defined knowledge domains and use communication technologies to make it easy for employees to find the appropriate expert in a company. Some knowledge network systems go further by systematizing the solutions developed by experts and then storing the solutions in a knowledge database as a best-practices or frequently asked questions (FAQs) repository (see Figure 10.15). Hivemine's AskMe provides stand-alone knowledge networking capabilities, and some knowledge networking capabilities can be found in the leading collaboration software suites.

Collaboration Tools and Learning Management Systems

We have already discussed the role of collaboration tools in information sharing and teamwork in Chapters 2 and 6. Social bookmarking and learning management systems feature additional capabilities for sharing and managing knowledge.

Figure 10.15
An Enterprise Knowledge Network System
A knowledge network maintains a database of firm experts, as well as accepted solutions to known problems, and then facilitates the communication between employees looking for knowledge and experts who have that knowledge. Solutions created in this communication are then added to a database of solutions in the form of frequently asked questions (FAQs), best practices, or other documents.

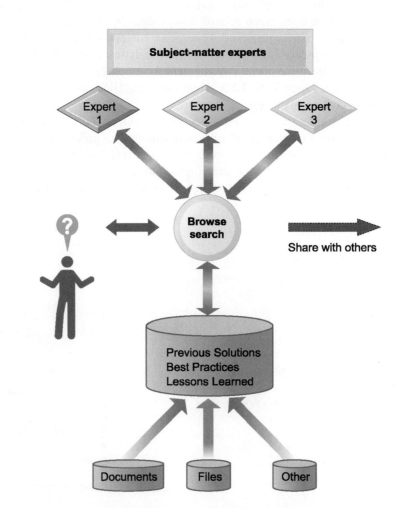

Social bookmarking makes it easier to search for and share information by allowing users to save their bookmarks to Web pages on a public Web site and tag these bookmarks with keywords. These tags can be used to organize and search for the documents. Lists of tags can be shared with other people to help them find information of interest. The user-created taxonomies created for shared bookmarks and social tagging are called **folksonomies**. Delicious and Digg are two popular social bookmarking sites.

Suppose, for example, that you are on a corporate team researching wind power. If you did a Web search and found relevant Web pages on wind power, you would click on a bookmarking button on a social bookmarking site and create a tag identifying each Web document you found to link it to wind power. By clicking on the "tags" button at the social networking site, you would be able to see a list of all the tags you created and select the documents you need.

Companies need ways to keep track of and manage employee learning and to integrate it more fully into their knowledge management and other corporate systems. A **learning management system (LMS)** provides tools for the management, delivery, tracking, and assessment of various types of employee learning and training.

For example, the Whirlpool Corporation uses CERTPOINT's learning management system to manage the registration, scheduling, reporting, and content for its training programs for 3,500 salespeople. The system helps Whirlpool tailor course content to the right audience, track the people who took courses and their scores, and compile metrics on employee performance.

KNOWLEDGE WORK SYSTEMS

The enterprise-wide knowledge systems we have just described provide a wide range of capabilities used by many, if not all, the workers and groups in an organization. Firms also have specialized systems for knowledge workers to help them create new knowledge for improving the firm's business processes and decision making. **Knowledge work systems (KWS)** are specialized systems for engineers, scientists, and other knowledge workers that are designed to promote the creation of knowledge and to ensure that new knowledge and technical expertise are properly integrated into the business.

Requirements of Knowledge Work Systems

Knowledge work systems give knowledge workers the specialized tools they need, such as powerful graphics, analytical tools, and communications and document management. These systems require great computing power to handle the sophisticated graphics or complex calculations necessary for such knowledge workers as scientific researchers, product designers, and financial analysts. Because knowledge workers are so focused on knowledge in the external world, these systems also must give the worker quick and easy access to external databases. They typically feature user-friendly interfaces that enable users to perform needed tasks without having to spend a lot of time learning how to use the computer. Figure 10.16 summarizes the requirements of knowledge work systems.

Knowledge workstations often are designed and optimized for the specific tasks to be performed. Design engineers need graphics with enough power to handle three-dimensional CAD systems. However, financial analysts are more interested in access to a myriad of external databases and technology for efficiently storing and accessing massive amounts of financial data.

Examples of Knowledge Work Systems

Major knowledge work applications include CAD systems (which we introduced in Chapter 3), virtual reality systems for simulation and modeling, and financial workstations.

Contemporary CAD systems are capable of generating realistic-looking three-dimensional graphic designs that can be rotated and viewed from all sides. Troy Lee Designs, which makes sports helmets, recently invested in CAD software that could create the

Figure 10.16
Requirements of Knowledge Work Systems
Knowledge work systems require strong links to external knowledge bases in addition to specialized hardware and software.

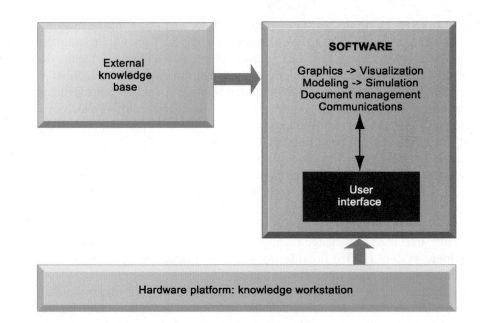

helmets in 3-D. The technology defined the shapes better than traditional methods, which involved sketching an idea on paper, hand-molding a clay model, and shipping the model to Asian factories to create a plastic prototype. Production is now about six months faster and about 35 percent cheaper, with Asian factories able to produce an exact replica after receiving the digital design via e-mail (Maltby, 2010).

Virtual reality systems use interactive graphics software to create computer-generated simulations that are so close to reality that users almost believe they are participating in a real-world situation. In many virtual reality systems, the user dons special clothing, headgear, and equipment, depending on the application. The clothing contains sensors that record the user's movements and immediately transmit that information back to the computer. For instance, to walk through a virtual reality simulation of a house, you would need garb that monitors the movement of your feet, hands, and head. You also would need goggles containing video screens and sometimes audio attachments and feeling gloves so that you are immersed in the computer feedback.

A virtual reality system helps mechanics in Boeing Company's 25-day training course for its 787 Dreamliner learn to fix all kinds of problems, from broken lights in the cabin to major glitches with flight controls. Using both laptop and desktop computers inside a classroom with huge wall-mounted diagrams, Boeing airline mechanics train on a system that displays an interactive Boeing 787 cockpit, as well as a 3-D exterior of the plane. The mechanics "walk" around the jet by clicking a mouse, open virtual maintenance access panels, and go inside the plane to repair and replace parts (Sanders, 2010).

Augmented reality (AR) is a related technology for enhancing visualization. AR provides a live direct or indirect view of a physical real-world environment whose elements are augmented by virtual computer-generated imagery. The user is grounded in the real physical world, and the virtual images are merged with the real view to create the augmented display. The digital technology provides additional information to enhance the perception of reality, making the surrounding real world of the user more interactive and meaningful. The yellow first-down markers shown on televised football games are examples of augmented reality as are medical procedures like image-guided surgery, where data acquired from computerized tomography (CT) and magnetic resonance imaging (MRI) scans or from ultrasound imaging are superimposed on the patient in the operating room. Other industries where AR has caught on include military training, engineering design, robotics, and consumer design.

Virtual reality applications developed for the Web use a standard called **Virtual Reality Modeling Language (VRML)**. VRML is a set of specifications for interactive, three-dimensional modeling on the World Wide Web that organizes multiple media types, including animation, images, and audio, to put users in a simulated real-world environment. VRML is platform independent, operates over a desktop computer, and requires little bandwidth.

DuPont, the Wilmington, Delaware, chemical company, created a VRML application called HyperPlant, which enables users to access three-dimensional data over the Internet using Web browser software. Engineers can go through three-dimensional models as if they were physically walking through a plant, viewing objects at eye level. This level of detail reduces the number of mistakes they make during construction of oil rigs, oil plants, and other structures.

The financial industry is using specialized **investment workstations** to leverage the knowledge and time of its brokers, traders, and portfolio managers. Firms such as Merrill Lynch and UBS Financial Services have installed investment workstations that integrate a wide range of data from both internal and external sources, including contact management data, real-time and historical market data, and research reports. Previously, financial professionals had to spend considerable time accessing data from separate systems and piecing together the information they needed. By providing one-stop information faster and with fewer errors, the workstations streamline the entire investment process from stock selection to updating client records.

LEARNING TRACKS

The following Learning Tracks provide content relevant to topics covered in this chapter:

1. Building and Using Pivot Tables

2. How an Expert System Inference Engine Works

3. Challenges of Implementing and Using Knowledge Management Systems

4. Business Intelligence

Review Summary

1 **What are the different types of decisions, and how does the decision-making process work?** Decisions may be structured, semistructured, or unstructured, with structured decisions clustering at the operational level of the organization and unstructured decisions at the strategic level. Decision making can be performed by individuals or groups and includes employees as well as operational, middle, and senior managers. There are four stages in decision making: intelligence, design, choice, and implementation.

2 **How do business intelligence and business analytics support decision making?** Business intelligence and analytics promise to deliver correct, nearly real-time information to decision makers, and the analytic tools help them quickly understand the information and take action. A business intelligence environment consists of data from the business environment, the BI infrastructure, a BA toolset, managerial users and methods, a BI delivery platform (MIS, DSS, or ESS), and the user interface. There are six analytic functionalities that BI systems deliver to achieve these ends: pre-defined production reports, parameterized reports, dashboards and scorecards, ad hoc queries and searches, the ability to drill down to detailed views of data, and the ability to model scenarios and create forecasts.

Management information systems (MIS) producing prepackaged production reports are typically used to support operational and middle management, whose decision making is fairly structured. For making unstructured decisions, analysts and "super users" employ decision-support systems (DSS) with powerful analytics and modeling tools, including spreadsheets and pivot tables. Senior executives making unstructured decisions use dashboards and visual interfaces displaying key performance information affecting the overall profitability, success, and strategy of the firm. The balanced scorecard and business performance management are two methodologies used in designing executive support systems (ESS).

3 How do information systems help people working in a group make decisions more efficiently? Group decision-support systems (GDSS) help people meeting together in a group arrive at decisions more efficiently. GDSS feature special conference room facilities where participants contribute their ideas using networked computers and software tools for organizing ideas, gathering information, ranking and setting priorities, and documenting meeting sessions.

4 What are the business benefits of using intelligent techniques in decision making and knowledge management? Expert systems capture tacit knowledge from a limited domain of human expertise and express that knowledge in the form of rules. The strategy to search through the knowledge base is called the inference engine. Case-based reasoning represents organizational knowledge as a database of cases that can be continually expanded and refined.

Fuzzy logic is a software technology for expressing knowledge in the form of rules that use approximate or subjective values. Neural networks consist of hardware and software that attempt to mimic the thought processes of the human brain. Neural networks are notable for their ability to learn without programming and to recognize patterns in massive amounts of data.

Genetic algorithms develop solutions to particular problems using genetically based processes, such as fitness, crossover, and mutation. Intelligent agents are software programs with built-in or learned knowledge bases that carry out specific, repetitive, and predictable tasks for an individual user, business process, or software application.

5 What types of systems are used for enterprise-wide knowledge management and knowledge work, and how do they provide value for businesses? Enterprise content management systems feature databases and tools for organizing and storing structured documents and semistructured knowledge, such as e-mail or rich media. Knowledge network systems provide directories and tools for locating firm employees with special expertise who are important sources of tacit knowledge. Often these systems include group collaboration tools, portals to simplify information access, search tools, and tools for classifying information based on a taxonomy that is appropriate for the organization. Learning management systems provide tools for the management, delivery, tracking, and assessment of various types of employee learning and training.

Knowledge work systems (KWS) support the creation of new knowledge and its integration into the organization. KWS require easy access to an external knowledge base; powerful computer hardware that can support software with intensive graphics, analysis, document management, and communications capabilities; and a user-friendly interface.

Key Terms

Artificial intelligence (AI), 346

Augmented reality, 358

Balanced scorecard method, 342

Business performance management (BPM), 343

Case-based reasoning (CBR), 348

Choice, 335

Data visualization, 339

Design, 335

Digital asset management systems, 356

Drill down, 343

Enterprise content management systems, 355

Enterprise-wide knowledge management systems, 355

Folksonomies, 357

Fuzzy logic, 348

Genetic algorithms, 350

Geographic information systems (GIS), 339

Group decision-support systems (GDSS), 345

Implementation, 335

Intelligence, 335

Inference engine, 346

Intelligent agents, 351

Intelligent techniques, 346

Investment workstations, 359

Key performance indicators (KPIs), 342

Knowledge base, 346

Knowledge management, 352

Knowledge network systems, 356

Knowledge work systems (KWS), 357

Learning management system (LMS), 357

Neural networks, 349

Pivot table, 341

Semistructured decisions, 334

Sensitivity analysis, 341

Social bookmarking, 357

Structured decisions, 334

Structured knowledge, 355

Tacit knowledge, 354

Unstructured decisions, 333

Virtual reality systems, 358

Virtual Reality Modeling Language (VRML), 358

Review Questions

1. What are the different types of decisions and how does the decision-making process work?
- List and describe the different decision-making levels and decision-making groups in organizations, and their decision-making requirements.
- Distinguish between an unstructured, semistructured, and structured decision.
- List and describe the stages in decision making.

2. How do business intelligence and business analytics support decision making?
- Define and describe business intelligence and business analytics.
- List and describe the elements of a business intelligence environment.
- List and describe the analytic functionalities provided by BI systems.
- List each of the types of business intelligence users and describe the kinds of systems that provide decision support for each type of user.
- Define and describe the balanced scorecard method and business performance management.

3. How do information systems help people working in a group make decisions more efficiently?
- Define a group decision support system (GDSS), and explain how it works and how it supports organizational decision making.

4. What are the business benefits of using intelligent techniques in decision making and knowledge management?
- Define an expert system, describe how it works, and explain its value to business.
- Define case-based reasoning and explains how it differs from an expert system.
- Define a neural network, and describe how it works and how it benefits businesses.
- Define and describe fuzzy logic, genetic algorithms, and intelligent agents. Explain how each works and the kinds of problems for which each is suited.

5. What types of systems are used for enterprise-wide knowledge management and knowledge work, and how do they provide value for businesses?

- Define knowledge management and explain its value to businesses.

- Define and describe the various types of enterprise-wide knowledge systems and explain how they provide value for businesses.

- Define knowledge work systems and describe the generic requirements of these systems.

- Describe how the following systems support knowledge work: computer-aided design (CAD), virtual reality, and investment workstations.

Discussion Questions

1. If businesses used DSS, GDSS, and ESS more widely, would they make better decisions? Why or why not?

2. Describe various ways that knowledge management systems could help firms with sales and marketing or with manufacturing and production.

3. How much can business intelligence and business analytics help companies refine their business strategy? Explain your answer.

Hands-On MIS Projects

The projects in this section give you hands-on experience designing a knowledge portal, identifying opportunities for business intelligence, using a spreadsheet pivot table to analyze sales data, and using intelligent agents to research products for sale on the Web.

MANAGEMENT DECISION PROBLEMS

1. U.S. Pharma Corporation is headquartered in New Jersey but has research sites in Germany, France, the United Kingdom, Switzerland, and Australia. Research and development of new pharmaceuticals is key to ongoing profits, and U.S. Pharma researches and tests thousands of possible drugs. The company's researchers need to share information with others within and outside the company, including the U.S. Food and Drug Administration, the World Health Organization, and the International Federation of Pharmaceutical Manufacturers & Associations. Also critical is access to health information sites, such as the U.S. National Library of Medicine and to industry conferences and professional journals. Design a knowledge portal for U.S. Pharma's researchers. Include in your design specifications relevant internal systems and databases, external sources of information, and internal and external communication and collaboration tools. Design a home page for your portal.

2. Applebee's is the largest casual dining chain in the world, with over 1,800 locations throughout the United States and 20 other countries. The menu features beef, chicken, and pork items, as well as burgers, pasta, and seafood. Applebee's CEO wants to make the restaurant more profitable by developing menus that are tastier and contain more items that customers want and are willing to pay for despite rising costs for gasoline and agricultural products. How might business intelligence help management implement this strategy? What pieces of data would Applebee's need to collect? What kinds of reports would be useful to help management make decisions on how to improve menus and profitability?

IMPROVING DECISION MAKING: USING PIVOT TABLES TO ANALYZE SALES DATA

Software skills: Pivot tables
Business skills: Analyzing sales data

This project gives you an opportunity to learn how to use Excel's PivotTable functionality to analyze a database or data list. Use the data file for Online Management Training Inc. described earlier in the chapter. This is a list of the sales transactions at OMT for one day. You can find this spreadsheet file at MyMISLab. Use Excel's PivotTable to help you answer the following questions:

- Where are the average purchases higher? The answer might tell managers where to focus marketing and sales resources, or pitch different messages to different regions.
- What form of payment is the most common? The answer could be used to emphasize in advertising the most preferred means of payment.
- Are there any times of day when purchases are most common? Do people buy are products while at work (likely during the day) or at home (likely in the evening)?
- What's the relationship between region, type of product purchased, and average sales price?

We provide instructions on how to use Excel PivotTables in our Learning Tracks.

IMPROVING DECISION MAKING: USING INTELLIGENT AGENTS FOR COMPARISON SHOPPING

Software skills: Web browser and shopping bot software
Business skills: Product evaluation and selection

This project will give you experience using shopping bots to search online for products, find product information, and find the best prices and vendors. Select a digital camera you might want to purchase, such as the Canon PowerShot S100 or the Olympus Stylus 7030. Visit MySimon (www.mysimon.com), BizRate.com (www.bizrate.com), and Google Product Search to do price comparisons for you. Evaluate these shopping sites in terms of their ease of use, number of offerings, speed in obtaining information, thoroughness of information offered about the product and seller, and price selection. Which site or sites would you use and why? Which camera would you select and why? How helpful were these sites for making your decision?

Video Cases

Video Cases and Instructional Videos illustrating some of the concepts in this chapter are available. Contact your instructor to access these videos.

Collaboration and Teamwork

Designing a University GDSS

With three or four of your classmates, identify several groups in your university that might benefit from a GDSS. Design a GDSS for one of those groups, describing its hardware, software, and people elements. If possible, use Google Sites to post links to Web pages, team communication announcements, and work assignments; to brainstorm; and to work collaboratively on project documents. Try to use Google Docs to develop a presentation of your findings for the class.

BUSINESS PROBLEM-SOLVING CASE

Zynga Wins with Business Intelligence

The world's fastest growing gaming company doesn't boast top-of-the-line graphics, heart-pounding action, or masterful storytelling. It doesn't make games for the PlayStation, Xbox, or Wii. The company in question is Zynga, and if you have a Facebook account, odds are you're already well aware of its most popular games. Zynga's explosive growth illustrates the potential of social gaming and the ability of social networks to provide critical data about a company's customers.

Founded in 2007 by Mark Pincus and a group of other entrepreneurs, Zynga is the leading developer of social network games, such as CityVille, Texas HoldEm Poker, and FarmVille. These games, along with Zynga's Empires & Allies game, are the four most frequently used applications on Facebook. Zynga's games have 250 million monthly active users, whose gaming keystrokes and clicks generate 3 terabytes of data every day. Since its inception, Zynga has put a priority on data analytics to guide the management of its games and the business decisions of the company.

The company relies heavily on its data to improve user retention and to increase collaboration among its gamers. In the words of Ken Rudin, chief of data analytics at Zynga, to be useful, data has "gotta be actionable"—it has to be information that allows Zynga to make noticeable improvements to its games. Generating and storing game data is only half of the battle. Zynga also uses a reporting team and an analytics team to work with the data and make concrete recommendations for business improvements based on that data.

There are three key metrics that drive the economics of social gaming: churn rates, the viral coefficient, and revenue per user. Churn, which we discuss in Chapter 8, is the loss rate of game players. Social gaming can have an extraordinarily high churn rate, about 50 percent per month on average. That means that half the new players signing up for a game today will be gone in a month.

The viral coefficient is a measure of the effectiveness of existing game players for drawing new players, an important capability for social network platforms. For example, if 100 FarmVille users are likely to cause 5 of their friends to sign up in a given month, that would result in a viral coefficient of 1.05.

Expected revenue per user is an estimate of the lifetime revenue that a game player will generate, based on an estimate of monthly revenue per user and the churn rate. For instance, if the average monthly revenue

is $5 per user and the churn rate is 50 percent, the expected revenue can be estimated as $5 the first month + $2.50 the second month + $1.25 the third month, and so forth, or approximately $20.

The first wave of social gaming applications on Facebook tried to increase the viral coefficient with wall postings advertising in-game actions by players. This approach created too much "wall spam," or game-related postings that made it difficult for social network users to identify posts by friends. Facebook and other social networking platforms then demanded that gaming firms reduce their wall spam.

As a result, Zynga turned to social graph analysis. For social games, the "social graph," or relationships between friends, is somewhat different from that for the social networking platform itself. For example, in Zynga's Mafia Wars game, players might have two types of friends—those who actively play the game and a more passive group that signed on to help expand a friend's Mafia organization and then left the game or played very infrequently. Players don't always interact the same way with these two groups, with gifts and offers of help more frequent within the active group. Guiding game players to communicate appropriately with these different types of relationships helps increase revenue and virality while reducing churn. A social gaming company such as Zynga will thus try to improve the player experience to make every aspect of the game more profitable.

Technology from Vertica Systems, an analytic database management company, helps solve this problem. Vertica's Massively Parallel Processing (MPP) architecture enables customers to deploy its analytics platform using industry-standard hardware or cloud solutions as building blocks called "nodes." Users can build clusters consisting of 1, 10, 100 or more nodes, putting thousands of processors, terabytes of computer memory, and petabytes of disk storage to work as a single parallel cluster. A small start-up company can deploy Vertica on a single node, adding new nodes as needed.

Vertica's data warehouse is columnar, meaning that data are stored in columns instead of rows. This allows Zynga's data to be more tightly compressed, at a rate of 10 to 1 (10 terabytes of data become 1 terabyte of compressed data). Vertica's data warehouse is able to work with this compressed data, which improves performance by reducing processor demands, memory, and disk input/output at processing time. Traditional database management systems can't work with compressed data. As a result, Zynga achieves rates of performance that are 50 to 100 times faster than the data warehouses used by other companies.

Vertica software is also able to manipulate the database for social graph analysis, transposing all of an individual user's interactions with other users into a single row, and it can do this quickly with database tables consisting of tens of billions of rows of data. Relational database platforms are unable to cope with the massive volume of data created by all the connections in a social graph.

Zynga's social graph-related data are streamed in real time to a dedicated Vertica cluster where the graph is generated on a daily basis. Every night, the models resulting from this graph are fed back into its games for use the next day. With this business intelligence solution, Zynga has been able to improve the targeting of items such as gifts to effectively increase the level of interaction between active players while minimizing spam to passive players. Zynga is now in a position to identify groups of users with similar behavior or common paths for even more precise targeting of game-related promotions and activities.

Zynga's revenue rose from $121 million in 2009 to $600 million and a $91 million dollar profit in 2010. Clearly, Zynga's methods are working. Traditional game makers like Activision Blizzard and Electronic Arts are noting Zynga's growth and success and have moved towards a similar business model. For example, Electronic Arts launched a free Facebook version of the classic game "The Sims." The game now has 40 million active monthly players and was Facebook's fastest growing app for much of 2011.

Zynga's business model is to offer free games geared towards a larger, more casual gaming audience, and to generate revenue by selling "virtual goods" in game. The idea of virtual goods has been around for years, most notably in Second Life and other virtual worlds, where users can buy apparel and accessories for their in-game avatars. But Zynga's attention to detail and ability to glean important information from countless terabytes of data generated daily by its users has set it apart. For example, product managers in Zynga's FishVille Facebook game discovered that players bought a certain type of fish in game, the translucent anglerfish, more frequently than the rest. Zynga began offering fish similar to the anglerfish for about $3 apiece, and FishVille players responded by buying many more fish than usual. Analytics have also shown that Zynga's gamers tend to buy more in-game goods when they are offered as limited-edition items. Zynga sells advertising, both in and around its games, but the vast majority of its revenue comes from its virtual goods sales.

Zynga also benefits from using Facebook as its game platform. When users install a Zynga application, they allow Zynga access to all of their profile information, including their names, genders, and lists of friends. Zynga then uses that information to determine what types of users are most likely to behave in certain ways. Zynga particularly hopes to determine which types of users are most likely to become "whales," or big spenders that buy hundreds of dollars of virtual goods each month. Though only 5 percent of Zynga's 150 million active users contribute to corporate revenue, that subset of users is so dedicated that they account for nearly all of the company's earnings.

Zynga's games make heavy use of Facebook's social features. For example, in CityVille, users must find friends to fill fictional posts at their "City Hall" to successfully complete the structure. All of Zynga's games have features like this, but Facebook hasn't always fully supported all of Zynga's efforts. Zynga's Facebook apps were formerly able to send messages directly to Facebook members, but they disabled the feature after complaints that it was a form of spam. Still, if your friends use Zynga's Facebook apps, chances are you've seen advertisements encouraging you to play as well in your News Feed.

Zynga's success has disrupted the video game industry. Traditional video game companies begin with an idea for a game that they hope players will buy and enjoy, and then make the game. Zynga begins with a game, but then studies data to determine how its players play, what types of players are most active, and what virtual goods players buy. Then, Zynga uses the data to get players to play longer, tell more friends, and buy even more goods.

Not everybody is thrilled with Zynga's data-driven approach to making games. Many game industry veterans believe Zynga's games are overly simplistic and have many of the same game elements. The company has also been the target of several lawsuits alleging that Zynga copied other companies' games. Even developers within Zynga have sometimes bristled at the company's prioritization of data analysis over creativity in game design. Some question Zynga's ability to prosper over the long term, saying it would be difficult for the company to create new games to replace old ones whose novelty is fading. Zynga's business model also assumes Facebook will continue to operate in the same manner and that customers will continue to expect the same quality of games. That may not always be the case.

In other words, Zynga's games lack artistry. But Zynga readily admits that its target audience is the segment of gamers that prefer casual games, and its goal is to make games that nearly anyone can play. Gamers that want a game requiring high levels of skill or sophisticated graphics can get their fix elsewhere. Zynga is using the measurability of Facebook activity to guide its game management, and this is helping the company create a finely tailored user experience that hasn't been seen before in gaming. Zynga's future is bright, but you can bet that they'll be poring over the data to find out how to make it even brighter.

Sources: Nick Wingfield, "Virtual Products, Real Profits," *Wall Street Journal*, September 9, 2011; "The Impact of Social Graphing Analysis on the Bottom Line: How Zynga Performs Graph Analysis with the Vertica Analytics Platform," www.vertica.com, accessed October 1, 2011; and Jacquelyn Gavron, "Vertica: The Analytics Behind all the Zynga Games," ReadWrite Enterprise, July 18, 2011.

Case Study Questions

1. It has been said that Zynga is "an analytics company masquerading as a games company." Discuss the implications of this statement.
2. What role does business intelligence play in Zynga's business model?
3. Give examples of three kinds of decisions supported by business intelligence at Zynga.
4. How much of a competitive advantage does business intelligence provide for Zynga? Explain.
5. What problems can business intelligence solve for Zynga? What problems can't it solve?

Building and Managing Systems

PART IV

Part IV shows how to use the knowledge acquired in earlier chapters to analyze and design information system solutions to business problems. This part answers questions such as these: How can I develop a solution to an information system problem that provides genuine business benefits? How can the firm adjust to the changes introduced by the new system solution? What alternative approaches are available for building system solutions? What broader ethical and social issues should be addressed when building and using information systems?

Building Information Systems and Managing Projects

CHAPTER

11

STUDENT LEARNING OBJECTIVES

After completing this chapter, you will be able to answer the following questions:

1. What are the core problem-solving steps for developing new information systems?

2. What are the alternative methods for building information systems?

3. What are the principal methodologies for modeling and designing systems?

4. How should information systems projects be selected and evaluated?

5. How should information systems projects be managed?

Chapter Outline

A NEW ORDERING SYSTEM FOR GIRL SCOUT COOKIES

Peanut Butter Petites, Caramel deLites, Thin Mints—Girl Scout Cookies are American favorites. Cookie sales are a major source of funding for the Girl Scouts, but collecting, counting, and organizing the annual avalanche of cookie orders has become a tremendous challenge.

The Girl Scouts' traditional cookie-ordering process depends on mountains of paperwork. During the peak sales period in January, each Girl Scout marked her sales on an individual order card and turned the card in to the troop leader when she was finished. The troop leader would transfer the information onto a five-part form and give this form to a community volunteer who tabulated the orders. From there, the orders data passed to a regional council headquarters, where they would be batched into final orders for the manufacturer, ABC Cookies. In addition to ordering, Girl Scout volunteers and troop members had to coordinate cookie deliveries, from the manufacturer to regional warehouses, to local drop-off sites, to each scout, and to the customers themselves.

The paperwork was overwhelming. Order transactions changed hands too many times, creating many opportunities for error. All the added columns, multiple prices per box, and calculations that had to be made by different people, all on a deadline.

© Michael Newman, 2011, PhotoEdit, Inc.

The Patriots' Trail Girl Scout Council, representing 65 communities and 18,000 Girl Scouts in the greater Boston area, was one of the first councils to tackle this problem. The council sells over 1.5 million boxes of cookies each year. The council initially investigated building a computerized system using Microsoft Access database management and application development tools. But this alternative would have cost $25,000 to develop and would have taken at least three to four months to get the system up and running. It was too time-consuming, complex, and expensive for the Girl Scouts. In addition to Microsoft Access software, the Girl Scouts would have to purchase a server to run the system plus pay for networking and Web site maintenance services so the system could be made available on the Web.

After consulting with management consultants Dovetail Associates, the council selected Intuit's QuickBase for Corporate Workgroups. QuickBase is a hosted Web-based software service for small businesses and corporate workgroups. It is especially well suited for building simple database applications very quickly and does not require a great deal of training to use. QuickBase is customizable and designed to collect, organize, and share data among teams in many different locations.

A Dovetail consultant created a working QuickBase prototype with some basic functions for the Girl Scouts within a few hours. It only took two months to build, test, and implement the entire system using this software. The cost for developing the entire system was a fraction of the Microsoft Access solution. The Girl Scouts do not have to pay for any hardware, software, or networking services because QuickBase runs everything for them on its servers. QuickBase costs about $500 per month for organizations with 100 users and $1,500 per month for organizations with up to 500 users. It is very easy to use.

The QuickBase solution eliminates paperwork and calculation errors by providing a clear central source of data for the entire council and easy online entry of cookie orders over the Web. Troop leaders collect the Girl Scouts' order cards and enter them directly into the QuickBase system using their home computers linked to the Web. With a few mouse clicks, the council office consolidates the unit totals and transmits the orders electronically to ABC Cookies. As local orders come in, local section leaders can track the data in real time.

The Patriots' Trail Girl Scouts also uses the QuickBase system to manage the Cookie Cupboard warehouse, where volunteers pick up their cookie orders. Volunteers use the system to make reservations so that the warehouse can prepare the orders in advance, saving time and inventory management costs. The trucking companies that deliver cookie shipments now receive their instructions electronically through QuickBase so that they can create efficient delivery schedules.

Since its implementation, the Patriots' Trail QuickBase system has cut paperwork by more than 90 percent, reduced errors to 1 percent, and reduced the time spent by volunteers by 50 percent. The old system used to take two months to tally the orders and determine which Scouts should be rewarded for selling the most cookies. Now that time has been cut to 48 hours.

Other Girl Scouts, councils have implemented similar QuickBase systems to track sales and achieved similar benefits. The Girl Scouts of Greater Los Angeles, serving Los Angeles County and parts of Kern and San Bernardino counties, has reduced the paperwork associated with the sales for 3.5 million boxes of cookies annually by 95 percent.

Sources: Liz McCann, "Texting + QuickBase Make Selling Girl Scout Cookies Easier in LA, "March 8, 2010, www.quickbase.intuit.com, www.girlscoutseasternmass.org/cookies, accessed July 15, 2011; and "Girl Scouts Unite Behind Order Tracking," *Customer Relationship Management*, May 2005.

The experience of the Patriots' Trail Girl Scout Council illustrates some of the steps required to design and build new information systems. It also illustrates some of the benefits of a new system solution. The Girl Scouts had an outdated manual paper-based system for processing cookie orders that was excessively time-consuming and error ridden. The Girl Scouts tried several alternative solutions before opting for a new ordering system based on the QuickBase software service. In this chapter, we will examine the Girl Scouts' search for a system solution as we describe each step of building a new information system using the problem-solving process.

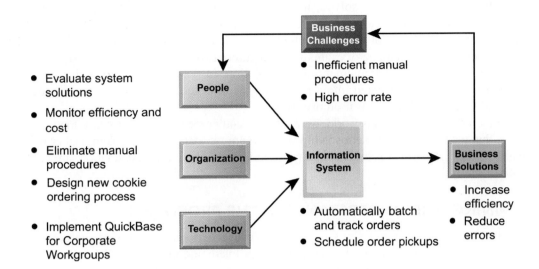

11.1 Problem Solving and Systems Development

We have already described the problem-solving process and how it helps us analyze and understand the role of information systems in business. This problem-solving process is especially valuable when we need to build new systems. A new information system is built as a solution to a problem or set of problems the organization perceives it is facing. The problem may be one in which managers and employees believe that the business is not performing as well as expected, or it may come from the realization that the organization should take advantage of new opportunities to perform more effectively.

Let's apply this problem-solving process to system building. Figure 11.1 illustrates the four steps we would need to take: (1) define and understand the problem, (2) develop alternative solutions, (3) choose the best solution, and (4) implement the solution.

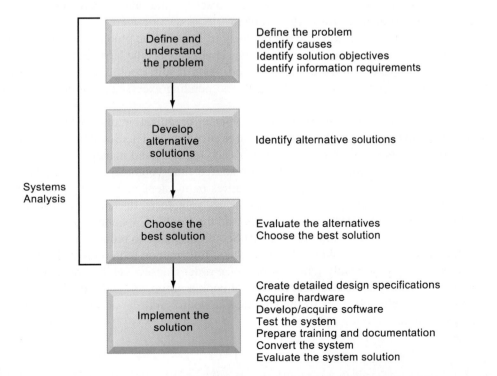

**Figure 11.1
Developing an
Information System
Solution**
*Developing an informa-
tion system solution is
based on the problem-
solving process.*

Before a problem can be solved, it first must be properly defined. Members of the organization must agree that a problem actually exists and that it is serious. The problem must be investigated so that it can be better understood. Next comes a period of devising alternative solutions, then one of evaluating each alternative and selecting the best solution. The final stage is one of implementing the solution, in which a detailed design for the solution is specified, translated into a physical system, tested, introduced to the organization, and further refined as it is used over time.

In the information systems world, we have a special name for these activities. Figure 11.1 shows that the first three problem-solving steps, where we identify the problem, gather information, devise alternative solutions, and make a decision about the best solution, are called **systems analysis**.

DEFINING AND UNDERSTANDING THE PROBLEM

Defining the problem may take some work because various members of the company may have different ideas about the nature of the problem and its severity. What caused the problem? Why is it still around? Why wasn't it solved long ago? Systems analysts typically gather facts about existing systems and problems by examining documents, work papers, procedures, and system operations, and by interviewing key users of the system.

Information systems problems in the business world typically result from a combination of people, organization, and technology factors. When identifying a key issue or problem, ask what kind of problem it is: Is it a people problem, an organizational problem, a technology problem, or a combination of these? What people, organizational, and technological factors contributed to the problem?

Once the problem has been defined and analyzed, it is possible to make some decisions about what should and can be done. What are the objectives of a solution to the problem? Is the firm's objective to reduce costs, increase sales, or improve relationships with customers, suppliers, or employees? Do managers have sufficient information for decision making? What information is required to achieve these objectives?

At the most basic level, the **information requirements** of a new system identify who needs what information, where, when, and how. Requirements analysis carefully defines the objectives of the new or modified system and develops a detailed description of the functions that the new system must perform. A system designed around the wrong set of requirements will either have to be discarded because of poor performance or will need to undergo major modifications. Section 11.2 describes alternative approaches to eliciting requirements that help minimize this problem.

Let's return to our opening case about the Girl Scouts. The problem here is that the Girl Scout ordering process is heavily manual and cannot support the large number of volunteers and cookie orders that must be coordinated. As a result, cookie ordering is extremely inefficient with high error rates and volunteers spending excessive time organizing orders and deliveries.

Organizationally, the Girl Scouts is a volunteer organization distributed across a large area, with cookie sales as the primary source of revenue. The Scouts rely on volunteers with little or no business or computer experience for sales and management of orders and deliveries. They have almost no financial resources and volunteers are strapped for time. The Girl Scout cookie-ordering process requires many steps and coordination of multiple groups and organizations—individual Girl Scouts, volunteers, the council office, the cookie manufacturing factory, trucking companies, and the Cookie Cupboard warehouse.

The objectives of a solution for the Girl Scouts would be to reduce the amount of time, effort, and errors in the cookie-ordering process. Information requirements for the solution include the ability to rapidly total and organize order transactions for transmittal to ABC Cookies; the ability to track orders by type of cookie, troop, and individual Girl Scout; the ability to schedule deliveries to the Cookie Cupboard; and the ability to schedule order pickups from the Cookie Cupboard.

DEVELOPING ALTERNATIVE SOLUTIONS

What alternative solutions are possible for achieving these objectives and meeting these information requirements? The systems analysis lays out the most likely paths to follow given the nature of the problem. Some possible solutions do not require an information system solution but instead call for an adjustment in management, additional training, or refinement of existing organizational procedures. Some, however, do require modifications to the firm's existing information systems or an entirely new information system.

EVALUATING AND CHOOSING SOLUTIONS

The systems analysis includes a **feasibility study** to determine whether each proposed solution is feasible, or achievable, from a financial, technical, and organizational standpoint. The feasibility study establishes whether each alternative solution is a good investment, whether the technology needed for the system is available and can be handled by the firm's information systems staff, and whether the organization is capable of accommodating the changes introduced by the system.

A written systems proposal report describes the costs and benefits, and advantages and disadvantages of each alternative solution. Which solution is best in a financial sense? Which works best for the organization? The systems analysis will detail the costs and benefits of each alternative and the changes that the organization will have to make to use the solution effectively. We provide a detailed discussion of how to determine the business value of systems and manage change in the following section. On the basis of this report, management will select what it believes is the best solution for the company.

The Patriots' Trail Girl Scouts had three alternative solutions. One was to streamline existing processes, continuing to rely on manual procedures. However, given the large number of Girl Scouts and cookie orders, as well as relationships with manufacturers and shippers, redesigning and streamlining a manual ordering and delivery process would not have provided many benefits. The Girl Scouts needed an automated solution that accurately tracked thousands of order and delivery transactions, reduced paperwork, and created a central real-time source of sales data that could be accessed by council headquarters and individual volunteers.

A second alternative was to custom-build a cookie-ordering system using Microsoft Access. This alternative was considered too time-consuming, expensive, and technically challenging for the Girl Scouts. It required $25,000 in initial programming costs, plus the purchase of hardware and networking equipment to run the system and link it to the Internet, as well as trained staff to run and maintain the system.

The third alternative was to rapidly create a system using an application service provider. QuickBase provides templates and tools for creating simple database systems in very short periods, provides the hardware for running the application and Web site, and can be accessed by many different users over the Web. This solution did not require the Girl Scouts to purchase any hardware, software, or networking technology or to maintain any information system staff to support the system. This last alternative was the most feasible for the Girl Scouts.

IMPLEMENTING THE SOLUTION

The first step in implementing a system solution is to create detailed design specifications. **Systems design** shows how the chosen solution should be realized. The system design is the model or blueprint for an information system solution and consists of all the specifications that will deliver the functions identified during systems analysis. These specifications should address all of the technical, organization, and people components of the system solution. Table 11.1 shows some of the design specifications for the Girl Scouts' new system, which were based on information requirements for the solution that was selected.

TABLE 11.1		
Design Specifications for the Girl Scout Cookie System		
	Output	Online reports
		Hard-copy reports
		Online queries
		Order transactions for ABC Cookies
		Delivery tickets for the trucking firm
	Input	Order data entry form
		Troop data entry form
		Girl Scout data entry form
		Shipping/delivery data entry form
	User interface	Graphical Web interface
	Database	Database with cookie order file, delivery file, troop contact file
	Processing	Calculate order totals by type of cookie and number of boxes
		Track orders by troop and individual Girl Scout
		Schedule pickups at the Cookie Cupboard
		Update Girl Scout and troop data for address and member changes
	Manual procedures	Girl Scouts take orders with paper forms
		Troop leaders collect order cards from Scouts and enter the order data online
	Security and controls	Online passwords
		Control totals
	Conversion	Input Girl Scout and troop data
		Transfer factory and delivery data
		Test system
	Training and documentation	System guide for users
		Online practice demonstration
		Online training sessions
		Training for ABC Cookies and trucking companies to accept data and instructions automatically from the Girl Scout system
	Organizational changes	Job design: Volunteers no longer have to tabulate orders
		Process design: Take orders on manual cards but enter them online into the system
		Schedule order pickups from the Cookie Cupboard online

Completing Implementation

In the final steps of implementing a system solution, the following activities would be performed:

- *Hardware selection and acquisition.* System builders select appropriate hardware for the application. They would either purchase the necessary computers and networking hardware or lease them from a technology provider.

- *Software development and programming.* Software is custom programmed in-house or purchased from an external source, such as an outsourcing vendor, an application software package vendor, or an application service provider.

The Girl Scouts did not have to purchase additional hardware or software. QuickBase offers templates for generating simple database applications. Dovetail consultants used the QuickBase tools to rapidly create the software for the system. The system runs on QuickBase servers.

- *Testing.* The system is thoroughly tested to ensure it produces the right results. The **testing process** requires detailed testing of individual computer programs, called **unit testing**, as well as **system testing**, which tests the performance of the information system as a whole. **Acceptance testing** provides the final certification that the system is ready to be used in a production setting. Information systems tests are evaluated by users and reviewed by management. When all parties are satisfied that the new system meets their standards, the system is formally accepted for installation.

The systems development team works with users to devise a systematic test plan. The **test plan** includes all of the preparations for the series of tests we have just described. Figure 11.2 shows a sample from a test plan that might have been used for the Girl Scout cookie system. The condition being tested is online access of an existing record for a specific Girl Scout troop.

- *Training and documentation.* End users and information system specialists require training so that they will be able to use the new system. Detailed **documentation** showing how the system works from both a technical and end-user standpoint must be prepared.

The Girl Scout cookie system provides an online practice area for users to practice entering data into the system by following step-by-step instructions. Also available on the Web is a step-by-step instruction guide for the system that can be downloaded and printed as a hard-copy manual.

- *Conversion* is the process of changing from the old to the new system. There are three main conversion strategies: the parallel strategy, the direct cutover strategy, and the phased approach strategy.

In a **parallel strategy**, both the old system and its potential replacement are run together for a time until everyone is assured that the new one functions correctly. The old system remains available as a backup in case of problems. The **direct cutover strategy** replaces

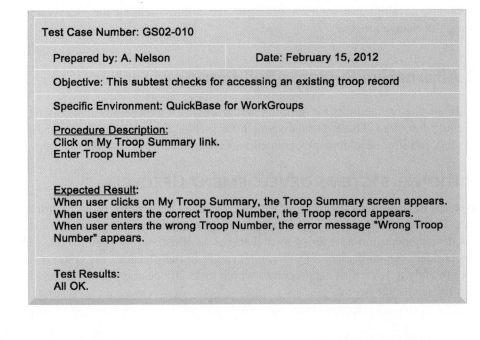

Figure 11.2
A Sample Test Plan for the Girl Scout Cookie System
When developing a test plan, it is imperative to include the various conditions to be tested, the requirements for each condition tested, and the expected results. Test plans require input from both end users and information systems specialists.

Test Case Number: GS02-010

Prepared by: A. Nelson   Date: February 15, 2012

Objective: This subtest checks for accessing an existing troop record

Specific Environment: QuickBase for WorkGroups

Procedure Description:
Click on My Troop Summary link.
Enter Troop Number

Expected Result:
When user clicks on My Troop Summary, the Troop Summary screen appears.
When user enters the correct Troop Number, the Troop record appears.
When user enters the wrong Troop Number, the error message "Wrong Troop Number" appears.

Test Results:
All OK.

the old system entirely with the new system on an appointed day, carrying the risk that there is no system to fall back on if problems arise. A **phased approach** introduces the system in stages (such as first introducing the modules for ordering Girl Scout cookies and then introducing the modules for transmitting orders and instructions to the cookie factory and shipper).

- *Production and maintenance.* After the new system is installed and conversion is complete, the system is said to be in **production**. During this stage, users and technical specialists review the solution to determine how well it has met its original objectives and to decide whether any revisions or modifications are in order. Changes in hardware, software, documentation, or procedures to a production system to correct errors, meet new requirements, or improve processing efficiency are termed **maintenance.**

The Girl Scouts continued to improve and refine their QuickBase cookie system. The system was made more efficient for users with slow Internet connections. Other recent enhancements include capabilities for paying for orders more rapidly, entering troop information and initial orders without waiting for a specified starting date, and receiving online confirmation for reservations to pick up orders from the Cookie Cupboard.

Managing the Change

Developing a new information systems solution is not merely a matter of installing hardware and software. The business must also deal with the organizational changes that the new solution will bring about—new information, new business processes, and perhaps new reporting relationships and decision-making power. A very well-designed solution may not work unless it is introduced to the organization very carefully. The process of planning change in an organization so that it is implemented in an orderly and effective manner is so critical to the success or failure of information system solutions that we devote the next section to a detailed discussion of this topic.

To manage the transition from the old manual cookie-ordering processes to the new system, the Girl Scouts would have to inform troop leaders and volunteers about changes in cookie-ordering procedures, provide training, and provide resources for answering any questions that arose as parents and volunteers started using the system. They would need to work with ABC Cookies and their shippers on new procedures for transmitting and delivering orders.

The Interactive Session on People provides another real-world example of the problem-solving process at work as Honam Petrochemical Corporation in South Korea develops a new management reporting system. As you read this case, observe how Honam handled these problem-solving activities: defining the problem, establishing information requirements, developing a solution, selecting technology, testing the new system, and managing the change process.

11.2 Alternative Systems-Building Approaches

There are alternative methods for building systems using the basic problem-solving model we have just described. These alternative methods include the traditional systems lifecycle, prototyping, end-user development, application software packages, and outsourcing.

TRADITIONAL SYSTEMS DEVELOPMENT LIFECYCLE

The **systems development lifecycle (SDLC)** is the oldest method for building information systems. The lifecycle methodology is a phased approach to building a system, dividing systems development into a series of formal stages, as illustrated in Figure 11.3. Although systems builders can go back and forth among stages in the lifecycle, the systems lifecycle is predominantly a "waterfall" approach in which tasks in one stage are completed before work for the next stage begins.

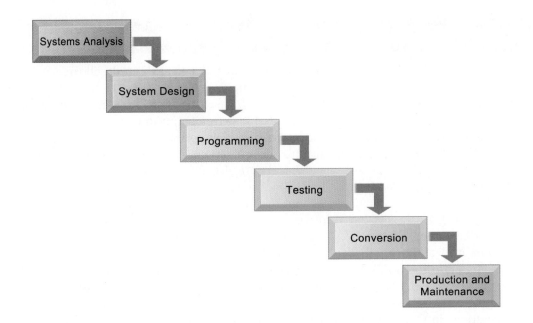

Figure 11.3
The Traditional Systems Development Lifecycle
The systems development lifecycle partitions systems development into formal stages, with each stage requiring completion before the next stage can begin.

This approach maintains a very formal division of labor between end users and information systems specialists. Technical specialists, such as system analysts and programmers, are responsible for much of the systems analysis, design, and implementation work; end users are limited to providing information requirements and reviewing the technical staff's work. The lifecycle also emphasizes formal specifications and paperwork, so many documents are generated during the course of a systems project.

The systems lifecycle is still used for building large complex systems that require rigorous and formal requirements analysis, predefined specifications, and tight controls over the systems-building process. However, this approach is also time-consuming and expensive to use. Tasks in one stage are supposed to be completed before work for the next stage begins. Activities can be repeated, but volumes of new documents must be generated and steps retraced if requirements and specifications need to be revised. This encourages freezing of specifications relatively early in the development process. The lifecycle approach is also not suitable for many small desktop systems, which tend to be less structured and more individualized.

PROTOTYPING

Prototyping consists of building an experimental system rapidly and inexpensively for end users to evaluate. The prototype is a working version of an information system or part of the system, but it is intended as only a preliminary model. Users interact with the prototype to get a better idea of their information requirements, refining the prototype multiple times. (The chapter-opening case describes how Dovetail Associates used QuickBase to create a prototype that helped the Patriots' Trail Girl Scout Council refine the specifications for their cookie-ordering system.) When the design is finalized, the prototype will be converted to a polished production system. Figure 11.4 shows a four-step model of the prototyping process.

Step 1: *Identify the user's basic requirements.* The system designer (usually an information systems specialist) works with the user only long enough to capture the user's basic information needs.

Step 2: *Develop an initial prototype.* The system designer creates a working prototype quickly, using tools for rapidly generating software.

Step 3: *Use the prototype.* The user is encouraged to work with the system to determine if the prototype meets his or her needs and to suggest improvements for the prototype.

INTERACTIVE SESSION: PEOPLE — Honam Petrochemical's Quest for Better Management Reports

You may soon hear more about Honam Petrochemical Corporation. Headquartered in Seoul, South Korea, this company manufactures and sells petrochemical products, such as synthetic resins, synthetic industrial materials, such as ethylene glycol and ethylene oxide for making polyester, automobile antifreeze solutions, benzene, propylene, and ethylene. Honam has about 2,200 employees and its 2010 revenues exceeded U.S. $6.75 million.

Honam's primary market is South Korea, but the company has set its sights on becoming a top-tier chemical company throughout Asia and achieving sales of U.S $10 billion. Honam plans to do this by strengthening its existing businesses, extending its overseas business and developing new businesses.

To manage far-flung operations in China, Hong Kong, Moscow, and New York City Honam needs reliable reports that are able to accurately measure management performance and provide useful, accurate information for increasing sales and reducing costs. Honam's existing systems provided managers with reports to guide their business decisions, but in many cases the data in the reports were outdated and "sanitized." Individual managers were processing and manipulating the data to make their departments "look better" to senior management. The report data were also somewhat outdated and presented periodically. Honam's top management wanted "anytime access" to current daily data to obtain an accurate and unbiased view of what was occurring in the sales office or on the plant floor. It did not wanted to be overloaded with unnecessary data so it could focus on the "watch-up indicators" it considered crucial to the business.

Executive decision-makers did not want to work with last quarter's numbers. They wanted up-to-the-minute reports that they could view quickly on their desktops. They also wanted access via the Web or their mobile devices. Finally, Honam executives wanted enterprise-wide data that could be accessed and shared easily across various business units and functions to support the company's expansion geographically and by product line.

These three requirements drove the technology selection process. Honam's information systems team reviewed a number of different software products and vendors and selected SAP BusinessObjects Dashboards and SAP BusinessObjects Web Intelligence. The company already had seven years' experience running SAP's ERP system, so this vendor seemed like an appropriate choice.

SAP BusinessObjects Dashboards is a drag-and-drop visualization tool designed to create interactive analytics for powerful, personalized dashboards based on SAP's BusinessObjects business intelligence platform. BusinessObjects software tools can be used for performance management, planning, reporting, query and analysis, and enterprise information management, and provide self-service access to data from databases and Excel spreadsheets. SAP BusinessObjects Web Intelligence is an ad hoc query, reporting, and analysis tool that is used to create queries or use existing reports, format retrieved information, and perform analysis to understand trends and root causes.

Once Honam's project team determined the business intelligence tools for the solution, its focus turned to determining which data and reports were required by the company's 200 high-level users of the new system. The information systems team started by asking executives to list existing reports they were already receiving and to assess the usefulness of each. The list was cut to a more manageable size and the executives were asked if there were any additional reports or data from which their organizational groups could benefit. These findings were very useful in determining the right set of reports and dashboards for Honam executives.

Once these user requirements were clarified, the information systems team designed a system that could extract data from a SAP NetWeaver Business Warehouse and present them to executives using the SAP BusinessObjects Dashboards software and SAP Crystal Reports, an application for designing and generating reports from a wide range of data sources. A highly intuitive Web-based user interface was created to make the system very accessible. This interface was so simple and well-designed that users required very little training on how to use the system or access data and reports.

To encourage users to start working with the system, members of the information systems department visited various manufacturing plants where the system was being rolled out and had in-depth discussions with executives about the systems' benefits as well as how to use it.

Honam's system went live in January 2011, and executives started immediately accessing reports and dashboards on a daily, weekly, and monthly basis. The system enables them to view key performance information such as manufacturing costs by plant, transportation costs, daily production and inventory rates, and global product price trends, and the information can be displayed visually in dashboards and management cockpits. Thirty executives tested mobile devices providing "anytime, anywhere" access to the new system. Delivery of the information is personalized and differentiated for high-level executives, middle managers, and front-line employees.

It is still too early to assess the long-term business impact of the system, but one benefit was immediate: Executives no longer are limited to "sanitized," stale data in an outdated presentation format. Management discussions and decisions are based on timely, consistent, and accurate company-wide data. Because the

system reduces the time required to collect, process, and track the data, executive decision making takes place more rapidly. Honam's information systems are now ready for global information-sharing as the company expands.

Sources: David Hannon, "Searching Beyond Sanitized Data," *SAPInsider PROFILES*, July 2011; David Steier, "Visualizing Success: Analytic User Interfaces that Drive Business," *Information Management*, July/August, 2011; and "Honam Petrochemical Strategy and Financial Highlights from ICIS," www.icis.com, accessed July 21, 2011.

CASE STUDY QUESTIONS

1. List and describe the information requirements of Honam's new management system. What problems was the new system designed to solve?

2. To what extent were "people" problems affecting management decision making at Honam? What were some of the people, organization, and technology issues that had to be addressed by the new system? How did the system's designers make the system more "people-friendly?"

3. What role did end users play in developing Honam's new system? How did the project team make sure users were involved? What would have happened to the project if they had not done this?

4. What were the benefits of the new system? How did it change the way Honam ran its business? How successful was this system solution?

MIS IN ACTION

Visit the Dashboard Insight Web site (dashboardinsight.com) and review the section on "Getting Started with Dashboards." Explain why digital dashboards are so useful to Honam's management and what "best practices" for building dashboards Honam followed.

Step 4: *Revise and enhance the prototype.* The system builder notes all changes the user requests and refines the prototype accordingly. After the prototype has been revised, the cycle returns to Step 3. Steps 3 and 4 are repeated until the user is satisfied.

Prototyping is especially useful in designing an information system's user interface. Because prototyping encourages intense end-user involvement throughout the systems development process, it is more likely to produce systems that fulfill user requirements.

However, rapid prototyping may gloss over essential steps in systems development, such as thorough testing and documentation. If the completed prototype works reasonably well, management may not see the need to build a polished production system. Some hastily constructed systems do not easily accommodate large quantities of data or a large number of users in a production environment.

END-USER DEVELOPMENT

End-user development allows end users, with little or no formal assistance from technical specialists, to create simple information systems, reducing the time and steps required to produce a finished application. Using fourth-generation languages, graphics languages, and PC software tools, end users can access data, create reports, and develop entire

Figure 11.4
The Prototyping
Process
The process of devel-
oping a prototype
consists of four steps.
Because a prototype can
be developed quickly
and inexpensively,
systems builders can
go through several itera-
tions, repeating steps
3 and 4, to refine and
enhance the prototype
before arriving at the
final operational one.

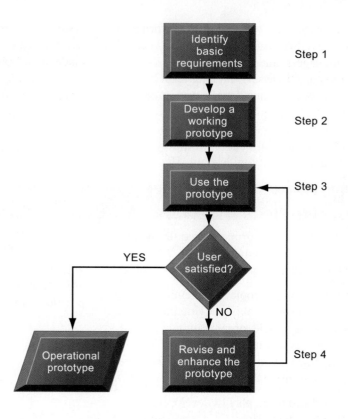

information systems on their own, with little or no help from professional systems analysts or programmers.

For example, Travel and Transport, the sixth-largest travel management company in the United States, used Information Builders' WebFOCUS to create an online self-service reporting system for monitoring and managing travel expenditures. More than 800 external clients are able to access information directly on their own to plan, track, analyze, and budget their travel expenses and benchmark them against similar companies, saving millions of dollars (Information Builders, 2011).

On the whole, end-user-developed systems are completed more rapidly than those developed with conventional programming tools. Allowing users to specify their own business needs improves requirements gathering and often leads to a higher level of user involvement and satisfaction with the system. However, fourth-generation tools still cannot replace conventional tools for some business applications because they cannot easily handle the processing of large numbers of transactions or applications with extensive procedural logic and updating requirements.

End-user development also poses organizational risks because systems are created rapidly, without a formal development methodology, testing, and documentation. To help organizations maximize the benefits of end-user applications development, management should require cost justification of end-user information system projects and establish hardware, software, and quality standards for user-developed applications.

PURCHASING SOLUTIONS: APPLICATION SOFTWARE PACKAGES AND OUTSOURCING

Chapter 4 points out that the software for most systems today is not developed in-house but is purchased from external sources. Firms may choose to purchase a software package from a commercial vendor, rent the software from a service provider, or outsource the development work to another firm. Selection of the software or software service is often based on a **Request for Proposal (RFP)**, which is a detailed list of questions submitted to external vendors to see how well they meet the requirements for the proposed system.

Application Software Packages

Most new information systems today are built using an application software package or preprogrammed software components. Many applications are common to all business organizations—for example, payroll, accounts receivable, general ledger, or inventory control. For such universal functions with standard processes that do not change a great deal over time, a generalized system will fulfill the requirements of many organizations.

If a software package can fulfill most of an organization's requirements, the company does not have to write its own software. The company saves time and money by using the prewritten, predesigned, pretested software programs from the package.

Many packages include capabilities for customization to meet unique requirements not addressed by the package software. **Customization** features allow a software package to be modified to meet an organization's unique requirements without destroying the integrity of the packaged software. However, if extensive customization is required, additional programming and customization work may become so expensive and time-consuming that it negates many of the advantages of software packages. If the package cannot be customized, the organization will have to adapt to the package and change its procedures.

Outsourcing

If a firm does not want to use its internal resources to build or operate information systems, it can outsource the work to an external organization that specializes in providing these services. Software service providers, which we describe in Chapter 4, are one form of outsourcing. An example is the Girl Scouts leasing the software and hardware from QuickBase to run their cookie-ordering system. Subscribing companies use the software and computer hardware of the service provider as the technical platform for their systems. In another form of outsourcing, a company hires an external vendor to design and create the software for its system, but that company operates the system on its own computers.

The outsourcing vendor might be domestic or in another country. Domestic outsourcing is driven primarily by the fact that outsourcing firms possess skills, resources, and assets that their clients do not have. Installing a new supply chain management system in a very large company might require hiring an additional 30 to 50 people with specific expertise in supply chain management software. Rather than hire permanent new employees, and then release them after the new system is built, it makes more sense, and is often less expensive, to outsource this work for a 12-month period.

In the case of offshore outsourcing, the decision tends to be driven by cost. A skilled programmer in India or Russia earns about U.S. $10,000 per year, compared to $70,000 per year for a comparable programmer in the United States. The Internet and low-cost communications technology have drastically reduced the expense and difficulty of coordinating the work of global teams in faraway locations. In addition to cost savings, many offshore outsourcing firms offer world-class technology assets and skills.

For example, Chaucer Syndicates, a specialist insurer for Lloyd's, the world's leading insurance market, contracted with Indian software and service provider Wipro Ltd. to develop a data warehouse and reporting system. Chaucer believed Wipro had the technical expertise, industry knowledge, and resources to quickly develop a solution that would meet its regulatory requirements and provide timely and improved analytics and management reports (Wipro, 2011).

There is a very strong chance that at some point in your career, you'll be working with offshore outsourcers or global teams. Your firm is most likely to benefit from outsourcing if it takes the time to evaluate all the risks and to make sure outsourcing is appropriate for its particular needs. Any company that outsources its applications must thoroughly understand the project, including its requirements, method of implementation, source of expected benefits, cost components, and metrics for measuring performance.

Many firms underestimate costs for identifying and evaluating vendors of information technology services, for transitioning to a new vendor, for improving internal software development methods to match those of outsourcing vendors, and for monitoring vendors to make sure they are fulfilling their contractual obligations. Outsourcing offshore incurs additional costs for coping with cultural differences that drain productivity and dealing with human resources issues, such as terminating or relocating domestic employees. These hidden costs undercut some of the anticipated benefits from outsourcing. Firms should be especially cautious when using an outsourcer to develop or to operate applications that give it some type of competitive advantage.

Figure 11.5 shows best- and worst-case scenarios for the total cost of an offshore outsourcing project. It shows how much hidden costs affect the total project cost. The best case reflects the lowest estimates for additional costs, and the worst case reflects the highest estimates for these costs. As you can see, hidden costs increase the total cost of an offshore outsourcing project by an extra 15 to 57 percent. Even with these extra costs, many firms will benefit from offshore outsourcing if they manage the work well.

MOBILE APPLICATION DEVELOPMENT

Developing applications for mobile platforms is quite different from development for PCs and larger computers. The reduced size of mobile devices makes using fingers and multi-touch gestures much easier than typing and using keyboards. Mobile apps need to be optimized for the specific tasks they are to perform, they should not try to carry out too many tasks, and they should be designed for usability. Saving resources—bandwidth, screen space, memory, processing, data entry, and user gestures—is a top priority.

There are three main platforms for mobile apps-iPhone/iPad, Android, and Windows Phone 7. Each of the platforms for mobile applications has an integrated development environment, such as Apple's iOS SDK (software development kit) for the iPhone/iPad, which provides tools for writing, testing, and deploying applications in the target platform environment. Larger companies or business owners with programming experience use these software development kits to create apps from scratch. App development can also be outsourced to specialized app development firms that charge as much as $20,000 to design and develop an app and additional fees to update the software.

A number of firms offer app templates for small businesses that require no programming knowledge. For example, Red Foundry lets owners use its templates to build and test an iOS app for free. Once the app is submitted to Apple, Red Foundry charges $9 to $599 per month and provides performance analytics for users paying $39 or more per month. The company is working on a platform for Android apps. The average time to create an app on this platform is 6 days, which includes editing images and other tasks. The actual time creating the app on Red Foundry's platform is about 4 hours.

Figure 11.5
Total Cost of Offshore Outsourcing
If a firm spends $10 million on offshore outsourcing contracts, that company will actually spend 15.2 percent in extra costs even under the best-case scenario. In the worst-case scenario, where there is a dramatic drop in productivity along with exceptionally high transition and layoff costs, a firm can expect to pay up to 57 percent in extra costs on top of the $10 million outlay for an offshore contract.

TOTAL COST OF OFFSHORE OUTSOURCING				
Cost of outsourcing contract			$10,000,000	
Hidden Costs	Best Case	Additional Cost ($)	Worst Case	Additional Cost ($)
1. Vendor selection	0.2%	20,000	2%	200,000
2. Transition costs	2%	200,000	3%	300,000
3. Layoffs & retention	3%	300,000	5%	500,000
4. Lost productivity/cultural issues	3%	300,000	27%	2,700,000
5. Improving development processes	1%	100,000	10%	1,000,000
6. Managing the contract	6%	600,000	10%	1,000,000
Total additional costs		**1,520,000**		**5,700,000**
	Outstanding Contract ($)	Additional Cost ($)	Total Cost ($)	Additional Cost
Total cost of outsourcing (TCO) best case	10,000,000	1,520,000	11,520,000	15.2%
Total cost of outsourcing (TCO) worst case	10,000,000	5,700,000	15,700,000	57.0%

RAPID APPLICATION DEVELOPMENT FOR E-BUSINESS

Technologies and business conditions are changing so rapidly that agility and scalability have become critical elements of system solutions. Companies are adopting shorter, more informal development processes for many of their e-commerce and e-business applications, processes that provide fast solutions that do not disrupt their core transaction processing systems and organizational databases. In addition to using software packages, application service providers, and other outsourcing services, they are relying more heavily on fast-cycle techniques, such as joint application design (JAD), prototypes, and reusable standardized software components that can be assembled into a complete set of services for e-commerce and e-business.

The term **rapid application development (RAD)** refers to the process of creating workable systems in a very short period of time. RAD includes the use of visual programming and other tools for building graphical user interfaces, iterative prototyping of key system elements, the automation of program code generation, and close teamwork among end users and information systems specialists. Simple systems often can be assembled from prebuilt components (see Section 11.3). The process does not have to be sequential, and key parts of development can occur simultaneously.

Sometimes a technique called **joint application design (JAD)** will be used to accelerate the generation of information requirements and to develop the initial systems design. JAD brings end users and information systems specialists together in an interactive session to discuss the system's design. Properly prepared and facilitated, JAD sessions can significantly speed up the design phase and involve users at an intense level.

The Interactive Session on Technology illustrates another approach for rapid development called Scrum. Software firm DST Systems needed a more agile and fast-paced method for developing its products in order to keep up with competitors. It adopted the Scrum methodology for software development. As you read this case, try to determine how Scrum provided a solution for DST.

11.3 Modeling and Designing Systems

We have just described alternative methods for building systems. There are also alternative methodologies for modeling and designing systems. The two most prominent are structured methodologies and object-oriented development.

STRUCTURED METHODOLOGIES

Structured methodologies have been used to document, analyze, and design information systems since the 1970s. **Structured** refers to the fact that the techniques are step by step, with each step building on the previous one. Structured methodologies are top-down, progressing from the highest, most abstract level to the lowest level of detail—from the general to the specific.

Structured development methods are process-oriented, focusing primarily on modeling the processes, or actions, that capture, store, manipulate, and distribute data as the data flow through a system. These methods separate data from processes. A separate programming procedure must be written every time someone wants to take an action on a particular piece of data. The procedures act on data that the program passes to them.

The primary tool for representing a system's component processes and the flow of data between them is the **data flow diagram (DFD)**. The data flow diagram offers a logical graphic model of information flow, partitioning a system into modules that show manageable levels of detail. It rigorously specifies the processes or transformations that occur within each module and the interfaces that exist between them.

Figure 11.6 shows a simple data flow diagram for a mail-in university course registration system. The rounded boxes represent processes, which portray the transformation of data.

Companies like DST Systems have recognized the value in Scrum development to their bottom lines, but making the transition from traditional developmental methods to Scrum development can be challenging. DST Systems is a software development company whose flagship product, Automated Work Distributor, increases back-office efficiency and helps offices become paperless. DST was founded in 1969 and its headquarters are in Kansas City, Missouri. The company has approximately ten thousand employees, 1,200 of whom are software developers.

This development group had used a mixture of tools, processes, and source code control systems, without any unified repository for code or single developer tool set. Different groups within the organization used very different tools for software development, like Serena PVCS, Eclipse, or other source code software packages. Processes were often manual and time consuming. Managers were unable to easily determine how resources were being allocated, which of their employees were working on certain projects, and the status of specific assets.

All of this meant that DST struggled to update its most important product, AWD, in a timely fashion. Its typical development schedule was to release a new version once every two years, but competitors were releasing versions faster. DST knew that it needed a better method than the traditional "waterfall" method for designing, coding, testing, and integrating its products. In the waterfall model of software development, progression flows sequentially from one step to the next like a waterfall, with each step unable to start until the previous step has been completed. While DST had used this method with great success previously, DST began searching for viable alternatives.

The development group started exploring Scrum, a framework for agile software development in which projects progress via a series of iterations called sprints. Scrum projects make progress in a series of sprints, which are timeboxed iterations no more than a month long. At the start of a sprint, team members commit to delivering some number of features that were listed on a project's product backlog. These features are supposed to be completed by the end of the sprint — coded, tested, and integrated into the evolving product or system. At the end of the sprint, a sprint review allows the team to demonstrate the new functionality to the product owner and other interested stakeholders who provide feedback that could influence the next sprint.

Scrum relies on self-organizing, cross-functional teams supported by a ScrumMaster and a product owner. The ScrumMaster acts as a coach for the team, while the product owner represents the business, customers or users in guiding the team toward building the right product.

DST tried Scrum with its existing software development tools and experienced strong results. The company accelerated its software development cycle from 24 to 6 months and developer productivity increased 20 percent, but Scrum didn't work as well as DST had hoped with its existing tools. Processes broke down and the lack of standardization among the tools and processes used by DST prevented Scrum from providing its maximum benefit to the company. DST needed an application lifecycle management (ALM) product that would unify its software development environment.

DST set up a project evaluation team to identify the right development environment for them. Key factors included cost-effectiveness, ease of adoption, and feature-effectiveness. DST wanted the ability to use the new software without significant training and software they could quickly adopt without jeopardizing AWD's development cycle. After considering several ALM products and running test projects with each one, DST settled on CollabNet's offering, TeamForge, for its ALM platform.

CollabNet specializes in software designed to work well with agile software development methods such as Scrum. Its core product is TeamForge, an integrated suite of Web-based development and collaboration tools for agile software development that centralizes management of users, projects, processes, and assets. DST also adopted CollabNet's Subversion product to help with the management and control of changes to project documents, programs, and other information stored as computer files. DST's adoption of CollabNet's products was fast, requiring only 10 weeks, and DST developers now do all of their work within this ALM platform. TeamForge was not forced on developers, but the ALM platform was so appealing compared to DST's previous environment that developers adopted the product virally.

Jerry Tubbs, the systems development manager at DST systems, says that DST was successful in its attempts to revamp its software group because of a few factors. First, it looked for simplicity rather than complicated, do-everything offerings. Simpler wasn't just better for DST, it was also much cheaper than some of the alternatives. DST also involved developers in the decision-making process to ensure that changes would be greeted enthusiastically. Lastly, by allowing developers to adopt ALM software on their own, DST avoided the resentment associated with mandating unwelcome change. DST's move from waterfall development to Scrum development was a success because the company selected the right development framework as well as the right software to make that change a reality and skillfully managed the change process.

Sources: Jerry Tubbs, "Team Building Goes Viral," *Information Week*, February 22, 2010; www.collab.net, accessed August 2, 2011; Mountain Goat Software, "Introduction to Scrum — An Agile Process," www.mountaingoatsoftware.com/topics/scrum, accessed August 2010.

CASE STUDY QUESTIONS

1. What were some of the problems with DST Systems' old software development environment?

2. How did Scrum development help solve some of those problems?

3. What other adjustments did DST make to use Scrum more effectively in its software projects? What people, organization, and technology issues had to be addressed?

MIS IN ACTION

Search the Internet for videos or Web sites explaining Scrum or agile development. Then answer the following questions:

1. Describe some of the benefits and drawbacks of Scrum development.

2. How does Scrum differ from other software development methodologies?

3. What are the potential benefits to companies using Scrum development?

The square box represents an external entity, which is an originator or receiver of information located outside the boundaries of the system being modeled. The open rectangles represent data stores, which are either manual or automated inventories of data. The arrows represent data flows, which show the movement between processes, external entities, and data stores. They always contain packets of data with the name or content of each data flow listed beside the arrow.

This data flow diagram shows that students submit registration forms with their names, identification numbers, and the numbers of the courses they wish to take. In Process 1.0, the system verifies that each course selected is still open by referencing the university's course file. The file distinguishes courses that are open from those that have been canceled or filled. Process 1.0 then determines which of the student's selections can be accepted or rejected. Process 2.0 enrolls the student in the courses for which he or she has been accepted. It updates the university's course file with the student's name and identification number and recalculates the class size. If maximum enrollment has been reached, the course number is flagged as closed. Process 2.0 also updates the university's student master file with information about new students or changes in address. Process 3.0 then sends each student applicant a confirmation-of-registration letter listing the courses for which he or she is registered and noting the course selections that could not be fulfilled.

Through leveled data flow diagrams, a complex process can be broken down into successive levels of detail. An entire system can be divided into subsystems with a high-level data flow diagram. Each subsystem, in turn, can be divided into additional subsystems with lower-level data flow diagrams, and the lower-level subsystems can be broken down again until the lowest level of detail has been reached. **Process specifications** describe the transformation occurring within the lowest level of the data flow diagrams, showing the logic for each process.

In structured methodology, software design is modeled using hierarchical structure charts. The **structure chart** is a top-down chart, showing each level of design, its relationship to other levels, and its place in the overall design structure. The design first considers the main function of a program or system, then breaks this function into subfunctions, and decomposes each subfunction until the lowest level of detail has been reached. Figure 11.7

Figure 11.6
Data Flow Diagram for Mail-in University Registration System
The system has three processes: Verify availability (1.0), enroll student (2.0), and confirm registration (3.0). The name and content of each of the data flows appear adjacent to each arrow. There is one external entity in this system: the student. There are two data stores: the student master file and the course file.

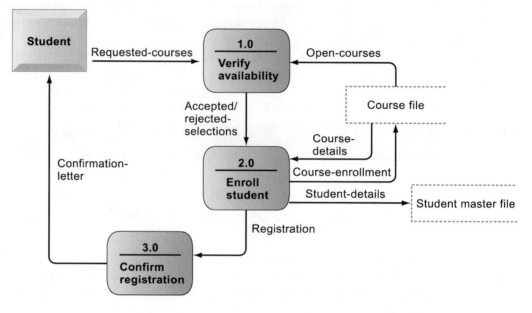

shows a high-level structure chart for a payroll system. If a design has too many levels to fit onto one structure chart, it can be broken down further on more detailed structure charts. A structure chart may document one program, one system (a set of programs), or part of one program.

OBJECT-ORIENTED DEVELOPMENT

Structured methods treat data and processes as logically separate entities, whereas in the real world such separation seems unnatural. Different modeling conventions are used for analysis (the data flow diagram) and for design (the structure chart).

Object-oriented development addresses these issues. Object-oriented development uses the object, which we introduced in Chapter 4, as the basic unit of systems analysis and design. An object combines data and the specific processes that operate on those data. Data encapsulated in an object can be accessed and modified only by the operations, or methods, associated with that object. Instead of passing data to procedures, programs send a message for an object to perform an operation that is already embedded in it. The system is modeled

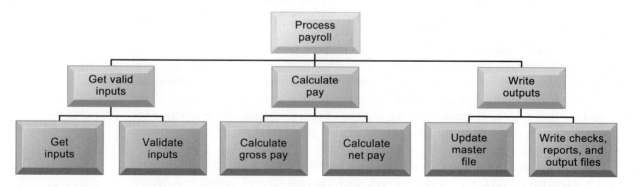

Figure 11.7 High-Level Structure Chart for a Payroll System
This structure chart shows the highest or most abstract level of design for a payroll system, providing an overview of the entire system.

as a collection of objects and the relationships among them. Because processing logic resides within objects rather that in separate software programs, objects must collaborate with each other to make the system work.

Object-oriented modeling is based on the concepts of *class* and *inheritance*. Objects belonging to a certain class, or general categories of similar objects, have the features of that class. Classes of objects in turn inherit all the structure and behaviors of a more general class and then add variables and behaviors unique to each object. New classes of objects are created by choosing an existing class and specifying how the new class differs from the existing class, instead of starting from scratch each time.

We can see how class and inheritance work in Figure 11.8, which illustrates the relationships among classes concerning employees and how they are paid. Employee is the common ancestor, or superclass, for the other three classes. Salaried, Hourly, and Temporary are subclasses of Employee. The class name is in the top compartment, the attributes for each class are in the middle portion of each box, and the list of operations is in the bottom portion of each box. The features that are shared by all employees (ID, name, address, date hired, position, and pay) are stored in the Employee superclass, whereas each subclass stores features that are specific to that particular type of employee. Specific to Hourly employees, for example, are their hourly rates and overtime rates. A solid line from the subclass to the superclass is a generalization path showing that the subclasses Salaried, Hourly, and Temporary have common features that can be generalized into the superclass Employee.

Object-oriented development is more iterative and incremental than traditional structured development. During systems analysis, systems builders document the functional requirements of the system, specifying its most important properties and what the proposed system must do. Interactions between the system and its users are analyzed to identify objects, which include both data and processes. The object-oriented design phase describes how the objects will behave and how they will interact with one other. Similar objects are grouped together to form a class, and classes are grouped into hierarchies in which a subclass inherits the attributes and methods from its superclass.

The information system is implemented by translating the design into program code, reusing classes that are already available in a library of reusable software objects and adding new ones created during the object-oriented design phase. Implementation may also involve the creation of an object-oriented database. The resulting system must be thoroughly tested and evaluated.

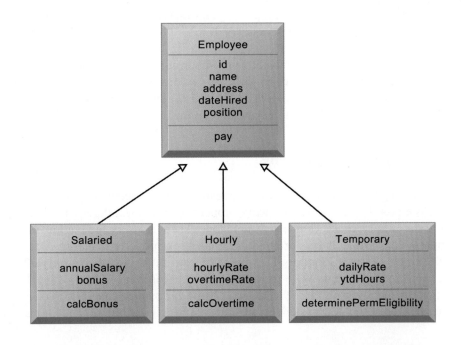

Figure 11.8
Class and
Inheritance
This figure illustrates how classes inherit the common features of their superclass.

Because objects are reusable, object-oriented development could potentially reduce the time and cost of writing software if organizations reuse software objects that have already been created as building blocks for other applications. New systems can be created by using some existing objects, changing others, and adding a few new objects.

Component-Based Development, Web Services, and Cloud-Based Development

To further expedite software creation, groups of objects have been assembled into software components for common functions, such as a graphical user interface or online ordering capability, and these components can be combined to create large-scale business applications. This approach to software development is called **component-based development**. Businesses are using component-based development to create their e-commerce applications by combining commercially available components for shopping carts, user authentication, search engines, and catalogs with pieces of software for their own unique business requirements.

Chapter 4 introduced Web services as loosely coupled, reusable software components based on Extensible Markup Language (XML) and other open protocols and standards that enable one application to communicate with another with no custom programming required. In addition to supporting internal and external integration of systems, Web services provide nonproprietary tools for building new information system applications or enhancing existing systems.

Platform as a service (PaaS), introduced in the Chapter 4 discussion of cloud computing, also holds considerable potential for helping system developers quickly write and test customer- or employee-facing Web applications. These online development environments come from a range of vendors, including Oracle, IBM, Salesforce.com (Force.com), and Microsoft (Azure). These platforms automate tasks such as setting up a newly composed application as a Web service or linking to other applications and services. Some also offer a cloud infrastructure service, or links to cloud vendors such as Amazon, so that developers can launch what they build in a cloud infrastructure.

COMPUTER-AIDED SOFTWARE ENGINEERING (CASE)

Computer-aided software engineering (CASE)—sometimes called computer-aided systems engineering—provides software tools to automate the methodologies we have just described to reduce the amount of repetitive work in systems development. CASE tools provide automated graphics facilities for producing charts and diagrams, screen and report generators, data dictionaries, extensive reporting facilities, analysis and checking tools, code generators, and documentation generators. CASE tools also contain features for validating design diagrams and specifications.

CASE tools facilitate clear documentation and coordination of team development efforts. Team members can share their work by accessing each other's files to review or modify what has been done. Modest productivity benefits are achieved if the tools are used properly. Many CASE tools are PC based, with powerful graphical capabilities.

11.4 Project Management

Your company might have developed what appears to be an excellent system solution. Yet when the system is in use, it does not work properly or it doesn't deliver the benefits that were promised. If this occurs, your firm is not alone. There is a very high failure rate among information systems projects because they have not been properly managed. The Standish Group consultancy, which monitors IT project success rates, found that only 32 percent of all technology investments were completed on time, on budget, and with all features and functions originally specified (McCafferty, 2010). Firms may have incorrectly assessed the business value of the new system or were unable to manage the organizational change required by the new technology. That's why it's essential to know how to manage information systems projects and the reasons why they succeed or fail.

PROJECT MANAGEMENT OBJECTIVES

A **project** is a planned series of related activities for achieving a specific business objective. Information systems projects include the development of new information systems, enhancement of existing systems, or projects for replacement or upgrading of the firm's information technology (IT) infrastructure.

Project management refers to the application of knowledge, skills, tools, and techniques to achieve specific targets within specified budget and time constraints. Project management activities include planning the work, assessing risk, estimating resources required to accomplish the work, organizing the work, acquiring human and material resources, assigning tasks, directing activities, controlling project execution, reporting progress, and analyzing the results. As in other areas of business, project management for information systems must deal with five major variables: scope, time, cost, quality, and risk.

Scope defines what work is or is not included in a project. For example, the scope of a project for a new order processing system might include new modules for inputting orders and transmitting them to production and accounting but not any changes to related accounts receivable, manufacturing, distribution, or inventory control systems. Project management defines all the work required to complete a project successfully, and should ensure that the scope of a project does not expand beyond what was originally intended.

Time is the amount of time required to complete the project. Project management typically establishes the amount of time required to complete major components of a project. Each of these components is further broken down into activities and tasks. Project management tries to determine the time required to complete each task and establish a schedule for completing the work.

Cost is based on the time to complete a project multiplied by the daily cost of human resources required to complete the project. Information systems project costs also include the cost of hardware, software, and work space. Project management develops a budget for the project and monitors ongoing project expenses.

Quality is an indicator of how well the end result of a project satisfies the objectives specified by management. The quality of information systems projects usually boils down to improved organizational performance and decision making. Quality also considers the accuracy and timeliness of information produced by the new system and ease of use.

Risk refers to potential problems that would threaten the success of a project. These potential problems might prevent a project from achieving its objectives by increasing time and cost, lowering the quality of project outputs, or preventing the project from being completed altogether. We discuss the most important risk factors for information systems projects later in this section.

SELECTING PROJECTS: MAKING THE BUSINESS CASE FOR A NEW SYSTEM

Companies typically are presented with many different projects for solving problems and improving performance. There are far more ideas for systems projects than there are resources. You will need to select the projects that promise the greatest benefit to the business.

Determining Project Costs and Benefits

As we pointed out earlier, the systems analysis includes an assessment of the economic feasibility of each alternative solution—whether each solution represents a good investment for the company. In order to identify the information systems projects that will deliver the most business value, you'll need to identify their costs and benefits and how they relate to the firm's information systems plan.

Table 11.2 lists some of the more common costs and benefits of systems. **Tangible benefits** can be quantified and assigned a monetary value. **Intangible benefits**, such as more efficient customer service or enhanced decision making, cannot be immediately quantified. Yet systems that produce mainly intangible benefits may still be good investments if they produce quantifiable gains in the long run.

To determine the benefits of a particular solution, you'll need to calculate all of its costs and all of its benefits. Obviously, a solution where costs exceed benefits should be rejected. But even if the benefits outweigh the costs, some additional financial analysis is required to determine whether the investment represents a good return on the firm's invested capital. Capital budgeting methods, such as net present value, internal rate of return (IRR), or accounting rate of return on investment (ROI), would typically be employed to evaluate the proposed information system solution as an investment. You can find out more about how these capital budgeting methods are used to justify information system investments in our Learning Tracks.

Some of the tangible benefits obtained by the Girl Scouts were increased productivity and lower operational costs resulting from automating the ordering process and from reducing errors. Intangible benefits included enhanced volunteer job satisfaction and improved operations.

The Information Systems Plan

An **information systems plan** shows how specific information systems fit into a company's overall business plan and business strategy. Table 11.3 lists the major components of such a plan. The plan contains a statement of corporate goals and specifies how information technology will help the business attain these goals. The report shows how general goals will be achieved by specific systems projects. It identifies specific target dates and milestones that can be used later to evaluate the plan's progress in terms of how many objectives were actually attained in the time frame specified in the plan. The plan indicates the key management decisions concerning hardware acquisition; telecommunications; centralization/decentralization of authority, data, and hardware; and required organizational change.

The plan should describe organizational changes, including management and employee training requirements, changes in business processes, and changes in authority, structure, or management practice. When you are making the business case for a new information system project, you show how the proposed system fits into that plan.

Portfolio Analysis and Scoring Models

Once you have determined the overall direction of systems development, **portfolio analysis** will help you evaluate alternative system projects. Portfolio analysis inventories all of the firm's information systems projects and assets, including infrastructure, outsourcing contracts, and licenses. This portfolio of information systems investments can be described as having a certain profile of risk and benefit to the firm (see Figure 11.9), similar to a financial portfolio. Each information systems project carries its own set of risks and benefits. Firms try to improve the return on their information system portfolios by balancing the risk and return from their systems investments.

Obviously, you begin first by focusing on systems of high benefit and low risk. These promise early returns and low risks. Second, high-benefit, high-risk systems should be examined; low-benefit, high-risk systems should be totally avoided; and low-benefit, low-risk systems should be reexamined for the possibility of rebuilding and replacing them with more desirable systems having higher benefits. By using portfolio analysis, management can determine the optimal mix of investment risk and reward for their firms, balancing riskier, high-reward projects with safer, lower-reward ones.

Another method for evaluating alternative system solutions is a **scoring model**. Scoring models give alternative systems a single score based on the extent to which they meet selected objectives. Table 11.4 shows part of a simple scoring model that could have been used by the Girl Scouts in evaluating their alternative systems. The first column lists the

TABLE 11.2

Costs and Benefits of Information Systems

IMPLEMENTATION COSTS
Hardware
Telecommunications
Software
Personnel costs

OPERATIONAL COSTS
Computer processing time
Maintenance
Operating staff
User time
Ongoing training costs
Facility costs

TANGIBLE BENEFITS
Increased productivity
Lower operational costs
Reduced workforce
Lower computer expenses
Lower outside vendor costs
Lower clerical and professional costs
Reduced rate of growth in expenses
Reduced facility costs
Increased sales

INTANGIBLE BENEFITS
Improved asset utilization
Improved resource control
Improved organizational planning
Increased organizational flexibility
More timely information
More information
Increased organizational learning
Legal requirements attained
Enhanced employee goodwill
Increased job satisfaction
Improved decision making
Improved operations
Higher client satisfaction
Better corporate image

criteria that decision makers use to evaluate the systems. Table 11.4 shows that the Girl Scouts attach the most importance to capabilities for sales order processing, ease of use, ability to support users in many different locations, and low cost. The second column in Table 11.4 lists the weights that decision makers attached to the decision criteria. Columns 3 and 5 show the percentage of requirements for each function that each alternative system meets. Each alternative's score is calculated by multiplying the percentage of requirements met for each function by the weight attached to that function. The QuickBase solution has the highest total score.

MANAGING PROJECT RISK AND SYSTEM-RELATED CHANGE

Some systems development projects are more likely to run into problems or to suffer delays because they carry a much higher level of risk than others. The level of project risk is influenced by project size, project structure, and the level of technical expertise of the information systems staff and project team. The larger the project—as indicated by the dollars spent, project team size, and how many parts of the organization will be affected by the new system—the greater the risk. Very large-scale systems projects have a failure rate that is 50 to 75 percent higher than that for other projects because such projects are complex and difficult to control. Risks are also higher for systems where information requirements are not clear and straightforward or the project team must master new technology.

Implementation and Change Management

Dealing with these project risks requires an understanding of the implementation process and change management. A broader definition of **implementation** refers to all the organizational activities working toward the adoption and management of an innovation,

TABLE 11.3

Information Systems
Plan

1. **Purpose of the Plan**
   Overview of plan contents
   Current business organization and future organization
   Key business processes
   Management strategy

2. **Strategic Business Plan Rationale**
   Current situation
   Current business organization
   Changing environments
   Major goals of the business plan
   Firm's strategic plan

3. **Current Systems**
   Major systems supporting business functions and processes
   Current infrastructure capabilities
      Hardware
      Software
      Database
      Telecommunications and the Internet
   Difficulties meeting business requirements
   Anticipated future demands

4. **New Developments**
   New system projects
      Project descriptions
      Business rationale
      Applications' role in strategy
   New infrastructure capabilities required
      Hardware
      Software
      Database
      Telecommunications and the Internet

5. **Management Strategy**
   Acquisition plans
   Milestones and timing
   Organizational realignment
   Internal reorganization
   Management controls
   Major training initiatives
   Personnel strategy

6. **Implementation of the Plan**
   Anticipated difficulties in implementation
   Progress reports

7. **Budget Requirements**
   Requirements
   Potential savings
   Financing
   Acquisition cycle

such as a new information system. Successful implementation requires a high level of user involvement in a project and management support.

If users are heavily involved in the development of a system, they have more opportunities to mold the system according to their priorities and business requirements, and more

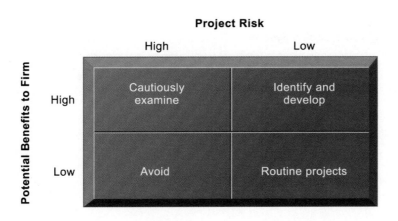

Project Risk

Figure 11.9
A System Portfolio
Companies should examine their portfolio of projects in terms of potential benefits and likely risks. Certain kinds of projects should be avoided altogether and others developed rapidly. There is no ideal mix. Companies in different industries have different information systems needs.

opportunities to control the outcome. They also are more likely to react positively to the completed system because they have been active participants in the change process.

The relationship between end users and information systems specialists has traditionally been a problem area for information systems implementation efforts because of differing backgrounds, interests, and priorities. These differences create a **user-designer communications gap**. Information systems specialists often have a highly technical orientation to problem solving, focusing on technical solutions in which hardware and software efficiency is optimized at the expense of ease of use or organizational effectiveness. End users prefer systems that are oriented toward solving business problems or facilitating organizational tasks. Often the orientations of both groups are so at odds that they appear to speak in different tongues. These differences are illustrated in Table 11.5.

If an information systems project has the backing and commitment of management at various levels, it is more likely to receive higher priority from both users and the technical information systems staff. Management backing also ensures that a systems project receives sufficient funding and resources to be successful. Furthermore, to be enforced effectively, all the changes in work habits and procedures and any organizational realignments associated with a new system depend on management backing.

Controlling Risk Factors

There are strategies you can follow to deal with project risk and increase the chances of a successful system solution. If the new system involves challenging and complex technology, you can recruit project leaders with strong technical and administrative experience. Outsourcing or using external consultants are options if your firm does not have staff with the required technical skills or expertise.

Large projects benefit from appropriate use of **formal planning and tools** for documenting and monitoring project plans. The two most commonly used methods for documenting project plans are Gantt charts and PERT charts. A **Gantt chart** lists project activities and their corresponding start and completion dates. The Gantt chart visually represents the timing and duration of different tasks in a development project as well as their human resource requirements (see Figure 11.10). It shows each task as a horizontal bar whose length is proportional to the time required to complete it.

Although Gantt charts show when project activities begin and end, they don't depict task dependencies, how one task is affected if another is behind schedule, or how tasks should be ordered. That is where **PERT charts** are useful. PERT stands for Program Evaluation and Review Technique, a methodology developed by the U.S. Navy during the 1950s to manage the Polaris submarine missile program. A PERT chart graphically depicts project tasks and their interrelationships. The PERT chart lists the specific activities that make up a project and the activities that must be completed before a specific activity can start, as illustrated in Figure 11.11.

TABLE 11.4

Example of a Scoring Model for the Girl Scouts Cookie System

Criteria	Weight	Microsoft Access System (%)	Microsoft Access System Score	QuickBase System (%)	QuickBase System Score
1.1 Order processing					
1.2 Online order entry	5	67	335	83	415
1.3 Order tracking by troop	5	81	405	87	435
1.4 Order tracking by individual Girl Scout	5	72	360	80	400
1.5 Reserving warehouse pickups	3	66	198	79	237
Total order processing			1,298		1,487
2.1 Ease of use					
2.1 Web access from multiple locations	5	55	275	92	460
2.1 Short training time	4	79	316	85	340
2.1 User-friendly screens and data entry forms	4	65	260	87	348
Total ease of use			851		1,148
3.1 Costs					
3.2 Software costs	3	51	153	65	195
3.3 Hardware (server) costs	4	57	228	90	360
3.4 Maintenance and support costs	4	42	168	89	356
Total costs			549		911
Grand Total			2,698		3,546

The PERT chart portrays a project as a network diagram consisting of numbered nodes (either circles or rectangles) representing project tasks. Each node is numbered and shows the task, its duration, the starting date, and the completion date. The direction of the arrows on the lines indicates the sequence of tasks and shows which activities must be completed before the commencement of another activity. In Figure 11.11, the tasks in nodes 2, 3, and 4 are not dependent on each other and can be undertaken simultaneously, but each is dependent on completion of the first task.

Project Management Software Commercial software tools are available to automate the creation of Gantt and PERT charts and to facilitate the project management process. Project management software typically features capabilities for defining and ordering tasks, assigning resources to tasks, establishing starting and ending dates for tasks, tracking progress, and facilitating modifications to tasks and resources. The most widely used project management tool today is Microsoft Office Project.

TABLE 11.5

The User-Designer Communications Gap

User Concerns	Designer Concerns
Will the system deliver the information I need for my work?	What demands will this system put on our servers?
Can we access the data on our iPhones, Blackberrys, tablets, and PCs?	What kind of programming demands will this place on our group?
What new procedures do we need to enter data into the system?	Where will the data be stored? What's the most efficient way to store them?
How will the operation of the system change employees' daily routines?	What technologies should we use to secure the data?

Overcoming User Resistance

You can overcome user resistance by promoting user participation (to elicit commitment as well as to improve design), by making user education and training easily available, and by providing better incentives for users who cooperate. End users can become active members of the project team, take on leadership roles, and take charge of system installation and training.

You should pay special attention to areas where users interface with the system, with sensitivity to ergonomics issues. **Ergonomics** refers to the interaction of people and machines in the work environment. It considers the design of jobs, health issues, and the end-user interface of information systems. For instance, if a system has a series of complicated online data entry screens that are extremely difficult or time-consuming to work with, users will reject the system if it increases their work load or level of job stress.

Users will be more cooperative if organizational problems are solved prior to introducing the new system. In addition to procedural changes, transformations in job functions, organizational structure, power relationships, and behavior should be identified during systems analysis using an **organizational impact analysis**.

MANAGING PROJECTS ON A GLOBAL SCALE

As globalization proceeds, companies will be building many more new systems that are global in scale, spanning many different units in many different countries. The project management challenges for global systems are similar to those for domestic systems, but they are complicated by the international environment. User information requirements, business processes, and work cultures differ from country to country. It is difficult to convince local managers anywhere in the world to change their business processes and ways of working to align with units in other countries, especially if this might interfere with their local performance.

Involving people in change, and assuring them that change is in the best interests of the company and their local units, is a key tactic for convincing users to adopt global systems and standards. Information systems projects should involve users in the design process without giving up control over the project to parochial interests.

One tactic is to permit each country unit in a global corporation to develop one transnational application first in its home territory, and then throughout the world. In this manner, each major country systems group is given a piece of the action in developing a transnational system, and local units feel a sense of ownership in the transnational effort. On the downside, this assumes the ability to develop high-quality systems is widely distributed, and that, a German team, for example, can successfully implement systems in France and Italy. This will not always be the case.

HRIS COMBINED PLAN–HR

Task	Da	Who
DATA ADMINISTRATION SECURITY		
QMF security review/setup	20	EF TP
Security orientation	2	EF JA
QMF security maintenance	35	TP GL
Data entry sec. profiles	4	EF TP
Data entry sec. views est.	12	EF TP
Data entry security profiles	65	EF TP
DATA DICTIONARY		
Orientation sessions	1	EF
Data dictionary design	32	EFWV
DD prod. coordn-query	20	GL
DD prod. coordn-live	40	EF GL
Data dictionary cleanup	35	EF GL
Data dictionary maint.	35	EF GL
PROCEDURES REVISION		
DESIGN PREP		
Work flows (old)	10	PK JL
Payroll data flows	31	JL PK
HRIS P/R model	11	PK JL
P/R interface orient. mtg.	6	PK JL
P/R interface coordn. 1	15	PK
P/R interface coordn. 2	8	PK
Benefits interfaces (old)	5	JL
Benefits interfaces (new flow)	8	JL
Benefits communication strategy	3	PK JL
New work flow model	15	PK JL
Posn. data entry flowsc	14	WV JL

RESOURCE SUMMARY

Name		Who	Oct	Nov	Dec	Jan	Feb	Mar	Apr	May	Jun	Jul	Aug	Sep	Oct	Nov	Dec	Jan	Feb	Mar
			2011			**2012**												**2013**		
Edith Farrell	5.0	EF	2	21	24	24	23	22	22	27	34	34	29	26	28	19	14			
Woody Vinton	5.0	WV	5	17	20	19	12	10	14	10	2								4	3
Charles Pierce	5.0	CP		5	11	20	13	9	10	7	6	8	4	4	4	4	4			
Ted Leurs	5.0	TL		12	17	17	19	17	14	12	15	16	2	1	1	1	1			
Toni Cox	5.0	TC	1	11	10	11	11	12	19	19	21	21	17	17	12	9				
Patricia Knopp	5.0	PC	7	23	30	34	27	25	15	24	25	16	11	13	17	10	3		3	2
Jane Lawton	5.0	JL	1	9	16	21	19	21	21	20	17	15	14	12	14	8	5			
David Holloway	5.0	DH	4	4	5	5	5	2	7	5	4	16	2							
Diane O'Neill	5.0	DO	6	14	17	16	13	11	9	4										
Joan Albert	5.0	JA	5	6			7	6	2	1				5	5	1				
Marie Marcus	5.0	MM	15	7	2	1	1													
Don Stevens	5.0	DS	4	4	5	4	5	1												
Casual	5.0	CASL		3	4	3			4	7	9	5	3	2						
Kathy Mendez	5.0	KM			1	5	16	20	19	22	19	20	18	20	11	2				
Anna Borden	5.0	AB						9	10	16	15	11	12	19	10	7	1			
Gail Loring	5.0	GL		3	6	5	9	10	17	18	17	10	13	10	10	7	17			
UNASSIGNED	0.0	X											9		236	225	230	14	13	
Co-op	5.0	CO		6	4				2	3	4	4	2	4	16			216	178	
Casual	5.0	CAUL									3	3	3							
TOTAL DAYS			49	147	176	196	194	174	193	195	190	181	140	125	358	288	284	237	196	12

Figure 11.10
A Gantt Chart
The Gantt chart in this figure shows the task, person-days, and initials of each responsible person, as well as the start and finish dates for each task. The resource summary provides a good manager with the total person-days for each month and for each person working on the project to manage the project successfully. The project described here is a data administration project.

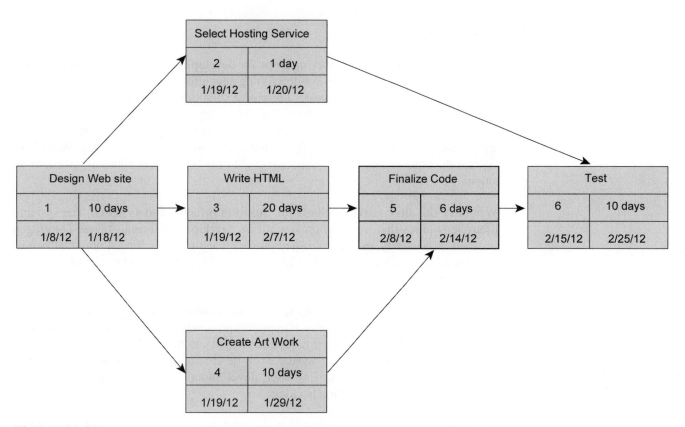

Figure 11.11
A PERT Chart
This is a simplified PERT chart for creating a small Web site. It shows the ordering of project tasks and the relationship of a task with preceding and succeeding tasks.

A second tactic is to develop new transnational centers of excellence, or a single center of excellence. These centers draw heavily from local national units, are based on multinational teams, and must report to worldwide management. Centers of excellence perform the business and systems analysis and accomplish all design and testing. Implementation, however, and pilot testing are rolled out to other parts of the globe. Recruiting a wide range of local groups to transnational centers of excellence helps send the message that all significant groups are involved in the design and will have an influence.

LEARNING TRACKS

The following Learning Tracks provide content relevant to topics covered in this chapter:

1. Capital Budgeting Methods for Information System Investments
2. Enterprise Analysis (Business Systems Planning) and Critical Success Factors (CSFs)
3. Unified Modeling Language (UML)
4. IT Investments and Productivity

Review Summary

1 **What are the core problem-solving steps for developing new information systems?** The core problem-solving steps for developing new information systems are: (1) define and understand the problem, (2) develop alternative solutions, (3) evaluate and choose the solution, and (4) implement the solution. The third step includes an assessment of the technical, financial, and organizational feasibility of each alternative. The fourth step entails finalizing design specifications, acquiring hardware and software, testing, providing training and documentation, conversion, and evaluating the system solution once it is in production.

2 **What are the alternative methods for building information systems?** The systems lifecycle requires that information systems be developed in formal stages. The stages must proceed sequentially and have defined outputs; each requires formal approval before the next stage can commence. The system lifecycle is rigid and costly but nevertheless useful for large projects.

Prototyping consists of building an experimental system rapidly and inexpensively for end users to interact with and evaluate. The prototype is refined and enhanced until users are satisfied that it includes all of their requirements and can be used as a template to create the final system. End-user-developed systems can be created rapidly and informally using fourth-generation software tools. End-user development can improve requirements determination and reduce application backlog.

Application software packages eliminate the need for writing software programs when developing an information system. Application software packages are helpful if a firm does not have the internal information systems staff or financial resources to custom-develop a system.

Outsourcing consists of using an external vendor to build (or operate) a firm's information systems. If it is properly managed, outsourcing can save application development costs or enable firms to develop applications without an internal information systems staff.

Rapid application design, joint application design (JAD), cloud-based platforms, and reusable software components (including Web services) can be used to speed up the systems development process.

3 **What are the principal methodologies for modeling and designing systems?** The two principal methodologies for modeling and designing information systems are structured methodologies and object-oriented development. Structured methodologies focus on modeling processes and data separately. The data flow diagram is the principal tool for structured analysis, and the structure chart is the principal tool for representing structured software design. Object-oriented development models a system as a collection of objects that combine processes and data.

4 **How should information systems projects be selected and evaluated?** To determine whether an information system project is a good investment, one must calculate its costs and benefits. Tangible benefits are quantifiable, and intangible benefits cannot be immediately quantified but may provide quantifiable benefits in the future. Benefits that exceed costs should then be analyzed using capital budgeting methods to make sure they represent a good return on the firm's invested capital.

Organizations should develop information systems plans that describe how information technology supports the company's overall business plan and strategy. Portfolio analysis and scoring models can be used to evaluate alternative information systems projects.

5 **How should information systems projects be managed?** Information systems projects and the entire implementation process should be managed as planned organizational change using an organizational impact analysis. Management support and control of the implementation process are essential, as are mechanisms for dealing with the level of risk in each new systems project. Project risks are influenced by project size, project structure, and the level of technical expertise of the information systems staff and project team. Formal planning and control tools (including Gantt and PERT charts) track the resource allocations and specific project activities. Users can be encouraged to take active roles in systems development and become involved in installation and training. Global information systems projects should involve local units in the creation of the design without giving up control of the project to parochial interests.

Key Terms

Acceptance testing, 384
Component-based
    development, 396
Computer-aided software
    engineering (CASE), 397
Conversion, 386
Customization, 390
Data flow diagram
    (DFD), 393
Direct cutover strategy, 386
Documentation, 384
End-user development, 389
Ergonomics, 405
Feasibility study, 383
Formal planning
    and tools, 405
Gantt chart, 405
Implementation, 404
Information
    requirements, 382

Information systems
    plan, 400
Intangible benefits, 400
Joint application design
    (JAD), 393
Maintenance, 386
Object-oriented
    development, 395
Organizational impact
    analysis, 405
Parallel strategy, 386
PERT charts, 405
Phased approach, 386
Portfolio analysis, 402
Process specifications, 394
Production, 386
Project, 397
Project management, 397
Prototyping, 388

Rapid application
    development (RAD), 392
Request for Proposal
    (RFP), 389
Scope, 397
Scoring model, 402
Structure chart, 394
Structured, 393
System testing, 384
Systems analysis, 382
Systems design, 383
Systems development
    lifecycle (SDLC), 387
Tangible benefits, 400
Test plan, 384
Testing, 384
Unit testing, 384
User-designer communi-
    cations gap, 404

Review Questions

1. What are the core problem-solving steps for developing new information systems?
   • List and describe the problem-solving steps for building a new system.
   • Define information requirements and explain why they are important for developing a system solution.
   • List the various types of design specifications required for a new information system.
   • Explain why the testing stage of systems development is so important. Name and describe the three stages of testing for an information system.
   • Describe the roles of documentation, conversion, production, and maintenance in systems development.

2. What are the alternative methods for building information systems?
   • Define the traditional systems lifecycle and describe its advantages and disadvantages for systems building.
   • Define information system prototyping and describe its benefits and limitations. List and describe the steps in the prototyping process.
   • Define end-user development and explain its advantages and disadvantages.
   • Describe the advantages and disadvantages of developing information systems based on application software packages.

- Define outsourcing. Describe the circumstances in which it should be used for building information systems. List and describe the hidden costs of offshore software outsourcing.
- Explain how businesses can rapidly develop e-business applications.

3. What are the principal methodologies for modeling and designing systems?
- Compare object-oriented and traditional structured approaches for modeling and designing systems.

4. How should information systems projects be selected and evaluated?
- Explain the difference between tangible and intangible benefits.
- List six tangible benefits and six intangible benefits.
- List and describe the major components of an information systems plan.
- Describe how portfolio analysis and scoring models can be used to establish the worth of systems.

5. How should information systems projects be managed?
- Explain the importance of implementation for managing the organizational change surrounding a new information system.
- Define the user-designer communications gap and explain the kinds of implementation problems it creates.
- List and describe the factors that influence project risk and describe strategies for minimizing project risks.
- Describe tactics for managing global projects.

Discussion Questions

1. Discuss the role of business end users and information system professionals in developing a system solution. How do both roles differ when the solution is developed using prototyping or end-user development?

2. It has been said that systems fail when systems builders ignore "people" problems. Why might this be so?

3. Why is building a system a form of organizational problem-solving?

Hands-on MIS Projects

The projects in this section give you hands-on experience evaluating information systems projects, designing a customer system for auto sales, and analyzing Web site information requirements.

MANAGEMENT DECISION PROBLEMS

1. The Warm and Toasty Heating Oil Company used to deliver heating oil by sending trucks that printed out a ticket with the number of gallons of oil delivered and that was placed on customers' doorsteps. Customers received their oil delivery bills in the mail two weeks later. The company recently revised its oil delivery and billing system so that oil truck drivers can calculate and print out a complete bill for each delivery and leave customers with the bill and a return envelope at the time the delivery takes place. Evaluate the business impact of the new system and the people and organizational changes required to implement the new technology.

2. Caterpillar is the world's leading maker of earth-moving machinery and supplier of agricultural equipment. The software for its Dealer Business System (DBS), which it licenses to its dealers to help them run their businesses, is becoming outdated. Senior management wants its dealers to use a hosted version of the software supported by Accenture Consultants so Caterpillar can concentrate on its core business. The system had become a de-facto standard for doing business with the company. The majority of the 50 Cat dealers in North America use some version of DBS, as do about half of the

200 or so Cat dealers in the rest of the world. Before Caterpillar turns the product over to Accenture, what factors and issues should it consider? What questions should it ask? What questions should its dealers ask?

IMPROVING DECISION MAKING: USING DATABASE SOFTWARE TO DESIGN A CUSTOMER SYSTEM FOR AUTO SALES

Software skills: Database design, querying, reporting, and forms
Business skills: Sales lead and customer analysis

This project requires you to perform a systems analysis and then design a system solution using database software.

Ace Auto Dealers specializes in selling new vehicles from Subaru in Portland, Oregon. The company advertises in local newspapers and is also listed as an authorized dealer on the Subaru Web site and other major Web sites for auto buyers. The company benefits from a good local word-of-mouth reputation and name recognition.

Ace does not believe it has enough information about its customers. It cannot easily determine which prospects have made auto purchases, nor can it identify which customer touch points have produced the greatest number of sales leads or actual sales so it can focus advertising and marketing more on the channels that generate the most revenue. Are purchasers discovering Ace from newspaper ads, from word of mouth, or from the Web?

Prepare a systems analysis report detailing Ace's problem and a system solution that can be implemented using PC database management software. Then use database software to develop a simple system solution. In MyMISLab, you will find more information about Ace and its information requirements to help you develop the solution.

ACHIEVING OPERATIONAL EXCELLENCE: ANALYZING WEB SITE DESIGN AND INFORMATION REQUIREMENTS

Software skills: Web browser software
Business skills: Information requirements analysis, Web site design

Visit the Web site of your choice and explore it thoroughly. Prepare a report analyzing the various functions provided by that Web site and its information requirements. Your report should answer these questions: What functions does the Web site perform? What data does it use? What are its inputs, outputs, and processes? What are some of its other design specifications? Does the Web site link to any internal systems or systems of other organizations? What value does this Web site provide the firm?

Video Cases

Video Cases and Instructional Videos illustrating some of the concepts in this chapter are available. Contact your instructor to access these videos.

Collaboration and Teamwork

Preparing Web Site Design Specifications

With three or four of your classmates, select a system described in this text that uses the Web. Review the Web site for the system you select. Use what you have learned from the Web site and the description in this book to prepare a report describing some of the design specifications for the system you select. If possible, use Google Sites to post links to Web pages, team communication announcements, and work assignments; to brainstorm; and to work collaboratively on project documents. Try to use Google Docs to develop a presentation of your findings for the class.

BUSINESS PROBLEM-SOLVING CASE

JetBlue and WestJet: A Tale of Two IS Projects

In recent years, the airline industry has seen several low-cost, high-efficiency carriers rise to prominence using a recipe of extremely competitive fares and outstanding customer service. Two examples of this business model in action are JetBlue and WestJet. Both companies were founded within the past two decades and have quickly grown into industry powerhouses. But when these companies need to make sweeping IT upgrades, their relationships with customers and their brands can be tarnished if things go awry. In 2009, both airlines upgraded their airline reservation systems, and one of the two learned this lesson the hard way.

JetBlue was incorporated in 1998 and founded in 1999 by David Neeleman. The company is headquartered in Queens, New York and flies to 63 destinations in 21 states and eleven countries in the Caribbean, South America and Latin America. JetBlue's goal has been to provide low-cost travel along with unique amenities like TV in every seat, and its heavy reliance on information technology throughout the business was a critical factor in achieving that goal. JetBlue met with early success and continued to grow at a rapid pace, consistently ranking at the top of customer satisfaction surveys for U.S. airlines.

Headquartered in Calgary, Canada, WestJet was founded by a group of airline industry veterans in 1996, including Neeleman, who left to start JetBlue shortly thereafter. The company began with approximately 40 employees and three aircraft. Today, the company has 7,800 employees and operates 420 flights per day to 71 destinations in Canada, the United States, the Caribbean, and Mexico. Earlier in this decade, WestJet underwent rapid expansion spurred by its early success and began adding more Canadian destinations and then U.S. cities for its flights. By 2010, WestJet held nearly 40 percent of the Canadian airline market, with Air Canada dropping to 55 percent.

JetBlue is slightly bigger, with 167 aircraft in use compared to WestJet's 88, but both have used the same low-cost, good-service formula that brought profitability in the notoriously treacherous airline marketplace. The rapid growth of each airline rendered their existing information systems obsolete, including their airline reservation systems.

Upgrading reservations systems carries special risks. From a customer perspective, only one of two things can happen: Either the airline successfully completes its overhaul and the customer notices no difference in the ability to book flights, or the implementation is botched, angering customers and damaging the airline's brand.

The time had come for both JetBlue and WestJet to upgrade their reservation systems. Each carrier had started out using a system designed for smaller start-up airlines, and both needed more processing power to deal with a far greater volume of customers. They also needed features like the ability to link prices and seat inventories to other airlines with whom they cooperated.

Both JetBlue and WestJet contracted with Sabre Holdings, one of the most widely used airline IT providers, to upgrade their airline reservation systems, The difference between WestJet and JetBlue's implementation of Sabre's SabreSonic CSS reservation system illustrates the dangers inherent in any large-scale IT overhaul. It also serves as yet another reminder of how successfully planning for and implementing new technology is just as valuable as the technology itself.

Sabre's newest system, SabreSonic CSS, performs a broad array of services for any airline. It sells seats, collects payments, allows customers to shop for flights on the airline's Web site, and provides an interface for communication with reservation agents. Customers can use it to access airport kiosks, select specific seats, check their bags, board, rebook, and receive refunds for flight cancellations. All of the data generated by these transactions are stored centrally within the system. JetBlue selected SabreSonic CSS over its legacy system developed by Sabre rival Navitaire, and WestJet was upgrading from an older Sabre reservation system of its own.

The first of the two airlines to implement SabreSonic CSS was WestJet. When WestJet went live with the new system in October 2009, customers struggled to place reservations, and the WestJet Web site crashed repeatedly. WestJet's call centers were also overwhelmed, and customers experienced slowdowns at airports. For a company that built its business on the strength of good customer service, this was a nightmare. How did WestJet allow this to happen?

The critical issue was the transfer of WestJet's 840,000 files containing data on transactions for past WestJet customers who had already purchased flights, from WestJet's old reservation system servers in Calgary to Sabre servers in Oklahoma. The migration required WestJet agents to go through complex steps to process the data. WestJet had not anticipated the transfer time required to move the files and failed to reduce its passenger loads on flights operating immediately after the changeover. Hundreds of thousands of bookings for future flights that were made before the changeover were inaccessible during the file transfer and for a period of time thereafter, because Sabre had to adjust the flights using the new system.

This delay provoked a deluge of customer dissatisfaction, a rarity for WestJet. In addition to the increase in customer complaint calls, customers also took to the Internet to express their displeasure. Angry flyers expressed outrage on Facebook and flooded WestJet's site, causing the repeated crashes. WestJet quickly offered an apology to customers on its site once it came back up, explaining why the errors had occurred. WestJet employees had trained with the new system for a combined 150,000 hours prior to the upgrade, but WestJet spokesman Robert Palmer explained that the company "encounter(ed) some problems in the live environment that simply did not appear in the test environment," foremost among them the issues surrounding the massive file transfer.

WestJet's latest earnings reports show that the company weathered the storm successfully, remained profitable, and ranks just below JetBlue and Southwest in airline customer satisfaction. Nevertheless, the incident forced the airline to slow down its rollout of a frequent flyer program, as well as code-sharing plans with other airlines, such as American Airlines and Cathay Pacific. These plans allow one airline to sell flights under its own name on aircraft operated by other airlines.

In contrast, JetBlue learned from WestJet's mistakes, and built a backup Web site to prepare for the worst case scenario. The company also hired 500 temporary call center workers to manage potential spikes in customer service calls. WestJet also ended up hiring temporary offshore call center workers, but only after the problem had gotten out of hand. JetBlue made sure to switch its files over to Sabre's servers on a Friday night, because Saturday flight traffic is typically very low. JetBlue also sold smaller numbers of seats on the flights that did take off that day.

JetBlue experienced a few glitches—call wait times increased and not all airport kiosks and ticket printers came online right away. In addition, JetBlue needs to add some booking functions. But compared to what WestJet endured, the company was extremely well prepared to handle these problems. JetBlue ended up using its backup site several times.

JetBlue had the advantage of seeing WestJet begin its implementation months before, so it was able to avoid many of the pitfalls that WestJet endured. But JetBlue had also experienced similar customer service debacles in the past. In February 2007, JetBlue tried to operate flights during a blizzard when all other major airlines had already canceled their flights. This turned out to be a poor decision, as the weather conditions prevented the flights from taking off and passengers were stranded for as long as ten hours. JetBlue had to continue canceling flights for days afterwards, reaching a total of 1,100 flights canceled and a loss of $30 million. JetBlue management realized in the wake of the crisis that the airline's IT infrastructure, although sufficient to deal with normal day-to-day conditions, was not robust enough to handle a crisis of this magnitude. This experience, coupled with the observation of WestJet's struggles when implementing its new system, motivated JetBlue's cautious approach to its own IT implementation.

Sources: Terry Maxon, "JetBlue, Southwest Top Annual Passenger Satisfaction Study," McClatch-Tribune News Service, June 20, 2011; Susan Carey, "Two Paths to Software Upgrade," *Wall Street Journal*, April 13, 2010; www.westjet.com, accessed August 4, 2011; www.jetblue.com, accessed June 25, 2011; Aaron Karp, "WestJet Offers 'Heartfelt Apologies' on Res System Snafus; Posts C$31 Million Profit," *Air Transport World*, Nov. 5, 2009; Ellen Roseman, "WestJet Reservation Change Frustrates," thestar.com, December 2, 2009; "JetBlue selects SabreSonic CSS for revenue and operational systems," Shepard.com, February 17, 2009; "Jilted by JetBlue for Sabre," Tnooz.com, February 5, 2010.

Case Study Questions

1. How important is the reservation system at airlines such as WestJet and JetBlue. How does it impact operational activities and decision making?

2. Evaluate the risks of the projects to upgrade the reservation systems of WestJet and JetBlue and key risk factors.

3. Classify and describe the problems each airline faced in implementing its new reservation system. What people, organization, and technology factors caused those problems?

4. Describe the steps you would have taken to control the risk in these projects?

Ethical and Social Issues in Information Systems

CHAPTER 12

STUDENT LEARNING OBJECTIVES

After completing this chapter, you will be able to answer the following questions:

1. What ethical, social, and political issues are raised by information systems?

2. What specific principles for conduct can be used to guide ethical decisions?

3. Why do contemporary information systems technology and the Internet pose challenges to the protection of individual privacy and intellectual property?

4. How have information systems affected everyday life?

CHAPTER OUTLINE

BEHAVIORAL TARGETING: YOUR PRIVACY IS THE TARGET

Ever get the feeling somebody is trailing you on the Web, watching your every click? Do you wonder why you start seeing display ads and pop-ups just after you've been searching the Web for a car, a dress, or cosmetic product? Well, you're right: your behavior is being tracked, and you are being targeted on the Web as you move from site to site in order to expose you to certain "targeted" ads.

So how common is online behavioral tracking? In a path-breaking series of articles in the *Wall Street Journal* in 2011, researchers examined the tracking files on 50 of the most popular U.S Web sites. What they found revealed a very widespread surveillance system. On the 50 sites, they discovered 3,180 tracking files installed on visitor computers. Only one site, Wikipedia, had no tracking files. Some popular sites such as Dictionary.com, MSN, and Comcast, installed more than 100 tracking files! Two-thirds of the tracking files came from 131 companies whose primary business is identifying and tracking Internet users to create consumer profiles that can be sold to advertising firms looking for specific types of customers. The biggest trackers were Google, Microsoft, and Quantcast, all of whom are in the business of selling ads to advertising firms and marketers. Google, given its dominance in search, knows more

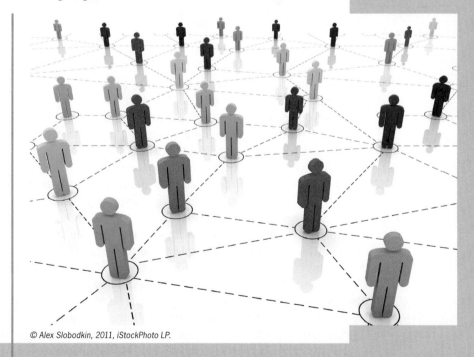

© Alex Slobodkin, 2011, iStockPhoto LP.

about you than your mother does. Another third of the tracking files came from database firms that gather and bundle the information and then sell it to marketers. Many of the tracking tools gather incredibly personal information such as age, gender, race, income, marital status, health concerns (health topics you search on), TV shows and movies viewed, magazines and newspapers read, and books purchased. Facebook does not need to put tracking programs on other Web sites, or its own Web site, because its social networking site is one giant tracking system already that remembers what you like, what your friends like, and whatever you reveal on your Wall. While tracking firms claim the information they gather is anonymous, this is true in name only. Scholars have shown that with just a few pieces of information, such as age, gender, zip code, and marital status, specific individuals can be easily identified.

The growth in the power, reach, and scope of behavioral targeting has drawn the attention of privacy groups and the Federal Trade Commission (FTC). Currently, there are no laws or regulations in the United States that prevent firms from installing tracking files on your computer or using that information in any way they please, but this situation is beginning to change. There is now considerable legislative and government interest in protecting the privacy of consumers, driven in part by public fear of the loss of privacy and the lack of transparency in the world of Web tracking.

In December 2010, the Federal Trade Commission issued a staff report that proposed a new balance between the privacy interests of consumers with continued innovation on the Web that relies on consumer information. The report argued that industry self-regulation had failed to protect consumer privacy. The Commission recommended consumers be given a simple way to opt out of tracking through a "Do Not Track" mechanism in the user's browser that would prevent Web sites from installing tracking software on the user's browser. In March, the White House issued a call for privacy legislation. In April 2011, Senators John Kerry and John McCain proposed bipartisan legislation that would create a "privacy bill of rights" to protect people from an unregulated, invasive commercial data-collection industry. Labeled the "Commercial Privacy Bill of Rights Act of 2011," the legislation would allow consumers, on a site-by-site basis, to demand, Web sites stop tracking them and selling their information online.

Sources: Julie Angwin, "Latest in Web Tracking: Stealthy 'Supercookies,'" by Julia Angwin, *Wall Street Journal*, August 18, 2011; Emily Steel, "WPP Ad Unit Has Your Profile," *Wall Street Journal*, June 27, 2011; "Do-Not-Track Online Act of 2011," Senate 913, U.S. Senate, May 9, 2011; Tanzina Vega, "Do Not Track Bill Appears in Congress," *New York Times*, May 6, 2011; Richard Thaler, "Show Us the Data. (It's Ours, After All)," *New York Times*, April 23, 2011; "Commercial Privacy Bill of Rights Act," Senate 799; U.S. Senate, April 13, 2011; "Protecting Consumer Privacy," Preliminary FTC Staff Report. Federal Trade Commission, March 10, 2011.

The growing use of behavioral targeting techniques described in the chapter-opening case shows that technology can be a double-edged sword. It can be the source of many benefits (by showing you ads relevant to your interests), but it can also create new opportunities for invading your privacy, and enabling the reckless use of that information in a variety of decisions about you. Moreover, you will not be informed of these uses or be able to amend the information about you. You have no enforceable legal rights vis-à-vis this personal information.

The chapter-opening diagram calls attention to important points raised by this case and this chapter. Online advertising titans like Google, Microsoft, and Yahoo are all looking for ways to monetize their huge collections of online behavioral data. While search engine marketing is arguably the most effective form of advertising in history, banner display ad marketing is highly inefficient because it displays ads to everyone regardless of their interests. As a result, these firms cannot charge much for display ads. However, by tracking the online movements of 232 million U.S. Internet users, they can develop a very clear picture of who you are, and use that information to show you ads that might be of interest to you. This would make the marketing process more efficient, and more profitable for all the parties involved.

But this solution also creates an ethical dilemma, pitting the monetary interests of the online advertisers and search engines against the interests of individuals to maintain a sense of control over their personal information and their privacy. Two closely held values are in conflict here. As a manager, you will need to be sensitive to both the negative and positive impacts of information systems for your firm, employees, and customers. You will need to learn how to resolve ethical dilemmas involving information systems.

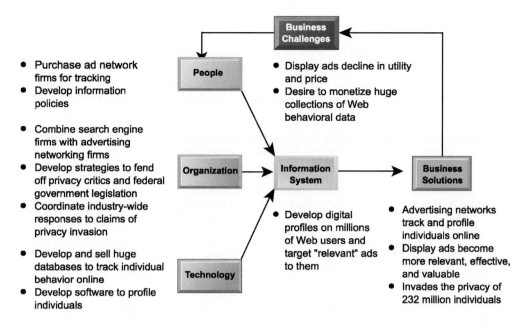

12.1 Understanding Ethical and Social Issues Related to Systems

In the past 10 years, we have witnessed, arguably, one of the most ethically challenging periods for U.S. and global business. Table 12.1 provides a small sample of recent cases demonstrating failed ethical judgment by senior and middle managers. These lapses in ethical and business judgment occurred across a broad spectrum of industries.

In today's new legal environment, managers who violate the law and are convicted will most likely spend time in prison. U.S. federal sentencing guidelines adopted in 1987 mandate that federal judges impose stiff sentences on business executives based on the monetary value of the crime, the presence of a conspiracy to prevent discovery of the crime, the use of structured financial transactions to hide the crime, and failure to cooperate with prosecutors (U.S. Sentencing Commission, 2004).

Although business firms would, in the past, often pay for the legal defense of their employees enmeshed in civil charges and criminal investigations, firms are now encouraged to cooperate with prosecutors to reduce charges against the entire firm for obstructing investigations. These developments mean that, more than ever, as a manager or an employee, you will have to decide for yourself what constitutes proper legal and ethical conduct.

Although these major instances of failed ethical and legal judgment were not masterminded by information systems departments, information systems were instrumental in many of these frauds. In many cases, the perpetrators of these crimes artfully used financial reporting information systems to bury their decisions from public scrutiny in the vain hope they would never be caught.

We deal with the issue of control in information systems in Chapter 7. In this chapter, we talk about the ethical dimensions of these and other actions based on the use of information systems.

Ethics refers to the principles of right and wrong that individuals, acting as free moral agents, use to make choices to guide their behaviors. Information systems raise new ethical questions for both individuals and societies because they create opportunities for intense social change, and thus threaten existing distributions of power, money, rights, and obligations. Like other technologies, such as steam engines, electricity, the telephone, and the radio, information technology can be used to achieve social progress, but it can also be used to commit crimes and threaten cherished social values. The development of information technology will produce benefits for many and costs for others.

Recent Examples of Failed Ethical Judgment by Senior Managers

Lehman Brothers (2008–2010)	One of the oldest American investment banks collapses in 2008. Lehman used information systems and accounting sleight of hand to conceal its bad investments. Lehman also engaged in deceptive tactics to shift investments off its books.
WG Trading Co. (2010)	Paul Greenwood, hedge fund manager and general partner at WG Trading, pled guilty to defrauding investors of $554 million over 13 years; Greenwood has forfeited $331 million to the government and faces up to 85 years in prison.
Minerals Management Service (U.S. Department of the Interior) (2010)	Managers accused of accepting gifts and other favors from oil companies, letting oil company rig employees write up inspection reports, and failing to enforce existing regulations on offshore Gulf drilling rigs. Employees systematically falsified information record systems.
Pfizer, Eli Lilly, and AstraZeneca (2009)	Major pharmaceutical firms paid billions of dollars to settle U.S. federal charges that executives fixed clinical trials for antipsychotic and pain killer drugs, marketed them inappropriately to children, and claimed unsubstantiated benefits while covering up negative outcomes. Firms falsified information in reports and systems.
Galleon Group (2011)	Founder of the Galleon Group sentenced to 11 years in prison for trading on insider information. Found guilty of paying $250 million to Wall Street banks, and in return received market information that other investors did not get.
Siemens (2009)	The world's largest engineering firm paid over $4 billion to German and U.S. authorities for a decades-long, worldwide bribery scheme approved by corporate executives to influence potential customers and governments. Payments concealed from normal reporting accounting systems.
IBM (2011)	IBM settled SEC charges that it paid off South Korean and Chinese government officials with bags of cash over a 10-year period.
McKinsey & Company (2011)	CEO Rajat Gupta heard on tapes leaking insider information. Currently under criminal investigation.
Tyson Foods (2011)	World's largest producer of poultry, beef, and pork agreed to pay $5 million in fines for bribing Mexican officials to ignore health violations.

Ethical issues in information systems have been given new urgency by the rise of the Internet and electronic commerce. Internet and digital firm technologies make it easier than ever to assemble, integrate, and distribute information, unleashing new concerns about the appropriate use of customer information, the protection of personal privacy, and the protection of intellectual property.

Other pressing ethical issues raised by information systems include establishing accountability for the consequences of information systems, setting standards to safeguard system quality that protects the safety of the individual and society, and preserving values and institutions considered essential to the quality of life in an information society. When using information systems, it is essential to ask, "What is the ethical and socially responsible course of action?"

A MODEL FOR THINKING ABOUT ETHICAL, SOCIAL, AND POLITICAL ISSUES

Ethical, social, and political issues are closely linked. The ethical dilemma you may face as a manager of information systems typically is reflected in social and political debate. One way to think about these relationships is shown in Figure 12.1. Imagine society as a more or less calm pond on a summer day, a delicate ecosystem in partial equilibrium with individuals

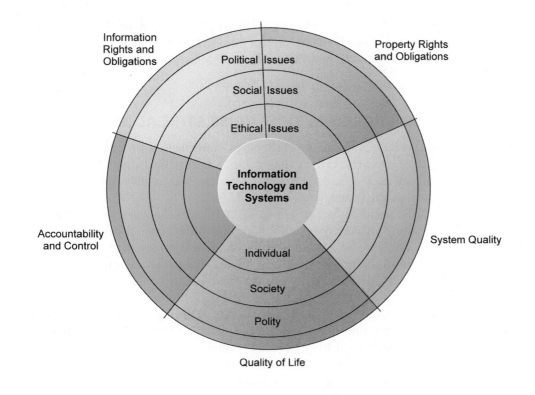

Figure 12.1
The Relationship Between Ethical, Social, and Political Issues in an Information Society
The introduction of new information technology has a ripple effect, raising new ethical, social, and political issues that must be dealt with on the individual, social, and political levels. These issues have five moral dimensions: information rights and obligations, property rights and obligations, system quality, quality of life, and accountability and control.

and with social and political institutions. Individuals know how to act in this pond because social institutions (family, education, organizations) have developed well-honed rules of behavior, and these are supported by laws developed in the political sector that prescribe behavior and promise sanctions for violations. Now toss a rock into the center of the pond. What happens? Ripples, of course.

Imagine instead that the disturbing force is a powerful shock of new information technology and systems hitting a society more or less at rest. Suddenly, individual actors are confronted with new situations often not covered by the old rules. Social institutions cannot respond overnight to these ripples—it may take years to develop etiquette, expectations, social responsibility, politically correct attitudes, or approved rules. Political institutions also require time before developing new laws and often require the demonstration of real harm before they act. In the meantime, you may have to act. You may be forced to act in a legal gray area.

We can use this model to illustrate the dynamics that connect ethical, social, and political issues. This model is also useful for identifying the main moral dimensions of the information society, which cut across various levels of action—individual, social, and political.

FIVE MORAL DIMENSIONS OF THE INFORMATION AGE

The major ethical, social, and political issues raised by information systems include the following moral dimensions:

- *Information rights and obligations.* What **information rights** do individuals and organizations possess with respect to themselves? What can they protect?
- *Property rights and obligations.* How will traditional intellectual property rights be protected in a digital society in which tracing and accounting for ownership are difficult and ignoring such property rights is so easy?
- *Accountability and control.* Who can and will be held accountable and liable for the harm done to individual and collective information and property rights?
- *System quality.* What standards of data and system quality should we demand to protect individual rights and the safety of society?

- *Quality of life.* What values should be preserved in an information- and knowledge-based society? Which institutions should we protect from violation? Which cultural values and practices are supported by the new information technology?

We explore these moral dimensions in detail in Section 12.3.

KEY TECHNOLOGY TRENDS THAT RAISE ETHICAL ISSUES

Ethical issues long preceded information technology. Nevertheless, information technology has heightened ethical concerns, taxed existing social arrangements, and made some laws obsolete or severely crippled. There are four key technological trends responsible for these ethical stresses and they are summarized in Table 12.2.

The doubling of computing power every 18 months has made it possible for most organizations to use information systems for their core production processes. As a result, our dependence on systems and our vulnerability to system errors and poor data quality have increased. Social rules and laws have not yet adjusted to this dependence. Standards for ensuring the accuracy and reliability of information systems (see Chapter 7) are not universally accepted or enforced.

Advances in data storage techniques and rapidly declining storage costs have been responsible for the multiplying databases on individuals—employees, customers, and potential customers—maintained by private and public organizations. These advances in data storage have made the routine violation of individual privacy both cheap and effective. Very large data storage systems capable of working with terabytes of data are inexpensive enough for large firms to use in identifying customers.

Advances in data analysis techniques for large pools of data are another technological trend that heightens ethical concerns because companies and government agencies are able to find out highly detailed personal information about individuals. With contemporary data management tools (see Chapter 5), companies can assemble and combine the myriad pieces of information about you stored on computers much more easily than in the past.

Think of all the ways you generate computer information about yourself—credit card purchases, telephone calls, magazine subscriptions, video rentals, mail-order purchases, banking records, local, state, and federal government records (including court and police records), and visits to Web sites. Put together and mined properly, this information could reveal not only your credit information but also your driving habits, your tastes, your associations, what you read and watch, and your political interests.

Companies with products to sell purchase relevant information from these sources to help them more finely target their marketing campaigns. Chapters 5 and 10 describe how companies can analyze large pools of data from multiple sources to rapidly identify

---

	Trend	Impact
TABLE 12.2 **Technology Trends That Raise Ethical Issues**	Computing power doubles every 18 months	More organizations depend on computer systems for critical operations.
	Data storage costs rapidly decline	Organizations can easily maintain detailed databases on individuals.
	Data analysis advances	Companies can analyze vast quantities of data gathered on individuals to develop detailed profiles of individual behavior.
	Networking advances	Copying data from one location to another and accessing personal data from remote locations are much easier.
	Mobile device growth Impact	Individual cell phones may be tracked without user consent or knowledge.

Credit card purchases can make personal information available to market researchers, telemarketers, and direct-mail companies. Advances in information technology facilitate the invasion of privacy.

© Marcus Clackson, 2011, iStockPhoto LP.

buying patterns of customers and suggest individual responses. The use of computers to combine data from multiple sources and create electronic dossiers of detailed information on individuals is called **profiling**.

For example, several thousand of the most popular Web sites allow DoubleClick (owned by Google), an Internet advertising broker, to track the activities of their visitors in exchange for revenue from advertisements based on visitor information DoubleClick gathers. DoubleClick uses this information to create a profile of each online visitor, adding more detail to the profile as the visitor accesses an associated DoubleClick site. Over time, DoubleClick can create a detailed dossier of a person's spending and computing habits on the Web that is sold to companies to help them target their Web ads more precisely.

ChoicePoint gathers data from police, criminal, and motor vehicle records; credit and employment histories; current and previous addresses; professional licenses; and insurance claims to assemble and maintain electronic dossiers on almost every adult in the United States. The company sells this personal information to businesses and government agencies. Demand for personal data is so enormous that data broker businesses such as ChoicePoint are flourishing. In 2011, the two largest credit card networks, Visa Inc. and MasterCard Inc., were planning to link credit card purchase information with consumer social network and other information to create customer profiles that could be sold to advertising firms. Visa processes 45 billion transactions a year and MasterCard processes 23 billion transactions. Currently, this transactional information is not linked with consumer Internet activities.

A new data analysis technology called **nonobvious relationship awareness (NORA)** has given both the government and the private sector even more powerful profiling capabilities. NORA can take information about people from many disparate sources, such as employment applications, telephone records, customer listings, and "wanted" lists, and correlate relationships to find obscure hidden connections that might help identify criminals or terrorists (see Figure 12.2).

NORA technology scans data and extracts information as the data are being generated so that it could, for example, instantly discover a man at an airline ticket counter who shares a phone number with a known terrorist before that person boards an airplane. The technology is considered a valuable tool for homeland security but does have privacy implications because it can provide such a detailed picture of the activities and associations of a single individual.

Figure 12.2
Nonobvious
Relationship
Awareness (NORA)
NORA technology can
take information about
people from dispa-
rate sources and find
obscure, nonobvious
relationships. It might
discover, for example,
that an applicant for a
job at a casino shares a
telephone number with a
known criminal and issue
an alert to the hiring
manager.

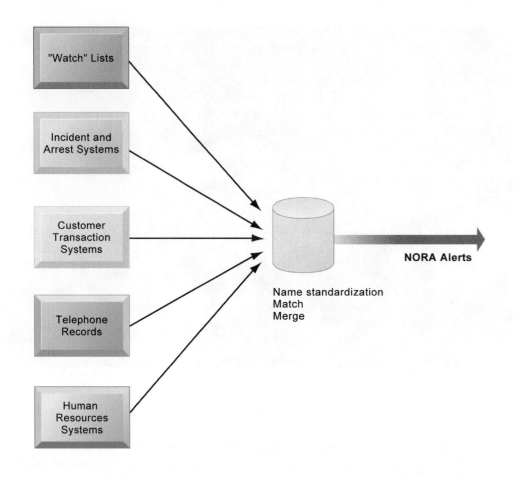

Finally, advances in networking, including the Internet, promise to greatly reduce the costs of moving and accessing large quantities of data and open the possibility of mining large pools of data remotely using small desktop machines, permitting an invasion of privacy on a scale and with a precision heretofore unimaginable.

12.2 Ethics in an Information Society

Ethics is a concern of humans who have freedom of choice. Ethics is about individual choice: When faced with alternative courses of action, what is the correct moral choice? What are the main features of ethical choice?

BASIC CONCEPTS: RESPONSIBILITY, ACCOUNTABILITY, AND LIABILITY

Ethical choices are decisions made by individuals who are responsible for the consequences of their actions. **Responsibility** is a key element of ethical action. Responsibility means that you accept the potential costs, duties, and obligations for the decisions you make. **Accountability** is a feature of systems and social institutions: It means that mechanisms are in place to determine who took responsible action, and who is responsible. Systems and institutions in which it is impossible to find out who took what action are inherently incapable of ethical analysis or ethical action. **Liability** extends the concept of responsibility further to the area of laws. Liability is a feature of political systems in which a body of laws is in place that permits individuals to recover the damages done to them by other actors, systems, or organizations. **Due process** is a related feature of law-governed societies and is a process in which laws are known and understood, and there is an ability to appeal to higher authorities to ensure that the laws are applied correctly.

These basic concepts form the underpinning of an ethical analysis of information systems and those who manage them. First, information technologies are filtered through social institutions, organizations, and individuals. Systems do not have impacts by themselves. Whatever information system impacts exist are products of institutional, organizational, and individual actions and behaviors. Second, responsibility for the consequences of technology falls clearly on the institutions, organizations, and individual managers who choose to use the technology. Using information technology in a socially responsible manner means that you can and will be held accountable for the consequences of your actions. Third, in an ethical, political society, individuals and others can recover damages done to them through a set of laws characterized by due process.

ETHICAL ANALYSIS

When confronted with a situation that seems to present ethical issues, how should you analyze it? The following five-step process should help:

1. *Identify and describe the facts clearly.* Find out who did what to whom, and where, when, and how. In many instances, you will be surprised at the errors in the initially reported facts, and often you will find that simply getting the facts straight helps define the solution. It also helps to get the opposing parties involved in an ethical dilemma to agree on the facts.

2. *Define the conflict or dilemma and identify the higher-order values involved.* Ethical, social, and political issues always reference higher values. The parties to a dispute all claim to be pursuing higher values (e.g., freedom, privacy, protection of property, and the free enterprise system). Typically, an ethical issue involves a dilemma: two diametrically opposed courses of action that support worthwhile values. For example, the chapter-ending case study illustrates two competing values: the need to improve health care record keeping and the need to protect individual privacy.

3. *Identify the stakeholders.* Every ethical, social, and political issue has stakeholders: players in the game who have an interest in the outcome, who have invested in the situation, and usually who have vocal opinions. Find out the identity of these groups and what they want. This will be useful later when designing a solution.

4. *Identify the options that you can reasonably take.* You may find that none of the options satisfy all the interests involved, but that some options do a better job than others. Sometimes arriving at a good or ethical solution may not always be a balancing of consequences to stakeholders.

5. *Identify the potential consequences of your options.* Some options may be ethically correct but disastrous from other points of view. Other options may work in one instance but not in other similar instances. Always ask yourself, "What if I choose this option consistently over time?"

CANDIDATE ETHICAL PRINCIPLES

Once your analysis is complete, what ethical principles or rules should you use to make a decision? What higher-order values should inform your judgment? Although you are the only one who can decide which among many ethical principles you will follow, and how you will prioritize them, it is helpful to consider some ethical principles with deep roots in many cultures that have survived throughout recorded history:

1. Do unto others as you would have them do unto you (the **Golden Rule**). Putting yourself into the place of others, and thinking of yourself as the object of the decision, can help you think about fairness in decision making.

2. If an action is not right for everyone to take, it is not right for anyone (**Immanuel Kant's Categorical Imperative**). Ask yourself, "If everyone did this, could the organization, or society, survive?"

3. If an action cannot be taken repeatedly, it is not right to take at all **(Descartes' rule of change)**. This is the slippery-slope rule: An action may bring about a small change now that is acceptable, but if it is repeated, it would bring unacceptable changes in the long run. In the vernacular, it might be stated as "once started down a slippery path, you may not be able to stop."

4. Take the action that achieves the higher or greater value **(Utilitarian Principle)**. This rule assumes you can prioritize values in a rank order and understand the consequences of various courses of action.

5. Take the action that produces the least harm or the least potential cost **(Risk Aversion Principle)**. Some actions have extremely high failure costs of very low probability (e.g., building a nuclear generating facility in an urban area) or extremely high failure costs of moderate probability (speeding and automobile accidents). Avoid these high-failure-cost actions, paying greater attention to high-failure-cost potential of moderate to high probability.

6. Assume that virtually all tangible and intangible objects are owned by someone else unless there is a specific declaration otherwise. (This is the **ethical "no free lunch" rule**.) If something someone else has created is useful to you, it has value, and you should assume the creator wants compensation for this work.

Actions that do not easily pass these rules deserve close attention and a great deal of caution. The appearance of unethical behavior may do as much harm to you and your company as actual unethical behavior.

PROFESSIONAL CODES OF CONDUCT

When groups of people claim to be professionals, they take on special rights and obligations because of their special claims to knowledge, wisdom, and respect. Professional codes of conduct are promulgated by associations of professionals, such as the American Medical Association (AMA), the American Bar Association (ABA), the Association of Information Technology Professionals (AITP), and the Association for Computing Machinery (ACM). These professional groups take responsibility for the partial regulation of their professions by determining entrance qualifications and competence. Codes of ethics are promises by professions to regulate themselves in the general interest of society. For example, avoiding harm to others, honoring property rights (including intellectual property), and respecting privacy are among the General Moral Imperatives of the ACM's Code of Ethics and Professional Conduct.

SOME REAL-WORLD ETHICAL DILEMMAS

Information systems have created new ethical dilemmas in which one set of interests is pitted against another. For example, many of the large telephone companies in the United States are using information technology to reduce the sizes of their workforces. Voice recognition software reduces the need for human operators by enabling computers to recognize a customer's responses to a series of computerized questions. Many companies monitor what their employees are doing on the Internet to prevent them from wasting company resources on non-business activities. Facebook monitors its 225 million American subscribers and then sells the information to advertisers and app developers.

In each instance, you can find competing values at work, with groups lined up on either side of a debate. A company may argue, for example, that it has a right to use information systems to increase productivity and reduce the size of its workforce to lower costs and stay in business. Employees displaced by information systems may argue that employers have some responsibility for their welfare. Business owners might feel obligated to monitor employee e-mail and Internet use to minimize drains on productivity. Employees might believe they should be able to use the Internet for short personal tasks in place of the telephone. A close analysis of the facts can sometimes produce compromised solutions that give each side "half a loaf." Try to apply some of the principles of ethical analysis described to each of these cases. What is the right thing to do?

12.3 The Moral Dimensions of Information Systems

In this section, we take a closer look at the five moral dimensions of information systems first described in Figure 12.1. In each dimension, we identify the ethical, social, and political levels of analysis and use real-world examples to illustrate the values involved, the stakeholders, and the options chosen.

INFORMATION RIGHTS: PRIVACY AND FREEDOM IN THE INTERNET AGE

Privacy is the claim of individuals to be left alone, free from surveillance or interference from other individuals or organizations, including the state. Claims to privacy are also involved at the workplace: Millions of employees are subject to electronic and other forms of high-tech surveillance (Ball, 2001). Information technology and systems threaten individual claims to privacy by making the invasion of privacy cheap, profitable, and effective.

The claim to privacy is protected in the U.S., Canadian, and German constitutions in a variety of different ways and in other countries through various statutes. In the United States, the claim to privacy is protected primarily by the First Amendment guarantees of freedom of speech and association, the Fourth Amendment protections against unreasonable search and seizure of one's personal documents or home, and the guarantee of due process.

Table 12.3 describes the major U.S. federal statutes that set forth the conditions for handling information about individuals in such areas as credit reporting, education, financial records, newspaper records, and electronic communications. The Privacy Act of 1974 has been the most important of these laws, regulating the federal government's collection, use, and disclosure of information. At present, most U.S. federal privacy laws apply only to the federal government and regulate very few areas of the private sector.

Most American and European privacy law is based on a regime called **Fair Information Practices (FIP)** first set forth in a report written in 1973 by a federal government advisory committee and updated most recently in 2010 to take into account new privacy-invading technology (FTC, 2010; U.S. Department of Health, Education, and Welfare, 1973). FIP

TABLE 12.3

Federal Privacy Laws in the United States

General Federal Privacy Laws	Privacy Laws Affecting Private Institutions
Freedom of Information Act of 1966 as Amended (5 USC 552)	Fair Credit Reporting Act of 1970
Privacy Act of 1974 as Amended (5 USC 552a)	Family Educational Rights and Privacy Act of 1974
Electronic Communications Privacy Act of 1986	Right to Financial Privacy Act of 1978
Computer Matching and Privacy Protection Act of 1988	Privacy Protection Act of 1980
Computer Security Act of 1987	Cable Communications Policy Act of 1984
Federal Managers Financial Integrity Act of 1982	Electronic Communications Privacy Act of 1986
Driver's Privacy Protection Act of 1994	Video Privacy Protection Act of 1988
E-Government Act of 2002	The Health Insurance Portability and Accountability Act of 1996 (HIPAA)
	Children's Online Privacy Protection Act (COPPA) of 1998
	Financial Modernization Act (Gramm-Leach-Bliley Act) of 1999

is a set of principles governing the collection and use of information about individuals. FIP principles are based on the notion of a mutuality of interest between the record holder and the individual. The individual has an interest in engaging in a transaction, and the record keeper—usually a business or government agency—requires information about the individual to support the transaction. Once information is gathered, the individual maintains an interest in the record, and the record may not be used to support other activities without the individual's consent. In 1998, the FTC restated and extended the original FIP to provide guidelines for protecting online privacy. Table 12.4 describes the FTC's Fair Information Practice principles.

The FTC's FIP principles are being used as guidelines to drive changes in privacy legislation. In July 1998, the U.S. Congress passed the Children's Online Privacy Protection Act (COPPA), requiring Web sites to obtain parental permission before collecting information on children under the age of 13. The FTC has recommended additional legislation to protect online consumer privacy in advertising networks that collect records of consumer Web activity to develop detailed profiles, which are then used by other companies to target online ads. In 2010, the FTC added three practices to its framework for privacy. Firms should adopt "privacy by design," building products and services that protect privacy. Firms should increase the transparency of their data practices. And firms should require consumer consent and provide clear options to opt out of data collection schemes (FTC, 2010). Other proposed Internet privacy legislation focuses on protecting the online use of personal identification numbers, such as social security numbers; protecting personal information collected on the Internet that deals with individuals not covered by COPPA; and limiting the use of data mining for homeland security.

Beginning in 2009 and continuing through 2011, the FTC extended its fair information practices doctrine to address the issue of behavioral targeting. The FTC held hearings to discuss its program for voluntary industry principles for regulating behavioral targeting. The online advertising trade group Network Advertising Initiative (discussed later in this section), published its own self-regulatory principles that largely agreed with the FTC. Nevertheless, the government, privacy groups, and the online ad industry are still at loggerheads over two issues. Privacy advocates want both an opt-in policy at all sites and a national Do Not Track list. The industry opposes these moves and continues to insist on an opt-out capability being the only way to avoid tracking. In May 2011, Senator Jay D. Rockefeller (D-WV), Chairman of the Senate Commerce Subcommittee on Consumer Protection, Product Safety, and Insurance, held hearings to discuss consumer privacy concerns and to explore the

TABLE 12.4

Federal Trade Commission Fair Information Practice Principles

1. Notice/awareness (core principle). Web sites must disclose their information practices before collecting data. Includes identification of collector, uses of data, other recipients of data, nature of collection (active/inactive), voluntary or required status, consequences of refusal, and steps taken to protect confidentiality, integrity, and quality of the data.

2. Choice/consent (core principle). There must be a choice regime in place allowing consumers to choose how their information will be used for secondary purposes other than supporting the transaction, including internal use and transfer to third parties.

3. Access/participation. Consumers should be able to review and contest the accuracy and completeness of data collected about them in a timely, inexpensive process.

4. Security. Data collectors must take responsible steps to assure that consumer information is accurate and secure from unauthorized use.

5. Enforcement. There must be in place a mechanism to enforce FIP principles. This can involve self-regulation, legislation giving consumers legal remedies for violations, or federal statutes and regulations.

possible role of the federal government in protecting consumers in the mobile marketplace. Rockefeller supports the Do-Not-Track Online Act of 2011, which requires firms to notify consumers they are being tracked and allows consumers to opt out of the tracking (U.S. Senate, 2011). Nevertheless, there is an emerging consensus among all parties that greater transparency and user control (especially making opt-out of tracking the default option) is required to deal with behavioral tracking.

Privacy protections have also been added to recent laws deregulating financial services and safeguarding the maintenance and transmission of health information about individuals. The Gramm-Leach-Bliley Act of 1999, which repeals earlier restrictions on affiliations among banks, securities firms, and insurance companies, includes some privacy protection for consumers of financial services. All financial institutions are required to disclose their policies and practices for protecting the privacy of nonpublic personal information and to allow customers to opt out of information-sharing arrangements with nonaffiliated third parties.

The Health Insurance Portability and Accountability Act (HIPAA) of 1996, which took effect on April 14, 2003, includes privacy protection for medical records. The law gives patients access to their personal medical records maintained by health care providers, hospitals, and health insurers, and the right to authorize how protected information about themselves can be used or disclosed. Doctors, hospitals, and other health care providers must limit the disclosure of personal information about patients to the minimum amount necessary to achieve a given purpose.

The European Directive on Data Protection

In Europe, privacy protection is much more stringent than in the United States. Unlike the United States, European countries do not allow businesses to use personally identifiable information without consumers' prior consent. On October 25, 1998, the European Commission's Directive on Data Protection went into effect, broadening privacy protection in the European Union (EU) nations. The directive requires companies to inform people when they collect information about them and disclose how it will be stored and used. Customers must provide their informed consent before any company can legally use data about them, and they have the right to access that information, correct it, and request that no further data be collected. **Informed consent** can be defined as consent given with knowledge of all the facts needed to make a rational decision. EU member nations must translate these principles into their own laws and cannot transfer personal data to countries, such as the United States, that do not have similar privacy protection regulations. In 2009, the European Parliament passed new rules governing the use of third-party cookies for behavioral tracking purposes. These new rules were implemented in May 2011 and require that Web site visitors must give explicit consent to be tracked by cookies. Web sites will be required to have highly visible warnings on their pages if third-party cookies are being used (European Parliament, 2009).

Working with the European Commission, the U.S. Department of Commerce developed a safe harbor framework for U.S. firms. A **safe harbor** is a private, self-regulating policy and enforcement mechanism that meets the objectives of government regulators and legislation but does not involve government regulation or enforcement. U.S. businesses would be allowed to use personal data from EU countries if they develop privacy protection policies that meet EU standards. Enforcement would occur in the United States using self-policing, regulation, and government enforcement of fair trade statutes.

Internet Challenges to Privacy

Internet technology has posed new challenges for the protection of individual privacy. Information sent over this vast network of networks may pass through many different computer systems before it reaches its final destination. Each of these systems is capable of monitoring, capturing, and storing communications that pass through it.

The Wall Street Journal in 2011 found 3,180 tracking files on 50 popular Web sites. Two-thirds of the tracking files came from 131 companies whose primary business is identifying and tracking Internet users to create consumer profiles that can be sold to advertising firms looking for specific types of customers. The biggest trackers were Google,

Microsoft, and Quantcast, all of whom are in the business of selling ads to advertising firms and marketers. Web sites track searches have been conducted, which Web sites and Web pages have been visited, the online content a person has accessed, and what items that person has inspected or purchased over the Web. This monitoring and tracking of Web site visitors occurs in the background without the visitor's knowledge. It is conducted not just by individual Web sites but by advertising networks such as Microsoft Advertising, Yahoo, and DoubleClick that are capable of tracking all browsing behavior at thousands of Web sites. Tools to monitor visits to the World Wide Web have become popular because they help businesses determine who is visiting their Web sites and how to better target their offerings. The commercial demand for this personal information is virtually insatiable.

Cookies are small text files deposited on a computer hard drive when a user visits Web sites. Cookies identify the visitor's Web browser software and track visits to the Web site. When the visitor returns to a site that has stored a cookie, the Web site software will search the visitor's computer, find the cookie, and know what that person has done in the past. It may also update the cookie, depending on the activity during the visit. In this way, the site can customize its content for each visitor's interests. For example, if you purchase a book on Amazon.com and return later from the same browser, the site will welcome you by name and recommend other books of interest based on your past purchases. DoubleClick, described earlier in this chapter, uses cookies to build its dossiers with details of online purchases and to examine the behavior of Web site visitors. Figure 12.3 illustrates how cookies work.

Web sites using cookie technology cannot directly obtain visitors' names and addresses. However, if a person has registered at a site, that information can be combined with cookie data to identify the visitor. Web site owners can also combine the data they have gathered from cookies and other Web site monitoring tools with personal data from other sources, such as offline data collected from surveys or paper catalog purchases, to develop very detailed profiles of their visitors.

There are now even more subtle and surreptitious tools for surveillance of Internet users. So-called "super cookies" or Flash cookies cannot be easily deleted and can be installed whenever a person clicks on a Flash video. These so-called "Local Shared Object" files are used by Flash to play videos and are put on the user's computer without their consent. Marketers use Web beacons as another tool to monitor online behavior. **Web beacons**, also called *Web bugs* (or simply "tracking files"), are tiny objects invisibly embedded in e-mail messages and Web pages that are designed to monitor the behavior of the user visiting a Web site or sending e-mail. The Web beacon captures and transmits information such as the IP address of the user's computer, the time a Web page was viewed and for how long, the type of Web browser that retrieved the beacon, and previously set cookie values. Web beacons

Figure 12.3
How Cookies Identify Web Visitors

Cookies are written by a Web site to a visitor's hard drive. When the visitor returns to that Web site, the Web server requests the ID number from the cookie and uses it to access the data stored by that server on that visitor. The Web site can then use these data to display personalized information.

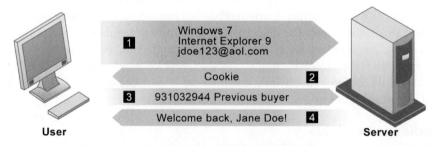

1. The Web server reads the user's Web browser and determines the operating system, browser name, version number, Internet address, and other information.
2. The server transmits a tiny text file with user identification information called a cookie, which the user's browser receives and stores on the user's computer hard drive.
3. When the user returns to the Web site, the server requests the contents of any cookie it deposited previously in the user's computer.
4. The Web server reads the cookie, identifies the visitor, and calls up data on the user.

are placed on popular Web sites by third-party firms who pay the Web sites a fee for access to their audience. Typical popular Web sites contain 25–35 Web beacons while some contain over 100 tracking programs.

Other **spyware** can secretly install itself on an Internet user's computer by piggybacking on larger applications. Once installed, the spyware calls out to Web sites to send banner ads and other unsolicited material to the user, and it can also report the user's movements on the Internet to other computers. More information is available about intrusive software in Chapter 7.

About 75 percent of global Internet users use Google search and other services, making Google the world's largest collector of online user data. Whatever Google does with its data has an enormous impact on online privacy. Most experts believe that Google possesses the largest collection of personal information in the world—more data on more people than any government agency. Table 12.5 lists the major Google services that collect user data and how Google uses these data.

After Google acquired the advertising network DoubleClick in 2007, Google has been using behavioral targeting to help it display more relevant ads based on users' search activities and to target individuals as they move from one site to another in order to show them display or banner ads. One of its programs enables advertisers to target ads based on the search histories of Google users, along with any other information the user submits to Google that Google can obtain, such as age, demographics, region, and other Web activities (such as blogging). An additional program allows Google to help advertisers select keywords and design ads for various market segments based on search histories, such as helping a clothing Web site create and test ads targeted at teenage females.

Google has also been scanning the contents of messages received by users of its free Web-based e-mail service called Gmail. Ads that users see when they read their e-mail are related to the subjects of these messages. Profiles are developed on individual users based on the content in their e-mail. Google now displays targeted ads on YouTube and on Google mobile applications, and its DoubleClick ad network serves up targeted banner ads.

Table 12.5

How Google Uses the Data It Collects

Google Feature	Data Collected	Use
Google Search	Google search topics Users' Internet addresses	Targeting text ads placed in search results
Gmail	Contents of e-mail messages	Targeting text ads placed next to the e-mail messages
DoubleClick	Data about Web sites visited on Google's ad network	Targeting banner ads
YouTube	Data about videos uploaded and downloaded; some profile data	Targeting ads for Google display-ad network
Mobile Maps with My Location	User's actual or approximate location	Targeting mobile ads based on user's zip code
Google Toolbar	Web-browsing data and search history	No ad use at present
Google Buzz	Users' Google profile data and connections	No ad use at present
Google Chrome	Sample of address-bar entries when Google is the default search engine	No ad use at present
Google Checkout	User's name, address, transaction details	No ad use at present
Google Analytics	Traffic data from Web sites using the Google Analytics service	No ad use at present

In the past, Google refrained from capitalizing too much on the data it collected, considered the best source of data about user interests on the Internet. But with the emergence of rivals such as Facebook who are aggressively tracking and selling online user data, Google has decided to do more to profit from its user data.

The United States has allowed businesses to gather transaction information generated in the marketplace and then use that information for other marketing purposes without obtaining the informed consent of the individual whose information is being used. U.S. e-commerce sites are largely content to publish statements on their Web sites informing visitors about how their information will be used. Some have added opt-out selection boxes to these information policy statements. An **opt-out** model of informed consent permits the collection of personal information until the consumer specifically requests that the data not be collected. Privacy advocates would like to see wider use of an **opt-in** model of informed consent in which a business is prohibited from collecting any personal information unless the consumer specifically takes action to approve information collection and use. Here, the default option is no collection of user information.

The online industry has preferred self-regulation to privacy legislation for protecting consumers. The online advertising industry formed the Online Privacy Alliance to encourage self-regulation to develop a set of privacy guidelines for its members. The group promotes the use of online seals, such as that of TRUSTe, certifying Web sites adhering to certain privacy principles. Members of the advertising network industry, including Google's DoubleClick, have created an additional industry association called the Network Advertising Initiative (NAI) to develop its own privacy policies to help consumers opt out of advertising network programs and provide consumers redress from abuses.

Individual firms like Microsoft, Mozilla Foundation, Yahoo!, and Google have recently adopted policies on their own in an effort to address public concern about tracking people online. AOL established an opt-out policy that allows users of its site to not be tracked. Yahoo follows NAI guidelines and also allows opt-out for tracking and Web beacons (Web bugs). Google has reduced retention time for tracking data.

In general, most Internet businesses do little to protect the privacy of their customers, and consumers do not do as much as they should to protect themselves. For commercial Web sites that depend on advertising to support themselves, most revenue derives from selling customer information. Of the companies that do post privacy polices on their Web sites, about half do not monitor their sites to ensure they adhere to these policies. The vast majority of online customers claim they are concerned about online privacy, but less than half read the privacy statements on Web sites. In general, Web site privacy policies require a law degree to understand, and are ambiguous about key terms. (Laudon and Traver, 2012).

In one of the more insightful studies of consumer attitudes towards Internet privacy, a group of Berkeley students conducted surveys of online users, and of complaints filed with the FTC involving privacy issues. Here are some of their results: people feel they have no control over the information collected about them, and they don't know who to complain to. Web sites collect all this information, but do not let users have access, the policies are unclear, and they share data with "affiliates" but never identify who the affiliates are and how many there are. Web bug trackers: they are ubiquitous and users are not informed of trackers on the pages users visit. The results of this study and others suggest that consumers are not saying "Take my privacy, I don't care, send me the service for free." They are saying "We want access to the information, we want some controls on what can be collected, what is done with the information, the ability to opt out of the entire tracking enterprise, and some clarity on what the policies really are, and we don't want those policies changed without our participation and permission." (The full report is available at knowprivacy.org.)

Technical Solutions

In addition to legislation, new technologies are available to protect user privacy during interactions with Web sites. Many of these tools are used for encrypting e-mail, for making e-mail or surfing activities appear anonymous, for preventing client computers from accepting cookies, or for detecting and eliminating spyware.

There are now tools to help users determine the kind of personal data that can be extracted by Web sites. The Platform for Privacy Preferences, an older technology solution known as P3P, proposed automatic communication of privacy policies between an e-commerce site and its visitors. **P3P** was intended to provide a standard for communicating a Web site's privacy policy to Internet users and for comparing that policy to the user's preferences or to other standards, such as the FTC's FIP guidelines or the European Directive on Data Protection. Users were supposed to select the level of privacy they wish to maintain when interacting with the Web site. While innovative, P3P did not work for lack of industry support and difficulties for users to understand the privacy settings. The privacy policies of Web sites are so disparate and incoherent that it is impossible to develop a common language or protocol to describe privacy policies.

With the failure of P3P, and mounting criticism of browser vendors as well as Google, Microsoft, and Yahoo, technology-based privacy efforts shifted to browsers. Microsoft's Internet Explorer easily permits private browsing (control over browsing history, and cookies) and private blocking of content that can track your history. Internet Explorer 9 also allows users to block tracking by creating a tracking protection list with Web addresses that the browser will visit only if a consumer clicks on a link or types in a Web address. This will provide scant protection for consumers who may want to click a link but not be tracked. Mozilla's Firefox 4 beta has implemented a "Do Not Track" option that allows users to click a "Do Not Track" box in the Privacy tab of Firefox's Options. When this option is selected, a header is sent to Web sites indicating that users want to opt out of online behavioral tracking. Unfortunately, most Web sites have no idea how to respond to this request, and are not set up to turn off tracking files based on consumer preferences. There is no online advertising industry agreement on how to respond to "Do Not Track" requests. Most consumers never visit the Options Privacy tab in Firefox.

The Interactive Session on Technology, Life on the Grid: iPhone Becomes iTrack, describes how mobile phones are used to track the location of individuals.

PROPERTY RIGHTS: INTELLECTUAL PROPERTY

Contemporary information systems have severely challenged existing laws and social practices that protect private intellectual property. **Intellectual property** is considered to be intangible property created by individuals or corporations. Information technology has made it difficult to protect intellectual property because computerized information can be so easily copied or distributed on networks. Intellectual property is subject to a variety of protections under three different legal traditions: trade secrets, copyright, and patent law.

Trade Secrets

Any intellectual work product—a formula, device, pattern, or compilation of data—used for a business purpose can be classified as a **trade secret**, provided it is not based on information in the public domain. Protections for trade secrets vary from state to state. In general, trade secret laws grant a monopoly on the ideas behind a work product, but it can be a very tenuous monopoly.

Software that contains novel or unique elements, procedures, or compilations can be included as a trade secret. Trade secret law protects the actual ideas in a work product, not only their manifestation. To make this claim, the creator or owner must take care to bind employees and customers with nondisclosure agreements and to prevent the secret from falling into the public domain.

The limitation of trade secret protection is that, although virtually all software programs of any complexity contain unique elements of some sort, it is difficult to prevent the ideas in the work from falling into the public domain when the software is widely distributed.

Copyright

Copyright is a statutory grant that protects creators of intellectual property from having their work copied by others for any purpose during the life of the author plus an additional

INTERACTIVE SESSION: TECHNOLOGY   Life on the Grid: iPhone Becomes iTrack

Do you like your smartphone? Living on the grid has its advantages. You can access the Internet, visit your Facebook page, get Twitter feeds, watch video, and listen to music all with the same "communication and media device." Less well known is that living on the grid means near continuous tracking of your whereabouts, locations, habits, and friends. At first the Web made it possible for you to search for and find products, and some friends. Now the mobile Web grid tracks you and your friends to sell you products and services.

A new technology based on smartphones can identify where you are located within a few yards. And there's a great deal of money to be made knowing where you are. Mobile technologies based on the smartphone make it possible to locate people throughout the day, to report this information to corporate data bases, retain and analyze the information, and then sell it to advertisers and others. A number of firms have adopted business models based on the ability of smartphones to report on your whereabouts, whether or not you choose to do so. Most of the popular apps report your location. Law enforcement agencies certainly have an interest in knowing the whereabouts of criminals and suspects, and of course divorce lawyers often want to document where a spouse might be located over long periods of time. There are, of course, many times when you would like to report your location either automatically or on your command. If you were injured, for instance, you might like your cell phone to be able to automatically report your location to authorities, or, if you were in a restaurant, you might want to notify your friends where you are and what you are doing. And there are occasions when you might not want anyone to know where you are. You'll have to recall your own examples, but we all have them, places we don't want others to know about.

Location data gathered from cell phones has extraordinary commercial value because advertising companies can send you advertisements, coupons, and flash bargains, based on where you are located. This technology is the foundation for many location-based services, which include smartphone maps and charts, shopping apps, and social apps that you can use to let your friends know where you are and what you are doing. The market for location-based services in 2011 is expected to be $2.9 billion, and will rise to $8.3 billion in 2014 according to Gartner.

But where does the location data come from, who collects it, and who uses it? In April 2011, the Wall Street Journal published the results of its research on smartphone tracking technology and individual private location data. The company discovered that both Apple's iPhone and Google's Android phones were collecting personal, private location data, for a variety of reasons. Both firms are advertising platforms, Google more so than Apple, but Apple is building a mobile advertising platform with its acquisition of AdMob. And both firms are building massive databases that can pinpoint your location. Advertising firms will pay Apple and Google for that information and for distributing their mobile ads. Apple transmits your location data back to central servers once every 12 hours, and it also stores a copy of your locations on the iPhone. Android phones transmit your location data continuously. Apple's files on the iPhone device can be stored for many months. Both Apple and Google say they do not share this information with third parties (at least not now), deny the information can identify individuals (as opposed to cell phones), and claim the information is being used only to identify the location of cell phones for Wi-Fi–connected phones, and to improve the customer experience of location-based services. Apple's technology reads the signal strength of nearby Wi-Fi transmitters, identifies and maps their location, and then calculates the location of the iPhone device. The result is a very large database of Wi-Fi hotspots in the United States, and a method for locating iPhones that is not dependent on GPS signals. Both companies say the location information is needed for them to improve their services.

Smartphone apps that provide location-based services are also sources of personal, private, location information based on the smartphone GPS capability. Foursquare, a 2009 start-up, is a popular mobile social application that allows users to check in to a restaurant or other location, and the app automatically lets friends on Facebook and other programs learn where you are. If you're in a new town, the app transmits your location and sends you popular spots close by, with reviews from other Foursquare users. After starting up Foursquare on a smartphone, you'll see a list of local bars and restaurants based on your cell phone's GPS position, select a location, and "check in," which sends a message to your friends. Foursquare has a widely accepted loyalty program. Each check-in awards users points and badges, which can be used later for discounts at various venues. Visitors to places compete to become "Mayors" of the venue based on how many times they have checked in over a month's time. Mayors receive special offers.

As the popularity of location-based services like Foursquare has grown, so too have concerns about the privacy of individual subscribers, and their friends on

Facebook and Twitter who may not be members. In 2011, many observers fear these services will operate automatically, without user permission or awareness. Certainly the revelation in 2011 that Apple and Google were surreptitiously and continuously collecting personal, private, and location data spurred privacy groups and Congress to launch investigations. Most cell phone users are unaware that their locations and travels are readily available to law enforcement agencies through a simple e-mail request, and without judicial review, and at the expense of the carriers. The number of such requests is not known or published.

To date, wireless location-based services remain largely unregulated. In 2011, the Federal Communications Commission in cooperation with the Federal Trade Commission sponsored a forum to discuss with industry and privacy groups the social impact of location-based services, both positive and negative. Industry representatives from Facebook, Google, and Foursquare argued that existing apps as well as corporate policies were adequate to protect personal privacy because they rely on user permissions to share location data (opt-in services). The industry argued as well that consumers get real benefits from sharing location data, otherwise they would not voluntarily share this data. Privacy experts asked if consumers knew they were sharing their location information and what kind of "informed consent" was obtained. Privacy advocates pointed out that 22 of the top 30 paid apps have no privacy policy, that most of the popular apps transmit location data to their developers after which the information is not well controlled, and that these services are creating a situation where government agencies, marketers, creditors, and telecommunications firms will end up knowing nearly everything about citizens including their whereabouts. The biggest danger they described are services that locate people automatically and persistently without users having a chance to go off the grid, and without being able to turn off the location features of their phones.

Sources: Noam Cohen, "It's Tracking Your Every Move and You May Not Even Know," *New York Times*, March 26, 2011; Robert Hotz, "The Really Smart Phone," *Wall Street Journal*, April 23, 2011; Peter Swire, "Wrap Up on Privacy and Location Based Services," Ohio State University, FCC Forum: "Helping Consumers Harness the Potential of Location Based Services," June 28, 2011; Matt Blaze, "Technology and Privacy," University of Pennsylvania, FCC Forum: "Helping Consumers Harness the Potential of Location Based Services," June 28, 2011; Julia Angwin and Jennifer Valentino-Devries, "Apple, Google Collect User Data," *Wall Street Journal*, April 22, 2011; "When a Cell Phone Is More Than a Phone: Protecting Your Privacy in the Age of the Smartphone," Privacy Rights Clearinghouse, http://www.privacyrights.org (undated).

CASE STUDY QUESTIONS

1. Why do cell phone manufacturers (Apple, Google, and BlackBerry) want to track where their customers go?

2. Do you think cell phone customers should be able to turn tracking off? Should customers be informed when they are being tracked? Why or why not?

3. Do you think cell phone tracking is a violation of a person's privacy?

MIS IN ACTION

1. Many privacy groups are calling for legislation to gain user consent as a condition of cell phone tracking. Go the FTC Web site. Read and summarize the testimony of privacy groups at the FTC Forum. Do you support these groups in their call for federal regulation of cell phone tracking? Why or why not?

2. Use a search engine to identify the positions of Google and Apple regarding cell phone tracking. What reasons do they give for tracking cell phones? What limitations do you think they might support?

70 years after the author's death. For corporate-owned works, copyright protection lasts for 95 years after their initial creation. Congress has extended copyright protection to books, periodicals, lectures, dramas, musical compositions, maps, drawings, artwork of any kind, and motion pictures. The intent behind copyright laws has been to encourage creativity and authorship by ensuring that creative people receive the financial and other benefits of their work. Most industrial nations have their own copyright laws, and there are several

international conventions and bilateral agreements through which nations coordinate and enforce their laws.

In the mid-1960s, the Copyright Office began registering software programs, and in 1980, Congress passed the Computer Software Copyright Act, which clearly provides protection for software program code and for copies of the original sold in commerce, and sets forth the rights of the purchaser to use the software while the creator retains legal title.

Copyright protects against copying of entire programs or their parts. Damages and relief are readily obtained for infringement. The drawback to copyright protection is that the underlying ideas behind a work are not protected, only their manifestation in a work. A competitor can use your software, understand how it works, and build new software that follows the same concepts without infringing on a copyright.

"Look and feel" copyright infringement lawsuits are precisely about the distinction between an idea and its expression. For instance, in the early 1990s, Apple Computer sued Microsoft Corporation and Hewlett-Packard for infringement of the expression of Apple's Macintosh interface, claiming that the defendants copied the expression of overlapping windows. The defendants countered that the idea of overlapping windows can be expressed only in a single way and, therefore, was not protectable under the merger doctrine of copyright law. When ideas and their expression merge, the expression cannot be copyrighted.

In general, courts appear to be following the reasoning of a 1989 case—*Brown Bag Software vs. Symantec Corp.*—in which the court dissected the elements of software alleged to be infringing. The court found that similar concept, function, general functional features (e.g., drop-down menus), and colors are not protectable by copyright law (*Brown Bag Software vs. Symantec Corp.*, 1992).

Patents

A **patent** grants the owner an exclusive monopoly on the ideas behind an invention for 20 years. The congressional intent behind patent law was to ensure that inventors of new machines, devices, or methods receive the full financial and other rewards of their labor and yet make widespread use of the invention possible by providing detailed diagrams for those wishing to use the idea under license from the patent's owner. The granting of a patent is determined by the United States Patent and Trademark Office and relies on court rulings.

The key concepts in patent law are originality, novelty, and invention. The Patent Office did not accept applications for software patents routinely until a 1981 Supreme Court decision that held that computer programs could be a part of a patentable process. Since that time, hundreds of patents have been granted and thousands await consideration.

The strength of patent protection is that it grants a monopoly on the underlying concepts and ideas of software. The difficulty is passing stringent criteria of nonobviousness (e.g., the work must reflect some special understanding and contribution), originality, and novelty, as well as years of waiting to receive protection.

Challenges to Intellectual Property Rights

Contemporary information technologies, especially software, pose severe challenges to existing intellectual property regimes and, therefore, create significant ethical, social, and political issues. Digital media differ from books, periodicals, and other media in terms of ease of replication; ease of transmission; ease of alteration; difficulty in classifying a software work as a program, book, or even music; compactness—making theft easy; and difficulties in establishing uniqueness.

The proliferation of electronic networks, including the Internet, has made it even more difficult to protect intellectual property. Before widespread use of networks, copies of software, books, magazine articles, or films had to be stored on physical media, such as paper, computer disks, or videotape, creating some hurdles to distribution. Using networks, information can be more widely reproduced and distributed. The Eighth Annual Global Software Piracy Study conducted by the International Data Corporation and the Business Software Alliance reported that the rate of global software piracy climbed to 42 percent in 2010, representing $59 billion in global losses from software piracy. Worldwide, for every

$100 worth of legitimate software sold that year, an additional $75 worth was obtained illegally (Business Software Alliance, 2011).

The Internet was designed to transmit information freely around the world, including copyrighted information. With the World Wide Web in particular, you can easily copy and distribute virtually anything to thousands and even millions of people around the world, even if they are using different types of computer systems. Information can be illicitly copied from one place and distributed through other systems and networks even though these parties do not willingly participate in the infringement.

Individuals have been illegally copying and distributing digitized MP3 music files on the Internet for a number of years. File-sharing services such as Napster, and later Grokster, Kazaa, and Morpheus, sprung up to help users locate and swap digital music files, including those protected by copyright. Illegal file sharing became so widespread that it threatened the viability of the music recording industry. The recording industry won the legal battles for shutting these services down, but it has not been able to halt illegal file sharing entirely. As more and more homes adopt high-speed Internet access, illegal file sharing of videos poses similar threats to the motion picture industry.

Technology has radically altered the prospects for intellectual property protection from theft, at least for music, videos, and television shows (less so for software). The Apple iTunes Store legitimated paying for music and entertainment, and created a closed environment where music and videos could not be easily copied and widely distributed unless played on Apple devices. Amazon's Kindle also protects the rights of publishers and writers because its books cannot be copied to the Internet and distributed. Streaming of Internet radio and Hollywood movies also inhibits piracy because the streams cannot be easily recorded on separate devices. Moreover, the large Web distributors like Apple, Google, and Amazon do not want to encourage piracy in music or videos simply because they need these properties to earn revenue.

The Digital Millennium Copyright Act (DMCA) of 1998 is also providing some copyright protection. The DMCA implemented a World Intellectual Property Organization Treaty that makes it illegal to circumvent technology-based protections of copyrighted materials. Internet service providers (ISPs) are required to take down sites of copyright infringers that they are hosting once they are notified of the problem. Microsoft and other major software and information content firms are represented by the Software and Information Industry Association (SIIA), which lobbies for new laws and enforcement of existing laws to protect intellectual property around the world. The SIIA runs an antipiracy hotline for individuals to report piracy activities, offers educational programs to help organizations combat software piracy, and has published guidelines for employee use of software.

ACCOUNTABILITY, LIABILITY, AND CONTROL

Along with privacy and property laws, new information technologies are challenging existing liability laws and social practices for holding individuals and institutions accountable. If a person is injured by a machine controlled, in part, by software, who should be held accountable and, therefore, held liable? Should a public bulletin board or an electronic service, such as America Online, permit the transmission of pornographic or offensive material (as broadcasters), or should they be held harmless against any liability for what users transmit (as is true of common carriers, such as the telephone system)? What about the Internet? If you outsource your information processing, can you hold the external vendor liable for injuries done to your customers? Some real-world examples may shed light on these questions.

Computer-Related Liability Problems

For a week in October 2011, millions of BlackBerry users around the world began experiencing disruption to their e-mail service, the most vital service provided by the smartphone maker Research in Motion (RIM). The three-day blackout of e-mail involved users in Asia, Europe, the Middle East, and the Americas, a substantial part of BlackBerry's installed base of 70 million users. The BlackBerry, until recently, had the dominant position in corporate smartphone market because it provided excellent e-mail security, and integrated well with corporate mail servers. The iPhone and Android smartphones championed by employees now account for nearly half of all new corporate mobile devices. The outage is expected to encourage more corporations to abandon the BlackBerry. On the positive side, police departments around the world report a significant drop in urban car accidents because drivers could no longer text or telephone using their BlackBerry (Austen, 2011).

After the outage, Research in Motion CTO for Software David Yach said a backlog of messages to Europe created a cascading outage effect around the world.

The company determined the root cause of the initial European BlackBerry e-mail service and said there was no evidence that a hack or security breach was involved.

RIM customers in Europe had been suffering from major outages for days, but it wasn't until the Americas caught the bug that BlackBerry customers started complaining on Twitter of mail delays and lack of access to their BlackBerry devices. Yach described the initial outage as a failure of one of RIM's core switches. However, the real trouble began when RIM's redundant systems failed as well. "The failover did not function as expected," Yach said, "despite the fact that we regularly test failover systems." This led to a significant backup of mail.

Who is liable for any economic harm caused to individuals or businesses that could not access their e-mail during this three-day period? If consumers pay for cell phone service, come to rely on it, and then are denied service for a significant period of time, is the cell phone provider liable to damages?

This case reveals the difficulties faced by information systems executives who ultimately are responsible for any harm done by systems they have selected and installed. Beyond IT managers, insofar as computer software is part of a machine, and the machine injures someone physically or economically, the producer of the software and the operator can be held liable for damages. Insofar as the software acts like a book, storing and displaying information, courts have been reluctant to hold authors, publishers, and booksellers liable for contents (the exception being instances of fraud or defamation), and hence courts have been wary of holding software authors liable for software.

In general, it is very difficult (if not impossible) to hold software producers liable for their software products that are considered to be like books, regardless of the physical or economic harm that results. Historically, print publishers, books, and periodicals have not been held liable because of fears that liability claims would interfere with First Amendment rights guaranteeing freedom of expression.

What about software as a service? ATM machines are a service provided to bank customers. Should this service fail, customers will be inconvenienced and perhaps harmed economically if they cannot access their funds in a timely manner. Should liability protections be extended to software publishers and operators of defective financial, accounting, simulation, or marketing systems?

Software is very different from books. Software users may develop expectations of infallibility about software; software is less easily inspected than a book, and it is more difficult to compare with other software products for quality; software claims actually to perform a task rather than describe a task, as a book does; and people come to depend on services essentially based on software. Given the centrality of software to everyday life, the chances are excellent that liability law will extend its reach to include software even when the software merely provides an information service.

Telephone systems have not been held liable for the messages transmitted because they are regulated common carriers. In return for their right to provide telephone service, they must provide access to all, at reasonable rates, and achieve acceptable reliability. But broadcasters and cable television stations are subject to a wide variety of federal and local constraints on content and facilities. In the United States, with few exceptions, Web sites are not held liable for content posted on their sites regardless if it was placed their by the Web site owners or users.

SYSTEM QUALITY: DATA QUALITY AND SYSTEM ERRORS

The debate over liability and accountability for unintentional consequences of system use raises a related but independent moral dimension: What is an acceptable, technologically feasible level of system quality? At what point should system managers say, "Stop testing, we've done all we can to perfect this software. Ship it!" Individuals and organizations may be held responsible for avoidable and foreseeable consequences, which they have a duty to perceive and correct. And the gray area is that some system errors are foreseeable and correctable only at very great expense, an expense so great that pursuing this level of perfection is not feasible economically—no one could afford the product.

For example, although software companies try to debug their products before releasing them to the marketplace, they knowingly ship buggy products because the time and cost of fixing all minor errors would prevent these products from ever being released. What if the product was not offered on the marketplace, would social welfare as a whole not advance and perhaps even decline? Carrying this further, just what is the responsibility of a producer of computer services—should it withdraw the product that can never be perfect, warn the user, or forget about the risk (let the buyer beware)?

Three principal sources of poor system performance are (1) software bugs and errors, (2) hardware or facility failures caused by natural or other causes, and (3) poor input data quality. A Chapter 7 Learning Track discusses why zero defects in software code of any complexity cannot be achieved and why the seriousness of remaining bugs cannot be estimated. Hence, there is a technological barrier to perfect software, and users must be aware of the potential for catastrophic failure. The software industry has not yet arrived at testing standards for producing software of acceptable but imperfect performance.

Although software bugs and facility catastrophes are likely to be widely reported in the press, by far the most common source of business system failure is data quality. Few companies routinely measure the quality of their data, but individual organizations report data error rates ranging from 0.5 to 30 percent.

QUALITY OF LIFE: EQUITY, ACCESS, AND BOUNDARIES

The negative social costs of introducing information technologies and systems are beginning to mount along with the power of the technology. Many of these negative social consequences are not violations of individual rights or property crimes. Nevertheless, these negative consequences can be extremely harmful to individuals, societies, and political institutions. Computers and information technologies potentially can destroy valuable elements of our culture and society even while they bring us benefits. If there is a balance of good and bad consequences of using information systems, who do we hold responsible for the bad consequences? Next, we briefly examine some of the negative social consequences of systems, considering individual, social, and political responses.

Balancing Power: Center Versus Periphery

An early fear of the computer age was that huge, centralized mainframe computers would centralize power in the nation's capital, resulting in a Big Brother society, as was suggested in George Orwell's novel 1984 italics. The shift toward highly decentralized computing, coupled with an ideology of empowerment of thousands of workers, and the decentralization of decision making to lower organizational levels, have reduced the fears of power centralization in government institutions. Yet much of the empowerment described in popular business magazines is trivial. Lower-level employees may be empowered to make minor decisions, but the key policy decisions may be as centralized as in the past. At the same time, corporate Internet behemoths like Google, Apple, Yahoo, Amazon, and Microsoft have come to dominate the collection and analysis of personal private information of all citizens. In this sense, power has become more centralized into the hands of a few private oligopolies.

Rapidity of Change: Reduced Response Time to Competition

Information systems have helped to create much more efficient national and international markets. Today's more efficient global marketplace has reduced the normal social buffers that permitted businesses many years to adjust to competition. Time-based competition has an ugly side: The business you work for may not have enough time to respond to global competitors and may be wiped out in a year, along with your job. We stand the risk of developing a "just-in-time society" with "just-in-time jobs" and "just-in-time" workplaces, families, and vacations.

Maintaining Boundaries: Family, Work, and Leisure

Parts of this book were produced on trains and planes, as well as on vacations and during what otherwise might have been "family" time. The danger to ubiquitous computing, telecommuting, nomad computing, and the "do anything anywhere" computing environment is that it is actually coming true. The traditional boundaries that separate work from family and just plain leisure have been weakened.

Although authors have traditionally worked just about anywhere (typewriters have been portable for nearly a century), the advent of information systems, coupled with the growth of knowledge-work occupations, means that more and more people are working when traditionally they would have been playing or communicating with family and friends. The work umbrella now extends far beyond the eight-hour day.

Even leisure time spent on the computer threatens these close social relationships. Extensive Internet use, even for entertainment or recreational purposes, takes people away from their family and friends. Among middle school and teenage children, it can lead to harmful anti-social behavior, such as the recent upsurge in cyberbullying.

Weakening these institutions poses clear-cut risks. Family and friends historically have provided powerful support mechanisms for individuals, and they act as balance points in a society by preserving private life, providing a place for people to collect their thoughts, allowing people to think in ways contrary to their employer, and dream.

Dependence and Vulnerability

Today, our businesses, governments, schools, and private associations, such as churches, are incredibly dependent on information systems and are, therefore, highly vulnerable if these systems fail. Secondary schools, for instance, increasingly use and rely on educational software. Test results are often stored off campus. If these systems were to shut down, there is no backup educational structure or content that can make up for the loss of the system. With systems now as ubiquitous as the telephone system, it is startling to remember that there are no regulatory or standard-setting forces in place that are similar to telephone, electrical, radio, television, or other public utility technologies. The absence of standards and the criticality of some system applications will probably call forth demands for national standards and perhaps regulatory oversight.

Computer Crime and Abuse

New technologies, including computers, create new opportunities for committing crime by creating new valuable items to steal, new ways to steal them, and new ways to harm others. **Computer crime** is the commission of illegal acts through the use of a computer or against a computer system. Computers or computer systems can be the object of the crime (destroying a company's computer center or a company's computer files), as well as the instrument of a crime (stealing computer lists by illegally gaining access to a computer system using a home computer). Simply accessing a computer system without authorization or with intent to do harm, even by accident, is now a federal crime. The Computer Security Institute's annual Computer Crime and Security Survey reported in 2011 that 46% percent of private firms experienced a computer security incident within the past year. The estimated cost of reported computer crime in 2010 was $559 million (National White Collar Crime Center and the Federal Bureau of Investigation, 2011). The true cost of all computer crime is estimated to be in the billions of dollars.

Although some people enjoy the convenience of working at home, the "do anything anywhere" computing environment can blur the traditional boundaries between work and family time.

© 2011, MBI / Alamy.

Computer abuse is the commission of acts involving a computer that may not be illegal but that are considered unethical. The popularity of the Internet and e-mail has turned one form of computer abuse—spamming—into a serious problem for both individuals and businesses. **Spam** is junk e-mail sent by an organization or individual to a mass audience of Internet users who have expressed no interest in the product or service being marketed. Spammers tend to market pornography, fraudulent deals and services, outright scams, and other products not widely approved in most civilized societies. Some countries have passed laws to outlaw spamming or to restrict its use. In the United States, it is still legal if it does not involve fraud and the sender and subject of the e-mail are properly identified.

Spamming has mushroomed because it costs only a few cents to send thousands of messages advertising wares to Internet users. The percentage of all e-mail that is spam is estimated at around 75 percent in 2011 (Symantec, 2011). After a period of decline, spam volume has resumed growth largely because of the greater number and sophistication of "spam zombies" and "bot networks," which consist of thousands of captured PCs that can initiate and relay spam messages. Spam is seasonally cyclical, and varies monthly due to the impact of new technologies (both supportive and discouraging of spammers), new prosecutions, and seasonal demand for products and services. Spam costs for businesses are very high (estimated at over $50 billion per year) because of the computing and network resources consumed by billions of unwanted e-mail messages and the time required to deal with them.

Internet service providers and individuals can combat spam by using spam filtering software to block suspicious e-mail before it enters a recipient's e-mail inbox. However, spam filters may block legitimate messages. Spammers know how to skirt around filters by continually changing their e-mail accounts, by incorporating spam messages in images, by embedding spam in e-mail attachments and electronic greeting cards, and by using other people's computers that have been hijacked by botnets (see Chapter 7). Many spam messages are sent from one country while another country hosts the spam Web site.

Spamming is more tightly regulated in Europe than in the United States. On May 30, 2002, the European Parliament passed a ban on unsolicited commercial messaging. Electronic marketing can be targeted only to people who have given prior consent.

The U.S. CAN-SPAM Act of 2003, which went into effect on January 1, 2004, does not outlaw spamming but does ban deceptive e-mail practices by requiring commercial e-mail messages to display accurate subject lines, identify the true senders, and offer recipients an easy way to remove their names from e-mail lists. It also prohibits the use of fake return addresses. A few people have been prosecuted under the law, but it has had a negligible impact on spamming in large part because of the Internet's exceptionally poor security and the use of offshore servers and botnets. In 2008, Robert Soloway, the so-called Seattle "Spam King" was sentenced to 47 months in prison for sending over 90 million spam messages in just three months off two servers. In 2011, the so-called Facebook "Spam King," Sanford Wallace, was indicted for sending over 27 million spam messages to Facebook users. He is facing a 40-year sentence because of prior spamming convictions.

Employment: Trickle-Down Technology and Reengineering Job Loss

Reengineering work is typically hailed in the information systems community as a major benefit of new information technology. It is much less frequently noted that redesigning business processes has caused millions of mid-level managers and clerical workers to lose their jobs. One economist has raised the possibility that we will create a society run by a small "high tech elite of corporate professionals . . . in a nation of the permanently unemployed" (Rifkin, 1993). In 2011, some economists have sounded new alarms about information and computer technology threatening middle class, white collar jobs (in addition to blue collar factory jobs). Erik Brynjolfsson and Andrew P. McAfee argue that the pace of automation has picked up in recent years because of a combination of technologies including robotics, numerically controlled machines, computerized inventory control, pattern recognition, voice recognition, and online commerce. One result is that machines can now do a great many jobs heretofore reserved for humans including tech support, call center work, x-ray examiners, and even legal document review (Brynjolfsson and McAfee, 2011; Arthur, 2011).

Other economists are much more sanguine about the potential job losses. They believe relieving bright, educated workers from reengineered jobs will result in these workers moving to better jobs in fast-growth industries. Missing from this equation are unskilled, blue-collar workers and older, less well-educated middle managers. It is not clear that these groups can be retrained easily for high-quality (high-paying) jobs. Careful planning and sensitivity to employee needs can help companies redesign work to minimize job losses.

Equity and Access: Increasing Racial and Social Class Cleavages

Does everyone have an equal opportunity to participate in the digital age? Will the social, economic, and cultural gaps that exist in the United States and other societies be reduced by information systems technology? Or will the cleavages be increased, permitting the better off to become even more better off relative to others?

These questions have not yet been fully answered because the impact of systems technology on various groups in society has not been thoroughly studied. What is known is that information, knowledge, computers, and access to these resources through educational institutions and public libraries are inequitably distributed along ethnic and social class lines, as are many other information resources. Several studies have found that poor and minority groups in the United States are less likely to have computers or online Internet access even though computer ownership and Internet access have soared in the past five years. Although the gap is narrowing, higher-income families in each ethnic group are still more likely to have home computers and Internet access than lower-income families in the same group.

A similar **digital divide** exists in U.S. schools, with schools in high-poverty areas less likely to have computers, high-quality educational technology programs, or Internet access availability for their students. Left uncorrected, the digital divide could lead to a society of information haves, computer literate and skilled, versus a large group of information have-nots, computer illiterate and unskilled. Public interest groups want to narrow this digital divide by making digital information services—including the Internet—available to virtually everyone, just as basic telephone service is now.

Health Risks: RSI, CVS, and Technostress

The most common occupational disease today is **repetitive stress injury (RSI)**. RSI occurs when muscle groups are forced through repetitive actions often with high-impact loads (such as tennis) or tens of thousands of repetitions under low-impact loads (such as working at a computer keyboard).

The single largest source of RSI is computer keyboards. The most common kind of computer-related RSI is **carpal tunnel syndrome (CTS)**, in which pressure on the median nerve through the wrist's bony structure, called a carpal tunnel, produces pain. The pressure is caused by constant repetition of keystrokes: in a single shift, a word processor may perform 23,000 keystrokes. Symptoms of carpal tunnel syndrome include numbness, shooting pain, inability to grasp objects, and tingling. Millions of workers have been diagnosed with carpal tunnel syndrome.

RSI is avoidable. Designing workstations for a neutral wrist position (using a wrist rest to support the wrist), proper monitor stands, and footrests all contribute to proper posture and reduced RSI. Ergonomically correct keyboards are also an option. These measures should be supported by frequent rest breaks and rotation of employees to different jobs.

RSI is not the only occupational illness computers cause. Back and neck pain, leg stress, and foot pain also result from poor ergonomic designs of workstations. **Computer vision syndrome (CVS)** refers to any eyestrain condition related to display screen use in desktop computers, laptops, e-readers, smartphones, and handheld video games. CVS affects about 90 percent of people who spend three hours or more per day at a computer (Beck, 2010). Its symptoms, which are usually temporary, include headaches, blurred vision, and dry and irritated eyes.

The newest computer-related malady is **technostress**, which is stress induced by computer use. Its symptoms include aggravation, hostility toward humans, impatience, and fatigue. According to experts, humans working continuously with computers come to expect other humans and human institutions to behave like computers, providing instant responses, attentiveness, and an absence of emotion. Technostress is thought to be related to high levels of job turnover in the computer industry, high levels of early retirement from computer-intense occupations, and elevated levels of drug and alcohol abuse.

Repetitive stress injury (RSI) is the leading occupational disease today. The single largest cause of RSI is computer keyboard work.

The incidence of technostress is not known but is thought to be in the millions and growing rapidly in the United States. with the rapid growth of mobile media and communication devices. Computer-related jobs now top the list of stressful occupations based on health statistics in several industrialized countries.

In addition to these maladies, computer technology may be harming our cognitive functions or at least changing how we think and solve problems. Although the Internet has made it much easier for people to access, create, and use information, some experts believe that it is also preventing people from focusing and thinking clearly. The Interactive Session on People highlights the debate that has emerged about this problem.

The computer has become a part of our lives—personally as well as socially, culturally, and politically. It is unlikely that the issues and our choices will become easier as information technology continues to transform our world. The growth of the Internet and the information economy suggests that all the ethical and social issues we have described will be heightened further as we move into the first digital century.

LEARNING TRACKS

The following Learning Tracks provide content relevant to the topics covered in this chapter:

1. Developing a Corporate Code of Ethics for Information Systems

2. Creating a Web Page

Review Summary

1 **What ethical, social, and political issues are raised by information systems?** Information technology is introducing changes for which laws and rules of acceptable conduct have not yet been developed. Increasing computing power, storage, and networking capabilities—including the Internet—expand the reach of individual and organizational actions and magnify their impacts. The ease and anonymity with which information is now communicated, copied, and manipulated in online environments pose new challenges to the protection of privacy and intellectual property. The main ethical, social, and political issues raised by information systems center around information rights and obligations, property rights and obligations, accountability and control, system quality, and quality of life.

2 **What specific principles for conduct can be used to guide ethical decisions?** Six ethical principles for judging conduct include the Golden Rule, Immanuel Kant's Categorical Imperative, Descartes' rule of change, the Utilitarian Principle, the Risk Aversion Principle, and the ethical "no free lunch" rule. These principles should be used in conjunction with an ethical analysis.

3 **Why do contemporary information systems technology and the Internet pose challenges to the protection of individual privacy and intellectual property?** Contemporary data storage and data analysis technology enables companies to easily gather personal data about individuals from many different sources and analyze these data to create detailed electronic profiles about individuals and their behaviors. Data flowing over the Internet can be monitored at many points. Cookies and other Web monitoring tools closely track the activities of Web site visitors. Not all Web sites have strong privacy protection policies, and they do not always allow for informed consent regarding the use of personal information. Traditional copyright laws are insufficient to protect against software piracy because digital material can be copied so easily and transmitted to many different locations simultaneously over the Internet.

INTERACTIVE SESSION: PEOPLE   TOO MUCH INFORMATION?

Do you think that the more information managers receive, the better their decisions? Well, think again. Most of us can no longer imagine the world without the Internet and without our favorite gadgets, whether they're iPads, smartphones, laptops, or cell phones. However, although these devices have brought about a new era of collaboration and communication, they have also introduced new concerns about our relationship with technology. Some researchers suggest that the Internet and other digital technologies are fundamentally changing the way we think—and not for the better. Is the Internet actually making us "dumber," and have we reached a point where we have too much technology? Is it possible that too much information (TMI) reduces the ability to think, and make decisions. Or does the Internet offer so many new opportunities to discover information that it's actually making us "smarter." And, by the way, how do we define "dumber" and "smarter" in an Internet age?

Wait a second, you're saying. How could this be? The Internet is an unprecedented source for acquiring and sharing all types of information. Creating and disseminating media has never been easier. Resources like Wikipedia and Google have helped to organize knowledge and make that knowledge accessible to the world, and they would not have been possible without the Internet. And other digital media technologies have become indispensable parts of our lives. At first glance, it's not clear how such advancements could do anything but make us smarter.

In response to this argument, several authorities claim that making it possible for millions of people to create media—written blogs, photos, videos—has understandably lowered the quality of media. Bloggers very rarely do original reporting or research but instead copy it from professional resources. YouTube videos contributed by newbies to come nowhere near the quality of professional videos. Newspapers struggle to stay in business while bloggers provide free content of inconsistent quality.

But similar warnings were issued in response to the development of the printing press. As Gutenberg's invention spread throughout Europe, contemporary literature exploded in popularity, and much of it was considered mediocre by intellectuals of the era. But rather than being destroyed, it was simply in the early stages of fundamental change. As people came to grips with the new technology and the new norms governing it, literature, newspapers, scientific journals, fiction, and non-fiction all began to contribute to the intellectual climate instead of

detracting from it. Today, we can't imagine a world without print media.

Advocates of digital media argue that history is bound to repeat itself as we gain familiarity with the Internet and other newer technologies. The scientific revolution was galvanized by peer review and collaboration enabled by the printing press. According to many digital media supporters, the Internet will usher in a similar revolution in publishing capability and collaboration, and it will be a resounding success for society as a whole.

This may all be true, but from a cognitive standpoint, the effects of the Internet and other digital devices might not be so positive. New studies suggest that digital technologies are damaging our ability to think clearly and focus. Digital technology users develop an inevitable desire to multitask, doing several things at once while using their devices. Unfortunately, the performance of the individual tasks declines. Researchers in 2011 found that multitasking and interruption impairs memory, especially among the elderly.

Although TV, the Internet, and video games are effective at developing our visual processing ability, research suggests that they detract from our ability to think deeply and retain information. Researchers in 2011 found that using Google reduces recall of information and enhances recall of where to find information. It's true that the Internet grants users easy access to the world's information, but the medium through which that information is delivered is hurting our ability to think deeply and critically about what we read and hear. You'd be "smarter" (in the sense of being able to give an account of the content) by reading a book rather than viewing a video on the same topic while texting with your friends.

Using the Internet lends itself to multitasking. Pages are littered with hyperlinks to other sites; tabbed browsing allows us to switch rapidly between two windows; and we can surf the Web while watching TV, instant messaging friends, or talking on the phone. But the constant distractions and disruptions that are central to online experiences prevent our brains from creating the neural connections that constitute full understanding of a topic. Traditional print media, by contrast, makes it easier to fully concentrate on the content with fewer interruptions.

A recent study conducted by a team of researchers at Stanford found that multitaskers are not only more easily distracted, but were also surprisingly poor at multitasking compared to people who rarely do so themselves. The team also found that multitaskers receive a jolt of excitement when confronted with a new piece of information or a new call, message, or e-mail.

The cellular structure of the brain is highly adaptable and adjusts to the tools we use, so multitaskers quickly become dependent on the excitement they experience when confronted with something new. This means that multitaskers continue to be easily distracted, even if they're totally unplugged from the devices they most often use.

Eyal Ophir, a cognitive scientist on the research team at Stanford, devised a test to measure this phenomenon. Subjects self-identifying as multitaskers were asked to keep track of red rectangles in a series of images. When blue rectangles were introduced, multitaskers struggled to recognize whether or not the red rectangles had changed position from image to image. Normal testers significantly outperformed the multitaskers. Less than 3 percent of multitaskers (called "supertaskers") are able to manage multiple information streams at once; for the vast majority of us, multitasking does not result in greater productivity.

Neuroscientist Michael Merzenich argues that our brains are being "massively remodeled" by our constant and ever-growing usage of the Web. And it's not just the Web that's contributing to this trend. Our ability to focus is also being undermined by the constant distractions provided by smartphones and other digital technology. Television and video games are no exception. Another study showed that when presented with two identical TV shows, one of which

had a news crawl at the bottom, viewers retained much more information about the show without the news crawl. The impact of these technologies on children may be even greater than the impact on adults, because their brains are still developing, and they already struggle to set proper priorities and resist impulses.

The implications of recent research on the impact of Web 2.0 "social" technologies for management decision making are significant. As it turns out, the "always-connected" harried executive scurrying through airports and train stations, holding multiple voice and text conversations with clients and co-workers on sometimes several mobile devices, might not be a very good decision maker. In fact, the quality of decision making most likely falls as the quantity of digital information increases through multiple channels, and managers lose their critical-thinking capabilities. Likewise, in terms of management productivity, studies of Internet use in the workplace suggest that Web 2.0 social technologies offer managers new opportunities to waste time rather than focus on their responsibilities. Checked your Facebook page today? Clearly we need to find out more about the impacts of mobile and social technologies on management work.

Sources: Randall Stross, "Computers at Home: Educational Hope vs. Teenage Reality," *New York Times*, July 9, 2010; Matt Richtel, "Hooked on Gadgets, and Paying a Mental Price," *New York Times*, June 6, 2010; Clay Shirky, "Does the Internet Make You Smarter?" *The Wall Street Journal*, June 4, 2010; Nicholas Carr, "Does the Internet Make You Dumber?" *Wall Street Journal*, June 5, 2010; Ofer Malamud and Christian Pop-Echeles, "Home Computer Use and the Development of Human Capital," January 2010; and "Is Technology Producing a Decline in Critical Thinking and Analysis?" *Science Daily*, January 29, 2009.

CASE STUDY QUESTIONS

1. What are some of the arguments for and against the use of digital media?

2. How might the brain affected by constant digital media usage?

3. Do you think these arguments outweigh the positives of digital media usage? Why or why not?

4. What additional concerns are there for children using digital media? Should children under 8 use computers and cell phones? Why or why not?

MIS IN ACTION

1. Make a daily log for 1 week of all the activities you perform each day using digital technology (such as cell phones, computers, television, etc.) and the amount of time you spend on each. Note the occasions when you are multitasking. On average, how much time each day do you spend using digital technology? How much of this time do you spend multitasking? Do you think your life is too technology-intense? Justify your response.

4 **How have information systems affected everyday life?** Although computer systems have been sources of efficiency and wealth, they have some negative impacts. Computer errors can cause serious harm to individuals and organizations. Poor data quality is also responsible for disruptions and losses for businesses. Jobs can be lost when computers replace workers or tasks become unnecessary in reengineered business processes. The ability to own and use a computer may be exacerbating socioeconomic disparities among different racial groups and social classes. Widespread use of computers increases opportunities for computer crime and computer abuse. Computers can also create health problems, such as RSI, computer vision syndrome, and technostress.

Key Terms

Accountability, 412
Carpal tunnel syndrome (CTS), 431
Computer abuse, 429
Computer crime, 428
Computer vision syndrome (CVS), 431
Cookies, 418
Copyright, 421
Descartes' rule of change, 414
Digital divide, 430
Digital Millennium Copyright Act (DMCA), 425
Due process, 412

Ethical "no free lunch" rule, 414
Ethics, 407
Fair Information Practices (FIP), 415
Golden Rule, 413
Immanuel Kant's Categorical Imperative, 413
Information rights, 409
Informed consent, 417
Intellectual property, 421
Liability, 412
Nonobvious relationship awareness (NORA), 411
Opt-in, 420
Opt-out, 420

P3P, 421
Patent, 424
Privacy, 415
Profiling, 411
Repetitive stress injury (RSI), 431
Responsibility, 412
Risk Aversion Principle, 414
Safe harbor, 417
Spam, 429
Spyware, 419
Technostress, 431
Trade secret, 421
Utilitarian Principle, 414
Web beacons, 418

Review Questions

1. What ethical, social, and political issues are raised by information systems?
   • Explain how ethical, social, and political issues are connected and give some examples.
   • List and describe the key technological trends that heighten ethical concerns.
   • Differentiate between responsibility, accountability, and liability.

2. What specific principles for conduct can be used to guide ethical decisions?
   • List and describe the five steps in an ethical analysis.
   • Identify and describe six ethical principles.

3. Why do contemporary information systems technology and the Internet pose challenges to the protection of individual privacy and intellectual property?
   • Define privacy and fair information practices.
   • Explain how the Internet challenges the protection of individual privacy and intellectual property.
   • Explain how informed consent, legislation, industry self-regulation, and technology tools help protect the individual privacy of Internet users.
   • List and define the three different regimes that protect intellectual property rights.

4. How have information systems affected everyday life?
   • Explain why it is so difficult to hold software services liable for failure or injury.
   • List and describe the principal causes of system quality problems.
   • Name and describe four quality-of-life impacts of computers and information systems.
   • Define and describe technostress and RSI and explain their relationship to information technology.

Discussion Questions

1. Should producers of software-based services, such as ATMs, be held liable for economic injuries suffered when their systems fail?

2. Should companies be responsible for unemployment caused by their information systems? Why or why not?

3. Discuss the pros and cons of allowing companies to amass personal data for behavioral targeting.

Hands-On MIS Projects

The projects in this section give you hands-on experience in analyzing the privacy implications of using online data brokers, developing a corporate policy for employee Web usage, using blog creation tools to create a simple blog, and using Internet newsgroups for market research.

MANAGEMENT DECISION PROBLEMS

1. USAData's Web site is linked to massive databases that consolidate personal data on millions of people. Anyone with a credit card can purchase marketing lists of consumers broken down by location, age, income level, and interests. If you click on Consumer Lists to order a consumer mailing list, you can find the names, addresses, and sometimes phone numbers of potential sales leads residing in a specific location and purchase the list of those names. One could use this capability to obtain a list, for example, of everyone in Peekskill, New York, making $150,000 or more per year. Do data brokers such as USAData raise privacy issues? Why or why not? If your name and other personal information were in this database, what limitations on access would you want in order to preserve your privacy? Consider the following data users: government agencies, your employer, private business firms, other individuals.

2. As the head of a small insurance company with six employees, you are concerned about how effectively your company is using its networking and human resources. Budgets are tight, and you are struggling to meet payrolls because employees are reporting many overtime hours. You do not believe that the employees have a sufficiently heavy work load to warrant working longer hours and are looking into the amount of time they spend on the Internet.

Each employee uses a computer with Internet access on the job. Review a sample of your company's weekly report of employee Web usage, which can be found in MyMISLab.

- Calculate the total amount of time each employee spent on the Web for the week and the total amount of time that company computers were used for this purpose. Rank the employees in the order of the amount of time each spent online.
- Do your findings and the contents of the report indicate any ethical problems employees are creating? Is the company creating an ethical problem by monitoring its employees' use of the Internet?
- Use the guidelines for ethical analysis presented in this chapter to develop a solution to the problems you have identified.

ACHIEVING OPERATIONAL EXCELLENCE: CREATING A SIMPLE BLOG

Software skills: Blog creation
Business skills: Blog and Web page design

In this project, you'll learn how to build a simple blog of your own design using the online blog creation software available at Blogger.com. Pick a sport, hobby, or topic of interest as the theme for your blog. Name the blog, give it a title, and choose a template for the blog. Post at least four entries to the blog, adding a label for each posting. Edit your posts, if necessary. Upload an image, such as a photo from your hard drive or the Web to your blog. Add capabilities for other registered users, such as team members, to comment on your blog. Briefly describe how your blog could be useful to a company selling products or services related to the theme of your blog. List the tools available to Blogger that would make your blog more useful for business and describe the business uses of each. Save your blog and show it to your instructor.

IMPROVING DECISION MAKING: USING INTERNET NEWSGROUPS FOR ONLINE MARKET RESEARCH

Software Skills: Web browser software and Internet newsgroups
Business Skills: Using Internet newsgroups to identify potential customers

This project will help develop your Internet skills in using newsgroups for marketing. It will also ask you to think about the ethical implications of using information in online discussion groups for business purposes.

You are producing hiking boots that you sell through a few stores at this time. You would like to use Internet discussion groups interested in hiking, climbing, and camping both to sell your boots and to make them well known. Visit groups.google.com, which stores discussion postings from many thousands of newsgroups. Through this site you can locate all relevant newsgroups and search them by keyword, author's name, forum, date, and subject. Choose a message and examine it carefully, noting all the information you can obtain, including information about the author.

- How could you use these newsgroups to market your boots?
- What ethical principles might you be violating if you use these messages to sell your boots? Do you think there are ethical problems in using newsgroups this way? Explain your answer.
- Next use Google or Yahoo to search the hiking boots industry and locate sites that will help you develop other new ideas for contacting potential customers.
- Given what you have learned in this and previous chapters, prepare a plan to use newsgroups and other alternative methods to begin attracting visitors to your site.

Video Cases

Video Cases and Instructional Videos illustrating some of the concepts in this chapter are available. Contact your instructor to access these videos.

Collaboration and Teamwork

Developing a Corporate Ethics Code

With three or four of your classmates, develop a corporate ethics code that addresses both employee privacy and the privacy of customers and users of the corporate Web site. Be sure to consider e-mail privacy and employer monitoring of worksites, as well as corporate use of information about employees concerning their off-the-job behavior (e.g., lifestyle, marital arrangements, and so forth). If possible, use Google Sites to post links to Web pages, team communication announcements, and work assignments; to brainstorm; and to work collaboratively on project documents. Try to use Google Docs to develop your solution and presentation for the class.

BUSINESS PROBLEM-SOLVING CASE

When Radiation Therapy Kills

When new expensive medical therapies come along, promising to cure people of illness, one would think that the manufacturers, doctors, and technicians, along with the hospitals and state oversight agencies, would take extreme caution in their application and use. Often this is not the case. Contemporary radiation therapy offers a good example of society failing to anticipate and control the negative impacts of a technology powerful enough to kill people.

For individuals and their families suffering through a battle with cancer, technical advancements in radiation treatment represent hope and a chance for a healthy, cancer-free life. But when these highly complex machines used to treat cancers go awry or when medical technicians and doctors fail to follow proper safety procedures, it results in suffering worse than the ailments radiation aims to cure. Overuse of radiation presents substantial harm. In the last decade, the number of CT scans in the United States has tripled, including CT scans of children. One study concluded that of the 72 million CT scans performed in 2007 alone, an estimated 29,000 future cancers and 14,500 future deaths could develop due to radiation exposure. A litany of horror stories underscores the consequences when hospitals fail to provide safe radiation treatment to cancer patients. In many of these horror stories, poor software design, poor human-machine interfaces, and lack of proper training are root causes of the problems.

The deaths of Scott Jerome-Parks and Alexandra Jn-Charles, both patients of New York City hospitals, are prime examples of radiation treatments going awry. Jerome-Parks worked in southern Manhattan near the site of the World Trade Center attacks, and suspected that the tongue cancer he developed later was related to toxic dust that he came in contact with after the attacks. His prognosis was uncertain at first, but he had some reason to be optimistic, given the quality of the treatment provided by state-of-the-art linear accelerators at St. Vincent's Hospital, which he selected for his treatment. But after receiving erroneous dosages of radiation several times, his condition drastically worsened.

For the most part, state-of-the-art linear accelerators do provide effective and safe care for cancer patients, and Americans safely receive an increasing amount of medical radiation each year. Radiation helps to diagnose and treat all sorts of cancers, saving many patients' lives in the process, and is administered safely to over half of all cancer patients. Whereas older machines were only

capable of imaging a tumor in two dimensions and projecting straight beams of radiation, newer linear accelerators are capable of modeling cancerous tumors in three dimensions and shaping beams of radiation to conform to those shapes.

One of the most common issues with radiation therapy is finding ways to destroy cancerous cells while preserving healthy cells. Using this beam-shaping technique, radiation doesn't pass through as much healthy tissue to reach the cancerous areas. Hospitals advertised their new accelerators as being able to treat previously untreatable cancers because of the precision of the beam-shaping method. Using older machinery, cancers that were too close to important bodily structures were considered too dangerous to treat with radiation due to the imprecision of the equipment.

How, then, are radiation-related accidents increasing in frequency, given the advances in linear acceleration technology? In the cases of Jerome-Parks and Jn-Charles, a combination of machine malfunctions and user error led to these frightening mistakes. Jerome-Parks's brain stem and neck were exposed to excessive dosages of radiation on three separate occasions because of a computer error.

The linear accelerator used to treat Jerome-Parks is known as a multi-leaf collimator, a newer, more powerful model that uses over a hundred metal "leaves" to adjust the shape and strength of the beam. The St. Vincent's hospital collimator was made by Varian Medical Systems, a leading supplier of radiation equipment.

Dr. Anthony M. Berson, St. Vincent's chief radiation oncologist, reworked Mr. Jerome-Parks's radiation treatment plan to give more protection to his teeth. Nina Kalach, the medical physicist in charge of implementing Jerome-Parks's radiation treatment plan, used Varian software to revise the plan. State records show that as Ms. Kalach was trying to save her work, the computer began seizing up, displaying an error message. The error message asked if Ms. Kalach wanted to save her changes before the program aborted and she responded that she did. Dr. Berson approved the plan.

Six minutes after another computer crash, the first of several radioactive beams was turned on, followed by several additional rounds of radiation the next few days. After the third treatment, Ms. Kalach ran a test to verify that the treatment plan was carried out as prescribed, and found that the multi-leaf collimator, which was supposed to focus the beam precisely on Mr. Jerome-Parks's tumor, was wide open.

The patient's entire neck had been exposed and Mr. Jerome-Parks had seven times the prescribed dose of radiation.

As a result of the radiation overdose, Mr. Jerome-Parks's experienced deafness and near-blindness, ulcers in his mouth and throat, persistent nausea, and severe pain. His teeth were falling out, he couldn't swallow, and he was eventually unable to breathe. He died soon after, at the age of 43.

Jn-Charles's case was similarly tragic. A 32-year-old mother of two from Brooklyn, she was diagnosed with an aggressive form of breast cancer, but her outlook seemed good after breast surgery and chemotherapy, with only 28 days of radiation treatments left to perform.

On the day of her 28th and final session, technicians realized that something had gone wrong. Jn-Charles's skin had slowly begun to peel and seemed to resist healing. When the hospital looked into the treatment to see why this could have happened, they discovered that the linear accelerator lacked the crucial command to insert the wedge, which must be programmed by the user. Technicians had failed to notice error messages on their screens indicating the missing wedge during each of the 27 sessions. This meant that Jn-Charles had been exposed to almost quadruple the normal amount of radiation during each of those 27 visits.

Ms. Jn-Charles's radiation overdose created a wound that would not heal despite numerous sessions in a hyperbaric chamber and multiple surgeries. Although the wound closed up over a year later, she died shortly afterwards.

It might seem that the carelessness or laziness of the medical technicians who administered treatment is primarily to blame in these cases, but other factors have contributed just as much. The complexity of new linear accelerator technology has not been accompanied with appropriate updates in software, training, safety procedures, and staffing. St. Vincent's hospital stated that system crashes similar to those involved in the improper therapy for Mr. Jerome-Parks "are not uncommon with the Varian software, and these issues have been communicated to Varian on numerous occasions."

Manufacturers of these machines boast that they can safely administer radiation treatment to more and more patients each day, but hospitals are rarely able to adjust their staffing to handle those workloads or increase the amount of training technicians receive before using newer machines. Medical technicians incorrectly assume that the new systems and software are going to work correctly, but in reality they have not been tested over long periods of time.

Many of these errors could have been detected if the machine operators were paying attention. In fact, many of the reported errors involve mistakes as simple and as egregious as treating patients for the wrong cancers; in one example, a brain cancer patient received radiation intended for breast cancer. Today's linear accelerators also lack some of the necessary safeguards given the amounts of radiation they can deliver. For example, many linear accelerators are unable to alert users when a dosage of radiation far exceeds the necessary amount to effectively damage a cancerous tumor. Though responsibility ultimately rests with the technician, software programmers may not have designed their product with the technician's needs in mind.

Further complicating the issue is the fact that the total number of radiation-related accidents each year is essentially unknown. There is no national medical patient medical record system, and doctors do not know how much radiation their patients have received in the past. No single agency exists to collect data across the country on these accidents, and many states don't even require that accidents be reported.

The lack of a central U.S. reporting and regulatory agency for radiation therapy means that in the event of a radiation-related mistake, all of the groups involved are able to avoid ultimate responsibility. Medical machinery and software manufacturers claim that it's the doctors' and medical technicians' responsibility to properly use the machines, and the hospitals' responsibility to properly budget time and resources for training. Technicians claim that they are understaffed and overworked, and that there are no procedures in place to check their work and no time to do so even if there were. Hospitals claim that the newer machinery lacks the proper fail-safe mechanisms and that there is no room on already limited budgets for the training that equipment manufacturers claim is required.

Currently, the responsibility for regulating these incidents falls upon the states, which vary widely in their enforcement of reporting. As a result of the dangers associated with ionizing radiation, the Centers for Medicare & Medicaid Services (CMS), a part of the U.S. Department of Health and Human Services, will require the accreditation of facilities providing advanced imaging services such as CT, magnetic resonance imaging (MRI), positron emission tomography (PET), and nuclear medicine, in non-hospital, freestanding settings beginning January 1, 2012. The state of California has mandated that facilities that furnish CT X-ray services become accredited by July 1, 2013. This California law also requires the documentation of the dose of each CT exam, annual verification of each dose by a medical physicist; and reporting dose errors to patients and physicians. In addition, in May, the American College of Radiology (ACR) launched its National Radiology Data Registry (NRDR), a registry database (the General Radiology Improvement Database [GRID]) that compares radiology facilities regionally and nationwide. For the first time, it will be possible to identify weak imaging facilities across the nation and take corrective action.

Sources: Walt Bogdanich, "Medical Group Urges New Rules on Radiation," *The New York Times*, February 4, 2010; "As Technology Surges, Radiation Safeguards Lag," *New York Times*, January 27, 2010; "Radiation Offers New Cures, and Ways to Do Harm," *New York Times*, January 24, 2010; and "Case Studies: When Medical Radiation Goes Awry," *New York Times*, January 21, 2010.

Case Study Questions

1. What concepts in the chapter are illustrated in this case? What ethical issues are raised by radiation technology?

2. What people, organization, and technology factors were responsible for the problems detailed in this case? Explain the role of each.

3. Do you feel that any of the groups involved with this issue (hospital administrators, technicians, medical equipment, software manufacturers, and government agencies) should accept the majority of the blame for these incidents? Why or why not?

4. How would a central reporting agency that gathered data on radiation-related accidents help reduce the number of radiation therapy errors in the future?

5. If you were in charge of designing electronic software for a linear accelerator, what are some features you would include? Are there any features you would avoid?

Glossary

3G networks High-speed cellular networks based on packet-switched technology, enabling users to transmit video, graphics, and other rich media, in addition to voice.

4G networks The next evolution in wireless communication is entirely packet switched and capable of providing between 1 Mbps and 1 Gbps speeds; up to ten times faster than 3G networks. Not widely deployed in 2010.

acceptable use policy (AUP) Defines acceptable uses of the firm's information resources and computing equipment, including desktop and laptop computers, wireless devices, telephones, and the Internet, and specifies consequences for noncompliance.

acceptance testing Provides the final certification that the system is ready to be used in a production setting.

accountability The mechanisms for assessing responsibility for decisions made and actions taken.

accumulated balance digital payment systems Systems enabling users to make micropayments and purchases on the Web, accumulating a debit balance on their credit card or telephone bills.

affiliate revenue model An e-commerce revenue model in which Web sites are paid as "affiliates" for sending their visitors to other sites in return for a referral fee.

agile development Rapid delivery of working software by breaking a large project into a series of small sub-projects that are completed in short periods of time using iteration and continuous feedback.

analytical CRM Customer relationship management applications dealing with the analysis of customer data to provide information for improving business performance.

Android Open source operating system for mobile devices developed by Google and the Open Handset Alliance. Currently the most popular smartphone operating system worldwide.

antivirus software Software designed to detect, and often eliminate, computer viruses from an information system.

applet Miniature program designed to reside on centralized network servers.

application controls Specific controls unique to each computerized application that ensure that only authorized data are completely and accurately processed by that application.

application proxy filtering Firewall screening technology that uses a proxy server to inspect and transmit data packets flowing into and out of the organization so that all the organization's internal applications communicate with the outside using a proxy application.

application server Software that handles all application operations between browser-based computers and a company's back-end business applications or databases.

application software Programs written for a specific application to perform functions specified by end users.

apps Small pieces of software that run on the Internet, on a computer, or on a mobile phone and are generally delivered over the Internet.

artificial intelligence (AI) The effort to develop computer-based systems that can behave like humans, with the ability to learn languages, accomplish physical tasks, use a perceptual apparatus, and emulate human expertise and decision making.

attributes Pieces of information describing a particular entity.

audio input Voice input devices such as microphones that convert spoken words into digital form for processing by the computer.

augmented reality Technology for enhancing visualization that provides a live view of a physical world environment whose elements are augmented by virtual computer-generated imagery.

authentication The ability of each party in a transaction to ascertain the identity of the other party.

authentication The ability of each party in a transaction to ascertain the identity of the other party.

authorization management systems Systems for allowing each user access only to those portions of a system or the Web that person is permitted to enter, based on information established by a set of access rules.

authorization policies Determine differing levels of access to information assets for different levels of users in an organization.

autonomic computing Effort to develop systems that can manage themselves without user intervention.

backbone Part of a network handling the major traffic and providing the primary path for traffic flowing to or from other networks.

balanced scorecard method Framework for operationalizing a firm's strategic plan by focusing on measurable financial, business process, customer, and learning and growth outcomes of firm performance.

bandwidth The capacity of a communications channel as measured by the difference between the highest and lowest frequencies that can be transmitted by that channel.

banner ad A graphic display on a Web page used for advertising. The banner is linked to the advertiser's Web site so that a person clicking on it will be transported to the advertiser's Web site.

behavioral targeting Tracking the click-streams (history of clicking behavior) of individuals across multiple Web sites for the purpose of understanding their interests and intentions, and exposing them to advertisements which are uniquely suited to their interests.

benchmarking Setting strict standards for products, services, or activities and measuring organizational performance against those standards.

best practices The most successful solutions or problem-solving methods that have been developed by a specific organization or industry.

biometric authentication Technology for authenticating system users that compares a person's unique characteristics such as fingerprints, face, or retinal image, against a stored set profile of these characteristics.

bit A binary digit representing the smallest unit of data in a computer system. It can only have one of two states, representing 0 or 1.

blog Popular term for Weblog, designating an informal yet structured Web site where individuals can publish stories, opinions, and links to other Web sites of interest.

blogosphere The totality of blog-related Web sites.

Bluetooth Standard for wireless personal area networks that can transmit up to 722 Kbps within a 10-meter area.

botnet A group of computers that have been infected with bot malware without users' knowledge, enabling a hacker to use the amassed resources of the computers to launch distributed denial-of-service attacks, phishing campaigns or spam.

broadband High-speed transmission technology. Also designates a single communications medium that can transmit multiple channels of data simultaneously.

bugs Software program code defects.

bullwhip effect Distortion of information about the demand for a product as it passes from one entity to the next across the supply chain.

bundling Cross-selling in which a combination of products is sold as a bundle at a price lower than the total cost of the individual products.

bus networks Network topology linking a number of computers by a single circuit with all messages broadcast to the entire network.

business A formal organization whose aim is to produce products or provide services for a profit.

business continuity planning Planning that focuses on how the company can restore business operations after a disaster strikes.

business intelligence (BI) Applications and technologies to help users make better business decisions.

business model An abstraction of what an enterprise is and how the enterprise delivers a product or service, showing how the enterprise creates wealth.

business process reengineering (BPR) The radical redesign of business processes, combining steps to cut waste and eliminating repetitive, paper-intensive tasks in order to improve cost, quality, and service, and to maximize the benefits of information technology.

business processes The unique ways in which organizations coordinate and organize work activities, information, and knowledge to produce a product or service.

business process management Business process management (BPM) is an approach to business which aims to continuously improve and manage business processes.

business strategy Set of activities and decisions that determine the products and services the firm produces, the industries in which the firm competes, firm competitors, suppliers, and customers, and the firm's long-term goals.

business-to-business (B2B) electronic commerce Electronic sales of goods and services among businesses.

business-to-consumer (B2C) electronic commerce Electronic retailing of products and services directly to individual consumers.

C A powerful programming language with tight control and efficiency of execution; is portable across different microprocessors and is used primarily with PCs.

cable Internet connections Use digital cable coaxial lines to deliver high-speed Internet access to homes and businesses.

call center An organizational department responsible for handling customer service issues by telephone and other channels.

campus area network (CAN) An interconnected set of local area networks in a limited geographical area such as a college or corporate campus.

capacity planning The process of predicting when a computer hardware system becomes saturated to ensure that adequate computing resources are available for work of different priorities and that the firm has enough computing power for its current and future needs.

carpal tunnel syndrome (CTS) Type of RSI in which pressure on the median nerve through the wrist's bony carpal tunnel structure produces pain.

case-based reasoning (CBR) Artificial intelligence technology that represents knowledge as a database of cases and solutions.

cathode ray tube (CRT) Electronic gun that shoots a beam of electrons illuminating pixels on a display screen.

CD-ROM (compact disk read-only memory) Read-only optical disk storage used for imaging, reference, and database applications with massive amounts of unchanging data and for multimedia.

CD-RW (CD-ReWritable) Optical disk storage that can be rewritten many times by users.

cellular telephones (cell phones) A device that transmits voice or data, using radio waves to communicate with radio antennas placed within adjacent geographic areas called cells.

central processing unit (CPU) Area of the computer system that manipulates symbols, numbers, and letters, and controls the other parts of the computer system.

centralized processing Processing that is accomplished by one large central computer.

change agent In the context of implementation, the individual acting as the catalyst during the change process to ensure successful organizational adaptation to a new system or innovation.

change management Giving proper consideration to the impact of organizational change associated with a new system or alteration of an existing system.

chat Live, interactive conversations over a public network.

chief information officer (CIO) Senior manager in charge of the information systems function in the firm.

chief knowledge officer (CKO) Responsible for the firm's knowledge management program.

chief privacy officer (CPO) Responsible for ensuring the company complies with existing data privacy laws.

chief security officer (CSO) Heads a formal security function for the organization and is responsible for enforcing the firm's security policy.

choice Simon's third stage of decision making, when the individual selects among the various solution alternatives.

Chrome OS Google's lightweight computer operating system for users who do most of their computing on the Internet; runs on computers ranging from netbooks to desktop computers.

churn rate Measurement of the number of customers who stop using or purchasing products or services from a company. Used as an indicator of the growth or decline of a firm's customer base.

clickstream tracking Tracking data about customer activities at Web sites and storing them in a log.

client The user point-of-entry for the required function in client/server computing. Normally a desktop computer, workstation, or laptop computer.

client/server computing A model for computing that splits processing between clients and servers on a network, assigning functions to the machine most able to perform the function.

cloud computing Web-based applications that are stored on remote servers and accessed via the "cloud" of the Internet using a standard Web browser.

coaxial cable A transmission medium consisting of thickly insulated copper wire; can transmit large volumes of data quickly.

COBOL (Common Business Oriented Language) Major programming language for business applications because it can process large data files with alphanumeric characters.

collaboration Working with others to achieve shared and explicit goals.

collaborative filtering Tracking users' movements on a Web site, comparing the information gleaned about a user's behavior against data about other customers with similar interests to predict what the user would like to see next.

co-location a kind of Web site hosting in which firm purchase or rent a physical server computer at a hosting company's location in order to operate a Web site.

community provider a Web site business model that creates a digital online environment where people with similar interests can transact (buy and sell goods); share interests, photos, videos; communicate with like-minded people; receive interest-related information; and even play out fantasies by adopting online personalities called avatars.

competitive forces model Model used to describe the interaction of external influences, specifically threats and opportunities, that affect an organization's strategy and ability to compete.

component-based development Building large software systems by combining pre-existing software components.

computer Physical device that takes data as an input, transforms the data by executing stored instructions, and outputs information to a number of devices.

computer abuse The commission of acts involving a computer that may not be illegal but are considered unethical.

computer crime The commission of illegal acts through the use of a computer or against a computer system.

computer forensics The scientific collection, examination, authentication, preservation, and analysis of data held on or retrieved from computer storage media in such a way that the information can be used as evidence in a court of law.

computer hardware Physical equipment used for input, processing, and output activities in an information system.

computer literacy Knowledge about information technology, focusing on understanding of how computer-based technologies work.

computer software Detailed, preprogrammed instructions that control and coordinate the work of computer hardware components in an information system.

computer virus Rogue software program that attaches itself to other software programs or data files in order to be executed, often causing hardware and software malfunctions.

computer vision syndrome (CVS) Eyestrain condition related to computer display screen use; symptoms include headaches, blurred vision, and dry and irritated eyes.

computer-aided design (CAD) system Information system that automates the creation and revision of designs using sophisticated graphics software.

computer-aided software engineering (CASE) Automation of step-by-step methodologies for software and systems development to reduce the amounts of repetitive work the developer needs to do.

consumer-to-consumer (C2C) electronic commerce electronic commerce Consumers selling goods and services electronically to other consumers.

controls All of the methods, policies, and procedures that ensure protection of the organization's assets, accuracy and reliability of its records, and operational adherence to management standards.

conversion The process of changing from the old system to the new system.

cookies Tiny file deposited on a computer hard drive when an individual visits certain Web sites. Used to identify the visitor and track visits to the Web site.

copyright A statutory grant that protects creators of intellectual property against copying by others for any purpose during the life of the author plus an additional 70 years after the author's death.

core competency Activity at which a firm excels as a world-class leader.

cost-benefit ratio A method for calculating the returns from a capital expenditure by dividing total benefits by total costs.

cost transparency The ability of consumers to discover the actual costs merchants pay for products.

cracker A hacker with criminal intent.

critical thinking Sustained suspension of judgment with an awareness of multiple perspectives and alternatives.

cross-selling Marketing complementary products to customers.

crowdsourcing Using large Internet audiences for advice, market feedback, new ideas and solutions to business problems. Related to the 'wisdom of crowds' theory.

culture Fundamental set of assumptions, values, and ways of doing things that has been accepted by most members of an organization.

customer decision-support systems (CDSS) Systems to support the decision-making process of an existing or potential customer.

customer lifetime value (CLTV) Difference between revenues produced by a specific customer and the expenses for acquiring and servicing that customer minus the cost of promotional marketing over the lifetime of the customer relationship, expressed in today's dollars.

customer relationship management (CRM) systems Information systems that track all the ways in which a company interacts with its customers and analyze these interactions to optimize revenue, profitability, customer satisfaction, and customer retention.

customization The modification of a software package to meet an organization's unique requirements without destroying the package software's integrity.

cybervandalism Intentional disruption, defacement, or even destruction of a Web site or corporate information system.

cyberwarfare State-sponsored activity designed to cripple and defeat another state or nation by damaging or disrupting its computers or networks.

cycle time The total elapsed time from the beginning of a process to its end.

data Streams of raw facts representing events occurring in organizations or the physical environment before they have been organized and arranged into a form that people can understand and use.

data administration A special organizational function for managing the organization's data resources, concerned with information policy, data planning, maintenance of data dictionaries, and data quality standards.

data center Facility housing computer systems and associated components, such as telecommunications, storage and security systems and backup power supplies.

data cleansing Activities for detecting and correcting data in a database or file that are incorrect, incomplete, improperly formatted, or redundant. Also known as data scrubbing.

data definition Specifies the structure of the content of a database.

data dictionary An automated or manual tool for storing and organizing information about the data maintained in a database.

data flow diagram (DFD) Primary tool for structured analysis that graphically illustrates a system's component process and the flow of data between them.

data management software Software used for creating and manipulating lists, creating files and databases to store data, and combining information for reports.

data management technology The software that governs the organization of data on physical storage media.

data manipulation language A language associated with a database management system that end users and programmers use to manipulate data in the database.

data mart A small data warehouse containing only a portion of the organization's data for a specified function or population of users.

data mining Analysis of large pools of data to find patterns and rules that can be used to guide decision making and predict future behavior.

data quality audit A survey and/or sample of files to determine accuracy and completeness of data in an information system.

data visualization Technology for helping users see patterns and relationships in large amounts of data by presenting the data in graphical form.

data warehouse A database, with reporting and query tools, that stores current and historical data extracted from various operational systems and consolidated for management reporting and analysis.

data workers People such as secretaries or bookkeepers who process the organization's paperwork.

database A group of related files.

database administration Refers to the more technical and operational aspects of managing data, including physical database design and maintenance.

database management system (DBMS) Special software to create and maintain a database and enable individual business applications to extract the data they need without having to create separate files or data definitions in their computer programs.

database server A computer in a client/server environment that is responsible for running a DBMS to process SQL statements and perform database management tasks.

decision-support systems (DSS) Information systems at the organization's management level that combine data and sophisticated analytical models or data analysis tools to support semistructured and unstructured decision making.

deep packet inspection (DPI) Technology for managing network traffic by examining data packets, sorting out low-priority data from higher priority business-critical data, and sending packets in order of priority.

demand planning Determining how much product a business needs to make to satisfy all its customers' demands.

denial of service (DoS) attack Flooding a network server or Web server with false communications or requests for services in order to crash the network.

Descartes' rule of change A principle that states that if an action cannot be taken repeatedly, then it is not right to be taken at any time.

design Simon's second stage of decision making, when the individual conceives of possible alternative solutions to a problem.

digital asset management systems Classify, store, and distribute digital objects such as photographs, graphic images, video, and audio content.

digital certificates Attachments to an electronic message to verify the identity of the sender and to provide the receiver with the means to encode a reply.

digital checking Systems that extend the functionality of existing checking accounts so

they can be used for online shopping payments.

digital dashboard Displays all of a firm's key performance indicators as graphs and charts on a single screen to provide one-page overview of all the critical measurements necessary to make key executive decisions

digital divide Large disparities in access to computers and the Internet among different social groups and different locations.

digital goods Goods that can be delivered over a digital network.

digital market A marketplace that is created by computer and communication technologies that link many buyers and sellers.

Digital Millennium Copyright Act (DMCA) Adjusts copyright laws to the Internet Age by making it illegal to make, distribute, or use devices that circumvent technology-based protections of copy-righted materials.

digital signature A digital code that can be attached to an electronically transmitted message to uniquely identify its contents and the sender.

digital subscriber line (DSL) A group of technologies providing high-capacity transmission over existing copper telephone lines.

digital video disk (DVD) High-capacity optical storage medium that can store full-length videos and large amounts of data.

digital wallet Software that stores credit card, electronic cash, owner identification, and address information and provides this data automatically during electronic commerce purchase transactions.

direct cutover A risky conversion approach where the new system completely replaces the old one on an appointed day.

disaster recovery planning Planning for the restoration of computing and communications services after they have been disrupted.

disintermediation The removal of organizations or business process layers responsible for certain intermediary steps in a value chain.

disruptive technologies Technologies with disruptive impact on industries and businesses, rendering existing products, services and business models obsolete.

distributed denial-of-service (DDoS) attack Uses numerous computers to inundate and overwhelm a network from numerous launch points.

distributed processing The distribution of computer processing work among multiple computers linked by a communications network.

documentation Descriptions of how an information system works from either a technical or end-user standpoint.

domain name English-like name that corresponds to the unique 32-bit numeric Internet Protocol (IP) address for each computer connected to the Internet.

Domain Name System (DNS) A hierarchical system of servers maintaining a database enabling the conversion of domain names to their numeric IP addresses.

domestic exporter Form of business organization characterized by heavy centralization of corporate activities in the home county of origin.

downtime Period of time in which an information system is not operational.

drill down The ability to move from summary data to lower and lower levels of detail.

DSS database A collection of current or historical data from a number of applications or groups. Can be a small PC database or a massive data warehouse.

DSS software system Collection of software tools that are used for data analysis, such as OLAP tools, datamining tools, or a collection of mathematical and analytical models.

due process A process in which laws are well-known and understood and there is an ability to appeal to higher authorities to ensure that laws are applied correctly.

dynamic pricing Pricing of items based on real-time interactions between buyers and sellers that determine what a item is worth at any particular moment.

e-government Use of the Internet and related technologies to digitally enable government and public sector agencies' relationships with citizens, businesses, and other arms of government.

electronic billing presentment and payment systems Systems used for paying routine monthly bills that allow users to view their bills electronically and pay them through electronic funds transfers from banks or credit card accounts.

electronic business (e-business) The use of the Internet and digital technology to execute all the business processes in the enterprise. Includes e-commerce as well as processes for the internal management of the firm and for coordination with suppliers and other business partners.

electronic commerce (e-commerce) The process of buying and selling goods and services electronically involving transactions using the Internet, networks, and other digital technologies.

electronic data interchange (EDI) The direct computer-to-computer exchange between two organizations of standard business transactions, such as orders, shipment instructions, or payments.

electronic mail (e-mail) The computer-to-computer exchange of messages.

electronic records management (ERM) Policies, procedures, and tools for managing the retention, destruction, and storage of electronic records.

employee relationship management (ERM) Software dealing with employee issues that are closely related to CRM, such as setting objectives, employee performance management, performance-based compensation, and employee training.

encryption The coding and scrambling of messages to prevent their being read or accessed without authorization.

end users Representatives of departments outside the information systems group for whom applications are developed.

end-user development The development of information systems by end users with little or no formal assistance from technical specialists.

end-user interface The part of an information system through which the end user interacts with the system, such as on-line screens and commands.

enterprise applications Systems that can coordinate activities, decisions, and knowledge across many different functions, levels, and business units in a firm. Include enterprise systems, supply chain management systems, customer relationship management systems, and knowledge management systems.

enterprise content management systems Help organizations manage structured and semistructured knowledge, providing corporate repositories of documents, reports, presentations, and best practices and capabilities for collecting and organizing e-mail and graphic objects.

enterprise software Set of integrated modules for applications such as sales and distribution, financial accounting, materials management, production planning, and human resources that allow data to be used by multiple functions and business processes.

enterprise systems Integrated enterprise-wide information systems that coordinate key internal processes of the firm. Also known as enterprise resource planning (ERP).

enterprise-wide knowledge management systems General-purpose, firmwide systems that collect, store, distribute, and apply digital content and knowledge.

entity A person, place, thing, or event about which information must be kept.

entity-relationship diagram A methodology for documenting databases illustrating the relationship between various entities in the database.

ergonomics The interaction of people and machines in the work environment, including the design of jobs, health issues, and the end-user interface of information systems.

e-tailer Online retail stores from the giant Amazon to tiny local stores that have Web sites where retail goods are sold.

Ethernet The dominant LAN standard at the physical network level, specifying the physical medium to carry signals between computers; access control rules; and a standardized set of bits to carry data over the system.

ethical "no free lunch" rule Assumption that all tangible and intangible objects are owned by someone else, unless there is a specific declaration otherwise, and that the creator wants compensation for this work.

ethics Principles of right and wrong that can be used by individuals acting as free moral agents to make choices to guide their behavior.

evil twins Wireless networks that pretend to be legitimate Wi-Fi networks to entice participants to log on and reveal passwords or credit card numbers.

exchanges Third-party Net marketplaces that are primarily transaction oriented and that connects many buyers and suppliers for spot purchasing.

executive support systems (ESS) Information systems at the organization's strategic level designed to address unstructured decision making through advanced graphics and communications.

expert systems Knowledge-intensive computer programs that capture the expertise of a human in limited domains of knowledge.

Extensible Markup Language (XML) A more powerful and flexible markup language than hypertext markup language (HTML) for Web pages.

extranets Private intranets that are accessible to authorized outsiders.

Fair Information Practices (FIP) A set of principles originally set forth in 1973 that governs the collection and use of information about individuals and forms the basis of most U.S. and European privacy laws.

fault-tolerant computer systems Systems that contain extra hardware, software, and power supply components that can back a system up and keep it running to prevent system failure.

feasibility study As part of the systems analysis process, the way to determine whether the solution is achievable, given the organization's resources and constraints.

feedback Output that is returned to the appropriate members of the organization to help them evaluate or correct input.

fiber-optic cable A fast, light, and durable transmission medium consisting of thin strands of clear glass fiber bound into cables. Data are transmitted as light pulses.

field A grouping of characters into a word, a group of words, or a complete number, such as a person's name or age.

file transfer protocol (FTP) Tool for retrieving and transferring files from a remote computer.

finance and accounting information systems Systems keep track of the firm's financial assets and fund flows.

firewalls Hardware and software placed between an organization's internal network and an external network to prevent outsiders from invading private networks.

FLOPS Stands for floating point operations per second and is a measure of computer processing speed.

folksonomies User-created taxonomies for classifying and sharing information.

foreign key Field in a database table that enables users to find related information in another database table.

formal planning and control tools Improve project management by listing the specific activities that make up a project, their duration, and the sequence and timing of tasks.

fourth-generation languages Programming languages that can be employed directly by end users or less-skilled programmers to develop computer applications more rapidly than conventional programming languages.

franchiser Form of business organization in which a product is created, designed, financed, and initially produced in the home country, but for product-specific reasons relies heavily on foreign personnel for further production, marketing, and human resources.

free/fremium revenue model an e-commerce revenue model in which a firm offers basic services or content for free, while charging a premium for advanced or high value features.

fuzzy logic Rule-based AI that tolerates imprecision by using nonspecific terms called membership functions to solve problems.

Gantt chart Visually represents the timing, duration, and human resource requirements of project tasks, with each task represented as a horizontal bar whose length is proportional to the time required to complete it.

general controls Overall control environment governing the design, security, and use of computer programs and the security of data files in general throughout the organization's information technology infrastructure.

genetic algorithms Problem-solving methods that promote the evolution of solutions to specified problems using the model of living organisms adapting to their environment.

geographic information systems (GIS) Systems with software that can analyze and display data using digitized maps to enhance planning and decision-making.

gigabyte Approximately one billion bytes.

Gramm-Leach-Bliley Act Requires financial institutions to ensure the security and confidentiality of customer data.

graphical user interface (GUI) The part of an operating system users interact with that uses graphic icons and the computer mouse to issue commands and make selections.

green computing Practices and technologies for producing, using, and disposing of computers and associated devices to minimize impact on the environment.

grid computing Applying the resources of many computers in a network to a single problem.

group decision-support system (GDSS) An interactive computer-based system to facilitate the solution to unstructured problems by a set of decision makers working together as a group.

hacker A person who gains unauthorized access to a computer network for profit, criminal mischief, or personal pleasure.

hertz Measure of frequency of electrical impulses per second, with 1 Hertz equivalent to 1 cycle per second.

high-availability computing Tools and technologies ,including backup hardware resources, to enable a system to recover quickly from a crash.

HIPAA Law outlining medical security and privacy rules and procedures for simplifying the administration of healthcare billing and automating the transfer of healthcare data between healthcare providers, payers, and plans.

home page A World Wide Web text and graphical screen display that welcomes the user and explains the organization that has established the page.

hotspots Specific geographic locations in which an access point provides public Wi-Fi network service.

HTML5 Next evolution of HTML, which will make it possible to embed images, video, and audio directly into a document without using add-on software.

hubs Very simple devices that connect network components, sending a packet of data to all other connected devices.

hypertext markup language (HTML) Page description language for creating Web pages and other hypermedia documents.

hypertext transport protocol (HTTP) The communications standard used to transfer pages on the Web. Defines how messages are formatted and transmitted.

identity management Business Processes and software tools for identifying the valid users of a system and controlling their access to system resources.

identity theft Theft of key pieces of personal information, such as credit card or Social Security numbers, in order to obtain merchandise and services in the name of the victim or to obtain false credentials.

Immanuel Kant's Categorical Imperative A principle that states that if an action is not right for everyone to take it is not right for anyone.

implementation Simon's final stage of decision-making, when the individual puts the decision into effect and reports on the progress of the solution.

inference engine The strategy used to search through the rule base in an expert system; can be forward or backward chaining.

information Data that have been shaped into a form that is meaningful and useful to human beings.

information appliance Device that has been customized to perform a few specialized computing tasks well with minimal user effort.

information asymmetry Situation where the relative bargaining power of two parties in a transaction is determined by one party in the transaction possessing more information essential to the transaction than the other party.

information density The total amount and quality of information available to all market participants, consumers, and merchants

information policy Formal rules governing the maintenance, distribution, and use of information in an organization.

information requirements A detailed statement of the information needs that a new system must satisfy; identifies who needs what information, and when, where, and how the information is needed.

information rights The rights that individuals and organizations have with respect to information that pertains to themselves.

information system Interrelated components working together to collect, process, store, and disseminate information to support decision making, coordination, control, analysis, and visualization in an organization.

information systems department The formal organizational unit that is responsible for the information systems function in the organization.

information systems literacy Broad-based understanding of information systems that includes behavioral knowledge about organizations and individuals using information systems as well as technical knowledge about computers.

information systems managers Leaders of the various specialists in the information systems department.

information systems plan A road map indicating the direction of systems development the rationale, the current situation, the management strategy, the implementation plan, and the budget.

information technology (IT) All the hardware and software technologies that a firm needs to use in order to achieve its business objectives.

information technology (IT) infrastructure Computer hardware, software, data, storage technology, and networks providing a portfolio of shared IT resources for the organization.

informed consent Consent given with knowledge of all the facts needed to make a rational decision.

input The capture or collection of raw data from within the organization or from its external environment for processing in an information system.

input devices Device which gathers data and converts them into electronic form for use by the computer.

instant messaging Chat service that allows participants to create their own private chat channels so that a person can be alerted whenever someone on his or her private list is on-line to initiate a chat session with that particular individual.

intangible benefits Benefits that are not easily quantified; they include more efficient customer service or enhanced decision making.

intellectual property Intangible property created by individuals or corporations that is subject to protections under trade secret, copyright, and patent law.

intelligence The first of Simon's four stages of decision making, when the individual collects information to identify problems occurring in the organization.

intelligent agents Software programs that use a built-in or learned knowledge base to carry out specific, repetitive, and predictable tasks for an individual user, business process, or software application.

intelligent techniques Technologies that aid decision makers by capturing individual and collective knowledge, discovering patterns and behaviors in very large quantities of data, and generating solutions to problems that are too large and complex for human beings to solve on their own.

Internet global network of networks using univeral standards to connect millions of different networks.

Internet Protocol (IP) address Four-part numeric address indicating a unique computer location on the Internet.

Internet service provider (ISP) A commercial organization with a permanent connection to the Internet that sells temporary connections to subscribers.

Internet telephony Technologies that use the Internet Protocol's packet-switched connections for voice service.

Internet2 Research network with new protocols and transmission speeds that provides an infrastructure for supporting high-bandwidth Internet applications.

internetworking The linking of separate networks, each of which retains its own identity, into an interconnected network.

interorganizational system Information systems that automate the flow of information across organizational boundaries and link a company to its customers, distributors, or suppliers.

intranets Internal networks based on Internet and World Wide Web technology and standards.

intrusion detection systems Tools to monitor the most vulnerable points in a network to detect and deter unauthorized intruders.

investment workstations Powerful desktop computers for financial specialists, which are optimized to access and manipulate massive amounts of financial data.

IPv6 New IP addressing system using 128-bit addresses. Stands for Internet Protocol version 6.

IT governance Strategy and policies for using information technology within an organization, specifying the decision rights and accountabilities to ensure that information technology supports the organization's strategies and objectives.

Java An operating system-independent, processor-independent, object-oriented programming language that has become a leading interactive programming environment for the Web.

Joint application design (JAD) Process to accelerate the generation of information requirements by having end users and information systems specialists work together in intensive interactive design sessions.

just-in-time Scheduling system for minimizing inventory by having components arrive exactly at the moment they are needed and finished goods shipped as soon as they leave the assembly line.

key field A field in a record that uniquely identifies instances of that record so that it can be retrieved, updated, or sorted.

key loggers Spyware that records every keystroke made on a computer.

key performance indicators Measures proposed by senior management for understanding how well the firm is performing along specified dimensions.

knowledge base Model of human knowledge that is used by expert systems.

knowledge management The set of processes developed in an organization to create, gather, store, maintain, and disseminate the firm's knowledge.

knowledge management systems (KMS) Systems that support the creation, capture, storage, and dissemination of firm expertise and knowledge.

knowledge network systems Online directory for locating corporate experts in well-defined knowledge domains.

knowledge work systems Information systems that aid knowledge workers in the creation and integration of new knowledge in the organization.

knowledge workers People such as engineers or architects who design products or services and create knowledge for the organization.

learning management system (LMS) Tools for the management, delivery, tracking, and assessment of various types of employee learning.

legacy systems System that have been in existence for a long time and that continue to be used to avoid the high cost of replacing or redesigning them.

liability The existence of laws that permit individuals to recover the damages done to them by other actors, systems, or organizations.

Linux Reliable and compactly designed operating system that is an open-source offshoot of UNIX and that can run on many different hardware platforms and is available free or at very low cost.

local area network (LAN) A telecommunications network that requires its own dedicated channels and that encompasses a limited distance, usually one building or several buildings in close proximity.

long tail marketing Refers to the ability of firms to profitably market goods to very small online audiences, largely because of the lower costs of reaching very small market segments (people who fall into the long tail ends of a Bell curve).

magnetic disk A secondary storage medium in which data are stored by means of magnetized spots on a hard or floppy disk.

magnetic tape Inexpensive, older secondary-storage medium in which large volumes of information are stored sequentially by means of magnetized and nonmagnetized spots on tape.

mainframe Largest category of computer, used for major business processing.

maintenance Changes in hardware, software, documentation, or procedures to a production system to correct errors, meet new requirements, or improve processing efficiency.

malware Malicious software programs such as computer viruses, worms, and Trojan horses.

managed security service providers (MSSPs) Companies that provide security management services for subscribing clients.

management information systems (MIS) The study of information systems focusing on their use in business and management..

manufacturing and production information systems Systems that deal with the planning, development, and production of products and services and with controlling the flow of production.

market creator An e-commerce business model in which firms provide a digital online environment where buyers and sellers can meet, search for products, and engage in transactions.

market entry costs The cost merchants must pay simply to bring their goods to market.

marketspace A marketplace extended beyond traditional boundaries and removed from a temporal and geographic location.

mashups Composite software applications that depend on high-speed networks, universal communication standards, and open source code and are intended to be greater than the sum of their parts.

mass customization The capacity to offer individually tailored products or services on a large scale.

menu prices Merchants' costs of changing prices.

metropolitan area network (MAN) Network that spans a metropolitan area, usually a city and its major suburbs. Its geographic scope falls between a WAN and a LAN.

microblogging Blogging featuring very short posts, such as using Twitter.

microbrowser Web browser software with a small file size that can work with low-memory constraints, tiny screens of handheld wireless devices, and low bandwidth of wireless networks.

micropayment Payment for a very small sum of money, often less than $10.

microprocessor Very large scale integrated circuit technology that integrates the computer's memory, logic, and control on a single chip.

microwave A high-volume, long-distance, point-to-point transmission in which high-frequency radio signals are transmitted through the atmosphere from one terrestrial transmission station to another.

middle management People in the middle of the organizational hierarchy who are responsible for carrying out the plans and goals of senior management.

middleware Software that connects two disparate applications, allowing them to communicate with each other and to exchange data.

midrange computers Middle-size computers that are capable of supporting the computing needs of smaller organizations or of managing networks of other computers.

minicomputers Middle-range computers used in systems for universities, factories, or research laboratories.

MIS audit Identifies all the controls that govern individual information systems and assesses their effectiveness.

mobile commerce (m-commerce) The use of wireless devices, such as cell phones or handheld digital information appliances, to conduct both business-to-consumer and business-to-business e-commerce transactions over the Internet.

model An abstract representation that illustrates the components or relationships of a phenomenon.

modem A device for translating a computer's digital signals into analog form for transmission over ordinary telephone lines, or for translating analog signals back into digital form for reception by a computer.

mouse Handheld input device with point-and-click capabilities that is usually connected to the computer by a cable.

MP3 (MPEG3) Standard for compressing audio files for transfer over the Internet.

multicore processor Integrated circuit to which two or more processors have been attached for enhanced performance, reduced power consumption and more efficient simultaneous processing of multiple tasks.

multinational Form of business organization that concentrates financial management and control out of a central home base while decentralizing production, sales, and marketing operations to units in other countries.

multitouch Interface that features the use of one or more finger gestures to manipulate lists or objects on a screen without using a mouse or keyboard.

nanotechnology Technology that builds structures and processes based on the manipulation of individual atoms and molecules.

natural languages Nonprocedural languages that enable users to communicate with the computer using conversational commands resembling human speech.

net marketplaces Digital marketplaces based on Internet technology linking many buyers to many sellers.

netbook Small low-cost lightweight subnotebooks optimized for wireless communication and Internet access.

network The linking of two or more computers to share data or resources, such as a printer.

network address translation (NAT) Conceals the IP addresses of the organization's internal host computer(s) to prevent sniffer programs outside the firewall from ascertaining them and using that information to penetrate internal systems.

network economics Model of strategic systems at the industry level based on the concept of a network where adding another participant entails zero marginal costs but can create much larger marginal gains.

network operating system (NOS) Special software that routes and manages communications on the network and coordinates network resources.

networking and telecommunications technology Physical devices and software that link various pieces of hardware and transfer data from one physical location to another.

neural networks Hardware or software that attempts to emulate the processing patterns of the biological brain.

nonobvious relationship awareness (NORA) Technology that can find obscure hidden connections between people or other entities by analyzing information from many different sources to correlate relationships.

normalization The process of creating small stable data structures from complex groups of data when designing a relational database.

n-tier client/server architecture Client/server arrangement which balances the work of the entire network over multiple levels of servers.

object Software building block that combines data and the procedures acting on the data.

object-oriented DBMS An approach to data management that stores both data and the procedures acting on the data as objects that can be automatically retrieved and shared; the objects can contain multimedia.

object-oriented development Approach to systems development that uses the object as the basic unit of systems analysis and design. The system is modeled as a collection o objects and the relationship between them.

object-relational DBMS A database management system that combines the capabilities of a relational DBMS for storing traditional information and the capabilities of an object-oriented DBMS for storing graphics and multimedia.

Office 2007 Microsoft desktop software suite with capabilities for supporting collaborative work on the Web or incorporating information from the Web into documents.

Office 2010 The latest version of Microsoft desktop software suite with capabilities for supporting collaborative work on the Web or incorporating information from the Web into documents.

offshore software outsourcing Outsourcing systems development work or maintenance of existing systems to external vendors in another country.

on-demand computing Firms off-loading peak demand for computing power to remote, large-scale data processing centers, investing just enough to handle average processing loads and paying for only as much additional computing power as they need. Also called utility computing.

online analytical processing (OLAP) Capability for manipulating and analyzing large volumes of data from multiple perspectives.

online processing A method of collecting and processing data in which transactions are entered directly into the computer system and processed immediately.

online transaction processing Transaction processing mode in which transactions entered on-line are immediately processed by the computer.

open source software Software that provides free access to its program code, allowing users to modify the program code to make improvements or fix errors.

operating system The system software that manages and controls the activities of the computer.

operational CRM Customer-facing applications, such as sales force automation, call center and customer service support, and marketing automation.

operational management People who monitor the day-to-day activities of the organization.

opt-in Model of informed consent permitting prohibiting an organization from collecting any personal information unless the individual specifically takes action to approve information collection and use.

opt-out Model of informed consent permitting the collection of personal information until the consumer specifically requests that the data not be collected.

organizational impact analysis Study of the way a proposed system will affect organizational structure, attitudes, decision making, and operations.

output The distribution of processed information to the people who will use it or to the activities for which it will be used.

output devices Device that displays data after they have been processed.

outsourcing The practice of contracting computer center operations, telecommunications networks, or applications development to external vendors.

P3P Industry standard designed to give users more control over personal information gathered on Web sites they visit. Stands for Platform for Privacy Preferences Project.

packet filtering Examines selected fields in the headers of data packets flowing back and forth between the trusted network and the Internet

packet switching Technology that breaks messages into small, fixed bundles of data and routes them in the most economical way through any available communications channel.

parallel processing Type of processing in which more than one instruction can be processed at a time by breaking down a problem into smaller parts and processing them simultaneously with multiple processors.

parallel strategy A safe and conservative conversion approach where both the old system and its potential replacement are run together for a time until everyone is assured that the new one functions correctly.

partner relationship management (PRM) Automation of the firm's relationships with its selling partners using customer data and analytical tools to improve coordination and customer sales.

patches Small pieces of software that repair flaws in programs without disturbing the proper operation of the software.

patent A legal document that grants the owner an exclusive monopoly on the ideas behind an invention for 17 years; designed to ensure that inventors of new machines or methods are rewarded for their labor while making widespread use of their inventions.

peer-to-peer Network architecture that gives equal power to all computers on the network; used primarily in small networks.

people perspective Consideration of the firm's management, as well as employees as individuals and their interrelationships in workgroups.

personal computer (PC) Small desktop or portable computer.

Personal digital assistants (PDA) Small, pen-based, handheld computers with built-in wireless telecommunications capable of entirely digital communications transmission.

personal-area networks (PANs) Computer networks used for communication among digital devices (including telephones and PDAs) that are close to one person.

personalization Ability of merchants to target their marketing messages to specific individuals by adjusting the message to a person's name, interests, and past purchases.

PERT chart Graphically depicts project tasks and their interrelationships, showing the specific activities that must be completed before others can start.

pharming Phishing technique that redirects users to a bogus Web page, even when the individual types the correct Web page address into his or her browser.

phased approach Introduces the new system in stages either by functions or by organizational units.

phishing A form of spoofing involving setting up fake Web sites or sending e-mail messages that look like those of legitimate businesses to ask users for confidential personal data.

pilot study A strategy to introduce the new system to a limited area of the organization until it is proven to be fully functional; only then can the conversion to the new system across the entire organization take place.

pivot table Spreadsheet tool for reorganizing and summarizing two or more dimensions of data in a tabular format.

podcasting Method of publishing audio broadcasts via the Internet, allowing subscribing users to download audio files onto their personal computers or portable music players.

pop-up ads Ads that open automatically and do not disappear until the user clicks on them.

portal Web interface for presenting integrated personalized content from a variety of sources. Also refers to a Web site service that provides an initial point of entry to the Web.

portfolio analysis An analysis of the portfolio of potential applications within a firm to determine the risks and benefits, and to select among alternatives for information systems.

prediction markets An analysis of the portfolio of potential applications within a firm to

determine the risks and benefits, and to select among alternatives for information systems.

predictive analysis Use of datamining techniques, historical data, and assumptions about future conditions to predict outcomes of events.

presentation graphics Software to create professional-quality graphics presentations that can incorporate charts, sound, animation, photos, and video clips.

price discrimination Selling the same goods, or nearly the same goods, to different targeted groups at different prices.

price transparency the ease with which consumers can find out the variety of prices in a market.

primary activities Activities most directly related to the production and distribution of a firm's products or services.

primary key Unique identifier for all the information in any row of a database table.

privacy The claim of individuals to be left alone, free from surveillance or interference from other individuals, organizations, or the state.

private cloud Proprietary network or data center that ties together servers, storage, networks, data, and applications as a set of virtualized services that are shared by users inside a company.

private exchange Another term for a private industrial network.

private industrial networks Web-enabled networks linking systems of multiple firms in an industry for the coordination of trans-organizational business processes.

process specifications Describe the logic of the processes occurring within the lowest levels of a data flow diagram.

processing The conversion, manipulation, and analysis of raw input into a form that is more meaningful to humans.

procurement Sourcing goods and materials, negotiating with suppliers, paying for goods, and making delivery arrangements.

product differentiation Competitive strategy for creating brand loyalty by developing new and unique products and services that are not easily duplicated by competitors.

production The stage after the new system is installed and the conversion is complete; during this time the system is reviewed by users and technical specialists to determine how well it has met its original goals.

production or service workers People who actually produce the products or services of the organization.

profiling The use of computers to combine data from multiple sources and create electronic dossiers of detailed information on individuals.

program Series of instructions for the computer.

programmers Highly trained technical specialists who write computer software instructions.

programming The process of translating the system specifications prepared during the design stage into program code.

project A planned series of related activities for achieving a specific business objective.

project management Application of knowledge, skills, tools and techniques to achieve specific targets within specified budget and time constraints.

protocol A set of rules and procedures that govern transmission between the components in a network.

prototyping The process of building an experimental system quickly and inexpensively for demonstration and evaluation so that users can better determine information requirements.

public cloud Cloud maintained by an external service provider, accessed through the Internet, and available to the general public.

public key encryption Uses two keys one shared (or public) and one private.

public key infrastructure (PKI) System for creating public and private keys using a certificate authority (CA) and digital certificates for authentication.

pull-based model Supply chain driven by actual customer orders or purchases so that members of the supply chain produce and deliver only what customers have ordered.

pure-play Business models based purely on the Internet.

push-based model Supply chain driven by production master schedules based on forecasts or best guesses of demand for products, and products are "pushed" to customers.

quality Product or service's conformance to specifications and standards.

query languages Software tools that provide immediate online answers to requests for information that are not predefined.

radio frequency identification (RFID) Technology using tiny tags with embedded microchips containing data about an item and its location to transmit short-distance radio signals to special RFID readers that then pass the data on to a computer for processing.

Rapid application development (RAD) Process for developing systems in a very short time period by using prototyping, fourth-generation tools, and close teamwork among users and systems specialists.

rationalization of procedures The streamlining of standard operating procedures, eliminating obvious bottlenecks, so that automation makes operating procedures more efficient.

reach Measurement of how many people a business can connect with and how many products it can offer those people.

records Groups of related fields.

recovery-oriented computing Computer systems designed to recover rapidly when mishaps occur.

referential integrity Rules to ensure that relationships between coupled database tables remain consistent.

relational database A type of logical database model that treats data as if they were stored in two-dimensional tables. It can relate data stored in one table to data in another as long as the two tables share a common data element.

repetitive stress injury (RSI) Occupational disease that occurs when muscle groups are forced through repetitive actions with high-impact loads or thousands of repetitions with low-impact loads.

Request for Proposal (RFP) A detailed list of questions submitted to vendors of software or other services to determine how well the vendor's product can meet the organization's specific requirements.

responsibility Accepting the potential costs, duties, and obligations for the decisions one makes.

revenue model A description of how a firm will earn revenue, generate profits, and produce a return on investment.

richness Measurement of the depth and detail of information that a business can supply to the customer as well as information the business collects about the customer.

ring networks A network topology in which all computers are linked by a closed loop in a manner that passes data in one direction from one computer to another.

ringtones Digitized snippets of music that play on mobile phones when a user receives or places a call.

risk assessment Determining the potential frequency of the occurrence of a problem and the potential damage if the problem were to occur. Used to determine the cost/benefit of a control.

Risk Aversion Principle Principle that one should take the action that produces the least harm or incurs the least cost.

router Specialized communications processor that forwards packets of data from one network to another network.

RSS Technology using aggregator software to pull content from Web sites and feed it automatically to subscribers' computers.

SaaS (Software as a Service) Services for delivering and providing access to software remotely as a Web-based service.

safe harbor Private self-regulating policy and enforcement mechanism that meets the objectives of government regulations but does not involve government regulation or enforcement.

sales and marketing information systems Systems that help the firm identify customers for the firm's products or services, develop products and services to meet their needs, promote these products and services, sell the products and services, and provide ongoing customer support.

Sarbanes-Oxley Act Law passed in 2002 that imposes responsibility on companies and their management to protect investors by safeguarding the accuracy and integrity of financial information that is used internally and released externally.

satellites The transmission of data using orbiting satellites that serve as relay stations for transmitting microwave signals over very long distances.

scalability The ability of a computer, product, or system to expand to serve a larger number of users without breaking down.

scope Defines what work is or is not included in a project.

scoring model A quick method for deciding among alternative systems based on a system of ratings for selected objectives.

search costs The time and money spent locating a suitable product and determining the best price for that product.

search engine marketing Use of search engines to deliver sponsored links, for which advertisers have paid, in search engine results.

search engine optimization (SEO) the process of changing a Web site's content, layout, and format in order to increase the ranking of the site on popular search engines, and to generate more site visitors.

search engines Tools for efficiently searching the Internet for information based on user queries (search engine arguments).

secondary storage Relatively long term, nonvolatile storage of data outside the CPU and primary storage.

Secure Hypertext Transfer Protocol (S-HTTP) Protocol used for encrypting data flowing over the Internet; limited to individual messages.

Secure Sockets Layer (SSL) Enables client and server computers to manage encryption and decryption activities as they communicate with each other during a secure Web session.

security Policies, procedures, and technical measures used to prevent unauthorized access, alteration, theft, or physical damage to information systems.

security policy Statements ranking information risks, identifying acceptable security goals, and identifying the mechanisms for achieving these goals.

Semantic web Collaborative effort led by the World Wide Web Consortium to make Web searching more efficient by reducing the amount of human involvement in searching for and processing web information.

semistructured decisions Decisions in which only part of the problem has a clear-cut answer provided by an accepted procedure.

semistructured knowledge Information in the form of less structured objects, such as e-mail, chat room exchanges, videos, graphics, brochures, or bulletin boards.

senior management People occupying the topmost hierarchy in an organization who are responsible for making long-range decisions.

sensitivity analysis Models that ask "what-if" questions repeatedly to determine the impact of changes in one or more factors on the outcomes.

sensors Devices that collect data directly from the environment for input into a computer system.

server Computer specifically optimized to provide software and other resources to other computers over a network.

service level agreement (SLA) Formal contract between customers and their service providers that defines the specific responsibilities of the service provider and the level of service expected by the customer.

service-oriented architecture (SOA) Software architecture of a firm built on a collection of software programs that communicate with each other to perform assigned tasks to create a working software application.

shopping bots Software with varying levels of built-in intelligence to help electronic commerce shoppers locate and evaluate products or service they might wish to purchase.

six sigma A specific measure of quality, representing 3.4 defects per million opportunities; used to designate a set of methodologies and techniques for improving quality and reducing costs.

smart card A credit-card-size plastic card that stores digital information and that can be used for electronic payments in place of cash.

smartphones Wireless phones with voice, messaging, scheduling, e-mail, and Internet capabilities.

sniffer A type of eavesdropping program that monitors information traveling over a network.

social bookmarking Capability for users to save their bookmarks to Web pages on a public Web site and tag these bookmarks with keywords to organize documents and share information with others.

social CRM Tools enabling a business to link customer conversations, data, and relationships from social networking sites to CRM processes.

social engineering Tricking people into revealing their passwords by pretending to be legitimate users or members of a company in need of information.

social graph Map of all significant online social relationships, comparable to a social network describing offline relationships.

social networking Online community for expanding users' business or social contacts by making connections through their mutual business or personal connections.

social search Effort to provide more relevant and trustworthy search results based on a person's network of social contacts.

social shopping Use of Web sites featuring user-created Web pages to share knowledge about items of interest to other shoppers.

software package A prewritten, precoded, commercially available set of programs that eliminates the need to write software programs for certain functions.

spam Unsolicited commercial e-mail.

spamming A form of abuse in which thousands and even hundreds of thousands of unsolicited e-mail and electronic messages are sent out, creating a nuisance for both businesses and individual users.

spoofing Misrepresenting one's identity on the Internet or redirecting a Web link to an address different from the intended one, with the site masquerading as the intended destination.

spreadsheet Software displaying data in a grid of columns and rows, with the capability of easily recalculating numerical data.

spyware Technology that aids in gathering information about a person or organization without their knowledge.

SQL injection attack Attacks against a Web site that take advantage of vulnerabilities in poorly coded SQL (a standard and common database software application) applications in order to introduce malicious program code into a company's systems and networks.

star network A network topology in which all computers and other devices are connected to a central host computer. All communications between network devices must pass through the host computer.

stateful inspection Provides additional security by determining whether packets are part of an ongoing dialogue between a sender and a receiver.

Storage area networks (SAN) High-speed networks dedicated to storage that connects different kinds of storage devices, such as tape libraries and disk arrays so they can be shared by multiple servers.

stored value payment systems Systems enabling consumers to make instant on-line payments to merchants and other individuals based on value stored in a digital account.

strategic information system Computer system at any level of the organization that changes goals, operations, products, services, or environmental relationships to help the organization gain a competitive advantage.

strategic transitions A movement from one level of sociotechnical system to another. Often required when adopting strategic systems that demand changes in the social and technical elements of an organization.

structure chart System documentation showing each level of design, the relationship among the levels, and the overall place in the design structure; can document one program, one system, or part of one program.

structured Refers to the fact that techniques are carefully drawn up, step by step, with each step building on a previous one.

structured decisions Decisions that are repetitive, routine, and have a definite procedure for handling them.

structured knowledge Knowledge in the form of structured documents and reports.

structured knowledge systems Systems for organizing structured knowledge in a repository where it can be accessed throughout the organization. Also known as content management systems.

Structured Query Language (SQL) The standard data manipulation language for relational database management systems.

supercomputer Highly sophisticated and powerful computer that can perform very complex computations extremely rapidly.

supply chain Network of organizations and business processes for procuring materials, transforming raw materials into intermediate and finished products, and distributing the finished products to customers.

supply chain execution systems Systems to manage the flow of products through distribution centers and warehouses to ensure that products are delivered to the right locations in the most efficient manner.

supply chain management (SCM) systems Information systems that automate the flow of information between a firm and its suppliers in order to optimize the planning, sourcing, manufacturing, and delivery of products and services.

supply chain planning systems Systems that enable a firm to generate demand forecasts for a product and to develop sourcing and manufacturing plans for that product.

support activities Activities that make the delivery of a firm's primary activities possible. Consist of the organization's infrastructure, human resources, technology, and procurement.

switch Device to connect network components that has more intelligence than a hub and can filter and forward data to a specified destination.

switching costs The expense a customer or company incurs in lost time and expenditure of resources when changing from one supplier or system to a competing supplier or system.

syndicators Business aggregating content or applications from multiple sources, packaging them for distribution, and reselling them to third-party Web sites.

system software Generalized programs that manage the computer's resources, such as the central processor, communications links, and peripheral devices.

system testing Tests the functioning of the information system as a whole in order to determine if discrete modules will function together as planned.

systems analysis The analysis of a problem that the organization will try to solve with an information system.

systems analysts Specialists who translate business problems and requirements into information requirements and systems, acting as liaison between the information systems department and the rest of the organization.

systems design Details how a system will meet the information requirements as determined by the systems analysis.

systems development The activities that go into producing an information systems solution to an organizational problem or opportunity.

systems development life cycle (SDLC) A traditional methodology for developing an information system that partitions the systems development process into formal stages that must be completed sequentially with a very formal division of labor between end users and information systems specialists.

systems integration Ensuring that a new infrastructure works with a firm's older, so-called legacy systems and that the new elements of the infrastructure work with one another.

T lines High-speed data lines leased from communications providers, such as T-1 lines (with a transmission capacity of 1.544 Mbps).

tablet computer Mobile handheld computer that is larger than a mobile phone, and operated primarily by touching a flat touch screen.

tacit knowledge Expertise and experience of organizational members that has not been formally documented.

tangible benefits Benefits that can be quantified and assigned a monetary value; they include lower operational costs and increased cash flows.

taxonomy Method of classifying things according to a predetermined system.

technostress Stress induced by computer use; symptoms include aggravation, hostility toward humans, impatience, and enervation.

teams Teams are formal groups whose members collaborate to achieve specific goals.

telepresence Telepresence is a technology that allows a person to give the appearance of being present at a location other than his or her true physical location.

terabyte Approximately one trillion bytes.

test plan Prepared by the development team in conjunction with the users; it includes all of the preparations for the series of tests to be performed on the system.

testing The exhaustive and thorough process that determines whether the system produces the desired results under known conditions.

text mining Discovery of patterns and relationships from large sets of unstructured data.

token Physical device, similar to an identification card, that is designed to prove the identity of a single user.

topology The way in which the components of a network are connected.

Total cost of ownership (TCO) Designates the total cost of owning technology resources, including initial purchase costs, the cost of hardware and software upgrades, maintenance, technical support, and training.

Total quality management (TQM) A concept that makes quality control a responsibility to be shared by all people in an organization.

touch point Method of firm interaction with a customer, such as telephone, e-mail, customer service desk, conventional mail, or point-of-purchase.

touch screen Device that allows users to enter limited amounts of data by touching the surface of a sensitized video display monitor with a finger or a pointer.

trade secret Any intellectual work or product used for a business purpose that can be classified as belonging to that business, provided it is not based on information in the public domain.

transaction fee revenue model An online e-commerce revenue model where the firm receives a fee for enabling or executing transactions.

transaction processing systems (TPS) Computerized systems that perform and record the daily routine transactions necessary to conduct the business; they serve the organization's operational level.

Transmission Control Protocol/Internet Protocol (TCP/IP) Dominant model for achieving connectivity among different networks. Provides a universally agreed-on method for breaking up digital messages into packets, routing them to the proper addresses, and then reassembling them into coherent messages.

transnational Truly global form of business organization where value-added activities are managed from a global perspective without reference to national borders, optimizing sources of supply and demand and local competitive advantage.

Trojan horse A software program that appears legitimate but contains a second hidden function that may cause damage.

tuples Rows or records in a relational database.

twisted wire A transmission medium consisting of pairs of twisted copper wires; used to transmit analog phone conversations but can be used for data transmission.

unified communications Integrates disparate channels for voice communications, data communications, instant messaging, e-mail, and electronic conferencing into a single experience where users can seamlessly switch back and forth between different communication modes.

unified threat management (UTM) Comprehensive security management tool that combines multiple security tools, including firewalls, virtual private networks, intrusion detection systems, and Web content filtering and anti-spam software.

Uniform Resource Locator (URL) The address of a specific resource on the Internet.

unit testing The process of testing each program separately in the system. Sometimes called program testing.

UNIX Operating system for all types of computers, which is machine independent and supports multiuser processing, multitasking, and networking. Used in high-end workstations and servers.

unstructured decisions Nonroutine decisions in which the decision maker must provide judgment, evaluation, and insights into the problem definition; there is no agreed-upon procedure for making such decisions.

up-selling Marketing higher-value products or services to new or existing customers.

user interface The part of the information system through which the end user interacts with the system; type of hardware and the series of on-screen commands and responses required for a user to work with the system.

user-designer communications gap The difference in backgrounds, interests, and priorities that impede communication and problem solving among end users and information systems specialists.

Utilitarian Principle Principle that assumes one can put values in rank order and understand the consequences of various courses of action.

utility computing Model of computing in which companies pay only for the information technology resources they actually use during a specified time period. Also called on-demand computing or usage-based pricing.

value chain model Model that highlights the primary or support activities that add a margin of value to a firm's products or services where information systems can best be applied to achieve a competitive advantage.

value web Customer-driven network of independent firms who use information technology to coordinate their value chains to collectively produce a product or service for a market.

virtual company Uses networks to link people, assets, and ideas, enabling it to ally with other companies to create and distribute products and services without being limited by traditional organizational boundaries or physical locations.

Virtual private network (VPN) A secure connection between two points across the Internet to transmit corporate data. Provides a low-cost alternative to a private network.

Virtual Reality Modeling Language (VRML) A set of specifications for interactive three-dimensional modeling on the World Wide Web.

virtual reality systems Interactive graphics software and hardware that create computer-generated simulations that provide sensations that emulate real-world activities.

virtual world Computer-based simulated environment intended for its users to inhabit and interact via graphical representations called avatars.

virtualization Presenting a set of computing resources so that they can all be accessed in ways that are not restricted by physical configuration or geographic location.

visual programming language Allows users to manipulate graphic or iconic elements to create programs.

Voice over IP (VoIP) Facilities for managing the delivery of voice information using the Internet Protocol (IP).

voice portals Capability for accepting voice commands for accessing Web content, e-mail, and other electronic applications from a cell phone or standard telephone and for translating responses to user requests for information back into speech for the customer.

war driving An eavesdropping technique in which eavesdroppers drive by buildings or park outside and try to intercept wireless network traffic.

Web 2.0 Second-generation, interactive Internet-based services that enable people to collaborate, share information, and create new services online, including mashups, blogs, RSS, and wikis.

Web 3.0 Future vision of the Web where all digital information is woven together with intelligent search capabilities.

Web beacons Tiny objects invisibly embedded in e-mail messages and Web pages that are designed to monitor the behavior of the user visiting a Web site or sending e-mail.

Web browsers Easy-to-use software tool for accessing the World Wide Web and the Internet.

Web hosting service Company with large Web server computers to maintain the Web sites of fee-paying subscribers.

Web mining Discovery and analysis of useful patterns and information from the World Wide Web.

Web server Software that manages requests for Web pages on the computer where they are stored and that delivers the page to the user's computer.

Web services Set of universal standards using Internet technology for integrating different applications from different sources without time-consuming custom coding. Used for linking systems of different organizations or for linking disparate systems within the same organization.

Web site All of the World Wide Web pages maintained by an organization or an individual.

Webmaster The person in charge of an organization's Web site.

Wide area networks (WANs) Telecommunications networks that span a large geographical distance. May consist of a variety of cable, satellite, and microwave technologies.

Wi-Fi Standards for Wireless Fidelity and refers to the 802.11 family of wireless networking standards.

wiki Collaborative Web site where visitors can add, delete, or modify content on the site, including the work of previous authors.

WiMax Popular term for IEEE Standard 802.16 for wireless networking over a range of up to 31 miles with a data transfer rate of up to 75 Mbps. Stands for Worldwide Interoperability for Microwave Access.

Windows 7 The successor to Microsoft Windows Vista operating system released in 2009.

Windows 8 Most recent Windows operating system.

Windows Server 2008 Most recent Windows operating system for servers.

wireless portals Portals with content and services optimized for mobile devices to steer users to the information they are most likely to need.

wireless sensor networks (WSNs) Networks of interconnected wireless devices with built-in processing, storage, and radio frequency sensors and antennas that are embedded into the physical environment to provide measurements of many points over large spaces.

wisdom of crowds The belief that large numbers of people can make better decisions about a wide range of topics or products than a single person or even a small committee of experts (first proposed in a book by James Surowiecki).

Word processing software Software for electronically creating, editing, formatting, and printing documents.

workflow management The process of streamlining business procedures so that documents can be moved easily and efficiently from one location to another.

workstation Desktop computer with powerful graphics and mathematical capabilities and the ability to perform several complicated tasks at once.

World Wide Web A system with universally accepted standards for storing, retrieving, formatting, and displaying information in a networked environment.

worms Independent software programs that propagate themselves to disrupt the operation of computer networks or destroy data and other programs.

References

CHAPTER 1

Arthur, W. Bryan. "The Second Economy." McKinsey Quarterly (October 2011).

BEA. "Table 5.5.5. Private Fixed Investment in Equipment and Software by Type." Bureau of Economics Analysis (2011).

Belson, Ken. "Technology Lets High-End Hotels Anticipate Guests' Whims." The New York Times (November 16, 2005).

Brynjolfsson, Erik. "VII Pillars of IT Productivity." Optimize (May 2005).

Bureau Of Labor Statistics. "Occupational Outlook Handbook 2010-2011 Edition." United States Department of Labor (2011).

Campbell, Don. "10 Red Hot BI Trends." Information Management Special Report (June 23, 2009).

Emarketer. "U.S. Advertising Spending: the New Reality" (April 2009).

FedEx Corporation. "SEC Form 10-K For the Fiscal Year Ended 2010."

Friedman, Thomas. The World is Flat. New York: Picador (2007).

Gartner Inc. "Insight CIO IT Investment Trends Study." (July 7, 2011).

Gurbaxani, Vijay, and Phillippe Jorion. "The Value of Information Systems Outsourcing Arrangements: An Event Study Analysis." Center for Research on IT and Organizations, University of California, Irvine, Draft (April 2005).

Ives, Blake, Joseph S. Valacich, Richard T. Watson, and Robert W. Zmud. "What Every Business Student Needs to Know about Information Systems." CAIS 9, Article 30 (December 2002).

Light, Joe. "Recent Business School Graduates Covet Technology Jobs-Again." The Wall Street Journal (July 18, 2011).

Pew Internet and American Life. "Daily Internet Activities," and "Internet Activities." (May 2011)

Ross, Jeanne W. And Peter Weill. "Four Questions Every CEO Should Ask About IT." The Wall Street Journal (April 25, 2011).

Tuomi, Ilkka. "Data Is More Than Knowledge." Journal of Management Information Systems 16, no. 3 (Winter 1999–2000).

U.S. Bureau of Labor Statistics. Occupational Outlook Handbook, 2008-2009 Edition. Washington D.C.: Bureau of Labor Statistics (2009).

U.S. Census. "Statistical Abstract of the United States 2011." Department of Commerce (2011).

Weill, Peter and Jeanne Ross. IT Savvy: What Top Executives Must Know to Go from Pain to Gain. Boston: Harvard Business School Press (2009).

CHAPTER 2

Alter, Allan. "Unlocking the Power of Teams." CIO Insight (March 2008).

Aral, Sinan, Erik Brynjolfsson; and Marshall Van Alstyne, "Productivity Effects of Information Diffusion in Networks," MIT Center for Digital Business (July 2007).

Banker, Rajiv D., Nan Hu, Paul A. Pavlou, and Jerry Luftman. "CIO Reporting Structure, Strategic Positioning, and Firm Performance ." MIS Quarterly 35. No. 2 (June 2011).

Bernoff, Josh and Charlene Li."Harnessing the Power of Social Applications." MIT Sloan Management Review (Spring 2008).

Broadbent, Marianne and Ellen Kitzis. The New CIO Leader. Boston, MA: Harvard Business Press (2004).

Cash, James I. Jr., Michael J. Earl, and Robert Morison. "Teaming Up to Crack Innovation and Enterprise Integration." Harvard Business Review (November 2008).

Chen, Daniel Q., David S. Preston, and Weidong Xia. "Antecedents and Effects of CIO Supply-Side and Demand-Side Leadership: A Staged Maturity Model."Journal of Management Information Systems 27, No. 1 (Summer 2010).

Connolly, P.J. "Video Conferencing Bucks Trend." eWeek (May 16, 2011).

Easley, Robert F., Sarv Devaraj, and J. Michael Crant."Relating Collaborative Technology Use to Teamwork Quality and Performance: An Empirical Analysis." Journal of Management Information Systems 19, no. 4 (Spring 2003)

Forrester Consulting, "Total Economic Impact of IBM Social Collaboration Tools" (September 2010).

Frost & White. "Meetings Around the World II: Charting the Course of Advanced Collaboration." (October 14, 2009).

Griffith, Terri L. "Tapping into Social-Media Smarts." The Wall Street Journal (April 25, 2011).

IBM Corporation. "Magnum Integrates Email and Document Management" (January 13, 2010).

IBM Institute for Business Value. "A New Way of Working."IBM Corporation (2010).

Johnson, Bradfor, James Manyika, and Lareina Yee. "The Next Revolution in Interactions," McKinsey Quarterly No. 4 (2005).

Kopytoff, Verne G. "Companies Staying in the Loop by Using In-House Social Networks." The New York Times (June 26, 2011).

Korolov, Maria. "Companies Explore Private Virtual Worlds." PC World (May 13, 2011).

Lardi-Nadarajan, Kamales. "Doing Business in Virtual Worlds." CIO Insight (March 2008).

Malone, Thomas M., Kevin Crowston, Jintae Lee, and Brian Pentland. "Tools for Inventing Organizations: Toward a Handbook of Organizational Processes." Management Science 45, no. 3 (March 1999).

McAfee, Andrew P. "Shattering the Myths About Enterprise 2.0." Harvard Business Review (November 2009).

Microsoft Corporation. "Sony Electronics Improves Collaboration, Information Access, and Productivity." (May 12, 2010).

Nolan, Richard, and F. Warren McFarland. "Information Technology and the Board of Directors." Harvard Business Review (October 1, 2005).

Perez, Dan. "The New Data-Driven U.S. Government." SIPA News (January 2010).

Poltrock, Steven and Mark Handel. "Models of Collaboration as the Foundation for Collaboration Technologies. Journal of Management Information Systems 27, No. 1 (Summer 2010).

Premier Global Services. "Evaluating Shift to Online Communication Tools."(2010).

Sarker, Saonee, Manju Ahuja , Suprateek Sarker and Sarah Kirkeby. "The Role of Communication and Trust in Global Virtual Teams: A Social Network Perspective." Journal of Management Information Systems 28, No. 1 (Summer 2011).

Saunders, Carol, A. F. Rutkowski, Michiel van Genuchten, Doug Vogel, and Julio Molina Orrego. "Virtual Space and Place: Theory and Test." MIS Quarterly 35, No. 4 (December 2011).

Siebdrat, Frank, Martin Hoegl, and Holger Ernst. "How to Manage Virtual Teams." MIT Sloan Management Review 50, No. 4 (Summer 2009).

Soat, John. "Tomorrow's CIO." Information Week (June 16, 2008).

Weill, Peter and Jeanne W. Ross. IT Governance. Boston: Harvard Business School Press (2004).

CHAPTER 3

Altinkemer, Kemal, Yasin Ozcelik, and Zafer D. Ozdemir. "Performance Effects of Business Process Reengineering: A Firm-Level Analysis." Journal of Management Information Systems 27, No. 4 (Spring 2011).

Andreesen, Marc. "Why Software Is Eating the World." The Wall Street Journal (August 20, 2011).

Bhatt, Ganesh D., and Varun Grover. "Types of Information Technology Capabilities and Their Role in Competitive Advantage." Journal of Management Information Systems 22, no.2 (Fall 2005).

Bughin, Jacques, Michael Chui, and Brad Johnson. "The Next Step in Open Innovation." The McKinsey Quarterly (June 2008).

Bunkley, Nick. "Piecing Together a Supply Chain." The New York Times (May 12, 2011).

Champy, James A. X-Engineering the Corporation: Reinventing Your Business in the Digital Age. New York: Warner Books (2002).

Champy, James. Outsmart: How to Do What Your Competitors Can't. Upper Saddle River, NJ: FT Press (2008).

Chen, Daniel Q., Martin Mocker, David S. Preston, and Alexander Teubner. "Information Systems Strategy: Reconceptualization, Measurement, and Implications." MIS Quarterly 34, no. 2 (June 2010).

Chen, Pei-Yu (Sharon), and Lorin M. Hitt. "Measuring Switching Costs and the Determinants of Customer Retention in Internet-Enabled Businesses: A Study of the Online Brokerage Industry." Information Systems Research 13, no.3 (September 2002).

Christensen, Clayton, Jeanne G. Harris, and Ajay K. Kohli. "How Do They Know Their Customers So Well?" Sloan Management Review 42, no. 2 (Winter 2001).

Christensen, Clayton. "The Past and Future of Competitive Advantage." Sloan Management Review 42, no. 2 (Winter 2001).

Copeland, Michael V. "The Mighty Micro-Multinational." Business 2.0 (July 28, 2006).

Davenport, Thomas H. and Jeanne G. Harris. Competing on Analytics: The New Science of Winning. Boston: Harvard Business School Press (2007).

El Sawy, Omar A. Redesigning Enterprise Processes for E-Business. New York: McGraw-Hill (2001).

Engardio, Pete. " Mom-and-Pop Multinationals." Business Week (July 3, 2008).

Fine, Charles H., Roger Vardan, Robert Pethick, and Jamal E-Hout. "Rapid-Response Capability in Value-Chain Design." Sloan Management Review 43, no.2 (Winter 2002).

Gilbert, Clark and Joseph L. Bower, "Disruptive Change." Harvard Business Review (May 2002),

Hammer, Michael, and James Champy. Reengineering the Corporation. New York: HarperCollins (1993).

Hammer, Michael. "Process Management and the Future of Six Sigma." Sloan Management Review 43, no.2 (Winter 2002).

Iansiti, Marco, and Roy Levien. "Strategy as Ecology." Harvard Business Review (March 2004).

Kauffman, Robert J., and Yu-Ming Wang. "The Network Externalities Hypothesis and Competitive Network Growth." Journal of Organizational Computing and Electronic Commerce 12, no. 1 (2002).

Koulopoulos, Thomas, and James Champy. "Building Digital Value Chains." Optimize (September 2005).

Lohr, Steve. "The Power of the Platform at Apple." The New York Times (January 29, 2011).

Luftman, Jerry. Competing in the Information Age: Align in the Sand,. Oxford University Press , USA; 2 edition (August 6, 2003).

Maltby, Emily. "Affordable 3-D Arrives." The Wall Street Journal (June 29, 2010).

Massie, Roy "Process Management: The Ideal Meeting Place for Business and IT." KM World (January 2008).

McAfee, Andrew and Erik Brynjolfsson. "Investing in the IT That Makes a Competitive Difference." Harvard Business Review (July/August 2008).

McLaren, Tim S., Milena M. Head, Yufei Yuan, and Yolande E. Chan. "A Multilevel Model for Measuring Fit Between a Firm's Competitive Strategies and Information Systems Capabilities." MIS Quarterly 35, No. 4 (December 2011).

Piccoli, Gabriele, and Blake Ives. "Review: IT-Dependent Strategic Initiatives and Sustained Competitive Advantage: A Review and Synthesis of the Literature." MIS Quarterly 29, no. 4 (December 2005).

Porter, Michael E., and Scott Stern. "Location Matters." Sloan Management Review 42, no. 4 (Summer 2001).

Porter, Michael. Competitive Advantage. New York: Free Press (1985).

_____. "Strategy and the Internet." Harvard Business Review (March 2001).

_____. "The Five Competitive Forces that Shape Strategy." Harvard Business Review (January 2008).

Prahalad, C.K.and M.S.Krishnan. The New Age of Innovation. Driving Cocreated Value Through Global Networks. New York: McGraw Hill (2008).

Shapiro, Carl, and Hal R. Varian. Information Rules. Boston: Harvard Business School Press (1999).

Shpilberg, David, Steve Berez, Rudy Puryear, and Sachin Shah. "Avoiding the Alignment Trap in Information Technology." MIT Sloan Management Review 49, no. 1 (Fall 2007).

Von Hippel, Eric, Susumu Ogawa, and Jeroen P.J. DeJong. "The Age of the Customer-Innovator." MIT Sloan Management Review 53, No. 1 (Fall 2011).

CHAPTER 4

Boehret, Katherine. "PC Downloads as Easy as an App." The Wall Street Journal (March 30, 2011).

Choi, Jae, Derek L. Nazareth, and Hemant K. Jain. "Implementing Service-Oriented Architecture in Organizations." Journal of Management Information Systems 26, No. 4 (Spring 2010).

Clark, Don and Tara Shibkin. "Intel Chips to Power Down." The Wall Street Journal (May 18, 2011).

Clark, Don. "HTML5: A Look Behind the Technology Changing the Web." The Wall Street Journal (November 11, 2011).

Currier, Guy. Cloud Spending: The Hidden Truth."CIO Insight (May 5, 2011).

Duvall, Mel. "Study Predicts Big Shift to Cloud By 2020." Information Management (June 10, 2010).

Glader, Paul and Don Clark. "IBM Launches Next Generation of Chips and Servers." The Wall Street Journal (February 7, 2010).

Greengard, Samuel. "Hybrid Clouds Roll into the Picture." Smarter Technology (November/December 2010).

IBM. "Seeding the Clouds: Key Infrastructure Elements for Cloud Computing." (February 2009).

Kopytoff, Verne G. and Ian Austen. "As PCs Wane, Companies Look to Tablets." The New York Times (August 19, 2011).

Lawinski, Jennifer. "Today's Data Center: More Cloud Less Mainframe" CIO Insight (April 6, 2011).

Leong, Lydia and Ted Chamberlin. "Magic Quadrant for Web Hosting and Hosted Cloud System Infrastructure Services (On Demand)." Gartner Inc. (July 2, 2009).

Lohr, Steve. "Netbooks Lose Status as Tablets Like the IPad Rise." The New York Times (February 13, 2011).

McAfee, Andrew. "What Every CEO Needs to Know about the Cloud." Harvard Business Review (November 2011).

McCafferty, Dennis. "Cloudy Skies: Public Vs. Private Option Still Up in the Air." Baseline (March/April 2010).

Mell, Peter and Tim Grance. "The NIST Definition of Cloud Computing" Version 15. NIST (October 17, 2009).

Mossberg, Walter. "Apple's Lion Brings PCs Into Tablet Era," The Wall Street Journal (July 21, 2011).

Plant, Robert. "To Cloud, or Not to Cloud." The Wall Street Journal (April 25, 2011).

Stone, Brad and Ashlee Vance. "Companies Slowly Join Cloud Computing," The New York Times (April 18, 2010).

Taft, Darryl K. "Will PAAS Solve All Developer Ills?" eWeek (March 28, 2011).

Vance, Ashlee. "The Cloud: Battle of the Tech Titans." Bloomberg Business Week (March 3, 2011).

Wingfield, Nick. "Microsoft Faces the Post-PC World." The Wall Street Journal (August 15, 2011).

CHAPTER 5

Cappiello, Cinzia, Chiara Francalanci, and Barbara Pernici. "Time-Related Factors of Data Quality in Multichannel Information Systems." Journal of Management Information Systems 20, no. 3 (Winter 2004).

Clifford, James, Albert Croker, and Alex Tuzhilin. "On Data Representation and Use in a Temporal Relational DBMS." Information Systems Research 7, no. 3 (September 1996).

Eckerson, Wayne W. "Data Quality and the Bottom Line." The Data Warehousing Institute (2002).

Gartner Inc. "'Dirty Data' is a Business Problem, not an IT Problem, Says Gartner." Sydney, Australia (March 2, 2007).

Hayler, Andy. "Building a Robust Business Case for High Quality Master Data." The Information Difference Company Ltd. (February 2010).

Hoffer, Jeffrey A., Mary Prescott, and Heikki Toppi. Modern Database Management, 10th ed. Upper Saddle River, NJ: Prentice-Hall (2011).

Hoover, J. Nicholas. "Search, Mobility BI Keys to Hotel Chain's Growth." Information Week (September 13, 2010).

Jinesh Radadia. "Breaking the Bad Data Bottlenecks." Information Management (May/June 2010).

Klau, Rick. "Data Quality and CRM." Line56.com, accessed March 4, 2003.

Kroenke, David M. and David Auer. Database Processing 12e. Upper Saddle River, NJ: Prentice-Hall (2012).

Lee, Yang W., and Diane M. Strong. "Knowing-Why about Data Processes and Data Quality." Journal of Management Information Systems 20, no. 3 (Winter 2004).

Loveman, Gary. "Diamonds in the Datamine." Harvard Business Review (May 2003).

McKnight, William. "Seven Sources of Poor Data Quality." Information Management (April 2009).

Pottie, G. J., and W.J Kaiser. "Wireless Integrated Network Sensors." Communications of the ACM 43, no. 5 (May 2000).

Redman, Thomas. Data Driven: Profiting from Your Most Important Business Asset. Boston: Harvard Business Press (2008).

Sharpe, Michael. "Mastering Master Data Management." Information Week (July 11, 2011).

Shen, George. "The Disconnect of Intelligence and Analytics." Information Management (January 20, 2011).

St. Clair, Scott and Keefe Bailey. "Prognosis: Opportunity." Information Week (March 8, 2010).

Teachy, Daniel. "Is Your Data Inhibiting Customer Relationships?" Information Management (April 12, 2011).

CHAPTER 6

Borland, John. "A Smarter Web." Technology Review (March/April 2007).

Bustillo, Maguel. "Wal-Mart Radio Tags to Track Clothing." The Wall Street Journal (July 23, 2010).

Cain Miller, Claire. "Seeking to Weed Out Drivel, Google Adjusts Search Engine." The New York Times (February 25, 2011).

Cheng, Roger. "AT&T Relabels Network as 4G." The Wall Street Journal (January 5, 2011).

ComScore. "comScore Reports May 2011 U.S. Mobile Subscriber Market Share." comScore, Press Release July 5, 2011.

Efrati, Amir. "Google's Search Cleanup Has Big Effect." The Wall Street Journal (February 28, 2011).

Eisenberg, Anne. "Keeping Tabs on the Infrastructure, Wirelessly." The New York Times (March 13, 2011).

eMarketer, Inc. "US Search Engine Users and Search Ad Users, 2010-2015." eMarketer, July 2011.

eMarketer. Inc. US Broadband Subscriptions, by Access Technology, June 2006-June 2010 (thousands). Chart." eMarketer, March 21, 2011.

Fish, Lynn A. and Wayne C. Forrest. "A Worldwide Look at RFID." Supply Chain Management Review (April 1, 2007).

Flynn, Laurie J. "New System to Add Internet Addresses as Numbers Run Out." The New York Times (February 14, 2011).

Hickins, Michael. "Google Rakes Content Farms." The Wall Street Journal (February 25, 2011).

Holmes, Sam and Jeffrey A. Trachtenberg. "Web Addresses Enter New Era." The Wall Street Journal (June 21, 2011).

ICANN. "ICANN Policy Update." 10, No. 9 (September 2010).

Lahiri, Atanu, I. "The Disruptive Effect of Open Platforms on Markets for Wireless Services." Journal of Management Information Systems 27, No. 3 (Winter 2011).

Lohr, Steve. "Can Microsoft Make You Bing?" The New York Times (July 30, 2011).

Miller, Claire Cain. "Google, a Giant in Mobile Search, Seeks New Ways to Make It Pay," The New York Times (April 24, 2011)

"More Internet Users Will Be Mobile by 2015: Report." CIO Insight (September 12, 2011).

Panko, Raymond. Business Data Networks and Telecommunications 8e. Upper Saddle River, NJ: Prentice-Hall (2011).

Shaw, Tony. "Innovation Web 3.0." Baseline (March/April 2011).

Schatz, Amy and Shayndi Raice. "Internet Gets New Rules of the Road." The Wall Street Journal (December 22, 2010).

Segal, David "The Dirty Little Secrets of Search." The New York Times (February 12, 2011).

"The Internet of Things." McKinsey Quarterly (March 2010).

The McKinsey&Company. "The Impact of Internet Technologies: Search (July 2011).

Wingfield, Nick and Amir Efrati. "Google Rekindles the Browser War." The Wall Street Journal (July 7, 2010).

Worthen, Ben and Cari Tuna. "Web Running Out of Addresses." The Wall Street Journal (Feb 1, 2011).

Xiao, Bo and Izak Benbasat. "E-Commerce Product Recommendation Agents: Use, Characteristics, and Impact." Mis Quarterly 31, No. 1 (March 2007).

CHAPTER 7

Bernstein, Corinne. "The Cost of Data Breaches." Baseline (April 2009)

Bray, Chad. "Global Cyber Scheme Hits Bank Accounts." The Wall Street Journal (October 1, 2010.)

Cavusoglu, Huseyin, Birendra Mishra, and Srinivasan Raghunathan. "A Model for Evaluating IT Security Investments." Communications of the ACM 47, no. 7 (July 2004).

Chen, Pei-Yu, Gaurav Kataria, And Ramayya Krishnan. "Correlated Failures, Diversification, and Information Security Risk Management." MIS Quarterly 35, No. 2 (June 2011).

Chickowski, Ericka. "Is Your Information Really Safe?" Baseline (April 2009).

D'Arcy, John and Anat Hovav. "Deterring Internal Information Systems Use." Communications of the ACM 50, no. 10 (October 2007).

Danchev, Dancho. "Malware Watch: Rogue Facebook Apps, Fake Amazon Orders, and Bogus Adobe Updates." ZD Net (May 19, 2010).

Dash, Eric. "Online Woes Plague Chase for 2nd Day." The New York Times (September 15, 2010).

Dash, Eric. "Citi Data Theft Points Out a Nagging Problem." The New York Times (June 9, 2011).

"Data Center Outages Rack Up Costs Quickly: Report." CIO Insight (May 16, 2011).

"Data Theft: Top 5 Most Expensive Data Breaches." Christian Science Monitor (May 9, 2011)

"Devastating Downtime: The Surprising Cost of Human Error and Unforeseen Events." Focus Research (October 2010).

Drew, Christopher and Verne G. Kopytoff. "Deploying New Tools to Stop the Hackers." The New York Times (June 17, 2011).`

El-Ghobashy, Tamer. "Columbia Is Hit with $4.5 Million Bank Fraud." The Wall Street Journal (November 29, 2010).

Ely, Adam. "Browser as Attack Vector." Information Week (August 9, 2010).

Feretic, Eileen. "Security Lapses More Costly."baselinemag.com, January 26, 2010.

Fowler, Geoffrey A. and Ben Worthen. "Hackers Shift Attack to Small Firms." The Wall Street Journal (July 21, 2011).

Galbreth, Michael R. and Mikhael Shor. "The Impact of Malicious Agents on the Enterprise Software Industry." MIS Quarterly 34, no. 3 (September 2010).

George, Randy. "Database Breaches: Lessons Learned from Real-World Attacks." Information Week Analytics (April 2011).

Glanz, James and John Markoff. "Vast Hacking by a China Fearful of the Web." The New York Times (December 4, 2010).

Gorman, Siobhan. "Broad New Hacking Attack Detected." The Wall Street Journal (February 18, 2010).

Hardy, Quentin. "Internet Architects Warn of Risks in Ultrafast Networks." The New York Times (November 14, 2011).

Ives, Blake, Kenneth R. Walsh, and Helmut Schneider. "The Domino Effect of Password Reuse." Communications of the ACM 47, no.4 (April 2004).

Javelin Strategy & Research. "2010 Identity Fraud Survey Report." (2010).

Kaplan, James, Shatnu Sharma and Allen Weinberg. "Meeting the Cybersecurity Challenge." McKinsey Quarterly (June 2011).

Lawinski, Jennifer. "Internet Security Threat Report: Mobile Attacks on the Rise." CIO Insight (April 7 2011).

Markoff, John. "Vast Spy System Loots Computers in 103 Countries." The New York Times (March 29, 2009).

McGraw, Gary. "Real-World Software Security." Information Week (August 9, 2010).

McMillan, Robert. "Microsoft: One in 14 Downloads Is Malicious." PC World (May 17, 2011).

Miller, Claire Cain. "For Hackers, the Next Lock to Pick." The New York Times (September 27, 2011).

Moerschel, Grant. "4 Strategies to Lower Mobile Device Risk." Information Week (January 9, 2011).

Moyle, Ed and Diana Kelly. "Cloud Security: Understand the Risks Before You Make the Move." Information Week Analytics (April 2011).

Murphy, Kate. "New Hacking Tools Pose Bigger Threats to Wi-Fi Users," The New York Times (February 16, 2011).

Panko, Raymond R. Corporate Computer and Network Security 2e. Upper Saddle River, NJ: Pearson Prentice Hall (2010).

Ponemon Institute. "Second Annual Cost of Cyber Crime Study." (August 2011).

Pug, Ivan P.L. and Qiu-Hong Wang. "Information Security: Facilitating User Precautions Vis a Vis Enforcement Against Attackers. "Journal of Management Information Systems 26, No. 2 (Fall 2009).

Richardson, Robert. "2010/2011 Computer Crime and Security Survey." Computer Security Institute (2011).

Richmond, Riva. "Security to Thwart Swindlers on Phones." The New York Times (February 23, 2011).

Roche, Edward M., and George Van Nostrand. Information Systems, Computer Crime and Criminal Justice. New York: Barraclough Ltd. (2004).

Rooney, Ben. "Mobile Devices and Social Networks Key Malware Targets." The Wall Street Journal (April 5, 2011).

Saif, Irfan. "A New World of IT Risks: Are CIO's Up to the Challenge?" CIO Insight (March 11, 2011).

Sample, Char and Diana Kelley. "Cloud Computing Security: Infrastructure Issues." Security Curve June 23, 2009).

Schwartz, Matthew J. "Should Businesses Track Employee Smartphones?" Information Week, May 27, 2011.

Schwerha, Joseph J., IV. "Cybercrime: Legal Standards Governing the Collection of Digital Evidence." Information Systems Frontiers 6, no. 2 (June 2004).

Sherr, Ian. "Fox Says Hackers Hit Twitter Feed." The Wall Street Journal (July 5, 2011).

Sophos. "Security Threat Report 2011." (2011).

Spears. Janine L. and Henri Barki. "User Participation in Information Systems Security Risk Management." MIS Quarterly 34, No. 3 (September 2010).

Steel, Emily. "Web Ad Sales Open Door to Viruses." The Wall Street Journal (June 15, 2009).

Symantec. "Symantec Internet Security Threat Report." (2011).

Vance, Ashlee. "Gadgets Bring New Opportunities for Hackers. "The New York Times (December 26, 2010).

Vance, Ashlee. "If Your Password is 123456, Just Make It HackMe." The New York Times (January 20, 2010).

Violino, Bob. "IT Downtime Carries a High Price Tag." CIO Insight (May 25, 2011).

Volonino, Linda and Stephen R. Robinson. Principles and Practice of Information Security. Upper Saddle River, NJ: Pearson Prentice Hall (2004).

Westerman, George. IT Risk: Turning Business Threats into Competitive Advantage. Harvard Business School Publishing (2007)

Worthen, Ben and Anton Troianovski. "Firms Come Clean on Hacks." The Wall Street Journal (June 17, 2011).

Worthen, Ben, Russell Adams, Nathan Hodge, and Evan Ramstad. "Hackers Broaden Their Attacks." The Wall Street Journal (May 31, 2011).

Wright, Ryan T. and Kent Marrett."The Influence of Experiential and Dispositional Factors in Phishing: An Empirical Investigation of the Deceived." Journal of Management Information Systems 27, No. 1 (Summer 2010).

CHAPTER 8

Aeppel, Timothy."'Bullwhip' Hits Firms as Growth Snaps Back." The Wall Street Journal (January 27, 2010).

Alison, Diana. "Social CRM Rush Projected for Enterprises." Information Week (March 4, 2011).

Barrett, Joe. "Whirlpool Cleans Up Its Delivery Act." The Wall Street Journal (September 24, 2009).

Bozarth, Cecil and Robert B. Handfield. Introduction to Operations and Supply Chain Management 2e. Upper Saddle River, NJ: Prentice-Hall (2007).

Chickowski, Ericka. "5 ERP Disasters Explained."www.5Baselinemag.com, accessed October 8, 2009.

D'Avanzo, Robert, Hans von Lewinski, and Luk N. Van Wassenhove. "The Link between Supply Chain and Financial Performance." Supply Chain Management Review (November 1, 2003).

Davenport, Thomas H. Mission Critical: Realizing the Promise of Enterprise Systems. Boston: Harvard Business School Press (2000).

Ferrer, Jaume, Johan Karlberg, and Jamie Hintlian."Integration: The Key to Global Success." Supply Chain Management Review (March 1, 2007).

Fleisch, Elgar, Hubert Oesterle, and Stephen Powell. "Rapid Implementation of Enterprise Resource Planning Systems." Journal of Organizational Computing and Electronic Commerce 14, no. 2 (2004).

Fournier, Susan and Jill Avery. "Putting the 'Relationship' Back into CRM." MIT Sloan Management Review 52, No. 3 (Spring 2011).

Garber, Randy and Suman Sarkar. "Want a More Flexible Supply Chain?" Supply Chain Management Review (January 1, 2007).

Goodhue, Dale L., Barbara H. Wixom, and Hugh J. Watson. "Realizing Business Benefits through CRM: Hitting the Right Target in the Right Way." MIS Quarterly Executive 1, no. 2 (June 2002).

Greengard, Samuel. "ERP, RIP" Baseline (May 2, 2011).

Henschen, Doug. "Data Drives Colgate Investment Decisions." Information Week (September 13, 2010).

Henschen, Doug. "ERP's Cool Again." Information Week (July 25, 2011).

Henschen, Doug. "Salesforce's Facebook Envy Goes Mobile." Information Week (September 13, 2010).

Hitt, Lorin, D. J. Wu, and Xiaoge Zhou. "Investment in Enterprise Resource Planning: Business Impact and Productivity Measures." Journal of Management Information Systems 19, no. 1 (Summer 2002).

Johnson, Maryfran."What's Happening with ERP Today." CIO (January 27, 2010).

Kalakota, Ravi, and Marcia Robinson. E-Business 2.0. Boston: Addison-Wesley (2001).

Kanakamedala, Kishore, Glenn Ramsdell, and Vats Srivatsan. "Getting Supply Chain Software Right." McKinsey Quarterly No. 1 (2003).

Kanaracus, Chris. "Biggest ERP Failures of 2010." CIO (December 17, 2010).

Klein, Richard and Arun Rai. "Interfirm Strategic Information Flows in Logistics Supply Chain Relationships." MIS Quarterly 33, No. 4 (December 2009).

Kopczak, Laura Rock, and M. Eric Johnson. "The Supply-Chain Management Effect." MIT Sloan Management Review 44, no. 3 (Spring 2003).

Krigsman, Michael. "Five Critical Points for ERP Success." Focus Research (2010).

Laudon, Kenneth C. "The Promise and Potential of Enterprise Systems and Industrial Networks." Working paper, The Concours Group. Copyright Kenneth C. Laudon (1999).

Lee, Hau, L., V. Padmanabhan, and Seugin Whang. "The Bullwhip Effect in Supply Chains." Sloan Management Review (Spring 1997).

Lee, Hau. "The Triple-A Supply Chain." Harvard Business Review (October 2004).

Liang, Huigang, Nilesh Sharaf, Quing Hu, and Yajiong Xue. "Assimilation of Enterprise Systems: The Effect of Institutional Pressures and the Mediating Role of Top Management." MIS Quarterly 31, no. 1 (March 2007).

Maleshefski, Tiffany. "140 Characters, but Numerous Social CRM Possibilities." Information Management (July 11, 2011).

Malhotra, Arvind, Sanjay Gosain, and Omar A. El Sawy. "Absorptive Capacity Configurations in Supply Chains: Gearing for Partner-Enabled Market Knowledge Creation." MIS Quarterly 29, no. 1 (March 2005).

Malik, Yogesh, Alex Niemeyer, and Brian Ruwadi. "Building the Supply Chain of the Future." McKinsey Quarterly (January 2011).

Mehta, Krishna."Best Practices for Developing a Customer Lifetime Value Program." Information Management (July 28, 2011).

Oracle Corporation. "Alcoa Implements Oracle Solution 20% below Projected Cost, Eliminates 43 Legacy Systems." www.oracle.com, accessed August 21, 2005.

Rai, Arun, Ravi Patnayakuni, and Nainika Seth. "Firm Performance Impacts of Digitally Enabled Supply Chain Integration Capabilities." MIS Quarterly 30 No. 2 (June 2006).

Ranganathan, C. and Carol V. Brown. "ERP Iinvestments and the Market Value of Firms: Toward an Understanding of Influential ERP Project Variables." Information Systems Research 17, No. 2 (June 2006).

Robey, Daniel, Jeanne W. Ross, and Marie-Claude Boudreau. "Learning to Implement Enterprise Systems: An Exploratory Study of the Dialectics of Change." Journal of Management Information Systems 19, no. 1 (Summer 2002).

Scott, Judy E., and Iris Vessey. "Managing Risks in Enterprise Systems Implementations." Communications of the ACM 45, no. 4 (April 2002).

Seldon, Peter B., Cheryl Calvert, and Song Yang. "A Multi-Project Model of Key Factors Affecting Organizational Benefits from Enterprise Systems." MIS Quarterly 34, no. 2 (June 2010).

Strong, Diane M. and Olga Volkoff. "Understanding Organization-Enterprise System Fit: A Path to Theorizing the Information Technology Artifact." MIS Quarterly 34, No.4 (December 2010).

Wailgum, Thomas. "Why ERP Is Still So Hard." CIO (September 9. 2009).

Wailgum, Thomas. "The Future of ERP." Parts I and II. CIO (November 20, 2009).

Wing, George. "Unlocking the Value of ERP." Baseline (January/February 2010).

CHAPTER 9

Bakos, Yannis. "The Emerging Role of Electronic Marketplaces and the Internet." Communications of the ACM 41, no. 8 (August 1998).

Bluefly, Inc. "Form 10K Report For the Fiscal Year Ended December 31, 2010." Filed with the Securities and Exchange Commission (February 20, 2011).

Brynjolfsson, Erik,Yu Hu, and Michael D. Smith."Consumer Surpus in the Digital Economy: Estimating the Value of Increased Product Variety at Online Booksellers." Management Science 49, no. 11 (November 2003).

Cain Miller, Claire. "Take a Step Closer for an Invitation to Shop." The New York Times (February 23, 2010).

Clemons, Eric K. "Business Models for Monetizing Internet Applications and Web Sites: Experience, Theory, and Predictions. "Journal of Management Information Systems 26, No. 2 (Fall 2009).

Clifford, Stephanie."Web Coupons Know Lots About You, and They Tell." The New York Times (April 16, 2010).

ComScore Inc. "The Network Effect: Facebook, Linkedin, Twitter & Tumblr Reach New Heights in May 2011." comScore Inc. (June 15, 2011),

ComScore. "Facebook Takes Lead In Time Spent." comScore Media Metrix. Press Release. (September 9, 2010).

eMarketer Inc. "US Internet Users and Penetration, 2009-2015." Chart. (January 25, 2011b).

eMarketer, Inc. "Net US Online Ad Revenues at Top 5 Ad-Selling Companies, 2009-2012 (billions)." Chart. (September 15, 2011).

eMarketer, Inc. "US Mobile Advertising 2010 to 2015" (October 2011).

eMarketer, Inc. "US Retail Ecommerce Forecast: Growth Opportunities in a Maturing Channel." (Jeffery Grau) eMarketer, (April 1, 2011a

eMarketer, Inc. "Virtual Goods and Currency: Real Dollars Ad Up." eMarketer. (July 25, 2011).

Evans, Philip and Thomas S. Wurster. Blown to Bits: How the New Economics of Information Transforms Strategy. Boston, MA: Harvard Business School Press (2000).

Fuller, Johann, Hans Muhlbacher, Kurt Matzler, and Gregor Jawecki. "Customer Empowerment Through Internet-Based Co-Creation." Journal of Management Information Systems 26, No. 3 (Winter 2010).

Hinz, Oliver , Jochen Eckert, and Bernd Skiera. "Drivers of the Long Tail Phenomenon: An Empirical Analysis." Journal of Management Information Systems 27, No. 4 (Spring 2011).

Hinz, Oliver, Il-Horn Hann, and Martin Spann. Price Discrimination in E-Commerce? An Examination of Dynamic Pricing in Name-Your-Own Price Markets." MIS Quarterly 35, No 1 (March 2011).

Koch, Hope and Ulrike Schultze. " Stuck in the Conflicted Middle: A Role-Theoretic Perspective on B2B E-Marketplaces." MIS Quarterly 35, No. 1 (March 2011).

Howe, Heff. Crowdsourcing: Why the Power of the Crowd Is Driving the Future of Business. New York: Random House (2008).

Internetworldstats.com. "Internet Usage Statistics: The Big Picture." Internetworldstats.com, (June 2010).

Jiang, Zhengrui and Sumit Sarkar. "Speed Matters: The Role of Free Software Offer in Software Diffusion." Journal of Management Information Systems 26, No. 3 (Winter 2010).

Kauffman, Robert J. and Bin Wang. "New Buyers' Arrival Under Dynamic Pricing Market Microstructure: The Case of Group-Buying Discounts on the Internet, Journal of Management Information Systems 18, no. 2 (Fall 2001).

Laseter, Timothy M., Elliott Rabinovich, Kenneth K. Boyer, and M. Johnny Rungtusanatham. "Critical Issues in Internet Retailing." MIT Sloan Management Review 48, no. 3 (Spring 2007).

Laudon, Kenneth C. and Carol Guercio Traver. E-Commerce: Business, Technology, Society, 8th edition. Upper Saddle River, NJ: Prentice-Hall (2012).

Leimeister, Jan Marco, Michael Huber, Ulrich Bretschneider, and Helmut Krcmar." Leveraging Crowdsourcing: Activation-Supporting Components for IT-Based Ideas Competition." Journal of Management Information Systems 26, No. 1 (Summer 2009).

Li, Xinxin and Lorin M. Hitt. "Price Effects in Online Product Reviews: An Analytical Model and Empirical Analysis." MIS Quarterly 34, No. 4 (December 2010).

Pavlou, Paul A., Huigang Liang, and Yajiong Xue. "Understanding and Mitigating Uncertainty in Online Exchange Relationships: A Principal-Agent Perspective." MIS Quarterly 31, no. 1 (March 2007).

Pew Internet & American Life Project. "Daily Internet Activities." (May 2011).

Piskorski, Mikolaj Jan."Social Strategies that Work." Harvard Business Review (November 2011).

Resnick, Paul and Hal Varian. "Recommender Systems." Communications of the ACM (March 2007).

Rosenbloom, Stephanie. "Cellphones Let Shoppers Point, Click, and Purchase." The New York Times (February 26, 2010).

Schoder, Detlef and Alex Talalavesky. "The Price Isn't Right." MIT Sloan Management Review (August 22, 2010).

Schultze, Ulrike and Wanda J. Orlikowski. "A Practice Perspective on Technology-Mediated Network Relations: The Use of Internet-Based Self-Serve Technologies." Information Systems Research 15, no. 1 (March 2004).

Smith, Michael D., Joseph Bailey and Erik Brynjolfsson."Understanding Digital Markets: Review and Assessment" in Erik Brynjolfsson and Brian Kahin, ed. Understanding the Digital Economy. Cambridge, MA: MIT Press (1999).

Smith, Michael D. and Rahul Telang. "Competing with Free: The Impact of Movie Broadcasts on DVD Sales and Internet Piracy." MIS Quarterly 33, No. 2 (June 2009).

Steel, Emily, "Exploring Ways to Build a Better Consumer Profile." The Wall Street Journal (March 15, 2010).

Steel, Emily."Marketers Watch Friends Interact Online." The Wall Street Journal (April 15, 2010).

Stross, Randall. "Just Browsing? A Web Store May Follow You Out the Door." The New York Times (May 17, 2009).

Surowiecki, James. The Wisdom of Crowds: Why the Many Are Smarter Than the Few and How Collective Wisdom Shapes Business, Economies, Societies and Nations. Boston: Little, Brown (2004).

United States Census Bureau. "E-Stats Report. Measuring the Electronic Economy." (May 27, 2010). www.census.gov.

Vance, Ashlee. "For An Online Marketplace, It's Better Late Than Never." The New York Times (November 20, 2010).

Wilson, H. James, PJ. Guinan, Salvatore Parise, and Bruce D. Weinberg. "What's Your Social Media Strategy?" Harvard Business Review (July 2011).

CHAPTER 10

Alavi, Maryam and Dorothy Leidner. "Knowledge Management and Knowledge Management Systems: Conceptual Foundations and Research Issues," MIS Quarterly 25, No. 1 (March 2001).

Alavi, Maryam, Timothy R. Kayworth, and Dorothy E. Leidner. "An Empirical Investigation of the Influence of Organizational Culture on Knowledge Management Practices." Journal of Management Information Systems 22, No.3 (Winter 2006).

Animesh Animesh, Alain Pinsonneault, Sung-Byung Yang, and Wonseok Oh. "An Odyssey into Virtual Worlds: Exploring the Impacts of Technological and Spatial Environments." MIS Quarterly 35, No. 3 (September 2011).

Anson, Rob and Bjorn Erik Munkvold. "Beyond Face-to-Face: A Field Study of Electronic Meetings in Different Time and Place Modes."

Journal of Organizational Computing and Electronic Commerce 14, no. 2 (2004).

Atre, Shaku. "Who in the World Uses Only Words and Numbers in Reports?" Information Management (April 7, 2011).

Bazerman, Max H. and Dolly Chugh. "Decisions Without Blinders." Harvard Business Review (January 2006).

Booth, Corey and Shashi Buluswar. "The Return of Artificial Intelligence," The McKinsey Quarterly No. 2 (2002).

Burtka, Michael. "Generic Algorithms." The Stern Information Systems Review 1, no. 1 (Spring 1993).

Clark, Thomas D., Jr., Mary C. Jones, and Curtis P. Armstrong. "The Dynamic Structure of Management Support Systems: Theory Development, Research Focus, and Direction." MIS Quarterly 31, no. 3 (September 2007).

Davenport, Thomas H. and Jim Hagemann Snabe. "How Fast and Flexible Do You Want Your Information, Really?" MIT Sloan Management Review 52, No. 3 (Spring 2011).

Davenport, Thomas H., and Lawrence Prusak. Working Knowledge: How Organizations Manage What They Know. Boston, MA: Harvard Business School Press (1997).

Davenport, Thomas H., Jeanne Harris, and Robert Morison. Analytics at Work: Smarter Decisions, Better Results. Boston: Harvard Business Press (2010).

Davenport, Thomas H., Laurence Prusak, and Bruce Strong. "Putting Ideas to Work." The Wall Street Journal (March 10, 2008).

Davenport, Thomas H., Robert J. Thomas and Susan Cantrell. "The Mysterious Art and Science of Knowledge-Worker Performance." MIT Sloan Management Review 44, no. 1 (Fall 2002).

Davis, Gordon B. "Anytime/ Anyplace Computing and the Future of Knowledge Work." Communications of the ACM 42, no.12 (December 2002).

Dennis, Alan R., Jay E. Aronson, William G. Henriger, and Edward D. Walker III. "Structuring Time and Task in Electronic Brainstorming." MIS Quarterly 23, no. 1 (March 1999).

DeSanctis, Geraldine, and R. Brent Gallupe. "A Foundation for the Study of Group Decision Support Systems." Management Science 33, no. 5 (May 1987).

Dhar, Vasant, and Roger Stein. Intelligent Decision Support Methods: The Science of Knowledge Work. Upper Saddle River, NJ: Prentice Hall (1997).

Earl, Michael. "Knowledge Management Strategies: Toward a Taxonomy." Journal of Management Information Systems 18, no. 1 (Summer 2001).

Franchesi, Katherine, Ronald M. Lee, Stelios H. Zanakis, and David Hinds. "Engaging Group E-Learning in Virtual Worlds." Journal of Management Information Systems 26, No. 1 (Summer 2009).

Griffith, Terri L., John E. Sawyer, and Margaret A Neale. "Virtualness and Knowledge in Teams: Managing the Love Triangle of Organizations, Individuals, and Information Technology." MIS Quarterly 27, no. 2 (June 2003).

Grover, Varun and Thomas H. Davenport. "General Perspectives on Knowledge Management: Fostering a Research Agenda." Journal of Management Information Systems 18, no. 1 (Summer 2001).

Henschen, Doug. "Next-Gen BI Is Here." Information Week (August 31. 2009).

Holland, John H. "Genetic Algorithms." Scientific American (July 1992).

Housel Tom and Arthur A. Bell. Measuring and Managing Knowledge. New York: McGraw-Hill (2001).

IBM Corporation."Extending Business Intelligence with Dashboards." (2010).

Hurst, Cameron with Michael S. Hopkins and Leslie Brokaw. "Matchmaking With Math: How Analytics Beats Intuition to Win Customers." MIT Sloan Management Review 52, No. 2 (Winter 2011).

Jander, Mary. "The Web 2.0 Balancing Act." Information Week (February 16, 2009).

Jarvenpaa, Sirkka L. and D. Sandy Staples. "Exploring Perceptions of Organizational Ownership of Information and Expertise."Journal of Management Information Systems 18, no. 1 (Summer 2001).

Jones, Quentin, Gilad Ravid, and Sheizaf Rafaeli. "Information Overload and the Message Dynamics of Online Interaction Spaces: A Theoretical Model and Empirical Exploration." Information Systems Research 15, no. 2 (June 2004).

Kankanhalli, Atreyi, Frasiska Tanudidjaja, Juliana Sutanto, and Bernard C.Y Tan."The Role of IT in Successful Knowledge Management Initiatives." Communications of the ACM 46, no. 9 (September 2003).

King, William R., Peter V. Marks, Jr. and Scott McCoy. "The Most Important Issues in Knowledge Management." Communications of the ACM 45, no.9 (September 2002).

Kiron, David And Rebecca Schockley. "Creating Business Value With Analytics." MIT Sloan Management Review 53, No 1 (Fall 2011).

Kuo, R.J., K. Chang, and S.Y.Chien."Integration and Self-Organizing Feature Maps and Genetic-Algorithm-Based Clustering Method for Market Segmentation." Journal of Organizational Computing and Electronic Commerce 14, no. 1 (2004).

Kwok, Ron Chi-Wai, Jian Ma, and Douglas R. Vogel."Effects of Group Support Systems and Content Facilitation on Knowledge Acquisition." Journal of Management Information Systems 19, no. 3 (Winter 2002-3).

Lanier, Jaron. "The First Church of Robotics." The New York Times (August 9, 2010).

LaValle, Steve, Michael S Hopkins, Eric Lesser, Rebecca Shockley, and Nina Kruschwitz. "Analytics: The New Path to Value." MIT Sloan Management Review and IBM Institute for Business Value (Fall 2010).

LaValle, Steve, Eric Lesser, Rebecca Shockley, Michael S. Hopkins and Nina Kruschwitz. "Big Data, Analytics, and the Path from Insights to Value." MIT Sloan Management Review 52, No. 2 (Winter 2011).

Leonard-Barton, Dorothy and Walter Swap. "Deep Smarts.' Harvard Business Review (September 1, 2004).

Lev, Baruch. "Sharpening the Intangibles Edge." Harvard Business Review (June 1, 2004).

Lohr, Steve. "When There's No Such Thing as Too Much Information." The New York Times (April 23, 2011).

Malone, Thomas. "Rethinking Knowledge Work: A Strategic Approach." McKinsey Quarterly (February 2011).

Maltby, Emily. "Affordable 3-D Arrives." The Wall Street Journal (July 29, 2010).

Markoff, John. "The Coming Superbrain." The New York Times (May 24, 2009).

Markoff, John. "A Fight to Win the Future: Computers vs. Humans." The New York Times (February 14, 2011).

Markus, M. Lynne. "Toward a Theory of Knowledge Reuse: Types of Knowledge Reuse Situations and Factors in Reuse Success." Journal of Management Information Systems 18, no. 1 (Summer 2001).

Maryam Alavi and Dorothy E. Leidner. "Knowledge Management and Knowledge Management Systems." MIS Quarterly 25, no. 1 (March 2001).

McKay, Lauren. "Decisions, Decisions." Customer Relationship Management (May 2009).

McKnight, William. "Predictive Analytics: Beyond the Predictions." Information Management (July/August 2011).

Nunamaker, Jay, Robert O. Briggs, Daniel D. Mittleman, Douglas R. Vogel, and Pierre A. Balthazard. "Lessons from a Dozen Years of Group Support Systems Research: A Discussion of Lab and Field Findings." Journal of Management Information Systems 13, no. 3 (Winter 1997).

Open Text Corporation. " Barrick Gold Turns to Open Text to Help Streamline Information Flow (2011).

Orlikowski, Wanda J. "Knowing in Practice: Enacting a Collective Capability in Distributed Organizing." Organization Science 13, no. 3 (May-June 2002).

Robertson, Jordan. "IBM Pursues Chips that Behave Like Brains" Associated Press (August 18, 2011).

Sadeh, Norman, David W. Hildum, and Dag Kjenstad."Agent-Based E-Supply Chain Decision Support." Journal of Organizational Computing and Electronic Commerce 13, no. 3 & 4 (2003)

Samuelson, Douglas A. and Charles M. Macal. "Agent-Based Simulation." OR/MS Today (August 2006).

Sanders, Peter. "Boeing 787 Training Takes Virtual Path" The Wall Street Journal (September 2, 2010).

Scanlon, Robert H. "A New Route to Performance Management." Baseline Magazine (January/February 2009).

Schultze, Ulrike and Dorothy Leidner."Studying Knowledge Management in Information Systems Research: Discourses and Theoretical Assumptions." MIS Quarterly 26, no. 3 (September 2002).

Schwabe, Gerhard. "Providing for Organizational Memory in Computer-Supported Meetings." Journal of Organizational Computing and Electronic Commerce 9, no. 2 and 3 (1999).

Simon, H. A. The New Science of Management Decision. New York: Harper & Row (1960).

Singer, Natasha. "Face Recognition Makes the Leap from Sci-Fi." The New York Times (November 12, 2011).

Singer, Natasha. "When Data Struts Its Stuff." The New York Times (April 2, 2011).

Softscape. " Dtac Selects Softscape's Learning Management Platform to Drive Employee Engagement." (October 20, 2009).

Sommer, Dan and Bhavish Sood. "Market Share Analysis: Business Intelligence, Analytics and Performance Management, Worldwide, 2010." Gartner Inc. (April 18, 2011).

Steel, Emily. "Modeling Tools Stretch Ad Dollars." The Wall Street Journal (May 18, 2009).

Turban, Efraim, Ramesh Sharda, and Dursun Delen. Decision Support and Business Intelligence Systems 9e. Upper Saddle River, NJ: Prentice Hall (2011).

Turban, Efraim, Ramesh Sharda, Dursun Delen, and David King. Business Intelligence 2e. Upper Saddle River, NJ: Prentice Hall (2011).

Ukelson, Jacob. "Trends in Knowledge Work." Information Management (May/June 2011).

Viaene, Stijn. and Annabel Van den Bunder "The Secrets to Managing Business Analytics Projects." Sloan Management Review 52, No. 1 (Fall 2011).

Wakefield, Julie. "Complexity's Business Model." Scientific American (January 2001).

Walczak, Stephen."An Emprical Analysis of Data Requirements for Financial Forecasting with Neural Networks." Journal of Management Information Systems 17, no. 4 (Spring 2001).

Wayner, Peter. "Illustrating Your Life in Graphs and Charts.: The New York Times (April 20, 2011).

Zack, Michael H "Rethinking the Knowledge-Based Organization." MIS Sloan Management Review 44, no. 4 (Summer 2003).

Zadeh, Lotfi A. "The Calculus of Fuzzy If/Then Rules." AI Expert (March 1992).

CHAPTER 11

Armstrong, Deborah J. and Bill C. Hardgrove. "Understanding Mindshift Learning: The Transition to Object-Oriented Development." MIS Quarterly 31, no. 3 (September 2007).

Aron, Ravi, Eric K.Clemons, and Sashi Reddi. "Just Right Outsourcing: Understanding and Managing Risk." Journal of Management Information Systems 22, no. 1 (Summer 2005).

Ashrafi Noushin and Hessam Ashrafi. Object-Oriented Systems Analysis and Design. Upper Saddle River, NY: Prentice-Hall (2009).

Avison, David E., and Guy Fitzgerald. "Where Now for Development Methodologies?" Communications of the ACM 41, no. 1 (January 2003).

Biehl, Markus. "Success Factors For Implementing Global Information Systems." Communications of the ACM 50, No. 1 (January 2007).

Brewer, Jeffrey and Kevin Dittman. Methods of IT Project Management. Upper Saddle River, NJ: Prentice-Hall (2010).

Chickowski, Ericka. "Projects Gone Wrong." Baseline (May 15, 2009).

Delone, William H., and Ephraim R. McLean. "The Delone and McLean Model of Information Systems Success: A Ten-Year Update. Journal of Management nformation Systems 19, no. 4 (Spring 2003).

Dibbern, Jess, Jessica Winkler, and Armin Heinzl. "Explaining Variations in Client Extra Costs between Software Projects Offshored to India." MIS Quarterly 32, no. 2 (June 2008).

Erickson, Jonathan. "Dr Dobb's Report: Agile Development." Information Week (April 27, 2009).

Esposito, Dino. "A Whole New Ball Game: Aspects of Mobile Application Development." Information Week (March 12, 2011).

Feeny, David, Mary Lacity, and Leslie P. Willcocks. "Taking the Measure of Outsourcing

Providers." MIT Sloan Management Review 46, no. 3 (Spring 2005).

Flyvbjerg, Bent and Alexander Budzier. "Why Your IT Project May Be Riskier Than You Think." Harvard Business Review (September 2011).

Gefen, David and Erarn Carmel. "Is the World Really Flat? A Look at Offshoring in an Online Programming Marketplace." MIS Quarterly 32, no. 2 (June 2008).

Goff, Stacy A. "The Future of IT Project Management Software." CIO (January 6, 2010).

Goo, Jahyun, Rajive Kishore, H. R. Rao, and Kichan Nam. The Role of Service Level Agreements in Relational Management of Information Technology Outsourcing: An Empirical Study." MIS Quarterly 33, No. 1 (March 2009).

Hahn, Eugene D., Jonathan P. Doh, and Kraiwinee Bunyaratavej. "The Evolution of Risk in Information Systems Offshoring: The Impact of Home Country Risk, Firm Learning, and Competitive Dynamics. MIS Quarterly 33, No. 3 (September 2009).

Hickey, Ann M., and Alan M. Davis. "A Unified Model of Requirements Elicitation." Journal of Management Information Systems 20, no. 4 (Spring 2004).

Hoffer, Jeffrey, Joey George, and Joseph Valacich. Modern Systems Analysis and Design, 6th ed. Upper Saddle River, NJ: Prentice Hall (2011).

Information Builders, "Travel and Transport Tracks and Analyzes Travel Expenses with WebFOCUS," www.informationbuilders.com, accessed August 6, 2011.

Jeffrey, Mark, and Ingmar Leliveld. "Best Practices in IT Portfolio Management." MIT Sloan Management Review 45, no. 3 (Spring 2004).

Kendall, Kenneth E., and Julie E. Kendall. Systems Analysis and Design, 8th ed. Upper Saddle River, NJ: Prentice Hall (2011).

Kettinger, William J., and Choong C. Lee. "Understanding the IS-User Divide in IT Innovation." Communications of the ACM 45, no.2 (February 2002).

Kim, Hee Woo and Atreyi Kankanhalli. "Investigating User Resistance to Information Systems Implementation: A Status Quo Bias Perspective." MIS Quarterly 33, No. 3 (September 2009).

Kirsch, Laurie J. "Deploying Common Systems Globally: The Dynamic of Control." Information Systems Research 15, no. 4 (December 2004).

Koh, Christine, Song Ang, and Detmar W. Straub. "IT Outsourcing Success: A Psychological Contract Perspective." Information Systems Research 15 no. 4 (December 2004).

Lapointe, Liette, and Suzanne Rivard. "A Multilevel Model of Resistance to Information Technology Implementation." MIS Quarterly 29, no. 3 (September 2005).

Levina, Natalia, and Jeanne W. Ross. "From the Vendor's Perspective: Exploring the Value Proposition in Information Technology Outsourcing." MIS Quarterly 27, no. 3 (September 2003).

Liang, Huigang, Nilesh Sharaf, Qing Hu, and Yajiong Xue. "Assimilation of Enterprise Systems: The Effect of Institutional Pressures and the Mediating Role of Top Management." MIS Quarterly 31, no 1 (March 2007).

Limayem, Moez, Mohamed Khalifa, and Wynne W. Chin. "Case Tools Usage and Impact on System Development Performance." Journal

of Organizational Computing and Electronic Commerce 14, no. 3 (2004).

Majchrzak, Ann, Cynthia M. Beath, and Ricardo A. Lim. "Managing Client Dialogues during Information Systems Design to Facilitate Client Learning." MIS Quarterly 29, no. 4 (December 2005).

McCafferty, Dennis. "What Dooms IT Projects." Baseline (June 10, 2010).

McGrath, Rita. "Six Problems Facing Large Government IT Projects (and Their Solutions)." Harvard Business Review Online (October 10, 2008).

McMahan, Ty. "The Ins and Outs of Mobile Apps." The Wall Street Journal (June 13, 2011).

Nelson, H. James, Deborah J. Armstrong, and Kay M. Nelson. Patterns of Transition: The Shift from Traditional to Object-Oriented Development." Journal of Management Information Systems 25, No. 4 (Spring 2009).

Overby, Stephanie. "The Hidden Costs of Offshore Outsourcing," CIO Magazine (September 1, 2003).

Rai, Arun, Sandra S. Lang, and Robert B. Welker. "Assessing the Validity of IS Success Models: An Empirical Test and Theoretical Analysis." Information Systems Research 13, no. 1 (March 2002).

Ravichandran, T., and Marcus A. Rothenberger. "Software Reuse Strategies and Component Markets." Communications of the ACM 46, no. 8 (August 2003).

Robey, Daniel, Jeanne W. Ross, and Marie-Claude Boudreau. "Learning to Implement Enterprise Systems: An Exploratory Study of the Dialectics of Change." Journal of Management Information Systems 19, no. 1 (Summer 2002).

Ryan, Sherry D., David A. Harrison, and Lawrence L Schkade. "Information Technology Investment Decisions: When Do Cost and Benefits in the Social Subsystem Matter?" Journal of Management Information Systems 19, no. 2 (Fall 2002).

Sharma, Rajeev and Philip Yetton. "The Contingent Effects of Training, Technical Complexity, and Task Interdependence on Successful Information Systems Implementation." MIS Quarterly 31, no. 2 (June 2007).

Silva, Leiser and Rudy Hirschheim. "Fighting Against Windmills: Strategic Information Systems and Organizational Deep Structures." MIS Quarterly 31, no. 2 (June 2007).

Sircar, Sumit, Sridhar P. Nerur, and Radhakanta Mahapatra. "Revolution or Evolution? A Comparison of Object-Oriented and Structured Systems Development Methods." MIS Quarterly 25, no. 4 (December 2001).

Smith, H. Jeff, Mark Keil, and Gordon Depledge. "Keeping Mum as the Project Goes Under." Journal of Management Information Systems 18, no. 2 (Fall 2001).

Taft, Darryl K. "Will PAAS Solve All Developer Ills? " eWeek (April 4, 2011).

Venkatesh, Viswanath, Michael G. Morris, Gordon B Davis, and Fred D. Davis. "User Acceptance of Information Technology: Toward a Unified View." MIS Quarterly 27, no. 3 (September 2003).

Wang, Eric T.G., Gary Klein, and James J. Jiang. "ERP Misfit: Country of Origin and Organizational Factors." Journal of Management Information Systems 23, No. 1 (Summer 2006).

Whitaker , Jonathan, Sunil Mithas and M.S. Krishnan. "Organizational Learning and Capabilities for Onshore and Offshore Business Process Outsourcing." Journal of Management Information Systems 27, No. 3 (Winter 2011).

Wipro Technologies. "Wipro Technologies wins engagement with Chaucer Syndicates, Specialist Insurer at Lloyd's." (June 2, 2011).

Wulf, Volker, and Matthias Jarke. "The Economics of End-User Development." Communications of the ACM 47, no. 9 (September 2004).

Xia, Weidong, and Gwanhoo Lee. "Complexity of Information Systems Development Projects." Journal of Management Information Systems 22, no. 1 (Summer 2005).

Zhu, Kevin, Kenneth L. Kraemer, Sean Xu, and Jason Dedrick. "Information Technology Payoff in E-Business Environments: An International Perspective on Value Creation of E-business in the Financial Services Industry." Journal of Management Information Systems 21, no. 1 (Summer 2004).

CHAPTER 12

Angst, Corey M. and Ritu Agarwal. "Adoption of Electronic Health Records in the Presence of Privacy Concerns: The Elaboration Likelihood Model and Individual Persuasion." MIS Quarterly 33, No. 2 (June 2009).

Austen, Ian. "With Apologies, Officials Say Blackberry Service is Restored." New York Times (October 13, 2011).

Baumstein, Avi. "New Tools Close Holes in Cam-Spam." Information Week (February 23, 2009).

Belanger, France and Robert E. Crossler. "Privacy in the Digital Age: A Review of Information Privacy Research in Information Systems." MIS Quarterly 35, No. 4 (December 2011).

Bilski v. Kappos, 561 US, (2010).

Brown Bag Software vs. Symantec Corp. 960 F2D 1465 (Ninth Circuit, 1992).

Business Software Alliance. "Eighth Annual BSA and IDC Global Software Piracy Study." (2011).

Carr, Nicholas. "Tracking Is an Assault on Liberty, with Real Dangers." The Wall Street Journal (August 7, 2010).

Clifford, Stephanie. "Web Coupons Know Lots About You, and They Tell." The New York Times (April 16, 2010).

Duffy, John. "Why Business Patent Methods." Stanford Law Review (June 2011).

Efrati, Amir, Scott Thurm, and Dionne Searcy. "Mobile-App Makers Face U.S. Privacy Investigation." The Wall Street Journal (April 5, 2011).

European Parliament. "Directive 2009/136/EC of the European Parliament and of the Council of November 25, 2009." European Parliament (2009).

FTC. "Protecting Consumer Privacy In an Era of Rapid Change." Federal Trade Commission (2010).

Harper, Jim. "It's Modern Trade: Web Users Get as Much as They Give." The Wall Street Journal (August 7, 2010).

Laudon, Kenneth C. and Carol Guercio Traver. E-Commerce: Business, Technology, Society 8th Edition. Upper Saddle River, NJ: Prentice-Hall (2012).

Lee, Dong-Joo, Jae-Hyeon Ahn, and Youngsok Bang. "Managing Consumer Privacy

Concerns in Personalization: A Strategic Analysis of Privacy Protection." MIS Quarterly 35, No. 2 (June 2011).

Lohr, Steve. "How Privacy Vanishes Online." The New York Times (March 16, 2010.)

Matt Richtel, "Hooked on Gadgets, and Paying a Mental Price," The New York Times, June 7, 2010.

National White Collar Crime Center and the Federal Bureau of Investigation. "Internet Crime Complaint Center. "2010 Internet Crime Report." (2011).

Pavlou, Paul A. "State of the Information Privacy Literature: Where Are We Now and Where Should We Go?" MIS Quarterly 35, No. 4 (December 2011).

Schwartz, Matthew J. "Sophos: U.S. Leads List of Spam Originators." Information Week (July 15, 2010).

Singer, Natasha. "Shoppers Who Can't Have Secrets." The New York Times (April 30, 2010).

Smith, Ethan and Geoffrey A. Fowler. "Ganging Up on Internet Pirates." The Wall Street Journal (July 8, 2011).

Smith, H. Jeff, Tamara Dinev, and Heng Xu . "Information Privacy Research: An Interdisciplinary Review." MIS Quarterly 35, No. 4 (December 2011).

Steel, Emily and Julia Angwin,"On the Web's Cutting Edge, Anonymity in Name Only." The Wall Street Journal (August 4, 2010).

Steel, Emily. "Marketers Watch Friends Interact Online." The Wall Street Journal (April 15, 2010)

Symantec. "Symantec Global Internet Security Threat Report: Trends for 2011." (April 2011).

Tarafdar, Monideepa, Tu, Qiang and Ragu-Nathan, T. S. "Impact of Technostress on End-User Satisfaction and Performance." Journal of Management Information Systems 27, No 3 (Winter 2011).

Brynjolfsson, Erik and Andrew McAfee. Race Against the Machine. Digital Frontier Press (2011).

Valentino-Devries, Jennifer and Emily Steel. "'Cookies' Cause Bitter Backlash." The Wall Street Journal (September 19, 2010).

Vascellaro, Jessica E. "Google Agonizes on Privacy as Ad World Vaults Ahead." The Wall Street Journal (August 10, 2010).

Xu, Heng, Hock-Hai Teo, Bernard C.Y. Tan, and Ritu Agarwal. "The Role of Push-Pull Technology in Privacy Calculus: The Case of Location-Based Services." Journal of Management Information Systems 26, No. 3 (Winter 2010).

Index

Subject Index

BUSINESS CASES AND INTERACTIVE SESSIONS

Here are the cases and Interactive Sessions you'll find in the tenth edition of Essentials of Management Information Systems. These cases and Interactive Sessions cover new developments in information systems and real-world company applications of systems.